MANAGING ORGANIZATIONAL BEHAVIOR
Achieving results through understanding and action

The Irwin Series in Management and The Behavioral Sciences

L. L. Cummings and E. Kirby Warren   *Consulting Editors*

John F. Mee   *Advisory Editor*

MANAGING ORGANIZATIONAL BEHAVIOR
Achieving results through understanding and action

CYRUS F. GIBSON

Vice President
Index Systems, Inc.
Formerly Associate Professor
Graduate School of Business Administration
Harvard University

1980

RICHARD D. IRWIN, INC.   Homewood, Illinois   60430
Irwin-Dorsey Limited   Georgetown, Ontario   L7G 4B3

ISBN 0-256-02237-2
Library of Congress Catalog Card No. 79–90545
Printed in the United States of America

1 2 3 4 5 6 7 8 9 0 MP 7 6 5 4 3 2 1 0

For Joanne, Kate, Tim, and Philip

PREFACE

The field of organizational behavior is bewilderingly diverse, as any teacher who has searched the literature to design a course and any manager who has sought helpful guides for practice will testify.

Over the last five years I have been in the position of both the teacher and the manager. First, as a teacher I designed and taught a course in organizational behavior for a particularly exciting group of students: middle-level managers, mostly in their 30s, in the 14-week Program for Management Development at the Harvard Business School. More recently, as a manager in a consulting firm, I felt the pressing need for ideas to help define and solve problems of work behavior so that results follow. This book is the product of that five-year odyssey.

As a teacher and academic I came to find some comfort with the various concepts and models of the subfields of organizational behavior, such as work-group theory, interpersonal relations, motivation, individual psychology, and organization structure, but was uneasy about how useful they were. As a manager, I found how incessant is the barrage of data on results and behavior. It does not come packaged to fit a concept or model. The book represents an effort to organize the field of organizational behavior within a broad conceptual framework and to provide guidelines for applying this so that data may be sifted and ordered and a process of problem defining and action taking can occur.

The primary organizing dimension of the book is conceptual, the secondary one is action taking. Each part and each chapter deal with topics covered (to a greater or lesser degree) by the literature in organizational behavior. Within each chapter the treatment deals first with concepts and models and then with practical implications and guidelines.

Part I is a presentation and elaboration of the overview model. The basic model is in the tradition of the sociotechnical school. It is elaborated upon as a framework for different forms of managerial influence and to account for the importance of organizational processes as well as static concepts. The action-oriented aspect of Part I is largely an approach to problem diagnosis using the overview model.

All the subsequent Parts, II through VI, build on key elements and processes in the overview model in Part I. The sequence is from the objective, structural, and global aspects of organization toward the subjective, people-specific, and individual aspects. Thus, Part II deals with the design and implementation of formal structure. Part III deals with work groups and managerial groups. Part IV deals with interpersonal relationships. Parts V and VI deal with individual issues in both the management of other individuals and of oneself. The cases have been selected and placed in each part so that the concepts of the preceeding chapter or chapters in that part have particular relevance to their understanding and solution.

It should be possible for the reader to fit his or her knowledge and experience within the overview model. Indeed, the experienced manager and the academician may find little that is conceptually new in the model itself. With such an all-inclusive model presented first, subsequent topics are a selection from the population of topics and cases which could have been taken up. For example, in Part II the focus is on formal structure, leaving out detailed treatment of administrative systems, technology, and strategy, all of which are elements in the overview model. The selection and elimination was based partly on what appeared to me to be the most important topics for managers today, and, inevitably, what I was most interested in and familiar with.

Despite the effort to provide coherence and order conceptually, the stance and treatment of topics has wide variation. There is, first of all, a deliberate juxtaposition in each chapter of descriptive treatment of the literature and prescriptive advice on how to do something in practice. Beyond that, however, the reader will find variation between pure acceptance of others' research and critique of research, and between critique and opinion. Part III and Part VI, on managerial politics and individual integrity, are particularly susceptible to the accusation that they represent the author's opinion more than documented fact, and so they do.

I trust that editorializing will be recognized when it crops up, and that selectivity of topics and variation in stance and treatment will contribute to the reader's debating and filtering what is here so that what is useful becomes integrated into his or her own perspective.

Acknowledgments

Although written in the singular, this book owes direct and indirect attribution to many others.

The substance of many chapters and cases was either initially written or thoroughly revised by colleagues at the Harvard Business School. In particular, Chapter 9 is a modest revision of a piece by John Gabarro. Pierre du Jardin and Margaret Lawrence wrote early drafts of most of Part III. Many of the concepts in Chapter 5 are based on a piece by Jay Lorsch. Renato Taguiri provided insightful suggestions on several chapters. Tony Athos contributed ideas and a personal model of care and attention to the student perspective on material.

The single greatest inspiration and influence on the book came from over a thousand students in Harvard's "Program for Management Development," sessions PMD29 through PMD34, and in the summer course, "Managing the Computer Resource." Their reactions in class to cases and chapters sent me back to the drawing board many times. Their sense of what was important to them and how they best learned was translated into criteria for selection and sequencing of topics.

Similarly, my colleagues at Index Systems, Inc., have unwittingly shaped much of the final revision. I owe special thanks to Tom Gerrity, president of Index, for encouraging me to finish the book on company time. Help in typing and editing came from Erica Davis, Krista Page, Frank Leonard, Jane Bass, Joan Homar, Alex Henry, Margo Clay, Laurie McEachern, Deborah Mayhew, and Jay Talbott. I am grateful to all of them.

Larry Cummings contributed invaluable substantive and editorial suggestions.

Joanne, Kate, Tim, and Philip provided the personal support, the needed goading, and the patience with the long period of evolution and writing by their husband and father. This book is dedicated to them.

February 1980   Cyrus F. Gibson

Contents

their strategies. Organizations and internal social forces. Summary. Basic forms of structure: *The functional form. The divisional form. The overlay form. The matrix form.* A practical approach to organization design: *Diagnosis of a structural problem. Analysis of structural design. Choice of form. Synthesis.*

On changing organizational structure. What implementation means. The phases of change: *Unfreezing. Moving. Refreezing.* Toward strategies of implementation: *Personal philosophies of change. The tops-down strategy. The bottoms-up strategy. A contingent philosophy of implementation. Diagnosis of setting for implementation. The choice of a strategy of implementation. Limitations to contingency of implementation.*

Part III
MANAGING GROUPS   **273**

6. **Understanding and managing work groups**   **275**

An illustrative situation. Formation and persistence of groups: *Input conditions to emergent work group formation. Why emergent groups form and persist.* Qualities of established emergent groups. Implications for management. Designing and managing work groups.

7. **Informal managerial groups and organizational politics**   **303**

Informal managerial groups: *Informal managerial groups and organizational results. Politics in organizations. The dilemmas of organizational politics. The dominant coalition.* Implications for managers: *Action guidelines. Influencing one's own group.*

8. **Managing decision-making groups**   **331**

Decision-making groups in the context of the overview model. Individuals versus groups for decision making. Field studies and normative approaches to managerial decision making: *Critique of the research. The nature of inputs to group decision making. The nature of results of group decision making.* The process of group decision making: *Meetings as forums for process. Purpose versus functions for meetings.* Influencing decision-making groups: *Influencing inputs. Influencing the group itself. Influencing individual group members.*

Conflict and communications problems: *Sources of conflict. Effective communication and good communication. One-way and two-way communications. Assumptions, perceptions, and feelings in communications.* An illustrative case: *An opportunity. A case of misunderstanding. Understanding the misunderstanding. Facilitating understanding in two-person relationships. Assumptions about communication which impede understanding. The tendency to evaluate and judge.*

What motivates people? *Motivation in the overview model. The path-goal theory of motivation.* Rewards people strive for: *The complexity of people.* How can I motivate people? *Specific actions to motivate others.* Management style: *Management style and the assumption sets. Human complexity and contingent style: The implications. Dealing with the challenges of contingent style.* Leadership.

Models of organizational results, behavior, and influence

What causes people to behave the way they do at work? How much does a manager really need to know about the causes of human behavior in order to be effective in achieving good organizational results? How can a manager get results through people? What are the limits on what a manager can do?

In Part I we address these questions. To do so we shall develop and elaborate an overview model of the causes of organizational results. Basically the model shows input elements and emergent relationships as determining the nature of individuals' *perspectives* in a work situation. An individual's perspective is the key antecedent of his or her behavior in organizations and behavior, in turn, is the most important cause of organizational results. The elements in this model can serve as a checklist of things a manager should look at in understanding the origins of forces and behavior which lead to results and in understanding the constraints on and channels for those forces.

In its development in Chapter 1 the model will be static. In Chapter 2 one kind of process dimension is added to the model, namely the process of managerial influence. Influence efforts will be defined in terms of what elements of the overview model they are aimed at. That is, whether the influence is direct on behavior, or semidirect or indirect, through causes of behavior.

In Chapter 3 another kind of process dimension is added. This refers to forces that occur naturally in organizations over time and which require management effort to control.

Throughout Part I and the book we shall concentrate on elements and forces which affect results and which the practicing manager can use to achieve desirable results.

The Ford-Knudsen case (Case 3–1) at the end of Part I is taken exclusively from published news articles. It illustrates virtually all the concepts and processes described in Chapters 1, 2 and 3.

Chapter 1

MANAGING ORGANIZATIONAL BEHAVIOR: AN OVERVIEW MODEL

In the literature on management and the manager, academicians and practitioners offer a variety of definitions of the management task.[1] A common theme is that management involves having responsibility for the achievement of some intended organizational ends or outcomes—that is, for getting results which meet or exceed performance expectations. Achieving results is of particular importance to the practicing manager in an organization. In this chapter we shall develop an overview model to explain how results come about. Our purpose is to provide a useful framework for practicing managers by drawing on a necessary minimum of concepts from academicians in organizational behavior.

In developing the overview model we shall focus initially on organizational results or *ends* rather than on the *means* of obtaining ends or on the processes which lead to them. In doing so our approach differs from that of many authors in the field of management and organizational behavior. For example, the traditional approach to management, as articulated by Fayol (1950), Gulick (1937), and others, emphasized the functions performed by management, such as planning, organizing, staffing, directing, and controlling. A more contemporary approach is that of Mintzberg (1973), who studied empirically

---

[1] For a thorough review of definitions of management, see Albanese (1975).

the behavior of managers at work and derived a set of concepts to describe ten roles managers fill, such as those of leader, liaison, entrepeneur, disturbance handler, and so on. None of these approaches denies the importance of results, and none is really incompatible with the others. They are basically different ways of conceptualizing managerial behavior in terms of the means by which managers strive to achieve results such as their personal ends and organizational ends. We shall also deal with means and processes, but we begin with results and we shall select concepts which are most relevant to explain how results come about.

Our emphasis on results is largely because our primary audience is intended to be practicing managers and managers in training. Our contact with managers in teaching executives, consulting, and doing field research leaves us with the distinct impression that achieving organizational results is uppermost in their minds. They are concerned much more with solving problems, that is, with correcting and improving performance results, than they are with purely understanding or theorizing about what causes their problems or about *why,* descriptively, things happen the way they do in their organizations. To put this another way, managers are more interested in information that is *prescriptive* or *normative* than information that is explanatory or *descriptive.* They have personal perspectives of performance and needs to use knowledge for action. For example, managers want to know how to get sales up, how to stop and reverse a decline in output per day, or how to "put out a fire" or smooth a crisis rather than to know why the situation is what it is. The knowledge of why is of interest to them only if it helps them decide what to do; knowledge beyond what is needed to reach a satisfactory solution is often considered superfluous. Nevertheless, many if not most managers need to understand more about these problems than they typically do in order to solve them quickly and permanently.

Behavioral scientists, by training and inclination, are—and probably ought to be—more interested in descriptive information of why organizations and the people within them behave the way they do. They are less interested in how to influence that behavior to achieve results. Theirs is a perspective of observation, contemplation, and knowledge building. Clearly, behavioral scientists and managers need each other. Ultimately, the behavioral scientist's work must have application in the world of action to be useful, and he or she should understand the manager's perspective in order to understand how organizations function. The manager's action can be improved in achieving its intentions if it is based on an improved understanding of what causes behavior and organizational results.

It is for the purpose of helping the manager that we begin with the topic of results and with the overview model of causes. Here we have a common ground of interest between the practitioners and the behavioral scientists.

In the model, results are the outcomes of an organizational system of causes. The model itself is largely descriptive, but in developing it we shall concentrate on concepts and relationships which have utility. In this chapter the basic model is developed by working *back*, starting with results or outcomes, then identifying the behavior of people which causes those results, and then back further to considering the several elements which cause behavior.

ORGANIZATIONAL RESULTS AND PERFORMANCE

What do we mean by *results?*

We consider results to be the outcomes of an organizational system, and particularly to be aspects of the behavior of people in organizations. The organizational system which produces any result may be an entire company or agency, a division, a department, a committee, or even two people in a relationship within a larger organization. The behavior of people in an organization, people acting and making decisions in their jobs, produces outcomes in the form of goods and services, events, decisions, attitudes, and potential future behavior. A *result* is an outcome which can be assessed according to some standard of comparison. Typical examples of results include the level of sales, profitability, return on investment, the trend in growth or market share, the quality level of widgets produced, the absenteeism and turnover of employees on the third shift, and so on. Clearly, there are an almost infinite number of specific kinds of results, depending on the particular organization and what management is interested in.

The way we have defined these terms says nothing about how good or bad any given result may be. Such a judgment or assessment is essential to management. The assessment of a result requires comparison of it to some standard or criterion. A standard which exists in advance of the occurrence of some result in a *goal* or *objective*. The assessment of performance consists of comparing a result, the outcome, with the goal or objective. Without some basis for comparison, such as an explicit or implicit goal, it is impossible to say with any validity whether a result is good or bad. Is a 15 percent return on investment good? Obviously it depends on what is needed, what the alternative opportunities are, and what return is expected. For a personal savings account, 15 percent sounds good in 1980. For the manufacture of calculators using a design and manufacturing process likely to be obsolete next year, 15 percent may not be enough to recover the investment before it is worthless.

Figure 1–1 shows the essential sets of elements of the overview

FIGURE 1-1
Simplified elements of the overview model

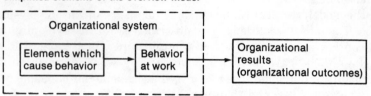

model presented so far. The manager in an organization is concerned with results, otherwise known as organizational outcomes. Results of interest to us here are the consequences of human behavior in organizations. Obviously, results can be affected by external and uncontrollable forces from outside the organization. While these are important to take into account, it is precisely because they are uncontrollable that a manager can do little about them. For purposes of managing for results, we shall confine our discussion to that cause of results which the manager can affect, namely human behavior in the organization. Organizational behavior, in turn, is caused by a complex set of elements in the organizational system. These elements will be described and separated out, first in this chapter in general categories and in a static sense in the overview model, and in more detail and with a dynamic or process orientation in later chapters.

When we say that a manager is "concerned" with results, we mean that manager must somehow assess or judge results to determine what action can or should be taken. To assess results is to determine the performance of the system. Assessment requires that there be criteria, such as goals or objectives, and that these be set ahead of time.

Let us turn now to a closer look at results as part of our overview model.

Criteria for assessing results

A way of thinking about results which is both general and useful is in terms of criteria for evaluating them. Rather than attempt to categorize results themselves or to categorize various types of organizations and their associated results, we shall use categories of criteria for assessing any given result in any given organization. The reader may notice that according to our earlier definitions and distinctions, the list of criteria we shall develop could be thought of as categories of organizational goals, inasmuch as we have defined goals in terms of their serving as the means to assess results. However, as we shall see below, the concept of organizational goals, although useful for establishing some criteria, is not sufficiently broad and is too suggestive of purposefulness and intention to serve our needs completely.

There are five categories of criteria for assessing organizational results. These are (1) efficiency, (2) effectiveness, (3) employee satisfaction, (4) adaptability to change, and (5) ability to acquire resources. Each of these is derived from or implied by different approaches in organizational theory. An expansion of this approach may be found in Scott (1977). Much of this section is drawn from Scott's treatment.

One theoretical approach to understanding organizations is to conceive of organizations as rational systems designed to achieve goals or, more broadly, to achieve purpose. It is from this school of thought that efficiency and effectiveness come:

Efficiency This is the degree to which an organization is able to achieve its goals of production of output relative to the amount of resource input that it uses. Efficiency can usually be measured quantitatively. Productivity is a common measure of efficiency, and typically means the amount of output per unit of input, such as, for example, the number of units produced per unit of raw material or per unit of labor used. Another measure of efficiency is the amount of output per unit of time required to produce it.

Effectiveness This is a measure of the quality of output results, that is, whether the units of output are sufficiently good to meet the needs of the customers or users, given their expectations. The term is also used in a broader context to assess the processes within an organization, whether or not a particular output has been achieved. Thus, a manager may ask, "Was that an effective meeting?" and be thinking of how good it was as a process of discussion leading toward some yet unrealized goal. In organization theory effectiveness is also used as a general term for organizational performance, in which instance all the other criteria we are discussing here fall under it. For our purposes, however, we shall confine the definition to a criterion of quality and processes leading to outcomes. Sometimes effectiveness can, like efficiency, be operationalized into measurements which are quantitative, but in many instances it can only be qualitative.

A basically different view of organizations is to see them as *natural systems*. This view emphasizes the basic purpose of *survival* as an organizational purpose and points to the fact that organizations are made up of people. As a criterion for assessing results, survival is too general for our purposes. However, it is important to recognize that as organiztions produce goods and services they also generate the precedents for subsequent impact on employees' perspectives. Therefore, a criterion is needed which will enable the manager to assess a result in terms of its human impact:

Employee satisfaction   This is the degree to which employees feel their personal goals or needs are met as a result of their participation as members of the organization. It is important to note that in general *needs* may be instrumental or ephemeral. That is, they may be needs which can be satisfied by the granting of some reward, such as pay or promotion or a pat on the back, or they may be intrinsic and purely subjective and personal, such as needs for fulfillment or feeling of mastery over work, results, or simply the process of working.

Another view of organizations is to think of them as *open systems* which engage in a constant interchange of materials, energy, and other resources with their environments.[2] In order to be efficient and effective in the short run, organizations must possess the ability to cope with the environment. From this school of thinking come our final two criteria, adaptability to change and ability to acquire resources.

Adaptability to change   This is the degree to which an organization's results affect its own structure and processes to increase or decrease its ability to absorb, reject, or otherwise deal with important changes in its environment. In the long run, adaptability is a key to the survival of the organization. This emphasis on adaptability is highlighted in an article by Weick (1977) in which it is argued that in general we should put more emphasis in organizations on internal processes which generate adaptive processes and structures.

Ability to acquire resources   This is the degree to which an organization's results make it more or less able to get scarce and valued inputs to do its work. Resources include not only money, raw materials, and labor, but also the commitment of employees to devote their energy to the organization's benefit. This criterion was first proposed in an article by Yuchtman and Seashore (1967).

At this point the reader should pause and think of two or three examples of specific results from organizations with which he or she is familiar. Next, think of the particular ways in which these results are measured by the organization, if they are measured at all. Finally, take each result and decide which one or more of the above five criteria the results fall under.

Theoretical and practical use of results criteria

The five criteria discussed above are intended to be what Scott (1977) calls a "universal set" of criteria. That is, they are meant to be general enough to be used to evaluate all organizational results. Scott has pointed out that there are several theoretical difficulties in any attempt to develop such a list. These include the fact that they are derived from different theoretical perspectives on organizations, as we have indicated, and they apply differently depending on the time

---

[2] This is the approach taken in Katz and Kahn (1966).

horizon and on what group or individual is doing the evaluation. Thus, for example, the stockholder interested in dividends might emphasize efficiency and effectiveness in the short run, the employee might emphasize employee satisfaction, and the community might emphasize adaptability that ensures survival of the organization and its ability to remain as an employer of the local labor force in the long run. For our purposes, these criteria are not intended to satisfy the need for theoretical nicety so much as the need for practical utility. While there are differences in which one or several criteria will be most important for any given group or individual, the list is nevertheless valid for any one group, and provides a basis for comparison among interested parties.

It must also be noted that the criteria may often be in conflict with one another. A production department which emphasizes only efficiency may run up against the problem of poor quality of output; the most satisfied worker may be inefficient; an organization which emphasizes flexibility and adaptability may have so much "slack" in resources that it is inefficient; an organization which aggressively captures resources may have too many resources to make it efficient in the short run. Obviously, the problem of putting the appropriate weight on criteria, over the appropriate period of time, is left for the particular manager using the criteria under the circumstances facing him or her.

We began this discussion of results and criteria with an emphasis on providing concepts which would be general and useful and which would serve as the first step in development of an overview model of the causes of results. Our intent was to speak in terms useful to the practitioner, the manager, but also to broaden out from a limited view to cover other suggestive ways of thinking about results in organizations. It should be noted that the order in which the criteria were presented corresponds roughly to the order of importance which managers generally place on results: efficiency and effectivness first, employee satisfaction next, adaptability and ability to capture resources last. In developing these criteria in this order we have drawn on theoretical views of organizations as rational instruments of purpose, as natural systems, and as open systems. The five results criteria should be applicable in practice regardless of which of these conceptual views one adopts.

ELEMENTS IN THE STATIC OVERVIEW MODEL

The static model: Behavior causes results

In our overview model organizational results come from the behavior at work of the members of an organization. Behavior at work includes all activities and decisions made by people in the organization. In a general sense, all behavior may be thought of as coming from decisions or *choices* made by individuals. This is the approach of authors in the "Carnegie school" represented in the work of Simon (1957), March and Simon (1958), Cyert and March (1963), and more recently, March and Olsen (1976). The choices may be visible, as in the case of a management decision, or they may be manifested in other activity, as when a person chooses to leave or chooses to join, or chooses to put in extra work effort over the alternative of not putting in that effort. We shall consider behavior at work to be the more concrete manifestations of "choice," namely activities and decisions which are relatively visible or which can be clearly identified.

Behavior at work includes not only activities and decisions directly associated with results, like running machines, keypunching, and so on, but also activities and decisions that are only indirectly related to total organizational results, such as attending meetings, training subordinates, writing reports, and the like. Moreover, social and nonwork behavior within the organization is also included in that it too can affect or lead to organizational results.

Behavior at work is the most important factor affecting results for the practicing manager to consider, at least from the point of view of things which he or she can affect to achieve goals. At the same time, as we have indicated earlier, results are also affected directly by extra-organizational forces and conditions as well as intra-organizational behavior. Indeed, for some organizational systems, particularly departments which are closely linked in their work with other departments, results may be more determined by those external forces than by controllable and manageable behavior within the unit for which the manager is responsible. When production is consistently late in shipping orders, sales' performance may suffer; when sales consistently underprices products, profits of the organization as a whole may suffer; when economic conditions deteriorate, sales may lag and costs escalate. Most organizations strive to eliminate or reduce to a minimum or take into account the influence of these uncontrollable factors in setting responsibility for their managers. This is a very important and appropriate effort to be undertaken, because it makes possible the creation of responsibility which can lead to accountability.

In many of the most complex tasks it is impossible to eliminate the effects of exogenous forces without diluting or detracting from the purpose of the unit in question. Consider, for example, the design of a new product which requires close collaboration between engineering and production and research and development. If each went off on its own, the final design might never be finished. Collaboration, cooperation, and give-and-take are required, and in a sense the manager of any one of the three departments is dependent on each of the others. In such instances, which are common, the manager's responsibility includes not only getting results from behavior of members of his or her own units, but also taking into account and trying to affect the behavior of people in other parts of the organization or even in other organizations. In our model, we should keep in mind that although we show only behavior at work within an organizational system as leading to organizational results, there often are important external causes of results which the manager may be responsible for and which must be taken into account when his or her results are assessed.

The two elements of the model presented thus far, organizational results and behavior at work, are summarized in Figure 1–2.

FIGURE 1–2
Behavior and results in the overview model

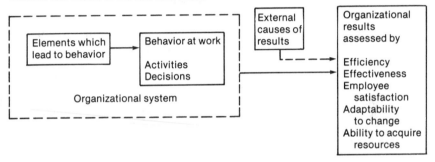

Results and behavior: An example

Let us illustrate with an actual example some of the concepts and relationships among concepts developed in our model thus far.

A plant manager we know became concerned recently with a decline in the production output of hourly employees in his plant, which was part of a large manufacturer of container packages for sale to packers of food and industrial products. He was alerted to this by comparison of weekly production reports over the last several months. On talking to his production manager he learned that quality control (QC) was also becoming a problem, and that the decline in efficiency was accompanied by poor quality. The plant manager's quality control manager reported directly to him, and when asked about this the QC manager in formed him that the QC inspectors were overworked and being blocked by production foremen in their efforts to sample output for testing. A few days later the plant personnel manager came in to tell the plant manager that several union grievances by hourly workers had cropped up unexpectedly in the past week, and that turnover among hourly production workers and quality control inspectors was at an all-time high. This had created a' problem in terms of being able to hire replacements.

As if this were not enough, at this time the plant manager got a phone call from his boss, informing him that his plant would have to absorb part of the production output of a new and unexpected order. The plant manager knew that the behavior and results problem he was having would make it very difficult for his organization to adapt to this change in expected work load.

Without digging any further, the plant manager had evidence that *work behavior* by production employees, quality control inspectors, and probably production foremen was affecting, directly or indirectly, the *efficiency,* product quality (*effectiveness*), *satisfaction* of some employees, ability to hire new people (*acquire resources*), and *adaptability to change* in production planning.

Although the plant manager would have to look further for the underlying cause of the behavior of his people and others, and then to take action, he had begun the process by looking at results and discovering which particular behavior was most immediately related to those results. In this case, the effects were severe and touched unfavorably on all the results criteria in our model. The situation was of crisis proportions.

Fortunately for our plant manager friend, his boss was responsive to his problems. Even before the fundamental problems were solved, the two of them reached agreement on the best possible schedule for the additional work that had to be assigned to the plant. This helped somewhat, but the plant manager was still expected to work out his own problems. He was responsible for the results.

At this point the reader is invited to think of specific examples of behavior by individuals in organizations with which he or she is familiar. Then, tie these behavioral examples to one or more of the five criteria by which the organizational results are judged. To what extent does each example of behavior lead to a result which is favorable or unfavorable? If your list does not have one, think of two or three behaviors which lead to results which are favorable on one criterion but unfavorable on another.

Intermediate variables: Perspective and emergent relationships

In discussing results, criteria for assessing results, and behavior at work, we have dealt with relatively concrete and observable variables. We have not strayed far from the terms familiar to most managers. As we move back now to define the elements which cause behavior, the intermediate variables in the overview model, we shall introduce concepts that are more abstract and "soft." These are the concepts of people's perspectives and of emergent relationships. In no direct way can these be seen or measured objectively. They are, rather, constructs with particular meanings from the behavioral science literature based on research and theory building. Their existence must be inferred from observable behavior, but familiarity with them is, perhaps for the very reason of their being less empirically evident, very important in the management of organizational behavior.

A person's *perspective* is the total conscious and implicit view held by that individual of the particular context or situation in which he or she is about to behave. This perspective is the state of mind and emotion which precedes and determines that person's behavior.[3] An individual's perspective in a situation consists of his or her *assumptions* or beliefs about the situation, his or her conscious *perceptions* of the situation (i.e., what the individual sees happening), and the *feelings* or emotions evoked by the situation itself or associated with the assumptions and perceptions.

Assumptions, perceptions, and feelings then are the subelements which make up perspective. At any given time a person may have a cluster of assumptions, perceptions, and feelings about any one particular topic or object, such as one's perspective on one's work, on one's family, or on national taxes or national political parties. One's assumptions, perceptions, and feelings may be conscious and recognized by the person or they may be preconscious or unconscious. An important implication of this should be recognized at this point. A manager can only partly understand the perspective of another by direct questioning of and discussion with the person involved. Moreover, in some instances, it may be inadvisable to directly discuss matters of a sensitive nature with the person involved. An example of this would be when a manager is trying to decide how to go about a necessary reduction in labor force. The manager may want to know what the employee's perspective is toward such a layoff, but open discussion before it has been decided how to do it may create unnecessary problems. Understanding another person's perspective (a topic that will be discussed in detail in Chapter 9) requires that the manager draw inferences from behavior and other sources which often do not come directly from conversation with the individual whom the manager is trying to understand.

The reader familiar with concepts in social psychology may recognize that perspective as described here includes a person's *attitude* toward any particular topic or object. Indeed, attitude may be defined as the predisposition to act (behave) toward some object or idea, which predisposition includes an emotional aspect (feeling) and cognitive as-

---

[3] This definition of perspective is based on the use of that concept by Becker et al. (1961).

pects (assumptions) toward the object. In this sense, perspective is the repository of a person's attitudes. Beyond that, perspective in our use of the term is the locus of high-order mental activities, cognitive processes, and ego functioning, which include perceiving, thinking, and problem solving.

The perspective which an individual has on a situation is the person's model or map of reality. One person's map at any given moment may be very different from that of another, even when both people have been exposed to the same recent experience. It may or may not be an accurate reflection of reality, either for lack of sufficient information or because the individual's own feelings and personal stakes in the situation have affected his or her perceptions of the information.

For example, imagine the effect of an announcement of a change in management to nonunionized employees of a profit center unit who know they are below their performance goals in a time of high unemployment and high inflation. Whatever management's reason for the change, employees are likely to perceive it leading to disruption and layoffs, a perspective which may lead to behavior which generates rumors and impedes effectiveness of the unit. Imagine further that the new manager's *own* perspective on the unit happens to be that poor profit performance has been due to misallocation of overhead costs and unrealistic transfer pricing. This may lead him to go right to work on the accounting department. The employees soon see cost analysts coming through this department. Their perception of this in view of their assumptions about the change in management may lead to a further worsening of work performance and the creation of a new problem with output. Achieving effective communications in organizations requires addressing the perspective of the receiver.

Individual perspective is the precursor of individual behavior. Every individual has a perspective, his or her own model or map, of every situation within which behavior is about to occur. If a person is very conscious, systematic, and thoughtful about an act, such as making a decision after full analysis, we may say that his or her perspective is the source or cause of the behavior. If, on the other hand, a person acts intuitively or on impulse, then his or her perspective has served more as a channel or mediating force on a deeper or preceding cause, such as a *need* or a *motive*. The state of one's perspective may either constrain or guide or directly cause that behavior, depending in part on the degree to which the elements of the perspective are consciously recognized. The perspective serves a crucial functional purpose in individual behavior, namely serving as a model of reality which makes possible economical interpretation of new events by means of a context of experience and personal needs. The function of perspective is to cause behavior which is consistent or rational to the individual.

A person's perspective on an object or situation may be relatively changeable or relatively permanent. We shall deal with the more changeable aspects in our discussion of interpersonal relationships in Chapter 9. Of particular importance to management is the employees' perspectives on their overall relationships to the organization. This is a relatively permanent thing, at least for employees who have been with the organization for some time, and it affects their perception and interpretation of specific events and decisions which come up. This overall perspective on the organizational relationship is sufficiently important that we shall give it a special name, the "psychological contract." Strictly speaking there are two sides to the psychological contract, that in the perspective of the individual employee, and that in the perspective of the managers who represent the organization to the employee. Thus, a full definition of the psychological contract is the set of expectations by the employee toward the organization, what is expected of the employee by the organization, and what each party perceives as the fair interchange of commodities among the things being exchanged.[4] Figure 1–3 presents examples of the typical commodities which make up the psychological contract, and is based on the examples first presented in Kotter(1973).

FIGURE 1–3
Examples of expectation and commodities in the psychological contract

What the individual may expect to receive and the organization may expect to give:	What the individual may expect to give and the organization may expect to receive:
a. Salary.	a. An honest day's work.
b. Personal development opportunities.	b. Loyalty to organization.
c. Recognition and approval for good work.	c. Initiative.
d. Security through fringe benefits.	d. Conformity to organizational norms.
e. Friendly, supportive environment.	e. Job effectiveness.
f. Fair treatment.	f. Flexibility and a willingness to learn and to develop.
g. Meaningful or purposeful job.	

The psychological contract in an employee's perspective is an important thing for management to assess and articulate, particularly when an organizational change is being contemplated which could change the terms of the contract. We shall make use of this in Chapter 5 in discussing the management of organizational change.

---

[4] For a full discussion of the psychological contract, see Thomas (1974).

As we warned at the outset of this section, the concept of perspective is an abstract one. On the one hand, perspective is the individual's mental trace, reflecting to the person the relevant external structures and forces in a particular situation. At the same time perspective is a reflection of the individual's inner personality structures and forces: motives, needs, and stored experiences. The term *motivation* refers to the strength of an individual's propensity to behave in order to gain some needed reward. As such, motivation may be thought of as a way of describing an individual's perspective. Motivation is dependent on both inner and external structures and forces. We shall deal further with motivation in Chapter 10.

One's perspective is also formed and changed by one's perceptions of organizational results and the behavior in the organization. In our evolving model this particular effect may be shown by a feedback loop. Figure 1–4 gives a summary of the elements of the model presented thus far.

FIGURE 1—4
Perspective in the overview model

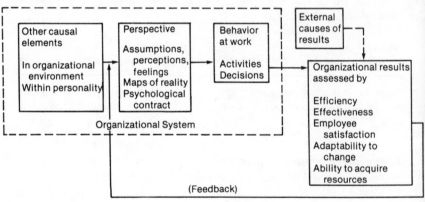

Emergent relationships

The next element in our model is the relationships which emerge between and among people in an organization. These are the social relationships—of friendship or hostility—which exist and which invariably strongly affect individuals' perspectives toward their work. Emergent relationships thus play a strong role in determining behavior at work.

In every organization of any size there are informal groups (or emergent groups) of people.[5] These exist at the clerical and blue-collar

---

[5] Most of the concepts discussed here pertaining to emergent relationships are based on Homans (1950).

levels and at the supervisory and managerial levels as well. Emergent groups of employees differ basically from departmental groups in that they are not formally sanctioned by the organization, although in fact an emergent group may form among members of a department. Just as organizational departments have a hierarchical structure of authority relationships and a set of formal rules affecting work behavior, so too may an emergent group have an informal "structure" and set of "norms" which group members implicitly recognize in their perspectives and which affect their behavior. Emergent group structure is based on differences in statuses and informal roles of group members. Norms are the emergent rules of what should and should not be done by members. A particularly important topic of conversation among emergent groups is what should be the proper relationship between an employee and the organization: what is an appropriate level of work, what is fair pay and fair treatment, and so on. In other words, the terms of the psychological contract in an individual's perspective is heavily affected by that person's membership in an emergent group. What individuals think about the organization often reflects what their peers think.

Emergent groups form among employees at all levels in organizations, including the top management in the hierarchy. The norms and status of members of managerial groups can affect their decision-making behavior as individuals. These effects can be for better or for worse. When a managerial group is highly cohesive and characterized by strong norms that members should conform and not rock the boat, the phenomenon of "group think" can arise, with poor decision making the result. We shall explore in more depth the ideas outlined here about emergent groups and implications for managing them in three chapters. Chapter 6 deals with so-called work groups among clerical and blue-collar employees. Chapter 7 deals with managerial groups, and Chapter 8 with decision making in managerial groups.

Emergent relationships in our model include not only groups but two-person relationships which develop as people work together. Key two-person relationships in organizations include those a person might have with his or her boss, secretary, each subordinate, individual members of other departments, and so on.

Two implications for managers

From a managerial perspective there are two important things to remember about emergent groups and emergent two-person relationships in organizations. First, while we have asserted that emergent relationships will form, we have not said what their effect will be in terms of organizational results. Emergent groups may be a good thing or a bad thing in terms of people's work behavior, getting the job done, feeling satisfied, being adaptable to change, and being capable of acquiring resources. What is generally true is that a person's relationship will often affect his or her perspective in terms of whether that person *should* or *should not* conform to organizational goals and results desired by management.

The second implication of emergent relationships is that the fact that they exist and often affect the perspectives of people who are members of the relationship must be taken into account by a manager in almost any action taken to affect behavior and results. The manager should examine not only the skills and personalities of members of an organization as individuals but also their perspectives as affected by their social relationships. Moreover, it is not enough to think of influencing behavior as a manager by means of formal organization structure, rewards, compensation, job assignment, and so on. Managers must also think how these formal aspects of the organization are perceived and interpreted by individuals wearing the spectacles of membership in an informal social system. In effect, all parts of the formal organizational system, which we shall refer to as the "inputs" in our overview model, are attenuated and interpreted by employees through their individual perspectives and through the effects on the perspectives which they get from their emergent relationships. These "intermediate variables" in our model represent the social and psychological aspects of the organizational system.

Input elements to the model

The overview model is shown in its complete form in Figure 1–5. In it are contained all the elements discussed so far (including emergent relationships), in addition to three broad categories of input elements. These three are the "outer environment," the "inner environment," and the "people." The reader will note that in Figure 1–5 we have drawn a boundary around all the elements except results and outer environment. Enclosed in the boundary are the elements which make up the organizational system.

Unlike the rather abstract and soft intermediate elements (perspective and emergent relationships), the input elements are relatively observable. These elements are terms which are familiar to most managers.

The input elements have both a direct and an indirect effect on individuals' perspectives, as indicated by the arrows coming from inputs in Figure 1–5. Their effect is direct in that inputs include characteristics of the people themselves, their personalities, skills and abilities, all of which provide basic aspects of their perspectives with regard to what they can do and what their inner needs and motives are. Moreover, the inner environment element will obviously shape

¬URE 1–5

¬e complete overview model

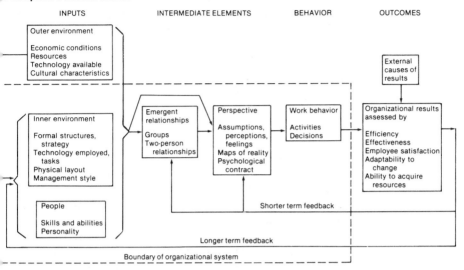

one's assumptions about what one's job is, what the rewards for work are, who the boss is, and so on. The effect of inputs on perspectives is indirect because they determine the nature of the emergent relationships which in turn help shape perspectives.

The three input elements are described below.

Outer environment

This category includes such things as conditions in the political and economic sector of the environment, the job market as it relates to jobs in the organization, competition or rivalry from other organizations, the nature of technology available to perform the organization's tasks, the availability of resources (money, material, people), and the cultural and social values of the society.

As we have already suggested, some of these conditions have a direct effect on organizational results. This is indicated by the separate box on the right, external causes of results.

Inner environment

This is the largest and most diverse category of inputs, and consists of subelements which are worthy of distinct discussion in their own right.

The *formal structure* and *strategy* of an organizational system includes an organization's explicit goals and statement of means for achieving these goals, its reporting relationships, job descriptions, systems of measurement and control, and the like. We shall be particularly interested in this book in the formal authority structure of organizations, a topic covered in Chapter 4, and in the process of managing the change of a formal structure and strategy—that is, organizational change—in Chapter 5. The design and changing of these elements is typically done with relative infrequency by top management. The design of an organization chart of control system requires that management assess the nature of the outer environment, the nature of the inner environment, and the nature of the strategy (i.e., purposes, goals, and policies for achieving those goals) pertaining to their organization.

The *technology employed* and *tasks* refers to the nature of the machines, data processing equipment, and the like in terms of the kinds of skills required to operate them, their implications for investment and depreciation as compared to labor costs, and whether they impose needs for continuous process, batch, or custom-built operation. Tasks are the required functions which must be performed, as dictated by the technology, by other aspects of the environment, and by the strategy and goals which are part of the formal structure input. These tasks are therefore the required tasks which must be accomplished; they are not the job descriptions for employees. Job descriptions and specific policies and procedures are an organization's response to meeting the required tasks.

The *physical layout* of an organization has a strong effect on how well the work can get done and particularly on who will come into relationship with whom.

Management style is considered an input from the inner environment of organizations because, to employees working under a particular manager, a manager's style is in effect a given characteristic of the inner environment. Management style may be defined as the characteristic pattern of behavior which a manager exhibits over time when attempting to influence directly other people's behavior. We shall say more about influence in Chapter 2 and about management style in Chapter 10.

People

Characteristics of the people constitute the human resources which are vital inputs to the organizational system. When they come to work people bring with them traits they were born with, traits they learned in childhood, and recent learning as well. Many of the traits may be quantified, such as age, educational level, test scores on qualification tests, and the like. Others may be assessed in a more subjective way, such as an interviewer's write-up. The characteristics which are included for people here are meant to include those basic skills and abilities and personality characteristics which they bring with them to their employment. These characteristics differ from the perspective an individual holds largely because perspective is the way the individual views his or her work or some other object, whereas the input characteristics are the more enduring aspects of the individual's makeup. In Chapter 11 we shall present and discuss several concepts to describe an individual personality, with particular reference to managers as members of the organization.

THE DYNAMIC NATURE OF ORGANIZATIONS: FEEDBACK LOOPS IN THE STATIC MODEL

The main emphasis in this chapter has been to describe a static model of organization which contains the elements which managers need to understand and to affect in order to achieve desired results. In addition to this static view, it is equally important to recognize the *dynamic* nature of how organizations function as they produce results. One suggestion of this is shown in Figure 1–5, where there are two feedback loops coming from results and behavior. The first of these is a shorter term feedback which affects individual perspective and emergent relationships. An example of this would be communication between two individuals. When one person communicates with another, or behaves in such a way as to transmit information in, say, the form of a written memo, it may have an immediate effect on the perspective of the person being communicated to. That effect may be to change the receiver's behavior in some way. Note that the loop does not come back *directly* to that person's behavior. Rather, the message is filtered through the individual's perspective: it is perceived by the person in what may be exactly what the sender intended or in what may be some different interpretation. This feedback from behavior and results may also be attenuated by the interpretation by the emergent group of the message to the sender who is a member of that group.

The longer term feedback loop suggests that organizations as systems modify their inputs as a result of information based on behavior and results. Left to its own devices, an organization will sometimes modify itself by means of feedback. It is in this sense a self-regulating system which at any given moment is in "dynamic equilibrium." An example of this is when an organization adjusts itself to poor performance, such as a loss of market share (a measure of effectiveness and perhaps also efficiency). Decisions may be made to reduce the work force (fewer people as inputs) and to automate production (adoption of a new technology) to correct the deviation in output from the desired standard.

In Chapter 2 we shall pay particular attention to managerial behavior, that is, action by a manager aimed at affecting elements in the model which cause behavior. These target elements are perspective, emergent relationships, and inputs. Managerial behavior is called for when the dynamic equilibrium is not leading to an improvement by management's standards in results.

As a whole, the model should be thought of as a connected set of elements which represent *structures* through which *forces* act to influence people's perspectives and behavior and ultimately organizational results. The categories and concepts of the model are a checklist of the total static framework leading to behavior and outcomes and are only partly descriptive of the processes or dynamic aspects of how things happen. In a sense, the model is the structural skeleton of channels through which processes occur. We shall elaborate on processes and dynamics in Chapters 2 and 3.

The model we have presented has been influenced by a number of authors in organization theory and systems theory in addition to those already cited. One feature is the integration of technical, formal, and social variables, an idea developed by writers from the Tavistock Institute[6] and elaborated upon by Seiler (1967) and Lorsch and Sheldon (1976). The idea of a sequential set of variables clustered separately as inputs, intervening variables, and outputs was applied to organizational behavior by Likert (1967). The idea of an organization as a self-regulating mechanism is discussed in Ashby (1960).

Using the model for problem diagnosis

For practical purposes the model should help *remind* a manager of aspects of a particular situation which need to be taken into account in defining a problem and suggesting solutions to it.

The process of problem definition begins with a diagnosis moving from right to left in Figure 1–5. The process begins with a recognition of *symptoms* or potential symptoms of difficulty in terms of organizational results: off-spec output, inordinate customer complaint, threat of a strike, or whatever. Note that in order to identify a symptom, a manager must have some standard by which to measure results. Typically, these standards are organizational objectives or the manager's own internalized personal goals and standards.

The diagnosis then proceeds to the question, "Is there an external force, other than the behavior of the organizational members, which is producing the results that are undesirable?" If so, it may be that nothing can be done or that the manager must attempt to change the result

---

[6] See, for example, Rice (1963).

by going outside the organizational system for which he has responsibility.

In any case, the next question is a key one: "What behavior by what individuals within the organization is contributing to or producing the results which are off-spec?" Here, the diagnostician should go back and check over all five criteria for organizational results to see if the behavior which is affecting one of them adversely may be affecting another positively. For example, it may be that a team of computer programmers has fallen behind in their schedule to build a system. It could turn out, however, that the team has slipped behind in the schedule because they have discovered a much more elegant way of writing their programs, a result which could enhance the effectiveness of the system. It may also be that they are highly enthusiastic about what they have done, have learned a lot which could be useful for their work in the future, and are highly motivated and satisfied as employees. The manager may decide that the benefits of the behavior offset the apparent problems and that no further diagnosis or eventual action is necessary, or that action must be taken to get the system done.

Having answered the questions in terms of results criteria and behavior, the manager has identified the symptoms which may be manifestations of a problem. That is, the manager has specified features which cannot be *directly* changed. To find the problem means to identify causes which can be corrected. To do so the manager must proceed with diagnostic questions addressed to each element to the left of "behavior" in the model.

The next question is, "What is the perspective of the individual or individuals whose behavior is leading to the off-spec result which must be corrected?" Here, an objective assessment of the view of the work *as the employee sees it* is called for. This can be a difficult thing to do inasmuch as the manager is involved with the matter, may even be a part of the problem, and most often is attempting to infer how others look at things without being able to ask them directly. In some instances direct questioning can help gain data to build the insight on others' perspectives, but such questioning may in itself affect people's perspectives and even, in some circumstances, make the problem worse. Nevertheless, the exercise of sifting available data and building a model of what others are assuming, perceiving, and feeling is a crucial diagnostic step. Managers who do it get consistently better at it.

Then, progressively, the diagnostic questions are addressed to the nature of the emergent relationships and each of the input elements. The net result of the diagnostic process is a problem definition which pinpoints all the elements which are contributing causes. It may be that only one element is the key: a single individual may be misinformed about how to do a job, a single person may be a misfit in terms of skills, the compensation system may be unfair and lead people to feel their psychological contract is being violated. In such cases the solution is rather straightforward, although the manager should be careful that correcting the single cause does not create an additional problem. The essence of the overview model is systemic: in one way or another, every element has an effect on every other. The astute manager takes this into account in planning action steps and in monitoring the second-order effects of action.

CONCLUSION

In this chapter we have presented a set of static elements and the suggestion of self-regulating feedback loops to describe the causes of organizational results. With the exception of elements required to describe the perspective of organizational members and emergent relationships, most of the concepts and ideas here are familiar to practicing managers. The practitioner often uses these terms in everyday discussion and often uses the elements intuitively in diagnosing problems. The approach here is one which assumes relatively simple cause-and-effect relationships among elements. It largely ignores the fact that there are processes which work through and around structural elements to affect results, and that there are results and behavior which may be virtually inexplicable. For an elaboration on the fact that this is so, and why it can be, the reader is referred to March and Olsen, *Ambiguity and Choice in Organizations* (1976).

The basic reason for the static and somewhat oversimplified approach is a matter of choice of what should come first and what should come later on in the book. We have attempted to start with as much of what managers already know as possible. Having presented the static model in this chapter, we move with Chapter 2 into management processes which can affect elements of the model. In Chapter 3 we elaborate on the static model further by contrasting it with another important model, that of March and Olsen (1976), used to explain organizational behavior and results. Other chapters are elaborations on key elements of the model.

QUESTIONS FOR STUDY AND DISCUSSION

1. Make a list of any courses in management or organizational behavior you have had in your educational experience. What elements of the overview model do the topics in these courses address?

   How do other courses which you have had dealing with management or administration fit into the overview model or relate to the model?

2. Without necessarily using the overview model, diagram your own existing theory of cause and effect for organizational results either in the organization in which you currently work, or for any organization in general. When you have done that go back to the overview model and see to what extent you are able to make a correspondence between the elements in your model and those in the overview model. What concepts or elements are contained in your model that are not covered by the overview model? Conversely, what elements of the overview model suggest to you important new elements for your own model?

3. "Perspective" is a complex element. In order to understand it better, describe your perspective on the course you are now taking, on a job you have had, or on an issue of concern to you.

4. Think of one or more symptoms of problems in the organization in which you are now a part, whether it be a business, government, or educational institution. Using the elements of the overview model presented in this chapter, draw a diagram beginning with results and working back to input. In each box of the model list the particular aspects which apply to the situation. Do any new aspects of the situation come to mind as you go through this exercise?

   Which one or more of the elements can you do something about? Which elements require action by others? Who in particular?

5. If possible, discuss with another person a problem or set of symptoms that require the analysis described in question 4. Conduct this analysis separately, and then compare and discuss your diagnosis and indication of people who must take action with those done by the other person.

Chapter 2

MANAGING ORGANIZATIONAL BEHAVIOR: POWER AND PROCESSES OF INFLUENCE

In Chapter 1 it was emphasized that managers in organizations are primarily interested in results, particularly those results that are caused by the behavior of members of the organization. An overview model of elements which lead to organizational results was developed.

The elements in the model are largely *structural* in nature. Taken alone, they do not explain the *processes* by which forces affect the perspectives of individuals and by which aspects of those structural elements themselves are changed over time. In Chapter 1 feedback loops were used to summarize some of these processes. In particular, the feedback loops represent processes of more or less automatic or natural adjustments in people's perspectives, in emergent relationships, and in input elements. As we shall see in Chapter 3, there are other natural processes in addition to feedback which also affect organizational functioning and results.

But what if the natural processes do not lead to adjustments in results that are favorable from a management point of view? How can management affect the functioning of the organization when there is a problem at hand or a problem to come and when the organizational system clearly is not going to adjust to it? Under such conditions management must exercise its own processes to achieve the desired results. In this chapter we shall identify these as influence processes, and describe them in terms of how they can be used to affect the

26

key elements of the overview model. In order for influence to occur, power must be available to the influencer with respect to the person or persons being influenced. Also in this chapter we begin a discussion of the sources of power which managers have available to them. In combination with the terms introduced in Chapter 1, power and influence are key concepts which will be used and elaborated on throughout the book.

In Chapter 1 the tone and stance was largely descriptive and static, but in Chapter 2 the tone and stance will be largely prescriptive and process oriented.

PROCESSES OF INFLUENCE

We shall think of all the processes of managerial action which affect the behavior of individuals in organizations as processes of influence. The term *influence* refers to any process acting on the perspective of an individual which leads to his or her behavior being different than it would have been without the influence effort. Thus, influence in general is behavior of one party which changes the behavior of another party. Managerial influence in particular is the behavior of one or more persons responsible for organizational results acting to change the behavior of organizational members in ways intended to change results. In short, we see the process of managing as the same thing as the exercise of influence by managers.

With reference to the overview model, influence as defined does not operate directly on organizational results or on individual behavior, but rather through individuals' perspectives. Influence directly on behavior might be called coercion or physical force. As we shall use the term, influence refers to all those processes initiated by others which act on and through perspective. Moreover, we are particularly interested in this chapter in action by a manager intended to affect the behavior of people in the organizational unit for which the manager has responsibility. These processes include, for example, the conditioning of an individual through modification of behavior by praise or punishment, direct and explicit persuasion, indirect influence through the input elements, such as new monetary incentives, different job assignments, and so on. In general, influence can also be *self*-influence. In this case the source is from within the personality or perspective of the person based on some stimuli from the environment which may or may not have been put there by another party. In this chapter we focus on influence originating from management external to the individual. In Chapter 12 we shall deal with self-influence in the context of a problem which many managers face in their careers, namely that of maintaining personal integrity.

There are three types of managerial influence in organizations. These are illustrated in Figure 2–1, in which the influence processes are superimposed on the overview model of causal structural variables leading to outcomes.

FIGURE 2–1
Types of management influence in the organization

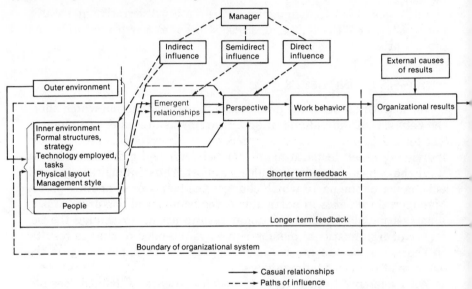

The most immediate type occurs when a manager acts directly on the perspective of the individual who is the target of influence. This is indicated in Figure 2–1 by the dotted arrow labeled "direct influence." This type involves communicating in one or more ways in order to achieve the intended behavior change. Direct influence can occur in any interpersonal relationship.

The second type of influence may be called "semidirect influence." As indicated by the arrow in Figure 2–1, this is exercised by a manager toward an emergent relationship. In semidirect influence the manager is attempting to affect the perspective of one member of a two-person relationship, or one or more members of a group, by changing the structure or functioning of the relationship itself rather than the person directly. When a manager engages in team building with a project group at the outset of its work, gives a speech to a department to improve morale, or breaks up a relationship to separate two people, the manager is exercising this semidirect type of influence.

The final type of influence is "indirect influence." In using this the manager does not communicate directly with an individual or group, but rather changes one or more of the input elements to the organizational system within which they work. Because employees' emergent relationships and perspectives are determined by inputs, indirect influence can change one or more individuals' perspectives and behavior. Examples of this type include change in organizational reporting relationships, hiring and firing people, changing job descriptions, bringing in new machines, and so on.

We turn now to a closer look at each of these three types of influence available to managers.

DIRECT INFLUENCE

In a recent survey of managerial behavior it was found that managers spend some 61 percent of their total work time in verbal communications and an additional 13 percent preparing written communications (du Jardin and Gibson, 1976). While much of this communication may be directed toward key people outside the organization (such as customers, suppliers, legislators), most of it is an effort by the manager to influence one or more individuals to behave in their work in some desired way. Direct influence is the most easily identifiable form of influence and under the right circumstances can be the most effective. In a crisis situation, direct influence may be the only type that can achieve behavior change in the necessarily short time available. It is important to understand the different means of exercising direct influence and the conditions necessary for it to be successful.

Direct influence encompasses a range of communications efforts. At one extreme is simply being present, without verbal or written communication occurring. Managers have a rich and largely untapped reservoir of means to influence others through nonverbal communication, which may include asking questions and asking for guidance as well as giving information and giving direction. Further along on the range from subtle to explicit direct influence is verbal communications which involve persuasion and, in the extreme, explicit promise of reward or threat of punishment. Thus, direct influence ranges in degree from gentle to forceful, with forms of communication from nonverbal and symbolic to explicit.

The success of an attempt to influence others directly will obviously depend on the receiver as well as the manager or sender. In general, an individual receiver will be more likely to accept the effort if he or she is expecting it, or wants or needs (is motivated to accept) the information or direction of the influence. In this easy case the target person's perspective is in a sense programmed to accept the influence.

For example, imagine a machine operator who is confronted with two separate jobs to work on next and does not know which one to do. Let us say the operator has a desire to work, but out of concern for getting into trouble finds it easy to do neither one and chooses instead to take a break and then "make work" by slowly filling out the work report. A supervisor who simply and politely tells the operator which job to start on has no problem influencing behavior. Conversely, if the individual's perspective is not expectant or is experiencing conflicting signals in the environment, the influence attempt is less likely to succeed.

Suppose that while on break the machine operator in our example happens to hear a story about operators who got into trouble because they did what their supervisor told them to do next but the department manager later "chewed them out" for it. When our operator meets the supervisor the operator's perspective on following instructions is likely to be more resistant. Hopefully, the two of them can talk about the job priorities and the work can go on. Notice that the operator may be able to exert direct influence on the supervisor here by informing the supervisor that the department manager has been known to contradict job priorities set by supervisors. It could lead to this supervisor checking with the department manager, which might not have been done otherwise. In any event, the operator's perspective in this instance has been affected by other information and he or she is likely to be less receptive. Such a state calls for more understanding and more effort on the part of the influencer to achieve what he or she wants.

Let us emphasize once again that influence of any type (direct, semidirect, or indirect) has occurred when the relevant behavior of an individual changes from what it would have been without the influence effort. Successful influence does not necessarily require that an individual's perspective must be changed. A manager may merely inform someone whose perspective is entirely congruent with the intended change and who is receptive to the information. In such a case the person's perspective undergoes no change—he or she just acts differently in light of information compatible with expectations.

The success or failure of direct influence is a function both of the particular form and substance of the communication sent and of the degree of receptivity of the receiver. Whenever an influence attempt is successful the influencer has demonstrated some measure of *power* over the receiver. This is true for indirect and semidirect as well as direct influence. *Power* is defined as the potential of one person to affect the behavior of another. In terms of receptivity, the lower the receptivity, the more power required for a given form and substance of direct influence to be successful. Thus, a manager with a great deal of power may be able to influence successfully with the most subtle form of symbolic communication, or by setting an example of the behavior desired without engaging in more explicit and forceful communications and persuasion. A manager with less power may have to resort to persuasion, promise of reward, or threat to get the same desired result.

The concept of power, its sources and its effects on people and organizations are important topics for management. As we have framed it, the job of managing means exercising influence to achieve some desired results. Since power makes influence possible, we shall devote attention later in this chapter to its sources and its effects in terms of interpersonal power (social-psychological approach)[1] and in terms of organizational power (a structuralist and sociological approach.)[2]

An important prescriptive implication should be noted with respect to direct influence. The person who would influence another needs to sense or recognize in advance whether his or her power is sufficient, given the receptivity of the individual, for the particular form of communication being used. The reason for this is that a direct influence attempt which fails may affect adversely the target person's perspective toward subsequent attempts. When an influence attempt fails, a resistance can develop, like an inoculation, and subsequent efforts will require that more power be acquired, that more forceful direct influence be used, or that other types of influence be used. The influencer needs to have a systematic or intuitive understanding of the perspective of the other person and of his or her own power in order to choose the adequate form and substance of direct influence.

To illustrate this point let us return to our example of the supervisor and the operator. Imagine that the operator learned from a friend that another operator had followed the supervisor's instructions and later got in trouble with the department manager. Also, let us assume the supervisor comes along and, being in a hurry, merely tells the operator quickly which job to work on. The operator may well perceive the supervisor's haste as evidence that the supervisor does not know what can happen, and it may drive the operator to further avoid starting on either job. Moreover, the operator may begin to think of reasons why avoidance of the job makes sense. Had the supervisor sensed the reluctance in the first place, the supervisor might have taken a little longer to probe, found out what worried the operator, and checked with the department manager. Of course, managers do not always have time to do this; the trick is to sense when the perspective of the other may be resistant and to work on the influence process a little longer in those situations.

On the other hand, the use of an excessively forceful approach can backfire. There is such a thing as using too much power. The manager with plenty of power who is too forceful may be successful but will diminish his or her power in the attempt. This can be understood as a misuse or abuse of power. Such a misuse, just as underuse, can arouse

---

[1] The social-psychological approach to power is illustrated in French and Raven (1968, pp. 259–69).

[2] The organizational approach to power is illustrated in Salancik and Pfeffer (1977).

potential resistance to further influence. Thus, the manager must select the appropriate use of influence, neither too little nor too much.

A manager's total power can be gradually increased under circumstances of repeated successful direct influence efforts. This typically results in an increase in trust, credibility, and respect toward the manager in the perspective of those he or she works with. As we shall see below, this base of power, known as personal power, is one of several bases for an individual's total power.

SEMIDIRECT INFLUENCE: THROUGH EMERGENT RELATIONSHIPS

As described in Chapter 1, emergent relationships consist of structures and norms which evolve over time among individuals in organizations. Semidirect influence occurs when the person initiating the influence successfully affects the behavior of another individual in either of two ways. The first is by exercising direct influence on a third party, an intermediary, who in turn exercises direct influence over another individual. The other way is by affecting the structure or norms of the emergent system of which the target individual is a member. These two kinds of semidirect influence are illustrated in Figure 2–2.

An example of the first way is when a manager communicates directly to an intermediary a desired behavior change and the inter-

FIGURE 2–2
Two kinds of semidirect influence

A. Semi-direct influence via two-person relationship

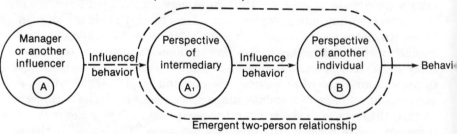

B. Semi-direct influence via emergent group

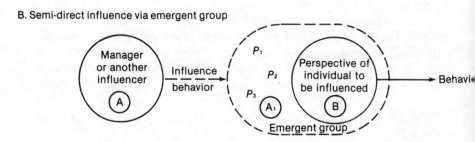

mediary in turn exercises direct influence on the target. The key difference between this and direct influence is that success is a function of
both power of the manager over the intermediary *and* the power of
the intermediary over the target person.

Semidirect influence is often used where the manager ((Ⓐ)) perceives
he or she may not have adequate power over the person to be influenced
((Ⓑ)), but that an intermediary ((Ⓐ₁)) does have that power and the
manager has the necessary power over the intermediary. An example
would be the manager who says, "Tom won't listen to me, but he and
Joe are great friends. Let me talk to Joe and see if he can get Tom to
do this."

An example of the second kind of semidirect influence would be
when a manager addresses an entire group about some substantive
issue, such as the need for greater output, or simply informs them
about the state of the business or where it is going. Such informative
sessions may be intended to influence specific behavior of specific
individuals, or they may be intended to affect perspectives by providing a kind of general sense of purpose to individuals. That is, they may
be largely symbolic and intended to have general beneficial effects on
work behavior of members of the group.

Another example of the second way is a manager or consultant
doing "process" work. This is communicating with a work group or
managerial group about its structure, norms, and patterns of behavior.
Group meetings or process discussions which raise norms or relationships among members as topics (e.g., the pecking order, problem-
solving methods) are examples of this process. Semidirect influence of
this type is most successful when the norms and patterns are still
unformed, when group members are new, or when all the members are
committed to process change. The term *team building* is used to describe this process effort, although much substantive job-related
discussion also occurs in team building.

The advantages of semidirect influence over direct influence include
the fact that if it is successful, the influence of the initiator continues
without the necessity for continual direct influence. In other words the
intermediary individual or the group internalizes the desired effect and
may continue to reinforce it. Moreover, more than one person can be
reached. In this sense, semidirect influence can lead to a change in
structures or norms of emergent relationships in such a way that the
influence effort becomes built into emergent social relationships.
The principal disadvantage is that a higher investment of time and
energy is required.

It is important to remember that in semidirect influence the influencer per se is not the immediate source of influence. With the possible
added leverage of acting through others comes the greater distance

from control over the individual to be influenced. Direct managerial control is supplemented by group or intermediary control. A rich literature exists on influence exerted toward processes of group functioning as the central approach to achieving organizational change.[3] To be sure, process change on the emergent system can affect perspectives in ways that can have permanent effects and can create means by which members contribute to creative solutions to organizational problems as they arise.

The effective use of semidirect influence through emergent relationships requires, as in the use of direct influence, an understanding of the perspectives, structures, and norms of the intermediary individual or group. The manager must be able to develop his or her own personal model of the situation to characterize these abstract but potent elements in the organizational system.

As mentioned, this type of influence takes time, and when the structure or norms of an existing emergent system are to be changed rather than built up at the start even more time and energy are required. The planning of the process of change itself, as well as the substance of the semidirect influence method, requires managerial attention. A useful approach to this has been described by Dalton (Dalton, Lawrence, and Greiner, 1970, pp. 230–58) based on Lewin's notion of three phases through which individuals and social systems must pass in order for a change in attitude and significant change in behavior to occur.[4] In our terminology, the phases are the *unfreezing of existing perspective,* the *moving or changing of perspective,* and the *refreezing of perspective.* We shall deal with this theory of change in greater depth in Chapter 5. For now, the point to be made is that semidirect influence, because it operates through emergent social relationships, typically requires more time and effort than direct influence and should be planned in such a way that it takes into account the nature of the structure and norms of those relationships as they change over time. We shall discuss one kind of semidirect influence in Chapter 6, on the management of work groups.

INDIRECT INFLUENCE: THROUGH THE INPUT VARIABLES

In organizations which are appropriately structured, there may be very little visible direct influence between managers and subordinates. Yet, in terms of the definition of influence as one party affecting the behavior of another, influence occurs. That is, management is influencing in the most indirect way: by having established the appropriate

---

[3] This literature is summarized in Katz and Kahn (1966, pp. 390–451).

[4] Lewin's concept is summarized in Hersey and Blanchard (1972, pp. 100–101).

organization and control systems, defined tasks, chosen a technology, and filled slots with people with the necessary skills and personal attributes. In short, this form of influence is functioning when there is a combination among these input elements which results in a good fit. In these circumstances forces act on the perspectives of organizational members which affect their behavior. As always, the test of this success is the behavior of the individuals; whether or not influence has occurred is defined as whether or not the intended behavior is different from what it would have been.

Formal organizations may be defined as social and technical systems which structure human relationships among members in ways which make indirect influence possible. Thus, organizations differ from other human relationships, in which only direct influence can occur. A good example of an input variable which permits indirect influence is the control and incentive system. When a production operation is established to pay an incentive to employees on a piecework basis, and it results in work effort which otherwise would not have occurred, management which installed the system has exercised indirect influence.

In a smoothly running organization in which fit among inputs is appropriate, employee behavior may continue indefinitely in the direction of desired outcomes without further intervention of management. Under such ideal, steady-state conditions the notion of management's role as one of planning, organizing, motivating, and controlling, words which imply continuous and often direct influence, is inadequate as a description of what management often does.

On the other hand, things are rarely ideal and static. Even with a steady environment, constant inputs, and stable requirements for results, organizations foster emergent systems which can alter, for better or for worse, the perspectives and behavior of members. Moreover, most organizations are confronted with changing environments which impose demands for changes in results and changes in the input variables to maintain acceptable levels of results. Environmental change typically requires adjustment in organizational strategy and structure inputs. The design or redesign of formal organizational structure is to be dealt with in Chapter 4.

Thus, in order to respond to a change in environment top management must periodically review and sometimes change inputs, particularly the formal structure. We shall refer to this process as organizational change and deal with it in Chapter 6. For our purposes we shall make distinctions among organizational change (change of formal structural inputs), process change aimed at a change in emergent structures to facilitate semidirect influence, and a change in individual perspective through direct influence.

It should be recognized, however, that organizational change, to be successful, also calls for simultaneous attention to process change and to individual change directly. Katz and Kahn (1966, pp. 390–451) have described total organizational change as including both process and formal structural elements. Leavitt (Dalton, Lawrence, and Greiner, 1970, pp. 198–212), using categories of elements of formal organizations similar to our input elements, points out the connectedness or systemic nature of them. When major change is undertaken, *all* the elements in our overview model, and their interconnections, must be taken into account in the planning.

Deliberate organizational change consists of planning and implementation. In the terminology used here, the goal is to establish successful indirect influence processes. But the processes of planning and implementation are themselves examples of direct influence or semidirect influence through emergent relationships. Thus, the manager working to reorganize must himself engage in direct influence, the exercise of power, to achieve agreement on the plan and to see that the plan is implemented.

On the whole, then, the practical problems managers face in exercising indirect influence are those of deciding what the particular mix of input variables should be and exercising influence to establish or implement the desired structure. The implementation of organizational change itself is a special case of the exercise of direct influence.

POWER AND ITS SOURCES

As we have indicated, power is a key concept in this discussion of the types of influence. If the would-be influencer or manager has no power then no effective action is possible. Being able to influence is the necessary characteristic of management; power is the ability to influence. Building and holding power are therefore essential for the successful manager. A very practical look at the process of gaining power and using it on an individual basis is given by Kotter (1977). What is sometimes overlooked in discussions of power is that it is complementary to and not a sufficient replacement for ability in performing tasks. In terms of the power required for organizational change, individual managers find it necessary to band together in groups. As discussed in Salancik and Pfeffer (1977), this process leads to the dominance of a coalition of managers at any given time, and to organizational politics. We shall deal with the topic of managerial groups and politics in Chapter 7. Power has many sources other than simply the power of authority. The particular perception of power by others and to some extent an appropriate fit between the source of power and the type of influence for which it is being used need to be understood by managers who would be effective.

A number of authors have discussed the bases or sources of power. In the organizational context we shall discuss four bases: position, referent, expertise, and personal.

Power based on *position* is simply that potential to influence others which derives from one's formal authority or the authority of office in an organizational setting. In this case the perception of power by subordinates or others derives from their sense of the legitimacy of the position holder's right to influence them in certain domains, a right which they implicitly or explicitly recognize as part of the psychological contract formed at the time of their entering, or possibly adapted and modified during their time at work in the organization. Although it has been argued that the position power in organizations is declining over time, and that there is an incompatibility between the trend toward greater individual education and freedom on the one hand and authority within an organization on the other, it may very well be that for most organizations and most relationships between managers and subordinates the power of authority is the most important single base of power today. Along with formal position itself we include the potential to reward and to punish, which French and Raven (1968) classify as a separate base of power. In business organizations another component of authority as a base of power which sometimes applies is ownership. The significant or controlling owner of a business holds power which may be the most influential of all.

Referent power is closely related to authority and consists of the power which one holds by virtue of being supported by powerful higher authority. In other words, going beyond the formal attributes of one's position is the support (or others' perception of it) one has of persons in higher positions. This is worth breaking out from authority power as a base, because while the potential to reward and/or punish generally inevitably goes with position, referent power may not. When subordinates perceive that managers have the full backing of higher officers, their power base can be considerably enhanced over the power of position alone.

The power of *expertise* is often overlooked in discussions of power. It refers to the power one holds by virtue of being successful in tasks and skills which others perceive as valuable and important to them in the work context. In his book *Power: How to Get It, How to Use It,* Korda (1975) implies that virtually all power derives from interpersonal relationships, and that the energy one expends toward getting a job done would better be expended on attaining that kind of power. We wish to expand the meaning of power well beyond the strictly image-building type. Considering power as a concept describing things one step removed from action, that is as the potential to influence, suggests that a greater variety of means to have power is possible. The power of expertise is in this respect one of the more distant from those bases which are developed only from interpersonal contact.

Finally, there is *personal* power. A manager can develop a power base over others by virtue of personal attractiveness to them, or what is referred to as *charisma*. The psychological base for this in the perspective of the target individuals is the identification which they have with the individual. Leadership may be defined as the power which a superior in a relationship holds by virtue of the development of personal power. In many organizational situations, personal power and its development are becoming more important for managers. This is because psychological contracts and union contracts, reflecting in part the prevailing environmental cultural values, have reduced the scope of acceptable use of formal or position power. Note that in personal power more than in any other base of power, it is the perception of the followers that determines the extent of a manager's personal power. Thus, in some cultures, within some organizations, the quiet leader may be most respected, in others the verbal and quick witted, and so on.

CONCLUSION

The theme of this chapter has been that the essence of organizational functioning is the exercise of influence, direct, semidirect, and indirect, of one individual or group on another. Appropriate managerial influence is that which seeks to affect the behavior of others toward organizational results. The successful accomplishment of influence requires an adequate amount of power in the face of others' receptivity. Power itself can and must be built up from a number of bases in organizations.

QUESTIONS FOR STUDY AND DISCUSSION

1. Make a list of three examples in your experience of each of the three types of influence described in Chapter 2. Which of these attempts were successful?

    For the unsuccessful ones, refer to the overview model to explain why you think they were unsuccessful.

2. Name two individuals with whom you interact in your current organization. Under each name list in order of importance the base of power which the individual has with respect to actual or potential attempts to influence your behavior.

    With reference to the bases of power described in Chapter 2, what other action could the two individuals take to build power in order to influence you?

3. For each of the individuals listed in question 2 list your own sources of power for influencing them. What other potential power could you build to influence them?

Chapter 3

UNMANAGED RESULTS AND NATURAL PROCESSES

Sometimes, things just don't work out . . . .

Henry Ford II
On announcing his firing of Bunkie Knudsen
from the presidency of Ford Motor Company.

In Chapters 1 and 2 we outlined the essential concepts to be used in this book. Our approach is to blend a managerial focus on results with a behavioral focus on understanding what leads to results. Thus far we have provided a descriptive overview model and a prescriptive treatment of influence processes. Basically, we have sketched out the elements of the model and types of influence as a framework for elaboration in subsequent chapters of the book.

One implication which could be drawn from what has been presented so far is that organizational results and human behavior leading to those results are largely predictable and controllable. A straightforward reading of the model and what can be done by managers might suggest that a manager who has power can influence people in such a way that desired goals are achieved. These implications are oversimplified, as any experienced manager will recognize immediately. Despite great effort at understanding, building power, and using it wisely, managers often find that things just do not work out.

In this chapter we shall reexamine our approach and some of the concepts of the first two chapters to suggest why things may go awry. Our purpose is to develop a richer understanding of ways alternative to ours for explaining organizational outcomes, and to suggest a sense of caution, care, and tolerance for ambiguity on the part of the manager with responsibility for results.

THE "CYCLE OF CHOICE" MODEL AND THE OVERVIEW MODEL

In their book, *Ambiguity and Choice in Organizations,* March and Olsen (1976) summarize the academic tradition of theories of individual choice by presenting a model referred to as the "complete cycle of choice." Their critique of the assumptions behind this model is the starting point for their presentation of a very different conceptualization intended to explain choice and organizational outcomes. In this section we shall present the cycle of choice model and their critique and compare both the model and the critique to the overview model in Chapter 1. As we shall see, the overview model can deal effectively with many of their criticisms of the cycle of choice model, but not with all of them.

The cycle of choice model

In the tradition of the rationalist, closed-system theorists of organizational behavior, organizational outcomes and organizational learning or adaptation are explained by a model consisting of four elements connected together. The model is reproduced in Figure 3–1.

FIGURE 3–1
The complete cycle of choice

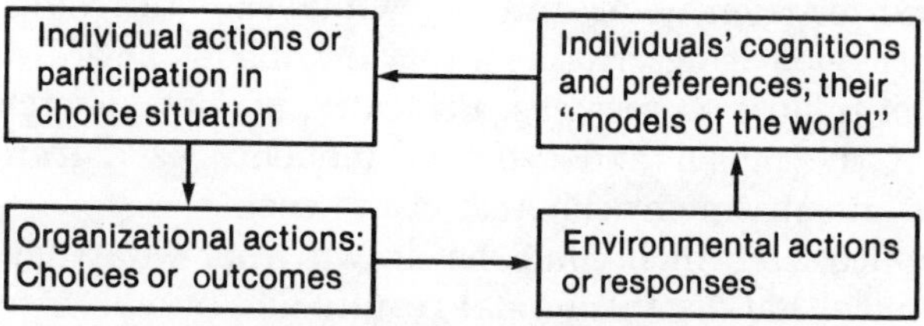

Source: J. G. March and J. P. Olsen, *Ambiguity and Choice in Organizations* (Bergen, Norway: Universitets Forlaget, 1976), p. 13.

With reference to this model, March and Olsen (1976, p. 13) state:

This conception of choice assumes a closed cycle of connections:

1. The cognitions and preferences held by individuals affect their behavior.

2. The behavior (including participation) of individuals affects organizational choices.
3. Organizational choices affect environmental acts (responses).
4. Environmental acts affect individual cognitions and preferences.

March and Olsen's critique of this model begins with an examination of the assumptions regarding the relationships among the elements, that is, with the arrows which connect each of them. They point out that empirically it can be observed that individuals' beliefs and preferences often in fact do not predict well their behavior, that organizational outcomes do not always follow from accumulated individual behavior, that relevant environmental responses to organizational outcomes often are unpredictable given only those outcomes, and that the state of cognitions and preferences varies widely from what one might expect given the environmental inputs. In part, March and Olsen argue, the weak relationships suggest that the four elements at best ought to be "loosely coupled" to take exogenous forces into account. In short, they point out that what goes on in organizations is much more ambiguous than the simple cause-effect relationships implied by the closed cycle of choice model.

The overview model revisited

The overview model presented in Chapter 1 closely resembles the closed cycle of choice which is the starting point for March and Olsen's critique of traditional theory. In Figure 3–2 we have redrawn the overview model such that its elements are arranged in the same way as March and Olsen's cycle of choice.

FIGURE 3–2
Adaptation of overview model to correspond to the cycle of choice

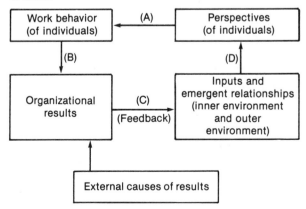

The similarities in the two models may be noted immediately. "Individual cognitions and preferences" corresponds to "individual perspective," "individual actions" corresponds to "behavior" and "organizational results," and "environmental actions" corresponds to the elements of "inputs" and "emergent relationships," all of which together make up the "environment" of the individual in the organization.

In our presentation and discussion of the overview model in Chapter 1, many of the weaknesses pointed out by March and Olsen in the cycle of choice model were accounted for. Let us take them one by one.

Regarding the connection between "perspective" and "behavior," we have argued that this is indeed a tight coupling, that every individual act of behavior (reflecting a "choice") is in fact predetermined by a state of that individual's perspective. In order for this to be valid, however, our definition of perspective has had to be much broader than "cognitions" and "preferences". Thus, in order to make the connection a simple cause and effect one, we deliberately broadened the definition of the cause. We have made perspective—a key concept in our model—a somewhat ambiguous concept. Perspective is defined as the state of an individual's assumptions, perceptions, and feelings which precedes any particular behavior.

Just how easy is it to know another's precise perspective, and thereby to predict his or her behavior? Very difficult indeed! As Sagan (1978) has pointed out, the total number of different combinations of circuits in the human brain is on the order of two raised to the power of ten to the thirteenth (10^{13}), or greater than the number of elementary particles (electrons, neutrons, etc.) *in the entire universe!* An important implication of this is that the manager attempting to predict behavior from perspective will be right only part of the time, given the difficulty of knowing another's perspective exactly and given the almost infinite number of states which a perspective can be in. Therefore, the manager assessing individuals' perspectives as a prelude to prediction or influence must recognize the probabilistic and changeable nature of perspectives and should strive to improve his batting average in anticipating behavior rather than attempt to get it right every time.

Regarding the connection between behavior and organizational results (arrow B in Figures 3–1 and 3–2), it will be noted that the overview model includes an input from the external environment. This has been described in Chapter 1 as a caution against the assumption that it is only the behavior of organizational members which affects results: some outcomes will be affected by the actions of customers or managers in other departments more than by one's own department. Beyond this, the March and Olsen critique can serve well to point out the complicated relationship between individual behavior and organizational outcomes. For one thing, not all individuals have an equal impact on the outcomes, so the net effect is not the simple summation of separate individual behaviors. This is a warning to the manager to *weigh* the various individuals in terms of their relative importance in achieving coordinated outcomes. Thus, for example, if all the members of a production department are performing well in producing widgets, productivity can still be affected by the absence of the shipping clerk, or by the inventory level of boxes into which the widgets are packed. Another way of putting this is in terms of influence and control of resources: an assessment of outcomes from individual behavior at work requires that the manager understand the relative influence of individuals over the outcome in question. The implication is that if possible the manager in turn should work to gain power over that particular individual or function.

An illustration of the problems of predictability of the behavior of others is the case of Bunkie Knudsen at Ford, described in the case at the end of this chapter. For his part, Knudsen's perspective on on becoming president of Ford appears to have been based on the same kinds of assumptions that had served him well as a division head at GM. He was working hard and believed positive results would follow. His sudden and surprising firing by Henry Ford would certainly suggest that unpredictable forces and processes were at work in his environment. From his perspective, a "rational" model of cause and effect was inadequate. At the time of his firing he might well have agreed with March and Olsen as to the essentially unpredictable and even idiosyncratic nature of organizational behavior.

But is the basic model really invalid in Knudsen's case? Our argument with some of the March and Olsen criticism of traditional models is that as a *practical* tool those models should not be taken as rigid cause-and-effect predictions. The user of the models must think carefully about all the assumptions that go into the boxes. Thus, Knudsen's view of how Ford operated did not adequately take into account the different inputs there compared to GM. These included, in particular, the power of the emergent group around Lee Iacocca (one of Ford's executive vice presidents) and the role and perspective of Mr. Ford. Having broadened and complicated his perspective, Knudsen may have been able to change his behavior in such a way that he influenced Iacocca, Ford, and others more positively. Of course, no amount of knowledge on his part could deal with all the eventualities. At the very least, a richer perspective by Knudsen would have reduced surprise and helped him take action to prepare for the worst.

Another complication arising from the relationship between individual behavior and organizational outcomes is the problem of coordinating or timing the work behavior of separate individuals. Even when the widget production department is working well and shipping and inventory are doing their job, the result necessary to meet some standard or goal may fall short if things do not happen in a fairly precise sequence. Clearly, the manager must exercise influence toward the structuring of organizational inputs which take this sequencing into account; in short, the manager must plan for the coordination of work behavior.

The relationship between organizational outcomes and environmental response, shown in our overview model as feedback loops and in Figure 3–2 as arrow C, is pointed out by March and Olsen to be too "organization centered." That is, the cycle model relationship paints too simplistic a picture of the organization as being the primary affect on environmental response. In the overview model we take this into account in part by showing the external environment as an input, in addition to the feedback loops (see Chapter 1, Figure 1–5). Indeed, it is at this point that the overview model takes into account an open systems view of organizations. As an open system, the elements within the organization are subject to change by forces outside the control of the individuals and managers within the organization. Clearly, such a source of ambiguity can be significant to the point of negating the usefulness of any simplified model. On the other hand, our purpose has been deliberately to simplify the world by means of an overview model which can be used as a starting point for a managerial perspective. All models, by definition, oversimplify reality. The caution to the manager is not to take the model as reality.

The greatest disparity between our overview model and the cycle of choice is contained in the "environment" box (Figure 3–1). In the simplified cycle model, environment refers to all those elements external to the individual perspective. In the overview model, the complications which March and Olsen describe as arising from mixed signals are accounted for to a large extent by the *several* elements external to the individual which affect his or her perspective. (Arrow D in Figure 3–2.) As we have defined perspective, it is the net result of forces and information acting on individuals. It is, in effect, more than cognitions based on perceptions of information. It also includes the feelings arising from individual personality and from the individual being a member of a social system of human relationships as well as from the individual being something of a "rational" information processor. In other words, we take an individual's perspective at any point in time to be the net resultant of personality, social forces, retained myths and quirks, and rational information processing. In an academic sense, the traditions behind the overview model include psychological, social, and cultural research as well as the rational choice models emphasized by March and Olsen.

On the whole then, we have seen that the overview model is both an adaptation of the traditional closed cycle choice model and a somewhat richer vehicle for explaining organizational results. The elaborations of the overview model which distinguish it from the cycle of choice also make it necessarily more complicated and more difficult to use than a purely closed system model. Managerial interpretation and inference are needed to identify the particular states of any given element at any point in time; judgment, experience, and intuition are needed. Indeed, one might say *luck* is needed for predictions to be accurate and for attempts at influence to be successful.

At the same time, the constructive side of the March and Olsen argument bears looking at, and its implications for the overview model as a descriptive metaphor (rather than a rigid guide) for organizational functioning needs to be elaborated.

THE PROCESS APPROACH TO ORGANIZATIONAL BEHAVIOR

Instead of looking first at structural elements or states as a model of organization and then at process as what happens between those elements, March and Olsen propose a model of organizations which *begins* with organizational processes. They continue to focus on individual and organizational choice (behavior) as the key events that occur, but propose thinking of such choice events themselves as ongoing needs or opportunities for choices to be made. "Choice opportunities" is thus one *stream of process* in their model. There are three other streams: problems, solutions, and participants. Each of these is seen as ongoing processes with characteristics of their own which may or may not be closely connected. An organization then becomes the channel through which these streams flow, and organizational outcomes are the result of planned *and unplanned* confluence of the streams. In their words:

> An organization is a set of procedures for argumentation and interpretation as well as for solving problems and making decisions. A choice situation is a meeting place for issues and feelings looking for decision situations in which they may be aired, solutions looking for issues to which they may be an answer, and participants looking for problems or pleasure. (March and Olsen, 1976, p. 25)

> What happens in the situation of interest to a student of choice depends on how that situation (and the participants in it) fit into a mosaic of simultaneous performances involving other individuals, other places, other concerns, and the phasing of other events. *What happens is the*

almost fortuitous result of the intermeshing of loosely-coupled processes.
(Emphasis added) (Ibid., p. 26)

The essentially separate running of the four processes over time and the haphazard nature of the confluence of the streams at any point in time has led March and Olsen to refer to their process model as a "garbage can" model. A specific choice opportunity is like a garbage can which at any moment will have in it the particular mix of participants with their various perspectives, problems which each participant sees as important (including problems of a personal nature as well as organizational problems), and the various solutions available and looking for problems to solve. Obviously, the likelihood is very low that there will be a perfect mix of the four when a given choice opportunity arises, a mix which would lead to an optimum solution to the problem at hand.

Diagramatically, we have characterized the March and Olsen approach with the diagram in Figure 3–3. The organization is shown as a

FIGURE 3–3
Schematic of the March and Olsen process approach

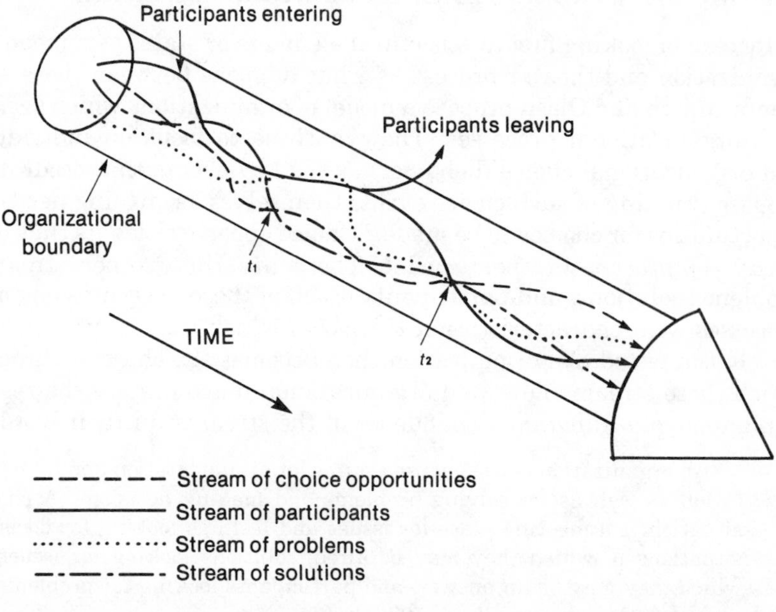

————— Stream of choice opportunities
——————— Stream of participants
·············· Stream of problems
—·——·—— Stream of solutions

hollow tube bounding the four streams as they flow over time. Participants enter and leave from time to time. It should be understood that the nature of *all* the streams change as well. Where two or more streams intersect may be thought of as a confluence of those particular processes conducive to some managerial goal. Thus, at point *t*, there is a good mix of participants, whose points of view lead to agreement on key problems, and there are solutions available that could solve the problems. However, there is no confluence of opportunity to make a choice; that is, in this instance, there is no call for or consensus that anything needs to be done with respect to those problems. Such a situation might be illustrated, for example, by a lack of communication among managers about their joint problems, or by top management not perceiving the need to act. Action may occur at point t, and some result come out, but it will not address the problems suited to the opportunity for action which is best at that time.

At point t_2 in the diagram, an unusual confluence of all streams has occurred. By pure chance, an organizational choice or behavior will be appropriate in the perspective of all relevant participants, given their joint definition of the organization's need at that time.

Unmanaged processes

We may think of a process approach to understanding how organizations function as an alternative to our overview model in two respects. First, process comes before structure and before the recognition of managed processes. In this respect, the approach we have taken puts structures first and then specifies management processes as operating through the structural elements of the overview model. Second, however, because the processes are essentially descriptive and do not include prescriptive or normative elements, we may characterize them as natural processes or "unmanaged" processes, to distinguish them from the processes of managerial influence.

An example of how an unmanaged process model fits reality may be seen from the example of the difficulties facing the plant manager described in Chapter 1. Rather suddenly a series of events occurred. These were a decline in output, drop in quality, increase in union grievances, increased turnover, conflict between the production and quality control departments, and a call from the boss requesting that the plant take on more production. To the plant manager at that time, these events had only slight and dimly understood connections. They were in fact manifestations of natural, largely unmanaged processes. In order to understand them, the manager worked with an experienced outside organizational consultant who conducted several interviews at all levels in the plant. The analysis which was developed was characterized by a historical view of events in the plant. In particular, the long period of conflict between production and quality control was traced back to the men who headed each department being rivals for the affection of one of the women working in quality control. Moreover, it appeared that much of the internal problems in the plant were the result of the plant manager having replaced a very popular predecessor only two months before. Indeed, it appeared that even the boss's phone call could be interpreted as a test of the new plant manager's strength in arguing against superior's demands, a practice which appeared to have ample precedent and acceptance as a norm in that company.

Thus, an adequate understanding of the plant manager's situation necessarily included a description of the processes that led up to recent events that affected the plant manager's results. Having understood matters a bit more in this light, the plant manager might well have been tempted to throw up his hands and bemoan the fates of unpredictability. He might well have seen himself being carried along in the turbulent organizational tube illustrated in Figure 3–3, and have chosen simply to wait for a propitious confluence in the process of which he was only a part. Had he done so he would have made the step between using a descriptive model for understanding and being seduced into limited or no action implied by a purely descriptive model, particularly a purely process model.

We shall return to the situation as it actually unfolded for this plant manager, but for the moment let us continue to develop a linkage between the March and Olsen model and our overview model.

The March and Olsen process approach is focused on the organizational level, as opposed to a broader macro level or an individual micro level. Examples of these additional natural process views should be kept in mind. An example of the macro view is that of Greiner (1976), who sees organizations as undergoing predictable phases or change over long periods of time. These phases alternate between periods of relative calm or evolution and briefer events or revolution. A similar view for the EDP function is given in Gibson and Nolan (1974). Of interest here is the fact that these long-range views imply certain inherent patterns within organizations, with growth and change following in part essentially natural and immutable laws of development. It is not claimed that these approaches explain all the variance in organizational outcomes. Rather, their utility lies in the fact that they provide long-term gross predictability and create constraints on efforts to manage. They are analogous to biological growth curves, to learning curves for organizations as a whole, and to the perspective of the individual as living through somewhat predictable stages in life.

The importance of the process view of organizations lies in the implication of there being more or less natural flows over time which have a kind of vigor and life of their own, which arise from individual motivation (people inputs), and which are sustained by the energy people bring with them to work every day. One utility of the process approach is to remind management of the potentially changeable nature of static elements and structures: modifications of elements "always" occur to some degree without management influence.

Another important implication is to recognize that management processes, particularly indirect and semidirect influences, are being imposed on an existing system which is essentially dynamic and flowing. The imposition of a change in formal structure may or may not be compatible with the streams at that time, either for individuals or for the achievement of results.

Indeed, some argue that the problem with many organizations is that they are *too* managed and that natural processes ought to be given more free reign. The benefit for organizational results would be greater employee satisfaction and organizational adaptability to change. An enticing exponent of this view is Weick (1977). As we have suggested in Chapter 1, these particular results criteria are important but are only two of five. The problem for management is to balance these needs, which may well call for less managerial control, against the typically more short-run needs for efficiency, effectiveness, and ability to acquire resources. Moreover, managerial behavior which permits natural processes to go unmanaged is still managerial influence by our meaning of that process. While a manager may choose to give up control in some particular situation, he or she is still exercising influence. The essence of management is influence, not necessarily managerial control.

An important conceptual similarity between the March and Olsen approach and our own is that at the outset both approaches attempt to provide a descriptive model. Beyond that, however, our approach adds *management* processes (influence) to the largely static overview model to provide a prescriptive approach.

In their book, March and Olsen do not carry their descriptive theory to the point of prescription or direct advice for managing organizations. They do recognize the need for managers to *act* on the knowledge of descriptive theory as well as to *understand* it:

> We would argue that there is a large class of significant situations within organizations in which the preconditions of the garbage can process probably cannot be eliminated. Indeed in some they should not be eliminated. The great advantage of trying to see garbage can phenomena together as a process is the possibility that the process can be understood, that organization design and decision-making can take account of its existence and that, to some extent, it can be managed. (March and Olsen, 1976, p. 37)

In the remainder of this chapter we shall suggest how theories of natural processes may be taken into account by elaboration of our overview model.

THE OVERVIEW MODEL IN A PROCESS FRAMEWORK

Given the importance of the unmanaged natural process approach as something which managers need to take into account, and the fact that our overview model and prescriptive processes of managerial influence have not taken them into account, it remains for us here to incorporate that approach.

The multistatic overview model

One may think of the static overview model of Chapter 1 as analogous to a blueprint, such as for an oil refinery, or as a photographic snapshot of an organization at one point in time. Like a blueprint, it shows the general elements and concepts, analogous to tanks and pipes, connected to each other. It provides no *specific* description of what is the state of what is in any particular organization at any one time. When such specific assessments are made, such as might be done by management or consultants, we add the pressure, temperature, and volumes of the vessels, that is, the *type* of formal structure, *nature* of emergent systems norms, and so on. When that is done for a given point in time, we have a snapshot of the specific state of the entire organizational system.

But a specific snapshot of a system shows at best what is connected to what, or what things upstream determine the state and nature of things downstream. It is a static view, and it will not show the previous state or the next state of any particular aspect of the system. To do this we need a sequence of snapshots taken over time intervals. Just as a family photo album can show the growth and change of people over time, sequential diagnostic static descriptions of organizations can show that the state of upstream variables at one time resulted in a change in state downstream at a later time. This is illustrated by the multistatic diagram in Figure 3–4.

Imagine, for example, an organization which has demotivated and dissatisfied employees under a highly centralized organizational structure and tight control system. Top management decides at a certain time to reorganize to a decentralized divisional structure and simultaneously introduces true management by objectives, management education programs, and active efforts at all levels to get people to understand and use the new systems. At the time of introduction a diagnosis of the state of the system would show the old poor results and the new decentralized systems and supportive activities occurring at the same time. It is only by looking at a state of the system later, perhaps as much as several years later for large organizations, that the effects of the change on behavior and outcomes can be adequately assessed.

One example of the state of an organization's results is that which is

FIGURE 3–4
Multistatic diagram showing sequence of change in elements of overview model resulting from a change in inputs*

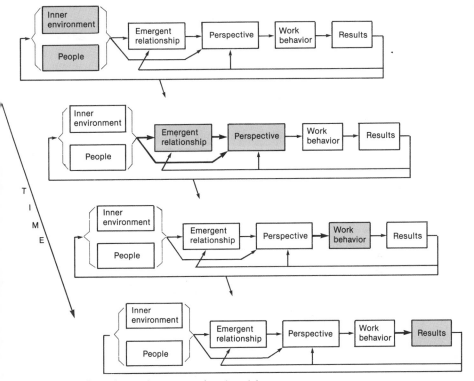

* For simplicity, effects of external environment have been left out.

taken annually and reflected in its financial statements. Of course, a multiple sequence of such static descriptions can be deceptive and incomplete. It is still basically a static look. A company could have a huge balloon payment of debt principal due January 1st. The balance sheet of December 31st would not in itself show the impending impact of this without the addition of explanatory notes. A firm which has just had a wildcat strike in three of its four plants might reflect in a description of its results an apparently inexplicable decline in performance unless there were additional explanations of what took place between periodic assessments of its organizational state.

Beyond this problem lies another limitation of static and multistatic views of organization. That is that they do not reflect the natural processes discussed above. These processes help explain what happens as one state leads to another, or precisely how a change in one variable among the inputs affects and interacts with an ongoing emergent sys-

FIGURE 3–5
Natural/unmanaged processes in conjunction with the overview model over time

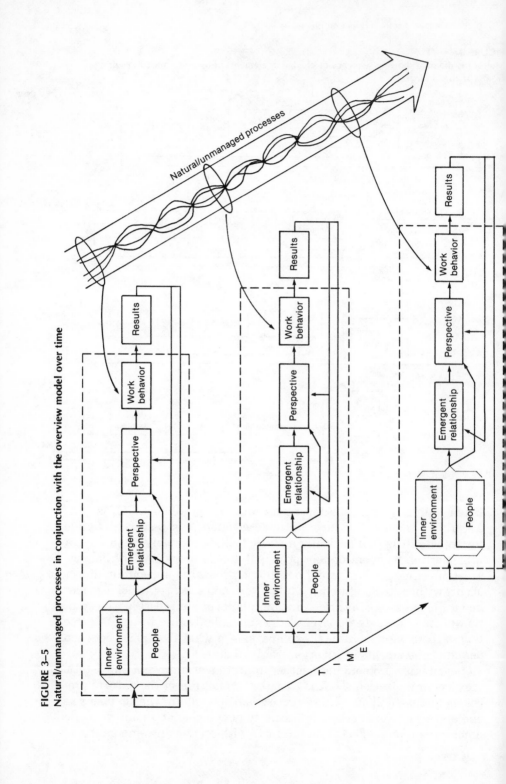

tem. To understand this we need to recognize that most of the parts of our overview model have a natural dynamism, sets of *internal* forces producing change and resisting change quite apart from deliberate influence attempts by management. It is the interplay, the mixing and interaction of natural or unmanaged processes, feedback processes, and managed processes which affect changes in organizational states. Our basically static overview model could take this into account by emphasizing the connecting arrows and feedback loops between the several conceptual boxes, inasmuch as the arrows suggest flows of energy and information which constitute forces affecting each element.

Let us use the connecting arrows and external environmental inputs in the overview model to represent the largely observable and manageable relationships. For the natural, unmanaged processes we shall connect the multistatic overview model by a heavy arrow of processes over time, representing effects on results that are beyond control at any point in time, and which affect elements in the overview model. This combination of models is illustrated in Figure 3–5. Here our static elements and our connecting causal arrows and feedback loops are indicated as cross sections within a thick natural unmanaged process arrow.

As an illustration of how these two models fit together usefully, let us return to the illustration of the plant manager whose crisis situation was described in Chapter 1 and earlier in this chapter. With the guidelines of a historical process framework, the plant manager and an outside consultant were able to understand the forces that led to the crisis situation. Both realized that this understanding was only useful as a basis for action, inasmuch as it was the plant manager's responsibility to gain control of the situation. It was at this point that they conducted an exercise in analysis of the static situation at that time. The consultant talked through the overview model as it pertained to each key subordinate and department. The emphasis was on the perspective of individuals and groups and on the elements of the model which could be influenced by the plant manager to change perspectives. It was recognized that the unmanaged processes had been allowed to run for so long that perspectives were focused on nonproductive personal vendettas and conflict rather than on useful organizational results.

In particular it was found that a strong emergent system, a clique, had built up under the production manager. The norms and values of its members, the production manager and five production supervisors, included a tough antiunion bias and a fierce pride in being harsh.

The plant manager sensed that his power was limited with respect to the production manager. He was concerned that if he fired this manager all the supervisors would quit, making a bad situation worse and very likely leading to his own firing.

The plant manager decided to try a long-term approach to change the emergent group by bringing in two additional supervisors from another plant of the company who were available. He was able to do this within his budget because the existing staff was short by two unfilled slots. Within two months, however, both these supervisors resigned.

Recognizing that a certain equilibrium had developed between production supervision and the union employees, at least up to the present crisis, the plant manager decided to attack first the immediate problem of conflict between the production department and quality control. On a Friday afternoon he informed the production manager and the quality control manager that he was considering having the latter report to the former, and that he expected each to bury their interpersonal differences. On the following Monday the wife of the production manager called to tell the plant manager that Sunday afternoon her husband had suffered a heart attack and would be out of work for at least six weeks.

At this point the reader should think through these events in terms of the overview model, the influence exercised by the plant manager, and the unmanaged processes at play in this rather serious situation. Quite clearly, a full understanding of the plant manager's plight requires that all these frameworks be used. He needed to understand the situation in terms of unmanaged forces and to recognize the inherent risk in taking any action. Nevertheless action was called for and had to be based on judgments of his power weighed against opposing forces out of his control. In fact his actions up to that point were not only unsuccessful but appeared to have been a partial cause of tragic personal damage to one of his own managers, an event singularly unpredictable.

As it turned out, the absence of the production manager was the beginning of improvement. His recuperation lasted ten weeks. During that time the plant manager directly managed production and imposed a very different style on the supervisory group. Two of them quit and were replaced by managers of the plant manager's choice. When the production manager returned, under medical advice to take it easy, the plant manager worked closely with him and was able to improve working relationships and, eventually, plant results.

CONCLUSION

Imbedded in this chapter and the first two chapters of this book are two explanations for why things often do not work out for managers.

The first of these is that managers do not use some model or theory for helping them understand and act with respect to people in organizations. It is an error of omission. In these instances actions are based exclusively on intuition. To alleviate this we have offered the overview model, the notions of influence and power and the idea of unmanaged processes within which a manager can function.

The second explanation is that managers may take their models *too* seriously. It is an error of commission. In this instance the manager expects an airtight explanation, counts on predictability of behavior, and ignores intuition in favor of systematic thought. No model of human behavior is valid enough or strong enough to stand up under these pressures.

In this chapter, we have attempted to relax somewhat the rationalistic, cause-effect tone of the first two chapters. The overview model should be thought of as a rough guide, a checklist, and a source of vocabulary. It is a metaphor for managers rather than a straight jacket. Neither this nor any other model can lead to 100 percent predictability of behavior.

The context which led to this modified view of our approach was the March and Olsen critique of traditional theory of choice, and particularly the assumptions of a closed system with full cause and effect. In its stead, they proposed a process model. We have argued that the overview model, given its somewhat imprecise definitions, and its recognition of complexity from environmental forces, meets many of the limitations of their closed cycle of choice model.

Nevertheless, we have also suggested that the alternative explanatory theory of March and Olsen, and others, can provide some substantive modifications to our model. They remind us that things change over time. A multistatic enhancement of the overview model was presented to take into account the fact that management influence at one point in time shows up in results only later. We adopt the approach that organizational results can best be described by a multistatic, open-system model with suggestive (rather than precise) definitions of elements, combined with managerial influence processes acting through the elements. Nevertheless, to explain the variance in results and the limitations of management, a combination of knowledge of natural processes and a managed organizational system over time is worth keeping in mind.

On a dimension of being descriptive versus being prescriptive or normative we deliberately lean in this book toward the normative end. Managers need to understand enough about the causes of results from descriptive theory to enable them to take effective action. We believe that to date there is little indication that an elaborate and complex description of natural and unmanaged organizational processes will, in and of itself, help the manager to know *what to do* about those processes to affect results.

As a normative matter, the manager should attempt to bring unmanaged processes under his or her control, but also to recognize and allow for the inevitable effects of those forces which cannot be managed. In an effort to improve understanding and the batting averages of managers in achieving results we offer, in the subsequent parts of the book, closer looks at major elements of the overview model and managerial implications of those examinations.

QUESTIONS FOR STUDY AND DISCUSSION

1. Can you describe a work situation in which there are "solutions looking for problems to which they may be the answer?"

2. What results criteria (see Chapter 1) are potentially beneficially affected by giving free rein to "natural" processes? How does this type of management fit in with the book's definition of management?

3. As a manager, what difference would the use of the overview model as opposed to the open-process model make to the way you performed your job?

4. Make notes on an organizational event you are familiar with that was unsuccessful. To what extent was this due to processes which were ongoing in the organization and which were not controlled by management?

   In what ways could management have prevented the failure by attention to these processes and through the use of systematic analysis and action? Be specific in this.

Case 3–1
The Ford-Knudsen case

In September 1969, the news broke that Semon E. Knudsen had been dismissed without notice from his position as president of the Ford Motor Company. Only 19 months earlier Mr. Knudsen, after resigning from General Motors, had accepted the presidency of the Ford company at the request of Henry Ford II.

Some observers saw the dismissal as the result of "a personality conflict" or a rivalry situation. Others were inclined to the view that Mr. Knudsen was ousted as the consequence of the combined efforts of younger executives working behind the scenes to advance the candidacy of Lee Iacocca for the top position under Mr. Ford. The episode may be seen as the outcome of a number of variables interacting in fairly predictable ways within an organizational system. Readers may debate the possibility of different outcomes if either Mr. Ford or Mr. Knudsen had foreseen the likelihood of disruptive consequences and had made special efforts to avoid them.

This case consists of extensive excerpts from news magazines and printed media. The first four excerpts are news and discussion of the dismissal. The next six are background material, mostly published before 1969. The case ends with a postscript, an article on the dismissal of Iacocca from Ford in 1978.

FORD DISMISSES KNUDSEN AS COMPANY'S PRESIDENT[1]

DETROIT, September 11—Semon E. Knudsen, who quit the General Motors Corporation 19 months ago to become the president of the Ford Motor Company, has been dismissed, Henry Ford 2d, the company's chairman, said today.

"Sometimes things don't work out," Mr. Ford said at a news conference today, but he refused to give any specific reasons for the dismissal of the president of the world's second largest automobile manufacturer.

Mr. Knudsen, 56 years old, also said he could not understand the reasons. But it is believed the strong-willed president, nicknamed "Bunkie," irritated lesser Ford executives, and, in turn, Mr. Ford, by running the company with a strong hand. The ouster is considered in Detroit as a victory for the home-grown Ford men, particularly Lee Iacocca, another strong man at the company, over an outsider.

---

[1] *The New York Times*, September 12, 1969. © 1969 The New York Times Company. Reproduced by special permission.

Disputes in past

Sources within Ford said there had been disputes between the two in the past and that Mr. Iacocca, an executive vice president, was winning some of these. The 44-year-old vice president, with sideburns down to his earlobes matching Mr. Ford's, appeared to have a hard time containing a grin—in fact, he could not contain it—as he sat with Mr. Ford and other sober-faced executives at a news conference in the Ford headquarters building in Dearborn, outside Detroit.

When a reporter asked Mr. Iacocca if he was sad to see Mr. Knudsen go, the dark-haired executive said, "I never said no comment to the press yet but I'll say no comment now."

The Knudsen name is closely tied to the automobile world and Ford. William ("Big Bill") Knudsen, Bunkie's father, was forced out of Ford in 1921 by the first Henry Ford. The late Mr. Knudsen then went to GM and headed the Chevrolet Motor division triumphing over Ford in the automobile market and rising to the presidency of GM.

His son also headed Chevrolet and was a GM executive vice president and the fourth-ranking executive at the world's largest manufacturer. But he quit early in 1968 after being bypassed for the top job at GM. Mr. Ford, the grandson of old Henry, made his old Detroit friend Ford president on Feb. 6.

When he hired Mr. Knudsen, Mr. Ford said that "the flow of history is reversed," meaning that a Knudsen was coming back to Ford—but instead history was just repeating itself.

The actual dismissal came on September 2. Mr. Ford walked into Mr. Knudsen's office and told him he was through at Ford, both men said today. But the news was kept secret until today, when the Ford board of directors met to confirm it.

Mr. Knudsen, defending his reputation, said: "During the time that I was at the Ford Motor Company Mr. Ford concurred with every important decision I made. Working as an executive team, we materially improved the condition of the company. He never indicated to me any dissatisfaction with my services or the direction the company was taking."

"I would be leaving"

On September 2, Mr. Ford just "walked into my office and informed me that I would be leaving; his explanation was that things had not worked out as he had hoped," Mr. Knudsen said at his news conference today, held in the Sheraton-Cadillac Hotel in downtown Detroit.

The former Ford president added: "In all fairness to my reputation and my family, I want to make clear that today's decision, in my opinion, is unwarranted, in view of the accomplishments the company has made during my brief tenure. Further, it is completely inconsistent with what Mr. Ford said to me at the time I was offered the presidency."

Mr. Knudsen, who is a millionaire, has a five-year $200,000-a-year contract with Ford and he said he had expected to be there ten years.

Mr. Knudsen said Mr. Ford "wished to be relieved of daily operating responsibilities."

Mr. Knudsen admitted he had some "difference of opinion" with Mr. Iacocca when he came to Ford a year and a half ago, but he said he thought these had been worked out.

"If I knew I was going to be there only 19 months, I certainly wouldn't have come," he said while denying he was bitter. But he also admitted that among some of his plans for Ford there were some "I had not discussed with Mr. Ford."

Phrase is repeated

Mr. Ford, in turn, kept repeating the phrase, "Sometimes these things don't work out." He denied there was any personality conflict or that Mr. Knudsen had taken too much power or that any Ford executives had threatened to leave if Mr. Knudsen stayed. But Mr. Ford indicated some had come to him with complaints about Mr. Knudsen.

Mr. Ford said he "talks to lots of people all the time" and the Knudsen dismissal "had a lot of input from a lot of people."

The ouster triggered a management shake-up at Ford. Mr. Ford remains chairman and chief executive officer; there will be no new president. Instead, Mr. Iacocca, who fathered the popular Mustang car five years ago and is the general architect of Ford's order of battle in the automobile war, retains his title of executive vice president but adds the title of President—Ford North American Automotive Operations.

New titles given

Robert Stevenson, who headed foreign operations, which Mr. Knudsen also was changing, gets the title of President—Ford International Automotive Operations. Robert J. Hampson, a vice president, gets the title President—Philco-Ford and Tractor Operations.

When Mr. Knudsen first came to Ford there was some feeling, even within the company, that a strong hand was needed. But in recent months Ford executives have grumbled about the strong hand that went into styling, into engineering, and into foreign operations. Mr. Knudsen also was reported to be more interested in pushing high-powered "super cars" of racing vehicles than Mr. Iacocca.

"I've been around for 30 years. Have you ever heard about my inability to get along with people?" Mr. Knudsen asked a reporter.

The dismissal comes just as Ford fortunes in the automobile market appeared to be turning upward. The company's new Maverick car is a good seller and Ford could catch up with Chevrolet, the nation's best-selling car line, in the coming model year because Chevrolet has no such car yet.

*   *   *   *   *

BUNKIE'S DOWNFALL[2]

Palace Revolt Forced Henry Ford to Remove Knudsen as President

Newcomer's Moves to Restyle 1972 Autos Brought Clash with Iacocca and Others

Old Hands Get Henry's Ear

DETROIT—Nineteen months ago, when Henry Ford hired Semon E. (Bunkie) Knudsen from rival General Motors Corp. and made him president of Ford Motor Co., Mr. Ford was credited with a brilliant corporate coup.

Now with Mr. Knudsen unceremoniously dumped, an industry veteran calls the Knudsen appointment "Henry's biggest mistake since the Edsel."

What happened in the interim?

The ill-concealed satisfaction of Lee A. Iacocca, one of Ford's executive vice presidents, at Mr. Knudsen's demise, shows that Mr. Knudsen stirred deep enmity within the Ford hierarchy. Talks with dozens of Ford officials, former Ford employees and informed outsiders show that Mr. Knudsen, a strong-willed executive, indeed did bruise some big and powerful egos within the company.

The fiefdoms

But the Knudsen episode reveals more than that. It emerges as a classic demonstration of what can happen when an outsider is placed at the helm of a vast, established organization with power centers jealously guarded by men who have spent their professional lives developing them.

These men, the ambitious "comers" in high executive ranks, also had developed intricate relationships with one another, with Mr. Iacocca most frequently mentioned as a possible future president.

---

[2] *The Wall Street Journal*, September 17, 1969. Reproduced by permission of the publisher.

When Mr. Knudsen appeared, says a top Ford executive, "The hard-chargers felt they had experienced a ten-year delay in their master plan."

The climactic battle between Mr. Knudsen and the old hands took place over crucial decisions on styling. The 1972 line was in the offing, and big questions had to be answered: How to style the cars, what prices to charge and how much money to spend in the effort.

"These are highly subjective decisions," says a Ford official. And here Bunkie ran head on into Mr. Iacocca, a cigar-chomping dynamo responsible for Ford's two great successes of recent years, the Mustang and the Maverick. Mr. Iacocca had private words with Mr. Ford about Mr. Knudsen, and rumor has it that he also aired his grievances at the July meeting of the Ford directors (Mr. Iacocca is a member of the board).

Mr. Ford has acknowledged that the decision to fire Mr. Knudsen was an "emotional" one. Indeed, he has been forced to renege on one of his own most important decisions, hiring Bunkie. But in early 1968 it seemed like an intelligent move.

Nagging problems

Ford was just regaining momentum after the longest and most costly strike in the company's history. The Philco-Ford appliance and defense contracting subsidiary had posted another losing year. European operations, especially in Germany, were lagging. The Taunus, a new model for European markets, hadn't excited buyers.

More than that, there was a mounting restlessness within the Ford organization over the seemingly perennial "poor second" relationship to GM. For years Ford had been trying without notable success to break GM's grip on the market for cars in the upper-middle price range (about $3,500 to $5,000), where profits are big. Moreover, Chrysler Corp. was offering Ford serious competition for the first time in a decade.

For Mr. Ford there was a personal motive. He seemed to be getting itchy after concentrating on the company's affairs for two decades. The Detroit riot of 1967 had turned his interests to social problems and the urban crisis in particular. Lyndon Johnson was asking him to take charge of the National Alliance of Businessmen, and there were rumors that he was a candidate for an eventual Cabinet post or a key ambassadorship.

Such prospects posed high-level problems at Ford. Over the years Mr. Ford had developed a management system that gave much autonomy to the operational executives, checked them through staff review and kept the veto power in his hands. The president, financially oriented Arjay Miller, hadn't been deeply involved in day-to-day affairs in the various operations.

Time was ripe

The time seemed ripe for bringing in a topnotch outsider. None of Ford's three executive vice presidents had experience in all of the company's problem areas, and elevating one would distress the others. Then Mr. Ford had a windfall. He heard that Mr. Knudsen, an executive vice president at GM, was upset at being passed over for the GM presidency and was about to quit the auto giant.

Mr. Knudsen seemed perfect for the Ford job. He is the son of a former GM president and had enormous prestige within the industry. He had established himself as a respected professional, rolling up successes as head of GM's Pontiac division, then as chief of Chevrolet and later moving to head GM's overseas operations, its appliance and other nonauto business and its defense programs, in that order. He was knowledgeable in all of Ford's problem areas.

President Knudsen got off to a smooth start, inspecting the facilities and familiarizing himself with the various operations. At first, he didn't seem like the kind of executive who would arouse powerful antagonism. "We looked for heads to roll," says one Ford official, "but they didn't." Comments another Ford executive: "We expected him to shake the organization to its teeth. He never did it."

On the other hand, he did attack one prominent problem, Philco-Ford, and in the process prompted some departures by executives. He brought in Robert Hunter, an old GM associate, to run the subsidiary and accepted the resignation of the old boss. Some other Philco-Ford men also left, but not many.

In time, some of Mr. Knudsen's other actions began to alienate people. As an activist with little respect for conventional organizational structure, he got deeply involved in operations that customarily had gotten only periodic review from the president and his staff.

Mr. Knudsen began to bear down on Ford's overseas problems, with particular reference to the troubles of the Ford Taunus and the success of GM's Opel in the European market. Robert Stevenson, executive vice president in charge of overseas activities, found himself under the gun.

"I think Steve thought he was going to be scrapped," says one company executive. "Bunkie was leaning on him pretty hard. Steve would take trips abroad every time it happened (to get out of the line of fire)." Informed sources say Mr. Knudsen was especially bearish about Ford's plans for the Capri, a sporty, cut-down version of the Mustang to be sold abroad. "He was predicting the Capri would be a failure," says one official.

But it was Mr. Knudsen's interest in styling and engineering that triggered the most resentment—and put him into conflict with Mr. Iacocca. If others were cowed by Mr. Knudsen's credentials and authority, Mr. Iacocca wasn't; he, in fact, was used to taking orders only from Henry Ford.

Messrs. Iacocca and Knudsen had tangled before, when Mr. Iacocca was in charge of the Ford division and Mr. Knudsen ran GM's competing Chevrolet division. Although Chevrolet maintained its sales leadership, Ford scored an impressive end run with the Mustang, a car that gave Ford the edge in a growing, profitable market.

With the Ford presidency in his grasp, Mr. Knudsen now had the initiative. He put his personal stamp on the 1970 models, even though they were pretty well "locked up," when he ordered an expensive last-minute change on the Thunderbird. He cut five inches from the front end, gave the car a pronounced snout similar to the Pontiac and redesigned the taillights. Mr. Iacocca, who had approved of the earlier version of the car, stood mute throughout the revisions.

On the 1971 models, Mr. Knudsen had the opportunity to dictate extensive sheet-metal changes—and did. "He played a dominant hand," recalls a Ford stylist. Mr. Iacocca became steadily more annoyed. "Lee resented Bunkie telling him how to style cars," says one Ford executive.

Feuding in the styling center led to a bizarre situation, say insiders. Mr. Knudsen would make his rounds—the "dawn patrols"—early in the morning. Mr. Iacocca would follow along the same route, questioning decisions made earlier. "They were literally redoing each other's work" says one source in the Ford styling staff. The design center staff members began to protect their own positions. "They were showing Knudsen things they weren't showing Iacocca, and the other way around," says the styling man.

Morale plunged. "There was a feeling of animosity," says one executive. "People spent more time worrying about the other guy than about their own jobs. It got to the verge of a palace revolt. There were personality conflicts among the top men—some imagined, some real. Bunkie tried to overcome them, but by then it was too late."

The tide started to turn against Mr. Knudsen. Mr. Ford quit his job as head of the National Alliance of Businessmen and began spending more time at Ford's Dearborn headquarters. Unhappy executives found it easier to get his ear than previously.

Programs planned before Mr. Knudsen's arrival began to thrive, strengthening the hand of their creators. The Capri, instead of flopping as Mr. Knudsen allegedly had predicted, "took off like a bird," says one Ford official. More than 115,000 have been sold since its introduction in February. The Maverick, Mr. Iacocca's project, also did well. Ford sold 115,478 of them in the first four months, in a fiercely competitive market.

These events set the stage for the battle over the 1972 models. Fundamental concepts were involved. "There was great disagreement on approach—real policy decisions," says one source. "Things like how to attack the intermediate market, whether you should get into markets or not, how much you spend on racing." In the end, Mr. Iacocca prevailed on most matters. The original 1972 program, approved by Mr. Knudsen, was held up for reconsideration by a committee of Mr. Ford and others, an unheard-of-event in recent years.

Henry Ford began to realize that he faced a far tougher decision—what to do about the growing discontent within the top echelons of his organization. This meant checking various stories to separate fact from fiction. "I know he checked and cross-checked to find out what was going on," says an executive.

Mr. Ford telephoned one executive well after midnight one night to discuss the man's relationship with Mr. Knudsen. The two men chatted for nearly an hour, bringing the Ford chieftain closer to an inevitable choice: He had to fire Mr. Knudsen or lose a number of top-level and talented executives, probably including Mr. Iacocca. He fired Bunkie.

*   *   *   *   *

WHY KNUDSEN WAS FIRED[3]

Stunned and aggrieved, Knudsen asked why he was being dismissed from his job, which paid him $580,952 last year. As Knudsen told the story, Ford replied only that "things did not work out as I had hoped" . . . .

A matter of personality

What did not work was Knudsen's concept of how a Ford president should operate. Ford's young executives have always admired GM's all-around management strength, but they were startled when a GM man was brought in to be their boss. Their dismay increased when they discovered that Knudsen, a gentlemanly but strong-willed executive, intended to run the company practically at the plant level. Instead of sitting in his office ruling on policy, he took to haunting the Ford design center, arriving there as early as 7:15 A.M. He ordered one change in the grille of the 1970 Thunderbird that made it resemble the Pontiac—a car produced by the GM division that Knudsen once headed. He also changed some personnel at the middle-management level without paying due respect to the wishes of other managers.

---

[3] *Time,* September 19, 1969. © Time, Inc., 1969. Reproduced by special permission.

All this stirred general resentment among Ford men, especially executive vice president Lee A. Iacocca, the assertive architect of Ford's highly successful Mustang and Maverick. Iacocca, a tough and ambitious marketing whiz whom Detroiters look on as chairman Ford's heir apparent, was shocked and disappointed when Knudsen was brought in, and later had several clashes with him. The two men held a peace parley last January, but if they came to an agreement, it did not last. Says one high executive who knows both well: "Lee had chewed his way through ten layers of management to get where he was, and he was determined to chew his way through anyone who was placed above him."

Ford's original idea in recruiting Knudsen, now 56, was to let him act as president for some years while Iacocca, 44, got some more seasoning. After Knudsen arrived at Ford, many executives concluded, to their surprise, that he was not really as shrewd or nimble as Iacocca. In his overeagerness to succeed, Knudsen committed a tactical error. He tried to make policy in parts of the company that Iacocca thought were his responsibility. Not long ago, Iacocca went to Henry Ford, who considers Iacocca his brightest protégé, and told him that he could no longer endure Knudsen's meddling. Apparently Knudsen's methods had not overly pleased Ford, either. The grandson of the founder of the Ford Motor Co. insists on maintaining absolute control of the business, and knows just about everything important that goes on in the company. As he said last week: "I am the chief executive officer of this company."

* * * * *

BEHIND THE PALACE REVOLT AT FORD[4]

Ouster of Semon Knudsen Shows Who's Boss—It's Definitely Henry Ford II—But the Plot Could Get a Lot Thicker

A motive?

This week, a puzzled Knudsen could only offer to *Business Week* his assumptions about Ford's actions. "When Mr. Ford asked me to come to Ford Motor Co., he said he wanted someone who had wide knowledge of the automotive business and who would take over the day-to-

---

day operations of the company. He had other activities then, such as the National Alliance of Businessmen, and I can only assume that his outside activities have diminished and he wants to run the company himself."

If Ford does intend to run the company himself, it will be consistent with his actions since the day in July 1960 when he said good-bye to another outgoing GM executive—one who had taught him much about business, Chairman Ernest R. Breech—with the casual words, "Ernie, I've graduated."

Since then, Ford Motor has had four presidents: Robert S. McNamara, John Dykstra, Arjay Miller, and Knudsen. Since 1965, Ford Div. has had four general managers, and Lincoln-Mercury has had three, while normal tenure for division heads in the auto business in three or four years. Houston Ford dealer John S. Osborne, referring to Ford's lectures to dealers about getting good men and keeping them, says: "The very thing they try to inspire in us, they're not doing themselves" . . . .

Ford's nonexplanation of the event is in vivid contrast to his garrulity on February 6, 1968, when he hailed Knudsen's arrival at Ford. He alluded to the departure of Knudsen's father for greener pastures at GM, and said: "Today, the flow of history is reversed. Another Mr. Knudsen, having left General Motors, has been elected president of the company his father helped to build. I am delighted to have him with us because I know him to be a strong and resourceful executive, brought up in a great automotive tradition, who will be a fine asset to top management of Ford."

Conflicts

With no adequate explanation of Knudsen's departure offered by Ford, speculation in Detroit has centered on the "strong and resourceful" qualities that Ford alluded to as a possible source of conflict with Ford. And then there are stories about Iacocca's "Chester gang," a group of four Ford vice presidents, including Iacocca and Mecke, as well as general managers John B. Naughton of the Ford Division and Matthew S. McLaughlin of the Lincoln-Mercury Division. All got their start in the company's Chester (Pa.) office.

One story has it that a number of Ford executives—perhaps as many as ten—prepared a dossier of Knudsen's real or imagined mistakes at the helm and confronted Ford with them after it became apparent that the Maverick, which was Iacocca's baby and not Knudsen's, was going to be an enormous success. It was "either he goes or we go," the story has it, and Knudsen's fate was sealed.

Other players

If this story is true, it does not necessarily prove that Iacocca himself was directly involved in the machinations. Although he and Knudsen had cool relations, and there were differences between them, both said last week that they patched up their quarrel in a meeting last January. The intrigues can be handled by minor players, as the circumstances surrounding the departure of newcomer James J. Nance in 1958 show.

Nance, a former president of Hotpoint, Inc., left General Electric Co. when he was passed over for the presidency, and was then named president of Packard Motor Car Co. Through the influence of Breech, he came to Ford as vice president of marketing with another unacknowledged role: backup man to Breech and the other older executives in case anything happened to them before the young "Whiz Kids" were ready to take over the company.

The men around one of them, Robert McNamara, already group vice president for cars and trucks and plainly an eventual presidential candidate, saw in Nance a threat to their future. While McNamara wasn't personally involved, some of his associates actually hired a consulting psychologist to suggest ways in which Nance could be harassed and embarrassed. Their triumph, if it can be called that, came in the office of Charles F. Moore, Jr., then vice president of public relations: Nance was fired for allegedly violating Ford's policy on executive press interviews.

Who's in charge?

Whether or not there was a repeat of the 1958 palace revolt, Ford would not have bowed to such a demand without a preconditioned sympathetic ear. After all, Ford's response to a similar ultimatum from Charles B. Thornton, who protested the hiring of Breech, was to fire Thornton. Thornton then went to build Litton Industries, Inc.

It is felt in Detroit that Knudsen may have inadvertently preempted Henry Ford's prerogatives as head of the company under the assumption that this was the job entrusted to him. Says a former top auto executive: "As Bunkie carried out authority, he limited options for other people such as Iacocca. He may have unwittingly taken product decisions away from Henry simply because by the time the final decision got to Henry his choices for change were limited."

This kind of misunderstanding is not the dramatic sort, but a day-to-day deterioration of the kind that happens when two people fail to communicate.

Matter of style

There were other strains. Knudsen's early morning visits to the design shops raised eyebrows in a company where the department heads have traditionally been allowed wide leeway. Grumped one Midwest dealer: "He took the Pontiac front end and put it on our T-Bird. We didn't go for that."

One cause of Knudsen's downfall seems to have been his inability to recognize the differences between the tone and style of doing things at Ford and at GM. "What he didn't realize was that Ford and Chevrolet are two very different organizations," said one Ford executive after the firing.

When Knudsen arrived at Ford, Henry Ford got just what he said he was getting: a strong executive. Knudsen first looked into engineering, styling, and international operations, his forte at General Motors, and made changes. He worked diligently "visiting plants around the world that haven't seen a major Ford executive in years," reports an auto insider.

Dilution

From Henry Ford's point of view, Knudsen's very strength may have been his weakness. The unassertive Miller was replaced by the assertive Knudsen, who in turn was replaced by a nonpresident: The office was abolished, for the time being, and in a stroke designed to avoid the appearance of a complete triumph for anyone, the office was made a trio.

Last year, Knudsen said that his main job at Ford was to train a number of men to succeed him. Last week, before he had the chance to do any training, he was succeeded by Iacocca as president of Ford North American automotive operations; Robert Stevenson as president of Ford International Automotive operations; and Robert J. Hampson as president of Philco-Ford and Tractor operations. Chairman and chief executive is still Henry Ford II.

For Henry Ford, the dramatic events of the past week do not change things all that much. He is still a leading member of the jet set, and head of the family that controls about 40 percent of the company's stock. The doubts raised by the Knudsen affair were posed by one well-versed management consultant: "If Ford permitted a palace revolt in the Knudsen case, that means two in the last ten years or so. Who's to say it can't happen again?" . . .

Up the ladder

Rarely without his cigar, and sporting long sideburns like his boss, Iacocca appears to be the sort of auto man Henry Ford II likes. His climb through the ranks has been marked by a combination of sheer brashness and shrewd commercial judgment.

Educated at Lehigh and Princeton, he joined the company in 1946. His first major triumph was the introduction of the sporty Mustang in 1964, while he was general manager of the Ford Division. Some disgruntled colleagues protested that he got more credit than he deserved for that success, but it was Lee Iacocca whose face appeared on the covers of *Time* and *Newsweek* simultaneously as the orginator of the Mustang. When the hot-selling Maverick compact was marketed this spring, the press quickly labeled it "Iacocca's baby."

One reason for the great personal publicity he has received is that, unlike most auto executives, he talks very freely, and pungently, with the press. It has been observed in Detroit that a reporter will ask Iacocca a question—and then listen, and listen, and listen.

Another personal quality that has helped his cause is a skill at inside maneuvering. During Arjay Miller's term as president, Iacocca frequently went around him to deal directly with the chairman.

Iacocca's turn at the top may come next. Of course, the big question is: Will the strong-minded chairman accept a president who is also tough and outspoken?

* * * * *

THE BIGGEST SWITCH[5]

One of the remarkable strengths of General Motors Corp. is its ability to hang on to key men through a system based on tradition, hefty salaries, and stratospheric but delayed bonuses subject to costly forfeit if a man quits. Automen were understandably astonished two weeks ago when Semon Emil ("Bunkie") Knudsen, GM's fourth-ranking officer, abruptly resigned as executive vice president and a company director. Even more stunning was last week's announcement that Knudsen had become the new president of Ford Motor Co., GM's archrival in one of the toughest competitions private enterprise has yet produced. . . .

---

[5] *Time,* February 16, 1968. © Time, Inc., 1968. Reproduced by special permission.

Blocked promotion

The record clearly belongs to Bunkie Knudsen, 55.[6] After 29 years as a GM executive, he was earning some $481,000 a year as boss of domestic nonauto and all overseas operations. But he was keenly disappointed at his failure to win GM's presidency last fall. Instead, his only obvious rival, Edward N. Cole, 58, won the job that Knudsen had coveted and courted for most of his life. Cole's ascension meant not only that Knudsen's road to promotion was blocked for at least another four years; it also meant that even if Knudsen did follow Cole to the top at GM, he would have so few years to serve before mandatory retirement at 65 that his age might deny him the chance to win the job at all. As a multimillionaire by inheritance as well as by his own labors—his 42,507 shares of General Motors stock alone are worth $3,257,000—Knudsen regarded his failure to move to a higher salary bracket with comparative indifference. But he looked on a dead-end career with dread.

While hiding his unhappiness in public, Knudsen told GM chairman James Roche and a few close friends that he would probably leave the auto industry or "look for another assignment" inside it. Word soon got to Henry Ford II, who started the nation's most audacious executive raid in years. "Sure I did it," Ford said last week. "Nobody but me—so I have to take the credit."

Ford moved with secrecy and circumspection. A month ago, while Knudsen was still on GM's payroll, Ford telephoned him at home and hinted at the presidency. "I made no commitment," recalled Knudsen last week, "nor were any details worked out. Then I told Mr. Roche that I had been approached." The next Saturday, Ford drove to Knudsen's home in Bloomfield Hills, and there the deal was clinched. Knudsen then phoned Roche. "He wished me well," says Knudsen, "and hoped we could be friendly competitors—and I assured him we could."

For another two weeks, while Knudsen wound up his affairs at General Motors and Ford called a directors' meeting to approve his decision, the arrangements remained one of autodom's best-kept secrets. Ford shuffled able but colorless president Arjay Miller, 51, to the new post of vice chairman. As such, Miller will run Ford's finances, legal department, public relations, Washington staff and long-range planning. Knudsen, as chief operating officer, will not only control sales, product development and plant operations, but will also assume full command of the company when chairman and chief executive Ford is absent.

Upsetting though the importation of an outsider was to other Ford executives, vice chairman Miller seemed almost relieved. No engineer,

---

[6] His father gave him the nickname as a boy. It is argot for military barracks mates who are buddies.

Miller has never worked on an assembly line or run an auto plant. In his five years as president, he found it difficult to keep some underlings under firm control, notably the brilliant but impulsive Lee Iacocca, 43, who heads Ford's North American automotive operations. Iacocca (*Time* cover, April 17, 1964) had been widely regarded as a candidate for the Ford presidency. Now, he presumably faces a decade of waiting under Knudsen—and one of Detroit's current speculations is what he may do . . . .

Reversing history

As Bunkie Knudsen cautiously allowed, "only time will tell" if he can reverse Chevrolet's lead. He likes to remember one of the few pieces of advice his father gave him: "In this business, the competition will bite you if you keep running; if you stand still, they will swallow you" . . . .

In the end, Knudsen missed the presidency [of General Motors] because of General Motors' tradition of always having at least two men ready to take over every job. And Ed Cole, three years his senior, with many of the same qualifications, had after all, run Chevrolet and become an executive vice president before him.

Abandoned options

By jumping to Ford, Knudsen forfeited some $674,000 of accrued but unpaid GM bonuses. He also abandoned options to buy at least 30,000 more shares of GM common stock, although he insisted that he would keep the 42,507 shares he already owns. For the time being, Knudsen's Ford pay remains undisclosed (under SEC rules, it must be divulged to stockholders in April before Ford's annual meeting).

Knudsen's impact in Ford's fight in the auto market could be considerable. Despite such trend-setting firsts as the sporty Mustang and the intermediate-sized Fairlane, Ford's share of domestic auto sales has slipped from 31 percent of U.S.-made cars in 1961 to no more than 28 percent since. Ford's latest strategy is to battle for the medium-priced market, which GM dominates with its Pontiacs, Oldsmobiles and Buicks. Obviously, Knudsen carries in his head much inside knowledge—from styling to engineering to marketing—of GM's future plans. Nor can he erase them from his mind. But as automen quickly recognized, this was hardly what Henry Ford sought. What counts is the disciplined insight Ford most can use: Knudsen's ingrained intimacy with the concepts and techniques (from cost control to dealer organization) that have long made General Motors, by common consent of both friends and foes, one of the world's best-managed corporations . . . .

* * * * *

KNUDSEN OF FORD[7]

. . . In one deft stroke, chairman Ford had reshaped the management of his company, remedying a managerial weakness and restyling the corporation's top executive structure, with a president to handle operations and a new vice chairman in charge of finance and public affairs. It was with good reason that a GM organization chart hung on the wall of Ford's office when he announced the move.

Knudsen could prove the key to Ford's recovery from a serious slump. Despite such spectacular coups as the Mustang at home and the Cortina abroad, Ford has not been able to mount a consistent challenge to GM in the automobile market. Ford's success has cropped up in fits and patches, but the company has lacked the balanced, across-the-board competitive power of General Motors. The weakness has been in the middle-priced field. Though there have been repeated efforts to remedy the situation—like the attempts to pep up the Mercury division—Ford has not been able to sustain its attack on that critical market. Weakness also shows up overseas, where Ford has lost a number of its top managers to rivals, and the major integration of European operations is running into difficulties. Earnings were down 43 percent in the first quarter of 1967, 32 percent in the second, 212 percent in the strike-ridden third quarter, and will be down again for the fourth. GM earnings, by comparison, slipped 34 percent in the first quarter, 4 percent in the second; they rose 49 percent in the third, and 2 percent in the fourth.

Ford's top management has been strong on cost control and systematic budgeting but weak on the production side. Arjay Miller, 52, who relinquished the presidency to take the new position of vice chairman, is a sound—even brilliant—financial executive, but was never at ease with problems of designing and merchandising—and production and salesmen were never quite at ease with him. He had been particularly hard pressed since the retirement last year of executive vice president Charles Patterson, the chief "plant man" on his team. Lee Iacocca, 43, head of North American automotive operations and the man behind the Mustang, is one of the bright young men of the industry—but he, too, lacks the long production experience Ford needed. He is well situated to be a future president. . . .

---

[7] *Fortune*, March 1968. Reprinted by special permission. *Fortune* Magazine © 1968, Time, Inc.

Despite predictions to the contrary, Knudsen is less likely to encounter resentment from his colleagues than an outsider normally would be when thrust into a top job in a giant company. For one thing, he is a straightforward and approachable man, although he carries the patina of reserve that GM executives seem to acquire. More important is the uniqueness of his situation, and the logic of the new executive assignments at Ford. Henry Ford II continues as chief executive, adamantly denying rumors that he would consider leaving for a government post. Knudsen is chief operating officer, with authority to serve as chief executive in Ford's absence. And vice chairman Arjay Miller is now in a job well suited to his talents: he heads financial and legal staffs, corporate development, and public information. In short, Henry Ford has himself quite a team.

$$* \quad * \quad * \quad * \quad *$$

CHIP OFF THE OLD ENGINE BLOCK
AUTOMAKER KNUDSEN[8]

One of the enduring mysteries of U.S. business is how a product can suddenly catch fire with consumers or, at times, just as suddenly lose favor. Nearly 30 years ago, General Motors' William S. Knudsen, a Danish immigrant bicyclemaker turned automan, was the one who lit the fuse under Chevrolet and sent it out ahead of Ford as the most popular U.S. car. His reward was the presidency of General Motors.

Three years ago, Big Bill Knudsen's son, Semon Emil Knudsen, took on a similar job: he was made boss of GM's sputtering Pontiac division, thus became, at 43, GM's youngest auto-division boss. Pontiac was the weakest of all the auto divisions, languishing in sixth place in overall U.S. car sales. Last week "Bunky" Knudsen's hot-rodding Pontiac was at the top of the medium-price field, with 30 percent of that market; sales were up (117 percent in April, 60 percent for the year), and Pontiac was in a nip-and-tuck race with lower-priced Plymouth for third place in overall standings. On GM's corporate-profit sheets, Pontiac stood second only to Chevrolet; around the GM building in Detroit there was quiet talk that Bunky Knudsen might well become GM president some day.

From the start, Bill Knudsen insisted that his son be on his own. When Bunky was 14, his father told him he could have a new (1927) Chevrolet if he would stop by the plant. Bunky hurried over—and found the car in several thousand pieces. "It took me a couple of months to assemble the darn thing," he says, "but I finally got it running."

---

[8] *Time*, May 23, 1959. © 1959, Time, Inc. Reproduced by special permission.

The challenge turned him into a car bug. It also made him determined to fill his father's oversized boots. A broad-shouldered (185 lbs., 6 ft.), soft-spoken young man, Knudsen had the single-minded drive of a piston. He worked in auto plants in summer, went to Dartmouth, then to M.I.T. ('36) for his degree in engineering.

After several years at other companies, he arrived at Pontiac, as a menial "tool chaser." He tried everything, just so it added another bit of experience: defense plant chief inspector, car-assembly superintendent, assistant master mechanic, boss of a new "process development" section searching to make products more efficiently. Says Knudsen: "As long as you're interested enough to take any job that comes along, you'll find something worthwhile to do, and it usually turns out to be a better job than the last one." By the time he was 43, he had performed chores in no fewer than 106 GM plants.

The top Pontiac job tied all the work together. Knudsen's first move after he became general manager was to go to the styling center. He knew what was wrong with Pontiacs; it had a "grandma image" in the customer's mind. He wanted to change it so "teen-agers would shout, 'Cool, man, real cool!'" The 1957 Pontiac was only 30 days from pilot production, just 60 days from volume production. Walking around the car, Knudsen announced abruptly: "Let's take the silver streaks off. That's the biggest change we can make." The stylists were shocked. They reminded the new boss that Big Bill Knudsen himself was the one who introduced the streaks, in 1935. But off they went, the first move to facelift grandma.

He reorganized the division (retirements and transfers were encouraged, "and we did some firing too," says Knudsen) and set out to redesign the Pontiac from the wheels up—and out—aiming to make it real cool by this year. His biggest change was to widen the car by 2½ inches and push the wheels out as well. The effect was spectacular. The car not only looked flashy, but also the wide-track wheels gave better balance and road ability. Equally important, says Knudsen, "it gave people something to talk about. They can see it and they can understand it." Where the average age of previous Pontiac buyers was around 45, today's buyer is between 30 and 35. Another sales lure: Knudsen cut the price of expensive models, held the line on the lower-priced models, so that Pontiac's top-selling Catalina costs less than a Chevrolet Impala.

For Bunky Knudsen, the rewards of success are a $100,000 annual salary, a sprawling, 12-room colonial farmhouse, with two tennis courts and a swimming pool, on 40 acres in suburban Birmingham, Michigan, where he lives with his wife Florence and their four teen-age children. Knudsen does not spend much time there. His work day is ten hours long, and part of every evening is spent slamming Pontiacs, a new one each day, around the roughest roads he can find. Knudsen, who fidgets when he hears his success mentioned, likes to recall one of the few pieces of advice his father gave him: "Before you tell someone how good you are, you must tell him how bad you used to be."

*   *   *   *   *

AT FORD EVERYONE KNOWS WHO IS THE BOSS

WILLIAM SERRIN[9]

. . . Handsomely clothed, impeccably manicured and combed, with a large head, slim hips and the beer gut of a tool-and-diemaker, Henry Ford II clearly knows who he is: one of America's richest men (his fortune has been estimated at anything from $200 million to $500 million), certainly its most prominent industrial boss, and the man who, by saving the Ford Motor Company, directed its greatest industrial comeback.

Ford is Midwest rich, not Eastern rich. Brusque, earthy, demanding, often profane—much like Lyndon Johnson, with whom he became friendly when Johnson was president and Ford was heading the National Alliance of Businessmen, charged with lining up 500,000 jobs for the hard-core unemployed. He swears, laughs hard at a good story, likes Scotch and knows a well-turned ankle or a well-drawn face when he sees one. He is hard-working—only a hard worker could have engineered the recovery of the Ford Motor Company, which was losing $9.5 million a month in 1945, and made it what it is today: America's third-largest corporation, with total assets of $9 billion, 435,500 employees in more than 33 countries and annual gross sales of more than $14 billion. Of all the automobile executives in Detroit, only Ford—and perhaps, his own flashy executive, ambitious Lee Iacocca, and GM's hip John DeLorean—has any real personal style, what with Fenn-Feinsten suits, earlobe-length sideburns and a discreet "HFII" on his shirt pockets and on the door of his Lincoln Continental.

Moreover, Ford is more a boss than any other major corporation chief in America, certainly more than the colorless James Roche, chairman of the General Motors Corporation, or Lynn Townsend, chairman of Chrysler Corporation. If any proof of that were needed, Ford provided it in September, when he stunned the American business world by walking into the office of Semon E. (Bunkie) Knudsen, whom he had hired from General Motors just 19 months before, and saying, "You'll

[9] *The New York Times Magazine,* October 19, 1969. © 1969 The New York Times Publishing Company. Reproduced by special permission of the publishers and William Serrin.

be leaving." Knudsen—a fabled automobile man in his own right—had lost a power struggle with Iacocca, but he had, just as importantly, shown too much authority for Ford, who, like his grandfather, wants to run the Ford Motor Company himself. Chatting over drinks with friends the night the firing was announced, Knudsen said: "I think Henry was afraid of losing his Tinker Toy." One thing was clear: control of the Ford Motor Company remains—and will remain—in the hands of Ford. "I am the chief executive of this company," says the best-known businessman in the nation's leading business.

Ford admits he is no intellectual. He is, instead, savvy, perceptive, confident, forceful and his own boss. His grandfather, who, with the assembly line, the Model T and the $5-day probably changed the face of America more than any other man, was the genius; Henry the younger is the manager. "I wouldn't want a genius in charge," he says. "A genius tends to be overbearing. He can't get along with people." And Ford is a powerful manager, as the Knudsen firing so graphically shows. A Detroit auto writer says, "In a sense, he's the last of the corporate dictators." He saved the company not by his own brilliance, nor even his knowledge of the automobile, but by surrounding himself with men ideally suited for their roles in the enterprise—John R. Davis, Charles R. (Tex) Thornton, Ernest R. Breech, Robert McNamara, Arjay Miller, Iacocca—and then taking their advice. It could be argued that it really took General Motors to save Ford, since Breech, the architect of the recovery, and a number of his top subordinates were GM men. Yet it was Ford who had the presence of mind—in a sense, the brilliance—to choose the men and accept their counsel . . . .

But his Navy career lasted little more than two years. In August 1943, Ford—then almost 26—was discharged at the direction of Secretary of the Navy Frank Knox. His job: save the Ford Motor Company . . . .

His task seemed impossible. One by one, top executives had left the company. There were no accounting systems, no balance sheets, no property books and for all practical purposes, no research or design departments. There had never been an audit in the company's history, more than 30 years. In one department, Ford recalled, invoices were weighted to compute costs. Another department, it was discovered after the war, was still producing propellers for the Ford Tri-Motor, which Ford had stopped manufacturing years before. In 1937, the Federal Trade Commission found that Ford was making a net profit of $5 a car, compared to $50 for Chevrolet and $39 for Plymouth. "The company was not only dying, it was already dead and rigor mortis was setting in," said one official.

Yet Ford's biggest problem was attempting to wrest control of the company from Bennett, the muscular ex-sailor and prize fighter who ran the dreaded Ford Service Department, a secret police force of gangsters and shady ex-policemen and football players. It was Bennett—who kept lions and tigers as pets, wore a size 17 collar and once shot the cigar from the mouth of a man violating a company ban against smoking—who led the charge against hunger marchers demanding Ford jobs in 1932 and who directed the company forces that fought off Walter Reuther and other United Auto Workers organizers in a bloody clash at Ford's River Rouge complex in 1937.

However, Henry Ford II was also tough—as tough as his grandfather. Many people saw him as the heir apparent; he had, after all, the Ford name, which Bennett did not, and he had the backing of both Clara, his grandmother, and Eleanor, his mother—plus cash reserves of more than $645-million. "I knew it could be turned around," he says. "It never occurred to me I couldn't do the job."

For several months, Ford was content to bide his time, trying to learn the automobile business. But early in 1944 he learned that his grandfather had drawn up a codicil to his will: at his death, control of the company would pass to a ten-member board of directors—not including Henry Ford II—for ten years. Ford was incensed; if the codicil could not be altered, he said, he would resign and inform all Ford dealers of the company's condition. But John Bugas, a Bennett aide who had become friendly with Ford, told him to wait. Bugas went to Bennett's office and persuaded Bennett to show him the codicil. Holding the document in his hand, Bennett set it on fire, letting the burning paper fall to the floor. Then he scraped up the remains and said, "You can take this back to young Henry." Later Bennett told I. A. Capizzi, the lawyer who had drawn up the codicil, that it was invalid. Ford had scribbled on it, he said, verses from the Bible; Capizzi concluded that Ford had never signed it. Whatever the case, the codicil moved the family to action. Ford and a few trusted executives—Bugas; John R. Davis, an ex-sales chief; and Meade Bricker, a production expert—met secretly at the Detroit Club to figure out, Ford says, "what to do with Bennett." Their decision: Henry Ford II had to take over the presidency.

Others felt the same way. Clara Ford had been urging her husband to transfer the presidency to Henry II. Then came the turning point: Eleanor Ford, Henry's mother, demanded that he be made president. "If this is not done," she told her father-in-law, "I will sell my stock." On September 20, 1945, Ford gave in. He summoned his grandson to Fairlane, his estate in Dearborn, and agreed to make him president; the next day Henry Ford II's assumption of the presidency was endorsed by the board of directors. After the meeting, he called Bennett to his office. "I told him he was through," Ford says. Bennett yelled: "You're taking over a billion-dollar company that you haven't contributed a thing to." But he was axed after 29 years at Ford, much of it as the real boss . . . .

Henry Ford stuck by his agreement to stay out of company affairs (he died at Fairlane in 1947), and his grandson slowly began salvaging the Ford Motor Company, all the time stamping it with his own personality. In the first several months, he fired more than 1,000 executives, including many Bennett cohorts and William J. Cameron, the old Ford "Voice of the Air" and editor of the anti-Semitic Dearborn Independent. He sold his grandfather's Brazilian rubber plantation, which had cost the company more than $20 million, plus the soybean farms, mineral and timber tracts and a number of other properties.

He also began hiring top-notch people who would serve as the company's leadership for the next 20 years. In November 1945, he received a telegram from Col. Charles B. (Tex) Thornton, who said a group of Air Force officers desired to work together and apply military management techniques to a civilian company. Ford hired all ten of them, later dubbed the "Whiz Kids" because they asked so many questions and seemed so intelligent. Among them were Robert M. McNamara, who later became Ford president, then left to become Secretary of Defense and now heads the World Bank; Arjay Miller, later a Ford president, now dean of the Graduate School of Business at Stanford University, and Thornton, now head of Litton Industries.

In July 1946—taking what was perhaps his most important step in the reconstruction—Ford hired Ernest Breech, who, as president of the Bendix Corporation, then a General Motors subsidiary, had tripled production in two years.

Breech brought much new blood into the company: Lewis D. Crusoe, a former GM assistant treasurer; Harold T. Youngren, chief engineer at Borg Warner Corporation; Delmar S. Harder, ex-production chief at GM; Albert J. Browning, director of the War Department's purchasing activities during World War II; and John Dykstra, another former GM executive. In January 1947, Crusoe, heading the Whiz Kids, reorganized and decentralized Ford in a pattern similar to that of General Motors. An audit system was established in 1946. Automation—the term was coined by Harder—was begun at Ford plants by the late 1940s and saved the company millions.

All this time, Ford was fighting to bring out a postwar car—a 1946 Ford, actually an improved 1942 model. But strikes slowed production and the company was experiencing heavy losses because of rising costs. In the first six months of 1946, for example, the loss was about $50 million. Now Henry Ford II took on the Office of Price Administration and its chief, Chester Bowles. He won two price increases and, in the confrontation with Bowles, emerged as a spokesman for the entire auto industry.

Losses were still mounting in September, so Ford officials decided to ask for another price hike. Breech, knowing that the OPA was expecting a request for $150, asked instead for a hike of just $80. The surprised OPA granted $61.50—$1.50 more than Breech's estimated break-even point, and the company ended the year with a $2,000 profit.

Meantime, the company was attempting to improve its labor relations, which had reached a dismal level under Henry Ford and Bennett (workers sometimes took to building rats in car doors). In January 1946, the company signed an agreement with the United Auto Workers for an 18-cent-an-hour raise, getting in return UAW guarantees against illegal strikes. Another contract in 1948 gave the workers a 15 percent wage hike. In 1947, foremen and supervisors were taken off the hourly rate system, and the old Henry Ford dictum was lifted, allowing employees to smoke in the plants for the first time. The old driver system, under which foremen and supervisors ruthlessly bossed men on the line, had all but disappeared from Ford.

In 1949, a contract with the UAW set up the auto industry's first pension plan, providing $100 monthly to each Ford worker with more than 30 years on the job. *Fortune* magazine reported: "No question about it, Ford is now doing a labor-relations job second to none in the tense Detroit area." And Henry Ford II was considered not merely a leader of the automobile industry, but a leader in improved labor relations as well.

In 1947 Breech made a bold move, deciding that Ford would build an all-new automobile for 1949, the first major postwar innovation in the American industry. It was introduced at the Waldorf-Astoria, where thousands jammed the showrooms. Although it was leaky and dusty— John Davis said it had 8,000 bugs—the model sold 806,766 units and Ford had its biggest year since 1929. In 1950 the company had a net profit of $265 million. In 1953, after three years of leveling off because of the Korean War, Ford moved past Chrysler into second place. In 1954 a new model with an overhead-valve V-8 engine sold 1.4 million units, putting Ford just 17,000 units behind Chevrolet.

Between 1945 and 1953, the company spent $1 billion on expansion. In January 1956, the Ford Motor Company, which had been started with a cash investment of $28,000, went public; the $690 million stock sale was the largest in history. The company, then 53 years old, was for the first time in its history a mature, well-structured enterprise, its recovery part of the legend of American industry.

In recent years, Ford has been the most innovative company in the auto industry, with Falcon, the Fairlane, the Mustang, the Maverick.

Unlike General Motors, it admits it is in racing in a big way, with a multimillion-dollar program that is the most extensive in the industry. Yet the company has problems, as Ford himself admits. It has one of the highest executive-turnover rates in American industry; it seems almost perpetually condemned to between 25 and 30 percent of the auto market; it has not beaten Chevrolet since 1959, and then its success was largely due to a steel strike; its Lincoln-Mercury division continually sells just about 5 percent of the market. And Ford has dumped more than $350 million into Philco Corporation, including the $94 million purchase price in 1961.

The Falcon—McNamara's car and the first of the Big Three compacts—came out in 1959 and sold 417,107 units, then an all-time first-year record. Then in 1964, recognizing that half of the American population is 27 or younger, Iacocca—a hard-driving man given to expensive black cigars, huge cuff links and expensive soft shoes that he is wont to prop on his desk—redesigned the Falcon and brought out the Mustang. (Ford wanted to call it T-Bird Two, but was outvoted.) It sold 417,811 units in its first year, surpassing the Falcon, and introduced the small, peppy car to America.

Last April, Iacocca scored again—and staked his claim to the No. 2 spot at Ford—when he came out with the Maverick, designed to compete primarily against foreign cars, which—led by Volkswagen—had taken 10 percent of the market in 1968. Out just six months, the Maverick has sold more than 150,000 units, a pace that could—given favorable seasonal sales fluctuations—put it over the Mustang record and perhaps push Ford past Chevrolet. It's also getting, according to Iacocca, about 15 percent Volkswagen trades. "I don't go in for superlatives," he says, "but it's fantastic."

In the last three years, the company has pumped $250 million into the Lincoln-Mercury Division in an attempt, says *Detroit News* auto writer Robert Irvin, to "get away from the image that Mercury is just a big Ford." And Henry Ford II says: "For the last several years . . . we've been doing everything we can to build up the Lincoln-Mercury division . . . and get a higher percentage of the intermediate class. We've got plans for them to grow even more—we want them to grow." Yet a Detroit auto observer says: "That division continually goes through flip-flops. They don't seem to be able to keep at a program. If it doesn't work immediately—change the manager and the program, just like a baseball team firing its manager if they don't win the pennant." One auto writer describes the Mercury as a "30-year failure," . . .

Since Robert McNamara left Ford in 1961 to become secretary of defense, the company had not really had a strong president, not even Miller, a "finance man" in the McNamara mold but not a "car man" in the Detroit tradition. It was against this background that Henry Ford—

amid rumors that he might take a high-level job in the Johnson Administration—hired Knudsen as Ford president.

Just back from a trip to Antigua, Ford, hearing that Knudsen had decided to quit GM after having been passed over for its presidency, drove—in an Oldsmobile to insure as little attention as possible—to Knudsen's home in Bloomfield Hills, a plush suburb much favored by General Motors brass, on a recruiting mission. Knudsen said he would come, and a week later they sealed the pact: Knudsen would receive a yearly salary and bonuses of $600,000—the same as Ford—and he would, he says, exercise a strong hand in the running of the company. A primary mission, it was clear, was to increase Ford's sales penetration in the middle- and upper-price car field, dominated by General Motors with Pontiac, Oldsmobile, Buick and Cadillac.

In the following months, Knudsen did indeed exercise a strong hand at Ford, especially in the area of styling and engineering. He made "dawn patrols" through the Ford Design Center and attended styling meetings at 7:15 A.M. He cut five inches off the Thunderbird and redesigned the front end, giving it a GM snout ("New Thunderbird Looks Like Old Pontiac," said a headline in *The Times*). Eugene Bordinat, the Ford styling chief and an Iacocca man, said: "Knudsen expresses a great interest in our vineyard and helps me toil-it. I think I mean that in both senses."

As Knudsen was fighting Iacocca, however, he was also making an enemy of Ford, who—like his grandfather—runs the company with nearly absolute control. He fired Knudsen, explaining that "sometimes things don't work out." It was history repeating itself, for in 1921 Ford's grandfather fired Knudsen's father, William S. (Big Bill) Knudsen, himself an automobile pioneer, who promptly went to GM and built Chevrolet . . . .

Iacocca is Henry Ford's man, and the reasons seem apparent. He is a winner: it was he who was behind both the Mustang and the Maverick. Moreover, he has caught the eyes of both Mrs. Edsel Ford, who, while living the life of a grande dame in Grosse Pointe Farms, is still influential in the company, and of William Clay Ford, who does not spend a great deal of time at the office, but still has his brother's ear. Just as much a part of Iacocca's success, however, is his ability to work with Henry Ford, which the forceful Knudsen lacked. Iacocca knows that it is Ford—not Iacocca, no matter how talented or ambitious he might be—who is the top man at the Ford Motor Company . . . .

While Ford denies that the company has an unstable management, it has lost a number of top executives in recent years—among them, Breech, McNamara, Miller and now Knudsen. Says Ford: "I think we've got good depth in management; I think we've got some very capable people." In reply to the unstable-management charges, he says: "I've heard that before. I heard that when Bob McNamara went to the Defense Department. I even heard it when John Dykstra retired. I'm not worried about that." Yet Knudsen's was not a unique case. Breech quit in 1961, saying, "Henry doesn't need me any more." And, as *Fortune* pointed out, Henry didn't—at least he didn't think so . . . .

The Ford Motor Company, which makes the family's lifestyle possible, is run by Henry Ford II through five major policy committees and what Iacocca calls the "key people," about 50 presidents and general managers.

Ford is a member of all committees and attends all their meetings when he is in Detroit, sometimes hiding his own views so other executives won't simply parrot his position: "I think the only way you learn something is by having open discussions and getting different points of view on the table."

He communicates with his top executives by an intercom or by telephone. "The less paper work the better, as far as I am concerned," he says, although he adds that he usually ends up taking papers home. "I don't say that I do everything every night, but I always take home enough so that if there is something I've got to read, I read it. I usually go to bed and read in bed." He tries to hold his temper, he says, but, "Sometimes I am pretty sharp, and tear up when I am sharp. I wrote a blistering son-of-a-bitch of a memorandum yesterday when I came in. I tore it up. I thought it was just going too far" . . . .

Life in the executive suite is not, however, an uninterrupted series of guffaws, even for Henry Ford II. Says Bordinat, the styling chief: "He makes the final decision. All committees are merely recommending agents to him. He has never come to a meeting when he hasn't been prepared . . . he loves a good scrap." Bordinat says Ford is "quite disappointed when there isn't another opinion," adding that if executives have "the guts" to put proposals on paper for Ford "they better have the guts to defend them."

Jacques Passino, the Ford racing chief, says the executives give Ford a list of questions about a proposal neatly typed on 3 × 5 file cards. "But he'll always come up with a question—a good question—that's not on the damn list."

Despite the modern management structure, there is still some of the old-fashioned seat-of-the-pants atmosphere at the Ford Motor Company, as Ford himself attests, describing how the Mustang was developed: "We had lots of discussions about it. Chevy had two products, Corvair and Chevy II, and we sat there with the Falcon. . . . So hell, I said, if they've got two, we're going to have two, or we are never going to be able to compete with them . . . . We considered the Falcon as the competition for the Chevy II, so we had to find something that would compete with the Corvair. That was the idea. And then Lee [Iacocca], who was then general manager of the Ford Division, went to work on it, and this got played around in all different kinds of ways." When the car was ready, Iacocca had to sell it to Ford, who at first was reluctant, believing it wouldn't sell. But Iacocca persevered and Mustang became an industry leader.

Says Iacocca, diligent in paying proper praise, "There could never have been a Mustang or a Maverick without a guy like Henry Ford." When the Mark III was developed, he recalls, some executives said, "My God . . . It's a plane!" Iacocca explains: "It's true; you can lose your ass if a car is too big, too small or, for whatever reasons, does not pique the public's interest." But Ford looks at it and says, "Wow, I'd like to drive that car home." It "turned him on," says Iacocca, and the Mark III—Henry's car—sold 22,306 units in its first 13 months, 30 percent more than the Cadillac Eldorado in its first year. . . .

"Somebody wrote an article the other day and said Ford—no pun intended—is the maverick of the business," says Iacocca. "When you have a big giant like GM . . . and you have another company under you that's small, you're sort of the middle guy." And being a maverick, according to Iacocca, is the Ford way of succeeding against General Motors. "They say that we over the years have done more innovative things, product and policy wise, than other companies have. That's probably true." He adds: "A lot of that is a tribute to the man, Henry Ford" . . . .

In a reflective moment, he [Mr. Ford] remarked last month: "I'd like for my epitaph—but I don't think I've accomplished it yet—an organization arrangement that will be stable enough and good enough—I'm not talking about individual people now, I'm talking about an organizational arrangement that anybody can fit into. That's the big thing General Motors has. I don't think we've accomplished that here yet." The present manufacturing system "works reasonably well," he says, "but it's not as good as I'd like to see it nor is it as puncture-proof as General Motors. That's what I hope to leave when I walk out the door the last time."

*   *   *   *   *

A NEW GENERATION OF WHIZ KIDS AT FORD

DAN CORDTZ[10]

If Ford's officials sometimes seem almost too inclined to measure their own performance in terms of General Motors', they do recognize that Ford is an entirely different creature—one that requires different

---

[10] Dan Cordtz, "A New Generation of Whiz Kids," *Fortune*, January 1967. Reproduced by special permission of *Fortune* Magazine, © 1967 Time, Inc.

organization and different policies. This seemingly obvious conclusion has not always been regarded as self-evident. In the early years of Ford's postwar rebirth, the efforts of its management were largely directed toward building the company in GM's image. Given the success of General Motors, this decision was understandable. But it overlooked the fact that GM's structure is almost an accident of history—a problem transformed into strength by managerial genius, General Motors came into being through the consolidation of several independent auto manufacturers. In the early years their lack of coordination created constant problems. Only Alfred P. Sloan Jr.'s development of the concept of centralized policy guiding decentralized operations made possible today's five separate car divisions blanketing the auto market. Even so, there are those who contend that the company's divisions still overlap and duplicate one another's facilities to a degree that is only partially offset by the benefits of internal competition.

Ford, by contrast found itself after World War II an enormous, shapeless, and unmanageable mess. To bring order out of chaos, the experienced executives Henry Ford hired—many of them veterans of GM service—not only applied General Motors methods but imposed a General Motors pattern on Ford. Ultimately the slavish copying led to serious troubles. At one point Ford had five separate car divisions of its own—some without enough volume to support the required overhead. The Edsel fiasco was in large measure caused by a conviction that the company had to match each and every one of GM's car lines with an offering of its own. At last Ford's top managers conceded, perhaps a little wistfully, that their company was not General Motors and that it required organizational solutions of its own. Since then, like a football coach who tailors his offense to his players, Ford has made countless large and small structural alterations—and Henry Ford says it has not attained its final shape yet.

The company shows no interest in running things by "the book"—that largely unwritten collection of precedents that many firms build up over the years. Ford leaders avoid any criticism of General Motors for an adherence to past practice. "That book has a lot of rigid things in it," observes Miller. But in their own company they clearly foster an iconoclastic attitude. This is not too surprising, of course. GM can hardly be expected to question its methods as long as they perform well. And Ford can hardly stand pat on any system that does not promise to narrow the lead of its giant rival.

"My name is on the building"

The personal force of individuals has an unusual impact on policies and operations at Ford. This undoubtedly reflects the fact that Henry

Ford II is in unchallenged command. The company has 400,000 stockholders, but the Ford family still holds a 40 percent interest. Everyone at Dearborn understands that the founder's grandson can impose his will whenever he chooses. As he sometimes remarks to settle an argument in his own favor: "My name is on the building." Nor does he hesitate to exercise his power. Other officers are baffled by the persistent legend entertained in the outside world that Henry Ford is just a playboy and their boss in name only. There have been times in the past when his interest in details of the business has flagged. In recent years, though, he not only has made the big decisions but has taken a direct hand in operations in a manner rare for the chairman of the board of a big, complex corporation.

A few subordinates—and executives no longer with the company—complain privately that he exercises too much control from the top. Specifically, they say that he intervenes at too many organizational levels. He himself stoutly maintains that he tries to avoid bypassing organizational lines. But he admits, for example, that when he heard a few years ago of Ford division plans for a seven-passenger limousine, he called general manager Donald M. Frey directly to tell him to forget the project—even though there are three men between him and Frey on the organization chart.

Other critics contend that one-man control has played a part in the departure from Ford of an undeniably large number of high-ranking executives before they reached retirement age. With no one to answer to, the charge goes, Henry Ford can be arbitrary and ruthless in his selection of men for promotion, demotion, or even dismissal; as a result capable men have been fired, and others have quit when they failed to get the rewards to which they felt entitled. "You don't see anything like that at General Motors," observes a former Ford executive. It is true that upper-level GM executives are better protected against the worst consequences of failure; dismissal is unheard of there. But neither does it seem possible at GM for an outstanding man to rise as rapidly as, for example, McNamara did with Henry Ford's blessing. And a defender of the Ford boss argues: "He certainly can't be too arbitrary in his personnel choices. The success of the company means too much to him."

Henry Ford does not conceal his central role in the selection of the company's top managers. Who gets what job, down to the third echelon of management, is a question whose answer he regards as very much his business. Nor does he deny that he sometimes overrules his officers in picking men for subordinate jobs. Consequently, the Ford management accurately reflects both his own complex personality and his insistence on a balance between brains and experience. It is a diverse group. Ford managers range from articulate intellectuals to taciturn self-taught engineers, from flamboyant tough guys to soft-spoken introverts, from youngsters not long out of school to oldtimers on the verge of retirement.

A thinker with gasoline in his blood

The variety can easily be demonstrated by a quick look at the mean at four levels below the chairman. . . .

Miller is alternate chief executive, with full powers to make and carry out large decisions in Henry Ford's absence. But his primary function is the future planning of Ford's marketing strategy, product design, facility requirements, even its public posture and role in society. For a onetime college professor who rose through the finance staff, it's a perfect match of skills and duties.

Directly below Miller is a 64-year-old Scotsman who personifies the up-from-the-ranks auto man. Executive Vice President Charles H. Patterson went to work for Ford in 1927 as a diemaker in the Rouge plant, climbed through a variety of manufacturing jobs, and after 36 years got his present title—and responsibility for all automotive operations in the United States and Canada. A stocky, bustling man who retains the accent of his native Edinburgh, Patterson is a nuts-and-bolts man who delights in getting into the plants and is likely to have a mockup of automobile innards in his office. But he is no stereotype; he is capable also of quoting four different poets in the course of an hour's conversation.

Reporting to Patterson as group vice president for cars and trucks is a man whose meteoric rise has been startling even in the atmosphere of opportunity that exists at Ford. Lee A. Iacocca, now 42, was barely 36 when he was jumped three levels and made boss of the Ford Division. There he fathered the phenomenally successful Mustang—an exploit that won him his present job two years ago. Iacocca's academic credentials are impeccable. He graduated with high honors from Lehigh, later won a master's degree at Princeton. But far from playing egghead, he frequently seems to work at concealing his thoughtfulness. He rather pointedly ignores grammatical niceties and delights in his reputation as a tough guy. An Iacocca admirer in the company says, "He's got more of the common-man perspective than anybody in the outfit. He knows pizzazz when he sees it. Some people at Ford are not so secure where to put the money, but he has a gut feeling about it."

This doesn't mean, however, that Iacocca is a throwback to the old seat-of-the-pants manager. "He's as brainy as any of them," declares a man who has worked closely with him. "Only he doesn't go in for the trappings—he doesn't wear it on his sleeve. In spite of his outward behavior and mannerisms he is a contemplative person. This is no snap judgment. People have gotten in trouble who took him literally. When he talks he seems to mesmerize himself, but decisions are not made on that basis."

Don Frey, Iacocca's successor as head of the Ford Division, almost brings the wheel back full circle. A Ph.D. who left the faculty at the University of Michigan to join Ford's scientific laboratory as a research metallurgist, Frey at 43 is so boyish in appearance that his ever present cigars are almost incongruous. Much more relaxed and informal than McNamara, he has much of his sharp intellect. Frey is a formidable conversationalist, bouncing readily from the car business to current events to historical anecdotes about scientific discovery to the psychology of human motivation. "He is not a 100 percent auto man," says a colleague. But Frey's interest in the business is as boundless as his curiosity about the world around him, and he is hard-working and demanding as his immediate boss, Iacocca. For all his own intelligence, Frey puts a higher premium on action than on thought. "Everybody knows somebody who can talk a lot about things but can never get anything done," he remarks. "So many intellectuals substitute the word for the deed."

Sharing the boss's ear

All these men, and a number of others equally various, have frequent direct contact with Henry Ford, and the interplay of the views—even of their styles—reflects itself through him in the company's policies and operations. One of the important differences between the Ford Motor Company of today and the company of six years ago can be measured in the number of men who have the chairman's ear. McNamara was the last company officer to exercise a dominant, single influence on Henry Ford and the company. Long before he was actually named president in late 1960, McNamara was recognized as the man on whom Henry Ford relied for advice on all the important decisions. With mingled admiration and ruefulness, veterans of those days recall that nobody in the top councils could stand up to the implacable logic of McNamara's arguments. "Even when you knew he was wrong," one many says, "he'd plow you under." Today, while Miller is clearly Henry Ford's first counselor, there are many others to whom the chairman listens with equal attention. For one thing, Miller—although hardly retiring—is not as forceful as McNamara. But more important, Henry Ford is now careful not to rely so heavily on one man—or even one kind of man. . . .

Ford executives vigorously contest the widely held notion that theirs is a Whiz Kid management. Unquestionably, it has attracted to Ford some highly intelligent young men who otherwise might not have looked in the auto industry's direction. But Miller frets about the frustrations that inevitably come to the fellow who believes a Phi Beta Kappa key, an M.B.A. from Harvard, and familiarity with the use of a computer constitute a quick and certain formula for success at judgment of what is needed at the moment," he says. "The car business is still a cut-and-try business. When you're tuning a car, you still need an old tin-bender out there."

It's really the myth about the Whiz Kids that bothers Miller, a myth that has continued to plague McNamara in Washington. What distinguished the group was not just intellectual brilliance, nor was it an over-reliance on computers to solve problems whose emotional content defied quantitative analysis (though critics at Ford still accuse McNamara of seeing the car market as made up of "economic men"). Basically, the hallmark of the Whiz Kids was their youth and their application of new tools and techniques to management problems. In that fundamental sense, it can reasonably be argued that the dominant tone of Ford's management today is set by men who are the spiritual descendants of the Whiz Kids.

The original ten Whiz Kids, however, were all essentially financial analysts. Of the three who are still with the company, one J. Edward Lundy, is now vice president in charge of the finance staff. And it is in the finance staff, with its impressive complement of "little McNamaras," where one can see that earlier era carried over in its purest form. Elsewhere in the company the fast-rising Ford manager is more likely to be an engineer with an advanced degree in industrial management or business administration than accountant or finance expert. . . .

Officials call the company's college recruitment program "the main source of Ford's management strength." No professional recruiters are used. Instead, every year some 280 managers of the company—at levels reaching all the way to Miller—each devote four or five days to visiting a campus and interviewing young men. This duty is rotated, so that virtually every Ford manager at one time or another is involved. From this effort, Ford obtains between 1,500 and 1,600 men annually. The middle levels of management are already heavily stocked with products of the 16-year-old program.

Once aboard, the Ford recruit is not treated like a trainee. The company had an unhappy experience with a formal training program a few years ago, and top officials now believe that "college boys must be productively occupied." In his first two years a recruit works in at least three different jobs. Here and there, supervisors grumble that the time these new men spend on each of their first jobs is so short that the efficiency of the operation suffers. The executives responsible for the program disagree. But, they add, if the problem arose, development of people would come ahead of short-term operating considerations.

In spite of Ford's intimidating size, there is little chance that a promising new man will get lost—or that a mediocrity will be able to hide. Every responsible manager in the company has to take a hard and continuing look at his subordinates, and to think seriously about how he can develop those with the greatest potential. He is required to keep a black loose-leaf notebook that contains profiles, records, performance appraisals, assessments of future potential, and specific plans for the promotion of the people under him. At least once a year the manager must rate each man—on a scale ranging from "unsatisfactory" to "outstanding"—and defend that rating both to the man himself and to his own superior. Henry Ford and Miller spend two weeks each year going over these fat notebooks with the divisional general managers and staff directors. . . .

*　*　*　*　*

HOW GM KEEPS ITS TOP RANKS STRONG[11]

Further Changes in Its Executive Echelon Show How the Company Carefully Grooms Its Management Talent and Allows for Flexible Organization Structure to Meet Changing Conditions

The world's largest manufacturing company this week put the finishing touches to an across-the-board realignment of its top management personnel. All the changes stem from the election last month of James M. Roche as president.

General Motors Corporation's executive committee last week announced eight changes in the top staff and divisional levels. This week, the board of directors finished the job by electing Edward N. Cole as the fourth of its executive vice presidents and naming Semon E. Knudsen and Edward D. Rollert to board membership. Also, two new car division general managers were elected vice presidents, a traditional title that goes with the job.

From the changes, some insights can be gained into the inner workings of giant General Motors, and its long-effective system of organization:

GM, though devoted to its system of centralized finance and policy control with decentralized operations, is far from inflexible in its orga-

---

nizational and manpower structure. Job patterns in the top echelons are altered from time to time to fit the talents and potential of its executives as well as current and future needs of the company. A GM executive, it becomes obvious, never ceases training on the job.

Those pegged for bigger things are watched carefully and nurtured as they climb the executive ladder so that GM's famous pool of management-in-depth never seems to run dry. Of all the auto companies, GM is the only one that, over the years, has rarely had to look outside for top personnel.

The organization is structured—and large enough—to provide ample opportunity and income to keep its managers happy until the time they are needed for different posts. Among the men promoted in the present shift, only one left the company after joining the organization to take another private industry job, (for a time, Rollert was manufacturing manager of the Elgin Watch Co. before returning to GM).

I. The pragmatic approach

If there is one word to describe General Motors, it is "practical." This goes for the way it handles its personnel, its executives, its own outlook, its research, and also its apparent refusal to follow traditional patterns when circumstances change.

This pragmatic approach to building and maintaining a high performing, cooperative team at the top is illustrated clearly in the shuffling of people and jobs the past month.

The favorites   Ever since John F. Gordon, who preceded James M. Roche as president, announced his retirement, speculation about his replacement swirled about the heads of a number of top GM executives. Among them was Executive Vice President James E. Goodman, who had the broad experience and manufacturing knowhow to complement the financial ability of Frederic G. Donner, chairman and chief executive officer.

But Roche, not Goodman, got the job. Roche did have some manufacturing experience, but his career had been largely in sales and marketing. On the other hand, he had been given responsibility for the company's overseas operations and, in addition, had a leg up on Goodman in terms of age. At 58 versus Goodman's 60—he will be in a position to take over when Donner retires.

Two-way bonus   In the shifts that followed Roche's election, however, Goodman got the recognition and the company got greater use of his talents through a logical change in former practice. This came about when Goodman, who is in charge of the automotive, body and assembly, and parts divisions, was named chairman of the administration committee.

This is one of the three major GM committees, made up of the principal officers as well as division general managers. Its function is the planning and review on a monthly basis of division activities. In recent years, it has been the president, as chief operating officer, who has also headed the administration committee. Now, it is Goodman's responsibility, making him clearly the third man in GM's hierarchy. As Goodman himself once told a Chevrolet national sales convention: "Although this is a big company, you can't get lost in it."

New duties In his new assignment, Goodman will be tackling the company's domestic operations and their problems. He mentioned some of those problems at a meeting of GM people earlier this year— among them are quality control, better methods of scheduling product mix to meet the proliferation of models and options, application of numerical control techniques for shorter lead times.

For his part, Roche, as president and also chairman of the executive committee, the No. 2 committee, will put his overseas knowledge to use and will handle broad public policies such as safety, air pollution, and antitrust.

Donner will continue as head of the No. 1 committee, finance.

II. Other shifts

This accommodation of the organization chart to broaden the responsibilities of those at the top—and thus enhance their value to the company as well as give recognition to past achievements—shows up in the other changes that took effect this week.

A new post, assistant to the president, was created for Louis C. Goad, who has been an executive vice president since 1951. This opened up a spot for Edward N. Cole, the new executive vice president who was among those suggested as Gordon's successor. He takes over Goad's duties in charge of staff operations.

Likely bets The triggering effect of General Motors' top-level changes plus shifts in the organization setup also give the company the opportunity to test the abilities and the potential of younger men, not only at the group but at the divisional level. Two of the top divisional vice presidents are immediately spotlighted as comers in the organization:

Semon E. Knudsen, 52, who successfully headed the Pontiac and then the Chevrolet divisions, is now the group vice president in charge of overseas and Canadian operations—a new position. Roche had been in charge of that group, as well as others, before becoming president.

Edward D. Rollert, 53, takes over from Cole as head of the car and truck group. He had been Buick's general manager.

On the ladder   Also tapped for bigger jobs, in GM's conscious effort to maintain management continuity from within, were:

E. M. (Pete) Estes, 49, who followed Knudsen as vice president and general manager of Pontiac and now follows him again as head of the company's biggest division, Chevrolet.

Robert L. Kessler, 50, Buick's general manufacturing manager, who replaces Rollert as vice president and general manager.

John Z. DeLorean, 40, who moves up from chief engineer to Pontiac vice president and general manager.

Thus, General Motors, looking down the road three years to the time of the next big scheduled change—the retirement of Donner as chief executive officer—has started younger men through the seasoning it has always demanded before they assume ever broader responsibilities.

At this stage, it is obviously futile to guess who will come out on top. About the only things you can be sure of are that the vast and efficient organization will (1) have the manpower where and when it needs it, and (2) not be bound by tradition—only by organization needs and individual performance—when change is necessary.

*   *   *   *   *

<h1 align="center">A Postscript:
Ford Fires Again[12]</h1>

At an informal luncheon several years ago, a reporter had a pointed question for Lee Iacocca, at that time Ford Motor Company's president, resident golden boy and unchallenged heir apparent to chairman Henry Ford II, "After Henry leaves," the reporter wondered, "who will take over as head of the company?" With an almost impish grin, Iacocca replied: "Anyone the family wants." At Ford Motor, the "family" is in fact Henry Ford, and last week the hard-driving Iacocca learned to his dismay just what Henry wanted: Iacocca's head.

As Ford himself is fond of remarking, his name is on the building—and in his 32-year reign as head of the company, he has sacked one chairman and two presidents in much the same manner. In Iacocca's case, Ford first won the consent of nine outside directors ostensibly gathered in Dearborn to view the company's upcoming new models and attend to other business at a regular monthly meeting. He then formally fired Iacocca—but didn't bother to tell the ousted president,

---

[12] *Newsweek*, July 24, 1978. Copyright © 1978 by Newsweek, Inc. All rights reserved. Reprinted by special permission.

who had joined Ford as an engineering trainee in 1946, a year after young Henry took control of the company from his grandfather. Iacocca actually got the first news of his dismissal when a trade-magazine publisher called him at his office. "There was supposed to be nothing to come out until Friday," a bitter Iacocca told *Newsweek's* James C. Jones in an interview after the dust had settled, "But somebody leaked the son of a bitch out here Wednesday night."

Later, Iacocca was summoned to Ford's office for the official word from the chairman. What did they talk about precisely? "Precisely?" the still-shaken Iacocca said to Jones. "Well, as best as I can recall it, you get to a point and it becomes, 'well, it's just one of those things.' Then I guess I held forth for quite a long time. You talk about your record, your credentials, where you are wrong, what you are doing right, that kind of thing. There was just nothing [specific]. We didn't have much of a discussion." One news report said that when Iacocca asked Ford what he'd done to deserve firing, the chairman shrugged. "I just don't like you." But Iacocca denied that. "There was no rancor. It was cordial," he told Jones. "I really can't embellish it. There's nothing to embellish." But Iacocca acknowledged the obvious. Henry Ford runs an "almost czarist company," he said with grudging admiration. "Henry is always the boss". . . .

As insiders tell it, Ford assembled all his directors, including Iacocca, for a Wednesday board meeting that lasted all afternoon; he then took only the outside directors to a top-floor dining room, where Iacocca's fate was first discussed. Next morning, the outside directors convened again. In the early afternoon, Iacocca got the unofficial word from his publishing friend—and a couple of hours later, Henry Ford, with brother William Clay Ford at his side, finally told Iacocca face-to-face that he was through.

The ousted president then returned to his office, and later that day and the next received dozens of supportive phone calls—many from Ford vice presidents as surprised and stunned as he. In fact, the first word many of them had of Iacocca's firing came from hallway scuttlebutt late Thursday afternoon. When the veeps left their offices and got into their cars in the basement garage of the executive office building, they found confirmation on their front seats—a note signed by Henry Ford instructing them that henceforth they would all report to Philip Caldwell.

Riches

For Iacocca, the blow was softened by the fact that he will leave Ford a very rich man. He earned nearly $1 million in salary and bonus last year alone. And while he will have no official duties after October 15, he will not formally resign until October of next year, when he turns 55, and thus will become eligible for additional millions in pension benefits and accrued bonuses. Beyond that point, he said last week, "I'm not thinking about anything yet, seriously. I don't know if I'd get into government or education or business." And whatever his shortcomings in Ford's eyes, Iacocca is confident he is leaving behind a healthy company. "We've got a lot going for us," he said. "We've got good people and, I think, spectacular products for 1979, '80 and '81. I think the company is going to make a lot of money."

If that happens, however, somebody else will be taking the credit. Within the next month or so, Henry Ford will choose his next president. Meanwhile, Philip Caldwell has plainly emerged as the new heir apparent to Henry Ford, who is scheduled to retire in four years at 65. But as Lee Iacocca now knows, Caldwell would be well advised to wait before ordering new business cards.

Establishing and implementing formal structure

In Part II we examine concepts and action related to the analysis and change of formal organizational structure. Structure in the form of organization charts is highly visible and important in determining perspectives of members, and the implementation of structural changes is a major undertaking for management.

In Chapter 4 we present a vocabulary and typology of structural forms and the different conditions and situations under which different forms are appropriate. Based on this knowledge, a practical process for the design and redesign of formal structures is then introduced.

In Chapter 5 we discuss the problem of implementation of organizational change from a behavioral perspective. Based on this perspective we develop an approach managers can use in selecting and carrying out the implementation of change.

The cases in Part II include several which deal specifically with organizational design (Case 4–1, Continental Can Company, and Cases 4–2 and 4–3, Texas Instruments), one which combines design with the process of implementation (Case 4–4, Centralized Information Services), two which highlight social problems in implementing change (Cases 5–1 and 5–2, Webster Industries), and a series on organizational design and implementation over an extended period of time (Cases 5–3 to 5–6, FNCB Operating Group, and Case 5–7, Project Paradise).

Chapter 4

UNDERSTANDING AND DESIGNING FORMAL ORGANIZATIONAL STRUCTURE

The right structure does not guarantee results.
But the wrong structure aborts results and smothers
even the best directed efforts.

Peter F. Drucker*

One of the most visible and recognized characteristics of organizations which affects the perspectives and behavior of its members is formal organizational structure. As defined by Albanese (1975, p. 285), "The design or structure of an organization is the relatively stable set of formally defined working relationships among the members of the organization." In terms of our overview model, formal structure is one of the input elements of the "inner environment." It is one of the key inputs available for the exercise of indirect influence on perspective and behavior. We shall use the phrase "formal organizational structure" to refer to the organization chart and the policies and procedures of administrative systems, such as those for planning, resource allocation, budgeting, and controlling.

In this chapter we focus particularly on the organization chart as an input. The chart is the form of the organization, a kind of skeleton of formal relationships among departments and individuals. In general,

---

* *Managing by Results* (New York: Harper & Row, 1964), p. 216.

the form of relationships shows how the organization creates a division of labor to accomplish its tasks, how the power of authority is distributed, what roles or jobs have general responsibility, and what the formal channels of communication are. Of course, the chart alone does not reveal the *total* power or specific responsibilities of a particular job, nor does it show the nature of emergent relationships such as the structures of informal groups. Still, as we shall argue below, discussing the chart and its design is a useful place to start our treatment of organizational elements which affect perspectives and behavior and which can be managed.

THE IMPORTANCE OF FORMAL STRUCTURE

One reason for treating formal organizational structure early in the book is that structure is already well recognized by managers. Many organizations have no explicit strategy, and many managers have no workable vocabulary or perspective on emergent social relationships, or management styles, or individual perspectives of employees. At the same time, most organizations have some kind of division of labor and administrative procedures, and virtually all managers recognize and talk about such formal structural things as who the boss is, to whom people report, what their responsibilities are, and so on.

This is not to imply that formal structure is necessarily the most important determinant of perspective, behavior, and performance results. Characteristics of formal structure do have effects on these elements. In a review of empirical research on these relationships, Cummings and Berger (1976) list seven particular aspects of structure which typically have been operationalized by researchers as independent variables. The list, shown in Figure 4–1, is a useful one to help clarify the aspects of formal structure, and particularly aspects of the

FIGURE 4–1
Aspects of formal organizational structure

1. The vertical level of the position held by an organizational member.
2. The nature of the authority (line versus staff) vested in the position.
3. The span of control (number of subordinates) of the position.
4. The size (number of members) of an organizational subunit—a department, for example.
5. The size of the total organization.
6. The number of levels of authority in the organization—whether its shape is relatively tall or flat.
7. The distribution of decision-making power across the levels of the organization—whether the organization is relatively centralized or decentralized.

Source: Cummings and Berger (1976), pp. 34–35.

organization chart. These specific aspects will be referred to throughout this chapter. Regarding the relationships between these and certain dependent variables, Cummings and Berger conclude, for example, that the higher one moves up the vertical hierarchy, the greater the satisfaction. Overall, they conclude that the research shows a few other weak direct relationships between features of structure and dependent variables. At the same time, they caution that these relationships are typically more complex than simple one-to-one covariance. In terms of our overview model and the discussion of natural processes (Chapter 3) we would expect this to be the case. As we have emphasized, *all* of the inputs and the emergent system of relationships, plus some forces from the external environment and internal processes, affect perspectives, behavior, and results.

Regardless of whether or not clear relationships between aspects of formal structure and results can be empirically validated by research, it is clear that as a practical matter formal structure is important in the *personal* perspectives of managers at middle and higher levels. There are two reasons for this. First, managers probably affect results and behavior of subordinates more through indirect influence arising from appropriate formal structuring than they do by exerting influence through the emergent system or face-to-face by direct influence. At least, as Perrow (1977) points out, managers *should* make use of this more. If formal structure is well designed and accepted as legitimate in the perspectives of employees, the need for managers to build bases of power and exercise other forms of influence is lessened. To put this another way, an appropriately designed organization reduces the need for management to be involved in the more routine, operational decisions and work and frees them to deal with the exceptions to the usual and with strategic decisions, longer-range planning, and structural change itself. Conversely, a poor formal structure makes for more managerial energy spent on direct and semidirect influence.

The second reason for the importance of formal structure to middle- and upper-level managers is a more personal one for them. As indicated, formal structure in general and formal organizational relationships in particular largely define the distribution of authority or formal power and the hierarchy of formal roles or jobs in an organization. Managers are concerned and interested in this not only to help them do their jobs, but also because it is so relevant to their careers. This seems quite obvious to most managers, but sometimes comes as a surprise to students and researchers of organizational behavior, whose training and experience may orient them to look strictly at intrinsic rewards (e.g., self-fulfillment) and overlook the importance to managers of promotion, formal power, and the attendant financial rewards that go with higher organizational jobs.

ORGANIZATIONAL FORMS: WHY SUCH VARIETY?

There is a wide variety of formal structures of work organizations. One might well expect the structure to change as an organization grows, reflecting a need for more hierarchical levels, or perhaps decentralization at some point. However, even for organizations of the *same* size and age the differences in structure from one to the next can be extreme. Some are extremely flat, with few levels and wide spans of control, others tall and pyramidal in shape, others with overlapping lines of authority. Moreover, subunits within the same organization often vary in form. Later in this chapter, we shall describe four basic structural forms, which capture in distinctive simplicity much of this observable variety. These are:

1. Functional (centralized).
2. Divisional (centralized and decentralized).
3. Overlay.
4. Matrix.

The fact that successful organizations exhibit different basic forms should lead to some thought. Why is it that Texas Instruments is so different in formal structure from General Motors, and they are different from McDonald's, the Jewel Companies, the Environmental Protection Agency, and so on? Why is it that different organizations, even successful ones of roughly the same size, have such very different formal structures?

Organizations and their external environments

The particular answers to this will probably fall into three categories of explanation. First, structures differ from one organization to another because organizations operate in different *external environments*. Different industries, for example, have different kinds of customers, different rates of growth and paces of change, different degrees of regulation, and different technologies available to firms which compete in them. Intuitively, one would expect these differences to be reflected over time in different organizational forms as firms adapt to the particular conditions of their environments. In one sense, organizations are like biological organisms which evolve by selective adaptation to their environments. Just as there are tremendous varieties of living animal species, presumably all evolved from the same simple forms of life, so too we would expect variety in organizational forms. This analogy suggests that organizations are organisms which evolve through selective adaptation to environmental conditions. They must change and adapt in order to survive. Using this explanation, it is unnecessary to imply any conscious action by managers or other decision makers to explain differences in structure. It is the "environmental imperative" explanation for variety of forms, and there is much truth in it.

One does not have to be a researcher in sociology to recognize the general causal relationship between outer environment and formal organizational structure. The relationship can be recognized intuitively. Nonetheless, researchers have confirmed what the astute practitioner knows. Moreover, researchers have developed some concepts and variables to measure and explain more carefully particular aspects of the environment, features of formal structure, and the relationships among them. For our purposes we shall make use of these concepts and relationships further along in this note as analytical tools for managers to further their understanding of formal organizations as adaptive entities in their environments, and to use in the process of organization design or redesign.

Pugh et al. (1969) present a conceptual scheme which specifies aspects of the external environment and of structural variables. As they point out, dealing with the question of what leads to different structural forms, as we are here, means considering aspects of structure as dependent variables resulting from environmental conditions. This is obviously a different point of view than asking what differences a given structure leads to in members' perspectives, behavior, and organizational results. Thus, the approach of this chapter is to focus on how structure is formed given some set of work perspectives which management wishes to create.

An important stream of research and theory on organization structure in relationship to external environment includes the work of Burns and Stalker (1961), Woodward (1965), Lawrence and Lorsch (1967), and Galbraith (1973). Although the research reported in some of these works includes large samples and statistical relationships, their most valuable contributions for our purposes are the conceptual developments. Woodward showed that the basic type of *technology adopted* by organizations from the available types on the environment was crucial in determining key aspects of structure. Lawrence and Lorsch saw the external environment as consisting of subenvironments, each with different importance to the different subunits of the organization. Thus, the subenvironment of available manufacturing technology might be a key one for the production department, the subenvironment of customers' key to sales, and so on. Lawrence and Lorsch used the concept *differentiation* to describe the relative extent of diversity of subenvironments and subunits, and *integration* to describe the level of coordination necessary among subunits. Consistent with this, Galbraith conceptualized the organization as an information processing organism. The key attribute of the environment is the degree of *uncertainty* of information relevant to the organization performing its key tasks. Uncertainty was defined as relative to the organizations' ability to process information. For Galbraith, the nature of formal structure, including the extent of differentiation and integrative devices used, is a product resulting from how the organization copes with uncertainty as it functions to achieve performance goals. We shall make use of these concepts as we develop our explanations of the four basic organizational forms.

This tradition of research has led to the basic recognition that the *appropriate* organizational structure is largely a function of aspects of the organization's environmental context. That is, there is no one best structure for all organizations, and not all structures are equally good. Rather, the question of appropriate structure is *contingent* on, most heavily, characteristics of the environment in which an organization is functioning. This general notion, "contingency theory", can be most useful for managers. We shall make use of the idea of contingency with reference not only to organizational design in this chapter, but also with respect to strategies for the implementation of organizational change (Chapter 5), choice of management style (Chapter 10), and elsewhere. The contingency approach reminds the manager of the need for diagnosis and analysis of situations and problems and the need for tailoring the organization, change approach, style, or whatever to fit the situation rather than to rely on some universal or currently popular form, approach, or style.

Organizations and their strategies

A second explanation for observed variety of formal structures is that different organizations have different purposes, goals, and ways of attaining those goals. That is, organizations have different *strategies*. Even for organizations of the same size and age and in the same environments we find differences in structure because different top management decisions lead to different strategies for dealing with that environment. In this explanation of variety we recognize that the organization is in part a consciously fashioned entity. From this perspective structure is the product or result of managerial decisions which reflect the purpose, choice of environments, and recognition of internal strengths and weaknesses. The strategy, in turn, leads the top decision makers to fashion a formal structure appropriate to that chosen strategy. An important reference substantiating this is Chandler's *Strategy and Structure* (1966), an account of historical studies of reorganizations at General Motors, du Pont, Standard Oil, and Sears-Roebuck. The concept of corporate strategy, and its development and implementation as the central task of top management, has been elaborated as a normative theory by Andrews (1971) and others from the business policy field at the Harvard Business School. The definition of strategy from that tradition reflects the broad but central importance of the concept:

> [Strategy is] the pattern of objectives, purposes or goals and major policies and plans for achieving these goals, stated in such a way as to define what business the company is in or is to be in and the kind of company it is or is to be. (Learned et al., 1965)

A concise approach to organization design as the product of a managerial decision-making process is contained in a pair of articles by Ansoff and Brandenburg (1971).

Strategy as a force on formal structure differs from external environment as a force in two ways. First, strategy as we have used it here is an explicit statement of what an organization is and what it intends to accomplish; it results from a managed process stimulated by basic questions like, "What business are we in?" Strategy setting requires understanding of the external environment. At the same time, much of the impact on strategy and structure by the external environment may result from forces which are not recognized and consciously reflected in strategic deliberations. Over long periods of time, most organizations respond to these forces incrementally, or in ways which could hardly be called deliberate. It is in this sense that the external environment acts as a natural or unmanaged process, as described in Chapter 3, and has effects on formal structure in ways that are essentially unmanaged.

The second distinction between strategy and the external environment as they affect formal structure is that strategy setting takes into account the *internal capabilities* of the firm. For example, a firm with a crackerjack research and development (R&D) department may choose a strategy which relies on new product development, and have the R&D group report as a unit to the chief executive officer (CEO). Another firm in the same industry may split up R&D and depend on relatively minor periodic enhancements.

Before leaving this part of the discussion we should emphasize that it is quite possible for an organization to have a strategy without setting strategy. Observers and analysts may infer what an organization is up to and how it seems to be going about it, but management of that organization may not have an explicit strategy.

Organizations and internal social forces

A third explanation for variety is that different organizations have different *internal social forces*. This category covers the effects on formal organizational structure which arise from the influence of an individual or department, as manifested by politics and bargaining among managers or departments or other coalitions within the organization. Company politics are processes of interaction and influence in which managers aim to build power and control. These efforts may or may not be in the best interest of the organization as a whole. Political battles are often most intense during the process of design and implementation of structural changes and other inputs including the implementation of new technologies, such as new computer applications, and the hiring and promotion of managers. In practice, as anyone familiar with formal organizational change knows, organizations as often as not are designed around key people, rather than the other way around. This is a reflection of the effects of these internal social forces.

Some recent research and observation has begun to recognize the importance of these internal social forces at managerial levels on the structure and functioning of organizations. For an approach to organization design which takes social forces into account, see Nystrom, Hedberg, and Starbuck (1976). The work of Hickson et al. (1974) and Salancik and Pfeffer (1977) suggests that this can be both beneficial and detrimental. It is beneficial for a group or department to grow in power relative to others if their function is a crucial one for the times and problems facing the organization. Thus, many firms were dominated by engineering and production during early phases of their growth, when they had a competitive edge due to a new product. As competitors came in, the marketing function became more important and it was beneficial for marketing managers to have more influence on top management decisions. The other side of the coin is that once in power, individuals and dominant coalitions like to stay there—human nature, if you will—and they may well stay beyond their usefulness. We shall take a close look at the process of politics in organizations in Chapter 7.

In terms of the concepts suggested earlier in this chapter, there are two appropriate ways for internal social forces to affect formal structure. First, an individual or managerial group should obtain and exercise power in the structure if they have the capability to cope with the external *uncertainty* in a key part of the external environment. Second, they should have such formal power if the unit they manage is crucial to the short-run functioning of the organization.

Summary

An understanding of the reason for variety in formal structure must include all three of the explanations discussed above. We are thinking here of formal structure as the *result* of other forces, the dependent variable, with the independent variables being outer environment, strategy, internal capabilities, and internal social forces. This discussion is summarized in Figure 4–2.

FIGURE 4–2
Elements and processes affecting formal structure

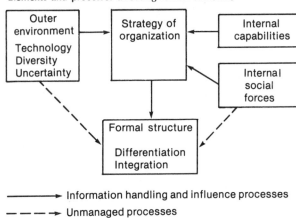

⟶ Information handling and influence processes

– – – ⟶ Unmanaged processes

Note that most of elements in Figure 4–2 can be matched up with or derived from elements in the overview model. "Internal social forces" may be thought of as a summary of the emergent relationships, particularly at managerial levels. The arrows represent processes of information flow, influence, and unmanaged forces. For the sake of brevity, the information and influence arrows do not show the elements of managerial perspective and behavior through which they operate.

According to the argument developed here, if two organizations evolve under identical patterns of these forces, they should develop identical structures. To the extent there are differences in the environments, strategies, and internal social forces of organizations, which there are, it follows that variety would evolve in the structures of organizations, which we observe. In the discussion in Chapter 1, formal structure was assumed to be fixed or static for purposes of explaining organizational behavior. In this chapter we focus on structure as the element subject to change.

In addition to providing a basis for understanding the major forces which affect formal structure, this discussion should serve to provide a checklist of factors to take into consideration in planning organizational design.

BASIC FORMS OF STRUCTURE

In order to understand the structure of any organization and alternatives to it, we shall describe four basic forms that organizational charts may take. These are functional, divisional, overlay, and matrix. Only a few organizations will have the precise skeletal form of one of these four types; in that sense these are ideal types. Most large, complex organizations are combinations of these.

There are common features of all of these forms. These include, first, that they have division of labor or differentiation. That is, all formal organizations larger than four or five individuals have some degree of specialization and separation of work. Second, all the forms have some means to achieve integration or coordination of the differentiated parts. Two things distinguish the forms from each other. The first is the particular rationale or dimension which is the basis for the differentiation; that is, whether the major subunits of the form are divided upon according to differences in functional tasks, or market orientation, or geographical location, or whatever. Second, the forms differ according to the way in which the necessary integration is achieved. We shall discuss the distinguishing features and the general strengths and weaknesses of each form.

The functional form

The most basic organizational form is one in which subunits (departments or groups of one or more employees) are each devoted to a different technical specialty or function and have distinctively different kinds of tasks to perform. In business firms the typical functions are R&D, production operations, and marketing, each reporting to the coordinating office (see Figure 4–3). Here, the primary focus or ratio-

FIGURE 4–3
The functional form

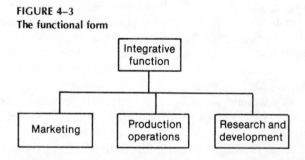

nale for differentiation is the fact that there are different technical or functional tasks to be performed. Each unit contributes its work effort to the product or service, and units efforts are integrated through planning, direction, and control by a *general management* function.

The fundamental advantage of the functional form over *no* division of labor, that is an arrangement of units and people in which everyone does all the different tasks required in the organization's work, is simply efficiency. By dividing up the tasks and specializing, individuals and functional units can become more proficient by moving up on the learning curve and employing machines, techniques, and procedures which take advantage of economies of scale. Organizational subunits which so specialize can become technical innovators at improving the ways their work is done. The fundamental advantages and principles underlying this form have been recognized in practice for thousands of years, and articulated by such writers as Adam Smith (1776) and Frederick Taylor (1923). These advantages hold about as well today as ever. A majority of large and successful work organizations make use of the functional form either as the primary means of formal organization or in combination with other formal structures. As we shall see in discussions of the other three forms, the functional form is often a common basic building block for other organization structures.

As a functional organization grows in size or the tasks become more complex, retention of the functional form requires increasing the levels of organizational hierarchy and the effort and investment in communications and coordination, that is, in integrative functions and activities. When this occurs there will often be an increase in the number of hierarchical levels (levels of authority) and/or an increase in average span of control. These aspects may be accompanied by a host of formal rules, policies, and procedures governing work behavior. These are characteristics of a *bureaucracy*. The principles and advantages of bureaucratic organization were elaborated by Max Weber.[1]

The disadvantages of the form, particularly as it becomes bureaucratic, are the considerable added overhead costs of these integrative roles and systems. Moreover, the flip side of the advantage of specialization of any kind is the potential narrowness of perspective of the specialists, who may not see the forest of overall organizational goals for the trees of their concentrated expertise. Specialization and investment in hierarchies can lead to a slowness of organizational adaptability and change.

When adopted for an entire organization the functional bureaucratic form is well suited to meeting overall strategy under conditions of environmental simplicity and low uncertainty. That is, this form can be the most efficient and effective and can also meet standards on the other results criteria when the relevant parts of the environment are not highly differentiated, not characterized by such aspects of uncertainty as unpredictability and rapid change. In these instances the functions may be defined in terms of routine subtasks, and the work may flow sequentially from one functional subunit to the next. The hierarchical levels serve to integrate the work flow by dealing with expectations to the preplanned routine. If uncertainty increases for

---

[1] A concise summary of Weber's work and of the problems with classical bureaucracy may be found in Shull, Delbecq, and Cummings (1970).

some reason (such as growth in size or greater environmental change), the organization may attempt to adapt by further subdivision and simplification of subtasks or by increasing the skills and competence of employees so that they may handle uncertainty at their levels, and correspondingly by using subunit goal setting rather than close control of the routinized work (Galbraith, 1973).

Analysts and critics of bureaucratic organizations in practice point out its frequent economic dysfunctions, in terms of efficiency and effectiveness, and the social and human costs in terms of employee satisfaction and adaptability. Some, notably Bennis (1966), have predicted the demise of bureaucracy in light of secular trends requiring that organizations be increasingly adaptable in order to survive the rising expectations for mankind for more challenging and meaningful work. Perrow (1974), while he appears sympathetic to the criticisms, has questioned whether in fact there are any significant trends in these respects, and observes that the basic bureaucratic form is still very much alive. Both Perrow (1977) and Blau (1955) have noted that under certain conditions autonomy of work and efficiency can be *retained* in bureaucratic situations.

The divisional form

Figure 4–4 shows the second basic form, the divisional. The primary focus or rationale for differentiation of units in the divisional form is

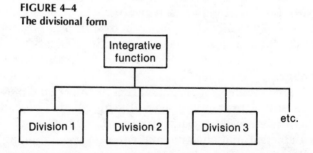

FIGURE 4–4
The divisional form

some task dimension *other* than functional task specialties. Divisions under the top integrative unit may be devoted to different geographical locations, different products, or different market segments. Each of these divisions contains within it the several technical functional specialties needed to research, produce, and market its product or service. Depending on how autonomous the divisions are with respect to the top integrative unit, the divisional form may be further categorized as *centralized* or *decentralized*. That is, the decision-making authority may be relatively more widely distributed or more centrally held.

Whereas the basic functional form is never fully decentralized, the divisional form may exist all along a continuum from tight centralization to a very loose decentralization.

In the smallest and simplest state of the divisional form, each of the basic subunits under the integrative unit consists of only a few members of each of the functional task specialties. The structure within units is very "organic," that is, flat, without many levels, and with wide spans of control. In large divisional organizations it becomes attractive to differentiate and coordinate *within* each division, and so the divisions themselves have more hierarchical levels and may themselves have characteristics of the functional form and of bureaucracies.

Thus, the divisional form differs from the functional primarily in that some task focus other than the required technical specialties has been used as the primary dimension for differentiation. The divisional form has the basic advantage of being more responsive and adaptable to different subenvironments, such as markets or businesses, than a functional form of equivalent total size. The divisional form is often an outgrowth of a functional form which has become large, has passed the peak of advantages of economies of scale for centralized technical functions, and/or whose products and customers are becoming more diverse. Comparing functional and divisional organizations of the same size, it should be noted that the functional form has differentiation according to technical task, whereas the divisional form makes coordination or integration easier among the technical tasks. Both of these forms suffer relative to the overlay form wth respect to responsiveness to need for short-term change.

The overlay form

Would it be possible to combine in a single organizational structure the advantages of the economies of technical division of labor of the functional form and product or geographical or market segment division of labor of the divisional form? The overlay form, shown in Figure 4–5, is the organizational attempt to do so.

Here, the basic subunit differentiation is the same as the functional form, but one of the functions becomes defined by a focus like that of a divisional form. This additional function, which may be set up to handle different customer accounts, products, customers grouped by industry, projects, programs, or whatever, becomes the locus of market-oriented integrative management. This form has been called the project management, program management, or matrix form. We shall follow the terminology of Davis and Lawrence in their book, *Matrix* (1977), and reserve the term *matrix* for a distinctively separate form.

There are three important distinguishing features of the overlay

FIGURE 4–5
The overlay form

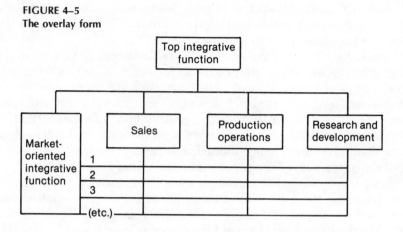

form. First, those individual employees within a function (those who reside along vertical lines) who are also members of a market-oriented group (those who reside along horizontal lines) in effect have two sets of responsibilities, one to their functional task unit (R&D, production/ operations, or sales) and the other to their project or program unit. The second feature is that the assignment of functional resources to the market project or program is intended to be temporary, lasting anywhere from a few weeks to a matter of years. And finally, the overlay structure is intended to reflect a *dominance* of one focus or rationale for the basic division of labor over the other. In practice, one of the two dimensions is invariably the functional technical specialties, and more often than not it is the dominant one, at least in the sense that more human and other resources go into it than the other dimension.

A major advantage of the overlay form is its flexibility to adjust to environmental changes, product life cycles, and whatever other potential threats due to obsolescence may exist in the firm's environment. When used for project management, for example, this form facilitates the coming and going of project team members as the requirements of different stages of the project task call for different resources of expertise and involvement. At the same time, the form permits structural recognition of a dominant focus, and in particular makes it possible to take advantage of centralized functional resources.

The major disadvantage of this form is that it requires acceptance, understanding, and ability among those organizational members who work under both the authority of a functional boss and the authority of a project boss to work with the realities of ambiguous reporting relationships, of conflicting pulls between functional loyalty and efficiency on the one hand and project or program success on the other. More energy and cost must go into coordination, training and development, and conflict resolution than would typically be the case in either pure functional or divisional forms.

The matrix form

The final form, which exists in relatively few organizations but typically in those dealing with the most uncertain environments, is the matrix form.

The matrix organization may be distinguished from the overlay, which it resembles with respect to dual (or more) boss-subordinate relationships, by the fact that two (or more) of the basic dimensions for primary differentiation are *equal* in importance. That is, in the matrix there is no dominance in importance of one base, such as the technical-functional, over another. This equality is reflected in the skeletal chart in Figure 4–6, following the convention of Davis and Lawrence (1977), by turning the rectangular shape of the overlay form onto a corner, giving the matrix a diamond shape.

But the matrix is different more than in degree of relative dominance. Each of the two basic dimensions of the diamond (e.g., functional and product) now has equal weight and power. The underlying role of the market-oriented project or program function in the overlay form was to marshall needed resources from the technical functions for temporary assignment, that is, to serve primarily as integrator, oriented toward some particular customer. In the matrix form, *both* the functional subunits *and* the product subunits, as examples, have their particular foci. Although neither could carry out its total mission without interaction with the other, there is need in the matrix for another unit to do the integration. Thus, the matrix adds a whole new dimension of coordinating effort at a relatively low organizational level. This is represented by the "business-oriented integrative function" unit in Figure 4–6.

In some instances major organizations find it necessary to impose a third basic dimension of focus onto the matrix form. A typical example is represented by Dow-Corning, which evolved over time three sets of dimensional foci, namely functions, products, and geographical distribution.[2] Other examples of organizations which have the basic matrix form are Texas Instruments, TRW Systems, and some parts of Citibank.[3]

The major advantages of the matrix form include the potentially highest degree of structural adaptability to changes in environment

---

[2] This description of the Dow-Corning organization is provided in Groggin (1974).

[3] Descriptions of these and other matrix organizations may be found in Davis and Lawrence (1977).

FIGURE 4–6
The matrix form

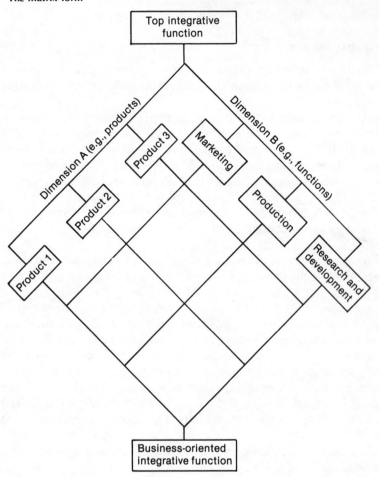

and strategy. In addition, once members become acclimatized to working in the difficult and complex matrix structure, the fact that coordination, planning, and control are of necessity truly pushed downward
can result in a situation of continual, on-the-spot structural adapta-
tions to external change. The major disadvantage of the matrix is implied in what was just said: the costs and efforts of coordination. It can
be an extremely difficult process to orient people's perspectives and
behavior to rapid change (uncertainty), and to the reality of the need to
continually confront conflict and differences of opinion in a manner
that will give rise to resolutions in the best interests of the organization
as a whole. A good illustration of the kind of requirements on manage-

ment style imposed by the overlay and matrix forms may be found in the case, "Product Management at United Brands" later in this book.

Where the cost of coordination can be borne, the management style found or developed, and perspectives oriented to ambiguity, matrix organizations are potent instruments for dealng with extremely changeable environments and for facilitating product and process innovations.

A PRACTICAL APPROACH TO ORGANIZATION DESIGN

It is important for managers to understand the advantages and disadvantages of the basic types of organizational forms, if for no other reason than to know how their own organization is supposed to work. Beyond that, however, top management is often confronted with the need to design an organization from scratch or, more frequently, to redesign an existing structure. The need to redesign may arise due to some present or anticipated problem in results and behavior which can be traced to deficiencies in the formal structure.

In the remainder of this chapter we shall present a sequence of steps and a normative approach to the process of organizational design. We shall treat this as a special case of basic problem solving. It consists of the steps of diagnosis, analysis, and synthesis. A final step, implementation of the design, is of such importance that it will be treated separately in Chapter 5.

What particular general guidelines can be suggested to management as they conduct the process of *diagnosis* of the need for structural design, *analysis* of the organizational requirements, and *synthesis* of these into a new or modified structure? We shall introduce several tools, concepts, and suggestions in each of these steps.

Diagnosis of a structural problem

An important question to ask at the outset of an effort to design or redesign structure is, "Who should be involved in the process?" The answer to this may vary widely, from only the one or a few managers at the level below which the change is to occur to a widespread participation of people at lower levels and from other organizational units. In this sense the choice can be treated like any decision-making process, where involvement of others is a function of how fast the job has to get done, how much others' involvement is needed to get their commitment, how much the management truly wants others' inputs, and so on.

In the case of structural design, it is often only the higher level of management which has the broad perspective necessary to see beyond intermediate problems and departmental special interests. As a general rule, the responsibility for design and major structural change ought to lie with top line management. Inputs of information about problems may come from lower levels, and expertise with respect to the substance of analysis, structural forms, and process may come from staff specialists or outside consultants. But the final and guiding word ought to be at or near the organizational level immediately above the units affected by the change.

The process of diagnosis of an organizational problem in general was described in Chapter 1. It consists, first, of the identification of current or anticipated organizational outcomes or results which are off-spec, and of the work behavior which precedes those results. These are the symptoms of the problem. Second, the diagnosis calls for developing a descriptive understanding, or model, of the perspectives of the individuals or group responsible for the behavior and results in question. This step is an inductive process which attempts to answer the question, "In the point of view of the people involved, what is the conception of the important issues and rewards to them which may be affecting their work behavior?"

Third, the diagnosis proceeds to an identification of the aspects of emergent relationships and formal inputs which are affecting perspectives. It is important to note that both the elements themselves and the *interaction* of elements affect perspectives. For example, there may be a strong emergent group with norms oriented toward cooperation and teamwork, and a management-by-objectives (MBO) system of formal incentives which rewards individual achievement and encourages competition. The combination of these may lead individuals to a cynical view of the formal system, or to discomfort leading to work alienation and below-standard effort and performance. The diagnostic step ends with a problem definition in terms of the inputs and emergent elements which can be changed by management action to alleviate the symptoms.

In the context of this general diagnostic process, formal structure and organizational form may be one of the elements which needs adjustment. It is that special case we are addressing here. In particular, a change in structural elements, including form and administrative support systems, is called for when there are problems whose symptoms are recurring, are growing in severity over time, or are of a particularly critical nature. When an organization is in crisis, when its survival is at stake, or when management needs to transmit strong signals for change is generally a time when significant structural change is needed and can be pulled off. Structural design and change ought to be considered only in conjunction with changes in other elements which are causes of work behavior. Structural change is an attempt to create a better form for indirect influence, but its conduct and success require that management exercise semidirect and direct influence, as these processes were defined in Chapter 2.

Top management and their advisors seem all too often to make one of two kinds of errors with respect to structural redesign. One is an avoidance of structural change when it is called for. The other is a total reliance on formal structural change to induce changes in work behavior when other elements and forces must inevitably be changed as well.

This discussion of diagnosis has focused on an existing organization, and leads to a problem definition suggesting corrective changes and *re*design. The reader should keep in mind that the same general process applies when management is considering future adverse symptoms or planning for a new organization with anticipated work behavior and perspectives, emergent relationships, and inputs which are as yet nonexistent.

Analysis of structural design

Having determined that an organizational problem requires a change in one or more structural elements, care should be taken to analyze the fundamental requirements which are imposed on the organization or which will be imposed if the problem relates to a new design. Basically the analysis involves having a statement of strategy and listing the key tasks or critical factors (Rockhart, 1979) which the organization must perform to carry out the strategy. These tasks are then prioritized and weighted and used to determine the nature of the basic rationale or dimensional focus for organizing the choice of basic form and to determine the key subtasks which different parts of the organization must accomplish. In other words, in terms of our discussion earlier in this chapter, the analysis step we advocate consists of a thorough look at the requirements (in terms of tasks) placed on an organization by its environment and its chosen strategy, but not by its internal social forces, and a choice of an ideal organizational form based on those requirements.

Listing and prioritizing the key tasks which an organization must accomplish is itself often quite difficult. The difficulty lies in defining tasks at a level of specificity which is neither too general to be operationally useful nor so specific as to require a total list that is unmanageably long. Saying that an existing profit center has the task of increasing its return on investment by 10 percent is too general to be useful for design purposes. Such a statement is more of an objective, requiring some time frame, than it is an operational task. On the other hand, saying that the unit has the task of increasing the utilization of production machinery in a particular plant by 50 percent may be useful to the plant, but is too specific to be helpful in thinking through structural organizational requirements. But saying that the profit center must improve the speed and effectiveness of communications between one or more field sales units and plants, in order to improve production planning, decrease machine downtime, and increase return on investment, is stating a task in terms that are useful and suggestive of an organizational structure issue.

The usefulness of a task description is also a function of the *level* of organizational design being considered. At a very high level, such as one which includes an entire multiproduct division, a general strategic task may be best, while at an operational level, such as the field sales force, a more specific, short-term task is more appropriate.

Eliminating the effects of politics and human resource strengths and weaknesses on organization design at this stage is intended to create a somewhat ideal and rational design. This approach is much in keeping with the approach of Ansoff and Brandenburg (1971). This will necessarily have to be modified in the synthesis and implementation steps as a result of the effects of those internal emergent human forces.

Choice of form

Choice of form (or check on existing form) depends on the answers to four analytical questions aimed at determining the implications of the prioritized *tasks* and also the *size* of the organization for requirements on organizational structure. These analytical questions are:

1. In light of prioritized tasks and the organization's size, what is the most important basic dimension or rationale for the horizontal division of labor (differentiation)?

From the discussion of forms, it will be recalled that this may be task functional, geographical, type of business, or some combination of these. The answer to this determines the essential form of organization; that is, functional, divisional, overlay, or matrix as described earlier. In general, the smaller the organization the less appropriate will be a matrix form.

2. In light of tasks, size, and basic form, what are the essential units of horizontal differentiation?

The answer to this question provides a finer cut on the division of labor, and leads to a clustering of subunits according to the functions or subtasks they are to carry out in accomplishing the tasks.

3. In light of the above, what are the essential units of vertical division of labor?

This seeks to determine the extent to which separation according to operational work (day-to-day) versus control work versus strategic planning is appropriate. These types of decision work have been elaborated by Anthony, Dearden, and Vancil (1976).[4] This deliberation seeks to determine the number of layers of hierarchy.

4. What purely integrative functions are required, and what structures other than hierarchical reporting relationships are necessary to carry out integration?

This is perhaps the most important analytical question in practice, particularly when the problem under study lies in inadequate coordination of effort among units rather than a poor basic division of labor. Once this fourth step is completed in a preliminary way, there should be an iteration through the other three steps again.

These four analytical questions lead to a preliminary determination of the ideal organizational structure.

Synthesis

The final step in the design process consists of synthesizing the elements of the basic form into a final design. This involves a process of simulation of the ideal structure and adjustments of it to take into account potential problems which may arise.

The essential question to be asked here is, "Given the ideal design, what will be the effects on the perspectives of groups and key individuals when the new structure is introduced?" The answers to this should lead to a final organization structure in which known individual managers and other employees are located on the chart, job descriptions are determined, manpower needs are listed, and an implementation plan is formulated. In effect, the synthesis step in organization design brings the abstraction of the ideal and rational structure resulting from the analysis step back down to earth. The resulting structure will necessarily represent a compromise between an ideal structure and the realities of anticipated expectations, political powers, and potential influence.

In closing, it should be evident that the step-by-step design process advocated here is itself highly idealized and oversimplified. The purpose of presenting the process has been to begin to fill the gap between the growing body of descriptive research on organizations, which has yielded valuable concepts and theories, and the important practical

---

[4] For an elaboration on alternative decision-making styles, see Tannenbaum and Schmidt (1973).

needs of managers for guidelines on how to conduct organizational design.

QUESTIONS FOR STUDY AND DISCUSSION

1. Sketch the organizational chart of your current organization, or one with which you are familiar. Which of the basic forms is it most like?
   What combinations of forms are in evidence?

2. Imagine a major need for change for your organization, such as the introduction of a new product by a competitor, the impact of a doubling in the cost of some raw material or service, or whatever.
   What changes in your current organization might be helpful in order to deal with this contingency in the long run?

3. Describe an industry and environment which would lend themselves to the bureaucratic (functional) form of organization.
   Can you cite examples of trends that might lead to the demise of the bureaucratic organization?

4. Would you prefer to work for an organization with an implicit or an explicit strategy? With a functional, divisional, overlay, or matrix organization? Why?

Case 4–1
Continental Can Company of Canada, Ltd.

By the fall of 1963, Continental Can Company of Canada had developed a sophisticated control system for use in its plants. This control system, begun in the years following World War II, stressed competition within the company as well as against other companies in the industry. Within its division at Continental, the can manufacturing plant at St. Laurent, Quebec, had become a preferred site for production management trainees as a result of its successful use of control systems. According to a division training executive:

> The St. Laurent people look at the controls as tools. They show trainees that they really work. The French-Canadian atmosphere is good too. In a French-Canadian family everything is open and above-board. There are no secrets. Trainees can ask anyone anything and the friendliness and company parties give them a feel for good employee relations.

PRODUCTS, TECHNOLOGY, AND MARKETS

Continental Can Company of Canada in 1963 operated a number of plants in Canada. The principal products of the St. Laurent plant were open top food cans, bottle caps and crowns, steel pails, and general line containers. Of these open top cans constituted the largest group. These were manufactured for the major packers of vegetable products—peas, beans, corn, and tomatoes—and for the soup manufacturers. Beer and soft drink cans were a growing commodity, and large quantities of general line containers of many different configurations were produced to hold solvents, paints, lighter fluids, waxes, anti-freeze, and so on. Several styles of steel pails of up to five-gallon capacity were also produced to hold many specialized products.

Most of the thousands of different products, varying in size, shape, color, and decoration were produced to order. Typical lead times between the customer's order and shipment from the plant were two to three weeks in 1963, having been reduced from five and one half to six weeks in the early 1950s, according to St. Laurent plant executives.

Quality inspection in the can manufacturing operation was critical, as the can maker usually supplied the closing equipment and assisted in or recommended the process to be used in the final packing procedure. In producing Open Top food cans, for example, the can body was formed, soldered, and flanged at speeds exceeding 400 cans per minute. After the bottom or end unit was assembled to the body, each can was air tested to reject poor double seams or poor soldering or plate inclusions that could cause pin holes. Both side seams and double seams underwent periodic destruction testing to ensure that assembly specifications were met. Although a number of measuring devices were used in the process, much of the inspection was still visual, involving human inspection and monitoring. The quality of the can also affected the filling and processing procedure: it had to withstand internal pressures from expansion of the product as it was heated and then it had to sustain a vacuum without collapsing when it was cooled. Costly claims could result if the container failed in the field and the product had to be withdrawn from store shelves.

Almost all of the containers required protective coatings inside and out, and the majority were decorated. The coating and decorating equipment was sophisticated and required sizable investment. This part of the operation was unionized, and the lithographers or press men were among the highest paid of the various craftsmen in the plant.

Most of the key equipment was designed and developed by the parent organization over many years. The St. Laurent plant spent substantial sums each year to modernize and renovate its equipment. Modernization and the implementation of new techniques to increase speed, reduce material costs, and improve quality were a necessity as volume increased. Over the years, many of the small run, handmade boxes and pails were discontinued and the equipment scrapped. Other lines were automated and personnel retrained to handle the higher mechanical skills and changeovers required. In spite of these changes, however, according to a general foreman, a production worker of the 1940s could return in 1963 and not feel entirely out of place. Many of the less skilled machine operators were required to handle several tasks on the higher speed equipment. In general, most of the jobs in the plant were relatively unskilled, highly repetitive, and gave the worker little control over method or pace. The die makers who made and repaired the dies, and machine repairmen and those who made equipment set-up changes between different products, were considered to possess the highest level of skill.

All production workers below the rank of assistant foreman were unionized; however, there had never been a strike at the plant. Wages were high compared to other similar industries in the Montreal area. The union was not part of the Master Agreement that governed all other plants in Canada and most of the plants in the United States, but management made every effort to apply equality to this plant. Output standards were established for all jobs, but no bonus was paid for exceeding standards.

The metal can industry was relatively stable with little product differentiation. The St. Laurent plant to some extent shipped its products throughout Canada although transportation costs limited its market primarily to Eastern Canada. While some of the customers were large and bought in huge quantities, (between 300–500 million cans) many were relatively small and purchased a more specialized product.

THE PLANT ORGANIZATION

Plant management

Andrew Fox, the plant manager at St. Laurent since 1961, had risen from an hourly worker through foreman up to plant manufacturing engineer in the maintenance of the business. He had developed an intimate first-hand knowledge of operations and was frequently seen around the plant, a cigar clenched between his teeth.

As plant manager, Fox had no responsibility for sales or research and development activities. In fact, both Fox and the district sales manager in his area had separate executives to whom they reported in the division headquarters and it was in the superior of these executives that responsibility for both sales and production first came together.

Fox commented about the working relationships at the St. Laurent plant:

> You will see that frequently two managers with different job titles are assigned responsibility for the same task. (He implied that it was up to them to work out their own pattern of mutual support and cooperation.) However, I don't have to adhere strictly to the description. I may end up asking a lot more of the man at certain times and under certain conditions than is ever put down on paper.
>
> In effect, the staff runs the plant.[1] We delegate to the various staff department heads the authority to implement decisions within the framework of our budget planning. This method of handling responsibility means that staff members have to be prepared to substantiate their decisions. At the same time, it gives them a greater sense of participation in and responsibility for plant income. We endeavor to carry this principle into the operating and service departments. The foreman is given responsibility and encouraged to act as though he were operating a business of his own. He is held responsible for all results generated in his department and is fully aware of how any decisions of his affect plant income.
>
> Our division personnel counsel and assist the plant staff and the plant staff counsel and assist the department foreman. Regular visits are made to the plant by our division manager and members of his staff. The principal contact is through the division manager of manufacturing and his staff, the manager of industrial engineering, the manager of production engineering and the manager of quality control. (There was no division staff officer in production control.)

---

[1] The personnel reporting directly to Fox. The organization chart (see Exhibit 1) was prominently displayed on the wall of the lobby. See Exhibit 2 for other information on personnel.

EXHIBIT 1
St. Laurent Plant, March 1, 1963

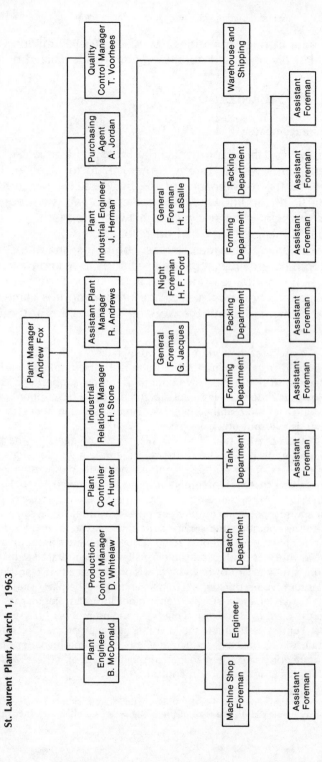

EXHIBIT 2
Information about certain personnel

Name	Position	Approximate Age	Approximate length of service		College education
			St. Laurent	CCC	
Andrew Fox	Plant manager	40–45	8	18	None
Robert Andrews	Assistant plant manager	35	3	8	Agricultural engineering
A. Hunter	Plant controller	50	15	23	None
D. Whitelaw	Production control manager ...	45	18	18	None
Harold Stone	Industrial relations manager ...	45–50	5	29	None
Joe Herman	Plant industrial engineer	30–35	1	10	Engineering
Tom Voorhees	Quality control manager	30	5	5	Engineering in Netherlands
G. E. Jacques	General foreman	45–50	25	25	None
Henri LaSalle	General foreman	50	18	18	None
L. G. Adams	District sales manager	45–50	18	18	None

However, the onus is on the plant to request help or assistance of any kind. We can contact the many resources of Continental Can Company, usually on an informal basis. That is, we deal with other plant managers directly for information when manufacturing problems exist without going through the division office.

Each member of the staff understands that we, as a plant, have committed ourselves through the budget to provide a stated amount of income, and regardless of conditions which develop, this income figure must be maintained. If sales are off and a continuing trend is anticipated, we will reduce expenses wherever possible to retain income. Conversely, if we have a gain in sales volume we look for the complete conversion of the extra sales at the profit margin rate. However, this is not always possible, especially if the increase in sales comes at a peak time when facilities are already strained.

Fox was assisted by Robert Andrews, the assistant plant manager. Andrews, promoted from quality control manager in 1961, was responsible for all manufacturing operations within the plant. Andrews appeared more reserved than Fox, talked intently, and smiled easily while working with the persons that reported to him. Fifteen salaried supervisors reported to Andrews and helped him control the three-shift operation of the plant and its 500 hourly workers. (During peak periods during the summer, the plant employed as many as 800 people; most of the additional workers were the sons and daughters of plant employees.)

Andrews noted:

> Our foremen have full responsibility for running their departments; quality, conditions of equipment, employee relations, production according to schedule, control of inventory through accurate reporting of spoilage and production, and cost control. He is just as accountable for those in his department as the plant manager is for the entire plant.

Andrews added that supervisory positions carried a good deal of status. Each supervisor had a personal parking spot and office and was expected to wear white shirts.[2] Andrews spoke of these symbols as an important aspect of the supervisor's position of authority. "He is no longer the best man with the wrench—he is the man with the best overall supervisory qualification."

Production control

D. Whitelaw, the production control manager, had worked all his 18 years with Continental Can at the St. Laurent plant. He was responsible

---

[2] The plant manager, management staff, foremen and clerks in the office all wore white shirts and ties but no coat. The union president (a production worker) wore a white shirt but no tie. All other personnel wore colored sports shirts.

for planning and controlling plant inventories and production schedules to meet sales requirements consistent with efficient utilization of facilities, materials and personnel. Whitelaw spoke quickly and chain-smoked cigarettes. According to him the main task of his job was "to try to achieve the maximum length of run without affecting service or exceeding inventory budgets."

Whitelaw was assisted by a scheduler for each major operating department and clerks to service the schedulers. The schedulers worked closely with the department foreman in the plant and were in frequent telephone contact with the sales offices. Whitelaw commented: "We in production control are the buffer between sales and operating people."

To facilitate their work, Whitelaw and Andrews headed bi-weekly production control meetings, each lasting about one hour. Fox, the plant manager, was a frequent observer. These meetings were attended by the two general foremen. Each production foreman and the production control scheduler working for his department came into the meeting at a prearranged time and when their turn came they reported on operations in their department and on problems they were encountering. Most of the questions as well as instructions given in the meeting came from Andrews. It was also he who usually dismissed one foreman/scheduler pair and called on the next. Questions from Andrews or Whitelaw were seldom clearly addressed to either the foreman or scheduler. They were answered more frequently by the scheduler than the foreman and often a scheduler would supplement comments made by the foreman. Generally the schedulers were younger but spoke with more self-assurance than the foremen.

In these meetings, there were frequent references to specific customers, their needs, complaints and present attitudes toward Continental Can. Both Whitelaw and Andrews tended to put instructions and decisions in terms of what was required to satisfy some particular customer or group of customers.

A recent meeting involving a foreman, Maurice Pelletier, and the scheduler for his department Dan Brown is illustrative of the process. It was observed that while Dan presented the status report Maurice shook his head in disagreement without saying anything. Dan was discussing his plan to discontinue an order being processed on a certain line on Friday to shift to another order and then to return to the original order on Tuesday.

Andrews: *I don't think your plan makes much sense. You go off on Friday and then again on Tuesday.*

Maurice: [*to Dan*] *Is this all required before the end of the year?* [This was asked with obvious negative emotional feeling and then followed by comments by both Andrews and Whitelaw.]

Dan: *Mind you–I could call sales again.*

Whitelaw: *I can see the point, Dan. It is sort of nonsensical to change back after so short a run.*

Maurice: *This would mean our production would be reduced all week to around 300 instead of 350. You know it takes four hours to make the changeover.*

Dan: *But the order has been backed up.*

Andrews: *It is backed up only because their* [sales] *demands are unreasonable.*

Dan: *They only asked us to do the best we can.*

Andrews: *They always do this. We should never have put this order on in the first place.*

Maurice: *If you want to we could . . . .* [Makes a suggestion about how to handle the problem.]

Andrews: *Production-wise, this is the best deal.* [Agreeing with Maurice's plan.]

Dan: *Let me look at it again.*

Andrews: *Production-wise, this is best; make the changeover on the weekend.*

Whitelaw: [Summarizes; then to Dan] *The whole argument is the lost production you would have.*

Maurice: *It'll mean backing up the order only one day.*

Andrews: [After another matter in Maurice's department has been discussed and there is apparently nothing further, Andrews turns to Dan and smiles.] *It's been a pleasure, Dan.*
[Dan then returned the smile weakly and got up to leave, somewhat nervously.]

As Whitelaw left the conference room after the meeting he was heard to comment: "Danny got clobbered as you could see. I used to stand up for him but he just doesn't come up here prepared. He should have the plans worked out with his foreman before they come up."

When discussing his job Whitelaw frequently commented on how he thought a decision or problem would affect someone else in the plant:

> If all you had to do was manage the nuts and bolts of production scheduling and not worry about the customer or how people were going to react, this would be the easiest job in the whole plant. You could just sit down with a paper and pencil and lay it out the best way. But because the customer is so important and because you've got to look ahead to how people are going to react to a given kind of schedule, it makes the whole job tremendously complicated. It isn't easy!

Other personnel and functions

Hunter, the plant accountant, reported directly to the plant manager, although he was functionally responsible to the division controller. The major tasks for Hunter's department were the development and application of many thousands of individual product costs and the coordination of the annual sales and income budget, developed by the responsible operating and staff groups. Explaining another of his duties Hunter noted: "We are the auditors who see that every other department is obeying rules and procedures. It is our responsibility to know all that is in the instruction manuals. There are 12 volumes of general instructions and lots of special manuals."

Joe Herman, the plant industrial engineer, explained the responsibilities of his department:

> We're active in the fields of time study, budgetary control, job evaluation, and methods improvement. Our company is on a standard cost system—that is, all our product costs are based on engineered standards, accurately measuring all labor, direct and indirect, and material that is expended in the manufacture of each and every item we make in our plants. All the jobs in the St. Laurent plant, up to and including the foreman, have been measured and standards set. However, all our standards are forwarded to division which checks them against standards in use at other plants. There are company-wide benchmarks for most standards, since most of the machinery is the same in other Continental Can plants.

Herman noted that the budgeted savings from methods improvement was approximately $600,000 for the year, and he expected to exceed that by a substantial amount.

Harold Stone, the industrial relations manager, was proud that the St. Laurent plant had never experienced a strike and that formal written grievances were almost unheard of. Stone ran training programs and monitored safety, absenteeism, and turnover data. The St. Laurent plant had an outstanding record in these areas. Stone attributed this to the high wages and fringe benefits of the plant. He also maintained campaigns on housekeeping and posted slogans and comments, in both French and English, on job security and industrial competition. Also he was responsible for the display of a five-foot chart on an easel near the main entrance which showed the manufacturing efficiency rating (actual production cost versus standard cost) of the previous month for each of the Continental Can Company plants and their standing within the division.

On Continental Can's personnel policy, Stone stated:

> We believe that it is important that the supervisor and the employee understand each other, that they know what the other person thinks about business, profit, importance of satisfying the customer and any other aspect of business. We also believe that rapport between the supervisor and the employee can be improved in the social contacts which exist or can be organized. For this reason we sponsor dances, bowling leagues, golf days, fishing derbies, picnics, baseball leagues, supervision parties, management weekends, and many unofficial get-

togethers. Over many years we have been convinced that these activities really improve management-labor relations. They also provide a means for union and management to work closely together in organizing and planning these events. These opportunities help provide a mutual respect for the other fellow's point of view.

It was Stone's responsibility to maintain the confidential file in connection with Continental's performance appraisal program for salaried employees. Procedures for handling the program were spelled out in one of the corporate manuals. Two forms were completed annually. One called for a rating of the employee by his supervisor, first on his performance of each of his responsibilities outlined in the Position Analysis Manual and then on each of 12 general characteristics such as cooperation, initiative, job knowledge and delegation. In another section the supervisor and the appraised employee were jointly required to indicate what experience, training or self-development would improve performance or prepare for advancement by the employee prior to the next appraisal. The appraisal was to be discussed between the supervisor and the employee; the latter was required to sign the form and space was given for any comments he might want to make. The second form was not shown to the employee. It called for a rating on overall performance, an indication of promotability, and a listing of potential replacements. It was used for manpower planning, and after comments by the supervisor of the appraiser, it was forwarded to the division office.

MANAGERIAL PRACTICES

Managing with budgets

Management at the St. Laurent plant coordinated their activities through a number of informal, as well as scheduled, meetings. Impromptu meetings of two or more members of management were frequent, facilitated by the close proximity of their offices. Among the formal meetings, the most important was the monthly discussion of performance against the budget. This meeting was attended by all of the management staff as well as production supervisors. Other regularly scheduled meetings included the production control meeting (twice weekly) and the plant cost reduction committee meetings.

In discussing the budget, Fox explained that the manufacturing plant was organized as a profit center. Plant income was determined by actual sales, not a transfer price. Therefore income was adversely affected when either sales failed to come up to the forecast on which the budget was based or sales prices were reduced to meet competition.

Fox also explained that sales managers also have their incentives based on making or exceeding the budget and that their forecasts had tended to be quite accurate. Overoptimism of one group of products had usually been offset by underestimation of sales on other products. However, because no adjustment was permitted in budgeted profit when sales income was below forecast, the fact that sales were running 3 percent below the level budgeted for 1963 was forcing the plant to reduce expenses substantially in order to equal or exceed the profit budgeted for the year.

When asked whether the budget was a straightjacket or if there were some accounts which left slack for reducing expenses if sales fell below forecast, Fox replied:

> We never put anything in the budget that is unknown or guessed at. We have to be able to back up every single figure in the budget. We have to budget our costs at standard assuming that we can operate at standard. We know we won't all the time. There will be errors and failures, but we are never allowed to budget for them.

Hunter agreed with Fox stating that "in this company there is very little opportunity to play footsy with the figures."

Fox conceded that there were some discretionary accounts like overtime and outside storage which involved arguments with the division. For example, "I might ask for $140,000 for overtime. The division manager will say $130,000, so we compromise at $130,000." As far as cost-reduction projects are concerned, Fox added that "we budget for more than the expected savings. We might have $100,000 in specific projects and budget for $150,000."

Fox went on to note that equipment repairs and overhauls could be delayed to reduce expenses. But even the overhaul schedule was included as part of the budget, and any changes had to be approved at the division level.

Robert Andrews complained that the budget system didn't leave much room for imagination. He felt that overly optimistic sales estimates were caused by the sales people being fearful of sending a pessimistic estimate up to the division. These estimates, according to Andrews, were a major source of manufacturing inefficiency.

Andrews was asked whether he was concerned about increasing production volume, and he replied:

> We have standards. So long as we are meeting the standards we are meeting our costs and we do not worry about increasing production. We don't tell the foreman that he needs to get more goods out the door. We tell him to get rid of the red in his budget. I'm content with a 100 percent performance. I'd like 105 percent but if we want more production it is up to Industrial Engineering [IE] to develop methods change.

Andrews talked about the necessary skills for a foreman:

> The foreman should be good at communications and the use of available control procedures. The foreman is expected to communicate effectively with all plant personnel, including staff heads. Our control procedures are easy to apply. In each department there is an engineered standard for each operation covering labor, materials and spoilage. Without waiting for a formal statement from accounting, a foreman can analyze his performance in any area and take corrective action if necessary. Then he receives reports from accounting to assist him in maintaining tight cost control. One is a daily report which records labor and spoilage performance against standard. The monthly report provides a more detailed breakdown of labor costs, materials and supplies use, and spoilage. It also establishes the efficiency figure for the month. This report is discussed at a monthly meeting of all my supervisors. Generally the plant industrial engineer and a member of the accounting staff are present. Each foreman explains his variances from standard and submits a forecast for his next month's performance.

The bonus plan

Andrew Fox indicated that the budget was also used in rewarding employees of Continental Can. The incentive for managers was based on performance of the plant compared to budget. According to Fox:

> The bonus is paid on the year's results. It is paid as a percentage of salary to all who are eligible—they are the ones on the organization chart (see Exhibit 1). There are three parts to it—one part is based on plant income, one on standards improvement or cost cutting, and the third on operating performance. We can make up to 20 percent by beating our plant income target and 25 percent on cost reduction and operating efficiency together. But we have to make 90 percent of our budgeted income figure to participate in any bonus at all.
>
> I think we have the 25 percent on efficiency and cost reduction pretty well sewn up this year. If we go over our budgeted income, we can get almost 35 percent bonus.

In years past, St. Laurent managers had made about 10 percent of their salaries from the bonus. The improved performance was the result of a change in the design of the bonus plan. Hunter explained the effect of the change:

> At one time the bonus plan was based on departmental results and efficiency. Under this there was a tendency for the departments to work at cross purposes, to compete rather than cooperate with each other. For the last seven or eight years, the emphasis has been on the plant, not the department. The latest plan is geared not only to the attainment of budgeted cost goals, but also the attainment of budgeted income. This is

consistent with the attention we are placing on sales. I think the company was disturbed by what they sensed was a belief that those at the plant level can't do much about sales. Now we are trying to get the idea across that if we make better cans and give better service, we will sell more.

FOREMEN AND PRODUCTION WORKERS

General foremen

Guillaume Jacques and Henri LaSalle were the general foremen on two of the three shifts. They described their jobs as working closely with both the assistant plant manager and the production control manager, but more with the latter. Jacques and LaSalle were asked how they balanced employee satisfaction with the requirements of the budget. Jacques commented:

> Management not only asks me to meet the budget but do better. So, you've got to make the worker understand the importance of keeping the budget. I get them in the office and explain that if we don't meet the budget we'll have to cut down somewhere else. It is mathematical. I explain all this to them; management has given me a budget to meet, I need them for this, they need me to give them work. We work like a team. I try to understand them. All supervisors work under tension. Myself, I ask the men to go out to have a beer with me, to go to a party. It relaxes them from our preoccupations. Right now, for example, there is this party with the foremen coming up. At these gatherings it is strictly against the rules to talk about work. These things are necessary.

LaSalle explained that while foremen have a copy of the budget for their department, the workers see only a machine operating standard. The standard was set so that if he works the machine at full capacity he achieves 110 percent of standard. LaSalle told of his way of handling workers.

> Well, there is usually some needling when a man is down below standard. He's told, "Why don't you get to be part of the crew?" It doesn't hurt anything . . . you only get a good day's work out of people if they are happy. We strive to keep our people happy so they'll produce the standard and make the budget. We try to familiarize them with what is expected of them. We have targets set for us. The budget is reasonable, but it is not simple to attain. By explaining our problems to the workers we find it easier to reach the budget.

Foremen

Most of the foremen were aware of, and accepted, the necessity of keying their activities to the work standards and budgets. One young, and purportedly ambitious, foreman commented about his job:

What I like about this department is that I am in charge. I can do anything I like as long as I meet with the budget. I can have that machine moved—send it over there—as long as I have good reasons to justify it. The department, that's me. I do all the planning and I'm responsible for results. I'm perfectly free in the use of my time (gives examples of his different arrival times during the past week and the fact that he came in twice on Saturday and once on Sunday for short periods).

While other foremen expressed dislike for some of the pressures inherent in their jobs, there was general satisfaction. One notable exception was a foreman with many years' service who said:

We have a meeting once a month upstairs. They talk to us about budgets, quality, etc. That's all on the surface; that's _____. It looks good. It has to look good but it is all bull. For example, the other day a foreman had a meeting with the workers to talk about quality. After that an employee brought to his attention a defect in some products. He answered, "Send it out anyway," and they had just finished talking to us about quality.

Foremen tended to view the production worker as irresponsible and interested, insofar as his job is concerned, only in his pay check and quitting time. One foreman said, "We do all the work; they do nothing." Even an officer of the union, speaking about the workers, commented:

They don't give a damn about the standards. They work nonchalantly and they are very happy when their work slows up. If the foreman is obliged to stop the line for two minutes everyone goes to the toilet. There are some workers who do their work conscientiously, but this is not the case with the majority.

Comments from workers

Several of the production workers expressed feelings of pressure although others declared they were accustomed to their work and it did not bother them. One said: "Everyone is obsessed with meeting the standards—the machine adjuster, the foreman, the assistant foreman. They all get on my nerves." One old-timer clearly differentiated the company, which he considered benevolent, from his foreman:

I can understand that these men are under tension as well as we are. They have meetings every week. I don't know what they talk about up there. The foremen have their standards to live up to. They're nervous. They don't even have a union like us. So if things go bad, well, that's all. They make us nervous with all this. But there's a way with people. We don't say to a man, "Do this, do that." If we said, "Would you do this?" it is not the same thing. You know a guy like myself who has been here for 35 years knows a few tricks. If I am mad at the foreman I could do a few little things to the machine to prevent it from keeping up with the standards and no one would know.

While some workers stated they would work for less money if some of the tension were relieved, the majority were quite content with their jobs.[3]

ENFORCING THE BUDGET

By November 1963, sales for the year had fallen below expectations and the management bonus was in jeopardy as a result.

One day in early November there was an unusual amount of activity in the accounting section. Fox came into the area frequently and he and Hunter from time to time would huddle with one of the accountants over some figures. Hunter explained that the extra activity was in response to a report on the October results that had been issued about a week before.

Fox decided to schedule a joint meeting of the management staff and the line organization to go over the October results. This was a departure from the usual practice of having the groups in separate meetings. Prior to the meeting Fox outlined what he hoped to accomplish in the meeting:

> Those figures we got last week showed that some of the accounts did what they were expected to do, some did more, and some did a good deal less. The thing we have to do now is to kick those accounts in the pants that are not making the savings they planned to make. What we've been doing is raising the expected savings as the time gets shorter. It may be easy to save 10 percent on your budget when you've got six months; but with only six weeks, it is an entirely different matter. The thing to do now is to get everybody together and excited about the possibility of doing it. We know how it can be done. Those decisions have already been made. It's not unattainable even though I realize we are asking an awful lot from these men. You see we are in a position now where just a few thousand dollars one way or the other can make as much as 10 percent difference in the amount of bonus the men get. There is some real money on the line. It can come either from a sales increase or an expense decrease, but the big chunk has to come out of an expense decrease.

Fox did not feel there would be a conflict in the meeting about who is right and who is wrong:

> We never fight about the budget. It is simply a tool. All we want to know is what is going on. There are never any disagreements about the budget itself. Our purpose this afternoon is to pinpoint those areas

---

[3] In a Harvard research study of 12 plants in the United States and Canada, the St. Laurent plant workers ranked highest of the 12 plants in job satisfaction.

where savings can be made, where there is a little bit of slack, and then get to work and pick up the slack.

Fox talked about his style in handling cost and people problems:

> When budgeted sales expenses get out of line, management automatically takes in other accounts to make up the losses. We'll give the department that has been losing money a certain period of time to make it up. Also, anytime anybody has a gain, I tell them I expect them to maintain that gain.
>
> The manager must make the final decisions and has to consider the overall relationships. But there are some things I can't delegate—relations with sales for example. The manager, and not production control, must make the final decisions.
>
> Larry Adams, the sales manager in our district, feels that the budget gets in the way of the customer's needs. He thinks the budget dominates the thinking and actions around here. Maybe he's right. But I have to deal with the people and problems here.
>
> The manager must be close to his people. I take a daily tour of the plant and talk to the people by name. My practice as a manager is to follow a head-on approach. I don't write many memos. When I have something to say I go tell the person or persons right away. That's why I'm holding a meeting this afternoon.

Bob Andrews commented on the methods used to pick up the projected savings:

> When you have lost money in one sector you have to look around for something else that you can "milk" to make up the difference. But we don't ask for volunteers, we do the "milking." Those guys just have to do what we say. How much we can save pretty much depends on how hard the man in the corner office wants to push on the thing. I mean if we really wanted to save money we probably could do it, but it would take a tremendous effort on everybody's part and Fox would really have to crack the whip.

Because of Fox's comments on relationships with sales, Larry Adams, the district sales manager, was asked about his feelings on working with the production people at the St. Laurent plant:

> The budget comes to dominate people's thinking and influence all their actions. I'm afraid even my salesmen have swallowed the production line whole. They can understand the budget so well they can't understand their customers. And the St. Laurent plant boys are getting more and more local in their thinking with this budget. They're not thinking about what the customer needs today or may need tomorrow, they just think about their _____ budget.
>
> If the customer will not take account of your shortcomings, and if you can't take account of the customer's shortcomings, the two of you will eventually end up at each other's throats. That's what this budget system

has built into it. Suppose, for example, you want to give a customer a break. Say he has originally planned for a two-week delivery date, but he phones you and says he really has problems and if you possibly could, he would like about four days knocked off that delivery date. So I go trotting over to the plant, and I say, "Can we get it four days sooner?" Those guys go out of their minds, and they start hollering about the budget and how everything is planned just right and how I'm stirring them up. They get so steamed up I can't go running to them all the time but only when I really need something in the worst way. You can't let those plant guys see your strategy, you know. It is taking an awful lot out of a guy's life around here when he has to do everything by the numbers.

Special budget meeting

The meeting was held in the conference room at 4:00 P.M. Fox and Hunter sat at the far end of the table, facing the door, with an easel bearing a flip chart near them. The chart listed the projected savings in budgeted expenses for November and December, account by account. The group of about 30 arranged themselves at the table so that, with only a couple of exceptions, the management staff personnel and general foremen sat closest to Fox and Hunter and the foremen and assistant foremen sat toward the foot of the table.

Fox opened the meeting and declared that performance against the budget for October would first be reviewed, followed by discussion of the November and December projections. He stated rather emphatically that he was "disappointed" in the October performance. Although money had been saved, it represented good performance in some areas but rather poor performance in others. The gains made in the areas where performance had been good must be maintained and the weak areas brought up, Fox declared.

He then turned the meeting over to Hunter who reviewed the October results, reading from the report which everyone had in front of him. Where performance was not good, he called on the individual responsible for that area to explain. The typical explanation was that the original budgeted figure was unrealistic and that the actual amount expended was as low as it could possibly be under the circumstances. Fox frequently broke into the explanation with a comment like, "Well, that is not good enough" or, "Can you possibly do better for the rest of the year?" or, "I hope we have that straightened out now." When he sat down, the person giving the explanation was invariably thanked by Hunter.

Next, Hunter, followed by Whitelaw, commented on the sales outlook for the remainder of the year. They indicated that for two months as a whole sales were expected to be about on budget. After asking for questions and getting one from a foreman, Fox said: "Well now, are there any more questions? Ask them now if you have them. Everybody sees where we stand on the bonus, I assume. Right?"

Fox then referred to the chart on plant expense savings and began to discuss it saying:

> The problem now is time. We keep compressing the time and raising the gain (the projected savings for the year had been raised $32,000 above what had been projected in October). You can only do that so long. Time is running out, fellows. We've got to get on the stick.

Several times Fox demanded better upward communication on problems as they came up. Referring to a specific example, he said: "This sort of thing is absolutely inexcusable. We've got to know ahead of time when these mix-ups are going to occur so that we can allow for and correct them."

As Hunter was covering manufacturing efficiency projections for November, he addressed Andrews: "Now we have come to you, Bob. I see you're getting a little bit more optimistic on what you think you can do."

Andrews replied:

> Yes, the boss keeps telling me I'm just an old pessimist and I don't have any faith in my people. I'm still a pessimist, but we are doing tremendously. I think it's terrific, fellows (pointing to a line graph). I don't know whether we can get off the top of this chart or not, but at the rate this actual performance line is climbing, we might make it. All I can say is, keep up the good work . . . .
> I guess I'm an optimistic pessimist.

During the discussion of projected savings for December in the equipment maintenance account, Hunter commented: "Where in the world are you fellows going to save $8,000 more than you originally said you would save?"

Jones responded:

> I'd just like to say at this point to the group that it would be a big help if you guys would take it easy on your machines. That's where we are going to save an extra $8,000—simply by only coming down to fix the stuff that won't run. You're really going to have to make it go as best you can. That's the only way we can possibly save the kind of money we have to save. You have been going along pretty well, but all I've got to say is I hope you can keep it up and not push those machines too hard.

Although Jones spoke with sincerity, a number of foremen sitting near the door exchanged sly smiles and pokes in the ribs.

Fox concluded the meeting at about 5:30 P.M., still chewing on his cigar:

There are just a couple of things I want to say before we break up. First, we've got to stop making stupid errors in shipping. Joe [foreman of shipping], you've absolutely *got* to get after those people to straighten them out. Second, I think it should be clear, fellows, that we can't break any more promises. Sales is our bread and butter. If we don't get those orders out in time we'll have no one but ourselves to blame for missing our budget. So I just hope it is clear that production control is running the show for the rest of the year. Third, the big push is on *now!* We sit around here expecting these problems to solve themselves, but they don't! It ought to be clear to all of you that no problem gets solved until it's spotted. Damn it, I just don't want any more dewy-eyed estimates about performance for the rest of the year. If something is going sour we want to hear about it. And there's no reason for not hearing about it! [Pounds the table, then voice falls and a smile begins to form.] It can mean a nice penny in your pocket if you can keep up the good work.

That's all I've got to say. Thank you very much.

The room cleared immediately, but Whitelaw lingered on. He reflected aloud on the just-ended meeting.

I'm afraid that little bit of advice there at the end won't make a great deal of difference in the way things work out. You have to play off sales against production. It's built into the job. When I attend a meeting like that one and I see all those production people with their assistants and see the other staff managers with their assistants, and I hear fellows refer to corporate policy that dictates and supports their action at the plant level, I suddenly realize that I'm all alone up there. I can't sit down and fire off a letter to my boss at the division level like the rest of those guys can do. I haven't got any authority at all. It is all based strictly on my own guts and strength. Now Bob is a wonderful guy, I like him and I have a lot of respect for him, but it just so happens that 80 percent of the time he and I disagree. He knows it and I know it; I mean it's nothing we run away from, we just find ourselves on opposite sides of the question and I'm dependent upon his tact and good judgment to keep from starting a war.

Boy, it can get you down—it really can after a while, and I've been at it for—god—20 years. But in production control you've just got to accept it—you're an outcast. They tell you you're cold, that you're inhuman, that you're a _____, that you don't care about anything except your schedule. And what are you going to say? You're just going to have to swallow it because basically you haven't got the authority to back up the things you know need to be done. Four nights out of five I am like this at the end of the day—just completely drained out—and it comes from having to fight my way through to try to get the plant running as smoothly as I can.

And Andrews up there in that meeting. He stands up with his chart and he compliments everybody about how well they are doing on efficiency. You know, he says, "Keep up the good work," and all that sort of stuff. I just sat there—shaking my head. I was so dazed you know, I mean I just keep saying to myself, "What's he doing? What's he saying? What's so great about this?" You know if I could have, I'd have stood up and I'd have said, "Somebody go down to my files in production control and pick out any five customer orders at random—and letters—and bring them back up here and read them—at random, pick any five." You know what they would show? Broken promises and missed delivery dates and slightly off-standard items we've been pushing out the door here. I mean, what is an efficient operation? Why the stress on operating efficiency? That's why I just couldn't figure out why in the world Andrews was getting as much mileage out of his efficiency performance as he was. Look at all the things we sacrifice to get that efficiency. But what could I do?

In early 1964 the report being sent by Fox to division would show, despite the fact that sales had fallen about 3 percent below budget, that profits for 1963 had exceeded the amount budgeted and that operating efficiency and cost reduction had both exceeded the budget by a comfortable margin. This enabled the managers and supervisors at the St. Laurent plant to attain the salary bonuses for which they had been striving.

Case 4-2
Texas Instruments Incorporated (A) (condensed)

On April 17, 1959, Texas Instruments Incorporated (TI) of Dallas, Texas, merged with the Metals and Controls Corporation (M&C) of Attleboro, Massachusetts. One of the fastest growing large corporations in the country, TI had achieved a compound annual growth from 1946 through 1958 of 38 percent in sales and 42 percent in net income. The president had publicly predicted that volume would more than double in 1959 to a sales level near $200 million. Almost half this growth, he added, might come through mergers, with M&C contributing $42 million to $45 million. To date, TI's principal business had been in electronic and electromechanical equipment services for oil, gas, and minerals.

So highly was TI regarded by the market that in May 1960, its common was selling at about 70 times the 1959 earnings of $3.59 a share.

M&C activities

Itself the product of a 1932 merger and a postwar diversification, M&C had three major groups of products: clad metals, control instruments, and nuclear fuel components and instrumented cores. The company had grown steadily, and in 1959 had plants in two U.S. locations and five foreign countries. Reflecting predecessor corporation names, the clad metal lines were known as General Plate (GP) products, and the control instrument lines were known as Spencer products. Included in the former were industrial, precious, and thermostat metals; fancy wire; and wire and tubing. Included in the latter were motor protectors, circuit breakers, thermostats, and precision switches. Among these Spencer lines there were some that utilized GP products as raw materials—i.e., GP thermostat bimetals and GP clad electrical contacts.

Apart from a portion of GP's precious metal products which went to the jewelry trade (where appearance and fast delivery from stock were key considerations), most GP and Spencer products had to be designed to specific customer requirements and produced to customer order. Thus, engineering know-how and close coordination between the sales and production departments on delivery dates were important. Owing to the technical nature of the products and also to their fast-changing applications, a company sales force with a high degree of engineering competence was essential. To serve its several thousand customers, many of whom purchased both Spencer and GP products, the company maintained a force of 50 men in the field, divided into Spencer and GP units.

With Spencer products facing important competition from four other firms in the $10 million to $40 million annual sales bracket, tight control of costs was important for securing the large orders generally placed by the kinds of customers to whom these products were sold. Buyers included manufacturers of fractional horsepower motors, household appliances, air conditioning, and aircraft and missiles. In contrast, GP industrial metals met no direct competition, although clad metals for industrial uses met with competition from alloys.

M&C's premerger organization

At the time TI took over M&C, a task force of four junior executives had just completed, at the acting president's request, a critical study of M&C's organizational structure. So far, its nuclear activities had been conducted by an entirely separate subsidiary, and the GP and Spencer activities had been organized as shown in Exhibit 1.

Under the acting president at the top level came a tier of predominantly functional executives (the vice presidents for marketing, engineering, and finance, the treasurer, and the controller). At the third and fourth levels of command, the structure increasingly showed a breakdown by product lines. For example, at the fourth level in man-

EXHIBIT 1
Premerger Metals and Controls organization

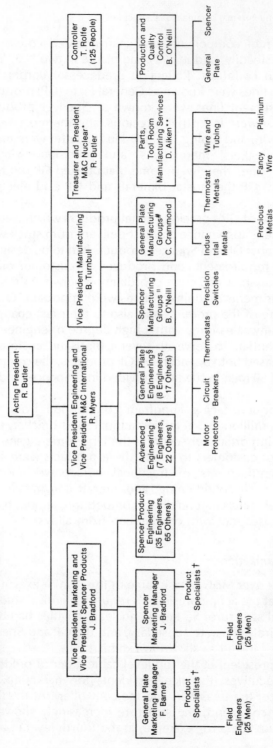

* Detail on M&C Nuclear not disclosed.

† Responsible for factory-customer coordination on specifications, prices, delivery, and new applications on different product lines (broken down about as shown in the manufacturing department).

‡ Responsible for long-range product development for GP lines.

§ Worked on new applications and process designs for GP lines.

‖ Principal operations in Spencer production departments were parts-making and assembly.

Principal operations in GP industrial, precious, and thermostat metal departments were bonding and rolling; in GP wire and fancy wire departments, drawing; and in GP platinum department, milting and refining. Some GP facilities were shared, and roughly 5 percent of direct labor hours for each GP department were devoted to work for other departments.

** Reporting to Aiken were units making two GP and three Spencer parts.

Source: Interviews and company records.

ufacturing there were four separate groups corresponding to the major Spencer lines, and six separate groups corresponding to the major GP lines. Approximately the same breakdown appeared among the fourth-level product specialists in marketing. Although there was no profit responsibility at this level, the controller had been sending marketing's product specialists a monthly profit and loss (P&L) by product line, in the hope of encouraging informal meetings among the people in marketing, engineering, and production who were working on the same lines.

Even at the second level, the predominantly functional division of responsibilities was neither complete nor unalloyed. Thus, the vice president for marketing was also the vice president of Spencer Products, and in this capacity he had reporting to him the Spencer engineers. As a result, the company's vice president of engineering was, in effect, the vice president only of GP engineering, although he also served in an other-than-functional role by acting as the vice president of M&C International. (In 1958 exports and other foreign sales totaled about $2 million.)

After confidential interviews with 140 people, members of the M&C task force reportedly concluded that this organizational structure was causing or contributing to a number of company problems. Accordingly, the task force recommended sweeping changes, first to the acting president by whom they had been appointed, then to his successor, Edward O. Vetter, a 39-year-old TI vice president brought in following the merger.

Vetter's review and appraisal

As soon as he arrived at M&C, Vetter spent most of four days in closed meetings with task force members. At the same time he scheduled public meetings with all executives; these sessions he devoted to general discussions of his aims for the organization and to reassurances that drastic changes would not be made.

From these discussions, Vetter learned that a great many people at M&C felt that the three major functional departments were not cooperating well enough in the exploitation of new product opportunities based on existing markets and skills. Although in a few isolated instances, marketing, engineering, and production personnel concerned with a particular product had formed small informal groups to work on common problems, the three departments had not been seen as working together with maximum effectiveness, particularly in new product development. To blame, besides top management's inattention and the absence of a comprehensive plan, was a lack of clear-cut responsibility and authority.

Other problems, too, provided additional evidence of the failure of functional groups to work together harmoniously and effectively. Thus, there was continued squabbling between process engineers and production supervisors, with neither group being willing to accept the other's suggestions for improvements in manufacturing methods. With both groups reporting to different vice presidents, conflicts too often came up for resolution at top levels. Here, many times, decisions were postponed and issues left unresolved.

Vetter was also told by many members of the organization that the personal influence of marketing's product specialists played too large a role in a company decisions. Formally assigned to coordinate certain aspects of factory-customer relations (see notes to Exhibit 1), these specialists were said to determine the amount of R&D time given to particular lines, with the result that some lines had grown quite strong while promising opportunities elsewhere were neglected. Similarly, personal relationships between product specialists and production personnel largely determined scheduling priorities.

After becoming familiar with these problems, Mr. Vetter decided that M&C provided a golden opportunity for applying TI's philosophy of organization by what TI called "product-customer centered groups." Basically, this plan involved putting a single manager in charge of sales, manufacturing, and engineering on a particular product line, and making this manager responsible for profits. This type of structure, Mr. Vetter noted, was what had been proposed by M&C's own task force on organization. According to TI's president, it offered advantages not only in managing existing lines but also in finding new opportunities for discerning and serving new customer needs.

As he was collecting information on M&C's organizational arrangements, Mr. Vetter had dictated the following set of notes for his own use:

It appears as if natural product groups already exist here. General Plate, Spencer and Nuclear have always been separate, and International sales are set apart under Richard Myers. Within these major groupings there is also a somewhat parallel division of the manufacturing and marketing facilities along product lines. There are ten production departments that are each organized to produce a particular product line, while there is an almost parallel organization of marketing product specialists under James Bradford.

Bringing together product managers and production supervisors for similar product lines would seem to be the logical implementation of TI's management philosophy. Of course, one problem would be the rearrangement of some of the production facilities in order to locate all the equipment under a product manager's control in one area. While we do have ten product-manufacturing departments, some of these share facilities and perform work for one another. In addition, the parts department performs fabrication operations for several production departments. In spite of this, there are no major pieces of equipment that would have to be physically relocated. We estimate that some duplicate equipment will have to be purchased if we go ahead with product-centered decentralization; in order to accomplish this about $1.5 million will have to be spent almost three years before it would otherwise have been committed.

I believe that the "inside" product specialist—the man at the factory who lives with both the manufacturing and the marketing problems for his line—is a key man. Our products are mainly engineered to customer order and, as such, require a great deal of coordination on delivery dates, specifications, and special applications. In addition to performing this liaison, the product managers could be the men who sense ideas for new product applications from their marketing contacts and then transmit these to the product engineering personnel at the factory.

These men would not be salesmen. A field sales force would still be needed to make regular calls on all of our clients and to cultivate the associations with our customers' engineering staffs. One significant question here is how to organize the sales force. These men are highly skilled and quite expensive to employ—each salesman should enter commitments of at least $1 million yearly in order to justify his expenses. Since our customers are spread all over the country, it would appear economical to assign field salesmen by geographical areas—each to sell all, or at least a number of, our products. Unfortunately, this system might take a good measure of the responsibility for the sales supervision. Our problem here is to leave sales responsibility at the product group level without having an undue duplication of field sales personnel.

The filtering down of responsibility and authority would mean that we would need more "management skill" in order for the product managers to be able to manage the little companies of which each would be in charge. The product manager must be capable of making sales, manufacturing, financial, and engineering decisions. He is no longer judged against a budget but becomes responsible for profits. We would need talented men to fill these positions—a shift in the organizational structure would undoubtedly force us to hire some new people. Nevertheless, there are tremendous benefits to be gained in terms of giving more people the chance to display their talents and in just plain better functioning of the M&C division.

The organization of engineering personnel brings up a whole hornet's nest of questions. First of all, there are two distinct engineering functions: product engineers, those concerned with current product designs and new applications for existing products; and advanced engineers, those who work on long-term product development. There is little doubt that the new application sales effort would benefit from placing the product engineering personnel in close organizational contact with the marketers. This would mean splitting engineering up among all the product groups and would probably make for a less efficient overall operation. Decentralization of the advanced engineering groups is easily as ticklish a problem. Again, it would probably receive a more marketing-oriented stimulus if it were placed under the supervision of the product manager. I wonder, however, if he might not be motivated to cut long-term development more drastically than top management normally would in times of business recession. Furthermore, I wonder if the economies of centralized advanced engineering and research in terms of combined effort and personnel selection are not so great as to make decentralization of this function an extremely poor choice. The basic question we have to answer here is to what degree should we sacrifice operating economy in order to give our engineering personnel a greater marketing orientation.

* * * * *

Scheduling has long been a bone of contention here wherever facilities are shared. Conflicts for priorities between product specialists are always occurring. If we decentralize, however, the amount of facilities that are shared will decrease substantially and this problem should be alleviated. Again, we have the basic choice of retaining the centralized scheduling groups or splitting the function up among the various product groups.

In addition to the above issues, Vetter was considering the proper timing for an organizational change. He was debating whether a change should be made by gradual steps or whether the transfer in corporate ownership provided a convenient opportunity for making radical changes with a minimum of employee resentment. In general, the M&C personnel expressed some regrets because the family that had founded the company was no longer associated with it. They recognized, however, that the continual top management conflict of recent years necessitated a change and were pleased by the fact that a recognized leader in the industry had taken over the company.

Case 4–3
Texas Instruments Incorporated (B)

In May 1960, Tom Pringle, the manager of the industrial metals product department at Texas Instruments Metals & Controls Division, was considering several courses of action in the face of his department's failure to meet forecasted sales and profits during the first four months of 1960. The rebuilding of inventories by M&C's customers, which had been expected as an aftermath of the settlement of the 1959 steel strike, had not materialized, and shipments from Pringle's product department were running about 12 percent below forecast. Furthermore, incoming sales commitments during these four months were 15 percent below expectations. The product department's direct profit, according to preliminary statements, was 19 percent below plan.

In light of these adverse developments, Pringle was studying the advisability of three specific moves which would improve his profit performance: (1) eliminating his $30,000 advertising budget for the latter half of 1960, (2) postponing the addition of two engineers to his engineering group until 1961, and (3) reducing further purchases of raw materials in order to improve his department's return on assets ratio. Until now, Pringle had been reluctant to make any concessions in his department's scale of operations since there was a very strong accent on rapid growth throughout the Texas Instruments organization. This attitude toward expansion also appeared to prevail in the new top management group in the Metals & Controls Division. The enthusiasm of the Texas Instruments' management had caught on at Metals & Controls with the formation of the product-centered decentralized organization.

THE 1959 REORGANIZATION

In June 1959, just three months after Metals & Controls Corporation had become a division of Texas Instruments Incorporated, Mr. Edward O. Vetter, the division vice president, instituted a product-centered organization. This decentralization was carried out in accordance with Texas Instruments' policy of placing ultimate responsibility for profitable operation at the product level. The framework that emerged was similar to that which existed elsewhere in the company.

Mr. Vetter organized four major product groups at Metals & Controls: General Plate, Spencer Controls, Nuclear Products, and International Operations. To augment these groups, six centralized staff units were organized at the division level: Research and Development, Legal, Industrial Engineering, Control, Marketing, and Personnel (Exhibit 1). The four managers of the product groups and the six managers of these staff departments, along with Mr. Vetter, comprised the Management Committee for the Metals & Controls Division. This committee was a sounding board for helping each responsible manager make the proper decision as required by his job responsibility. In the case of profit performance, the ultimate responsibility for the division was Vetter's.

Within each product group, several product departments were established. The General Plate Products Group, for example, included the Industrial Metals, Electrical Contacts, Industrial Wire, and Precious Metals departments (Exhibit 2). The manager of each of these depart-

EXHIBIT 1
Organization chart, Metals & Controls Division*

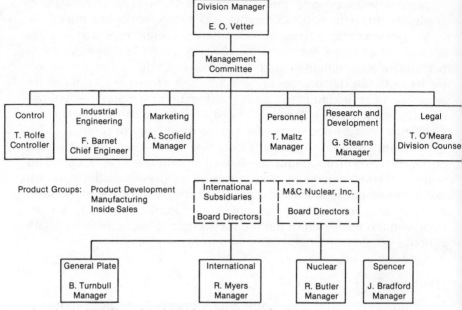

* Chart shows relationships only and not relative importance of positions.

EXHIBIT 2
Organization chart, General Plate Products Group*

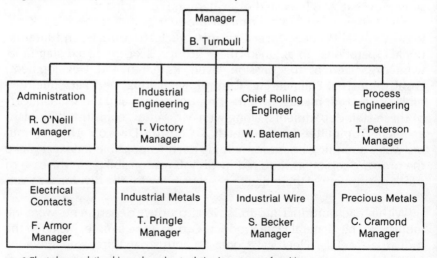

* Chart shows relationships only and not relative importance of positions.

ments was responsible for its "profit performance." He was supported by staff units such as Industrial Engineering and Administration which reported directly to the group manager (Burt Turnbull for General Plate products). The expense of these staff units was charged to the individual product departments proportionally to the volume of activity in the various departments as measured by direct labor hours or by sales dollars less raw materials cost. The product departments were also charged with those expenses over which the manager and his supervisory group were able to exercise direct control, such as labor and materials.

The field sales force of 50 men was centralized under the manager for marketing, Al Scofield (Exhibit 1). These men were divided about evenly into two major selling groups: one for General Plate products and the other for Spencer products. The 25 salesmen assigned to General Plate and the 25 salesmen assigned to Spencer were shared by the four General Plate and four Spencer product departments. Each individual product department also maintained "inside" marketing personnel who performed such functions as pricing, developing marketing strategy, order follow-up, and providing the field sales engineers with information on new applications, designs, and product specifications for its particular line.

THE INDUSTRIAL METALS DEPARTMENT

Tom Pringle was manager of the Industrial Metals department of the General Plate Products group. Sales of this department in 1959 were approximately $4 million.[1] Pringle was responsible for the profitability of two product lines: (1) industrial metals, and (2) thermostat metals. His department's sales were split about evenly between these lines, although industrial metals had the greater growth potential owing to the almost infinite number of possible clad metals for which an ever-increasing number of applications was being found. He was in charge of the marketing, engineering, and manufacturing activities for both these lines and had six key subordinates (see Exhibit 3).

The function of the marketing managers in the Industrial Metals department (Bud Sabin and Joe Brackman) was to supervise the "inside selling units." These units were responsible for developing marketing strategy, pricing, contacting customers on special requests and factory problems, for promotional activities, and for coordinating product development and sales. In May 1960, in addition to its regular work, the Industrial Metals inside selling unit was developing a manual of special

---

[1] All figures have been disguised.

EXHIBIT 3
Industrial Metals Department

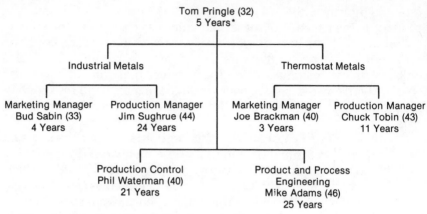

Tom Pringle (32)
5 Years*

Industrial Metals   Thermostat Metals

Marketing Manager   Production Manager   Marketing Manager   Production Manager
Bud Sabin (33)   Jim Sughrue (44)   Joe Brackman (40)   Chuck Tobin (43)
4 Years   24 Years   3 Years   11 Years

Production Control   Product and Process
Phil Waterman (40)   Engineering
21 Years   Mike Adams (46)
                                          25 Years

* Years of service with the Metals & Controls organization.

applications for its products which it hoped would improve the ability of the field sales force to envision new uses. The production managers had line responsibility for the efficient use of manufacturing facilities, for meeting delivery promises to customers, and for expenses incurred in producing the department's products. The product and process engineering group had responsibility for designing new products and devising new production processes. The production control manager formulated guidelines to aid the foremen in scheduling work through the plant, supervised the expediters and clerks who served as a clearing house for information on delivery dates, and was responsible for ordering raw material and maintaining a balanced inventory.

In accordance with Texas Instruments' policy of placing ultimate responsibility for profitable operation at the product level, Tom Pringle's performance was measured, to a large extent, by the actual profits earned by the Industrial Metals department. The old M&C system of evaluating performance according to fixed and variable departmental budgets had been supplemented by the establishment of these "profit centers." Although the system passed actual profit responsibility to the product department manager level, Texas Instruments' top management had always retained some control over the "profit centers" by requiring each manager to formulate a one-year plan which was subject to review by higher management. As a result, profit planning was instituted whereby each manager set forth a detailed plan for the year's operations under the direction of the Management Committee. His actual performance was continually being evaluated against the plan.

FORMULATION OF THE PROFIT PLAN

In October 1959, Tom Pringle began to prepare his department's profit plan for 1960. This was part of a company-wide effort in which all department managers participated. The first step in the process was to prepare a detailed estimate of expected sales for the year. These estimates were gathered from two sources: the inside selling units and the field sales force. Management felt that one would serve as a good check on the other, and furthermore believed that widespread participation in preparing the plan was one way to insure its effectiveness. Accordingly, Bud Sabin and Joe Brackman began to prepare estimates of 1960 sales by product lines, with the help of the individual product specialists within the inside marketing group. Sabin and Brackman were also aided by the Texas Instruments' central marketing group, which prepared a report which estimated normal growth for their product lines. Pringle suggested that they prepare their estimates by subdividing the market into three parts: sales resulting from normal industry growth at current levels of market penetration; increased sales resulting from further penetration of the market with existing products; and increased sales from new products detailed by specific customers. At the same time, Herb Skinner, the manager of the General Plate field sales force, asked the field engineers to predict the volume of orders that each Industrial Metals customer would place in 1960, without referring to the reports being readied by the product marketing groups. In this way, the marketing managers made forecasts by product line and field force made forecasts by customer.

The field selling force came up with estimated thermostat metal sales of $2.35 million for 1960, and the inside group estimated sales of $2.42 million. Pringle felt that these two estimates were in reasonably good agreement. On the other hand, Bud Sabin, the industrial metals marketing manager, estimated sales of $3.05 million, while Skinner's group predicted only $2.5 million. Sabin predicted that 20 percent of the increase would come from normal growth, 50 percent from increased market penetration with existing products, and 30 percent from new products. Sales for Sabin's group had been $1.4 million in 1958 and $2.1 million in 1959. Pringle felt that the disparity between the two estimates was significant, and he discussed the matter with both men. All three men finally decided that the sales force had submitted a conservative estimate and agreed that Sabin's figure was the more realistic goal.

Once the sales estimate of $5.47 million was agreed upon by Pringle and his marketing managers, the process of estimating manufacturing costs began. The manufacturing superintendents, Chuck Tobin and Jim Sughrue, were furnished the thermostat and industrial metals sales estimates and were instructed to forecast direct labor costs, supervisory salaries, and overhead expenses. These forecasts were to be made for each manufacturing area, or cost center, under their supervision. Sughrue was responsible for five cost centers and Tobin for four, each of which was directly supervised by a foreman. These expenses were to be forecast monthly and were to be used as a yardstick against which the actual expense performance of the manufacturing personnel could later be measured.

Jim Sughrue had previously calculated the hourly labor cost and the output per hour for each of his cost centers for 1959. To estimate 1960 salaries and wages, he then increased 1959 expenses proportionately to the expected sales increase. He followed the same procedure in determining 1960 overhead expenses such as expendable tools, travel, telephone, process supplies, and general supplies. Chuck Tobin's task was somewhat simpler since the sales projection for his cost centers required a level of output that exactly matched the current production level. For salaries and wages, he merely used as his 1960 estimate the actual cost experience that had been reported on the most recent monthly income statement he received. For overhead, he applied a historical percent-of-sales ratio and then reduced his estimate by 3 percent to account for increased efficiency. In discussing the overhead estimate with his foremen, Tobin informed them that he had allowed for an 8 percent efficiency increase.

Since this was the first time any attempt at such detailed planning had been made at M&C, and since the M&C accounting system had recently been changed to match Texas Instruments', very little historical information was available. For this reason, Pringle did not completely delegate the responsibility for the various marketing and manufacturing estimates to his subordinates. Instead he worked in conjunction with them to develop the forecasts. He hoped that his participation in this process would insure a more accurate forecast for the year. Furthermore, he hoped to develop the ability of his supervisors to plan ahead.

Pringle estimated direct materials cost and consumption factors himself. Since it was impossible to predict what all the various strip metal prices would be, he calculated the ratio of materials expense to sales for 1959 and applied it to the 1960 sales projections for each of the product lines in his department.

The marketing, administration, and engineering groups that serviced Pringle's Industrial Metals group forecast their expenses by detailing their personnel requirements and then applying historical ratios of expenses to personnel to estimate their other expenses. From these dollar figures, Pringle was able to estimate what proportion of these amounts would be charged to his department.

With the various forecasts in hand, Pringle estimated a direct profit of $1.392 million on a sales volume of $5.47 million. Once this plan had been drawn up, it was reviewed by the Division Management Committee in relationship to the specific profit and sales goals which it had established for the division. When the plans of each product department were reviewed in terms of the specific group goals, it became obvious that the combined plans of the General Plate product departments were not sufficient to meet the over-all goal, and that, based on market penetration, new product developments and other factors, the planned sales volume for Industrial Metals should be revised upward to $6.05 million and direct profit to $1.587 million (Exhibit 4). This was discussed among Vetter, Turnbull, Scofield, and Pringle, and was agreed to as a difficult but achievable plan.

EXHIBIT 4
Industrial Metals department initial and revised profit statements for 1960*

	Initial ($ thousands)	Revised ($ thousands)
Sales	$5,470	$6,050
Direct labor	435	480
Direct material	1,920	2,115
Overhead	875	968
Marketing	305	346
Administration	161	161
Engineering	382	393
Direct profit	1,392	1,587

* All figures have been disguised.

ACTUAL PERFORMANCE, 1960

On May 10, Tom Pringle received a detailed statement comparing the actual performance of his department for January through April with his budget (Exhibit 5). Sales were 12 percent below plan and direct profit was 19 percent below plan.

In addition to these figures, manufacturing expenses by cost centers were accumulated for Pringle. He passed these along to the production superintendents after he had made adjustments in the budgeted expense figures to allow for the sales decline. Pringle had devised a variable budget system whereby he applied factors to the forecast expenses to indicate what an acceptable expense performance was at sales levels other than the planned volume. Chuck Tobin and Jim Sughrue then analyzed the actual expenses and, one week later, held meetings with their foremen to discuss the causes of both favorable and unfavorable variances. The most common explanation of favorable

EXHIBIT 5
Comparison of actual and budgeted performance—January–April 1960*

	Budgeted ($ thousands)	Actual ($ thousands)
Sales	$2,020	$1,780
Direct labor	160	142
Direct material	704	593
Overhead	322	287
Marketing	100	116
Administration	54	55
Engineering	126	136
Direct profit	554	448

* All figures have been disguised.

manufacturing variances was either extremely efficient utilization of labor or close control over overhead. Unfavorable variances most frequently resulted from machine delays which necessitated overtime labor payments.

Specific problems

Pringle was currently faced with three specific problems. In light of his department's poor performance these past months, he was considering the effects of eliminating his $30,000 advertising budget for the remainder of 1960, postponing the addition of two new engineers to his staff for six months, and reducing raw materials purchases in order to decrease inventory and thus improve his department's return on assets performance.

He had discussed the possibility of eliminating the advertising budget with Bud Sabin and Joe Brackman but had not yet reached a conclusion. Advertising expenditures had been budgeted at $30,000 for the final six months of 1960. The Industrial Metals department ads were generally placed in trade journals read by design engineers in the electrical, automobile, and appliance industries. Pringle did not know for certain how important an aid these advertisements were to his sales force. He did know that all of his major competitors allocated about the same proportion of sales revenue for advertising expenditures and that Industrial Metals' ads were occasionally mentioned by customers.

In late 1959, Pringle had made plans to increase his engineering staff from eight men to ten men in mid-1960. He felt that the two new men could begin functioning productively by early 1961 and could help to revise certain processes which were yielding excessive scrap, to develop new products, and to assist the field engineers in discovering new applications for existing products. Pringle estimated that postponing the hiring of these men for six months would save $20,000 in engineering salaries and supporting expenses.

Pringle also knew that one of the important indicators of his performance was the department's ratio of direct profit to assets used. This figure had been budgeted at 40 percent for 1960, but actual results to date were 31 percent. Pringle was considering reductions in raw materials purchased in order to decrease inventories and thus improve performance. He had discussed this possibility with Phil Waterman, the production control manager for Industrial Metals. Pringle knew that significant improvements in the overall ratio could be made in this way since raw materials inventories accounted for almost 20 percent of total assets and were at a level of ten months' usage at present consumption ratios. He recognized, however, that this course of action required accepting a greater risk of running out. This risk was important to assess since most customers required rapid delivery and Pringle's suppliers usually required four months' lead time to manufacture the nonstandard size metals in the relatively small lots required for Industrial Metals' cladding operation.

THE PURPOSE OF THE PROFIT PLAN

The degree to which the plan was used as a method for evaluating performance and fixing compensation was not completely clear to Pringle. Everyone seemed to recognize that this first effort was imperfect and had errors built in because of inadequate historical data. He had never been explicitly informed of the extent to which top management desired product performance. Pringle stated that during the months immediately following the initiation of the plan he had concluded that short-term performance was much less significant than long-run growth and that he had preferred to concentrate on the longer-run development of new products and markets.

Pringle knew that the Metals & Controls Operating Committee met every Monday to review the performance of each product department from preliminary reports. Customarily Burt Turnbull, the manager of the General Plate group, discussed both Pringle's incoming sales commitments and actual manufacturing expenses with him before each meeting. Pringle also knew that each manager was given a formal appraisal review every six months by his superior. It was common knowledge that the department's performance in relation to its plan was evaluated at both these sessions. Furthermore, Pringle was aware of the fact that Turnbull's performance as product group manager would be affected by his own performance with Industrial Metals. Over a period of months, Pringle had learned that the Management Committee utilized the comparison of actual and planned performance to pinpoint trouble spots. On occasion Vetter had called him in to explain any significant deviations from plan, but normally he was represented at these meetings by Burt Turnbull. It was Pringle's impression that Vetter had been satisfied with the explanation he had given.

In their day-to-day decisions, Pringle's subordinates seemed to be influenced only in a very general way by the profit plan. They reviewed their monthly performance against plan with interest, but generally tended to bias their decisions in favor of long-run development at the expense of short-run deviations from the plan. More recently, however, Pringle realized that top management was not satisfied with his explanations of failure to meet plans. The message, though not stated explicitly, seemed to be that he was expected to take whatever remedial and alternate courses of action were needed in order to meet the one-year goals. He was certain that real pressure was building up for each department manager to meet his one-year plan.

In commenting on the use of planning at M&C, Vetter, the division vice president, stated four major purposes of the program:

1. To set a par for the course. Vetter believed that performance was always improved if the manager proposed a realistic objective for his performance and was informed in advance of what was expected of him.
2. To develop management ability. Vetter believed that the job of manager was to coordinate all the areas for which he was given responsibility. He saw the planning process as a tool for improving these managerial skills.
3. To anticipate problems and look ahead. Vetter felt that the planning process gave the department managers a convenient tool for planning personnel requirements and sales strategy. It also set guideposts so that shifts in business conditions could be detected quickly and plans could be altered.
4. To weld Texas Instruments into one unit. The basic goals for each division were formulated by Vetter in recognition of over-all company goals as disseminated by Haggerty, the company president. These were passed down to the product department level by the Product Group Manager at each Texas Instruments division. Profit planning was thus being carried out by the same process by every department manager in the corporation.

Vetter recognized, however, that many reasons could exist for performance being either better or worse than planned. He stated that in his experience, extremely rigid profit plans often motivated managers to budget low in order to provide themselves with a safety cushion. In his view, this made the entire profit planning process worthless.

Case 4–4
Centralized Information Services*

On October 31, 1976, Mr. Brad T. Jackson, president of Centralized Information Services (CIS), an affiliate of the Serve-Master Corporation, was driving from the Catskills to his home in Stamford, Connecticut. Jackson had just concluded a productive off-site weekend meeting with 12 managers of CIS in which there had been agreement to implement "Tier I" of a major reorganization.

The Catskills meetings were the culmination of the first part of the reorganization work which had been initiated by Jackson three months earlier. He had asked Mr. Gus Simonides, his Vice President of Planning, to head up the study and Mr. David Lieberman, a CIS staff officer who normally was responsible for consulting work to other affiliate companies of the Serve-Master Corporation, to work with Simonides. Jackson had asked for an assessment of the current organization and for plans for reorganization if it proved necessary. The project arose because of Jackson's concern for the ability of CIS to meet long-term, strategic goals, his desire to improve internal efficiency, and because of some recent personnel problems in Operations that had come to his attention.

Jackson had been impressed with the speed and quality of the work of his staff in relating problems and needs to organizational issues and in planning the reorganization. Moreover, the Catskills meetings had resulted in a high degree of consensus among his managers on changes in organizational responsibility, authority and personnel. The most visible change had been the matter of taking Operations out from Data Processing Services and having Pete Giliam report directly to him instead of through Wes Hicks. (See Exhibit 1 and Exhibit 2.)

Despite his satisfaction, however, Jackson was bothered by an uncertainty. "I wonder if it will work," he thought. "I wonder if by February of 1977 we can say to ourselves, 'We should have laid it out *this* way and gone about it *that* way rather than the way we did.' How does one predict that sort of thing? What other steps should I take now?"

BACKGROUND ON CENTRALIZED INFORMATION SERVICES

CIS was founded in 1968 as a result of a study by a consulting firm recommending the centralization of electronic data processing (EDP) hardware and service units of the Serve-Master Corporation. The mis-

---

* All names have been disguised.

EXHIBIT 1
Organization early in 1976*

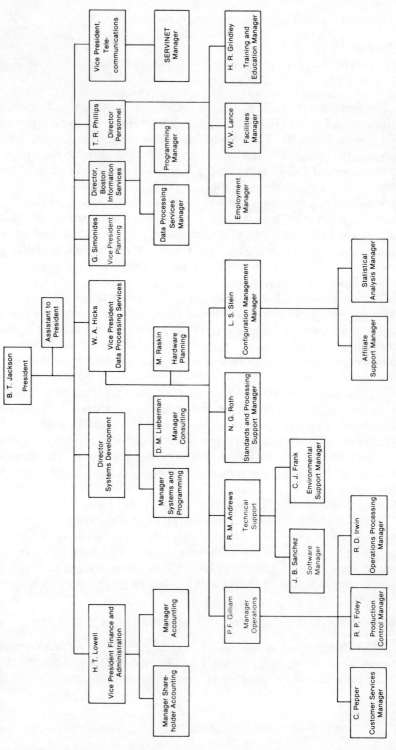

* Note: Names have been left on this chart for individuals mentioned in the case and for several whose titles or reporting relationships were changed by the 1976 reorganization (see Exhibit 2).

sion of CIS was to provide a consolidated base of data processing support and technical advice in information processing and communications to the affiliate companies of Serve-Master, and to become an innovative center of information processing which would help the corporation's affiliates gain a competitive edge in their respective businesses. Brad Jackson was hired from IBM, where his experiences had involved supervision of technical data processing functions, to head up CIS at its founding.

CIS was set up originally as a cost center and "division" of the corporation and was located in New York City. It became an affiliate in 1973 although unlike other affiliates, all of which were profit centers, it continued to be a cost center. The budget for 1976 was at $12 million. CIS employed some 210 people including 185 categorized as nonexempt. Virtually all employees were located in the company's headquarters or machine rooms in New York City.

Serve-Master Corporation was a diversified service company of 20 highly autonomous companies. Corporate headquarters were in Boston. In 1976 Serve-Master was to report revenues in excess of $2.5 billion, and earnings of $115 million. The corporation had reported increases in assets, revenues and stock dividends for some 15 consecutive years. The businesses in which affiliates were engaged included: life insurance, property and casualty insurance, consumer finance, title insurance and travel.

CIS had been created by the consolidation of parts of five previously separate computer organizations of affiliates in the New York area, the largest of which had come from the life insurance company. Brought together had been the hardware and software, operating personnel and most of the technical specialists of each computer organization. Left with the affiliates had been applications analysts, applications programmers and some technical specialists.

Day to day services of CIS to affiliate users occurred through transfers of input data and deliveries of output to and from the machine room, through interaction of an RJE facility in Boston, and through interaction by time sharing, particularly by the use of some 300-plus terminals. Aside from these contacts, relationships for other purposes were carried out by meetings of committees of officers at three distinct levels. These committees had been established over the years to discuss, recommend and in some instances make decisions on matters of planning, policy, and hardware and software purchase. These committees were:

1.   The Electronic Data Processing Technical Committees, of which there were two, one with 12 members for New York and one with 9 members for Boston. Their purpose was "to coordinate the technical development of consolidated EDP activities for major users." Members

EXHIBIT 2
Organization on November 1, 1976*

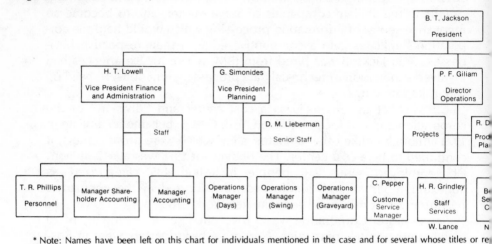

* Note: Names have been left on this chart for individuals mentioned in the case and for several whose titles or re
relationships were changed by the 1976 reorganization (see Exhibit 1).

were individuals holding positions of vice president of line functions or
very high staff positions in their respective organizations. CIS representation in 1976 included Wes Hicks, Vice President of Data Processing
Services, Gus Simonides, Vice President of Planning, and Harry Lowell,
Vice President of Finance and Administration.

2.   The Council of Presidents, which included Brad Jackson and the
presidents of four other Serve-Master affiliates, three of which had
been among the organizations located in New York from which CIS had
been formed in 1968. Its purpose was to "to coordinate the development of consolidated EDP activities providing intercorporate data processing services for EDP operations in New York.

3.   The Joint Planning Committee, a four-person group of vice presidents, including Harry Lowell of CIS. This committee served the Council of Presidents by developing recommendations "for equipment and
operating systems changes, budgetary information and other matters
as assigned."

4.   The Board of Directors of CIS was the highest level group. Its
membership included the president and CEO of Serve-Master Corporation, four other corporate-level officers and the chairman and CEO of
the largest affiliate and user of CIS services, Megalith Insurance Company.

In 1976 CIS was located in the Megalith Insurance Company complex. There was one building of 33 floors and two others approximately
one third that size, all connected by enclosed corridors. The tallest
building, very distinct on the New York skyline, had large neon letters

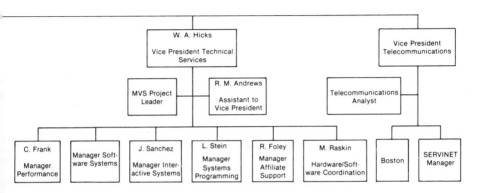

spelling out Megalith on each side at the top. The offices of Jackson and his vice presidents of CIS were on the 24th floor of this building, and the machine rooms and other offices were on the 6th floor of the most distant of the two smaller buildings, a five- to ten-minute trip on foot and by elevators. The computer facilities consisted of two IBM 370/168 machines and a number of second generation computers and peripheral equipment. Both the 168 systems were supported by OS/RJE under VS 2 release 1.7. The computers were linked by a shared HASP spooling technique and supported time sharing (TSO).[1]

In 1976 some 70 percent of total computer utilization at CIS was devoted to batch processing of applications programs, many of which provided output critical to the day-to-day operations of affiliate users. Among these were the daily life insurance policy accounting for Megalith offices and agents throughout the country, and the daily loading and flight schedules for an airline affiliate.

ANTECEDENTS TO REORGANIZATION

By August of 1976 there were a number of indicators of satisfactory performance and accomplishment of mission by CIS. It was becoming

---

[1] OS/RJE refers to the particular IBM operating system that makes possible the use of remote job entry, or the submission of jobs from a distant location. VS 2 further describes the operating system as supporting a virtual storage capability, enabling a job to use more memory locations than are actually physically available on the computer and to make more efficient use of it.

clear that 1976 would become the fourth consecutive year in which CIS would meet or beat a flat budgeted cost target. Much of the improvement was attributed to the efforts of Harry Lowell, Vice President of Finance and Administration, who had come in from Serve-Master Corporation in 1974 and had worked closely with his colleagues in CIS to bring about major changes in the chargeout system and better control over expenses.

An improved expense picture had also resulted from technical work and decisions. For example, at one time CIS had run an IBM 360/145, fully loaded, at its Boston facility. Through optimization efforts the utilization of the machine had been improved to the point where it was only half loaded, whereupon it had been sold at a profit and space rented on a 145 belonging to another company. This had resulted in a 40 percent savings in costs to users. Then in 1975 these applications were put into the 168 systems of CIS in New York and another 40 percent reduction in costs to users was achieved. Thus, for the same or better service, CIS had reduced those users' computing costs by some 64 percent in a two-year period.

While these improvements in control and efficiency, highly visible to affiliate users and the corporation, were taking place several affiliates who had retained or were developing their own EDP capabilities had experienced large overruns of anticipated costs.

In 1976 CIS began to be called upon by affiliates more often than had been the case before for consulting services relating to EDP and information systems decisions. CIS had won an important approval from the Council of Presidents committee and its Board of Directors for capital to continue a project for introducing MVS into its 168 operating system.

Yet, by the strategy and criteria for long-run performance for CIS which Jackson and his top managers believed in, there were problems which had not been solved. Management had believed 1976 would be a good year to attend to internal organizational matters, and discussions had been underway from time to time. Then, some unexpected events revealed the existence of other problems of which top management had not been fully aware.

One night in July an angry confrontation occurred between a black operator and the white lead man and the supervisor on the graveyard shift, resulting in the operator walking off the job. A few days later Jackson learned that CIS was threatened with a class action suit in which it was charged that there was discrimination against the individual by his immediate bosses, citing violations of rights specified in the Equal Employment Opportunity Act.

Jackson called a meeting to discuss the case with the company's lawyer and the supervisory and managerial personnel representing the layers of organization between him and the man in question. He noted that there were no less than seven supervisors and managers beside himself in the room, which struck him as symptomatic of there being too many organizational layers for effective communications to occur up and down the line. It seemed to Jackson that the supervisors had not been provided the training necessary to deal with their complex problems.

As an immediate follow-up to the incident CIS management commissioned an outside consulting firm to conduct a series of employee opinion surveys and follow-up group discussions among lower level employees.

Steps were taken right away to alleviate some of the complaints revealed by the survey. The dress code for machine room employees was relaxed. Programs of training in communications and leadership were initiated for supervisors. Nevertheless, the tenor of the survey raised management concerns about the morale of the employees.

Jackson believed these current people problems might have something in common with a problem he had wrestled with for several years, or at least that both problems might be attacked at the same time. This was what he referred to as "organizational rigidity." As far back as 1972, Jackson had asked that line management take steps to increase the capability for more RJE, anticipating at that time an increasing environment of multiple products and services as opposed to strictly batch production for users in New York. There had been little in the way of response:

> We couldn't get change, couldn't get the systems which would represent flexibility in our operations and potentially provide us with new products. It seemed as though we had levels of people in the middle in operations who were emphasizing attention to day-to-day and traditional work and seemed to be unable to initiate or accept change.

In 1976 Jackson's concern over organizational rigidity was a reflection of his evolving strategic thinking with respect to future decisions that would have to be made on such matters as continued investment in large machines versus minicomputers:

> I think we will see some people, existing users and new ones, that will look to CIS for services before they buy the mini. Maybe we can't compete with the mini; we are watching that closely. But what we have decided is that small users cannot afford programming. We think the small users are going to have to go with packages, with time sharing and with turn-key jobs. They just cannot afford the kind of applications development effort that a Megalith can.
>
> So we are trying to get ourselves in a position where we provide time sharing, we provide RJE and I think that is going to be a bigger part of our operations work load.

Discussions among CIS managers about the problems of rigidity at the middle levels often centered around the sense of incentive and loyalty of employees in Operations. Most of them were thought to "get their strokes" from users as opposed to their own line managers in CIS. A number of individuals, including some supervisors, had been in Operations since before the formation of CIS, and approximately 70 percent of nonexempt employees had been with CIS for more than five years.

CIS top management had also discussed that there was inefficiency in the way work was done on projects and in staff work, resulting in and related to inefficiency in the functioning of Operations itself. There were no reliable concrete measures of performance other than the usual ones of job reruns, on time delivery and the like. The problem was seen as stemming from a lack of division between line work and staff work. Virtually every manager in Data Processing Operations was believed to be working on several development projects. Indeed, some were on so many that most top managers doubted there was any way any particular project would get done.

Believing that "managers should manage," Jackson had wanted for some time to separate out staff and project work from line work. Such an approach, requiring lateral movement of individuals and an organizational change, was expected to make it possible to discover where and by whom projects were initiated, another difficulty experienced by top management. In one instance, for example, Jackson received a request for approval of a project which he asked some questions about. Looking into it, it was found that the project was already underway and that some 40 percent of the time budget he was being asked to approve had already been expended on it. At other times, management found there were no "discretionary resources" at their disposal to carry out high priority tasks which had come to the attention of the top. It appeared that project initiation was occurring internally, or at the request of a user, without management of CIS having control and without the capability to initiate projects on their own.

With the immediate and longer-standing problems in mind Jackson called a weekend off-site meeting at a resort on Long Island at the end of August. Present besides Jackson were all his immediate subordinates and staff and all the third-level managers who reported to Lowell and Hicks, some 16 individuals in all. The meetings resulted in an articulation of the symptoms and problems and a consensus that some form of consulting study of the organization was called for.

THE REORGANIZATION PROCESS

In the week following the Long Island meeting Jackson determined that the best approach would be to use his own management and staff to study, plan and implement the reorganization. There was a need to do the job quickly—he hoped by the end of the year—and outside consultants would invest considerable time just learning the organization. Jackson asked Simonides and Lieberman to head up the work. They were chosen because, as Jackson put it:

> They knew the organization, had consulting skills and were thoroughly versed in the technology and operations of CIS. At the same time they were not line managers and therefore would bring an element of objectivity to evaluation of units and to any consideration of changes of responsibility or resources from one part of the organization to another.

The three recognized at the outset that the process would be one of "learning as we go" and "pulling ourselves up by our bootstraps," as there were no universally appropriate ideal organizational structures for EDP and virtually no books or articles sufficiently specific to be of value to them. They agreed that a participative and team approach was best, one which would involve as many of the managers as possible in the study and planning consistent with the reality that everyone was busy.

Simonides and Lieberman conceived of their work as taking place in several distinct phases or tiers. Tier I would be an assessment of the current organization and if it proved necessary the design of a new one. Tier I would end with the announcement of any organizational changes. Tier II would be the implementation of change, and was to be carried out by the line managers affected and who had been involved in the process. Tier II would end with an assessment of the extent to which objectives were being achieved.

Based on the discussions that had taken place over the recent months, a list of objectives for the study part of Tier I was drawn up. In the words of Simonides and Lieberman:

> The principal objectives of the CIS organization study . . . are to provide Mr. Brad T. Jackson, President, with an assessment of the current organization with regard to:
>
> 1. The degree of internal flexibility and creativity available to make the changes which are demanded by external and internal factors.
> 2. Adequacy of the current structure to maximize resources to meet changing environments.
> 3. The ability to communicate information throughout the organization reliably and validly.
> 4. The ability of individuals and work units to understand organizational goals and create and monitor plans to achieve same.
> 5. The ability to create, monitor and react to performance measurements as well as provide necessary checks and balances to insure effectiveness.

The two men devoted full time to the project, and at their request Jackson created a task force consisting of Lowell and Hicks to assist them.

As a starting point for their assessment of the current organization, it was decided by the task force to develop, on the one hand, a statement of existing and potential products and product strategies for CIS and, on the other hand, a set of job descriptions of all current supervisors and managers, including staff as well as line. Lieberman worked up the strategy and product statement in conjunction with other task force members. Getting the job descriptions proved to be more difficult.

At the Long Island meeting in August all managers with subordinates had been asked to write up job descriptions for their organizations. By October less than half had come in and those which did were judged by Simonides and Lieberman to be "inadequate and incomplete." In response to this Lieberman sent a memorandum to the 16 managers who attended the Long Island meeting, with a copy to Jackson. "Once again," the memo began, "you are going to be asked to prepare job descriptions." The memo stressed the utility of job descriptions to "both performance measurement as well as adequate appraisals," and mentioned that "turnaround time (for submitting the completed job descriptions) is of the utmost importance." Attached to the memo was a two-page guide of categories and topics to be written in for each position described, and two completed examples.

The results of the memo were still disappointing. Simonides and Lieberman saw that the only way they would get good job descriptions would be to fill them out themselves, but they recognized that this would be an advantage in giving them an opportunity to talk to middle and lower level management. During late September and October they interviewed individually each of the 30 or so managers in CIS. The question of duties and responsibilities became just the starting point for these interviews; they tried to learn as much as they could about the nature of organizational problems and potential as well. Additional work with senior managers, particularly Wes Hicks and Pete Giliam, who between them had nearly half the managers and well over half the total personnel in CIS, resulted in a complete set of job descriptions and a set of "task descriptions." The task descriptions were of the functions or missions which were being carried out and were written without particular reference to a division of labor into individual positions.

PLANNING FOR KEY STRUCTURAL CHANGES IN OPERATIONS

In mid-October Simonides and Lieberman, working closely with Jackson and the task force, drew up a new "functional" organizational chart. It showed boxes with task functions but no individual names. Two particularly important organizational changes from the existing organization were shown, both of which pertained to the Operations function.

The first change was that Operations was taken out from Data Processing and shown reporting directly to the President of CIS. The remaining function was renamed Technical Services. Wes Hicks, Vice President of Data Processing Services and member of the task force, endorsed the change.

The other important change was that all employees in line operations functions under Pete Giliam would report to him directly through the shift supervisors rather than through the three managers of separate functions. As indicated in Exhibit 1, these functions were Customer Services, Production Control and Operations Processing.

Simonides and Lieberman were aware that these plans for changes had interesting precedents. Prior to 1972, for example, the operations function had been separated in the CIS organization. A manager hired from outside CIS in 1970 with a strong technical background had been instrumental in achieving a combination of operations and technical functions under himself. When this man left CIS for another position in 1975, Wes Hicks inherited the job. Thus, this particular Tier I change was a return back to the original organization.

Beginning in 1974 and extending through 1976 a significant reorganization at the supervisory level had been carried out by Pete Giliam. Operations in 1974 had been structured in what Giliam described as "a fairly traditional way." The units reporting to him had been "operations" (pre-processing, data entry, output processing and console operation), "data control" (staging of equipment and tape mounting on the input end) and "scheduling" (maintenance of a 24-hour process control schedule of jobs). The 1974 organization is shown in Exhibit 3. At that time there were some 45 people working in the three shifts under

EXHIBIT 3
CIS Operations in 1974

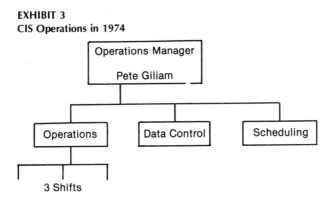

operations. A particular feature of the work was the rotation among them, in conjunction with their shift supervisors, of job assignments, including console operation. Although only a few were trained and qualified for console operation, over time a large number came to earn the level of pay and rank associated with the highest skill job.

Giliam's reorganization in 1974 separated the "people intensive" and relatively low skill jobs away from the console operation function. A new unit known as "operations processing" took the functions of tape mounting, input processing and output processing and organized the employees doing those jobs under the shift supervisors. Console operators went to a new unit known as "production control." Another new unit, "customer service" was created to handle user contact and some input preparation. The reorganization thus introduced by Giliam in operations was as it appears in Exhibit 1.

THE INTRODUCTION OF THE TIER I REORGANIZATION

By the end of October, after two months of intensive work, Simonides and Lieberman had accumulated a large volume of findings, had developed the skeleton of the new organization and had worked closely with Jackson and the members of the task force (Lowell and Hicks) so that there was full endorsement from them for the changes outlined in the new organization. The particular changes in Operations had also been discussed with Pete Giliam.

On Thursday and Friday, October 21 and 22, key managers met in the CIS headquarters offices with members of the task force to determine the specific new organization of functions and of changes of people. In the meeting the names of every CIS manager who would potentially be changed were put on separate cards. An outline of the new functional organization was put up on a corkboard and as a group the managers discussed placement of people. The discussion centered on assessments of each individual's technical abilities and how those could best be fitted to the task and functional needs. Jackson played an active role in the decision making. This work came to be known as "the card game." There was lively discussion about placement of people. At the end of the meetings the new organization chart was completed (Exhibit 2).

The final steps in Tier I of the reorganization took place at the off-site meetings in the Catskills over the weekend at the end of October 1976. Present were all the members of the task force plus the line managers who would be affected by the reorganization, 12 people in all. In response to the presentations by Simonides and Lieberman, the consensus was that a number of benefits would be achieved by "taking out a layer" of the organization and moving Operations up. For one, it would *raise* the people below and provide them additional stature in the hierarchy. This was seen as a step in the direction of dealing positively with the morale issue.

The task force recommended that two middle level people be "surplussed." Both these individuals had been involved heavily in staff project assignments. There was widespread support for the decision.

The managers present readily endorsed the summary of product strategies and products prepared earlier by Lieberman and the task force.

Most of the discussion at the Catskills meetings centered on the recommendations of what was to be achieved and on the new organization chart itself. The complete list of recommendations as presented is given in Exhibit 4. The reorganization and assignments of individuals was accepted without major dissent by all the CIS managers present.

EXHIBIT 4
Recommendations for Tier I reorganization

a. Separate Data Processing Operations from Technical Services and elevate the management level of operations to Director level.

b. Create staff functions within both Data Processing Operations and Technical Services to give cognizance to the separation of line and staff functions and responsibilities as well as establishing a mechanism for project control.

c. Reduce the reporting levels in Data Processing Operations and Technical Services to increase the span of control and shorten lines of communication.

   More specifically, provide for Shift Managers to report directly to the Director of Operations, and Technical Services Managers to report directly to the Vice President, Technical Services.

d. Increase the responsibility of Shift Managers, in order that they may assume more direct control of total operations. Incorporate within the Shift Managers' span of control those functions previously performed by the separate Production Control units.

e. Combine the staff functions of Training and Education, Systems and Procedures and Facilities into a Staff Services unit. Principal activities of this unit should provide direct support to the operational area and report to the Director of Operations.

f. Create a Boston Service Center unit whose construction reflects the planned environment of RJE and Interactive Services and support. This function should report to the Director of Operations.

g. Give cognizance to separation of measuree from measurer by the establishment of a performance unit within Technical Services.

h. Combine previous organizational units and staff activities associated with affiliate support, in order to maximize effective use of like skills and eliminate artificial boundaries. Achievement of this recommendation requires disbursement of previous Configuration Management components and Interactive Service functions.

EXHIBIT 4 (*continued*)

   i. Change reporting structure of Systems and Programming to Technical Services, in order to maximize use of like skills and project control.

   j. Retain current structure and reporting relations of Telecommunications. However, coordination of plans and activities are required to achieve integration necessary to meet future goals.

   k. Establish, within Finance and Administration, a staff function to provide business planning activities which encompass both traditional financial planning and budgeting as well as establishment and evaluation of measurements.

   l. Transfer the Personnel function to Finance and Administration, in order to combine control and information sources.

   m. Retain the senior staff function of Planning which is specifically devoted to evaluation of long-term technological trends and plans.

   n. Retain the senior staff function associated with Affiliate Systems Consulting and augment this activity with internal CIS assignments.

   o. Establish an "organizational development" function reporting directly to the President.

On Monday, October 25, a memorandum was distributed to all CIS supervisory and managerial personnel announcing the reorganization. It went into effect on Monday, November 1.

Chapter 5

IMPLEMENTING ORGANIZATIONAL CHANGE

No matter how rational and ideal a new organizational structure may seem to the designers, as often as not after it is introduced the desired results, if they ever come, are much longer than expected in coming. In many instances this is because insufficient attention has gone into the *implementation* of the change: it is as often *how* an organizational change is conducted more than the logic of *what* is being done that determines success or failure.

In many if not most instances in which management attempts to change organizational results attention is paid exclusively to a change of one or more of the manageable input elements in the overview model, such as the formal organizational structure and a change of a few management personnel in key positions in the structure. The reason for the failure of this approach should be apparent if one reconsiders the overview model presented in Chapter 1 and the discussion of unmanaged or natural processes in Chapter 3. Of course, in those instances where external forces and internal unmanaged processes are pushing so strongly in the direction of perpetuating poor results, no organizational structure, no matter how carefully implemented, can reverse the tide. Our discussion in this chapter is confined to that class of situations where there is good promise that change can be effected if it is well carried out.

ON CHANGING ORGANIZATIONAL STRUCTURE

Since manageable results are caused by individuals' work behavior, in any effort to improve results it is ultimately work behavior which must be changed. And since behavior is mediated and caused by individuals' perspectives, that must be changed. Thus, it is only if the balance of total forces on perspectives is changed in the desired direction that change in behavior and results will occur. Formal organizational structure is but one element acting on perspectives. To the extent that other inputs are not changed simultaneously and efforts are not made to exercise semidirect influence on emergent relationships and direct influence on perspectives, it is likely that people will continue to work in old patterns no matter how logical and rational the new organization may seem to its management creators.

In a few rare instances it may be that organizational structure is the primary element *preventing* a desirable change in behavior. It may be clear to everyone that something has to be done, such as decentralization of authority. Perspectives may already be oriented toward new patterns of work behavior, with reinforcement from informal relationships and most formal inputs. But in the vast majority of cases the opposite is true. From the top management perspective, organizations seem to have great inertia in their response to organizational change.

Let us look more closely to the sources of organizational inertia, at methods of assessing the state of receptivity to change, and at strategies for dealing with different degrees of receptivity.

WHAT IMPLEMENTATION MEANS

We shall define *implementation* as the process by which a change in one or more formal organizational inputs is introduced and carried out. There are several features of this definition worth noting and comparing to other uses of the term *implementation*. First of all, note that we include any and all of the formal organizational inputs as the substance of what can be changed and implemented. These include not only organizational structure, the design of which was discussed in the previous chapter, but also strategy, job descriptions, policies and procedures, measurement and control systems, and adopted technology, such as applications of computerized data processing.

Moreover, in this definition the implementation process does *not* include the act of change in the input, for example the redesign of organizational structure. Rather, this definition suggests that implementation begins where design leaves off. In this respect, just as the design process, discussed in Chapter 4 with respect to formal organizational structure, consists of the phases of diagnosis, analysis, and synthesis, so too do these phases apply to the implementation process. This

FIGURE 5–1
Alternative meanings of implementation

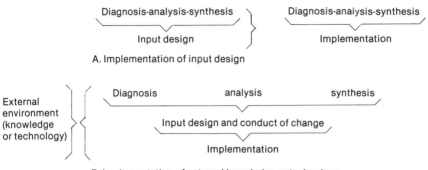

A. Implementation of input design

B. Implementation of external knowledge or technology

is illustrated in the upper half of Figure 5–1. We believe this use of the term is more familiar to managers than the alternative one, which would include within a broader meaning of the implementation process the design of the input as well as the introduction of it. This is illustrated in the lower half of Figure 5–1.

This distinction between our definition and a broader definition of implementation derives in part from a difference in what is being implemented. In our definition it is explicitly the implementation of changed organizational inputs. In the broader definition, it is frequently the implementation of some body of knowledge or available technology from the external environment which is being referred to. For example, it is this broader use of the term which is employed in referring to the introduction of applied mathematics, operations research, and management science techniques into organizations.[1] Under these circumstances, implementation may come to mean not only the adaptation of external technology, but the decision on what technology to apply. Of course, no matter which meaning of implementation one uses, the organizational problem of introducing change remains the same. It is this particular aspect of implementation, involving the need for diagnosis (analysis) of emergent relationships and perspectives, and the setting of strategy (synthesis) for the change process, which we shall address here.

THE PHASES OF CHANGE

Successful implementation of organizational changes requires an understanding of and strategy to deal with emergent relationships and

---

[1] For a very readable approach to this type of implementation, see Keen and Scott-Morton (1978).

individual perspectives. The whole tone and approach of organizational change in our discussion thus far suggests the *imposition* of change *onto* the relationships and perspectives of people in such a way that the change is accepted and leads to a change in people's behavior. This is generally a necessary and appropriate stance for management. It implies that the implementation of organizational change is essentially a process of management, that is, a process of influence.

At the same time, it should be recognized that changes in people's social relationships, perspectives and behavior at work and elsewhere occur rather frequently *without* management having anything to do with it. It would be useful for our purposes to understand how these unmanaged or natural changes take place, inasmuch as an understanding can improve the planning and likelihood of success of implementation.

The most valuable descriptive theory of social and individual change was proposed by Kurt Lewin (1952) who conceived of behavioral change as resulting from three phases of alteration of what we have called the individual's perspective. Lewin's basic framework, originally based on emergent groups was expanded by Schein (1961) to apply to individuals as well. Useful elaborations of this theory may be found in Dalton (1970) and in Kolb and Frohman (1970). The phases are (1) the *unfreezing* of an existing perspective; (2) the *moving* or *changing* toward a new perspective; and (3) the *refreezing* of the new perspective, accompanied by new behavior. Let us look at each of these phases and some of their implications for the implementation of organizational change.

Unfreezing

As a practical matter, change in behavior does not occur in a vacuum of *no* prior behavior or prior perspective. To the extent that the new is different from the old and the old had value to the individual, then the old patterns of perspective and behavior must first give way before the new can be adopted. Unfreezing of perspective implies a questioning and doubting of existing assumptions and feelings. For most change which is significant, the unfreezing requires a loosening of emotional as well as intellectual forces. It is for lack of adequate unfreezing before the introduction of new information that much organizational change fails. An individual or group may well understand intellectually what a new organizational arrangement is supposed to accomplish, and may even agree to it, only to resist it when the time comes for changed behavior. We may say that in these instances unfreezing has not been accomplished.

In unmanaged change of individuals alone and in groups, unfreezing of perspectives may come about from an unexpected and shocking event. Examples include the death of a friend or spouse, or feedback that is suddenly disconfirming and humiliating, such as unexpected criticism in a performance appraisal of some work behavior one had assumed was acceptable. In other instances the individual may perceive in someone else or in some new method of working a behavior pattern which they prefer over their present one. This might be provided by a mentor or teacher or effective salesperson. Although in these cases there is perhaps more positive incentive than negative self-evaluation, the individual still has to deal psychologically with the issue that what one has been doing is undesirable relative to some new way.

Many institutions implicitly recognize the nature of a necessary phase of unfreezing in rites of initiation and other symbolic and ritualistic events which serve to devalue the individual's past self-concept in preparation for new ways of thinking and behaving. Examples include brainwashing, hazing, boot camp, an overload of work at the outset of an educational program, and the like.

For the purposes of managing organizational change, it is very important to assess the need for unfreezing. Such an assessment is the essence of the diagnostic stage of implementation, to be discussed below.

Moving

In the moving or changing phase the individual is ready for new behavior and a change in perspective. It is important that he or she have an opportunity to build by experimentation new patterns of behavior and new assumptions, perceptions, and feelings. It is a time of trial-and-error learning, characterized by ambiguity and tentativeness. This phase is typically one of careful guidance by an authority, of learning the pieces of a new pattern of behavior before the whole can be conceived.

It is a quite possible for new behavior to be tried before the full old perspective has been replaced. Indeed, as a practical matter in organizational change it may be impossible to fully unfreeze old behavior or to know when the unfreezing has ended. In a sense, a temporary investment in guiding and closely controlling behavior required for a new organizational change, for example, is called for during this phase. In any event this period of learning is crucial to the establishment of new skills as well as new perspectives and psychological commitment. It clearly takes more time to accomplish this psychological movement than it takes merely to present the statement of new required behavior to those who are to change.

Refreezing

The final phase involves the establishment of a new perspective compatible with and leading to the new behavior. In effect, the new part of one's total perspective is now established and integrated so that it fits the whole. This makes it possible for the new behavior to be accomplished as a matter of course. This is the period in which the individual or group begin to enjoy the rewards for the new behavior, either extrinsically in the form of social approval, monetary reward, and the like or intrinsically in the form of ego satisfaction, sense of mastery, and self-fulfillment. With successful refreezing goes a heightened sense of self-confidence. Depending on how central to one's identity the change has been, refreezing may involve a new self-concept.

The test of successful organizational change does not come until the people are left, after implementation, to conduct the new required work behavior and to produce the new results. It is often only at this point, when problems arise, that some earlier error in not adequately providing for change of the entire system, or for unfreezing or training or refreezing of groups and individuals, is discovered. Examples of this include the changed organization in which employees revert to reporting to the previous boss, or the new computer system or the new forms which are used once and then ignored. Management tales of the instances of such recidivism abound.

We turn now to a prescriptive approach to the diagnosis and strategy setting for the implementation of change in which we make use of this descriptive theory of the three phases of individual and social change.

TOWARD STRATEGIES OF IMPLEMENTATION

Personal philosophies of change

Ask any experienced manager how organizational change should be implemented and you are likely to get an earful. Most managers who have been responsible for implementation have developed personal perspectives consisting of assumptions and strong feelings about how change should be introduced. These personal philosophies, or strategies, of implementation tend to fall into one of two camps, either "tops-down" or "bottoms up."

The tops-down strategy

The advocates of the tops-down strategy believe that in general people resist change and require direction and structure for their well-being as well as to work efficiently and effectively. The basic psychological contract between employees and management, it is assumed, is one in which the employee provides work effort and commitment and expects in return pay, benefits, and a clear definition of what is expected to be done. It follows that it is management's responsibility to design the changes it deems appropriate and to implement these thoroughly but quickly by directive from the top. When confronted with descriptive evidence from the behavioral sciences, such as the Lewinian phases, these managers are likely to smile knowingly, comment on the gap between behavioral science in the ivory tower and the realities of their problems, and remind the questioner that what they know is that their approach *works,* at least for them. Theirs is a results- and efficiency-oriented approach, and indeed it does work—at least for them, at least sometimes.

The bottoms-up strategy

The advocates of this approach profess what to them is a more enlightened view of human nature. They argue that people welcome change and the opportunity to contribute to their own productivity, especially if the change gives them more variety in their work and more autonomy. These managers assume people have a psychological contract which includes an expectation that they be involved in designing change as well as implementing it. Commitment to change, they say, follows from involvement in the total change process and is essential to successful implementation. They take the descriptive theory of Lewin as virtually a *normative* theory, which suggests strongly that change be gradual and in an environment of social and psychological support. Consultation, planning, design, and implementation ought to be from the bottom upward. Theirs is an effectiveness- and satisfaction-oriented approach to change. And it works—at least for them, at least sometimes.

At this point we invite the reader to pause and critique these two philosophies. Which is the more correct? Is the question of correctness the right question to ask? What is *your* philosophy of change?

A contingent philosophy of implementation

If your answer to the question was, in effect, "the correct strategy of change depends on the circumstances," you are in agreement with the currently very popular contingency school.

As we pointed out in Chapter 4 with reference to the design of organizational structure, the best form depends on an analysis of certain elements in the situation. The same philosophy is also useful as an approach to implementation of organizational change. Let us examine the relevant elements and variables here, and in so doing attempt to lay out a practical guide to the development of a strategy of change which fits a given situation. Then, in closing, we shall take a critical look at the limitations of this approach itself.

Diagnosis of setting for implementation

We shall assume that the manager who wishes to implement an organizational change has some idea in mind of the kind of thing to be implemented. Although we have argued in Chapter 4 that the primary responsibility for organizational design should lie with top management, in the case of some other formal inputs and in some organizations, it may well be advisable not to have a definitive design in mind before looking at the implementation strategy. This is for two reasons. First, much evidence suggests that certain formal inputs, such as major computer applications, virtually require the involvement of the user of the system in the design process as well as the implementation. Although this is less likely to be the case with formal organizational structure, since we stated in Chapter 4 that an initial design by top management and staff should not be cast in stone. It is legitimate and appropriate for the design to be debated and perhaps modified by virtue of the political processes, at least at managerial levels.

The second reason for flexibility of design prior to implementation is simply that the recommended implementation strategy may well turn out to be participative and bottoms-up. While it is intended here that we address the implementation process independent of the design process, and therefore that a participative implementation could be conducted even with a predetermined design, it is likely that a situation which calls for a participative implementation could provide for an improvement in the design through a similar process. In general, however, we advocate some prior definition of the organizational design or parameters for the redesign of inputs prior to the diagnosis of the implementation setting.

Whereas the design of new organizational structures and some other formal inputs may appropriately be carried out primarily by staff advisors, outside consultants, and top management, it is line management, particularly those who are deemed to be key for achieving the intended results from the change, who should engage in the exercise of implementation diagnosis and setting of implementation strategy.

The implementation diagnosis consists of *assessing* eight independent variables or factors in the organization. These are shown in the upper part of Figure 5–2, where each variable is given a continuum of

FIGURE 5–2

Variables for diagnosis and strategy setting of implementation of organizational change

	Diagnostic (independent) variables	
1. Time available	Short ————————	Long
2. Clarity of crisis or need for change	Clear to all ————————	Clear to few
3. Size of organization	Small ————————	Large
4. Effects of existing controls and incentives	Encourage initiative ————	Encourage focus
5. Organizational concentration of relevant knowledge	Concentrated at top ————	Concentrated at bottom
6. Expectations of people regarding involvement in implementation ..	None ————————	Extensive
7. Potential resistance	Small ————————	Great
8. Total power base of change agent	Great ————————	Small
	Implementation strategy (dependent) variables	
1. Pace	Fast ————————	Slow
2. Use of power	Tops-down ————————	Bottoms-up
3. Management style	Directive ————————	Participative

potential values.[2] Based on the diagnosis which evolves, the basic implementation strategy will consist of *selecting* values along the continua for the three dependent variables as shown at the bottom of Figure 5–2.

The ends of the continua for each variable have been located such that answers to the diagnostic for the independent variables which fall toward the left tend to dictate a change strategy toward the left of the dependent variables, and a pattern of diagnostics falling toward the right tend to dictate a strategy toward the right on the dependent variables. Thus, for example, if there is very little time available, the crisis or need for change is clear to all, it is a small organization, and so on, the appropriate change strategy is tops-down, directive, and fast.

The list of variables in Figure 5–2 bears some explanation. Each of the eight diagnostic variables represents an item or topic to be checked by management in the particular organization in which change is contemplated. Variables 1 and 2, time available and clarity of crisis or need for change, respectively, are aspects of the problem at hand. For situations where time is relatively short, such as a serious erosion of production efficiency or a decline in sales, very often there will also be visibility of the problem to those who would be affected by the change. Quite typically, the psychological contract of employees includes the

---

[2] Much of this discussion is adapted from Lorsch (1974).

implicit expectation that management has a prerogative to act more or less unilaterally in such instances. Of course, what may be perceived as a crisis by management may not be recognized as such by employees whose perspective on their jobs or whose political and ideological perspective are very different. Indeed, top management's notion that it is a crisis that productivity is down and absenteeism is up in a unionized plant may be perceived as justice and compensation for some unexpressed grievance by the employees. An important part of the diagnostic exercise is the ability to see matters through the eyes of others in the organization. Depending on the answers to questions raised about these first two variables, some immediate managerial action may be called for even before a full diagnosis is complete. Suppose, for example, that an assessment suggests that the time available for an organizational change is very short, but that the need for change is not widely perceived by the employees who would be affected by it. Management should consider an early campaign of "selling" the facts of the situation in as objective a manner as possible, while they proceed with the full diagnosis.

Variable 3, size of organization, refers to the number of employees in the organizational system which will be subjected to the change.

Variable 4, effects of existing controls and incentives, calls for an assessment of whether or not there exists encouragement of the kind of on-the-spot initiative so often required during the implementation of change. To the extent there is a tight control system which encourages a focus on specific, steady state efficiency and to the extent these same employees are expected to implement changes, management should undertake a slower process or reconsider the need for employee involvement in implementation.

Variables 5 and 6 are key ones for determining whether employee involvement is or is not required in the implementation. To the extent that knowledge relevant to the change is concentrated at lower levels, such as might be the case in a highly skilled and labor-intensive customer service organization like a social work agency, reorganization or automation will almost certainly require involvement of those individuals. Similarly, where the psychological contract leads to expectations for involvement in implementation, this should be carefully recognized by management. An interesting example of major change which is done tops-down with little difficulty is the annual model changeover on automobile assembly lines. Although many of the workers are highly skilled, their knowledge is not relevant to the change, nor do they expect to be involved in the implementation diagnostic process, at least not in most traditional capital-intensive automotive assembly line operations. Rather, the changeover is conducted as fast as possible without the help of most production employees, who return to work on a Monday morning to find most specific jobs unchanged but a different product being turned out. Incidentally, this is an illustration of how product design can be influenced by an implementation strategy that is given in advance: the product is designed to minimize changes in employees' work behavior.

Variable 7 asks for the judgment of the implementing management of the likely resistance to change to be encountered. The question might be phrased as follows: "Suppose we introduced this change quickly and without consultation with employees. Is there likely to be resistance that could adversely affect our results?" The answer to this is extremely subjective and tests the ability of management to sense potential employee reaction.

The final assessment question, dealing with variable 8, asks about the total power available to the change agents, normally the line managers who will be implementing the change. Note that all the bases of power discussed in Chapter 2 should be taken into account. Personal credibility in the eyes of employees and the "referred" power which comes from top management backing are as important as the formal authority of the manager. The entire assessment process really hinges on the judgment as to whether the power available is adequate compared to the power needed to carry out the change successfully.

In any particular situation there will be a mixed pattern of answers to the diagnostic questions raised by the checklist of independent variables in Figure 5–2. What is clearly necessary is for at least a qualitative weighting to be placed on some or all the variables. These weights will differ from one situation to another. Here again, the checklist can remind the manager of points to cover, but it cannot and should not be used as a substitute for judgment.

The choice of a strategy of implementation

With the diagnostic assessment done, managers responsible for implementation may now select a strategy as defined by the three independent variables in the lower part of Figure 5–2. These are the pace of implementation, how the power is exercised during change, and the management style employed. The options fall along the continua which define the tops-downs versus the bottoms-up philosophies. In general, to the extent the weighted answers for the assessment variables are to the left of those continua, then the strategy should be toward the tops-down end; and for assessments toward the right, a strategy toward the bottoms-up end. This, in essence, is the contingent approach as applied to implementation.

Limitations to contingency of implementation

We have deliberately left off one very important diagnostic variable from the list in Figure 5–2, and we have done so in order to emphasize its importance. That is the personality and preferred management style of the line manager or managers responsible for the implementation.

There is an assumption in the presentation of the assessment and strategy that the managers themselves can change their style to fit the circumstances. To the extent this is true, then the contingent scheme applies. That is, to the extent the implementor is able to adjust his or her style to fit the dictates of the situation, or at least to carry out the change without having to reveal a style which may be very different from the manner in which the implementation is being conducted, then the above scheme may be applied in all its pragmatic glory. However, most implementation requires an intense involvement of the managers with other people in the exercise of direct and semidirect influence. To the extent their management style is, say, either directive and highly output-oriented on the one hand or participative and people-oriented on the other, it will be difficult for them to be effective as the implementors of a change strategy which calls for an incompatible style.

Of course, it might also be possible for top management to change managers to fit the needs of the implementation strategy. Particularly in crisis situations which call for rapid turnarounds, companies and government agencies often make a change of management the first step to tops-down organizational change.

In any event, this question of preferred management style by the managers at hand should be factored into the assessment process. We shall have more to say about the whole subject of management style in Chapter 10, and about the problems which can arise for an individual who engages different styles as the circumstances dictate in Chapter 12.

CONCLUSION

This chapter on implementation should be thought of as closely related to Chapter 4 on formal organizational design. It is useful conceptually to think of design and implementation as separate, and we have argued that it is useful to create as a first cut a rational or ideal organization structure and then modify it to fit the social forces of political groups which would inevitably modify it. Nevertheless, thought about implementation and attention to the forthcoming requirements of implementation strategy ought to begin during the design phase. This is particularly true where the preferred implementation strategy is one of bottoms-up involvement, inasmuch as management may well prefer to delegate some of its power to include the design itself. Thus, in closing we may modify our diagram from the top of Figure 5–1, earlier in this chapter, to Figure 5–3. Here design and implementation are shown as potentially, although not necessarily, overlapping and highly interactive over time.

FIGURE 5–3
Design and implementation processes for formal organizational inputs

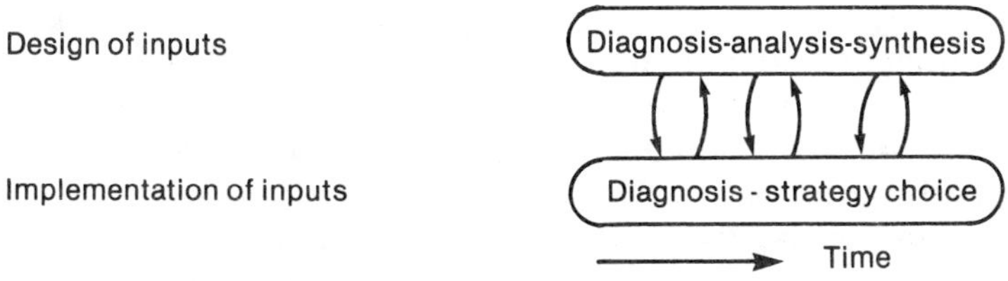

Design of inputs   Diagnosis-analysis-synthesis

Implementation of inputs   Diagnosis - strategy choice

Time

QUESTIONS FOR STUDY AND DISCUSSION

1. Referring back to the organizational design change developed in answer to questions at the end of Chapter 4, make a list of the specific action steps you would take in implementing the design. Take into account the need for communications with employees, training for new roles and responsibilities, and measures to ensure the success of the new organization.

2. Which of the basic styles of implementation most nearly fits your own style? What in your personality or training or experience makes this so?

   What would you do if your boss asked you to implement a change in a way which ran counter to your preferred method?

3. Think of the implementation of an organizational change, new administrative procedure, computer system, or other technology which you have experienced. Using the checklist of situational variables contained in this chapter indicate what the situation was for each variable. Which variables were most important in terms of the weight that should be placed on them?

   What does the analysis suggest as to the appropriate method of implementation? How did this differ from the actual method of implementation?

   What changes in implementation, if any, would you recommend for similar situations in the future? (Be as specific as possible in terms of the actions that were taken or should be taken.)

4. Organizational unfreezing is generally not as dramatic as the individual unfreezing precipitated by death of spouse, or negative assessment by another of personal performance one thought to be acceptable. Comment on the experience of instances of unfreezing in your own life. What methods can organizations use to unfreeze attitudes?

Case 5-1
Webster Industries (A)*

On Friday, October 17, 1975, Bob Carter, a 32-year-old graduate of the Amos Tuck School, was observing his first anniversary as Manufacturing Manager in the Fabrics Division of Webster Industries. Excluding two years spent earning his MBA, he had been with Webster for ten years. Carter was very satisfied with his Webster experiences. Before being selected for his current position, he had spent two years as a plant production superintendent, three years as a plant manager, and two as assistant to the President, Abe Webster. On a day that should have been one of celebration, Carter sat at home in a very somber mood and started on his third martini of the afternoon.

Earlier in the day Ike Davis, head of the Fabrics Division, had told Carter that Fabrics would have to reduce its personnel by 20 percent and that the manufacturing department, in particular, would have to make a cut of 15 percent at the managerial level. This meant that Carter would have to trim his 289 managers by 43 individuals. Davis' request stemmed from reduction plans presented to him by Abe Webster. Because Abe had set the following Friday as the deadline for the submittal of termination lists, Davis wanted his top divisional managers as a group to begin a review on the preceding Wednesday of all proposed Fabrics separations. Davis had concluded his conversation with Carter by listing the five guidlines that Abe had provided:

1. No one with over 20 years of Webster service and 50 years of age should be terminated without review by the President.
2. Since the last reduction approximately one year ago had impacted primarily on hourly and weekly workers, this "go-around" was to focus on managerial levels.
3. Seniority was not to be a major determining factor as to who would be separated.
4. Early retirement should not be counted upon as a mechanism for meeting reduction targets.
5. Blacks, women, and other minorities were not to be terminated more aggressively than other employees.

After speaking with Davis, Carter went home to ponder the situation.

Carter spent the afternoon in his den thinking about the task before him. He remembered the first time he had terminated a subordinate. Early in his career he had fired a secretary—it had taken him a week to muster enough courage to do it and a week to recover. However, since that experience he had found each successive termination increasingly easy. But never before had he been involved in releasing so many

---

* All names have been disguised.

individuals at once, especially so many people with whom he had worked and developed social relationships. Though he had been in his present position for only a year and had no previous experience in the Fabrics Division, Carter knew most of his managers by name and considered several to be friends. Further, he and his family interacted with many of these individuals and their families in various community and civic activities. In addition to the likelihood of having to recommend the termination of personal and family friends, Carter worried about the possibility of having to release employees with significant service. He knew that any person with over ten years of Webster employment would be very surprised by termination. While pondering the possible consequences of the reductions, Carter became more and more anxious as he realized that he had few firm ideas on how the cuts should be made. The only certainty was that he must conform to Abe's guidelines.

GENERAL INFORMATION ON WEBSTER INDUSTRIES

Location   Located on 17 acres of rolling red Georgia hills at the northern outskirts of Clearwater, Georgia, Webster's headquarters resembled a college campus with plantation-like buildings. Top management was housed in the refurbished "Big House" of the old Webster Plantation, while middle level corporate managers were situated in a modern three-story office building that was known as the "Box." Built a thousand yards from the Big House, the modern structure appeared out of place in the plantation setting. The Big House and the Box comprised the heart of one of America's most successful textile companies.

Clearwater was unabashedly a company town. Of its population of about 35,000, half the employed residents worked for Webster, one third engaged in "serious farming," and the remainder labored in several small factories around the town. Not only was Webster the dominant employer, Websterites held all "important" community positions. The company stressed community involvement and encouraged its people to accept civic responsibilities.

Because Webster attracted highly educated employees from a variety of places, Clearwater differed from the typical small, rural Georgia town. For example, Georgia educators ranked its school system ahead of Atlanta's. The town had experienced much success in attracting quality teachers through the offering of generous salary schedules and excellent facilities. Another unique feature of the town was a thriving set of cultural and entertainment events, from regular appearances by the Atlanta Symphony and various theater groups to exhibition games featuring the Atlanta professional athletic teams. As one Clearwaterite put it, "Clearwater is not your run-of-the-mill mill town."

Company history   Colonel Jeremiah Webster, an officer in the Confederate Army, founded the company after the Civil War. When the

Colonel retired from the operations, his youngest son assumed the leadership. He in turn was followed by his oldest male offspring, Mark Webster, who presided over the company from 1941 to 1960. Under Mark's tenure, Webster grew and branched into other fabric markets. By 1960 the company produced fibers for carpeting and for home and industrial furnishings. Sales rose from $150 million in 1941 to approximately $900 million in 1960. During this period Webster opened its first plants outside of Clearwater. Growth and geographical dispersion of operations greatly strained the company's management.

In the 50s Mark recognized his company's need for skilled management. Convinced of the importance of management for the future of Webster, in 1955 he set out to attract MBAs to his organization. Though trained as a lawyer, he had considerable respect for "professional" business education. This respect had been fostered by consulting relationships with professors from some of the leading national and regional business schools. Also, Mark encouraged his son, Abe, to attend the Wharton School.

After earning his MBA at Wharton, Abe served five "experience years" before assuming the presidency. Up to that point in time, Webster's president had also served as chairman of the Board of Directors. However, after Abe's five years of experience, Mark decided to split the jobs. Abe became president and Mark concentrated on the chairmanship. Mark still kept regular hours, but emphasized that Abe was run-

EXHIBIT 1
Partial Webster Industries corporate organization chart

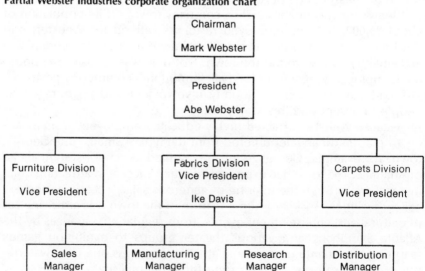

ning the business. Under Abe the company continued to grow, primarily through diversification by acquisition of several small furniture and carpet manufacturers. Following these acquisitions, Webster's management adopted a divisional structure. (See Exhibit 1.)

Despite its diversification Webster was very much a textile company. Of its present sales of approximately $1.7 billion, 70 percent came from the Fabrics Division. The carpet and furniture lines each accounted for 15 percent.

The Fabrics Division's products were categorized as fibers for apparel, home furnishings, carpeting, and industrial furnishings. Organizationally, Fabrics had a functional structure of sales, manufacturing, distribution, and research. Within sales, the organization was by markets; the sales force was organized around the different fiber classifications. Comparable to sales, the manufacturing plants were grouped by markets with three in apparel and two in each of the other areas. Each group reported to a production manager, who in turn reported to the Assistant Production Superintendent, Cecil Stevens. (See Exhibit 2.)

Organizational climate   Websterites described the company as a "first class" place to work. Employees took great pride in the company's nationally known products and frequently remarked, "You can tell Webster fabrics from a mile away!" The organization consistently won industry awards for superior products which were displayed in the Big House lobby. Webster also maintained excellent relations with its employees.

Management spared little in its efforts to make work at Webster rewarding and productive. The organization's facilities and working conditions excelled by far those of its competitors. Webster's pay and fringe benefits systems offered attractive financial packages and served as models for several firms located throughout the country. Further, because of its rapid growth, Webster had been able to provide its people with challenging work and opportunities for advancement. The company pioneered in establishing a Human Resources Division which performed the regular personnel functions along with a number of activities intended to facilitate the employees' growth and development. As part of its development projects the Human Resources Division designed both a performance appraisal system (PAS) and an information system capable of tracking each employee's career and development. Top management gave the division much credit for the fact that no Webster plant was unionized.

Company officials also pointed to the firm's paternalism as another factor contributing to good employee relations. These individuals used the term *constructive paternalism* when describing the organization's attitudes and activities.

EXHIBIT 2
Fabrics Manufacturing Department organization chart

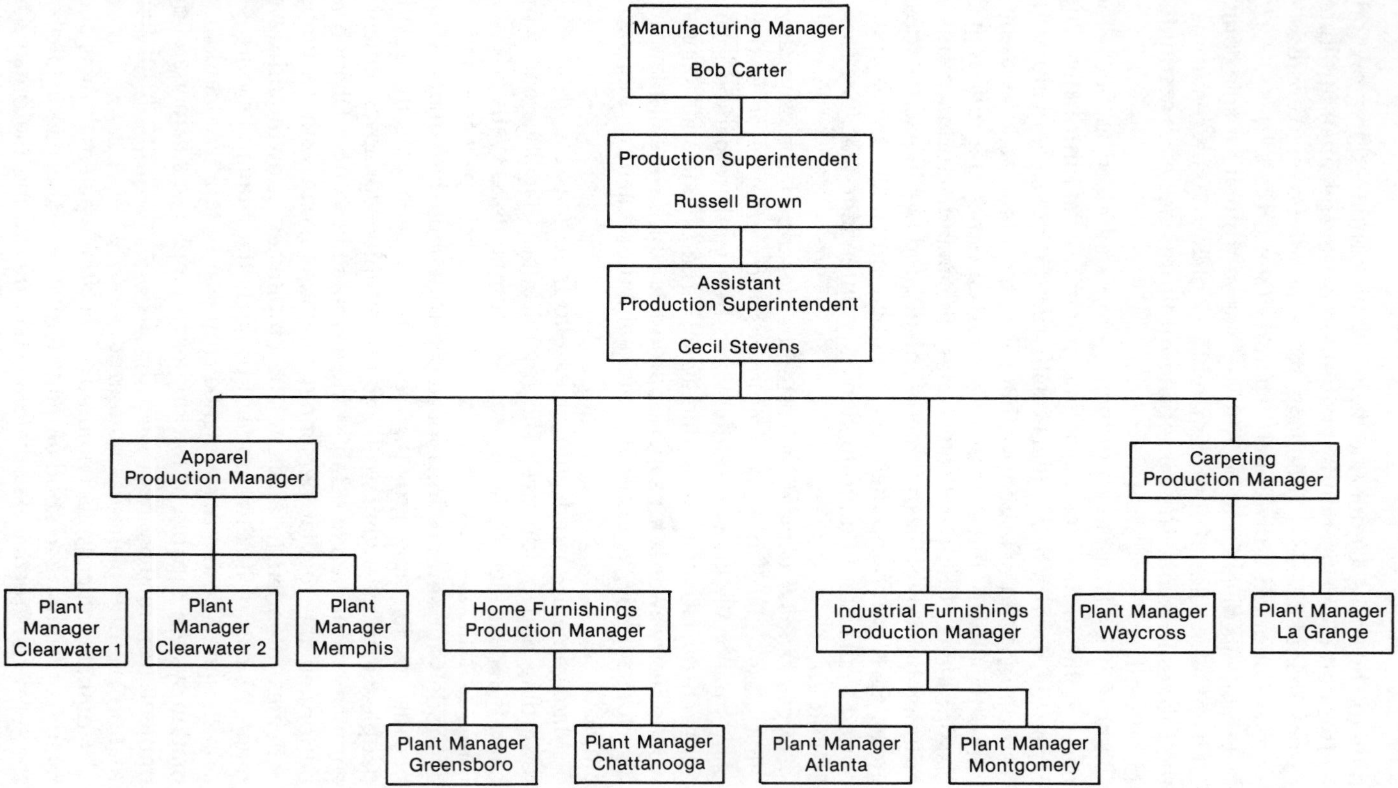

For example, there were the annual company picnics, luncheons, dinners, and parties around special occasions. The employees' "belief structure" reflected paternalism. Typically, the Webster employee believed, "If you make it through the tenth year, you can be reasonably assured that Webster always will have a place for you." Many employees expected this reciprocal agreement to hold even for individuals who had developed drinking and/or emotional problems. In more than one instance Webster had kept an employee long after alcoholism had impaired his effectiveness, primarily because top management's feeling that the person had no other place to go. Similarly, the company had paid the psychiatric bills of several employees, rather than dismiss them as ineffective performers. Some viewed the open door policies of the chairman and the president as another illustration of paternalism. All decisions could be appealed to the highest levels. A few managers expressed concern that employees with the appropriate connections had tended to use the open door policies to secure undeserved promotions. Finally, the company on several occasions had financed the education of local youths—obviously with hopes that they would return to Clearwater and Webster, but also with no strings attached. Two benefactors of this practice were the present Montgomery plant manager (Harvard: BA, MBA) and the chief corporate counsel (Yale: AB, JD). Neither had ever worked for any other organization.

Clearwaterites openly spoke of the firm's paternalism. In the words of one plant controller,

> There is a sense of family here. An expectation that if you are loyal to the company, it will be loyal to you. An expectation that if you have a problem, you can take it to Poppa Webster [the company] and it will be at least seriously considered. Twelve years ago, a tornado came through and fiercely hit Clearwater. The company stepped in and gave considerable aid. Those new houses you see along Webster Drive are a result of the company's generous response.
>
> I could go on and on. Fringe benefits also reflect how the company takes care of its people. The whole fringe benefits package is oriented toward taking care of the employee's family. We were the first to ensure the education of a worker's children should he or she die. We continually upgrade retirement benefits to offset inflation. The company's hiring and promotion practices are also paternalistic. The offspring of employees always have first shot—if they are qualified—at openings. Webster—along these same lines—promotes from within. Rare is the case of someone being hired from the outside for a top position.
>
> What more is there to say? Webster is a darn good company.

The Webster employees Webster's managerial employees came from several areas of the United States. Typically, they had received degrees from schools on the East Coast. The MBAs were from the top

national and regional schools. Managers without MBAs had sophisticated technical training. The backgrounds of Webster's managers differed significantly from those of its typical plant laborers, who tended
to come from the area around the plant and to have at least a high
school diploma or at most an associate degree from a community college. Despite these differences, Webster had experienced little class
conflict. Most attributed this harmoney to the Human Resources Division, the many opportunities for advancement, and Webster's practice
of having MBAs (especially those in manufacturing) spend some time in
low-level plant positions.

Manufacturing in the Fabrics Division had 1,787 people located at
headquarters and in the nine plants. Of these, 289 served as managers.
Managers worked either at corporate headquarters on the manufacturing manager's staff or functioned in a managerial, supervisory, or staff
capacity at one of the plants. The background of manufacturing managers was similar to that described above for Webster managers in
general. Of the 289 managers, 160 lived in and around Clearwater.

WEBSTER'S CURRENT TROUBLES

The symptoms that set off the alarm at Webster were second quarter
earnings of less than 50 percent of the prior year's earnings and a
threatened cash position. The economy and Webster's sloppy growth
habits contributed to each of these difficulties.

The economy, especially the slowdown in the construction industry,
hit Webster's furniture and carpeting businesses hard. The softening of
the demand for furniture and carpeting caused Webster's sales to decline from a 1973 peak of $2.1 billion. Simultaneously, inflation exerted
upward pressure on costs. The dips in sales and earnings reduced
Webster's cash flow considerably, so much so that money became extremely tight for the first time in 35 years. Though Mark and Abe Webster had expected the current earnings and cash troubles, they were
unnerved by the extent of the problems. In addition to the economy
the firm's phenomenal growth had complicated matters further.

The plant production manager in the largest Clearwater plant offered
the following observations:

> We grew too fast. We wanted diversification but were not ready to
> handle it. With the acquisitions of the sixties we became a different
> company almost overnight. Truthfully, we definitely were not prepared
> to break the billion-dollar level in sales. We grew too fast to consolidate.
> Only now are we learning the basics of managing a multi-business enter-
> prise. Controls were poor, especially in some of the plants we acquired.
> Staffing was done sloppily, so we ended up with a lot of fat. Plus we
> were—in my opinion—lax in our evaluation of performance.

The economy and the problems of diversification combined to slow Webster's growth and to threaten its financial integrity.

Bob Carter's evening

By 6:00 P.M. Carter began to overcome his initial shock and to realize that, while painful, the reduction was probably needed and probably best for the company. He had known for some time that his department had "fat" at the managerial levels. Just six months earlier he had sought to demote three individuals—including his second in command. In denying his recommendation Davis had told Carter, "These men have too much service to be treated as you have proposed." So Carter was stuck with them; at least that had been the case until today. Carter reasoned that one benefit of the reduction in force would be an opportunity to make some long needed changes. He perceived his task as that of making the best reductions possible in the least painful manner.

After dinner Carter returned to his den to address the issue of how to cut 43 individuals from his managerial payroll. Because of his relatively brief tenure, he wanted to consult at least one other individual. The logical choices were the number two and three persons in his hierarchy. However, Carter wanted to demote the Production Superintendent, Russell Brown, and to promote the Assistant Production Superintendent, Cecil Stevens. He had been impressed with Stevens and had decided some time back that he should have Brown's job. The reduction presented an opportunity to make the change.

Carter concluded that Stevens should be involved initially and perhaps others later on some basis. At 8:30 P.M. he called Stevens, who lived four miles away, and asked him to come over to discuss a "critical" situation. Cecil arrived an hour later. Carter informed him of the reduction plans and of his intention to recommend him for promotion to production superintendent. Predictably, Stevens was delighted by his promotion and shocked by the magnitude of the proposed separations. After relating details of his session with Davis, Carter asked Stevens to aid him in developing a strategy for determining the individuals to be released. Specifically, he requested that Stevens be prepared by Monday morning to identify and discuss issues that should be considered in formulating a reduction plan.

Carter and Stevens spent about 45 more minutes discussing their perceptions of the company's situation and the need for the reduction. Also, they raised some questions about Webster's performance appraisal system (PAS). Stevens wondered how much weight should be given to performance ratings. Carter admitted that he had not gotten around to using PAS on a regular basis, but indicated that he would be interested in hearing Stevens' perceptions of the system and its usage in the department. Stevens asked if they should consider inviting others to the session on Monday morning. After some discussion they agreed to invite the production managers with the exception of the home furnishing manager, who was a likely candidate for demotion or termination. Carter and Stevens ended their meeting by agreeing on a time table.

Monday, 8:00 A.M.—Develop strategy.

Monday, 1:00 P.M.—Begin to implement strategy.

Wednesday, 2:00 P.M.—Present list to divisional managers.

The Monday morning meeting

On Monday morning Carter, Stevens, and three of the four production managers met as planned. Stevens began the meeting by presenting his thoughts on possible criteria for developing a termination list. His remarks are reproduced in part below.

> The following represents my thinking on possible options open to us. I see five.
>
> The first is *seniority*. Though guidelines prohibit much of this criterion, there are a few individuals who might be receptive to offers of early retirement.
>
> The second is *fairness*. Should this be a criterion? Operationally, I do not know what it means except that we would not do anything that would be perceived as grossly unfair. I do know, however, that our people will expect fairness.
>
> The third is *fat*. The list would be determined by the elimination of fat or excess positions. This approach has legitimacy. The difficulty, however, is that some good people are in fat positions. The use of this criterion alone could result in a net quality downgrading of manufacturing personnel.
>
> The fourth is *performance*. The basic question here is, "How do we measure performance?" How much weight do we give to PAS data? Some individuals feel that the PAS data are hopelessly biased, because of the managers' tendency to give everyone "good" ratings. How much weight do we give to the personnel audit data?[1] If we were to give significant weight to the audit data, would we be compromising the future effectiveness of the auditor? When making field visits, the auditor not only gathers data on performance from managers, but also talks to individuals about their careers and problems. Many employees have been very frank with the auditors. If we use audit data as input in making termination decisions, the employees may feel betrayed and become reluctant to trust the

---

[1] Personnel auditors from the Human Resources Division visited each manager at least once a year to discuss his or her subordinates' performance. During these discussions they obtained a performance rating for each employee. This process was separate from Webster's performance appraisal system (PAS).

auditors in the future. This would be especially likely if managers tried to make the auditors scapegoats. I can hear a manager telling a terminated employee, "I wanted to keep you, but our auditor Jack had too strong a case against you."

Finally, to what extent are we constrained by past practices? In the past few managers have been diligent and responsible in talking with their people about performance; as a consequence, many employees are not aware of their relative standing with respect to performance. If these individuals are terminated, they will likely be shocked and feel that they have been treated unfairly. Can we fairly terminate on the basis of performance?

The fifth is *potential*. Again, the basic questions are around measurement and the weights to be given to PAS and audit data. How do we measure potential? How much weight do we give to PAS Data? Audit data? Should we terminate an individual with little potential but capable of doing his or her present job fully satisfactorily? I am thinking about one plant controller in particular. He is an excellent assistant plant controller, but does not have the potential to advance further. Would he be a candidate?

I consider this large reduction to be a one-shot deal. As such, the reduction represents a beautiful crisis opportunity to make moves that would be difficult under normal circumstances. We can seize the opportunity not only to meet our termination target, but also to upgrade our department. Other divisions are releasing competent people. Some will be better than those that we will propose to keep. This means that we could upgrade by reducing a larger number than our target, and then hiring replacements from our sister divisions' terminations. For example, our target is 43. If after meeting this target we identified 5 available individuals who were better than persons we were planning to keep, we could terminate 48 and hire the 5 former employees of the other divisions. However, if we are to seize this opportunity, we will have to develop sound ways of evaluating performance and potential.

A lively discussion of PAS and the personnel audit followed Stevens' remarks. During these deliberations the group relied heavily on Stevens' memorandum on performance appraisal at Webster. (See Exhibit 3.)

EXHIBIT 3
Memorandum on performance appraisal

MEMORANDUM

To: Bob Carter

From: Cecil Stevens

Re: Performance Appraisal at Webster

Date: October 20, 1975

Since leaving your home on Friday evening, I have had an opportunity to talk with a number of individuals. Specifically, I saw Ed Johnson, the designer of our PAS system, at the Club and had a good conversation; talked with Jack Bryant, our personnel auditor, about his work with the division; and spent two hours after church discussing the reduction with the manufacturing managers of the other divisions. Immediately below are my impressions of PAS and also the personnel audit function of the Human Resources Division.

PAS

Bob, PAS was designed three years ago and has been used primarily on a voluntary basis. My discussion of the system is based primarily on conversations with its designer, Ed Johnson.

Purpose

The system is intended to help the manager act as a:

1. Manager responsible for attaining organizational goals.
2. Judge responsible for evaluating individual performance and making decisions about salary and promotability.
3. Helper responsible for developing subordinates.

One problem in the past has been a failure to recognize the three roles cited above, or a tendency to emphasize one over the others. PAS is based on the assumption that each role is equally important and is intended to help the manager do justice to each.

Components

PAS components are three in number: management by objectives (MBO), a developmental review, and an evaluation and salary review.

MBO   This component focuses on results and is intended to help the manager realize organizational goals. Though each manager is expected to adapt MBO to his or her situation, there are typically six steps.

1. *Identification of objectives.* Here, objectives are identified and prioritized. Also, review periods are set.

EXHIBIT 3 (*continued*)

2. *Establishment of measurement criteria.* The basic question here is, "What monetary measures, percentages, and/or other numbers will be used to measure the achievement of objectives?" For example, if we in manufacturing were to establish "greater production effectiveness" as one of our objectives, we would have to decide how to measure the extent of achievement. Total unit costs? Total direct labor unit costs? Total production?

3. *Planning.* Plans are made for achieving the identified objectives. What is to be done? Who is to do it? When is it to be done? How is it to be done?

4. *Execution.* Plans are implemented.

5. *Measure.* Secure actual monetary figures, percentages, and/or other numbers so that results may be reviewed.

6. *Review results.* Compare actual measurements to plan. The frequency of measurement and review will depend on the number of review points within a year. Typically, the entire MBO cycle is repeated once a year, with intermittent reviews in between.

MBO is essentially a system for identifying what is to be done and ensuring that it is done. As such, MBO has a major weakness in terms of the managerial role: It does not aid the manager in observing, evaluating, or improving the behavior of subordinates. If the manager is to help his employees improve their behavior, he will need a behavior-oriented tool. The developmental review was designed to meet this need.

The developmental review As indicated above, the review is intended to help the manager observe, analyze, and improve subordinate behavior. There are three subcomponents: the Performance Description Questionnaire, the Performance Profile, and the Developmental Interview.

1. *Performance Description Questionnaire.* The questionnaire contains 100 questions. Each question has been determined through research to be descriptive of a behavior associated with a component of effectiveness at Webster. Examples of the components covered are openness to influence, priority setting, formal communications, organizational perspective, decisiveness, delegation/participation, support for company, unit productivity, and conflict resolution. The manager is asked to complete a questionnaire for each subordinate. He or she is asked to indicate on a 6-point rating scale how descriptive the statement is of the employee's actual behavior. Also, under each statement is space for the recording of any critical incidents supporting the manager's judgment. (See Attachment 1.) The performance profile is produced by computer from the questionnaire data.

2. *Performance Profile.* The profile is intended to serve as a tool to help managers discriminate among a subordinate's performances on a number of performance dimensions. An individual's profile shows net strengths or weakness for each dimension in terms of the person's own average. The profile line represents the average of the employee's ratings on all performance dimensions. The number and location of Xs show the extent to which the employee's score for a particular dimension is below or above his or her average for all dimensions. Dimensions with Xs to the left of the profile line are those where the individual is relatively weak (compared to his or her average). Dimensions with Xs to the right are those where the subordinate is relatively strong. The number of Xs indicates the extent of the weakness or strength. (See

EXHIBIT 3 (*continued*)

ATTACHMENT 1

Sample Items from Performance Description Questionnaire

1. Involves subordinates in
   decision-making process. _____
2. Makes a special effort to
   explain Webster policies
   to subordinates. _____
3. Molds a cohesive work
   group. _____
4. Fails to follow up on
   work assignments given
   to others. _____
5. Works closely with
   subordinates who lack
   motivation. _____

6. Selects and places
   qualified personnel. _____
7. Person's subordinates
   accomplish a large
   amount of work. _____
8. Objects to ideas before
   explained. _____
9. Is accurate in
   work. _____

10. Gives poor
    presentations. _____

RATINGS

Number	Definition
1	Strongly agree
2	Agree
3	Somewhat agree
4	Somewhat disagree
5	Disagree
6	Strongly disagree

Attachment 2.) The tool is designed to facilitate analysis of a subordinate's performance and is not valid theoretically for comparison of individuals.

    3. *Developmental Interview.* The purposes of the developmental interview are
to provide the subordinate with a performance analysis based on the performance
questionnaire and profile, to identify areas of weaknesses, and to translate these
weaknesses into an appropriate developmental program. Tools are available to help
the manager and subordinate in designing developmental plans.

    The reasoning behind the design of the Developmental Review was a hope that
the Performance Description Questionnaire and Profile would help the manager and
his subordinates distinguish development from MBO and evaluation, and thereby
reduce subordinate defensiveness that typically characterizes feedback sessions
where developmental and evaluative issues are handled simultaneously.

    Evaluation and salary review This review is separate from the
MBO and developmental reviews. Its basis is a form which asks the manager to rate
the employee's overall performance and his or her potential. (See Attachment 3.) The
overall rating should reflect the MBO sessions and the Developmental Review data
and interview. In short, the two other components of PAS provide important inputs for

EXHIBIT 3 (*continued*)

ATTACHMENT 2

Sample Profile Interpretations

Dimension	A		B		C	
1. Openness to influence	xx		xxxxx		xx	
2. Priority setting		xx		xxx		xxxxxx
3. Formal communications ..		xx		xxx	xxxxxx	
4. Organizational perspective	xx		xxxxxxxxxx			xx
5. Decisiveness		xx		xx		xx
6. Delegation/participation ...	xx			xx	xxxxxx	
7. Support for company		xx	xx			xxxxxx
8. Unit productivity	xx			xxx	xx	
9. Conflict resolution		xx	xx			xx
10. Team building	xx			xxx	xx	
11. Control		xx		xx		xxx

A. Implication is that this manager is well balanced *dimensionally.*
B. Implication is that this manager has one *very* significantly weak *dimension,* another relatively
     weak *dimension,* contrasted to the remaining favorably balanced *dimensions.*
C. Implication is that this manager has two relatively weak dimensions, two relatively strong
     dimensions, with remaining *dimensions* relatively balanced.
     Caution: Remember that you are only comparing the individual to self and *not* with other
     people. If an individual is "well balanced dimensionally," it means there is not much difference
     between what that person does best and poorest; it does *not* necessarily mean the person is a
     "well-balanced manager."

ATTACHMENT 3

DETACH AND SEND TO: PRIVATE

POSITION PREFERENCE: DATE _____

EMPLOYEE NAME _____   EMPLOYEE NUMBER _____

DIVISION _____   LOCATION _____

POSITION _____   SUPERVISOR _____

     Supervisor and subordinate develop *together.* Indicate below subsequent positions
for your subordinate *that you both can agree* are realistic, appropriate, and interesting.
Specify both functional area (e.g., sales, personnel, etc.) and, whenever possible, type
of job.

ORDER OF PREFERENCE FOR NEXT JOBS:

Short term
     First choice:

     Second choice:

EXHIBIT 3 (*continued*)

Long term (within next five years)
First choice:

Second choice:

SUPERVISOR'S SUMMARY: Supervisor fills in by self *after* developmental interview. Subordinate should be shown these ratings after supervisor has coordinated ratings with *second*-level supervisor.

A. *CHANGE OF STATUS:* Indicate by your choice of statements below (check one) change of status you recommend for this person during next 12 months.

_____ Should be separated as soon as possible. (SEP)

_____ Should be reassigned to position with decreased responsibility. (DEM)

_____ Should be reassigned to position with similar level of responsibility. (LAT)

_____ Needs more experience before reassignment can be considered. (EXP)

_____ Should be reassigned to position with more responsibility. (RDY)

_____ Should remain in present position. (STA)

B. *CAREER POTENTIAL:* Based on current knowledge, indicate in spaces below (check one) level this person has greatest probability of achieving. Note: Potential ratings do *not* imply person's readiness for promotion now.

_____ Potential devision manager or equivalent. [Must be Group 50 or above.] (Blue)

_____ Potential to higher supervisory/managerial level. (Green)

_____ Potential best utilized within specialty or as individual performer. (Brown)

_____ Good performer; no indication to date of potential for higher level. (Yellow)

_____ Questionable performance. (Red)

C. *OVERALL JOB PERFORMANCE* during the past 6 to 12 months may be characterized as: (check scale)

| Unsatisfactory | Fair | Satisfactory | Excellent | Outstanding |

D. *COMMENTS:*

ENDORSEMENT OF SECOND LEVEL SUPERVISOR:

_____ I agree with all of above recommendations.

_____ I disagree with some (or all of above recommendations) and would make following recommendations:

_____
                                    Signature

EXHIBIT 3 *(continued)*

the Evaluation Review. Possible overall ratings are unsatisfactory, fair, fully satisfactory, excellent, and outstanding.

Once the overall rating has been given, the salary matrix may be used as a *guide* in determining recommendations for salary adjustments. The matrix approach is straightforward and used by several organizations. Under this method salary adjustments are a function of the subordinate's rating and the relative standing of the employee's salary within his or her pay range. (See Attachment 4.)

ATTACHMENT 4

Salary Matrix

(Max.) 1.20					
	6%	4%	2%	—	—
1.10					
	8%	6%	4%	—	—
1.00					
	10%	8%	6%	—	—
0.90					
	12%	10%	8%	6%	—
(Min.) 0.80	Outstanding	Excellent	Fully satisfactory	Fair	Poor

Comparative ratio (vertical axis)

Ratings

Note: Comparative ratio equals actual salary divided by mid-point of individual's salary range. Salary adjustment is function of individual's ratio and rating. Employee with 0.85 ratio and rating of excellent would receive adjustment of 10 percent.

Usage of PAS

Bob, as I indicated earlier, the system has been used on a voluntary basis so far. In the corporation as a whole, the usage rate is 29 percent; in manufacturing it is 40 percent. The only group using it 100 percent is Fabrics' sales force.

THE PERSONNEL AUDIT

In addition to PAS the Human Resources Division is also responsible for conducting the personnel audit. The purposes of the audit are to secure performance data that will facilitate corporate manpower planning, to encourage and improve communica-

EXHIBIT 3 *(continued)*

tions between superiors and subordinates, and to provide career development counseling. There is a potential conflict among the purposes in that the auditor is required
to perform both evaluative and counseling roles. Some individuals who "pour out
their souls" to the auditors are unaware of their evaluative function.

Our auditor, as you know, is Jack Bryant. At least once a year Jack visits each
manager and talks about their subordinates. He also talks with subordinates about
their development and their perceptions of where they stand. Where there are
discrepancies between a subordinate's perception and what his or her manager has
said, Jack works with the manager in developing a plan for correcting the employee's
misperceptions. Jack, however, has no enforcement power; consequently, some
managers fail to give accurate—if any—feedback to their employees. The audit has
been very successful in securing information for the central corporate data bank, but
has had somewhat less success in getting managers to be honest with subordinates.
Though individual employees may see their central file, few avail themselves of the
opportunity; consequently, many subordinates remain in the dark as to how they are
actually perceived by their bosses. I, however, understand that a computer based
system capable of providing each employee with performance data has been designed and implemented below managerial levels. Reportedly, the system annually
provides each employee with a printout showing—among other things—
performance ratings and career history. April 1, 1976, is the target date for full
implementation in the managerial ranks.

Currently, the form used by the auditors asks for a rating of the individual's
performance and potential. There also are sections dealing with the employee's
strengths and weaknesses and the manager's recommendations for future reassignments. (See Attachment 5.)

I have checked with Jack, and he has assured me that there are audit ratings on file
for at least 97 percent of our personnel.

Bob, hopefully these remarks on PAS and the personnel audit will stimulate discussion leading to an appropriate reduction plan.

ATTACHMENT 5

Employee name _____ Supervisor name _____ Date _____

        PERFORMANCE   (see definitions below)   *POTENTIAL*
   1   2   3   4   5   NR   (circle one)   (circle one)   1   2   3   4   5   NR
        COMMENTS: (Supervisor should define significant strengths and weaknesses [de-
              velopment needs] and accomplishments.)

EXHIBIT 3 *(concluded)*

CHANGE OF STATUS: (for the next 12 months) (check one)

1. _____ Should be separated as soon as possible (termination).

2. _____ Should be reassigned to position of decreased responsibility (demotion).

3. _____ Should be reassigned to position with similar level of responsibility (lateral move).

4. _____ Needs more experience before reassignment can be considered (not ready).

5. _____ Should be reassigned to position of more responsibility (promotion).

6. _____ Will probably remain in present position indefinitely (leveled).

Which function(s)   (comment)
_____
_____

Which function(s)   (comment)
_____
_____

Which function(s)   (comment)
_____
_____

Performance

Number	Definition
5	Outstanding
4	Excellent
3	Fully satisfactory
2	Fair
1	Unsatisfactory

Potential

Color	Number	Definition
Blue	5	Potential division manager or equivalent (for individuals currently at "A" payroll level).
Green	4	Potential to higher supervisor position.
Brown	3	Potential best utilized within specialty or as individual performer.
Yellow	2	Good performer; no indication to date of potential for higher level.
Red	1	Questionable performer.

Case 5–2
Webster Industries (B)*

In October 1975, Webster Industries found it necessary to reduce its managerial personnel by 20 percent. Bob Carter, Manufacturing Manager of the company's Fabrics Division, was charged with making a 15 percent reduction in his department. Webster Industries (A) provides company background data and a description of Carter's reaction upon receiving his assignment. This case relates how the reduction was accomplished and its impact upon the department.

THE PROCESS

Bob Carter described the sequencing of events as they occurred on Monday, October 20, 1975:

> After discussing Cecil Stevens' memorandum on performance appraisal, we formulated our approach.[1] This was around noon. We broke for lunch before beginning implementation of our plans. During lunch someone remarked that Production Superintendent Russell Brown, who was scheduled to be demoted, had the longest managerial tenure in the department and probably would be able to provide invaluable input.
>
> We all agreed that Russ was an example of the Peter Principle, that he had been an excellent plant manager before being promoted to production superintendent. We decided to offer him a demotion to a plant manager position. After lunch I made the offer to Russ who—to my surprise—expressed shock *and* relief. It was as if he had wanted the burden lifted. Russ also agreed to participate in our deliberations.
>
> I guess you can describe what we did later in four steps: (1) reorganization, (2) staffing of new organization, (3) a second review of personnel, and (4) an upgrading review. We decided that we would do what was best for the business. Our thinking was centered around three basic questions: What are our departmental objectives and tasks? How do we have to go about accomplishing these objectives and tasks? What positions are needed to accomplish these tasks and objectives? Based on our answers to these questions, we reorganized the department. Among other actions this involved the closing of one apparel plant and the elimination of the home furnishings production manager position. The home furnishings plants were made the responsibility of the industrial furnishings production manager. [See Exhibits 1 and 2.]
>
> After the reorganization, we wanted to staff the positions with the *best* possible people. Here, we called in Jack Bryant and his audit data. He served as a useful check on our perceptions. Typically, an individual's name would come up and we would all voice our opinion. It was a time of

---

* All names have been disguised.

[1] Stevens' memorandum is presented in Exhibit 3 of Webster Industries (A).

EXHIBIT 1
Old Fabrics Manufacturing Department organization chart

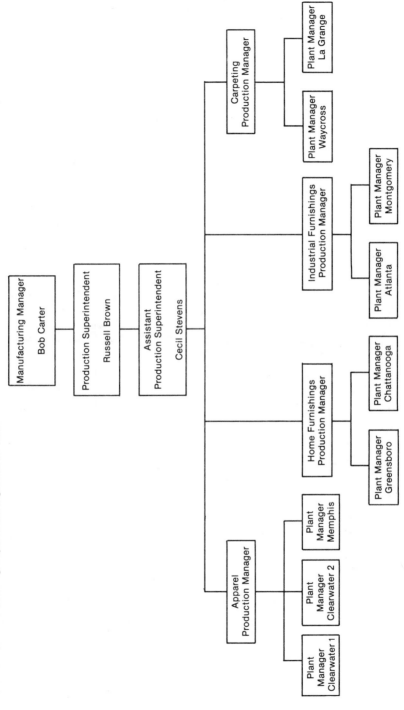

EXHIBIT 2
New Fabrics Manufacturing Department organization chart

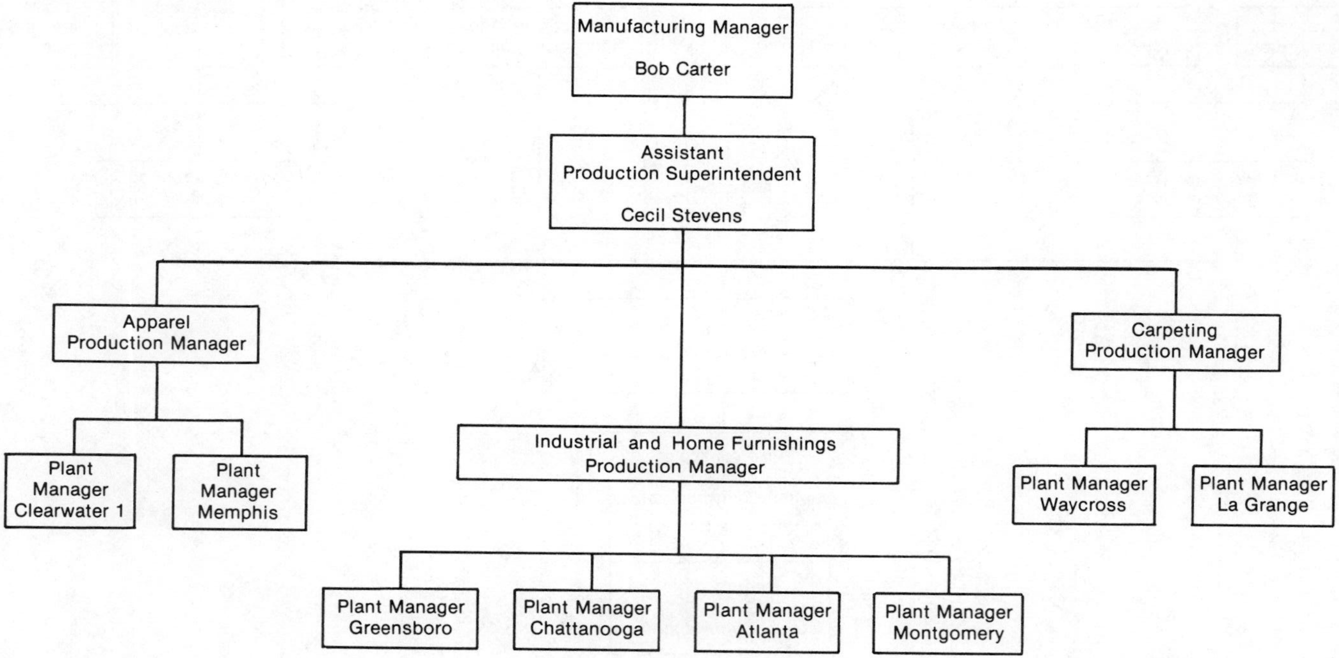

Manufacturing Manager
Bob Carter

Assistant
Production Superintendent
Cecil Stevens

Apparel
Production Manager

Plant
Manager
Clearwater 1

Plant
Manager
Memphis

Industrial and Home Furnishings
Production Manager

Plant Manager
Greensboro

Plant Manager
Chattanooga

Plant Manager
Atlanta

Plant Manager
Montgomery

Carpeting
Production Manager

Plant Manager
Waycross

Plant Manager
La Grange

truth telling. I feel that the input was realistic and fair. Where our perceptions did not jibe with his audit data, Jack would quickly let us know. Between the audit data and our comments, I think we got some good assessments. PAS data where available was thrown in by Jack; however, little weight was given to it. We just did not trust it.

During the staffing the basic issue was, "Who is the best person for this position." Decisions were based on assessments of individuals' performance and potential. It is difficult for me to say which received the greater weight. What was clear, however, was that an individual with both performance and potential was better off then one with either of the two. After staffing the positions, the "excess" employees were our prime candidates for separation. We referred to this as our "excess list."

The excess list was reviewed. We wanted to make certain to the extent possible that we did not release anyone better than the people we were keeping. Again, Jack was very helpful. We did make several changes, especially where an excess individual was broad enough to qualify for more than one position. At this point our tentative list was 5 over our reduction guideline of 43.

Before finalizing the list I asked Jack to learn who was available from the other divisions. From Jack's list we identified seven people superior to individuals we were proposing to retain. We added to our reduction list accordingly and made offers to the seven former employees of our sister divisions. Our final list was comprised of 55 names.

Because of our long working hours—until 10:00 P.M. on Monday and Tuesday nights, I was able to present our list at 2:00 P.M. on Wednesday to the other divisional managers. They disagreed with 3 of our recommendations; consequently, our final list was down to 53. In addition six individuals were demoted to the weekly payroll.

I am finding it difficult to describe the trauma we experienced. What I have told you sounds too cold. It does not capture the intense sensitivity we had to human pain and suffering. One case in particular comes to mind.

We terminated a plant engineer, Ray Pearson, who had been with Webster 23 years and was 52 years old. He had three children—one of whom was just entering law school. Though his performance had been unsatisfactory for at least the last ten years, he was not given any negative feedback until the fall of 1974. Concerned that he would be paying for the sins of his past managers, we really agonized over his case. Because we all knew Ray and had worked with him in various community settings, we found our decision to be especially difficult. But we had no other choice, he simply was not performing. Abe [Webster's president] reluctantly agreed with our action. Unfortunately, Ray's case was not unique.

The community has been very understanding of the company's position. Generally, the feeling is that Webster did the right thing. Abe did a good job of presenting our case. Drastic action was required to preserve our financial integrity.

Attitudes toward the process

The attitude of the top manufacturing managers was that the process had not been perfect, but had been done as well as possible—"given human frailties." Cecil Stevens, the new Production Superintendent, remarked:

> We did the best we could under the circumstances. I would have liked more time; I did not like the "rush-rush" atmosphere. We let some *good* people go. My guess is that 75 percent of those released were at least "satisfactory" employees. My misgivings about the process have been somewhat mitigated by the success that some former employees have experienced in getting new jobs at significantly higher pay.
>
> When put in a situation like we were, one eventually begins to play God. And even to believe eventually that he is God. During the process a feeling of doing the right thing had prevailed. After all, God does not make mistakes. After the fact, however, we realized that we were still mortals and that mortal decisions had been made. Nevertheless, I do feel that the department is much, much, stronger than before. We came out of it well.

The apparel production manager who participated in the process offered these thoughts:

> My belief in the rightness of the macro decision made it easier for me to participate in the micro decision making. My greatest concern was that too many people had to pay for the mistakes of their managers. These employees had either no business being in their positions or no inkling of their relative standing in terms of performance and potential. Also, there were too many instances of individuals having been retained long after they had ceased to be effective. All of this represented poor management of performance.

IMPACT OF THE REDUCTION IN FORCE

The most frequently cited impact was the shattering of the Webster belief structure. Bob Carter considered the shattering to be very important:

> The Webster employee had been laboring under the assumption that "if I make it past my tenth year and remain loyal to the company, the company will take care of me." This was the basic premise of the belief structure that was shattered by the large reduction.
>
> A belief structure is what you believe even in the absence of supporting evidence. It is what keeps you going. And it is necessary—just to get out of bed each morning. Our task as managers is to foster the development of a replacement that will be supportive of the company. We want to reinforce those beliefs supportive of the company and discourage those that would be dysfunctional.

If we were to encourage the belief that "loyal" individuals will be safe for life, we would be dishonest—for this simply is not true. It cannot be true. Loyalty is important and will be returned in kind, but it is not all encompassing. Employees can not expect absolute loyalty, neither can the company. To do so would be destructive and incongruent with business realities.

In addition to the loyalty belief, the expectation of continuous unparalleled growth was shattered. To me this is not disastrous. For this expectation to have continued to prosper would have been destructive. We now must work toward a realistic and functional belief structure.

A production engineer and a quality control specialist were among those commenting on the effects of the shattering:

Whatever the company had with its employees before the reduction rift is gone. Consider my case. I looked around and saw men and women with twice my years of service being dismissed, men and women with children entering college and graduate school, men and women with all kinds of advanced degrees, men and women who never had worked for any other company. My conclusion? It could happen to me! My sheer sense of loyalty to the corporation used to make me do things beyond the call of duty. The loyalty I had has been greatly reduced. I am gravely concerned for my family and myself. When I reach 45 or 50, the company may kick me out. I saw good people with years of service go out the door. This signaled to me that Webster is no longer a "cradle to the grave" organization. I would like to feel reasonably comfortable that if I am doing a good job, I am safe. I would like some assurance that if I should peak out after a good career, I will be working here as long as I am doing my job well. The reduction did not give me that assurance. I saw the dismissal of individuals who had leveled off, *but who were doing fully satisfactory work in their position*. Does this company have a place for a good, solid performing, "peaked-out," middle-aged employee? I once thought it did, but now I am no longer certain. [Production Engineer]

The reduction has resulted in growing uncertainty, anxiety, and cynicism. Morale is low. Webster gave the individuals who survived no hope of promotions and, indeed, demoted several managers. On top of this the company established a salary freeze. Those of us who remain are concerned that the company will not admit its mistakes. For example, in several cases Webster dismissed the "wrong" people but refused to rehire them. There is also a general belief—rightly or wrongly—that everybody terminated got more money in their new jobs. Many survivors are now beginning to wonder just how well off are they here at Webster. Cynicism toward personnel policies and practices is unbelievably high. A sign reading "Up your MBO and all that" was placed on one of the bulletin boards. [Quality Control Specialist]

Most of the manufacturing managerial personnel agreed with Carter that the reduction and the shattering of the belief structure were positive factors. One plant manager in particular viewed the belief shattering as very beneficial:

> I think maybe many of us were getting too comfortable. I am really a firm believer that an employee should not get too secure, but ought to always be a little afraid of losing his or her job. Employees should never get *too* comfortable—either because of seniority or performance. This holds for everybody! Security leads to performance below potential. I've seen it happen. People start arriving late in the morning and leaving early in the evening. Of course, uncertainty should not be carried to the extreme. A person should not have to come to work uncertain as to whether he or she will have a job at the day's end. However, some uncertainty is definitely in order.

The most frequent question asked by terminated employees was, "Why me?" This was especially true if he/she had a record of "good" performance or had received few formal appraisals. In several instances, separated employees reportedly were told in essence, "There was a meeting and your name came up on the list. I'm sorry, but I do not know any more." What disturbed those terminated most was their inability to place the dismissals in a performance context. Unable to relate their separation to poor performance, many concluded that other factors were involved—for example, politics, membership in the right groups, and/or ability to keep selling oneself.

Reportedly, wives felt betrayed by the dismissals of their husbands. One manager commented:

> Wives were much more bitter than their separated husbands. A typical reaction was, "Here we go again. After all you have done for the company, this [separation] is the thanks you get. And this is the thanks I get for being a camp follower."

Despite their puzzlement over the reduction decision-making process, terminated employees and their families were happy with the services provided by the Human Resources Division. The division in effect became a placement center offering a number of services: training in the writing of resumes; circulation of job information; arrangement of car pools to Atlanta for visits with regional and national recruiters; and locations of facilities for "head hunters" who wanted to recruit in Clearwater. Most of the released employees gave Webster an "A" in the area of "services rendered after termination." One individual reported, "I got more from personnel after I was separated than when I was employed."

Performance appraisal

The common denominator underlying the various reactions to the reduction in force was a strong feeling that "something had to be done about performance appraisal." This sentiment was pervasive at all levels of the organization. Abe Webster spoke on the topic at the monthly meeting of divisional vice presidents.

> The fact that many individuals terminated did not know where they stood in their managers' eyes reflected poor managerial practice. My position is that every Webster employee has a right to know where he or she stands and to be helped in his or her development. Managers must develop the capability of telling the employee "how it is." If he or she is doing well, the manager should communicate his satisfaction. Similarly, if the individual is doing poorly, the manager should make it known. The employee should be told, "If you do not do (a) . . . , (b) . . . , (c) . . . , and (d) . . . , you will be asked to leave." We owe it to our people—especially the young people we bring on board—to give them honest and clear feedback and assistance.

Mark Webster (chairman of the company's Board) concurred with son Abe except that he believed the individual should always be given hope, so that he or she would remain motivated. Abe was in agreement with the psychology of his father's perspective, but thought that it could lead to some poor decisions. He felt that motivational considerations should be handled separately from the feedback process. His position was, "The truth should be told."

There was some opinion at Webster that managerial resistance to PAS stemmed from concerns about its design. In particular, some complained about the tying of salary to MBO and the developmental review. The contention was that this link encouraged managers to play games in order to get top salary adjustments for their people. On the other hand, the Human Resources Division staff argued that each manager was allocated a certain amount for salary adjustments in total and was expected to adhere to his allotment, and that as a consequence the opportunity for playing games was considerably reduced.

Another complaint was that the system was so complex that it often was misused. One example cited was the Performance Profile. Reports were plentiful that the Profile, though not designed for comparative purposes, was being used to rank employees.

Jasper Calhoun, a personnel auditor who was involved in the designing of PAS, believed the problem to be external to the system.

> Our managers simply are not cold-blooded enough . . . [pause] I guess objective is a better word than cold-blooded. Right? . . . [pause] In any event our managers are not objective enough to tell an individual how he or she is doing. We're going to have to squeeze the managers to get them to use PAS. Our young people deserve to be told how they are doing and how they can improve.
>
> We need a monitoring system that will ensure usage. Monitoring could be done by keeping track of each manager's percentage of comple-

tions and the extent to which he or she follows through on recommendations from the Human Resources Division. The monitoring system also
could be used to track the promotions process to ensure that promotions
are based on appraisals. To work, the monitoring system must have *teeth!*
There should be some punishment for failure to use PAS.

The danger of such a monitoring system is that the manager will feel so
controlled that PAS will be viewed more as an imposition from above,
than as a potentially useful tool. I firmly believe that PAS—like any performance appraisal system—is a necessary tool for fulfillment of managerial responsibility.

Carter's new task

Approximately two weeks after the reduction, Ike Davis—the head
of the Fabrics Division—approached Carter about attaining 100 percent
utilization of PAS. Davis informed Carter that the Human Resources
Division was soliciting suggestions as to how full utilization might be
realized. Reportedly they were open to recommendations on design
changes and implementation strategy. Davis wanted Carter to represent the Fabrics Division next week at an off-site "brainstorming" session. The purpose of the meeting would be to formulate an implementation plan for PAS.

Case 5–3
First National City Bank Operating Group (A)

John Reed paced along the vast glass walls of his midtown Manhattan office, hardly noticing the panorama of rooftops spread out below
his feet, baking in the September sun. One of 41 senior vice presidents
of the First National City Bank, Reed, at 31, was the youngest man in the
bank's history to reach this management level. Reed headed the bank's
"Operating Group" (OPG)—the back office, which performed the
physical work of processing Citibank's business transactions and designing its computer systems, as well as managing the bank's real estate
and internal building services. Today, musing to himself about the
forthcoming 1971 operating year and his plans for the next five years,
John Reed was both concerned and angry.

He was concerned that his recent reorganization of the Operating
Group, though widely recognized as a success, was not sufficient. His
area still followed the traditional working procedures of the banking
business, and OPG continued to be seen by the rest of the bank as a

"necessary evil" which, given enough tolerance by its more intelligent brethren, should "muddle along" the way it always had. After a year with the Group and five months as its head, he still had few concrete measures of its performance. But most of all, John Reed was concerned that his initial concept of what the Group needed—massive new computerized systems for coping with a growing mountain of paper-based transactions—might be both impractical and irrelevant. Reed's new staff assistant, Bob White, had been pushing hard for a change in management approach, to emphasize budgets, costs, and production efficiency instead of systems development.

And, uncharacteristically, John Reed was angry. He looked again at the management report he had received the day before. Here it was, September of 1970, and he was only now learning that his manpower had grown by 400 people in July and August. Maybe Bob White really had something in his stress on control and management.

First National City Bank

The Operating Group was one of the major divisions established in a reorganization of Citibank at the end of 1968. The five market-oriented divisions, shown in the organization chart in Exhibit 1, gener-

EXHIBIT 1
Institutional organization—1970

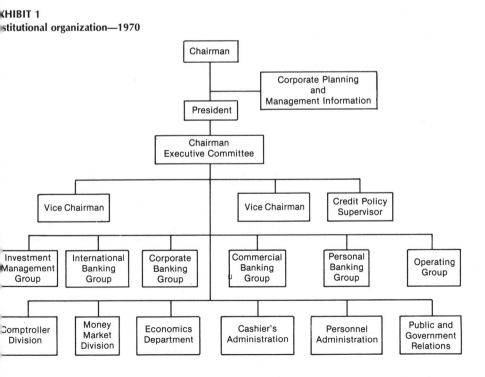

ated varying demands for OPG services; all of them were looking forward to continued growth in 1971, and all were pressing for improved performance by the Operating Group.

Citibank's Personal Banking Group, (PBG) with 181 branches and 6,000 employees, provided a full range of services to consumers and small businesses in the metropolitan New York area. As the area's leading retail bank, PBG projected a 3 percent annual growth in checking account balances, and a 2 percent annual growth in savings accounts over the next several years; in addition to an increase in number of accounts, PBG anticipated continuation of the recent trend toward more activity *per* account.

The Investment Management Group, with 1,700 employees, managed assets for personal and institutional investors, and provided full banking services to wealthy individuals. In this latter category, the group currently carried some 7,000 accounts, and hoped to increase its customers by 25 percent in the next four years.

The Corporate Banking Group, itself subdivided into six industry-specialist divisions, served big business (generally, companies with more than $20 million in annual sales), financial institutions, and government accounts within the United States. CBG aimed at an annual growth rate over 5 percent, but qualified its ambitions: in order to gain market share in the increasingly competitive world of the major corporations, the bank would have to improve both its pricing structures and the quality of its services. Operating Group errors, CBG said, had irritated many major accounts, and their reputation for slow, inaccurate service made expansion of market share very difficult.

The Commercial Banking Group operated 16 Regional Centers in the New York area to serve medium-sized companies, most of whom did not employ their own professional finance executives and thus relied upon the bank for money advice as well as banking services. The fastest growing group of the bank, Commercial Banking projected an annual growth rate of about 10 percent.

The International Banking Group operated some 300 overseas branches in addition to managing several First National City Corporation subsidiary units concerned with foreign investments, services, and leasing. Although IBG conducted its own transaction processing at its overseas centers, still its rapid growth would present new demands on the Operating Group in Manhattan. All business originating in New York was handled by John Reed's people, and the IBG complement of 160 New York-based staff officers was expected to double in five years.

Worldwide, First National City Corporation had shown assets of $23 billion in its financial statement of December 31, 1969. Earnings had been $131 million, after taxes (but before losses on securities traded). The corporation employed 34,000 people, having doubled its staff in the previous ten years, while tripling its assets. Citibank's published goals for financial performance presented another source of pressure for improvement in the Operating Group: Board Chairman Walter B. Wriston had recently committed the bank to an annual growth rate of 15 percent in earnings per share of common stock. President William Spencer had made it clear to John Reed that OPG was expected to contribute to this gain in earnings.

The Operating Group's functions

As the bank had grown, so had its back office. Increases in services offered, in customers, in volume per customer, and in staff all meant added transactions to be processed by the Operating Group. As the volume of paper flowing through the bank increased, so did the staff and budget of the back office. In 1970, John Reed had some 8,000 people on his group payroll, and would spend $105 million on the direct production of the bank's paperwork. For several years, transaction volume had increased at an annual rate of 5 percent; the Operating Group's total expenditures had grown faster, at an average of 17.9 percent per year since 1962.

Operating Group's headquarters was a 25-story building at 111 Wall Street, several miles south of the bank's head offices at 399 Park Avenue. The volume and variety of work flowing through this building was impressive; in a typical day, OPG would:

- ☐ Transfer $5 billion between domestic and foreign customers and banks.
- ☐ Process $2 billion worth of checks—between 1.5 and 2 million individual items. (A stack of 1.5 million checks would stand as tall as a 66-story building.)
- ☐ Start and complete 900 jobs in the data processing center, printing 5 million lines of statements, checks, and other reports.
- ☐ Process $100 million worth of bill and tax payments for major corporations and government agencies. (And during the 16 weeks between February 1 and May 30, the group also processed 50,000 income tax returns per day for the City of New York.)
- ☐ Handle 102,000 incoming and outgoing telephone calls and 7,000 telegrams and cables.
- ☐ Mail out 30,000 checking account statements and 25,000 other items, accounting for $10,000 a day for postage.

Operating Group organization

In 1968, John Reed had transferred into OPG from the International Banking Group, to become a vice president of the bank and to set up a task force pointed toward reorganization of the group. He had assembled a team of young, technically oriented managers (most of them relatively new to OPG) to analyze and rearrange the basic functions of the group. Systematically, this task force had examined the structure and function of each OPG subdepartment, working with the line managers to question where the subgroups fit in the organization; to whom their managers reported and why; what processes and technologies they shared with other groups; and how the physical output of each group affected the operation of the next sequential processing step. The result of this study was a complete realignment of reporting responsibilities, pulling together all those groups doing similar work, and placing them under unified management.

A leading member of OPG's "systems management" team during this reorganization effort was Larry Small, who had followed John Reed from the planning staff at the IBG in 1969. Small, a 1964 graduate of Brown University (with a degree in Spanish literature), set the keynote for the task force approach with his concept of basic management principles. Small elaborated:

> Managing simply means understanding, in detail—in *meticulous* detail—where you are now, where you have to go, and how you will get there. To know where they are now, managers must measure the important features of their systems. To know where they are going, managers must agree on their objectives, and on the specific desired values of all those measured factors. And, to know how to get there, managers must understand the processes which produce their results. Significant change demands the participation of the people involved, in order to gain the widespread understanding required for success. Management is essentially binary; all change efforts will be seen as either successes or failures. Success follows from understanding.

Few major changes in equipment or physical space were required by the new organization, and the approach characterized by Larry Small's statement made the transition an easy one. By late 1969, the Operating Group was running smoothly under a four-area structure as shown in Exhibit 2.

Area I was the high volume operating part of Operating Group. Here were the people who processed the transactions which constituted much of the bank's "retail" business. Area I operated many of the computer systems, processed checks for collection from other banks, posted the accounts for Citibank's customers, transferred funds from one customer to another, and prepared customers' bank statements.

Area II encompassed system design and software for computer operations. It was the "intellectual" side of Operating Group, developing new computer systems for the use of others, particularly Area I. The subgroups in charge of operations analysis, management information

EXHIBIT 2
Basic organization

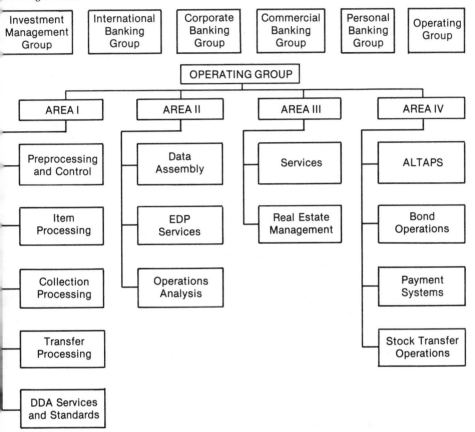

systems, and data control also belonged to Area II, as did the programming group in charge of "ALTAPS," a new automated loan and time payment processing system.

Area III, quite removed from the paper-oriented processing groups in Operating Group, was a free-standing organization in charge of Citibank's real estate, physical facilities, and building services. (When he was not concerned about processing transactions in the back office, John Reed could worry about the quality of cafeteria food, and the cleanliness of the bathrooms.)

Area IV was composed of the relatively low-volume, high-value transaction processing departments—stock transfer, corporate bonds, corporate cash management, mutual funds, and government services.

In addition to the routine of day-to-day operations, Reed was responsible for the long-range development of both hardware and software systems. For several years, a subsidiary of the bank, with operations in Cambridge, Massachusetts, and in California, had been working on the kind of on-line systems and terminals which would be required to support the "checkless society" which the financial community expected would replace paper-based record processing in the long-range future. Reed had decided to maintain the separation of this advanced research and development activity from the Operating Group. "Let's face it," he said, "the computer systems we have now will never evolve into the systems needed for point-of-sale transaction processing. When those new systems come, they'll come as a revolution—a total replacement of existing technology. We should develop the new systems, sure. But we shouldn't let them screw up the systems we need today and tomorrow in the meantime."

In September of 1970, John Reed, feeling comfortable with the overall structure of OPG but impatient with its lack of measured progress, had assigned Larry Small to head Area IV. Small's demonstrated skills in management of change held out the promise that this highly sensitive area, where any errors could cause major problems for the bank's most important customers, would soon be under more effective control. Now Reed was considering the future course of Area I, where even more people and dollars were involved.

Area I: The Demand Deposit Accounting system

The largest single job performed by the Operating Group was Demand Deposit Accounting (DDA), the complex process of handling the physical flow of paper and communications, posting transactions, distributing processed items, and producing the bank's daily statement of condition. Some 2,000 employees of OPG's Area I performed this work. The process was composed of three parts: The "front end," which received, encoded, and read transactions onto magnetic computer tapes; the data center, which sorted the data and printed statements; and the "back end," which microfilmed and filed the checks of Citibank's own customers, prepared and mailed their statements, and handled accounting exceptions.

Around the clock, mail sacks containing checks, deposit slips, traveler's checks, transfer vouchers, credit memos, and other paper transaction records arrived in the eighth floor receiving room at 111 Wall Street to enter the front end of the Demand Deposit Accounting system. The first step of that process was to weigh the bags, in order to gauge the volume of work coming in: one pound of mail equaled about 300 items to be processed.

Each incoming mailbag contained a control sheet, listing the various bundles of checks in that shipment and the aggregate totals of the bundles. As each sack was opened, its contents were checked against its control sheet, to ensure that all the bundles listed were actually received. This marked the first step in Citibank's system for proving the books; from this point onward in the DDA system, each batch of material was signed for whenever it moved from one area of responsibility to another. The records of these transfers, together with any changes in batch totals as discrepancies were discovered or generated, were accumulated by a "proof clerk" on each operating shift. The following morning, these proof worksheets were consolidated into the bank's daily report of its operating condition, as required by the Federal Reserve System.

Materials arriving from other banks and check clearinghouses were already partly processed, but items from domestic Citibank branches, the head office, mail deposits, and lockboxes had to be encoded with machine-readable information. These papers were distributed to one of the 150 magnetic ink encoding machines, where operators would key the dollar amounts into a keyboard. The machines would print these amounts on the checks, accumulating batch totals for each 300 checks processed. Some machines had several pockets, and sorted the work into different pockets for different kinds of media, adding up separate control totals for each pocket. As the pockets filled up, the paper was unloaded into conveyor trays, to be transported to the next operation, where the checks were read by machines and sorted by their destination, while the information from them was recorded on computer tape.

Encoder operators were generally women, who worked on an incentive pay arrangement and processed 800 to 1,100 items per hour. No direct record of keypunching accuracy was kept, and operators were not penalized for errors.

At the read/sort machines, on the floor above, the paper media were sorted into two major classifications. "On-us" checks—those written against the accounts of Citibank's own customers—were directed to the "back end" of the DDA system; "transit" checks, written on other banks, were directed to the various check clearinghouses and exchanges. Firm deadlines held for these exchanges. For example, the major Manhattan banks met at ten each morning to trade checks with each other, and to settle the differences between the checks paid and collected for other banks. This meeting had been a New York tradition for well over a hundred years ; banks were not late for the exchange.

About 600,000 checks each day entered the back end of Citibank's process, where they were microfilmed, screened for exceptions, and filed by customer for rendition and mailing of statements.

Overdrafts, stop payment orders, and "no-post" items were listed by the computer and referred to exception clerks, who searched through the incoming paper for the offending items, in order to route them to the proper offices for special handling. No-posts were especially troublesome; about 1,300 items per day, with an average value of $1,000 each, would flow into the back end, destined for accounts which had been closed, or were burdened by attachments, or had invalid numbers, or belonged to recently deceased owners, or were suspected of fraudulent activity. On a typical day, the exception clerks would fail to find between 50 and 100 of these checks, and the cases would be referred to the investigations unit.

In the filing and signature checking section, women worked at 158 large filing machines, where each operator was responsible for 5,000 to 7,500 accounts. In addition to simply filing the day's flow of checks, each operator handled telephoned check-cashing authorizations; reconciled "full sheets" (the first pages of multi-page monthly statements); compiled the daily activity of medium-volume accounts (between 25 and 125 items per day) into "SMUT listings"[1]; and ruled off the accounts scheduled for next-day statement rendition.

Nine clerks in the breakdown section received the checks for tomorrow's statements from the filing clerks, collated them with the statements arriving from the computer printer, and prepared the work for the rendition group the next day. The 60 women in rendition confirmed the count of checks to go with each statement, observed special mailing instructions, and sorted the outgoing mail into heavy, medium, and lightweight classifications.

Throughout the DDA process, errors could be generated in a variety of ways. Any of the machines could eat a check if the machine were out of adjustment. Multi-pocket encoders could add a check into the total for one pocket, but sort the paper into a different pocket, creating a shortage in one batch of material and a corresponding overage in another. Conveyor trays could be spilled, and loose paper could be stored in desk drawers, or shoved under furniture, or swept out in the trash. The bank's proofing systems recorded variances in all the processing steps, and accumulated the errors in the "difference and fine" account—commonly called the "D&F."[2]

The Operating Group staff

By tradition, the Operating Group was a service function to the customer-contact divisions of the bank. Citibank's top management

---

[1] The Citibank executives interviewed for this background material were generally young men who had served with OPG for only two or three years. They did not know the antecedents of the acronym "SMUT-list."

[2] Similarly, the source of the name "D&F" for the variance account was obscure— although one manager thought there might once have been a monetary fine levied against the bank which failed to balance its accounts perfectly.

attention was directed outward—toward the market. Operations was expected to respond to change as generated and interpreted by the customer-contact offices. As a consequence, tradition held that the career path to the top in banking led through line assignments in the market-oriented divisions. "The phrase 'back office' is commonly assumed to mean 'backwater'," said John Reed. "Operations is a secure haven for the people who have grown up in it; it's a place of exile for people in the other divisions."

In 1970, most of the Operating Group's management was made up of "career men" who had spent 15 to 25 years with OPG, often beginning their service with several years of clerical level work before advancing to supervisory jobs. Through years of contact with "their" outside divisions of the bank, managers had built up rich personal acquaintanceships with the people they served. Frequent telephone contacts reinforced these relationships. Dick Freund, OPG's vice president for administration and a veteran of 42 years' service with the group, commented on the close interaction between OPG people and the customer-contact offices:

> Problem solving here is typically done on a person-to-person basis. For example, an account officer in International Banking, faced with tracing some amendment to a letter of credit, would know that Jerry Cole, an assistant vice president on the 22d floor, could find the answer. He'd call Jerry, and yes, Jerry would get him an answer. Whatever else Jerry was doing in the Letter of Credit Departments could wait; when a customer needs an answer, our men jump. They're proud of the service they can give.

Recruits for the managerial ranks of the bank typically came directly from the college campus. Dick Freund described the process:

> We hire people straight out of college—most of them without business experience—and shuttle them around in a series of low-level jobs while they learn the bank. The Yale and Princeton and Harvard types eventually settle in the customer-contact offices; the Fordham and St. John's and NYU types come to Operating Group. We don't have the glamorous jobs that IBG and Corporate can offer, but even so there's a lot of prestige to working for First National City, and the security we offer means a lot to some of these people. I know one officer who bases his whole employment interview on security. "You come to work for us," he says, "and put in a good day's work, and you'll never have to worry about your job. Never."

While management ranks remained stable, the characteristics of the clerical staff had changed dramatically over the previous decade. Through the 1950s OPG relied on the local parochial high schools as a source of well-trained clerical applicants. Those women would typically work for one to five years before leaving to raise a family; some stayed on to form the experienced core of the staff. By 1970, however, applicants for work in lower Manhattan were predominantly black and Puerto Rican.

Management succession and the changing role of Operating Group

Dick Freund traced the recent succession of top managers at the Operating Group:

> From 1964 to 1968, when he retired, we had a top man who convinced the Policy Committee that our operating capabilities were becoming more and more important—that we simply couldn't afford to take them for granted. There was a tidal wave of paperwork coming—the same wave that swamped so many brokerage houses in '68—and we had to pay attention. Until 1968, nobody cared much.
>
> The first clear signals that management attitudes toward the Operating Group were changing came in 1968, when Bill Spencer was appointed executive vice president in charge of Operations. Mr. Spencer was generally regarded as a prime candidate for the bank's presidency. It was plain that his appointment wasn't some form of punishment. He had to be here for a reason, and the reason had to be that Operations was, after all, an important part of the corporation.

It was Mr. Spencer who recruited John Reed to move from the International Banking Group to Operations, and who promoted Reed to senior vice president, later in 1969.

"And that was another sign that things were changing," Reed said. "For one thing, nobody my age had ever made SVP before. But more important, I wasn't a 'banker' in the traditional sense. Most of Operations' management had been in the group for 15 to 30 years; I'd only been with Citibank for 5, and none of that was with OPG."

John Reed's undergraduate training had been in American literature and physical metallurgy. After a brief job with Goodyear Tire and Rubber, and a tour in the U.S. Army, he had taken a master's degree in management at MIT, and then joined the IBG planning staff, where he applied systems concepts to the international banking field with impressive results. That his rise in the organization was atypical was illustrated by the following comments from other bank officers:

> I've spent all my life in the bank [said a gray-haired senior vice president from the Corporate Banking Group]. I was trained by assignment to different departments every two years; then, when I went into a line position, I had enough experience to correct something by doing it myself. At the very worst, I always knew people in the other departments who could straighten out any problem.

I started with Citibank as a night clerk in Personal Banking [said a PBG vice president]. It was ten years before I reached supervisory ranks, and by then I'd had a lot of experience in credit and in operations as well.

I joined the bank as a naive liberal arts graduate, and spent three years in clerical work before making first-line supervision [said a newly appointed assistant vice president in the Operating Group]. After eight years as a supervisor, you get a pretty good feeling for what's happening around you.

In May 1970, to the surprise of no one, William Spencer was named president of First National City Corporation. John S. Reed—youth, nonbanking background, and all—was selected to head the Operating Group.

Operating Group costs

By tradition, the method of meeting increased work loads in banking was to increase staff. If an operation could be done at the rate of 800 transactions per day, and the load increased by 800 pieces per day, then the manager in charge of that operation would hire another person. It was taken for granted. Financial reports would follow, showing in the next month-end statement that expenses had risen, and explaining the rise through the increased volume of work processed.

But in the late 1960s the work load began to rise faster than the hiring rate could keep up, and in addition there was a decrease in productivity per operator. Backlogs of work to be done would pile up in one OPG department or another, and would require overtime work in order to catch up. Even with extensive reassignment of people and with major overtime efforts, some department would periodically fall behind by two or even three weeks, generating substantial numbers of complaints from customers. Three or four times a year, special "task forces" would be recruited from other branches of the bank to break the bottlenecks of these problem departments. Trainees, secretaries, junior officers, and clerks would be drafted for evening and weekend work, at overtime pay rates. "The task force approach is inefficient, annoying, and expensive, but it gets us out of the hole," said Dick Freund. "A lot of these people don't *want* to work these hours, but it has to be done." In 1970, OPG spent $1,983,000 on overtime pay.

There were other sources of expense in the Operating Group, which did not show up on financial reports. John Reed described a major area of hidden costs:

If we have cashed a $1,000 check drawn on the Bank of America in California, we are going to be out $1,000 until we send them the check. If we miss sending the check out today, it will wait until tomorrow's dispatches to the West Coast, and we'll wait a day longer for that $1,000. There are rigid deadlines for each of the clearinghouses; even a relatively small number of checks missing these deadlines can cost us a great deal of money. If each day only 3 percent of the $2 billion we handle is held over, then we will lose the interest on $60 million for one day. That turns out to be something like $3 million a year in lost earnings. We call it "lost availability."

That's a big number. Yet, until a few months ago we were making no effort to reduce it, or even to measure it. No one had thought of it as a cost. Check processing has always been treated as a straight-line operation, with bags of checks going through the line as they were received. Whatever wasn't processed at the end of the day was held over, and cleaned up the following day. It was just another clerical operation.

In 1970, lost availability amounted not to 3 percent of the value of checks processed, but to 4.

Operating Group quality

"Quality is something we really can't measure," said Dick Freund. "But we can get perceptions that the level of service we're providing isn't acceptable. For all our outlay of expenses, it seems we are not improving, or even maintaining our performance."

Indications of poor service came to the Operating Group in the form of customer complaints, usually voiced through Account Officers from the market-contact divisions of the bank. Failures could take many forms, including loss of checks after they had been posted, late mailing of statements, mis-coding of checks, payment of checks over stop orders, mis-posting of transfers, and, on occasion, loss of whole statements. Since any kind of error could cause inconvenience to the customer, the people in direct touch with the market were highly sensitive to quality. These Account Officers frequently assumed the role of problem solvers on the customer's behalf, traveling to the 111 Wall Street office to work directly with Operating Group staff to remedy specific errors affecting their accounts. A separate section had been set up to analyze and correct errors in customer accounts; its backlog of unsolved inquiries was a major indicator to management of OPG's quality level. In the fall of 1970, this investigations department faced a backlog of 36,000 unsolved cases.

The importance of error-free operation to the customer-contact officers was pointed out by several officers from outside the Operating Group:

> Sure, I know the volume of paper has gone up [said a vice president from Corporate Banking Group]. I know we have 750,000 accounts, and most of them are handled for years without a mistake. But Operations has

to perform at 100 percent, not at 99 percent. Errors can be terribly embarrassing to the customer; repeated errors can lose customers for us. I have 600 checks missing from last month's statement for a major government account . . . and there were 400 missing from the previous month's statement. Now, how can I sell additional services to that account, when we can't even produce a correct monthly statement for him?

We tell the customer that the cancelled check is a legal receipt [said an assistant vice president from Personal Banking], and then we lose the check. What am I supposed to tell the customer then? I can get a microfilmed copy of the check, but that's not very useful as a legal document, is it?

Just getting a simple transfer through the books can generate a whole family of problems [said an Account Officer in International Banking Group]. Here's a typical case. A translator at 111 Wall Street miscodes the original transaction (it was written in Portuguese), and the transfer goes to the wrong account. When that customer inquires, we trace the error and reverse it. But before the correction goes through, a follow-up request comes in from Brazil; it's a duplicate of the first request, and our people don't catch the fact it's a follow-up, so they put through another transfer. Now the same item has gone through twice. Where does it all end? My customer is tired of writing letters about it.

If our operations were perfect [sighed a CBG vice president], we'd have a tremendous tool to go out and sell against the competition.

The "technological fix"

"The customer-contact side of the bank," said John Reed, "and to some extent the top management group, shows a natural tendency to press in the direction of great, massive, new, total computer systems—bringing the ultimate promise of technology into instant availability. It has been natural for all of us to blame mistakes and daily operating problems on inadequate systems; after all, if the systems were perfect, those mistakes would be impossible. But maybe we've all been brainwashed. Maybe we expect too much."

Fifteen years before, Citibank had acquired its first computer—a desk-sized Burroughs machine used to calculate interest on installment loans. For the four years following, the Operating Group had cooperated in an extensive research program on automated check processing, based on equipment developed by International Telephone and Telegraph to encode and sort mail in European post offices. This experimental system had progressed to the point of pilot use on the accounts of First National City's own employees when, in 1959, the American Banking Association adopted Magnetic Ink Character Recognition (MICR) as an industry-wide standard approach to check processing.

Citibank immediately dropped the ITT system, and installed MICR equipment.

Although the computer facilities had grown immensely in the ensuing decade, the basic process performed by the Operating Group remained the same. "For example," said Reed, "people used to verify names and addresses against account numbers by looking them up in paper records. Now they sit at cathode-ray tubes instead, but they're still doing the same operation."

Reed's computer people had reported to him that Citibank's use of machines was already highly efficient. Operating Group was—and had been for several years—at the state-of-the-art level of computer usage. A new survey by the American Bankers Association seemed to verify this conclusion: Where the average large bank spent over 30 percent of its back-office budget on machine capacity, OPG spent less than 20 percent, because it had already invested in computer-based automation.

Reed paused beside his corner window. "Think about this for a minute," he said. "We've been running this operation as if it were a computer center. We've been hoping for some Great Mother of a software system to come along and pull the family together. Well, she's slow. None of us children has heard one word from her. Maybe she's not coming.

"What if it's *not* a computer center we have here? What other point of view could we take that would result in running the Operating Group differently? Better?"

Reed turned. "What if it's a *factory* we've got here?

The "factory" concept

Through much of August 1970, John Reed had worked with Larry Small and Bob White to develop the implications of viewing the Operating Group as a high-speed, continuous process production operation. White, working without an official title, had just joined Reed's staff after six years' experience with Ford Motor Co., most recently as manager of engineering financial analysis for Ford's Product Development Group. At the age of 35, with an Ohio State Bachelor of Science degree and an MBA from the University of Florida behind him, Bob White brought to the Operating Group a firm conviction that the McNamara philosophy of budgets, measurements, and controls was the only way to run a production operation.

Now, in early September, Reed was trying some of these ideas on Dick Freund to get a sense of their impact on the traditional banker. Freund, with more than four decades in the organization, was serving as a sounding board; Reed had almost decided to carry a new program to the Policy Committee of the Bank, and wanted to anticipate their reactions:

> We know where we want Operating Group to be in five years' time. For 1971 and 1972 we want to hold expenses flat; in spite of the rising transaction volumes we'll keep the same $105 million expense level as this year, and after that we'll let costs rise by no more than 6 percent a year. By 1975, that will mean a $70 million annual saving compared to uncontrolled growth at 15 percent. At the same time, we want to improve service, and eliminate our bottlenecks and backlogs, like the jam-up in investigations.
>
> To accomplish those goals, though, we will have to put over a fundamental change in outlook. We must recognize the Operating Group for what it is—a factory—and we must continually apply the principles of production management to make that factory operate more efficiently.
>
> It is not important for the people in the factory to understand banking. We'll take the institutional objectives and restate them in terms of management plans and tasks that are quite independent of banking. The plain fact is that the language and values we need for success are not derived from banking, and we couldn't achieve what we want in terms of systems development and operations if they were.
>
> To control costs, we must think in terms of costs. That means bringing in management people trained in production management—tough-minded, experienced people who know what it is to manage by the numbers and to measure performance against a meaningful budget. We have to infuse our management with a new kind of production-oriented philosophy, and the process has to start with new, outside points of view. Good production people in here can provide a seed crystal and the present management staff can grow around the seed. Some of them will make it; others won't. Our headhunters can find the top factory management people to start the reaction. From there on, it's up to us.
>
> Our costs are out of control because we don't know what they are, let alone what they should be. Our quality is criticized when we don't have any idea what quality really is, or how to measure what we're already doing. Our processes run out of control and build up backlogs because our efforts are aimed at coping with transactions instead of understanding what made them pile up in the first place.
>
> I'm not talking about turning the Operating Group *into* a factory. I'm talking about recognizing that it *is* a factory, and always has been. The function isn't going to change, but the way we look at it and manage it must.

Reed turned to Dick Freund, who has been listening intently. "What will they say to that, Dick?"

Freund smiled, and his eyes sparkled.

> They'll go for the stable budget idea, and in spite of skepticism they will hope you can do it. They'll love the idea of improved service, but

they'll know you can't pull that one off if you're holding costs down. And the factory management idea?

There's one other bit of history you should know, John. The first engineer we ever hired came to work here in 1957, the year after we bought our first little computer. He was an eager guy, really impressed by the challenge of managing back-office operations. He poked around for a few days, and then came back to the head office to declare that this wasn't a bank at all. It was a factory, he said. Nothing but a goddam paperwork factory.

That was after just two weeks on the job.

It was his last day on the job, too.

Reed grinned broadly, and turned to face Bob White. "Are you ready to move out of the office, Bob? This concept is going to fly, and we're going to need someone down at Wall Street who can make it happen. Why don't you get yourself ready to take over Area I?"

Case 5–4
First National City Bank Operating Group
(A–1)

Robert B. White, vice president of First National City Bank and head of Area I in the bank's Operating Group, looked around the small conference room at his new management team. It was August of 1971, and outside the OPG office building Wall Street steamed in the late summer sun. In the conference room an aura of indecision and hesitation resisted the air conditioner's efforts to clear the atmosphere.

"We've all heard people say it's too big a change to pull off [said Bob White]. But those same people can't tell us *why* it can't be done. And we've put months of study into how it *can* be done. Let's look at what we've accomplished over the past ten months. . . .

We set out to spend no more money in 1971 than we did in 1970, and we know now that we'll hit that target. We're measuring expenses for personnel, for equipment, and for overtime, and we're controlling those expenses better than ever before. We've cut out 15 percent of the people and a third of the overtime. Lost availability will be down to about 2 percent by the end of the year. And we have new managers; you people are now in positions where you're personally responsible for the measurements and the results.

The systems and procedures group has studied the DDA process and organization to the point of exhaustion. We've had team meetings to analyze flows and controls, and we've charted and documented this operation as it's never been done before. The last team meeting took three days for how many—15 people? 20?—and the whole thing contributed practically nothing to our knowledge about the process in DDA. Sure, we lack a lot of detail in the analysis of flows. But we're not going to learn *all* the details until we start changing things.

We know where we are. We have a traditional functional operation which has grown so large and cumbersome it defies management. We have a huge pipeline down there on the eighth floor, with all kinds of paper pouring into it at random; whatever comes in the door first gets processed first, and all the different kinds of items are mixed together throughout the process. Now, we know where we want to go. We've decided to break the front end process down into chunks that you men can understand and control.

We're now part of the way toward accomplishing that goal. We've identified six basically different sources of all that paper coming in the door, and we've appointed you three to take full responsibility for the different input streams. Effectively, we're breaking that one huge pipeline down into several smaller, independent pipes. (See Exhibits 1 and 2 for a graphic representation of the existing and proposed flows.) Cavaiuolo is responsible for all the input arriving from the Fed and the

EXHIBIT 1
Functional organization: Pipelines

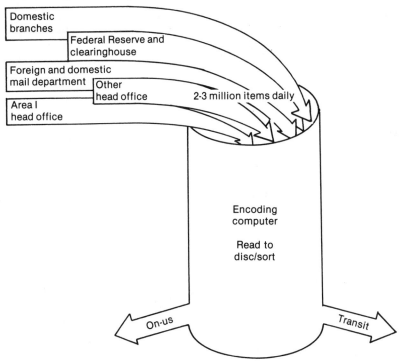

EXHIBIT 2
Product/process organization: Pipelines

Domestic Branches I	Domestic Branches II	Federal Reserve clearinghouse incoming exchange	Area I head office IMT, DMT collection L/C	Foreign mail day	Head office evening	Domestic mail night
Encode computer	Encode computer	Encode computer	Encode computer	Encode computer	Encode computer	Encode computer
Read to disc/ sort	Read to disc/ sort	Read to disc/ sort	Read to disc/ sort	Read to disc/ sort	Read to disc/ sort	Read to disc/ sort
Reconcilement, reject, repair, dispatch, and breakdown	Reconcilement, reject, repair, dispatch, and breakdown	Reconcilement, reject, repair, breakdown	Reconcilement, reject, repair, dispatch, and breakdown	Reconcilement, reject, repair, dispatch, and breakdown	Reconcilement, reject, repair, dispatch, and breakdown	Reconcilement, reject, repair, dispatch, and breakdown
Transit	Transit		Transit	Transit	Transit	Transit
On-us	On-us	On-us	On-us	On-us	On-us	On-us

Filing and rendition

exchanges; Whelan is in charge of all the paper coming in from our own branches; and Stoiber has the four smaller input streams—domestic mail, foreign mail, lockbox receipts, and head office transactions. You have gone through the manning process on schedule, and you have agreed that the right skills are matched to your requirements.

But we've stalled on the final step of the reorganization. We still have that one huge pipeline running, and you men will *never* get control of your operations until you have your own physical space, your own equipment, and your own independent processing lines. We've ordered the new peripheral gear for you, and it's still sitting here in crates.

All we need to finish the job is just the simple decision to do it—to get the moving crews in here to set up your individual shops. I recognize that some people are uneasy about that. But we've planned how to meet every specific objection that's come up. There's no way to plan around vague statements that somebody is uncomfortable. We've laid out the jobs, and we could go on training for *ever*. Now, do *any* of you see anything *specific* that we've overlooked?

No?

Then let's go. If the riggers come in Friday evening, we can be in business Monday morning.

Case 5–5
First National City Bank Operating Group (B)

Picture a high-pressure pipeline, five feet in diameter, carrying money to dozens of different distribution pipelines. Your job is to make a lot of plumbing changes in the pipes, but you can't shut off the flow of money while you work. If anything goes wrong and the pipe breaks, all those dollars are going to spill out on the floor. In a week's time, you'll be wading around in $10 billion. You'll be up to your eyebrows in money. Other people's money.

John S. Reed, one of six executive vice presidents of Citibank and the officer in charge of the bank's Operating Group, was reflecting on the process of change in a continuous-process, high-volume production operation. It was January of 1973, and Reed was reviewing the accomplishments of the past two and a half years. On the surface, it was easy to document progress; the Operating Group had numbers to show for its efforts. But Reed was anticipating criticism, too, as he prepared for the Policy Committee meeting at the end of the month. After all, the Group's performance hadn't been perfect; the money pipeline had broken, for the second time, only four months ago. Several customer-contact divisions still complained that service and quality levels in OPG were going downhill, in spite of numeric measurements that showed substantial improvement. And John Reed's fellow executive vice presidents and division heads on the Policy Committee had tenacious memories.

Added to his other concerns was a new situation, highly visible to the bank as a whole. Organizers for the Office and Professional Workers Union were handing out thousands of leaflets to workers at 111 Wall Street, OPG's office building. Citibank's pay scales were competitive with other Manhattan employers' rates, but there were some indications of dissatisfaction in the work force. The previous year, for example, 125 women had walked off the job with a list of grievances; bringing the situation back to normal had required four months' full-time effort of one of OPG's most experienced assistant vice presidents. There was little feeling among top management that unionization was an immediate threat, but still the OPWU leaflets couldn't be ignored.

How, Reed wondered, could changes in the bank's "back office" be evaluated in terms of their impact on the rest of the institution? How could the new nonbanking approach of the Operating Group be made meaningful to the traditional bankers from the market-oriented divisions? For that matter, how could Reed himself picture the full impact of his changes on the Operating Group and on the bank?

He stood at the window of his Manhattan office, high above the early-morning traffic on Park Avenue. Behind him on his huge desk lay the two documents he had studied the night before. One was a draft of a speech which Robert B. White, senior vice president in charge of the production areas of the Operating Group, would soon deliver to the American Bankers Association. The speech outlined the management approaches Citibank had applied to its back-office operations over the previous two years. Citibank's success in gaining control of its paperwork had attracted industry-wide attention; in 1971 and 1972, OPG had handled substantial increases in volume of work while reducing its expenditures below the 1970 level. The chairman of the First National City Corporation had been widely quoted as crediting the Operating Group for a major share of the bank's increased earnings. Judging by the numbers, John Reed had few reasons for concern.

The second document on his desk, however, seemed to tell a different story. It was a consultant's report, which Reed had commissioned in order to hear an outside viewpoint on the effects of the changes he and his colleagues had engineered in the past two years. The report was based largely on interviews the consultants had conducted with some 70 officers of the bank, both inside OPG and in the market-contact divisions; it focused sharply on some undesirable side effects of OPG's changes. The imposition of tight control policies, the report suggested, could lead to anxiety and insecurity in middle management. These fears could lead, in turn, to establishment of unrealistic goals (as an effort to please the new bosses), and to increased resistance to change (as middle management's effort to protect itself). The consequence of these two factors could be poor performance, seen as missed deadlines and crises, and as a sensed need by top management for still tighter controls. It was a classic vicious circle.

Placed side by side, the two documents made interesting reading. Reed wondered how OPG could learn from the comparison—how they could avoid unanticipated consequences of change in the future.

Change in the Operating Group, 1970–1972

Soon after his promotion to head OPG, in May of 1970, John Reed had faced the question of defining just what OPG was. Was it, as banking tradition dictated, simply a mechanical support group for the customer-contact offices of the bank? Or could it be seen as an independent, high-volume production operation—a factory—which designed and controlled its own processes and products in the style of a manufacturing organization.

Operating Group, Reed decided, was a factory. As such, it badly needed managers who knew how to run factories—men skilled in planning and controlling mass production processes. Dick Freund, OPG's vice president for administration and a veteran of 45 years' service with the bank, described the group's first effort to recruit professional production management:

> What industries do you think of when you want examples of outstanding factory management? Well, automotives have to be close to the top of the heap. And what companies do you think of? The winners: General Motors and Ford. The first headhunter Reed turned loose on the job happened to have his foot in the door at Ford. You should have seen the first man who came to interview; we really went all the way to impress him. Reed had the fellow out to his home to talk, and so did Mr. Spencer (the bank's president). The guy was obviously impressed, and went back to Detroit to think it over. Then he told us "no." His family was well established in their present home, and he didn't want to bring them to New York. His kids had put on a very convincing flip-chart presentation, he told us. Can you imagine it? Reed and Spencer were just incredulous—couldn't believe it. Here's a really top guy, and he lets his kids decide what he's going to do. We were flabbergasted.

Succeeding efforts at recruiting production-oriented executives were more fruitful, and OPG began to fill its management ranks with young, aggressive talent. One of the early arrivals was Bob White, who left Ford Motor Company to work as John Reed's assistant. For several months, the two men worked intensively to build a specific action framework around the 1971 goals of OPG. Then White, supported by other newly recruited executives (three of them from Ford), moved into the line organization to take charge of the transaction processing responsibilities of OPG's Area I.

Tops-down management

The draft of Bob White's speech for the ABA explained how the change process began with a fundamental look at the group's whole philosophy of management:

> In general terms, we can say that "administering" connotes a passive mode, while "managing" bespeaks an active mode. An administrator is, in a sense, a bystander, keeping watch on a process, explaining it if it goes awry. But managing means understanding your present world, deciding what you would like it to be, and making your desired results happen. A manager is an agent of the future, of change.
>
> The fact is that, traditionally, banking operations are not really managed at all. In a sense, the people in charge are running alongside the processing line, instead of being on top of it pressing the process levers. All you can do in such a situation is react. At Citicorp, we decided that this was unacceptable. We wanted to manage our back office, not administer it.
>
> There are two critical prerequisites for this: conviction, and orientation toward results. Each manager must be absolutely convinced that he *can* control *all* factors relevant to his operation. That conviction must begin at the top, and must carry with it a willingness to spend for results. I am talking about spending in terms of change to the organization, its structure, its fabric. About the amount of top management time and energy expended, and about the type of people you are willing to accept in your culture.
>
> To ensure an environment that will foster the kind of dedication and commitment we need, we use a pass/fail system as a management incentive. A manager passes or fails in terms of result objectives he himself has set within the top-down framework. He is rewarded or not rewarded accordingly. No excuses or rationalization of events "beyond one's control" are accepted . . . .[1]

> *I've been treated better in the past three years than in all of the previous nine years.*

> *Reed has been very fair with everybody who has produced, in a salary sense. . . .*

---

[1] (*Note to the reader:* Italicized quotations are used throughout this case to interject representative comments of *other* managers who were involved in or affected by the OPG reorganization, as reported to the consultants whom Reed had hired. These quotations, of course, did not appear in the ABA speech.)

The feeling was we should do things, especially make or beat budget, and that if we didn't we should expect to be out.

The ABA speech continued:

The style of management we sought was tops-down management. Each manager sets his own objectives for his own level in translating objectives set from above. Although people felt initially constrained by a tops-down approach, I am fully convinced that it is the ONLY approach. Each manager is not only free to exercise his vision—he is expected to do so. He is unfettered by what is traditional, by what is the norm. Nothing is sacred. The real problem is that the tops-down system "strains" people, but it does not "constrain" them. "Good" people thrive in such an environment. . . .

This job is exciting, like working for a glamour company, almost like having your own company. I really like being a "maverick". . . .

I like the opportunity to work for change, and to have responsibility for it. What I don't like is the incompetence of those who resist. . . .

I work 10 to 12 hours a day. I guess Reed works 24. . . .

OPG has lived in crisis for the past six years, but it's worse now, especially the hours and pressure that everyone is under. I spent the whole summer working six days a week, and never saw the kids. Finally got up the courage to tell my wife I was working Labor Day weekend. She put it to me . . . said . . . well, I called and said I wasn't coming in. The guys I used to work with say to me now, "congratulations," even though my new job isn't a promotion. They see me as being better off, just to be out of that place.

If you start your management process with the first-line supervisors and accumulate upward, you are assuming that the smartest people and the strategic direction for the business come from the bottom of the management pyramid . . . if this is true, we need to reverse the present salary structure so that the first-line people are paid the most money. It is not a question of brightness or ability, it is rather that top management has a better view of the overall organization, its direction, goals, strengths, weaknesses, and so forth. . . .

The speech went on to outline the basic management theories which Operating Group had formalized and applied to its functions in the past three years. "Management 101," it was called, and it was simply stated as "knowing WHERE WE ARE, WHERE WE WANT TO BE, and HOW WE PLAN TO GET THERE." Each responsible manager was expected to know, in formal terms, the current state of his world and all the processes that were producing his current results; the *desired* state of his area and the processes that would produce *those* results; and finally the changes he would make to today's processes, to turn them into tomorrow's processes. "It is not results we are managing, but processes that achieve the results." After defining the 1970 situation of the Operating Group and its three goals for 1971 (flat costs, improved service, and elimination of the investigations backlog), the speech proceeded:

> What was left was to design the action plan—the processes that would get us to the results we wanted. [See Figure 1, which reproduces a slide shown to the audience at this point in the speech.]

FIGURE 1

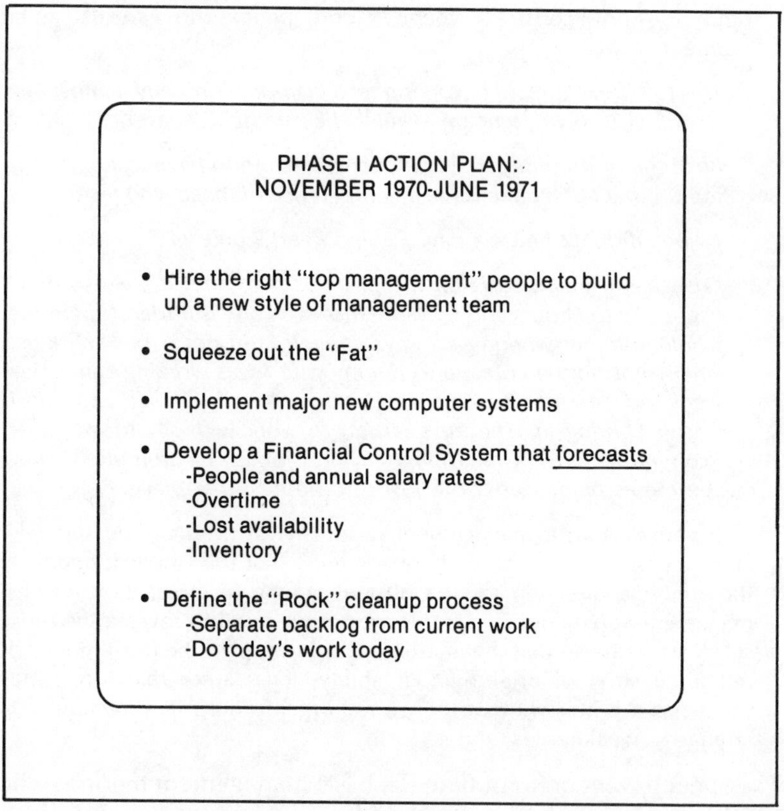

PHASE I ACTION PLAN:
NOVEMBER 1970-JUNE 1971

- Hire the right "top management" people to build up a new style of management team

- Squeeze out the "Fat"

- Implement major new computer systems

- Develop a Financial Control System that forecasts
  -People and annual salary rates
  -Overtime
  -Lost availability
  -Inventory

- Define the "Rock" cleanup process
  -Separate backlog from current work
  -Do today's work today

We planned to build a strong management team, to hire managers who had the conviction and motivation to control their own operations with "management" skills as opposed to "administrative" skills.

We planned in 1971 to cut out all the "fat" accumulated during the prior ten years of 18 percent annual cost rises—at that rate we knew there *was* some fat.

We planned to develop and install a financial control system, emphasizing simplicity and the major cost elements; (1) people, (2) overtime, (3) process float, or lost availability, and (4) equipment and computers.

We planned to define a process for cleaning up rocks, such as the 36,000 backlogged investigations, so that we could come out from under the crisis environment and get control of our processing. This meant designing the techniques to separate rocks out from current work so that we could both dissolve the rock *and* do today's work today so that the "rock" would not grow.

In fact, the real significance of the Phase I action plan was that it enabled us to get a handle on the operating environment. With this program, we started to get on top of the back office so as to control and manage it.

The whole management team was brought in cold, predominantely from Ford. So you had this whole new team applying industrial concepts to paper flow. It has worked. But people took affront that these bright young stars were coming along and changing the whole new world.

The number of people actually severed from the bank was actually very small for the organization . . . only 179 . . . but the image is very negative. . . .

The fear of a cut–a layoff–wasn't a very realistic one. In fact, there have been very few–but the perception of it was the important thing.

The key issue in the bank today is job security. . . .

There was a language problem. The buzz words used by the new guys differed from the language the old managers used and understood.

Lots of people close to retirement retired early. People at the AVP level are running scared. . . .

The bank no longer offers "security" to old-timers. My chance to become a VP is almost nil, regardless of performance; I just don't have the right background. . . .

People have really put out in this place . . . some of them have really worked. But when some old-timers were pushed out, it hurt a lot of us. We said, "Is that what's in store for us if we keep going here?" Also, when the old timers who knew other parts of the bank left, we lost a way to get a lot of contacts with the other groups.

To gain control of costs, it was necessary to forecast what our expenditures would be *before* we were committed. We developed a one-page expense summary report based on forecast, rather than on history. [See Exhibit 1.] The manager is in control of all his variables. We do not recog-

EXHIBIT 1

Operating Group—1973 expense forecast ($ 000)

AREA	AREA I	DIVISION		DDA RECAP		DATE		EXHIBIT	

	Month of January			Month of February			March-December			Full Year 1973			
	Actual	Actual (O)/U budget	Actual (O)/U forecast	Actual (O)/U 1972 actual	Forecast	Forecast (O)/U budget	Forecast (O)/U 1972 actual	Forecast	Forecast (O)/U budget	Forecast (O)/U 1972 actual	Forecast	Forecast (O)/U budget	Forecast (O)/U prior forecast	Forecast (O)/U 1972 actual

SALARIES
Official and nonofficial
Part-time
Fringe benefits
Overtime
Temporaries
Severance

Subtotal salaries

OTHER OPERATING (incl. 799s)
Education and training
Computer time - outside vendors
Consultants
Computers
Furniture and equipment
Insurance and legal
Postage
Stationery and supplies
Telephone, telegrams and cables
Travel membs. and subs.
Business, promotion and entertainment
Food
Operating losses and losses not insured
Difference and fine
Lost availability
Rent
Rental income
OPC occupancy expense
Real estate taxes
Building depreciation
Utilities
Freight and cartage
Other
1972 related expense
Provisions

Subtotal other operating

TOTAL EXPENSE

nize any type of expense as uncontrollable or institituional. Forecasts are updated monthly and are met.

We have a tendency now to try to meet due dates at all *costs. . . .*

Due dates for changes are in most cases absurd. Time commitments are ridiculous, and the consequences of not meeting due dates aren't made known beforehand.

People try to be optimistic to please the boss. When they miss the milestones, they get screwed.

But when we set about implementing new computer-based systems, we learned a very important lesson: we hadn't gone back to basics enough. We found we did not really understand the present processes completely.

And so a second action plan, Phase II, was devised in June of 1971. We called it the Performance Criteria System, PCS. What we were aiming at was breaking up the operations into manageable, controllable, understandable pieces. These were the key approaches to defining the back-office dynamics.

1. Define the products/services as recognized by the customer.
2. Develop a customer-to-customer flowchart and procedures for processing each product/service.
3. Develop the organization to match and support the product definition and process flow on a customer-to-customer basis.
4. Develop our physical layout into a closed-room/one-floor layout that matched the flows, procedures, and organization so as to enhance control and minimize movement.
5. Decentralize all peripheral equipment.
6. Incorporate support functions into the responsible line organization.

Our processing had always been conceived of in functions, rather than in system processes. All the work flowed into one pipeline of processing functions; for example: preprocessing, encoding, read-to-tape, sorting, reconcilement, repair, and dispatch. You can visualize the functions along a vertical axis, and the people and time-frame along a horizontal axis (see Exhibit 2), giving us a very wide pipe carrying 2 to 3 million transactions per day. If the one pipe breaks, all the work in the pipe before the break stops or spills out. That shouldn't happen often, but when it does, the whole operation stops.

We aimed to break down that pipeline into several smaller lines, each carrying a different product and each supervised by a single manager who controlled every aspect of the process, from the time a customer originates a transaction all the way through a straight line until we dispatch the results back to the customer. (For an example of this straightline flow, see Exhibit 3.)

We began by breaking the operations out on the basis of six separate input streams: two flows from our domestic branches, separate domestic

EXHIBIT 2
Functional organization: Pipelines

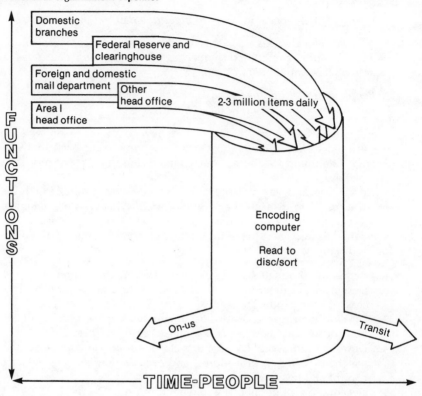

and international mail deposit flows, one flow from our head office department and one from incoming exchanges. Each of these became a separate processing line. (See Exhibit 4.) These flows are not mere theory; they exist in documented fact.

> *In came flowcharting and the product line concept. We had a flowchart that stretched across the room and back. White had an incredible ability to understand the whole thing—to point to something and just ask the critical question about how something worked, or why it was part of our activity and not somewhere else. The result was a definition of 11 different products, and a full reorganization in one month. It's the only way to run a bank.*

> *Changes were viewed differently by different people. People started flowcharting everything, and Bob White was going over everything, step-by-step. But lots of people got the feeling that they didn't know what to do. They didn't "fit" in this new environment. . . .*

EXHIBIT 3
Night mail deposit—Floor plan, South Street

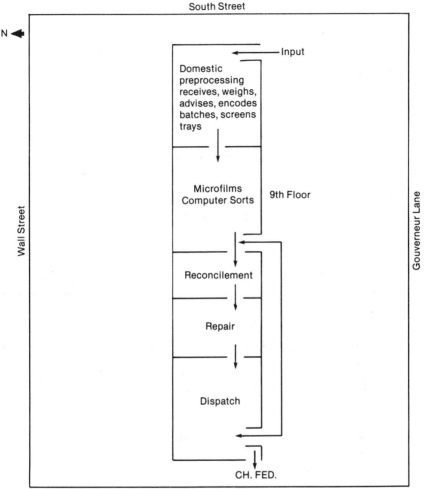

The blowup: September 1971

In August of 1971, Bob White decided it was time to act on the new organization of Area I. "We had been talking a lot abour reorganizing the flows," he said, "but nothing was actually happening. We had spent months with people, talking about implementation, and we thought they understood. It was time to move."

On a hot September Friday evening, when the regular working shift

EXHIBIT 4
Product/process organization: Pipelines

Domestic Branches I	Domestic Branches II	Federal Reserve clearinghouse incoming exchange	Area I head office IMT, DMT collection L/C	Foreign mail day	Head office evening	Domestic mail night
Encode computer	Encode computer	Encode computer	Encode computer	Encode computer	Encode computer	Encode computer
Read to disc/sort	Read to disc/sort	Read to disc/sort	Read to disc/sort	Read to disc/sort	Read to disc/sort	Read to disc/sort
Reconcilement, reject, repair, dispatch, and breakdown	Reconcilement, reject, repair, dispatch, and breakdown	Reconcilement, reject, repair, breakdown	Reconcilement, reject, repair, dispatch, and breakdown	Reconcilement, reject, repair, dispatch, and breakdown	Reconcilement, reject, repair, dispatch, and breakdown	Reconcilement, reject, repair, dispatch, and breakdown
Transit	Transit		Transit	Transit	Transit	Transit
On-us	On-us	On-us	On-us	On-us	On-us	On-us

FUNCTIONS

Filing and rendition

Personal A/Cs

Business A/Cs

went home, equipment crews began the job of rearranging the facilities of 111 Wall Street. By Monday morning the physical layout was set up for six separate lines, each with its own full complement of peripheral equipment, ready to begin work. And, soon after the work force reported on Monday, it became clear that the Demand Deposit Accounting system had problems. Equipment had been moved and connected, but technicians had not had time to check its operation before it went back into service; some of the machines refused to operate at all. Machine operators, informed on Friday that they would still have their same machines but they would be in different locations on Monday, arrived at work with questions, and there were not enough supervisors to answer them. Leftover work from Friday's processing, tucked away in accustomed corners by machine operators, was nowhere to be found; the customary corners were gone.

The money pipeline creaked and groaned under the strain.

As the week wore on new problems came to light. The three proofing clerks who had handled three shifts of consolidated front-end operations could not keep up with the load generated by decentralized work streams. With new people in charge of new areas, proof clerks did not know whom to call to resolve apparent discrepancies; the "Difference and Fine" (D&F) account of accumulated variances began to grow alarmingly. By the end of the week, it was apparent the Citibank's problems were greater than just "de-bugging" a new system. OPG's managers were inventing new systems on the spot, attempting to recover. By the second weekend of September, the disturbance had grown to tidal wave proportions. The D&F account hit $1.5 billion on each side of the ledger before heroic weekend work by the group's middle managers brought it back down to $130,000,000. First National City Bank failed to meet the other New York bankers at the 10:00 A.M. exchange, and failed to file its Federal Reserve reports.

The money pipeline had burst.

Geoffrey MacAdams, the grey-haired head of the proofing operation, walked into the computer room, waving his hands in the air. "Stop the machines," he said haltingly to the computer operations head. "Stop the machines. It's out of control."

"I remember walking through the area and finding a pile of work, out on a desk-top, with a note on the top saying, 'This is out by a million and I'm just too sleepy to find it'," said one manager. "There was maybe $20 or $30 million in the stack. At least the girl was good enough to put a note on it. We were learning, the hard way, not to put papers like that into desk drawers."

Larry Stoiber, operations head for four of the six processing lines, looked up slowly one morning when Bob White greeted him, and delayed several seconds before showing signs of recognition. Stoiber had been at work for 55 hours without a break. White sent him home in a Citibank car, with instructions not to let him back into the bank until he was coherent.

In two weeks' time the new production processes began to work. Within a month of the change, routine operations on̄ce more ran rou-

EXHIBIT 5

Memorandum to: Messrs.

J. Cavaiuolo, Operations Head
L. Stoiber, Operations Head
F. Whelan, Operations Head

Effective Tuesday, August 31, I would like a report (attached) from each of you showing Lost Availability and deferred Debits and Credits for each of your operations:

Branch—Whelan
Domestic mail—Stoiber
Foreign mail—Stoiber
Head office—Stoiber
Lock box—Stoiber
Exchanges—Cavaiuolo

The first Lost Availability report should cover the period from the first City Country deadline on Monday to the New York, New Jersey deadline on Tuesday. The deferred debits and credits report should be based on one DDA update to the next.

The report should be completed and on my desk by 1:45 P.M. daily. Initially the report will be in addition to the regular Lost Availability daily report—I assume you will ensure the report will tie. You are now each *personally* responsible for ensuring that all lost availability is measured. I would rather not *ever* find anymore "undiscovered" lost availability.

If you have any questions or any problems in meeting this deadline, see me today. If not, I will expect the first report at 1:45 P.M. on Tuesday.

Bob

Robert B. White
Vice President

August 30, 1971

---

tinely (note the difference between the Bob White memo of August 30 and the status report on October 6 on lost availability, Exhibits 5 and 6). But it was five months before the backlog of work and problems generated by the DDA blowup were resolved.

In early October, as the DDA system began to return to normal and its managers turned their attention to the problems of cleaning up the side effects of the blowup, John Reed visited the Wall Street building to talk to Larry Small and Bob White. "I wanted to be the first to tell

EXHIBIT 6
Excerpt from October 8, 1971, internal report on status of "rocks" in Demand Deposit Accounting system

Float statistics for the month of September were not available due to incomplete data as a result of procedural changes caused by the recent reorganization. A data-capturing network has now been developed and implemented; and reliable and complete data was reported on October 1 and thereafter, indicating an average 3.2 percent lost availability for the three-day period October 1–5.

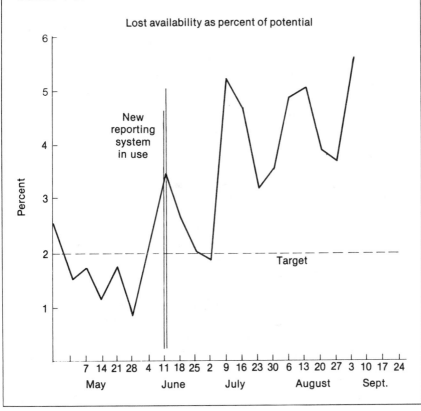

Lost availability as percent of potential

you this news," he said. "The Promotions Committee met this morning. You have both been named senior vice presidents of the bank." He smiled broadly, "Congratulations."

> The design for change from the top just cannot anticipate all the problems that are going to arise at the first-line supervisor level; those people have to know more than just the before and after job description. . . .
>
> I'll tell you why people didn't protest the change, or question their instructions. We were scared—afraid of losing our jobs if we didn't seem to understand automatically.
>
> The changes were accompanied by a great fear that people would get fired. Most lower managers and clerical workers felt management—that's AVP level and above—was highly insensitive to people. . . .
>
> Reed and White and the new guys know what they're doing; they're good at setting up cost and quality measures, and conceptualizing the system. But at the practical level, things haven't worked. In the past, new instructions would be questioned, and worked through until they were either understood, or the designer was convinced there was a problem. For example, if I go out there and tell Mary to start writing upside down and backwards on what she is doing, she'll look at me and say "why?," because she knows me and to her it doesn't make sense. If one of the new guys tells her to write upside down and backwards, she'll do it and not say a word. If anything a little unusual starts to happen, she won't know why it's important, and she won't say a word about it. When the Ford kids say do it, people do it. But they're scared.
>
> It hurt us, credibility-wise, with the rest of the bank. The sharks smelled blood in the water, and came at us from all directions. But things are better now—an order of magnitude better.

Just a year later, in September of 1972, the Demand Deposit Accounting system blew up again, this time centered in the back end of the process, where the filing and telephone authorization process was being changed to anticipate the installation of computer voice answer-back equipment. The changes altered the way accounts were "ruled off" in preparation for statement rendition, making it impossible for the file clerks to select the proper checks to match with the computer-printed last pages of customers' statements. Unlike the 1971 crisis, this blowup affected customers directly and immediately. "The problem looked critical to the branch people, who had customers standing in line at the tellers' windows waiting for answers that never came. And it seemed critical to account officers in corporate banking, who couldn't get statements for their customers. But it was actually much less serious than the 1971 episode, because it didn't involve the proofing system," said Bob White. "We were able to react much more quickly, and we were pretty much recovered from it within a month and a half."

Achievements in the Operating Group

The draft speech for the American Bankers Association summarized the results of Operating Group's improvement efforts in two charts which would be reproduced as full-color slides (see Exhibits 7 and 8).

EXHIBIT 7
Slides, copies from ABA speech

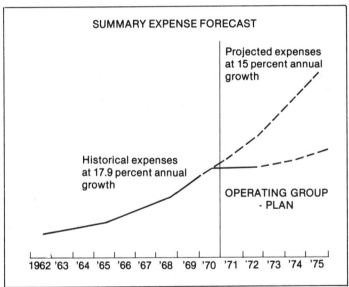

By the end of 1973, according to the forecast, personnel in the group would be reduced by 30 percent from 1970 levels; overtime would be down by 71 percent; lost availability would be down by 75 percent; and the backlog of investigations would be shrunk from 36,000 to 500 cases—one day's load. The speech would elaborate:

> The real achievement here, though, is that we forecasted what we would achieve and then made it happen. Moreover, we *did* put together the kind of management team we wanted, and we *did* get hold of the processes within our shop. At the same time, we developed a control system to measure the two facets of service to our customers: quality and

EXHIBIT 8

	RESULTS					
	HEADCOUNT		OVERTIME		LOST AVAILABILITY	
Year	Number of employees	Cumulative percent decrease from 1970	$000	Cumulative percent decrease from 1970	$millions	Percent of potential
1970	7,975	–	1,983	–	56.4	4.0%
1971	6,610	17%	1,272	35%	32.8	2.0%
1972	5,870	26%	845	57%	26.5	1.8%
1973	5,528	30%	564	71%	14.2	0.5%

timeliness. Quality measures error rate; it is the number of errors as a percentage of the total work processed on a daily basis.

We currently measure 69 different quality indicators, and we are meeting the standards 87 percent of the time. When a given indicator is met or beaten consistently, we tighten the standard; we expect to continue this process indefinitely.

Timeliness is the percentage of work processed in a given time period—generally a 24-hour time period. At the moment, we have defined 129 different standards for timeliness, and we expect that number to continue to grow. Today, we are meeting 85 percent of these standards. Moreover, we also continually tighten these standards as soon as we prove they can be consistently met. I think it is fair to say that our service performance has improved greatly since we began to hold costs flat—if for no other reason than that we now *really* know what we are doing.

> In order to make progress, we had to be firm with the other divisions of the bank. We used to interrupt anything in order to handle a special request. No more. We've consciously shut them out, so we could work on the basic processes here. Now we have no people wandering in here to distract our clerks.

From outside the Operating Group, changes were also evident. Three officers from the customer-contact divisions commented as follows:

> My frustration is I wish there were more old-time bankers in there, and fewer systems and organization types. There is a huge loss of old guys I can turn to for help in getting things done, people who know banking. Maybe they should keep just a few. Some. A few cents a share might well be worth it.

People over here do say that if those guys are so good, why do they keep screwing up. You'd think they'd learn something in two years. . . .

In the old days, when the old guys were running things, you knew who to go to. Now we don't know. Even if we find somebody, he's faced with a process where he couldn't give special service even if he wanted to.

Bob White's speech concluded:

These, then, were the achievements of two years of fundamental change. They are, I think, substantial, and they provide us with the solid base we need to focus in on the future.

One of John Reed's magazine articles that came around said something about people being replaceable, like machines. That hurt. You lose solidarity.

Somebody asked me once if I liked it that we were working in what Reed called a factory. That really struck home. So, maybe it is like a factory. Why do they have to say it?

Case 5–6
First National City Bank Operating Group (B–1)

John S. Reed and Robert B. White sat on the stage of a small auditorium at the Harvard Business School, looking far more comfortable than their audience of over 300 MBA candidates. It was March 1974, and the two senior men of Citibank's Operating Group had spent the day visiting six of the ten MBA sections. Now the students who had not enjoyed the chance to question Reed and White in class had their chance. Questions came quickly, beginning with probes into the posture of the bank's top management during OPG's periods of crisis:

On top management support

We were lucky, of course, in having a chief executive like William Spencer—but then, we would not have been in a position to make these changes if Spencer had not understood our problems. He is an immensely perceptive, sophisticated investment banker. He cried for 30 days when he himself was assigned to head OPG, but he understood in his guts that the back office was a point of vulnerability: it could bring the whole bank down. Spencer placed his bets on change when he appointed Reed to take over the Operating Group. He took the heat when the process blew up, and he insisted on playing the hand out.

On basic management guidelines

We assumed from the start that OPG could be managed, and that managers had to be accountable for the performance of their operations. The pass-fail system we installed gave us benchmarks for holding people responsible. Nobody is penalized under that system for failing, but people who hide failures, or lie about them, have no room in OPG. Men who cannot meet realistic targets are moved to jobs where they *can* succeed. If you're not failing at something, some of the time, then you aren't doing anything; you're not shooting high enough. People in OPG can and do admit to failures and ask for help.

On the lifestyle expected of OPG managers

RBW: *For me, it's normal to spend 12 to 16 hours a day on work. Sure, I'm exhausted emotionally by the time I get home at night—but I'm always fresh and eager to get at it in the morning.*

We're not looking for total dedication to the bank from our people. The job mustn't be all there is to a man's life. But it's common for our people to spend 10 to 11 hours a day at it. And sometimes more.

JSR: *I don't want to see any suicides among our people—either literally, through feelings of outright failures , or figuratively, through sticking in misfit positions where people can't be effective, and where they die by inches. I remember telling one of our people, who was near retirement age, to just stay home and continue drawing his full salary until his boy graduated from college, and then to retire. I told him, "Staying here and being useless would kill you; we can handle the financial problems without strain . . . until retirement, just don't come in to the office."*

On the reaction of the old culture to the new

Most—maybe 85 percent—of the old management was obsolete. They achieved their positions by being expert in handling transactions, not by proficiency in managing processes. Their fear came from their *realizing* they were inadequate.

Keep in mind, too, that there were some people in the old organization who suffered because they were misfits in *that* atmosphere. We had some people who really blossomed when they had a chance to take responsibility and prove themselves.

On the exodus of old-line management

We just told the people, "This is a different ball game; come and play in it if you want to." We made no effort to minimize departures. Actually, we worked hard to find these people other jobs—jobs better fitted to where they were individually. One of our old top people is now revolutionizing the banking industry in Brazil, and he's far happier there, in a technology appropriate for the 1960s, than he'd have been here, trying to get into the 1980s.

Nobody with more than five years' service left the bank. Transfers and reassignments took care of almost everybody. Only about 300 people hit the street.

On the warning signals of impending doom

Sure, we had some people warn us we'd blow the place up. We just didn't believe them. How much faith do you put in the advice of people who are content with 20 years of stagnation?

Parallel running of the new process wouldn't have helped us. We would have picked the process we knew best to experiment with, and it wouldn't have uncovered the problems we didn't know about.

If we'd really known what was coming, we might not have had the guts to do it. And if we'd waited long enough to fully understand the whole DDA system, we probably would have grown accustomed to its mode of operation.

On the rate of change in OPG

We took a quick shock, rather than slowly bleeding to death. The pace of change didn't seem fast at the time. We just came to work every day, and did what we had to do. We saw change as inevitable, so we did it. Now, of course, we can see we zapped the place. But we achieved more results, in less time, than we could have if we'd taken an understanding approach.

If anything, the rate of change was too slow, not too fast. Our real problems came because people tried to hold on to pieces of the old processes.

On results

We lost no customers because of problems generated by the blowups. We contributed to higher earnings, in spite of the crises. We have ten times more managers in DDA now than we did in 1970, even though total employment there has dropped from 2,000 to 1,200. Our managers are better paid than the rest of the bank, where they used to earn 20 to 30 percent less. Our people are in demand for promotions to other parts of the bank; turnover is still a problem with us, but it's because our guys are growing fast, and ready to take on other fields. We promoted 50 people to officerships in other branches of the bank in 1972, and 60 in 1973, and 20 more in the first quarter of this year. We've gone from a total of 8,400 people to 4,400 now, and we'll be down to 1,000 or 2,000 in another five years.

We'd do the same thing all over again if we had to.

Case 5–7
Project Paradise

In March 1975, Robert B. White, executive vice president of Citicorp and head of the Operating Group of Citibank, was concerned about the progress of a major reorganization of his group. The reorganization effort, called Project Paradise, had been initiated by White in 1974. The first phase of Project Paradise, which involved the detailed planning of the reorganization by members of White's executive staff unit, had gone smoothly and was completed ahead of schedule. However, now that the actual implementation of the planned reorganization was well under way, involving changes in responsibility and authority at middle management levels in several parts of the Operating Group, there was evidence of a slowdown. In view of the significance he placed on the success of Project Paradise, White wanted to understand the reasons for the slowdown and to take whatever action was necessary to insure the accomplishment of its purposes.

OVERVIEW

Overview of the Project Paradise reorganization

In 1974 Citicorp had revenues of nearly $5 billion and earnings of $312 million. Its business came predominantly from its principal subsidiary, Citibank. The Operating Group (known as OPG) of Citibank was one of the six groups which reported to the president, Mr. William Spencer. (See Exhibit 1.) Each of the other five groups served the banking needs of a particular market segment. Thus, the International Banking Group (IBG) maintained offices throughout the world and served individual "retail" banking customers and smaller corporations; the World Corporate Group (WCG) served major international corporations; the National Banking Group (NBG) served large corporations

EXHIBIT 1
Citibank group organization, 1975

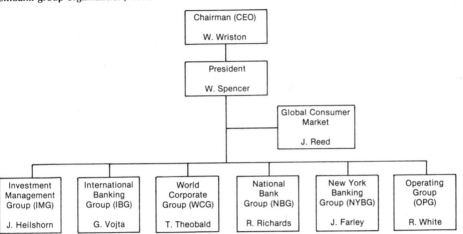

which did business primarily in the United States; and the New York Banking Group (NYBG) served the retail and smaller corporate customers through its system of branches in the New York City area. Traditionally the groups functioned with a great deal of autonomy. Top management of Citicorp, including all the individuals named in Exhibit 1 plus three other officers, made up the "Policy Committee." This body met weekly to discuss matters affecting more than one group or having broad institutional impact.

One result of Project Paradise would be a change in the organization of the Operating Group from a product organization to a market organization. Previously the organizational units which reported to White (known as "Areas") differed from one another in the nature of the products and services for which they were responsible. For example, Area I was the highly automated check processing and demand deposit accounting (DDA) unit, and Area IV conducted a variety of transaction processing activities, including record keeping for loans, stock and bond services, domestic and international payments and money transfers, and corporate cash management. The transactions processed by Area IV could be characterized as high in value per transaction and low in volume compared to Area I, which worked with low-value, high-volume paper. The Area structure of overall product and service responsibilities had been in existence for four years. (See Exhibit 2.)

The Project Paradise reorganization would result in most of the managers of units reporting to White being responsible for all the different operations, products, and services provided to customers in a

EXHIBIT 2
Basic OPG organization, 1970–1974

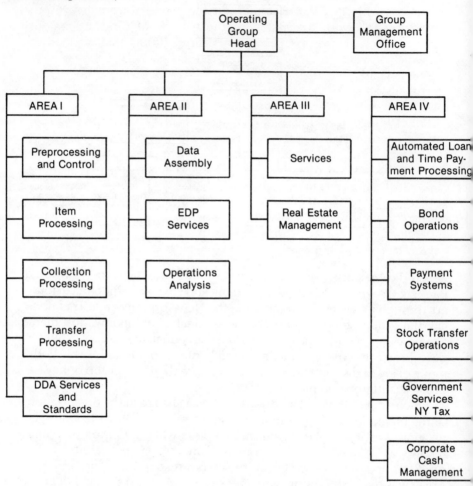

market segment. In particular, the new OPG units would do operations for five market segments served by the other Citibank groups. For example, there would be an OPG unit called "International Banking Group Services Management" to do the operations for customers of the IBG, another unit called "World Corporate Group Services Management" for customers of the WCG, and so on.

Thus, the Project Paradise reorganization within OPG involved splitting up the operations formerly accomplished in the old Area structure and rearranging the pieces so that different operations for the same customer group were structured together. Under the old organization all corporate cash management operations were in one subunit of Area IV. When Project Paradise was completed, a part of cash management operations which served customers of the World Corporate Group would be organized together with those parts of other operations (such as stock processing, check processing, money transfer, and so on) which also served WCG customers in the new WCG Services Management Unit. Similarly, those parts of the same operations which served customers of the National Banking Group would be together in NBG Services Management, and so on.

Bob White expected Project Paradise to lead to the achievement of several important goals. First, it was expected to reduce problems of communications that had existed for some years between the production-oriented operations specialists in OPG and their market-oriented counterparts in the banking groups. White and others in OPG perceived that a kind of cultural gap had developed between OPG and the rest of the bank. He hoped that by organizing OPG so that its units corresponded to (or "faced off" to) the banking group organization, better mutual understanding could be gained and more effective customer service provided. Second, White had long believed in the concept of taking relatively large, unified operations for each product or service and breaking them down into smaller pieces which could be managed independently. It had been the OPG experience in recent years that change based on this concept had led to greater cost efficiencies due to the benefits of improved controllability of operations. This had been true despite the need to duplicate equipment and in some instances increase personnel when a large, unified operation was broken down into identical independent streams. White expected the dramatic lowering of cost of minicomputer technology at that time to help hold down the cost of the new organization, which would require many more separate and smaller computer facilities compared to the old organization.

But the long-range purposes of Project Paradise extended beyond reorganization within OPG itself. White hoped that as the different market-oriented units within OPG were established they could be decentralized away from OPG and placed under the management control of the respective banking groups. Thus, an ultimate purpose of Project Paradise was to achieve the full integration of operations with the banking groups. Indeed, one new OPG unit, the New York Banking Group Services Management unit, had, as of February 1975, already been placed in a matrix relationship between the New York Banking Group and OPG. That is, NYBG had a solid line responsibility over that new operations unit and OPG maintained a kind of staff responsibility for such things as approval of major technical innovations and equipment purchases. However, the speed and ease with which the NYBG Services

Management unit had been reorganized and decentralized under Project Paradise was thought of as the exception rather than the rule. Although reorganization of other units within OPG was planned for completion by the end of 1975, decentralization of these units to the banking groups would come later.

In summary, Project Paradise was a major reorganization affecting virtually all the operations functions of OPG. The Project potentially could be extended to include the decentralization of OPG into the banking groups. Its purposes were to make operations more effective in satisfying the needs of banking group users and their customers, while at the same time at least maintaining the existing cost efficiencies of operations.

The particular problem

Bob White's particular concern in March 1975, was that an important deadline in part of the internal OPG reorganization was about to be missed. The deadline was the intended date of transfer of responsibility of some operations channels from a manager in Area IV to another manager in the new International Banking Group Services Organization elsewhere in OPG. Missing the deadline would represent a "fail" to White and to the managers involved, inasmuch as OPG prided itself on meeting deadlines.

Moreover, this potential schedule fail would lead to other delays. Bob White wanted the IBG Services Management unit to be created on time because he had discussed its formation with George Vojta, the EVP who headed the International Banking Group. The two men had planned that as soon as the IBG Services Management unit was up and running within OPG, Vojta would transfer a group of 80 customer service assistants from IBG to the new unit. It was seen as a logical consolidation into a single unit of the tasks of operations service performance and contact with customers about that service. If the deadline were missed, the date for this transfer of personnel from IBG would have to be put off. Such a delay would be potentially embarrassing to OPG because, unlike most other aspects of the Paradise reorganization within OPG, this one had immediate effects on another banking group.

It was evident to Bob White that this particular problem was not an isolated incident but one of several incidents in a general slackening in the pace of Project Paradise. It was important that he decide how to deal with this one and other current and future slips in the schedule. One option would be to let the schedule slip and be reset. He would have to explain the situation to Vojta in IBG and ask him to readjust his plans accordingly. As a second option, he could permit expenditures over the budget while insisting that schedules be met. This might entail, for example, permitting additional overtime expense. Finally, he could "tops-down" the problem by insisting that the schedule and the budget be met, and leave it to the line managers involved to work out how they did it. He knew that this would require considerable further personal effort from his line managers, most of whom were already working 10- and 12-hour days, and he knew that this kind of pressure increased the risk of an operational "blowup."

BACKGROUND ON CHANGE IN OPG

Project Paradise represented the latest phase in a long history of planned organizational changes within OPG. These changes had totally altered OPG and its relationships with other groups in Citibank. The internal OPG Project Paradise reorganization represented the culmination of many of these changes. The potential decentralization of OPG which Bob White had begun as an extension of Project Paradise represented the beginning of a new phase with impetus deeply rooted in this history.

Creation of the cultural gap, 1964–1970

Before 1964 there was no centralized operating group in Citibank. Bank office operations services were performed by employees working closely with those in contact with customers for their banking needs. For example, it was common for an operations officer to accompany a lending officer in a visit to an important corporate account. While the lending officer negotiated loan terms the operations officer would talk to accountants and others in the company responsible for handling transactions. Almost every officer had some experience in his department's operations function. As one officer put it, "In those days there wasn't any distinction between operations and banking. We all thought of ourselves as bankers."

By 1964 the volume of paperwork for most transactions and services had grown to the point where further specialization and efficiency were clearly necessary. The number of clerks and officers handling operations and services grew in proportion to volume and grew faster than those handling the credit side of the business. Specialization of people had begun, and what was subsequently described as a "cultural gap" was created. In 1964 this was recognized formally by the creation of the Operating Group as a centralized entity. Communications and relations between OPG and customers and users remained good, however. This was due in part to the fact that OPG was still physically located with the rest of the bank in the uptown headquarters building at 399 Park Avenue.

In 1968, OPG moved to its own building downtown at 111 Wall Street. There the latest in computers and processing technology was installed. As top OPG managers described it in 1975, this move led to a further widening of the cultural gap with the rest of the bank at that time. OPG employed more clerks and hourly employees of relatively low skill than the rest of the bank, and people in OPG began to be seen as lower status. It was widely recognized that career opportunities were more promising through the credit side. Differences in opportunity were even reflected in the colleges from which potential officers came: OPG typically got its management trainees from Fordham, St. John's or NYU, while the banking groups attracted the Ivy League graduates.

In the late 60s OPG employed some 8,300 people. Management was seen as very "people-oriented" and sought to have satisfied workers and middle managers. Although a budgeting and control system existed, officers were not held rigidly accountable for performance results. Within OPG job security was emphasized, and many middle managers were quite explicit about their desire for job security. Managers provided personalized service to customers and old friends in other parts of the bank. OPG management felt it was important to provide responsive service and to maintain relatively stable ranks of middle-level officers. Higher positions were typically filled from within OPG itself, with seniority and experience given heavy weight in promotion decisions.

About this time top management of Citicorp became concerned over the need for controlling costs in operations. It was realized that the traditional approach to dealing with increases in paperwork, which was to add clerical employees in proportion to increases in volume, would no longer suffice. The volume of transactions being processed was rising at 5 percent to 10 percent a year, while Operating Group expenses were rising at a rate of 18 percent per year. William Spencer, seen by many as the next Citicorp president, was brought from another group and made head of OPG. This was widely recognized as an indication of the importance being given to the operations function.

Spencer became president of Citicorp in 1970. He was succeeded as head of OPG by John Reed who, like Spencer, had come into OPG from another part of the bank. Thirty years old in 1969, he became the youngest senior vice president and subsequently the youngest executive vice president in Citicorp history. Reed recruited Robert White from his job as director of financial planning in the engineering division of the Ford Motor Company, making him a member of his group staff. This small staff, known as the Group Management Office (GMO), included officers responsible for overall personnel policy, development of new control systems, gathering information for periodic performance review meetings with line managers, design and planning of organizational changes, and the like. Offices of the GMO and the OPG head were in the Park Avenue headquarters of Citicorp.

In 1969 Reed reorganized OPG along functional lines, grouping together the processing of transactions which required similar machine technology and similar clerical skills. Even prior to changes in organization structure, the management of OPG had kept abreast of the latest in computerization and technology for paper processing as it had become available. OPG expenditures for machines as opposed to salaries were in line with or slightly higher than the banking industry as a whole.

The 1969 reorganization resulted in five Areas reporting to Reed. It was basically the same organization in terms of assigned functions to Areas which White inherited when he became head of OPG in 1974. (See Exhibit 2.) Area I handled the high-volume, low-dollar value per transaction processing, including, particularly, the check processing and demand deposit accounting functions. Area II did systems analysis and systems development services for other Areas and ran an extensive data processing and time-sharing system for the bank and some outside customers. Area III was distinct from the other three, with responsibility for maintaining buildings and providing general services. It had little contact with the other Areas. Area IV processed the low-volume, high-dollar value per transaction items such as stock transfer, corporate bond transfer, corporate cash management, and domestic and international funds transfers. It also provided services to the City of New York in processing city income tax returns. In addition to these, Reed was responsible for the somewhat independent research and development unit known as Transaction Technology Incorporated (TTI), a subsidiary which had been purchased to develop new hardware and software technologies in electronic funds transfer.

Despite his reorganization of OPG and the up-to-date machine technology employed, however, Reed became increasingly concerned in 1969 and 1970 as OPG costs continued to rise and as complaints from customers and other groups in the bank over service quality appeared to grow with the increase in volume. Moreover, the pressures to hold the line on costs and improve quality of services were such that Reed concluded it unlikely that a major technological breakthrough could be accomplished in time to be the solution to the problem. As he put it, the "Great Mother of a software system" that would automate their processing and eliminate the principal source of increase in expenses, namely payroll, probably just wasn't going to come in time.

An internal gap develops, 1970–1972

The path Reed chose to deal with the continuing problem of costs was to give line responsibility to a new breed of young managers like

Bob White. These people and a handful of their own recruits were not thoroughly familiar with OPG processes or people. Unlike their line predecessors in OPG they insisted on quantitative measurements and indicators of efficiency and quality results, on the introduction of systems to control the processes to improve those results, and on a detailed understanding of the flows and objectives of each operating entity.

In September of 1970 Reed moved White from his position as group controller in the Park Avenue headquarters to the line position in the operations building downtown at 111 Wall Street as head of Area I. His charge was to run the day-to-day operations and to restructure his Area to implement the necessary management systems to achieve better cost control and quality. As one specific goal, the men agreed that their aim was to hold OPG costs flat for the period 1971 and 1972, then to allow costs to rise at a rate not to exceed 6 percent per year if volume warranted for 1973 to 1975.

Reed conceived of Area I, which employed 3,500 people, as a paper processing "factory."[1] He knew that to make it a well-run production unit would require revolutionary changes in attitude of the existing ranks of middle managers, changes which would further widen the cultural gap with the rest of the bank and which would make communications and understanding even more difficult. In *The Wall Street Journal* article in 1975 Reed was quoted on his role during this period:

> I held a cultural umbrella over White's head so he wouldn't have to realize he was working in a bank. If he knew it would have scared the hell out of him. I protected him from the bankers. If we had to lay anybody off, I said, "Do it," and let the personnel office run up and down my back with spikes on.

Area I offered the greatest potential for savings and the greatest challenge to the introduction of change. It processed millions of items per day, and its results were highly visible. Thousands of personal and corporate checking account statements were mailed out monthly to customers of all other groups in Citicorp. Balances due from and owed to other New York banks were settled daily in a New York clearing house meeting that began promptly at 10:00 A.M. There were also strict reporting requirements from the Federal Reserve system that required that precise balances or "proofs" be kept on the DDA processing line.

White hired several young managers from outside the bank to help him understand, introduce changes and manager Area I. This team had in common a faith in a systems approach to management; a belief that

---

[1] For a full documentation of the development of this conception and the details of changes in Area I during this period see the cases, First National City Bank Operating Group (A), (A—1), (B), and (B—1).

it was necessary to actively "manage" their activities instead of passively "administering" them; and energy and ambition for career progress. None had extensive line experience in managing large numbers of subordinates, and few understood all the complexities of the products they turned out in OPG. As they set to work to understand the Area I processes they imposed a new and different language on the generally older middle managers who now reported to them. In retrospect, OPG management saw that an *internal* cultural gap between upper and middle management in OPG was created during this period, in addition to the gap between OPG and the rest of the bank.

By June of 1971, White's team had developed a new concept of organization for Area I which they saw as a necessary first step to bring that massive processing system under manageable control. Until that time all checks to be processed had been handled at input identically by a functional system regardless of whether they were to be drawn on Citibank or other banks, or whether the account was large or small. Thus, all the microencoder machines were together, all the proofing was done by a group of proof clerks, and so on. The new concept was to break down the input stream at the "front end" and organize the process into separate flows or channels according to the type of customer. In this way, each of the several channels could be managed separately and a manager held accountable for efficiency and quality of products that were for similar customers. During this planning White had originally attempted to involve those managers with longer experience in OPG in the planning process. Meeting resistance and lack of understanding, he increasingly came to rely on his new team of managers.

After extensive planning White pressed for the physical changes necessary to break out the front-end flows in Area I. This was done over a weekend in September of 1971. When work began on Monday it was soon evident that there were problems. Some machines were not operating properly. Some clerks arrived at work with questions about their new assignments but found that there were not enough supervisors to answer them. Pieces of work which had been tucked away in familiar corners at the close of work on Friday could not be found on Monday. The three proof clerks who had handled three shifts of consolidated front-end operations could not keep up with the load generated by decentralized streams. The variance account, an indicator of the extent to which funds were in balance between sources and uses, hit a record high $1.5 billion two weeks after the change, before intensive weekend work by some managers brought it back to $130 million. The Citibank representative was late for meetings with the other New York bankers for the daily exchange, and the bank failed to file some required Federal Reserve reports.

It took two weeks to get the new processes to work, and a month before operations were under control again. It took five months to chase down the backlog of problems generated by the blowup. There was an uproar of complaints from customers and other banking groups. However, during the height of the problems Bob White was promoted to senior vice president, a move widely seen as support for his ideas and an indication of the continuing commitment of top management to change in OPG.

A year later, in September of 1972, Area I experienced another blowup. This occurred on the "back end" of the process, during a change aimed at providing on-line exception processing (stop payments, overdrafts, etc.). This blowup affected customers directly, some of whom received statements with checks missing and out of balance, but it was less serious in terms of financial impact. Corrections were instituted more quickly, and the Area recovered in less than two months.

As they reflected on the blowups, Reed and White came to believe that the problem had not been in the concept or planning of the changes themselves, but in the planning and execution of the implementation of those changes. The internal cultural gap had led to the imposition of new approaches and concepts by a new group of managers on an existing culture of middle managers who did not fully understand the changes and whose warnings were not understood by the new managers at the top.

Despite these blowups, Area I and all of OPG achieved its goal of holding operating costs flat in 1971. The same was achieved in 1972 and 1973. The total employment of OPG actually declined by 30 percent, from 8,300 in 1970 to 5,550 in 1973. Cost of overtime was reduced 70 percent. "Lost availability," or the opportunity cost of float, was reduced from $56.4 million in 1970 to $14.2 million in 1973.

In a speech before the American Banking Association in 1972, Bob White summarized how these achievements had come about and where OPG stood:

> The real achievement here is that we forecasted what we would achieve and then made it happen. Moreover, we did put together the kind of management team we wanted and we did get hold of the processes within our shop. At the same time, we developed a control system to measure the two facets of service to our customers: quality and timeliness. Quality measures error rate; it is the number of errors as a percentage of the total work processed on a daily basis.
>
> We currently measure 69 different quality indicators, and we are meeting the standards 87 percent of the time. When a given indicator is met or beaten consistently, we tighten the standard; we expect to continue this process indefinitely.

Timeliness is the percentage of work processed in a given time period—generally a 24-hour time period. At the moment, we have 129 different standards for timeliness, and we expect that number to continue to grow. Today, we are meeting 85 percent of these standards. Moreover, we also continually tighten these standards as soon as we prove they can be consistently met. I think it is fair to say that our service performance has improved greatly since we began to hold costs flat—if for no other reason than we now really know what we are doing.

Closing the cultural gaps, 1972–1974

In 1972 White and Reed could point to clear improvements in control of costs and efficiency in Area I and the rest of OPG. Nevertheless, there were symptoms of continuing problems both within OPG and in relationships with the banking groups. Internally, much of the attitude and language of the new breed of higher managers had not rubbed off on middle management. There was a lack of enthusiasm and responsiveness in the ranks. In the spring of 1972 there was a union organizing drive among clerical workers at 111 Wall Street. Although it did not succeed, Reed and White were concerned that low-level line managers might not be representing an accurate picture of the intention to create a stable as well as productive work environment.

Externally, there was continual sniping and misunderstanding between OPG and several banking groups. Because of the tighter management and continuing change in OPG, the old informal channels of communication with banking groups had been closed off. From the perspective of OPG, a minor operational problem with a customer would get exaggerated out of proportion by a banking officer and pushed up to senior levels. There it would be used as evidence against the changes being made in OPG. Proud of its achievement in improving its cost and timeliness results, OPG management would present their numbers to senior managers only to have them argue that complaints from key customers about service were *increasing*. As one OPG manager described it in 1975:

> We would show them our charts and statistics on costs, quality and timeliness and how we were improving. They would say "Those are lies. The numbers don't mean anything. The costs to us of services are rising. Besides, we don't deal in averages, we deal in customers. You may get 95 percent perfect, but if a big corporate customer is one of the 5 percent, it's a disaster for us."

In late 1972 and early 1973 Reed and White took steps to begin to lower the "cultural umbrella" around OPG that had protected it from the outside during the major changes. It was judged that OPG was now strong enough to withstand whatever shocks might result, and that further isolation could be dysfunctional to the bank as a whole. Two new officers were hired for White's staff. Richard Matteis was told to study the problem of "external integration" and Arthur Kirsch to study "internal integration." As Kirsch later explained it:

> What we were supposed to do was not entirely clear. There I was, with no one working under me, trying to define a problem that could be solved to improve the climate within OPG. I spent five months writing papers and talking to a lot of people, especially White, and gradually some handles began to emerge.

Matteis was given a small staff and the job of conducting monthly meetings with senior officers in what later became the National Banking Group. These monthly management review meetings were aimed at achieving mutual understanding of OPG's measures of results and the others' problems with OPG services. In 1973 Matteis was given responsibility for the corporate market "product management" group, a unit which was transferred into OPG from one of the banking groups. OPG initiated a series of newsletters and bulletins designed to acquaint account managers and service assistants with the people, organizations and functions within OPG.

After several months Art Kirsch was given responsibility for personnel in OPG. Although strictly speaking a "staff" position, Kirsch had reporting to him personnel officers in each of the OPG Areas at Wall Street. He began to institute new approaches for management by objectives and performance appraisal. A significant innovation was the introduction of an additional level of management to the existing five levels between the clericals and group head. These new line managers were primarily responsible for the implementation of change, including making certain that problems foreseen by the lower managers were made clear to the higher levels of line and staff.

During 1973, White was given responsibility over all the OPG production operations when Larry Small, who had successfully introduced changes in Area II and Area IV, was promoted into a new position in the NYBG.[2] With these additional responsibilities, White was in a position to plan for organizational changes across the entire OPG which would represent the next phase in closing the external gap and reintegrating OPG into the bank.

---

[2] In 1974 Small became the head of personnel of Citicorp. Following him into other positions of high responsibility throughout the bank were to be a number of the new breed of successful OPG managers. In fact, OPG became a net supplier of management talent to the bank. In 1975 it was found necessary in OPG to restrict the outflow for fear of decimating its own supply of management talent.

PROJECT PARADISE AND ITS IMPLEMENTATION

White was officially made head of OPG in July of 1974 when John Reed moved up to work on worldwide consumer marketing for Citicorp. During the very next week Project Paradise was announced.

Art Kirsch, who moved to head White's GMO staff in 1975, explained the meaning of the name "Project Paradise":

> I wrote a paper which described the feelings of the first line managers at 111 Wall Street. I suggested that these managers were alienated and felt they were in "hell or purgatory," forgotten by the bank and seeing no escape from their concerns. The feeling went back to 1968 when they were initially separated from the rest of the bank and continued through all subsequent changes. At least one objective of Project Paradise is to bridge the gap between OPG and the marketing groups and give our people the feeling of being an accepted part of the bank again. Compared to where they've been, that will be Paradise!
>
> OPG has used a lot of negative reinforcement. Bob really cracked down on or moved out people who weren't performing. Negative reinforcement creates quick learning and performance which was appropriate to the task of achieving substantial change in a short time frame. We're changing our image, organization and style of management. Now there is more positive reinforcement.

In a discussion draft document to his senior staff dated March 15, 1974, White provided the basic rationale for Project Paradise:

> We believe the importance of our contribution (efficiency) has been understood by top management, but because our approach has been counter to the conventional wisdom that says "you have to spend money to provide good service," and because it has had negative impact on the security of people, and because it has stretched some of the bank's heritage and bruised its culture, it has been misunderstood or unappreciated by the rest of the bank.
>
> We believe we have built an infrastructure of management, processes, procedures, and systems that will continue to achieve optimum operational efficiency for the next five to seven years. This is a machine-intensive operation that will keep costs flat by being on the computer learning curve rather than on the labor-intensive 6–8 percent a year automatic cost increase curve.
>
> We now want to change the thrust of our strategy to one of effectiveness in Institutional Service rather than efficiency in Operations. We have hired and trained the right people, developed the management disciplines and procedures to provide better support to the marketing groups. The key is to move away from our posture of planning and producing average products for an average customer.
>
> Additionally we would now like to provide increased employment security for our staff to provide them with the atmosphere they need to

help us positively implement the new systems and organization. Although few people have actually left the bank as a result of layoffs or firing, the continuing possibility has kept our staff tense and less receptive to change than if we had a full employment policy.

White elaborated on why he was willing to turn over or share with other groups the management of operations:

> I'm trying to structure OPG so that the banking groups can take over their service functions if they have the inclination and management expertise necessary. Right now the profit potential on the services side is small and the banking groups should be concerned primarily with their credit business. In the long run, however, the profit potential on the services side is enormous but it will be a different business than the one we have now.
>
> What I want to do is to finish facing off my service operations with the banking groups. This will give me a customer base. Then I want to get the terminals and systems into the corporate treasurer's office. The terminal will do a full DDA accounting service and money transfer. Then I want to start doing all his back office work. He has the same problems I had, and we can do that job better today than almost anyone else. We've started this in a way. We've taken over Korvette's customer credit operation. The potential for services is unlimited.

By the end of 1974 the thrust of Project Paradise was becoming reflected in the OPG organization chart (Exhibit 3). Area I under Charles Long was relatively less affected, as it already served primarily the retail and commercial customers of the NYBG. Area II, then headed by Dick Matteis, was to become the services unit for both the World Corporate Group and the International Banking Group. In early 1974, most of these operations were still being handled in Area IV under Dick Kane. Ultimately, Kane would retain only those services corresponding to the National Banking Group, in what would be called NBG Services Management.

There were two Areas which would not be reorganized under Project Paradise. These were General Services (Hal Deford), and Area VI (Wade Coleman). Area VI was deeply involved in "Project Mustang," the project which would enable corporate customers of the bank to bypass much of the paperwork involved in transactions by having a computer terminal in corporate treasurers' offices. Statements of balances, transfers, and most other typical transactions could be handled directly and instantly by electronic transaction and computer. To the extent it was successful, the system could substantially reduce the cost of transaction processing and error rates while providing the customer more timely information on his resource position. However, income from the system was to be from fees rather than the interest earned by requiring minimum balances. By reducing the levels of balances re-

EXHIBIT 3
Partial organization chart for OPG, December 1974

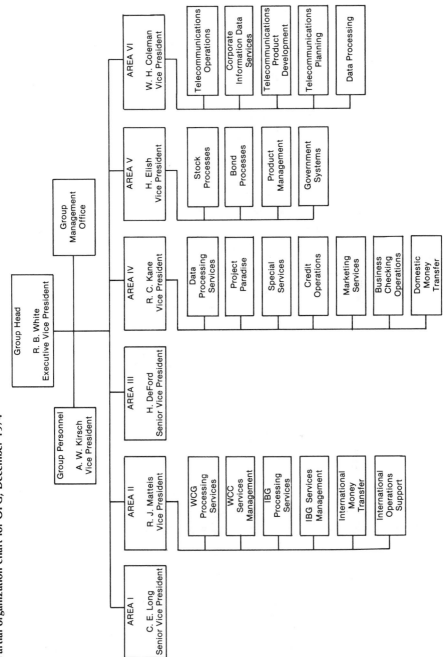

Group Head
R. B. White
Executive Vice President

Group Personnel
A. W. Kirsch
Vice President

Group Management Office

AREA I
C. E. Long
Senior Vice President

AREA II
R. J. Matteis
Vice President

WCG Processing Services

WCC Services Management

IBG Processing Services

IBG Services Management

International Money Transfer

International Operations Support

AREA III
H. DeFord
Senior Vice President

AREA IV
R. C. Kane
Vice President

Data Processing Services

Project Paradise

Special Services

Credit Operations

Marketing Services

Business Checking Operations

Domestic Money Transfer

AREA V
H. Elish
Vice President

Stock Processes

Bond Processes

Product Management

Government Systems

AREA VI
W. H. Coleman
Vice President

Telecommunications Operations

Corporate Information Data Services

Telecommunications Product Development

Telecommunications Planning

Data Processing

quired of customers the bank would eventually have to seek new ways of raising capital to cover reserve requirements and loan demand. The full development of this system was to be "the banking of the future" and a means by which OPG could establish a mechanism for selling many services to corporate customers.

Regarding the role of Project Mustang in the evolution of OPG, Art Kirsch commented:

> The ultimate integration of operations into the bank is through technology. We can all go back to being bankers and eliminate operations as a specialization. Bob believes we're on the threshold of putting the specialization or knowledge of how to perform transaction processing into the computer and putting the data entry function as close to the customer as possible—right in their offices.

The intended organization chart for OPG for later in 1975 is shown in Exhibit 4. In February, in a memo sent out jointly by White and James

EXHIBIT 4
Partial organization chart for OPG, May 1975 (as projected in February 1975)

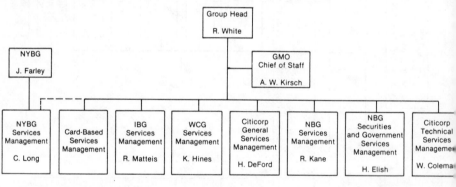

Farley, it was announced that the New York Banking Group Services Management unit (formerly Area I) was being transferred to NYBG under Farley, with White retaining a matrix responsibility over it.

The Paradise Project plan within OPG

When Bob White had taken over the old Area I in 1970 he changed what had been a functional organization in which all the work flowed into one large pipeline of processing functions into one which was broken down into several smaller lines. Each of these lines (channels) carried a product for a different type of customer, and each could be supervised by a single manager who controlled almost every aspect of his process. After taking over the rest of OPG, White found it was necessary to have his newly acquired production areas "channelize" their operations before he could fully implement adequate control and accountability systems, and before he could start Project Paradise. He reflected on this process:

> We channelized those operations (outside Area I) and didn't blow them up. It's getting to be old hat. What's really important though is the story told by comparing performances. The old Area I—DDA—that I channelized in 1971 just keeps getting better. We bit the bullet and bled hard and fast. Now it just gets better and better. The operations that weren't channelized in 1971 still haven't worked out all their problems.

The initial plan for implementing Project Paradise consisted of three phases. Phase one was to be a study of all 27 of the OPG channels by special teams. Four teams were created, each consisting of individuals with proven skills in planning OPG organizational changes and at least one individual with line experience in managing channels. Team members were predominately staff personnel, however. The entire phase was known as the "Staff Study Phase" and was headed up by Wade Coleman, who at that time was head of GMO staff. The objective of phase one was to study and divide on paper the processing work done by every channel throughout OPG into three parts: that which pertained to IBG customers, that for WCG customers, and the "residual."

Then, on paper, the phase one study would estimate what additional manpower and machines would be required if each of the three pieces for each channel was moved into a new market-oriented unit. The study would result in a notebook for each channel, and summaries of estimates of the volumes and resources required to accomplish the reorganization. As they studied each channel, the study teams were to be guided by the checklist of "processes and results" which had originated with White and had evolved over the years into the basic model for management in OPG. (The elements of this model are given in Exhibit 5.)

Phase two was planned as the "vertical breakout." Using the phase one studies, line managers, assisted by staff officers, would plan and conduct the actual physical separation of channels in place. That is, new equipment and people would be brought in if necessary, but the breakouts would remain under the line managers who had been responsible for them. All the bugs were to be ironed out under those managers' responsibilities.

Phase three was to be the "horizontal breakout" in which smoothly running channels for WCG, IBG and other customers were physically moved to separate floors. Line responsibilities would then fall to managers in each of the new face-off organizations.

EXHIBIT 5
The management model: Results/processes

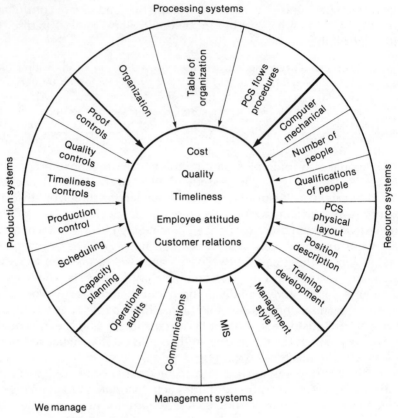

We manage
- within 4 systems
- under 19 disciplines
- for 5 results

to make things happen

Very early in the process White made it clear that he expected there to be no additional expenses or investments added to the OPG budget due to Project Paradise. Any necessary incremental costs were to be covered from new savings achieved during the same period. OPG managers knew from the outset that they would have to conduct the Paradise reorganization while at the same time striving for the usual stringent budget targets. Achieving these targets involved results improvement projects, such as the automation of channels and minor reorganizations quite apart from Project Paradise.

Moreover, these managers knew that their MBO objectives were based in part on achieving these savings and other results targets. The degree to which objectives were met, missed or exceeded became the primary determinant of a year-end ranking of all managers. A manager's position in this rating list determined directly the amount of merit increase in salary he would receive. In addition, the rating list was used to help decide who should get bonuses and how much they should be. Thus, if a manager simply met all his objectives he would not be ranked as high as those who exceeded theirs, and would likely receive less of a raise and bonus than they. By basing ratings and compensation on a curve the system was intended to encourage a healthy competitiveness among managers and reduce the likelihood that a manager would meet his objectives early in the year and then "coast."

Although the MBO system provided a clear statement of what was expected of a manager, many managers in OPG felt that Bob White's personal style was to be deliberately ambiguous, and to give different or conflicting signals to different managers. While they believed this was painful at times, on the whole they thought it was effective. They saw tension and positive conflict being created by White's insistence to some to maintain schedule and budget, while others were told to proceed carefully and to watch out for blowups. At the outset of Project Paradise White commented on this observation and on his experience in building the OPG organization:

> I may give different signals unconsciously in the sense that I think each manager's understanding of his world and his background and the management language that he is familiar with might be different. For the people that have experienced the blowups I don't need to remind them to be careful and touch all bases. The others that have only heard about those episodes I probably think need understanding of the processes emphasized rather than scheduled and speed.
>
> It's incredible how long it takes to build an organization. We had to build up both the people and the information necessary to even think about a Project Paradise. We have people available now who know how to change this organization, who didn't know before, and we have information we didn't have before. We've developed the ability to communicate and this is really an important change. We have a common language system, and that management model is in everybody's mind, down to a certain level in the organization. All the people reporting to me are "my people"; they are all hand picked and know they are part of the team. After you go down a few levels that distinction starts to cloud. It's a difficult and time-consuming process in a big organization to transmit your beliefs down through the managerial layers to the people on the processing line.

Actual implementation of Project Paradise

The phase one studies began on time and were completed within the scheduled three weeks. Coleman and his teams worked exceptionally long days, with what was seen as enthusiasm and thoroughness. One team member recalled White's reaction when the 27 volumes, one for each OPG channel, were presented to him:

> White said that he usually wasn't surprised with the work that people produced because in the past everyone had really come through to give him what he wanted. This time he said, "I'm really impressed." I've known him now for over three years and I've never heard him give a compliment like that.

As phase two got under way, however, a problem arose. Some of Coleman's staff team members actually began arranging for physical changes. This came to light in September 1974, when Art Kirsch received a call from one of his personnel officers at 111 Wall Street. Kirsch explained what happened:

> The staff was actually implementing changes. One of the team guys was furiously racing around making space allocations and telling my people to get ready to move. This was supposed to be a staff study and all of a sudden I'm getting requests for office construction!
>
> I thought the implementation was premature, especially without the line involved. I was scared and went to see Wade Coleman. I told him it would be a disaster, but I didn't get anywhere. Wade had not been through the Area I blowups before, and moreover this was Area IV. You can really lose money faster in international money transfer than you can by blowing up DDA. With DDA the paperwork is around, you just have to find it. In IMT you could lose track of millions of dollars in the International transfer system and never locate it.
>
> Well, I and a number of line managers blew the whistle. We had a big meeting with Bob to review the whole situation. He questioned us very closely and got a good understanding of what was happening. He slowed it down.
>
> The next day when I came to work I found a little printed sign on my door that read, "A SHADOW IN PARADISE."

As a result of White's involvement in phase two it was formally announced for the first time that Dick Kane, head of Area IV, would be responsible for the implementation of Paradise through phases two and three.

Phase two proceeded with the decision to break out physically the WCG pieces from each channel first, then proceed to the IBG. At about this time, however, White had the luncheon meeting with George Vojta, head of IBG, to explain the Project Paradise concept. As a result,

White switched the priority, telling his managers to work on the IBG pieces first. In October 1974, White explained what had occurred:

> George Vojta wanted to get all nondirect customer contact activities out of his staff and concentrate solely on the customer field contact side of the business. He thought that this would be a great opportunity to do it. He will transfer almost 80 people to OPG and be left with no service activity.
>
> I thought it was opportune also, since it was consistent with what I was trying to do. By getting all the services into OPG, we can reorganize the *total* aspect of the support business to face off to the banking side of IBG.

As phase two progressed, evidence of the slowdown began to surface. Despite the fact that line managers had "signed off" on the phase one studies and had given their agreement to the breakouts and schedules for change, there seemed to be resistance when the actual changes began. One of the staff members who was ultimately to take line responsibility over several channels in the IBG Services Management unit described this as follows:

> It became clear we were not getting the support of line management in making these changes. They had signed off on the books that everything was in order but we still didn't get any cooperation. This happened in September, three-quarters of the way through the year and they had their goals and objectives for the year to meet. Then we came along and said that we wanted to change their world. Certain cost savings projects had to be shelved, others postponed, and so on.

A line manager saw the situation this way:

> I was just getting rolling with a big automation job in my channel, a project which had just been approved by my boss, when these staff guys from uptown come in with their notebooks. I ask them, "Where are you going to get the money to split out this channel?" and they say, "From your automation project." Like hell they are. . . .

Bob White's summary of this issue in October of 1974 was the following:

> Up until the time we started to split out the IBG pieces the whole project had been planning. Now we were ready to do it, but the line managers weren't. What happened was that the line people knew the study was going on because they all agreed to it—but they forgot about it while the study teams were in operation. We were ready to move and everyone in the line wanted to know what was happening. They just didn't keep on top of it.
>
> Coleman really couldn't implement the project in Kane's shop. The implementation really has to be done by the line, but the line can't do the initial study because they don't have the time or resources.

So we had to go through another stage of handing responsibility from the planning unit to another implementation unit. What seems to happen is that you plan what you're going to do and how to do it, and then start all over again planning, organizing, directing, and controlling the implementation with a different group of people.

Ideally you would like to keep up the intensity. Some people worked very hard for three or four weeks and got sick and took vacation because of the intensity. There has been a letdown and it has probably cost us a couple of months.

The situation in March 1975

As a result of these problems, the implementation of the planned changes was delayed. Where the original schedule called for the completion of the IBG breakout by January 31, 1975, in February it had been reset to April 1, 1975.

Then, in March, Bob White learned about the potential slip in the deadline for the phase three transfer of several channels from Area IV to Area II, where the new IBG Services Management unit was being created. White knew the transfers of responsibility in Project Paradise had taken their toll in terms of time, and that some slippage in the schedule had had to occur. The high degree of commitment and enthusiasm that characterized the study phase had appeared to wane as the leadership had shifted to the line. White had sensed the change of pace but felt now that some of it was probably inevitable. He also knew the line managers were getting extremely careful about receiving channels into the new organization, not wanting to be in charge if a blowup occurred.

Even though it was early in the year, there had already been a number of arguments over how much the receiving manager was to take of the responsibility for 1975 results improvement projects. Line managers in Area IV were busy with phase two breakouts as well as day-to-day operations. They argued it was unfair to charge them with a monthly proportion of targeted annual goals. The receiving managers argued that they should not be expected to make up more than, at most, a time-proportioned part of the targets. All the while, it was important that IBG Services Management be established and running smoothly when the transfer of Vojta's 80 customer service people took place. If there was delay beyond April 1, that arrangement might have to be changed.

Reflecting back on the evolution and planned change of OPG, White attached great importance to Project Paradise. Ironically, some of the very reasons for it to be possible to reintegrate operations into the bank, namely the tight control system, finely tuned and efficiently running operations, and motivated managers, now seemed to be blocking the way. He wanted to resolve problems of schedule slips, budget and target attainment and potential blowups in ways which would be consistent with the management control systems and management practices in OPG, would not impose unreasonable burdens on his people and would insure that Project Paradise was completed successfully.

Managing groups

One of the most pervasive of the several elements affecting the perspective and behavior of people in organizations is the emergent group.

In Chapter 6 concepts are discussed which can help a manager understand the structure and dynamics of groups and their effects on members. These concepts from the behavioral sciences provide a general vocabulary and framework, applicable to any group at any organizational level. In Chapter 6 these concepts are illustrated by application to a work group in which the manager is not a member and over which he or she has some authority. Guidelines are presented for taking action to change the behavior of one or more work-group members.

In Chapters 7 and 8 the concepts are extended to cover managerial groups. Chapter 7 focuses particularly on informal, emergent coalitions of managers, most similar to lower level work groups, and on the political behavior of such managerial groups. Chapter 8 focuses on managerial groups which are officially recognized by the organization and whose primary task is decision making. Although they are formal in this sense, it will be argued that the success of these groups and one's effectiveness as a member depends on recognition and management of subtle informal forces.

The cases in Part III include Case 6–1, The Slade Company, an old classic on work groups which is as relevant today as it was when written in the early 1960s. Cases on managerial politics are hard to come by. Cases 7–1 and 7–2, Dave Melton, present one individual's perspective on his personal political battle. Case 8–1, Textile Corporation of America, is also one person's view, but important inferences can be drawn about the managerial context. Cases 8–2 to 8–5, Bay Markets, provide the views of all parties in a major organizational shakeup.

Chapter 6

UNDERSTANDING AND MANAGING WORK GROUPS

Managers often overlook the impact of social forces generated by work groups on employees. In part this is because the social group is not part of the formal organization; it appears on no organization chart. In fact, group members themselves may be only dimly aware of the existence of group forces and informal rules. We may also overlook the importance groups because, as Leavitt (1975) has pointed out, our organizations are typically designed around individuals and we may not see the effects of emergent group forces on individuals because formal structures point our attention toward individuals.

The manager unfamiliar with the phenomenon may naturally assume an individual's attitude and behavior are the product of forces other than those deriving from the social aspects of the work group. Managers who are sensitive to the workings of these particular forces are in a much better position to understand the causes of a problem of morale or performance arising from individuals in a work group. Moreover, through the judicious management of the conditions promoting social work groups and of the communications with the members of such groups a manager has a potent means of influencing an employee's perspective, behavior, and work performance.

The phenomena of social work-group dynamics is as prevalent for groups of managers themselves as it is for employees at lower levels in organizations. In this chapter we ask the reader to consider the concepts and applications as though he or she were responsible for the group's performance but was not a member of the group. Nevertheless, the concepts apply to groups of managers such as might be found on a task force team, a high-level committee, or a board of directors. Managerial groups will be taken up in Chapters 7 and 8.

An illustrative situation

Imagine that you have just been given responsibility over the Design Department. This is a definite promotion over your previous job as manager of customer relations. Your predecessor was promoted to Product Development three weeks ago. Your new boss has just taken you to your new (and larger) office and introduced you to your new secretary and the five designers.

The designers work in the "bull pen" down the hall from your office, in half-partitioned cubicles around a central open space. As you met them you noticed that in their room there was a meeting table scattered with sketches and specifications, a blackboard, assorted slip charts and corkboards, a drafting table, a computer terminal, and in a corner a small refrigerator with a coffee maker on top. Due to the chronic shortage of office space your new secretary's desk is in this same room, just by the door into the hall which is the only entrance and exit.

As your boss introduced you to the designers you noted that he stumbled with the names of all but George and Jon. The other three, Margaret, David, and Reuben, were noticeably younger (in their 20s) than George and Jon. George was wearing a company tie pin for 20 years of service.

You are delighted to get Diana as a secretary. She is known as a no-nonsense "old timer" who knows everyone and gets things done. In your new office for the first time, you called Diana over the intercom to the bull pen and asked quite politely for coffee for you and your boss. Ten minutes later, as your boss was leaving, she came in and, without a word, left two cups on the lamp table by the door. " 'No-nonsense Diana,' " you thought.

About all your boss could tell you about the department was that George had been there eight years, having transferred from another division, and John had been there four years. He knew these two because from time to time they had made presentations to the New Products Committee. Otherwise, he expressed satisfaction with the work of the department up to now. He admitted with some pride that inasmuch as things had gone so well he had been content to run things strictly through your predecessor, now thousands of miles away. As he left, he pointed out that your most immediate task would be to finish the design of the new "Veritas" line of products on time, i.e., in two months.

Because George had the most seniority, you called him in and asked him to give you a briefing the next day on the substance and current status of the Veritas job. You noticed that George appeared nervous, but he agreed to do it.

The next day George's presentation was a shocking disappointment. Again he was obviously uneasy. After a while he showed you some of the designs on the Veritas line and spoke briefly about the problems encountered so far. When you questioned him on schedules and deadlines, his answers were vague. He reported there was not much of a formal schedule, and could only say, with a tense determination that sounded like a challenge, "We'll make it."

You ended the discussion with George, feeling frustrated, slightly bewildered, and more than a little concerned about the project and what to do next. Your confidence and enthusiasm were momentarily undermined. "What's going on?" you asked yourself. Reluctant to take further action without a little more thought, you decided to take George's personnel file home for study. You were about to call Diana to get it for you when a mental picture of the bull pen crossed your mind: everyone around that table, probably talking about . . . . On an impulse, you decided to take the files on all *six* people home for study, and to get them from personnel yourself.

FORMATION AND PERSISTENCE OF GROUPS

Most managers know from experience that whenever employees are required to work closely with one another, the individuals in time develop attitudes and exhibit behavioral patterns differing from what they would have if they worked alone. These perspectives and behavior are also different from the behavior required of them by the organization to do their jobs. These perspectives and behavior patterns emerge from or are facilitated by the physical proximity of the people, the jobs they are required to do, the way they are treated by their supervisors, the incentives of the control and reward systems, and their individual personalities and skills. Although we may identify and assess these given conditions or inputs, taken singly or collectively they are inadequate to explain the persistence of emergent perspectives and behaviors. In order to explain them, we refer to the collection of individuals as an emergent group.

Input conditions to emergent work group formation

The input or background conditions which set the stage for the formation of emergent work groups in organizations may be clustered into three conceptual categories. These have been presented in our overview model in Chapter 1.

1. The outer environment of the organization.
2. The inner environment, consisting of the formal strategy, policies, authority structure, control systems, and management practices within the organization; and the nature of the technology, tasks, and physical layout of the factory, offices, or other work place.
3. The characteristics of the individual members of the group themselves: their skills; personalities; and whatever perspective of assumptions, perceptions, and feelings they may bring to the job.

Whether or not an emergent work group develops and how strong its influence over its members is a function of these three input conditions. We will not go into a detailed description of these input conditions. This is available elsewhere, particularly in Homans (1950) and Athos and Coffey (1968). For practical purposes, we want however to emphasize a number of aspects of these conditions.

Regular face-to-face contact is obviously necessary for the formation and continuation of an emergent group. This is typically determined for work groups by the physical layout. But even where people can see each other and communicate, the strength and nature of the group's influence on its members will depend on whether the required jobs its members perform are interdependent or independent and whether or not the work and the supervision permit communication and joint decision making among the employees. Note that in the case of the Design Department both the physical layout and the nature of the job are highly conducive to communications and mutual help. There is also evidence that there has been very little formal supervision of the design group: the boss's office is physically separated and down the hall, the group has no formal leader, and the boss's boss (your new boss) has let things run without feeling the necessity for much involvement of his own. This combination of layout, task, and supervision virtually ensures that an emergent group will form. It does not, of course, suggest whether the group will exhibit emergent behavior which is productive or wasteful, from management's viewpoint.

The personal characteristics of potential group members will also influence the structure of the emergent group and the way it functions. Suppose that as you reviewed the personnel files of your six subordinates in the Design Department you found the information given in Figure 6–1. Looking at readily available data such as these, a manager should ask to what extent these individuals have characteristic skills and motivations that promote or inhibit a strong emergent group. Note, for example, that there is the wide range in age, experience, and tenure with the company, and that the three younger individuals have a great deal in common. Moreover, note that the range of training and experience is somewhat inversely related: the oldest member of the

FIGURE 6–1
Selected information on Design Department personnel

Diana—secretary: 52, with company 20 years, in Design Department 8 years, widowed, three grown children, secretarial high school.

George: 50, with company 22 years, in Design Department 8 years, three grown children, very active in community affairs, technical school certificate in design.

Jon: 42, with company 10 years, in Design Department 4 years, divorced and now living alone, studying for MBA in night school, degree in industrial administration.

Margaret: 25, hired into Design Department 2 years ago, married, master's degree in design.

David: 23, hired into Design Department 1 year ago right out of college, master's degree in design, single.

Reuben: 27, with company 3 years, transferred to Design Department from Engineering two years ago, married, degree in design.

---

designers, George, has the least education and the younger members have full or advanced degrees. This might suggest some degree of incompatibility, at least initially, among the individuals as a total group, as well as the possible formation of a *subgroup* by the younger and newer members. Nevertheless, you also know the group has worked together for some time, in a closed setting. This suggests that differences among them which would lead to conflicts would either have been settled in some way, would have upset the work output, or would have caused people to leave.

Given that your boss expressed satisfaction with the work performance of the Design Department and that there has been no turnover, we can assume that in this case none of the potential dysfunctional outcomes resulting from certain apparent individual incompatibilities have become permanent. It would be safe to infer that the Design Department comprises a strong emergent group in which the people have learned to handle their differences. Moreover, the fact that the work requires the designers to collaborate and that there may be important *complementary* skills among these individuals suggest that these people would be very likely to have formed such a strong emergent group.

Why emergent groups form and persist

Up to this point we have more or less asserted that emergent groups often form in organizations and that they have important effects on the perspectives and behavior of their members. But why is this so? Where does the influence among peers come from?

To answer this we shall look more closely at the third category of input conditions, the individual members themselves. Using our illustrative example, we have discussed the effects on group formation of individuals' skills and some characteristics which a manager can readily learn about. It is important to note that people bring not only their skills to the work place, but their whole personality, including psychological needs and motivations. It is to this level that we must turn to explain why groups emerge when conditions in the work place permit it and why they often have such a persistent pervasive effect on their members.

In terms of Maslow's need hierarchy (as described, for example, in McGregor's *The Human Side of Enterprise,* 1960), social groups can most obviously serve to fulfill *social* needs. Membership in a group can, however, be very valuable in satisfying to some extent *all* the needs in Maslow's list. When the combined group effort contributes to the successful accomplishment of the task—in organization terms—it is likely that individual members will be rewarded by management through salary increases, promotion possibilities, etc. Members can thus increase the satisfaction of *material* and *security* needs. *Ego* and *self-fulfillment* needs can also be satisfied through the group. For instance, members may show respect to each other for the particular complementary skills, abilities, and so on they bring to the group. Or, they may encourage and help each other to develop those capabilities which each person considers to be essential to self-fulfillment. Thus, the emergent social group in organizations can serve the function of satisfying the personal needs of members. The reason for the existence of these groups is rooted in human psychology, and this fact helps explain the persistence and pervasiveness of the group as a force affecting individual behavior. (We shall discuss concepts for understanding individual personality more fully in Chapter 11.)

Emergent groups may also serve the important function of helping individuals cope with their environment. Under conditions of an oppressive boss, or a very difficult and demanding job, people band together to share sentiments and develop implicit and explicit joint tactics for dealing with the environment.

Thus, the emergent group in an organization comes about as a means for individuals to achieve some personal ends, namely psychological need satisfaction or coping. In some instances these needs will differ and may even conflict, as when two members both seek ego-fulfillment through informal leadership power in a group. In other instances needs may be complementary, as when two members seek satisfaction of a need for emotional security or coping in a highly stressful job by banding together to provide mutual reassurance and support. In view of such differences in individual members' needs, not to mention the wide differences in the other input condition categories, it is little wonder that different emergent groups go through different processes of evolution and have very different characteristics once established.

Although it is virtually impossible to predict in advance the precise behaviors and characteristics of emergent groups, we can say with certainty that whenever the input conditions make it at all feasible, emergent groups will develop and will have strong effects on their members.

We invite the reader to turn again to Figure 6–1 and to make some hypotheses about what the needs and motivations of the people in the Design Department might be. Which of these could best be satisfied by membership in a strong and cohesive emergent work group? As an example let us take Jon. Being divorced and now living alone, we can assume that a socially cohesive group would provide him with an opportunity to satisfy some of his social needs, like belonging and giving and receiving friendship. From his degree in industrial administration and the fact that he is taking MBA classes in night school, we could conclude that he sees himself as more of an administrator than a designer. The Design Department could then represent the particular context in which he tries out his management skill. If this skill is recognized by the other members of the group as being useful and complementary to their own interests, it is likely that Jon will gain respect and recognition (satisfaction of ego-needs) for his contributions and at the same time be encouraged to develop this ability further and grow in his ability and mastery as an administrator (satisfaction of self-fulfillment needs).

Although each of the three input conditions has to be described and assessed separately with respect to its impact on the formation of emergent groups, it is the extent of fit *among* the conditions which is most important. Thus, an incompatible collection of individuals with widely different skills and needs may nevertheless form a strong group when given a challenging task which interests them and cannot be performed easily alone. Conversely, if the task and working conditions do not promote it, individuals with similar backgrounds may become competitive, failing to form a cohesive, compatible group.

A manager seeking to understand such things as whether an emergent group exists, who is getting what out of it, and whether it is beneficial to performance faces a messy analytical challenge. Achieving a useful understanding requires at least as much intuitive guesswork as systematic, logical reasoning. The manager must be content with forming and testing hypotheses rather than drawing permanent conclusions. Being good at this kind of process is in itself an acquired managerial skill.

At this point the reader should work through the three input conditions outlined above in the context of a particular experience he or she has had or observed. What characteristics of each condition contributed to or prevented the creation of a strong emergent group? What interactions among the conditions added to or detracted from the net effect of these forces on creating and sustaining a strong group?

QUALITIES OF ESTABLISHED EMERGENT GROUPS

What characteristics of emergent groups should interest a manager who seeks to understand the influence such groups have on their members and who wants to affect the behavior of members?

As a group forms and develops over time, certain unwritten rules or *norms* come about to regulate the behavior of the members. Most often norms are not explicitly stated and operate almost on an unconscious level. They represent the "way things are done around here," how members of the group "should" behave. Group members make these norms quite clear to a newcomer, and there is often a process of socialization or joining up for newcomers who must learn the norms before they are accepted as full-fledged members. Some examples of norms are: one helps out others when they get behind in their work; we do not gossip about each other; don't talk religion; finish work at ten minutes to five; stay late for an occasional rush job; only do so much work each day; work in shirt-sleeves without a tie; and so on.

All emergent groups also have an *internal social structure* or "pecking order." Each of the membership slots has an implied status, and incumbents may be expected to play certain roles. The status and roles may be very different from that given by the formal organization. One or occasionally two members of the group become the informal leaders and have great influence in establishing and enforcing the norms. The higher status of informal leaders is derived from their characteristics and capabilities in terms of things the group values, such as seniority, expertise in their task, educational background, championship of the local bowling team, or whatever. Other people are "regular" members. Still others are "marginal members," living on the edges of the group, not fully participating in the group's life, even violating some norms. "Deviants" and "rate busters" are examples of marginal members of the internal social structure.

Thus, a group member's perspective on work and his or her behavior on the job is heavily affected by the person's position in the internal social structure and by the norms of the group. The stronger or more *cohesive* the group the more pervasive and encompassing these effects are. In the strongest of work groups the effects extend to social and recreational activities off the job as well as to work-related perspectives and behavior.

Returning once again to our illustration of the Design Department, it should be evident at this point that the input conditions are very conducive to the creation of a rather strong emergent group, with its own norms and internal social structure. Coming in from the outside, it is virtually impossible for you, the new manager, to be aware of the norms and pecking order within the Design Department. Most emergent groups develop norms on how to deal with their formal supervisor. Being in the dark about these as well, you may have—with the best of intentions—unwittingly violated some norms which the group had been applying to its previous manager.

It might well be, for example, that in the Design Department a norm existed that "everybody, including the boss, gets his own coffee." It probably takes Diana little time to straighten that out with most newcomers. Her delay and behavior in delivering your coffee might well have been a subtle way of trying to enforce the norm on a special newcomer, the new boss. Hopefully you have not touched a nerve so sensitive that she is now considering a sex discrimination grievance.

When you asked George for the presentation on the status of the Veritas product line, you did so out of the logic that he had the most seniority. Suppose however that either administrative skills or design creativity and not seniority are the criteria by which status is granted in the Design Department group. If that is the case and if we assume that Jon is the one with the administrative skills and, say, Margaret is the most creative designer, it would follow that George is more likely to be a regular or marginal member of the group and that quite possibly Jon and Margaret are the informal leaders. One can't be totally certain, but in retrospect George's reaction to your request suggests that he was the wrong person to ask. It may well be that George was uneasy because he did not want to upstage Jon, for example, or it may be that George really is not tuned in and simply is not up on the work. His parting phrase, "We'll make it," could be taken as an indication that he is tuned in but feels he is the wrong person to make the report.

IMPLICATIONS FOR MANAGEMENT

A manager cannot know all there is to know about the nature of emergent group norms and the internal structure. Moreover, one can never be absolutely certain that one's inferred, qualitative description of norms and relationships is valid. What is certain is that emergent groups are very often put there and are powerful forces in organizations. As Leavitt (1975, p. 70) puts it:

Groups are natural phenomena, and facts of organizational life. They can be created but their spontaneous development cannot be prevented. The problem is not shall groups exist or not, but shall groups be planned or not?

Knowledge about these groups and understanding of them is often of great importance, but just the first step for a manager who wishes to influence individuals in groups and to make use of groups for getting results.

To make practical use of our knowledge about groups it should be clear first of all that a group has enormous influence on its members. The group has the power to reward and punish its members, particularly those members who value their association with the group highly. In an organizational sense, the group exercises *control* over some significant part of the behavior of its members. This informal control varies in its intensity and exists in addition to formal organizational control. This means that the emergent norms can supplement the formal rules as well as compete or conflict with them. From a management perspective therefore, group influence can be either desirable or undesirable.

Another implication is that when members of a highly cohesive work group engage in certain activities, task related or not, they frequently do so with more energy and motivation than if they were acting alone. A strong group offers potential for productive synergistic effort sustained over time without the need for elaborate formal controls. The total effect of peer pressure can be very powerful indeed. The other side of this promising potential is that the energy may well not be directed toward goals that are congruent with those of management. Moreover, it should be noted that a group member can feel coercion from peer pressure as well as exhilaration from belonging.

Another implication is that emergent groups may be unstable over time. This is partly because their norms and structure are controlled by the group itself, rather than by formal organizational rules and structures, and partly because the purpose of such groups is typically as much social and coping as it is task related. For these reasons, a group may change its orientation toward work. From management's viewpoint, there needs to be careful understanding of the nature of a particular group's purpose, norms, and structure to predict these shifts in work performance and to take them into account.

Finally, the emergent group can be a source of valuable creativity, particularly when the task requires a creative solution and the members of the group collectively have the necessary skills and knowledge to tackle it. This creativity may be directed toward solving a complex problem which affects the group or some of its members, in figuring out ways to beat the system, and so forth. Whatever the group's purpose or goals, creativity becomes a resource at the group's disposal which does not exist when individual members act alone.

Should a manager responsible for organizational outcomes consider emergent groups as beneficial or as detrimental? By now, it should be clear that this depends on whether the group's norms, its goals, and the impact on the behavior of members contribute to or detract from organizational goals, both now and in the future. Seashore (1954) provided a useful way of thinking about the potential problems or benefits of strong, cohesive emergent work groups, as illustrated in Figure 6–2.

FIGURE 6–2
Relationship of peer-group loyalty to average productivity of group members

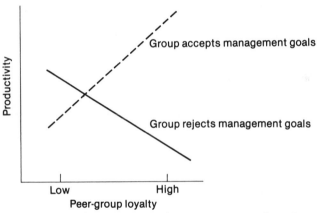

Source: Rensis Likert, *New Patterns of Management,* (New York: McGraw-Hill, 1961), p. 32.

The graph suggests that when emergent work groups accept management goals (i.e., their norms incorporate management goals) productivity increases in a way directly related to the extent of peer-group loyalty (or group cohesiveness). In other words, the more members of an emergent work group value group norms and internal social structure and the more they consider the organizational outcomes defined by management as desirable goals for their group, the higher their productivity (see dotted line). The reverse occurs when the group rejects management goals: in that case the greater peer-group loyalty or cohesiveness, the lower group pressure for productivity. In short, when a cohesive group is "with" management it can be very productive, and when it is against management it can be horrid!

Let us return to our Design Department and develop two short scenarios to illustrate this point. Suppose that your group of new subordinates has developed a set of work-related norms which puts a premium on good quality designs and which say one should either take work home or stay overtime when target dates have to be met. Suppose also that it has an internal social structure which allows its members to contribute their respective skills to doing a good job. Contrast this to a scenario in which the norms encourage members to work just hard enough to avoid management's suspicion and to keep one's best ideas to oneself, and a social structure in which status is derived from skill at avoiding work. As the new manager of the group, you would certainly want to know which of these was closer to the truth before you did anything that might seriously upset the group's functioning.

DESIGNING AND MANAGING WORK GROUPS

The cohesive work group's potential for improving productivity and quality and promoting the satisfaction and growth of its members has been widely recognized. Efforts are underway today in many organizations to encourage the development of emergent work groups which have goals compatible with management's aims. These efforts are variously known as job enrichment, work restructuring, or organizational development. The Volvo program, using teams to assemble automobiles, is perhaps the most widely recognized example. For a review of that and some other efforts, see Walton (1975).

What guidelines can help a manager whose task it is to achieve organizational results through emergent workgroups? The managerial task here is to influence the behavior of the members of one or more work groups, whether they be new or already in existence.

A manager can influence the behavior of group members by making use of one or more of the three forms of influence described in Chapter 2: direct influence, semidirect influence, and indirect influence. These correspond to attention to individuals, to the group as a whole, and to the inputs to the group. Let us examine each of these in turn.

By communicating with individual members one-on-one, a manager may affect that individual's behavior. For all the importance of pervasive social forces affecting group members, it should not be forgotten that individuals can also be influenced directly. This would be the preferred approach if it were clear that that individual was the source of a problem hurting the work group from management's point of view, or if the individual were the leader of the group.

Second, communication aimed at influencing behavior can be directed to the group as a whole. This general approach puts the manager in the "intervention" role and constitutes the approach of the "organizational development" school. The typical scenario is an informal group meeting, in which the partial or complete topic for discussion is not the work itself. Rather, the topic is either the strategy or general approach to the work which the group is using or wants to use, or the nature of the interpersonal relationships among group members. Hackman and Kaplan (1974) have pointed out that it is unusual for a group to engage in discussing these topics on their own. This may be because the typical perspective of members is "to get the job done," and therefore to ignore the potential usefulness of talking about how to plan and proceed (strategy) or what interpersonal conflicts may be blocking group work.

It is important to note that a discussion about interpersonal conflict and relationships can be very tension producing and quite possibly dysfunctional to the group's work. An emergent group which has been left to its own devices inevitably develops norms about how the matter of interpersonal difficulties are dealt with. They *may* have evolved ways of confronting and discussing openly their differences, but that would be very unusual. More often, such issues are avoided or suppressed or handled in subtle ways, such as by just the right touch of humor with a "needle." The clear implication of this is that an interventionist should only open this kind of topic if he or she is thoroughly familiar with the norms, if the work-related problem which calls for intervention can be traced to problems of relationships, and if the interventionist is skilled and patient enough to invest the energy that will be required to rework some of the central norms.

The time for this kind of semidirect influence, intervention, or organization development effort is toward the beginning of the group's life. For example, a project team may make use of meetings in which the purpose is partly to discuss how they will proceed with the work. Such team-building sessions can be valuable ways of getting the work group off on the right start, and an opportunity for the manager to share what he or she knows about the work. Even here, however, we believe the starting point for discussion should be the task itself and strategies for dealing with the task. Only secondarily should the topic of relationships be a focus.

Finally, management may influence a group in an indirect way, through the design, selection, and modification of the key inputs. Hackman (1977) provides a very practical guide to analysis and design of work for groups. The key guidelines which apply to inputs in our overview model are the following:

1. Pay considerable attention to the design of the work or task which the group is to perform. It obviously makes little sense to have a group responsible for something if the technology or work itself is not suited to group work, just as it would make no sense to mass produce a simple part, needed in small quantities, which was going into inventory and could be turned out on a single machine. Hackman has

pointed out elsewhere, in an article entitled, "On the Coming Demise of Job Enrichment," (1975), that the movement of job enrichment based on groups may die for the wrong reasons, including the fact that work is not restructured to fit what groups are capable of doing better than individuals.

2. As much as possible, adapt the formal inputs and structures to the group level rather than the individual level. This includes, particularly, the compensation system. Pay rewards which are intended as incentives or merit increases should be contingent on the performance of the group as a whole, rather than individuals within it. Leavitt (1975, p. 72) has put it this way:

> Just what does it mean to design organizations around groups? . . . One approach to an answer is simply to take the things organizations do with individuals and try them out with groups. The idea is to raise the level from the atom to the molecule, and *select* groups rather than individuals, *train* groups rather than individuals, *pay* groups rather than individuals, *promote* groups rather than individuals, *design jobs* for groups rather than individuals, *fire* groups rather than individuals, and so on down the list of activities which organizations have traditionally carried on in order to use human beings in their organizations.

3. Another important design issue is the autonomy of the group, that is, the extent to which members feel they truly have control over the work and are free to make certain decisions about it. One particular issue is the behavior of the group's immediate supervisor. In many of the group-oriented job enrichment schemes which are currently being tried, problems arise in retraining foremen and other managers in direct contact with the work group. Their role must be less one of day-to-day close supervision and more one of "managing the boundary" of the group. That is, the supervisor's role becomes one of providing resources, managing the relationships between the work group and other parts of the organization, and in effect being a source of support rather than formal control for the group.

In taking action toward work groups, a manager should consider all these options, including simultaneous action which is a combination of all three forms of influence.

As a final note, managers should have in mind a model of the particular characteristics of the group they are in charge of, using the concepts of input conditions contributing to emergent group formation and the concepts of norms and internal social structure discussed in this note. The refining of such a model must be continuous and carefully done both because most of the data are indirect, qualitative, and judgmental and because emergent work groups are subject to considerable change over time. Key questions for diagnosis and model building include the following:

1. What behavior of group members is desirable, given organizational goals?
2. What group norms are or will be consistent or inconsistent with the achievement of those goals?
3. What individual needs are being satisfied or will be satisfied if the members of the emergent work group conform to the norms?
4. How can we replace members' satisfaction from conforming to the group norms, in case these norms result in behavior dysfunctional to organizational goals?
5. Is management as a whole and in individual instances, powerful enough to influence the group directly?

CONCLUSION

In view of their potential power, perhaps the word which best summarizes a guiding approach for the management of emergent groups is *patience*. This is particularly important in those instances where a work group has been cooperative with management but where changes in the technology, the market, or the company's overall strategy require changes in behavior. In such an instance change can be encouraged and can be expected to evolve in time.

QUESTIONS FOR STUDY AND DISCUSSION

1. What are some of the means a manager can make use of to promote the formation of constructive emergent group norms and status?
2. What kind of training and experience should a manager have in order to identify and deal with the phenomenon of emergent groups?
3. The best time for intervention to influence groups is at the beginning of their formation. How can a new manager react to and affect an already established group?
4. List the names of at least three other people with whom you interact at work or socially at least once a week. What would you say are the norms of the group that are most important in influencing members' perspectives and behavior?
   What behavior, rewards, and activities does the group value most?
   What is the primary task which the group is required to carry out either as a direct mandate from an organization or in terms of its own purposes?
   To what extent do the norms and values support or inhibit the accomplishment of the group's task?
5. For the group which you described in question 4, list the roles or functions of a formal and informal nature which at least three of the members fulfill.
   What would you say is the pecking order or hierarchy of status of these members? Does the status order relate constructively or destructively to

the roles and functions in terms of their importance in carrying out the group's tasks?

How would you rate the quality of your group's communications with each other? If you think the communications need improvement, make a list of specific steps you or others in the group could take to improve these communications through a discussion of that problem within the group.

Case 6–1
The Slade Company*

Ralph Porter, production manager of The Slade Company, was concerned by reports of dishonesty among some employees in the Plating Department. From reliable sources, he had learned that a few men were punching the time cards of a number of their workmates who had left early. Mr. Porter had only recently joined the Slade organization. He judged from the conversations with the previous production manager and other fellow managers that they were, in general, pleased with the overall performance of the Plating Department.

The Slade Company was a prosperous manufacturer of metal products designed for industrial application. Its manufacturing plant, located in central Michigan, employed nearly 500 workers, who were engaged in producing a large variety of clamps, inserts, knobs, and similar items. Orders for these products were usually large and on a recurrent basis. The volume of orders fluctuated in response to business conditions in the primary industries which the company served. At the time of this case, sales volume had been high for over a year. The bases upon which The Slade Company secured orders, in rank of importance, were quality, delivery, and reasonable price.

The organization of manufacturing operations at the Slade plant is shown in Exhibit 1. The departments listed there are, from left to right, approximately in the order in which material flowed through the plant. The diemaking and setup operations required the greatest degree of skill, supplied by highly paid, long-service craftsmen. The finishing departments, divided operationally and geographically between plating and painting, attracted less highly trained but relatively skilled workers, some of whom had been employed by the company for many years. The remaining operations were largely unskilled in nature and were characterized by relatively low pay and high turnover of personnel.

The plating room was the sole occupant of the top floor of the plant. Exhibit 2 shows the floor plan, the disposition of workers, and the flow of work throughout the department. Thirty-eight men and women worked in the department, plating or oxidizing the metal parts or preparing parts for the application of paint at another location in the plant. The department's work occurred in response to orders communicated by production schedules which were revised daily. Schedule revisions, caused by last-minute order increases or rush requests from customers, resulted in short-term volume fluctuations, particularly in the plating, painting, and shipping departments. Exhibit 3 outlines the ac-

---

* All names have been disguised.

EXHIBIT 1
Manufacturing organization

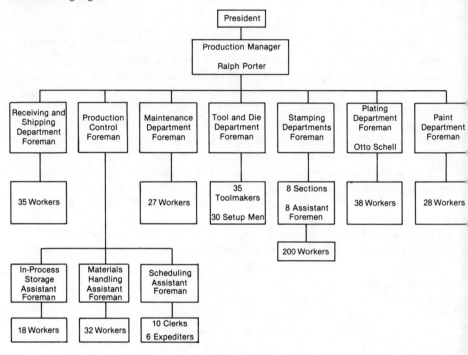

tivities of the various jobs, their interrelationships, and the type of work in which each specialized. Exhibit 4 rates the various types of jobs in terms of the technical skill, physical effort, discomfort, and training time associated with their performance.

Activities in the plating room were of three main types:

1. Acid dipping, in which parts were etched by being placed in baskets which were manually immersed and agitated in an acid solution.
2. Barrel tumbling, in which parts were roughened or smoothed by being loaded into machine-powered revolving drums containing abrasive, caustic, or corrosive solutions.
3. Plating—either manual, in which parts were loaded on racks and were immersed by hand through the plating sequence; or automatic, in which racks or baskets were manually loaded with parts, then carried by a conveyor system through the plating sequence.

Within these main divisions, there were a number of variables, such as cycle times, chemical formulas, abrasive mixtures, and so forth, which distinguished particular jobs as they have been categorized in Exhibit 3.

XHIBIT 2
lating room layout

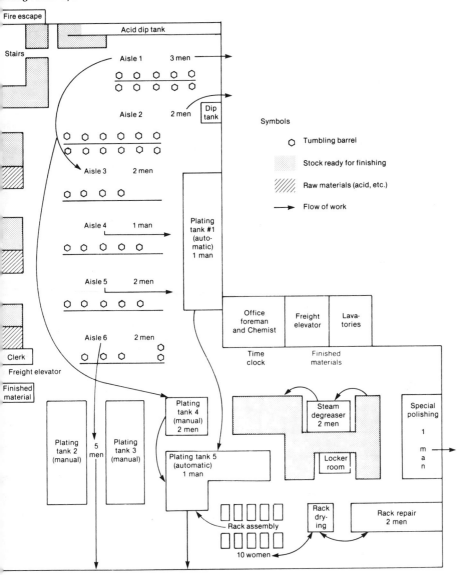

The work of the plating room was received in batch lots whose size averaged 1,000 pieces. The clerk moved each batch, which was accompanied by a routing slip, to its first operation. This routing slip indicated the operations to be performed and when each major operation on the batch was scheduled to be completed, so that the finished product

EXHIBIT 3
Outline of work flow, plating room

Aisle 1: Worked closely with Aisle 3 in preparation of parts by barrel tumbling and acid dipping for high-quality plating in Tanks 4 and 5.* Also did a considerable quantity of highly specialized, high-quality acid-etching work not requiring further processing.

Aisle 2: Tumbled items of regular quality and design in preparation for painting. Less frequently, did oxidation dipping work of regular quality, but sometimes of special design, not requiring further processing.

Aisle 3: Worked closely with Aisle 1 on high-quality tumbling work for Tanks 4 and 5.

Aisles 4, 5: Produced regular tumbling work for Tank 1.

Aisle 6: Did high-quality tumbling work for special products plated in Tanks 2 and 3.

Tank 1: Worked on standard, automated plating of regular quality not further processed in plating room, and regular work further processed in Tank 5.

Tanks 2, 3: Produced special, high-quality plating work not requiring further processing.

Tank 4: Did special, high-quality plating work further plated in Tank 5.

Tank 5: Automated production of high- and regular-quality, special- and regular-design plated parts sent directly to shipping.

Rack assembly: Placed parts to be plated in Tank 5 on racks.

Rack repair: Performed routine replacement and repair of racks used in Tank 5.

Polishing: Processed, by manual or semimanual methods, odd-lot special orders which were sent directly to shipping. Also, sorted and reclaimed parts rejected by inspectors in the shipping department.

Degreasing: Took incoming raw stock, processed it through caustic solution, and placed clean stock in storage ready for processing elsewhere in the plating room.

* Definition of terms: *High or regular quality:* The quality of finishes could broadly be distinguished by the thickness of plate and/or care in preparation. *Regular or special work:* The complexity of work depended on the routine or special character of design and finish specifications.

EXHIBIT 4
Skill indices by job group*

Jobs	Technical skill required	Physical effort required	Degree of discomfort involved	Degree of training required†
Aisle 1	1	1	1	1
Tanks 2–4	3	2	1	2
Aisles 2–6	5	1	1	5
Tank 5	1	5	7	2
Tank 1	8	5	5	7
Degreasing	9	3	7	10
Polishing	6	9	9	7
Rack assembly and repair	10	10	10	10

* Rated on scales of 1 (the greatest) to 10 (the least) in each category.
† The amount of experience required to assume complete responsibility for the job.

could be shipped on time. From the accumulation of orders before him, each man was to organize his own work schedule so as to make optimal use of equipment, materials, and time. Upon completion of an order, each man moved the lot to its next work position or to the finished material location near the freight elevator.

The plating room was under the direct supervision of the foreman, Otto Schell, who worked a regular 8:00 A.M. to 5:00 P.M. day, five days a week. The foreman spent a good deal of his working time attending to maintenance and repair of equipment, procuring supplies, handling late schedule changes, and seeing that his people were at their proper work locations.

Working conditions in the plating room varied considerably. That part of the department containing the tumbling barrels and the plating machines was constantly awash, alternately with cold water, steaming acid, or caustic soda. Men working in this part of the room wore knee boots, long rubber aprons, and high-gauntlet rubber gloves. This uniform, consistent with the general atmosphere of the "wet" part of the room, was hot in the summer, cold in winter. In contrast, the remainder of the room was dry, was relatively odor-free, and provided reasonably stable temperature and humidity conditions for those who worked there.

The men and women employed in the plating room are listed in Exhibit 5. This exhibit provides a certain personal data on each department member, including a productivity-skill rating (based on subjective and objective appraisals of potential performance), as reported by the members of the department.

The pay scale implied by Exhibit 5 was low for the central Michigan area. The average starting wage for factory work in the community was about $1.25. However, working hours for the plating room were long (from 60 hours to a possible and frequently available 76 hours per week). The first 60 hours (the normal five-day week) were paid for on straight-time rates. Saturday work was paid for at time and one half; Sunday pay was calculated on a double-time basis.

As Exhibit 5 indicates, Philip Kirk, a worker in Aisle 2, provided the data for this case. After he had been a member of the department for several months, Kirk noted that certain members of the department tended to seek each other out during free time on and off the job. He then observed that these informal associations were enduring, built upon common activities and shared ideas about what was and what was not legitimate behavior in the department. His estimate of the pattern of these associations is diagrammed in Exhibit 6.

The Sarto group, so named because Tony Sarto was its most respected member and the one who acted as arbiter between the other members, was the largest in the department. The group, except for Louis Patrici, Al Bartolo, and Frank Bonzani (who spelled each other

EXHIBIT 5 Plating room personnel

Location	Name	Age	Marital status	Company seniority (years)	Department seniority (years)	Pay	Education*	Familial relationships	Productivity-skill rating†
Aisle 1	Tony Sarto	30	M	13	13	$1.50	HS	Louis Patrici, uncle Pete Facelli, cousin	1
	Pete Facelli	26	M	8	8	1.30	HS	Louis Patrici, uncle Tony Sarto, cousin	2
Aisle 2	Joe Iambi	31	M	5	5	1.20	2 yrs. HS		2
	Herman Schell	48	S	26	26	1.45	GS	Otto Schell, brother	8
Aisle 3	Philip Kirk	23	M	1	1	0.90	College		—‡
	Dom Pantaleoni	31	M	10	10	1.30	1 yr. HS		2
Aisle 4	Sal Maletta	32	M	12	12	1.30	3 yrs. HS		3
	Bob Pearson	22	S	4	4	1.15	HS	Father in tool and die dept.	1
Aisle 5	Charlie Malone	44	M	22	8	1.25	GS		7
Aisle 6	John Lacey	41	S	9	5	1.20	1 yr. HS	Brother in paint dept.	7
	Jim Martin	30	S	7	7	1.25	HS		4
	Bill Mensch	41	M	6	2	1.10	GS		4
Tank 1	Henry LaForte	38	M	14	6	1.25	HS		6
Tanks 2, 3	Ralph Parker	25	S	7	7	1.25	HS		4
	Ed Harding	27	S	8	8	1.20	HS		4
	George Flood	22	S	5	5	1.15	HS		5
	Harry Clark	29	M	8	8	1.20	HS		3
Tank 4	Tom Bond	25	S	6	6	1.20	HS		4
	Frank Bonzani	27	M	9	9	1.25	HS		2
	Al Bartolo	24	M	6	6	1.25	HS		3
Tank 5	Louis Patrici	47	S	14	14	1.45	2 yrs. college		1
Rack assembly	10 women	30–40	9M, 1S	10 (av.)	10 (av.)	1.05	GS (av.)	6 with husbands in company	4 (av.)
Rack maintenance	Will Partridge	57	M	14	2	1.20	GS	Tony Sarto, nephew	7
	Lloyd Swan	62	M	3	3	1.10	GS	Pete Facelli, nephew	7
Degreasing	Dave Susi	45	S	1	1	1.05	HS		5
	Mike Maher	41	M	4	4	1.05	GS		6
Polishing	Russ Perkins	49	M	12	2	1.20	HS		4
Foreman	Otto Schell	56	M	35	35	n.a.	HS	Herman Schell, brother	3
Clerk	Bill Pierce	32	M	10	4	1.15	HS		4
Chemist	Frank Rutlage	24	S	2	2	n.a.	2 yrs. college		6

* HS = High school, GS = Grade school.

XHIBIT 6
nformal groupings in the plating room

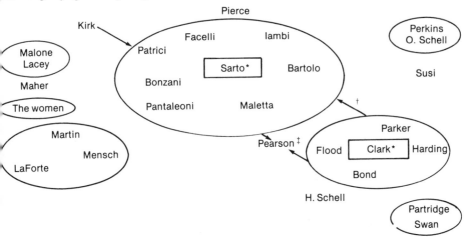

Pierce

Kirk

Facelli Iambi

Perkins
O. Schell

Malone
Lacey

Patrici

Maher

Bonzani

Sarto* Bartolo

Susi

The women

Pantaleoni Maletta

†

Parker

Martin

Pearson ‡

Flood Clark* Harding

Mensch

LaForte

Bond

H. Schell

Partridge
Swan

* The boxes indicate those men who clearly demonstrated leadership behavior (most closely personified the values hared by their groups, were most often sought for help and arbitration, and so forth).

† While the two- and three-man groupings had little informal contact outside their own boundaries, the five-man roup did seek to join the largest group in extraplant social affairs. There were relatively infrequent.

‡ Though not an active member of any group, Bob Pearson was regarded with affection by the two large groups.

during break periods), invariably ate lunch together on the fire escape near Aisle 1. On those Saturdays and Sundays when overtime work was required, the Sarto group operated as a team, regardless of weekday work assignments, to get overtime work completed as quickly as possible. (Few department members not affiliated with either the Sarto or the Clark groups worked on weekends.) Off the job, Sarto group members often joined in parties or weekend trips. Sarto's summer camp was a frequent rendezvous.

Sarto's group was also the most cohesive one in the department in terms of its organized punch-in and punch-out system. Since the men were regularly scheduled to work from 7:00 A.M. to 7:00 P.M. weekdays, and since all supervision was removed at 5:00 P.M., it was possible almost every day to finish a "day's work" by 5:30 and leave the plant. What is more, if one man were to stay until 7:00 P.M., he could punch the time cards of a number of men and help them gain free time without pay loss. (This system operated on weekends also, at which times members of supervision were present, if at all, only for short periods.) In Sarto's group the duty of staying late rotated, so that no man did so more than once a week. In addition, the group members would punch a man in in the morning if he were unavoidably delayed. However, such a practice never occurred without prior notice from the man who expected to be late and never if the tardiness was expected to last beyond 8:00 A.M., the start of the day for the foreman.

Sarto explained the logic behind the system to Kirk:

> You know that our hourly pay rate is quite low, compared to other companies. What makes this the best place to work is the feeling of security you get. No one ever gets laid off in this department. With all the hours in the week, all the company ever has to do is shorten the work week when orders fall off. We have to tighten our belts, but we can all get along. When things are going well, as they are now, the company is only interested in getting out the work. It doesn't help to get it out faster than it's really needed—so we go home a little early whenever we can. Of course, some guys abuse this sort of thing—like Herman—but others work even harder, and it averages out.
>
> Whenever an extra order has to be pushed through, naturally I work until 7:00 P.M. So do a lot of the others. I believe that if I stay until my work is caught up and my equipment is in good shape, that's all the company wants of me. They leave us alone and expect us to produce—and we do.

When Kirk asked Sarto if he would not rather work shorter hours at higher pay in a union shop (Slade employees were not organized), he just laughed and said: "It wouldn't come close to an even trade."

The members of Sarto's group were explicit about what constituted a fair day's work. Customarily, they cited Herman Schell, Kirk's work partner and the foreman's brother, as a man who consistently produced below that level. Kirk received an informal orientation from Herman during his first days on the job. As Herman put it:

> I've worked at this job for a good many years, and I expect to stay here a good many more. You're just starting out, and you don't know which end is up yet. We spend a lot of time in here; and no matter how hard we work, the pile of work never goes down. There's always more to take its place. And I think you've found out by now that this isn't light work. You can wear yourself out fast if you're not smart. Look at Pearson up in Aisle 4. There's a kid who's just going to burn himself out. He won't last long. If he thinks he's going to get somewhere working like that, he's nuts. They'll give him all the work he can take. He makes it tough on everybody else and on himself, too.

Kirk reported further on his observations of the department:

> As nearly as I could tell, two things seemed to determine whether or not Sarto's group or any others came in for weekend work on Saturday or Sunday. It seemed usually to be caused by rush orders that were received late in the week, although I suspect it was sometimes caused by the men having spent insufficient time on the job during the previous week.
>
> Tony and his group couldn't understand Herman. While Herman arrived late, Tony was always half an hour early. If there was a push to get out an extra amount of work, almost everyone but Herman would work

that much harder. Herman never worked overtime on weekends, while Tony's group and the men on the manual tanks almost always did. When the first exploratory time study of the department was made, no one in the aisles slowed down, except Herman, with the possible exception, to a lesser degree, of Charlie Malone. I did hear that the men in the dry end of the room slowed down so much you could hardly see them move; but we had little to do with them, anyway. While the men I knew best seemed to find a rather full life in their work, Herman never really got involved. No wonder they couldn't understand each other.

There was quite a different feeling about Bobby Pearson. Without the slightest doubt, Bob worked harder than anyone else in the room. Because of the tremendous variety of work produced, it was hard to make output comparisons, but I'm sure I wouldn't be far wrong in saying that Bob put out twice as much as Herman and 50 percent more than almost anyone else in the aisles. No one but Herman and a few old-timers at the dry end ever criticized Bobby for his efforts. Tony and his group seemed to feel a distant affection for Bob, but the only contact they or anyone else had with him consisted of brief greetings.

To the men in Tony's group the most severe penalty that could be inflicted on a man was exclusion. This they did to both Pearson and Herman. Pearson, however, was tolerated; Herman was not. Evidently, Herman felt his exclusion keenly, though he answered it with derision and aggression. Herman kept up a steady stream of stories concerning his attempts to gain acceptance outside the company. He wrote popular music which was always rejected by publishers. He attempted to join several social and athletic clubs, mostly without success. His favorite pastime was fishing. He told me that fishermen were friendly, and he enjoyed meeting new people whenever he went fishing. But he was particularly quick to explain that he preferred to keep his distance from the men in the department.

Tony's group emphasized more than just quantity in judging a man's work. Among them had grown a confidence that they could master and even improve upon any known finishing technique. Tony himself symbolized this skill. Before him, Tony's father had operated Aisle 1 and had trained Tony to take his place. Tony in his turn was training his cousin Pete. When a new finishing problem arose from a change in customer specifications, the foreman, the department chemist, or any of the men directly involved would come to Tony for help, and Tony would give it willingly. For example, when a part with a special plastic embossing was designed, Tony was the only one who could discover how to treat the metal without damaging the plastic. To a lesser degree, the other members of the group were also inventive about the problems which arose in their own sections.

Herman, for his part, talked incessantly about his feats in design and finish creations. As far as I could tell during the year I worked in the department, the objects of these stories were obsolete or of minor importance. What's more, I never saw any department member seek Herman's help.

Willingness to be of help was a trait Sarto's group prized. The most valued help of all was of a personal kind, though work help was also important. The members of Sarto's group were constantly lending and borrowing money, cars, clothing, and tools among themselves and, less frequently, with other members of the department. Their daily lunch bag procedure typified the "common property" feeling among them. Everyone's lunch was opened and added to a common pile, from which each member of the group chose his meal.

On the other hand, Herman refused to help others in any way. He never left his aisle to aid those near him who were in the midst of a rush of work or a machine failure, though this was customary throughout most of the department. I can distinctly recall the picture of Herman leaning on the hot and cold water faucets which were located directly above each tumbling barrel. He would stand gazing into the tumbling pieces for hours. To the passing, casual visitor, he looked busy; and as he told me, that's just what he wanted. He, of course, expected me to act this same way, and it was this enforced boredom that I found virtually intolerable.

More than this, Herman took no responsibility for breaking in his assigned helpers as they first entered the department, or thereafter. He had had four helpers in the space of little more than a year. Each had asked for a transfer to another department, publicly citing the work as cause, privately blaming Herman. Tony was the one who taught me the ropes when I first entered the department.

The men who congregated around Harry Clark tended to talk like and copy the behavior of the Sarto group, though they never approached the degree of inventive skill or the amount of helping activities that Tony's group did. They sought outside social contact with the Sarto group; and several times a year, the two groups went "on the town" together. Clark's group did maintain a high level of performance in the volume of work they turned out.

The remainder of the people in the department stayed pretty much to themselves or associated in pairs or triplets. None of these people were as inventive, as helpful, or as productive as Sarto's or Clark's groups, but most of them gave verbal support to the same values as those groups held.

The distinction between the two organized groups and the rest of the department was clearest in the punching-out routine. The women could not work past 3:00 P.M., so they were not involved. Malone and Lacey, Partridge and Swan, and Martin, La Forte, and Mensch arranged within their small groups for punch-outs, or they remained beyond 5:00 P.M. and slept or read when they finished their work. Perkins and Pierce went home when the foreman did. Herman Schell, Susi, and Maher had no punch-out organization to rely upon. Susi and Maher invariably stayed in the department until 7:00 P.M. Herman was reported to have established an arrangement with Partridge whereby the latter punched Herman out for a fee. Such a practice was unthinkable from the point of view of Sarto's group. It evidently did not occur often because Herman usually went to sleep behind piles of work when his brother left or, particularly during the fishing season, punched himself out early. He constantly railed against the dishonesty of other men in the department, yet urged me to punch him out on several "emergency occasions."

Just before I left The Slade Company to return to school after 14 months on the job, I had a casual conversation with Mr. Porter, the production manager, in which he asked me how I had enjoyed my experience with the organization. During the conversation, I learned that he knew of the punch-out system in the Plating Department. What's more, he told me, he was wondering if he ought to "blow the lid off the whole mess."

Chapter 7

INFORMAL MANAGERIAL GROUPS AND ORGANIZATIONAL POLITICS

In the last chapter we saw how the perspectives and behavior of individuals in organizations are affected by their membership in work groups. Although it was not stated explicitly, the examples used and the research cited suggested that work groups were composed of blue-collar, clerical, or other first-line nonprofessional employees. However, to the extent that professionals, managers, and top executives participate in emergent groups, they are affected by the same dynamics as work groups.

Despite the fact that managerial groups have a potentially greater impact on results than other work groups, there has been less research on how these groups function. In an attempt to provide useful concepts and guidelines for practical action, it will be necessary in this chapter not only to review what research conclusions there are, but to critique and extend them beyond existing findings.

It is useful to think of two distinctly different kinds of managerial groups: the "informal" and the "decision making." Informal managerial groups, discussed in this chapter, can be thought of as the managerial equivalent of the emergent work group discussed in the previous chapter. Only a few additional concepts are needed to understand how they function, but special attention needs to be placed on their exercise of political influence.

Decision-making managerial groups are distinctly different. They are established by management and charged with the responsibility for achieving a set of corporate results. They may even appear on an organization chart. Membership is formally sanctioned and to an extent can be controlled by the organization. Decision-making managerial groups include such bodies as boards of directors, standing committees, and ad-hoc problem-solving groups. They are informal in the sense that members are not necessarily in permanent interaction. Participation in a decision-making group is frequently undertaken in addition to a manager's on-going responsibilities. Members may or may not be evaluated on their contribution to the group. For these reasons, such groups often amalgamate a variety of different individual perspectives and may, themselves, exercise a subtle influence on the perspectives of members. Chapter 8 deals with these groups.

INFORMAL MANAGERIAL GROUPS

Just as workers on the shop floor or clerks in the office will form an emergent social group when certain minimum conditions are met in the work environment and in their individual skills and personalities, so too will managers and professionals. The emergence of groups which can exert strong forces on members' perspectives and behavior is a phenomenon independent of the level of education, organizational position, social and economic class, and so on. Informal managerial groups will emerge when the opportunity for interaction is present, such as when offices are conveniently close, when brought together by a common task or even a commonality as basic as their belonging to the same organization, or when the work or a common boss creates a sense of common purpose, enthusiasm, uncertainty, or anxiety, and when the organizational controls and their own personalities do not create conflict or competition among them. In short, the conditions conducive to their formation are as easy to meet as is the case with work groups. Informal managerial groups may be composed of members who all belong to the same organizational subunit, such as sales or production, but equally important are "coalitions," which are informal groups composed of members from several departments. The bond that ties coalition members together is often stronger than their formal organizational alignments. This creates particular problems and opportunities for management, as we shall see.

Informal managerial groups and organizational results

As with emergent work groups, norms and social structure of informal managerial groups can affect members' perspectives and work behavior in ways which may contribute to or detract from the attainment of good organizational results. Not only may the attitude of a professional or manager (a lab researcher, a cost accountant, the head of marketing, etc.) toward the job be positively or negatively affected by the prevailing perspective of the peer group, but the translation of that attitude into work behavior should have greater long-term impact on organizational performance because these people have greater responsibility for attaining organizational results. Moreover, the effects of this typically will be harder to see and deal with than similar effects at the work-group level. When there is a poor attitude on the shop floor arising from some shared sentiment, the impact in terms of lower quality or increased absenteeism and grievances is almost immediately visible. When the engineering design group is down on the company, the effects on their work may be mediated somewhat by the professionalism or other personal ethic of individual members, but its effects are longer in becoming manifest. Moreover, they can be more costly and may show up in turnover of human resources which are expensive to replace. Thus, the extent to which informal managerial groups have congruence with organizational goals will affect their members' behavior and this in turn may have more serious effects on organizational performance. The fact that this is so lends importance to understanding how these groups function and how they can be influenced.

Informal managerial groups can affect organizational outcomes in two other ways. First, in addition to affecting its own members, the spirit and perspective of a managerial group has a direct and powerful effect on individuals and groups which are organizationally subordinate to the members. In ways which are more often symbolic and subtle, employees pick up the enthusiasm, or the depression, or what not, of their superiors. Informal managerial groups are major setters of that amorphous but important condition known as organizational "climate."

Second, the *presence* of a cohesive managerial group represents a repository of power and source of indirect influence in organizations, whether or not that power is exercised explicitly in the form of behavior of one or more members. The deliberations of top management and formally sanctioned decision-making groups are often affected by informal managerial groups. A group's opinion carries weight only because the members can potentially exercise influence, either by working in destructive but undiscoverable ways, by avoiding collaboration, by merely "doing their job" to the letter and not going beyond that, or by leaving the organization en masse. The effects of this kind of power are part of what is commonly known as "politics" in organizations.

An excellent example of the power and influence of an informal managerial group is contained in accounts of events leading to the firing of Bunkie Knudsen from his job as president of Ford Motor Company by Henry Ford II. (See Case 3–1, Ford-Knudsen.) Some journalists attributed much of the cause to the machinations of a group of old Ford hands, known as the "Chester Gang" (because many of them had begun their careers with Ford as salesmen in Chester, Pennsylvania). This informal group had as its leader Lee Iacocca, the brilliant and outspoken young manager whose ambitions were clearly to become president of the company. When Knudsen was brought in, many observers saw Iacocca's game plan set back by several years. A key factor in Knudsen's abrupt dismissal by Henry Ford only 17 months after coming in was conflict with Iaccoca and implicit threat to Henry Ford that some or all of the Chester Gang might leave.

What goes on behind the scenes at Ford or any other company or government agency is almost never known beyond the certainty of speculation. At the same time we should recognize that frictions of this kind in organizations, both public and private, are probably more the rule than the exception. These kinds of inside political activities are only the most dramatic and newsworthy manifestations of the presence and workings of informal managerial groups.

Thus, informal managerial groups have much in common with emergent work groups, except that their impact on organizational outcomes is greater. The goals of work groups may vary widely, and they function to serve a variety of coping needs as well as social needs for their members. In the case of managerial groups, these same general needs are served, with a particular emphasis on the concern of individual members over career status and career advancement. What is also distinctive about managerial groups is the closer relationship between their goals and activities and organizational goals and strategy. Thus, a group of young MBAs may represent a force for more explicit decision making and more rapid advancement; a legal department may be pushing for one of their members to move into line authority; a coalition of older salesmen and production managers may want to continue to emphasize traditional products rather than new ones; and so on. Managerial groups and coalitions do not differ *conceptually* from work groups, but rather in the *degree* to which their activity and nature (norms and structure) reflect alternatives for the formal organization's strategy, structure, procedures, and the like.

Politics in organizations

Before turning from this discussion of informal managerial groups, an elaboration on our discussion of politics is in order. We see politics as the behavior toward the amassing of power and influence by managerial groups toward goals set implicitly or explicitly by those groups. In many organizations political rivalries consume all too much of the productive energies of managers. In many cases this climate is created and encouraged by a weak and indecisive top management or reflects an emphasis on attaining *personal* power rather than *organizational* power by a key senior officer. When ego dominates over organizational purpose, it would appear the subordinate levels are induced to political fighting in two ways. First, individuals are themselves likely to follow that pattern set by senior management, serving as it does as "modeling." Second, ego-centered and, what is often its corollary, erratic, leadership by superiors leads subordinates to band together as a mechanism to deal with the anxieties created by this type of leadership. A group which forms for such a purpose, divorced as it is from explicit necessities of organizational functioning, is likely to shift from this coping to proactive and destructive political infighting.

As a normative matter, however, politics in appropriate measure is not a bad thing. To understand this, consider the nature of the essential general task of management at higher organizational levels. Let us adopt the notion that this task is one of decision making, following the approach of March and Simon (1958), and in particular the making of *strategic* decisions, as opposed to decisions dealing with matters of *control* (predominately the general task at middle levels) or with matters of *operations* (predominately the task at lower levels.[1] Strategic decisions or policy-making decisions are by nature important ones for the success and survival of the business or public agency. They may be characterized by relatively high *uncertainty* or relatively high *complexity*, or both. Uncertainty is the extent to which outcomes of decision-making choices are unknown. Complexity is the extent to which a variety of elements or input information is required to make decisions. Strategic decisions thus are heavily subjective in nature, often deal with uncontrollable and difficult-to-predict events in the environment of the organization, and typically require information and judgment possessed by different individual managers or staff specialists representing separate parts of the organization. It follows from this that there will be and should be differences of opinion on the validity of and weight to be placed on information going into the decision-making process. Given that strategic decisions by definition affect the direction or mission of parts of the organization, it also follows that top management must take into account the commitment and ability of parts of the organization to successfully implement the decisions at the time the decision choice is made.

These aspects of strategic decisions require, in effect, that managers exercise influence as they participate in the process. In addition, the

---

[1] This general ordering of decision-making tasks was suggested by Anthony (1965) and has been elaborated on by Scott-Morton (1971).

limited information-processing capability of top management and the need for appropriate parties to be heard requires an assessment of the quality of the advocate or source and his or her capability for implementation, that is, the ability to get results. In effect, then, strategic decisions require that influence be exercised at high levels in organizations. This process, in short, is a political process. Strategic decision making or policy setting calls for politics to be played by the participants. Our metaphors for top management decision making should reflect this. They should recognize the gamelike quality required as well as the explicitly rational quality.

The dilemmas of organizational politics

Given that politics is thus recognized as an integral part of the organization's decision-making process, let us elaborate on how these ideas fit into the overview model presented in Chapter 1 and the processes of managerial influence explained in Chapter 2. This is shown in Figure 7–1. The figure consists of two general parts, aspects of ele-

IGURE 7–1

he functions and dysfunctions of organizational politics

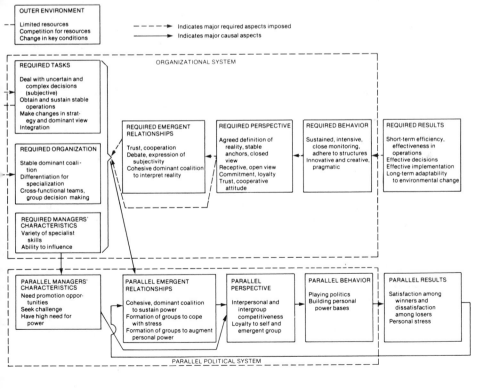

ments which are required by the environment and by typical results criteria, and a set of aspects of elements which are produced in parallel. The purpose of this section is to show in these general terms how politics become a necessary but also potentially dysfunctional part of managerial behavior.

At opposite ends of the model are the elements external to the organization, namely required results and outer environment. On the one hand, the outer environment is characterized by competition for limited resources and conditions that are constantly changing, more or less rapidly. The outer environment imposes uncertainty and complexity of the managerial tasks, namely the decision-making processes. On the other hand, in terms of required results, organizations must balance the desire for short-term efficiency and effectiveness in ongoing operations with the need to adapt to environmental change over a relatively longer period of time. These requirements, in turn, impose other requirements on elements to the left in the model. In terms of work behavior, short-term efficiency requires sustained, intensive work, close monitoring, and adherence to structures and procedures designed to achieve results, assuming a given state of environmental conditions and a predetermined organizational strategy. At the same time, managers must behave in innovative, creative ways to meet the need for adaptability. The tension between the two different types of behavior) steady, sustained, and focused versus innovative and creative) has implications for the perspectives of managers and emergent relationships.

Although both types of behavior call for commitment and loyalty, stable and sustained behavior requires a perspective of agreement on reality, on goals, and on desirable work behaviors. Innovative behavior and creative problem solving require a perspective where disagreement and discussion are encouraged within an atmosphere of trust, cooperation, and mutual respect. In addition, the two conflict needs— short-term efficiency and long-term adaptability—have several specific implications for the formal and people inputs to the organizational system. First, the need for short-term efficiency implies the separation of the overall goals of the organization into differentiated, specialized subunits or functions. This, in turn, requires managers with specialized skills and with the ability to influence others. Because people have limited information-processing capacity, the need to make complex and uncertain decisions regarding goals or outcome which cannot be delegated to specialized subunits within the organization requires *group* decision making. The groups must be made up of specialists whose efforts are coordinated or integrated to contribute to these important decisions.

The dominant coalition ·

In order to make decisions in an uncertain, unstable environment while still maintaining necessary stability, a "dominant coalition" which can order this environment, define reality, and lead the organization toward desired results is necessary. This group may be a department or managerial type that will define the organizations' operative model of reality, that is, how results can be achieved, for the short run at least. These managers must have the ability to influence fellow managers to achieve their ends. They can deliver the goods. Part of their ability to do so stems from control of promotion opportunities and other rewards. This dominant coalition is an emergent relationship, necessary if the organization is to achieve required results. Certain characteristics of emergent relationships are also implied as part of a successful dominant coalition: trust, cooperation, debate, and free expression of opinion. These norms are prerequisites to the creative and innovative behavior required to make complex decisions in an uncertain and unstable environment.

The need for a dominant coalition, in an environment of motivated and career-oriented managers, inevitably leads to the parallel need for strong emergent groups of managers who constantly seek to exercise influence and build a base of power to reinforce their status as a dominant coalition. Because of the tensions in the organizational system, the status of a dominant coalition will rarely reach equilibrium. In addition, the personal stress created by this type of environment strengthens the emergent group since it fills a role as a coping mechanism for individual managers. The unsteady state of the organizational system inevitably gives rise to several such parallel emergent groups (would-be dominant coalitions). The game of politics is begun in earnest, and a whole political system (as illustrated in the diagram), working in parallel to the system and intended to achieve required results, develops within the organization. When the energy of managers is diverted too much from achieving results to competing with other political groups or building personal or group power bases, the required perspective of cooperation and trust between managers becomes impossible and politics becomes dysfunctional.

In any given organization some decisions will be more judgmental, subjective, or requiring of participant involvement and commitment than others. These will generally more appropriately require political processes. In different organizations, operating in different environments, the requirements will also vary. Even the most important decisions for an organization in a stable environment over which that organization is able to exercise control will require less politics than decisions for an organization undergoing change resulting from its engagement in a dynamic and uncontrollable environment. Another way of looking at this is to say that organizations themselves are engaged in a game with their environments, that some games have higher risks and push the limits of rationality greater than do others, and that this in turn requires a political game *internally* to produce the decisions required for the organization to deal effectively with its environment.[2]

While politics are in part necessary, let us once again point out that politics can be dysfunctional if played for purposes other than to represent legitimate organizational ends.

Thus, the nature of the managerial task at high levels is political. Because informal managerial groups help their members perform their tasks more effectively in a political environment they will arise almost spontaneously in organizations. The question for managers is not how to eliminate politics, but how to manage the process of decision making to encourage a healthy and illuminating, rather than destructive, use of the motivation, creativity, and information generation which can evolve from groups engaged in playing the political game.

IMPLICATIONS FOR MANAGERS

It is important for managers simply to recognize the phenomenon of informal managerial groups and to be alert to the fact that they may be affecting the behavior of individual managers for better or for worse with respect to organizational goals. It is very easy to assume that since work behavior is generally observable only for individuals one at a time, that the causes of behavior are exclusively personal, or that formal organizational incentives and structures or interpersonal relationships are the only extrapersonal causes of individual behavior. As we have emphasized in our overview model, the perspective of the individual is indeed his or her own personal predisposition. Nevertheless, the causes or forces affecting an individual's perspective and behavior include not only personal characteristics and the more obvious influences but the subtle effects of norms and social roles which emerge from informal managerial groups. A mere recognition of this can help managers understand and act more effectively to influence their own behavior and that of other managers. Let us examine the practical implications of informal managerial groups and the action choices which follow from them.

Once a manager recognizes the possibility that the behavior of an-

---

[2] This idea closely parallels the notion of "requisite variety" described by Ashby (1960).

other manager may be affected by that person's membership in an informal managerial group, it should become evident that direct, face-to-face communications with that individual alone will be perceived by him or her in the context of that membership. Thus, an attempt to influence the work behavior of a member of a managerial group, when that behavior falls within the group's purview of norms, is at the least going to create conflict within the individual and may ultimately lead to a reaction against the change effort by the entire group. This same line of reasoning applies to work groups at any level. What is different is that informal managerial groups have more power in the organization, and that the manager who would introduce some change affecting a group's members is more dependent on their support to carry out his goals.

Action guidelines

In terms of action, it follows that the manager in question needs to be more careful and perhaps more subtle in dealing with a managerial group than with a work group. The less advantageous balance of power in this instance means that the option of breaking up an informal managerial group can rarely be justified or attempted. Rather, the manager is obliged to work on change in group norms in an effort to redirect the perspectives of members by dealing individually with leaders and members and discussions and influences on the group itself. However, in the case of these groups, the manager who is superior in position to some or all members may have the tool of reward power— the potential to promote, in particular—which may be more potent here than with work groups. Moreover, managers are typically in a better position to influence individuals through their personal relationships, inasmuch as social and friendship bonds that transcend the work place are more likely to occur with fellow managers.

Unlike the situation managers face with work groups, they should consider creating countervailing power through political processes. Thus, working behind the scenes with one's own peers, including especially the bosses of members of a group, a manager may indirectly affect the perspectives of members toward some new direction on a particular issue. Finally, the perspectives imposed on its members by an informal managerial group are if anything closer to and more attuned to the formal structural aspects of the organization than are the personal perspectives of members alone. Thus, these members can be influenced more effectively in the short run by changes in organization structure, task assignments, and compensation and promotion changes. The implications of such changes are apt to be perceived quickly. While it may be more difficult to break up a managerial group, a change in its composition and dynamics can become part of a manager's plan for organizational change. Conversely, whenever an organizational change is contemplated, the composition and mix of the managerial group involved should be analyzed and its behavior taken into account.

It is the nature of emergent informal groups that members typically are unaware of the pressures of norms and the extent to which their own opinions and attitudes are affected by group forces as compared to their awareness of formal organizational forces. A manager who would change member behavior by working with a group to change its norms should keep this in mind. In general, as with work groups, it is easier and more effective to shape norms at the outset of a managerial group's formation than after it has formed. The natural process of formation can take up to six months. Management can affect formation or change of informal group norms by means of interventions. In practice these activities are variously known as team building or part of the activity of organizational development. The intervention, so called because the manager or other change agent is not typically a member of the group, should be aimed at improving task behavior, rather than raising the awareness of group members to the process of pressures which the members are experiencing. Such raised awareness may indeed become a by-product of the exercise, and a useful one to the extent the group can subsequently engage on its own in discussions of the process of their interactions. But for reasons of efficiency and a prevailing focus on organizational results, it is appropriate that the interventionist have as an agenda attention to substantive work issues rather than informal group process issues per se.

All groups affect members' perspectives. Informal managerial groups in particular affect members' processes of interpretation of events and other sources of information from the environment. When such information conflicts with group norms or structure, there is the potential for these norms or structures to change. When such inputs are manipulated and managed by a responsible manager outside the group, and the effects are, over time, to change norms or social structures of the group in question, one may say that management has induced "organizational learning" at the managerial level.

A final implication to the manager of groups is to watch the politics. In the earlier discussion we indicated the balance required between too much and too little managerial energy being spent on political activity within an organization. Whether the organization be the state legislature, where policy setting is the central task and political activity a legitimate process for the assurance of justice in a democracy, or a rigid bureaucracy of a stable electric utility in a fully developed, nonchanging economic region, there is a particular balance in each organization between too little and too much politics being played by managers. Responsible top management will make efforts to be aware of the extent of politics, to remain sufficiently above the battles to know when it is too much or too little, and to take action with regard to tightening or loosening rules and structures to increase or decrease the amount of internal political activity.

Influencing one's own group

Thus far in the discussion of managerial implications we have focused on the management of groups by persons who are not full-fledged members of the group. But what about management of a group by a member of the group? What are the processes and aspects of being a part of an informal group and trying to affect its development and its impact on the behavior of other members?

As is the case throughout much of this book, the first rule in implications involving behavioral processes of which one is an active part is "be aware." Managers often learn only by experience that there is more than one way to look at problems, and that their present opinions, attitudes, and behavior may be largely affected and reinforced by their friends and colleagues at work and might well be different to a large extent if they were in a different group. One should recognize the essential relativism of influence by an informal group, distinguish group pressure from what may be right or appropriate by some other standard (legal, moral, organizational, or personal), and act as an individual as well as a member of a group. At the same time one should recognize the importance of being committed to a larger cause and identity than just the personal and individual level. Commitment implies the risk of losing self-awareness, of giving up something personal for the sake of the advantages which may accrue personally by virtue of membership in groups or organizations. The trick, of course, is to enter into commitments wholeheartedly and still to be able to distance oneself mentally and emotionally from those commitments. This is a matter of "self-management," which we shall return to as a topic in the final chapter.

Becoming an effective member of an organization, it should be recognized, involves much more than doing one's job and getting paid for it. As this chapter indicates, this is particularly true for managers. On joining an organization one should assess the explicit and relatively visible aspects of the employment relationship, comparing what one will give and get against one's skills, monetary needs, and professional desires. To the extent possible, one should also make an effort to assess the climate by inferring the organization's prevailing informal norms, informal social structure, and shared perspectives. These aspects should be compared to one's personal values and the risk of changing, over time, one's own identity and modifying one's values as a result of intense involvement as a member of an informal managerial group. This framework of choice is well illustrated in Texcorp case (Case 8–1) in which a young MBA complex has gone to work for a formal organization is confronted with a complex informal managerial system (several competing informal groups and coalitions engaged in active political struggles) which he is all but explicitly invited to become a part of.

CONCLUSION

Emergent managerial groups are as pervasive as emergent work groups in organizations and can be understood with basically the same concepts. However, because of the added organizational power of managers, the effects of the managerial group on the work behavior of its members are more important as determinates of organizational results. It follows that managers at all levels need to become sensitive to the phenomenon of managerial groups and adept at influencing them, both for reasons of personal gain and achievement of organizational results.

In this chapter we have argued that politics at managerial levels is an inevitable by-product of behavior required to achieve results and the phenomenon of emergent managerial groups. Moreover, political behavior in proper doses can be a positive thing for organizations, stimulating as it does forces of motivation for managers.

The actions needed to influence managerial groups are similar to those needed to influence work groups. Such action is made more difficult, however, by the fact that the manager may be a member of the group or a representative of another competitive group. The difficulty of exercising influence calls for a greater sensitivity of the effects of group pressures on members and on results, and greater self-awareness of the effects on one's own values and identity.

QUESTIONS FOR STUDY AND DISCUSSION

1. Discuss some of the differences between blue-collar and managerial emergent groups.
2. How can top management best foster the enthusiasm and commitment of middle management and professional groups, in view of their importance in achieving organizational results?
3. In what ways has your own perspective been affected by your participation in an emergent group? Have you affected the group to some degree?
4. Describe at least one example of political behavior by an individual or managerial group in an organization with which you are familiar.

What positive and negative effects, if any, were produced by this political activity?

To what extent could the negative aspect of the activity be discussed by managers affected by them?

What reasons are there for any limitations on the problems being discussed? Do you consider these valid reasons, or not? Why?

5. Are you currently engaged in activity which could be described as political as defined in this chapter?

What personal or informal group purposes and goals are being served by this activity?

If these purposes and goals were achieved, what organizational purposes would be served? What organizational purposes would be hindered? What individuals other than yourself or your group would be affected and in what ways?

Case 7–1
Dave Melton (A)*

Dave Melton sat in his office pondering the series of events that had led to his contemplating resigning from his position at National Paper, Inc., where he had been employed for over 11 years. The incident that had forced him to make a decision on whether or not to resign was his recent removal as head of the black recruitment effort at National Paper, and the subsequent installing of a white counterpart into his former position. Dave mused at how quickly the word had spread that he was upset with National. A few days after the change, he had received job offers from two large corporations to head up their black recruitment effort. The salaries in both offers were somewhat higher than he was making at National.

Early life

Dave Melton was born and raised in the small town of Summer Falls, Illinois. When he was born, in 1930, the town contained only three Black families, one of which was very self-contained and did not associate with the other two. The other two families, including Melton's family, had a great deal of interaction, partly because both had migrated from the same section of North Carolina, where, in addition to knowing each other, they had provided the black leadership for their area. Dave described his early life as follows:

> I had two brothers, one older and one younger. But the younger one died in infancy and I don't remember him at all. My mother and father were separated when I was three years old, for reasons which were standard for black families at that time; my father was unable to find work, but my mother could—so a matriarchy developed. However, my father would not accept the position of being supported by his wife, nor the role he was forced to play by her, so they separated. We went to live with my father's parents. My grandfather died when I was young, nine or ten, and grandmother became head of the household. She continued to manage the matriarchy and even today she feels she runs the household, at 88 years of age. She and my father still live together.
>
> My relationship with my grandmother has always been strong. She taught me her moral values which were strict southern black Baptist—no drinking, no smoking, no running around with women. However, today, I do all three to some extent and she understands that I do. But I still do not drink in her presence.

---

* All names have been disguised.

Unlike many blacks at that time, Melton felt that his education in the Summer Falls school system was quite adequate. He attributes this to the overwhelming interest that the town's large Jewish population had in the quality of their children's education. One of the attitudes held by the townspeople was their expectation that blacks participate in high school athletics. Both Dave and his older brother participated in athletics during their high school years. However, Dave never rivaled the skill of his brother in sports.

The casewriter asked Dave about his attitude toward whites during his high school years:

Melton: *In my freshman and sophomore years of high school, I viewed whites as friends and competitors since most of my social interaction was in athletics. In my junior and senior years, I recognized the social difference, but it did not bother me since the discrimination was not overt. My first exposure to blatant discrimination came earlier in my life, during the war, when a large military base was established nearby. Southern soldiers there were extremely cruel verbally, and, at one point, I was assaulted by one. I was just 11 years old at that time. However, I did not regard the soldiers as townspeople; hence there was no conflict in my mind about whites.*

Casewriter: *What did you do after high school?*

Melton: *I had to drop out of high school when I was 16 to help support the family. The job situation at that time was very bad, but since I had spent the previous summers refinishing floors for people in the community, I decided to start my own floor refinishing business. I had developed a very good reputation during the summers for dependability, so I soon found myself with more work than I could handle. In order to keep the contracts, I hired two older men as helpers. Strange as it may seem, my hiring helpers was the cause of all my problems because then I had to meet a weekly payroll and I soon ran into cash flow problems. The problem was mainly caused by my large customers, often contractors, who would not pay me for my work until they had completed the entire contract.*

Being young and inexperienced, I could not force my customers to pay me on time, nor could I secure short-term loans from the local bank. In order to keep my business afloat I would have to work eight hours during the day on big jobs with my helpers and then work an additional eight hours at night on smaller, individual jobs from which I demanded cash upon the completion of the job. After seven months the constant physical strain was really getting me down, but by that time the family's financial situation had improved so I gave up my business to go back to high school and complete my education.

About a year after I graduated from high school I married a girl who was attending a college near Summer Falls. She came from a southern family that was considered well off by black standards while my family was poor. As a result, I was less concerned with socializing then she was and more concerned with work. Our married life could be characterized as a long period of acquiring things—houses, cars, etc., and wondering what to purchase next to appear as good as our neighbors and our peer social group. I considered it nonsense and made it obvious that I did so. In retrospect, I believe our marriage was destroyed because of my unwillingness to fall into a matriarchal situation, along with my unwillingness to make adjustments that would prevent me from pursuing goals that I thought would make my life successful. The long separation during military service destroyed the marriage for all practical purposes and after that it was only a matter of time before the formal separation and divorce.

The army

In 1951, at the age of 21, Dave was drafted by the army. Unlike many young men, Dave found the army to be a tremendous learning experience but he also felt that his experience was a little different from that of others.

The first thing that I recall is that both the army and I considered Dave Melton to be a misfit right from the start. In addition to the normal problems of adjustment, the army was the first time in my life that I came face to face with American racism. During the time I was a private, this racism was articulated in the form of an abnormal amount of menial assignments being shoved my way, and many degrading comments by the noncommissioned officers who, for the most part, were crude and not very bright. In an effort to get out from under the hammer, I decided to become an officer and applied for OCS. I passed the necessary exams and was accepted at OCS at Ft. Sill. It was tough and I wanted to quit on many occasions, but I remembered how much tougher it was being a private, so I stayed with it and graduated at the top of the class.

I had to fight to do it, but all the people I've known that have succeeded were fighters. I was able to compete successfully in athletics because I was tough-minded as well as physically tough. I was successful at OCS and in Korea also because I was tough-minded as well as being physically tough.

After graduation from OCS, I was sent to Korea as one of the first black artillery officers assigned to the First Cavalry Division. As an example of what my tour of duty was to hold for me, when I arrived in Korea, my commanding officer became so flustered at seeing a black man as one of his new officers that he introduced himself to me as "Dave Melton."

During my entire tour of duty I was ostracized by all but the most Junior officers. The officer corps being like a college faculty, the Junior officers had to stick together in order to survive and there weren't enough of us to allow my white counterparts the luxury of discrimination. However, the Senior officers never had anything to do with me socially. I was never invited to any of the parties given by a Senior officer even though the white Junior officers were invited. On the other hand, when it came to technical ability, they were surprised that unlike most Junior officers, I was an expert at gunnery. Eventually, I was recognized as having the best battery in the entire command and we were always assigned to shoot the more important missions.

After leaving Korea Dave chose to stay in the army because of the "competition and the challenges." However, his feelings toward the service were gradually reversed after he served as trial counsel at "many court-martials and witnessed first hand the workings of the army's archaic legal system." He was also bothered by his inability to defend himself against an unwarranted, derogatory verbal attack by a white Senior officer. By 1956 Dave had decided to give up his commission and leave the service. He described his decision as follows:

> I was disturbed by the attitudes I could see developing in the Senior officers. The officer's club became the social center and "happy hour" was the most important part of the day. I began to suspect that I liked the army because of the security and the easy job; that worried me. Besides, the social activities, which included catering to wives of generals and colonels, was just not my cup of tea. Many of the officers I talked with, who had 10 to 15 years of service, regarded the military service not as an occupation but as a total way of life. I felt that they had little knowledge or concern for what was going on outside, so I decided it wasn't the life I wanted and got out.

National Paper, Inc.

In 1956, Dave obtained a job in the area of personnel with National Paper, Inc. Even though there were very few blacks working for National at that time, Dave did not experience any difficulty in obtaining his job. He attributes this to the fact that his older brother had been working for National for four years and had a good record with the company. He was also fortunate enough to be interviewed by a member of his old army unit.

After initially working a short time in Trenton, New Jersey, Dave arranged a transfer to Philadelphia to work toward a college degree in the evening division of Temple University. At that time, his job assignment was in the area of personnel recuirtment advertising. After attending Temple for one year, Dave became bored with school and quit. His disappointment over school, however, was offset by a new job assignment which dealt with personnel planning, an area that Dave indicated started him looking beyond strictly personnel issues and achieving a managerial perspective. Still feeling that he needed a college education, Dave enrolled in Lasalle University's Night Division one year later, but once again dropped out after another year, this time because he seemed to find himself working for a "union card" instead of knowledge. His discussions with faculty members at Lasalle developed this idea. One faculty member refused to grade him because he said "he would not grade talent." After that time, however, Dave continued to enroll in courses offered in night school that he felt were interesting or related in some way to his job. When asked if his lack of a college degree had hurt his career at National, Dave responded by saying:

> No, initially it did, but not anymore. Anybody who challenges me on my lack of a degree is only taking a cheap shot that can be easily handled. If I am at a meeting and a guy tries to show me up by quoting from a college textbook or something, I have enough book knowledge to refute his point by quoting several academic references on the issue. Education and a college degree are not synonymous. As a matter of fact, one of my career goals is to become a corporate vice president. That should show that I am not at all worried about not having a college degree.
>
> You know, it was after I made an analysis of my ability to learn in this company that I decided I could probably be a vice president. I also felt that the times would someday be on my side. This may not come to pass, and I will not see it as a sharp disappointment if it does not. However, if the opportunity is there, I want it and I am going to do what I can to make it.

The next five years saw Dave continue in his position in personnel planning with steady advancement but without any really significant promotions. Dave said of this period:

> Along with gaining experience in my area, I also started to see how the corporate game is played. I began making a habit of listening to my white counterparts when they would discuss their career goals, their personal problems and hangups, and other topics with me, and I made mental notes of these conversations for my future use. You know, I never invited these little chitchats, but I guess my counterparts just did not see me as being smart enough to be an opponent, so they didn't care what they told me. However, some of that uninvited information has been very useful to me during my years at National.

Black recruitment

In 1963 National initiated an extensive recruiting effort at black colleges throughout the country in an attempt significantly to increase the number of blacks working for the company. Dave Melton was chosen to head up this effort and was also given "carte blanche" authority to select his team from anywhere in the company.

Melton: *Actually, I was picked to be the project leader over the administrative assistant to the corporate Director of Personnel, who was also black, because management felt that the other black was too aggressive, too hard to get along with and too hard to control. However, interestingly enough, I later found out that a senior manager in the company had made a comment to the effect that: "Six months ago, you would not have even known that Dave Melton was around, but now you can't keep his mouth shut."*

The first problem that I faced was the actual selection of my project team. I wanted to get a team of blacks who held relatively high positions in the company so that when we talked to black job applicants about the potential for growth and advancement in National, the jobs being held by my recruiting team would serve to give that statement credibility. I was very pleased with the team I got. For example, one member was the manager of the Scientific Lab in Chester, Pa., another was a product manager in the International Services Division, and another was the administrative assistant to the Director of Personnel. I would say that my team was probably the best recruiting team ever assembled at National. The statistics just tell part of the story. We always surpassed our numerical objectives for each year and the number of blacks that we recruited into the company increased by over 100 percent in each of the five years that we were in operation. While the company-wide acceptance rate from people being offered jobs was around 50 percent, our acceptance rate was never below 80 percent and one year got to 95 percent.

Casewriter: *How did your team members relate to you as the head of the project?*

Melton: *Well, our record speaks for itself; however, I was working with some pretty high-powered people and naturally there had to be some conflict.*

Some of the conflict revolved around a policy which I initiated that gave me the final say on whether or not an applicant should be considered and, if he was considered, where he would be assigned. Many of the conflicts were caused by resistance to my theory that the company-wide screening test must be given to all black applicants and a B or better grade be attained, by these applicants, on the exam. (A B or better score was the cutoff point for all white applicants.) Many of the blacks on my team felt that the test should not be used in the case of black applicants because (1) black people have historically been underachievers on IQ tests and (2) the tests were oriented toward white middle-class applicants and therefore were irrelevant and incorrect when it came to judging the ability of black applicants. I prevailed because I felt we were underestimating the black talent and we could not afford to reinforce the stereotype. My position was that I had to maximize the possibility of success of blacks hired in the training program in order to forestall the development of an "I told you so" attitude by whites in the company, and having the base data from the tests was the only way that I could do this. I now feel that my position on the test score was correct, because during my team's existence, the washout rate for the blacks that we recruited into the company was very low [comparable to whites].

Additional conflicts arose when other members of the team, upon finding a very promising applicant, would try to get that applicant to work for them. Many times, I would overrule my team members and reassign those applicants to jobs or locations where I felt they would be better suited or where the manpower need was greater.

Casewriter: *Why was your team so successful in recruiting black college graduates?*

Melton: *I think that you could safely say that our entire approach was different than that exhibited by most corporation recruiters. For one thing, we looked upon ourselves as being the interface between the colleges and National, so therefore we gave ourselves the title of College Relations Specialists. Also unlike most corporation recruiters who are usually just starting with a company and therefore* *"wet behind the ears,"* no member of my team had less than five years' experience with the company. This experience level was a big help when my guys would sit down and tell an applicant what National was all about and what he could expect as a black working for a big corporation.

Furthermore, they told the truth—they talked about discrimination in the company, the forms that it usually took and the way that it had affected their careers. They also told the good side of the story, the potential for growth in National, the pay, the advancement and the other good points. As a matter of fact, I had to can one of my recruiters because he was going around telling these college kids that National was heaven and that there was no discrimination in the company. This kind of recruiting is unfair to both the company and the applicant because it can only lead to disillusionment on the part of both parties.

Casewriter: *Did you have any other problems with your recruiters?*

Melton: Yes, right at the start of our effort, two of the guys took to renting Cadillacs, throwing $300 cocktail parties for faculty members at the schools and getting involved in the coed scene. Now, I knew that it was going to be hard for any guy to stay away from the coed scene, but I also felt that since we were new faces on these campuses that we couldn't afford that kind of image, so I dropped those two guys from the team.

Casewriter: *How was your team received by the colleges involved?*

Melton: As I stated before, our approach was unique. Many times our first trip to the campus would be a nonrecruiting effort. If a recruiter was a chemist, let's say, he would often visit the chemistry department first and just talk shop with some of the professors. Many times this tactic would lead to our guys holding special seminars on their field for a certain department in the school. By talking shop, we would also get requests for lab equipment, literature and things like that. If National had a surplus of the needed items, my guys would shop around the company until they found the items and then send it to the school involved. Eventually, the schools looked upon us not just as recruiters, but as a valuable resource. We also made no attempts to sell the schools our products and services, even though there was often a need at these schools. However, I must admit that we did try to "plant a seed" in the minds of the college administrators so that the request for our salesmen to call on them would come from the colleges and not from us.

Casewriter: *Why was this approach to the faculty at the colleges necessary?*

Melton: We realized right from the start that if we went into these schools offering students more money than the large majority of the faculty was making without somehow smoothing the way, that we would pretty soon meet a lot of opposition from the faculty. You must also realize that the only concerns recruiting at black colleges in those days were the government and school boards, so we also had to give everyone at the colleges a chance to find out what we were all about and what we had to offer. In line with that policy, I was the only member of the team who dealt with the administrators and Senior Deans at schools. We did this to create an illusion of a hierarchy. In other words, the top man at National in charge of black recruitment would talk to the top people at the colleges. The fact that I was black enhanced the company's image and helped us to establish rapport with the administrators and Senior Deans in a very short period of time.

Casewriter: *Did your team employ any special techniques with the students?*

Melton: *We realized that we were also a new animal to the students. For one thing, the student applicants were scared, they knew very little about the business world. So when we talked to them we had to first gain their confidence and then we had to do a good job in explaining National and the industry to them. This is where the experience level of my men and their telling the truth helped.*

Another method we used was that when we made an offer to an applicant, the guy on my team who had talked to the student would be notified by my office. My guy would then call the student and explain the position being offered, the career paths that he could follow if he accepted and any other details that the applicant was interested in learning. This tactic boosted our acceptance rate because it showed that my guys were really interested in the individual applicants, which they were.

We also initiated a summer program where my guys would pick one or two promising sophomores or juniors and offer them jobs at locations for the summer. This helped to orient the students to working in industry. In addition, when these students went back to their campuses in the fall, they became our messengers and would spread the word around voluntarily that ours was a good company to work for. Because of the success of the student summer programs, the company set up a similar program for the faculty members at these schools. However, my guys were not in charge of the selection process and whoever was in charge selected the "bottom of the barrel" from these schools so the program naturally failed.

Before we change the subject, I think I should talk about the fantastic cooperation that I received from my guys. Even though there was some conflict, overall the team pulled very hard for the success of the project because they felt a deep personal involvement and did not want to see their effort fail. This commitment was absolutely necessary because I was not given a clerical staff and without the support of my team members and the efficiency of my secretary, I would not have been able to carry out my duties. Even with my teammates' help, I still had to work many 16-hour days and 7-day weeks in order to complete the processing of applications immediately after they had been submitted by team members.

Replacement as head of the team

Dave was quite proud of his record in black recruitment and was disappointed with National's decision to replace him as head of the minority recruitment. However, Dave seemed very calm to the casewriter as he talked about his removal.

Casewriter: *Given the success of your efforts in the area of black recruitment, Dave, why was the job taken from you?*

Melton: *I believe that the corporate intent at the time was to include the recruitment of blacks into the regular recruiting program and to phase out our operation. I think they thought they could give the effort to personnel people and have them multiply our efforts and really make hay in getting at this source of talent.*

Casewriter: *Well, what happened to change that plan?*

Melton: *I can only give you my perception of the events that took place, so keep that in mind. About the time that the people in corporate headquarters were thinking about phasing us out, a white personnel officer by the name of Dick Pringle became the volunteer to the Plans for Progress Youth Motivation and Advisory Group in Washington, D.C. Since the Plan for Progress Group deals with black employment, Pringle became informed about our operation. I think that Pringle saw equal opportunity employment as his road to the top of the corporate heap, and was just waiting for a chance to take over our operation.*

Casewriter: *How did Pringle finally pull off the coup?*

Melton: *It so happened that a few months earlier we had interviewed the son of a wealthy black businessman for a job. However, the son had already accepted another job before he interviewed with us. As it turned out, this kid really wanted to work for us but he was in a quandary about his previous job commitment and telephoned me for advice. Naturally, I told him that the decision was his to make and I did not try to pressure him one way or the other. He subsequently made the decision, and I think it was the right one, to stick by his previous commitment. Several weeks later the father was a guest speaker at a National seminar in Washington, D.C., which was also attended by Dick Pringle. After his speech he happened to tell Dick Pringle that his son had really wanted to work for National but that we hadn't offered him a position.*

Pringle then went into our files and pulled this kid's application which was naturally very impressive. However, what Pringle did not have were the notes that I had taken on all of my phone conversations with this young man. Without consulting me, Pringle took the file and the father's story to my boss as an example of how my team was failing to recruit highly qualified blacks. Again without consulting me, Pringle and my manager took his story straight up the corporate ladder.

Casewriter: *What was the reaction to Pringle's story upstairs?*

Melton: *Well, before they got a chance to hear my side of the story, they had already bought Pringle's and I suppose they had made a commitment to him concerning his heading up the black recruitment effort. The announcement was made last week; he's the new head and I'm to be under him. He's given me my first assignment, to lay out objectives for the number of recruits the office should get next year.*

Casewirter: *Did they ever hear your side of the story?*

Melton: *Well, yes, but by that time, so many higher ups had become involved I guess it was impossible for them to admit that they had all been wrong. They took the attitude of "How could Melton's team possibly be doing better than we could do?"*

Casewriter: *Is that when you decided to resign?*

Melton: *I haven't decided to resign yet. I'm not sure if Pringle will be able to handle the job. He doesn't understand that recruiting black kids from black colleges is a hell of a lot different than recruiting at Princeton or Penn. I don't think there are many anywhere in the company who do, although they are committed to black recruitment because they've seen how it pays off. If I could pull through this and* *regain my job, I would gain a lot of respect throughout the company for my ability to meet the problem head on.*

Another one of my alternatives would be to stay and go along with the company's decision. However, I really feel wronged in this matter and to simply acquiesce would be a bitter pill to swallow. Finally, I still have the two job offers pending, but I really have to study them to see what potential those companies are offering in terms of advancement. Until now, they have only talked to me about setting up their minority recruiting programs and nothing beyond that, as far as my future career, has been discussed.

Dave then went on to explain that he felt the need to make a decision very soon because the two companies that had made him job offers wanted his answer within five days.

Case 7–2
Dave Melton (B)*

As the casewriter sat in the reception area, waiting to interview Dave Melton, he thought to himself that an awful lot had happened to Dave during his last two years with National. The last time the casewriter and Dave had talked, Dave was thinking about resigning from the company because he had been removed as head of National's black recruitment effort. However, Dave did not resign but stayed with National and worked under Dick Pringle, the man who succeeded Dave as head of the company's black recruitment effort. Since that time, the job had been given back to Dave, who went on, once again, to attain the black recruitment objectives. The casewriter wanted to talk to Dave about his decision to stay and also about his new position with National's Urban Coordination staff.

The decision

As Dave began talking, he explained why he made his decision to remain with National:

Melton: *Sure, I was angry enough to think about leaving but I felt that any change in companies, at that time, would not afford me the same opportunities that I would have at National. As you remember, two large corporations wanted me to head up their minority recruiting programs, but I asked myself the question, "Am I*

---

* All names have been disguised.

being offered this job because I can set up a good black recruitment program or because I could make valuable contributions to the company in that and in other areas as well?"

To me, the answer was obvious, I was wanted by these other firms solely for my experience in setting up a good minority recruiting program. Well, that stopped me, because there will never be a corporate executive vice president for black recruitment and if some company did create that position, I wouldn't want the job anyway because it would just be a sham. I could see no long-term future in being a black recruitment specialist.

Casewriter: Was that the only reason that you decided to stay with National?

Melton: No, another reason, to put it simply: it was just too good a fight to run away from. Pringle had to lose because he never realized what he was getting into. In addition, whereas I could not watch him, Pringle could gain nothing more from attacking me, so I held all the aces, so to speak. I adopted the relationship with Pringle of a Shakesperian play. I remember thinking to myself, "You can run or think that you are running this department any way you want to, and I'll be in the audience watching you every step of the way."

Casewriter: Why do you now say that Pringle had to lose?

Melton: He never figured the job to be as tough as it was. Looking back, I now realize that he had a poor opinion of me and of the requirements of the job. I think this stemmed from the way that I ran the program, from my telephone.

Another thing that probably deceived him is that for some reason or another, I would always have a pile of forms of papers stacked up on my desk. Now, most of the times these were copies of job application forms which I was going over after I had processed and sent the originals to personnel. One of the policies around here is that all job applications be processed immediately, so Pringle probably said to himself, "This job must be easy because he's always at his desk talking to someone on the phone, he doesn't even get his applications processed right away, but yet he seems to be accomplishing his objectives."

Pringle also never perceived the difference in dealing with blacks and black colleges as opposed to normal recruiting at white institutions and he was not prepared for the reaction from blacks when it came.

Casewriter: What blacks are you referring to and what was their reaction?

Melton: The reaction of the colleges was that National was running the same old game of "once a program is successful, give it to Charlie." Now, at the same time, the students were hitting all the white recruiters with the attitude of "where were you yesterday, white man"? Even though I would categorize these as being the expected responses from the schools and students, Pringle never saw it and he blew the ball game on his first trip to one of the larger black schools; Pringle adopted the attitude of "I am here, I am God, I will arise on Easter." Naturally, this attitude went over like a lead balloon, and the word quickly spread to the other schools that were involved in the black recruitment effort. So Pringle immediately had his back up against the wall.

Another thing that Pringle never understood about the schools was that it was very important to maintain the proper level of contact between National and the colleges. Now, there are people in National who can walk into a college campus and say, *"You should build this facility, set up this program, etc."* However, what Pringle didn't realize was that the college administrators knew what needed to be done but they were working under extreme budget constraints. So when Pringle, who never had to worry about money at National, would start to shell out this high-powered advice it just served to prove to the schools that these guys did not understand black colleges.

The guys who were on my team were also assigned to Pringle on a part-time, as their workload allowed, basis. However, for some reason, they all became very busy at their own jobs and did not have that much time to spare for recruiting. They would also no longer make the extra effort, like going to a school on Friday afternoon in order to talk to people at the colleges and do some ground work for that Monday's recruiting appointment. Now, they would simply make the trip on Monday morning and Pringle could not criticize them for it because he didn't know any better. I feel they did this because they were disappointed, not because they were disloyal.

Casewriter: *What finally caused Pringle's downfall?*

Melton: It's a long story, but basically Pringle began to panic. When he first took over the operation, he gave me the task of deciding on our numerical objectives for the coming year. So what I did was to set and justify the objectives at twice what I thought Pringle could attain as far as the number of blacks recruited into the company. Before I set the quota, I had to ask myself, *"Am I lying to the company?"* I finally decided that, *"No, it can be done and it should be done."* That answered my personal concern about my loyalty. Company objectives had to be met and I could meet them while remaining loyal to the company. It turned out that my judgment was correct and Pringle could never seem to come close to *"his"* objectives that he had passed on to the vice president of personnel. So, naturally, the guy was behind the eight-ball all the way and as his record grew worse and worse, he started looking for a scapegoat and the scapegoat that he wanted was me.

Somehow, a survey form on black recruitment that had been sent out two years previous to Pringle's arrival was mailed in by its original recipient. The form was just lying on my desk and Pringle got a hold of it. Knowing that he had not authorized such a survey, Pringle thought that he had found conclusive evidence that I was doing things *"behind his back."* In an effort to make sure that he had a good case against me, Pringle went and asked our senior survey researcher a lot of questions about who could authorize a survey without telling this researcher why he was asking the questions. Now, the researcher wasn't suspicious so he informed Pringle that only people from the Director of Personnel on up can authorize surveys. Pringle then took his case all the way to a corporate vice president before everyone realized that he was once again attacking me unjustly.

It just so happened that the survey researcher that Pringle had questioned was a friend of mine—and one day as we were riding home together I happened to tell him about the survey incident. Well, my friend was fit to be tied because he realized that Pringle had duped him. In fact, he was so upset that he complained upstairs about Pringle's trickery and he was high enough in the company to make it hurt.

In retrospect, however, it wasn't just the survey incident that caused Pringle to be removed but a combination of things. His dismal record left him open to attack anyhow and with the black colleges' complaints and those of blacks within the company finally reaching management's ears, Pringle had to go.

Casewriter: What happened then?

Melton: I was again put in charge of black recruitment and together with my old team we achieved the objectives for that year.

I also ran the program for one more year but my team's intent at that time was to make an orderly transition so that the black colleges would come under the regular recruitment effort. We felt that the schools had learned enough about recruiting at black colleges and universities to make the move more feasible.

After that last year, my team was permanently disbanded and I was informed that I was in line for a plant personnel manager's position in Washington, D.C. I had a preliminary interview with the Washington plant manager while he was visiting one of our plants in the Philadelphia area. After this first interview, I was under the impression that I would be offered the plant personnel manager's position after a final interview at the actual job location in Washington. However, when I traveled to D.C. for the final interview, I was given a verbal runaround and was not offered the job. I later found out that the reason for the misunderstanding was that National was afraid of the consequences if I failed as a personnel manager. Right after that, I had a chance to join the Urban Coordination Staff and I took it.

Casewriter: Given the fact that you do not want to be looked upon as specialist in black recruitment, how does your present position with the Urban Coordination staff relate to your personal goals?

Melton: I still feel that in order to attain my goal of becoming a corporate vice president, I will have to do a stint in line management, probably as a personnel manager of one of our larger plants. I guess you could say that getting line management experience is a mechanical step in my career path.

My present job is a big step up for me because it is a corporate staff position. More important than that, however, is the wide scope of our efforts. The Urban Coordination Staff (UCS) devises, implements and manages all of the programs aimed at upgrading people belonging to minority groups. For example, one of our biggest manufacturing facilities is near the town of Chester, Pennsylvania, and employs a large percentage of that town's work force. Historically, conditions for minotiry groups in Chester have not been very pleasant, as is the case throughout many areas of this country. So when the UCS staff wanted to do something for minority groups in Chester, we could not just launch a minority hiring effort but we also had to look at the problems facing these people in the areas of health, housing and education in order to do a really effective job.

To answer your question directly, even though I am still somewhat of a specialist in social action programs, my interest has been broadened greatly and I plan to concern myself with other areas as soon as possible. In order for my efforts to be appreciated by more people, I have to get them to identify with what I am doing.

Casewriter: How do you plan to do this?

Melton: *If I could expand into the areas of, let's say, ecology and education, that would be one way. Another thing that I am doing is working with poor whites in Appalachia. If I can first get the people in the company to appreciate the problems of white people in Appalachia, then I can transfer that same concern to the problems of the poor people in our cities. By doing this, I can avoid all the heat and emotion that comes into play when you talk about helping blacks or other minority groups in the cities, because then the issue of racism comes into the picture.*

To show you what I mean, the UCS group has to maintain a very low profile on what we are doing and our accomplishments. This is done because all of the polls show that over 50 percent of the country feels that too much is already being done for minorities. That 50 percent is also present at National, so if we start tooting our horn, the company would risk alienating a large percentage of its work force and they are not going to take that chance. The reason that we go along with the low-profile concept is because we don't want to crystallize that large "silent majority" into a large, vocal opponent. Then again, most of the programs with a lot of publicity really are not accomplishing very much in terms of helping poor people.

The National Alliance of Businessmen, for example, is perpetrating a cruel hoax upon the people it is supposed to be helping. To assume that uneducated and desperate minority group members can be adequately trained in a short period of time and shoved into a highly efficient work organization is ridiculous. These workers usually turn out to be unprofitable and, as soon as a company can, they will get rid of them. This is exactly what happened with the car manufacturers, who recently laid off thousands of their people who had come into those concerns as hard-core unemployed. This stems from all the attention that has been focused on the lower rungs of the ladder. You know that a black guy with a degree could always get a job even if it was with the post office, but when Watts erupted, all the attention was shifted to the people on the lower rungs of the socio-economic ladder. Therefore, the people in the middle were left in the lurch. Take the Job Corps, for example. The entire concept behind the Job Corps is that it is better to drop out of high school, join Job Corps and learn a skill than it is to get your diploma. The Job Corps should be moved to the post high-school level because too many kids go all the way through school before they discover that they do not possess any skills, that the system has failed them. These are the people who have started all of the riots, the people in the middle, the people who have been left in the lurch. The people on the lower rungs need better health care and psychological help before we can start to place them in an organization that is so socially structured that you need a sixth sense in order to make it.

It's also interesting that companies will donate $250,000 to the Urban Coalition, which has done nothing and is staffed by a bunch of opportunists, but at the same time will express grave doubts about giving a paltry $25,000 to the NAACP Legal Defense Fund, which has constantly won victories for minority groups in this country. It seems that these companies perceive organizations that are accomplishing something as threats to their existence.

Black capitalism is another sham. The notion that I can go into a ghetto, hire

150 people and then compete with a large corporation is nonsense. What the proponents of black capitalism are doing is shuttling a lot of sharp, young black people into an impossible isolated effort. Blacks have got to start making the system work for them instead of trying to alter it. The system is set up in such a delicate manner that it will include blacks to avoid being changed. However, if we try to destroy the system, it will crush us.

Chapter 8

MANAGING DECISION-MAKING GROUPS

Managers and others at high levels in organizations often work together for purposes which are recognized as official or "formal" by the organization, even though often they do not appear on the organization chart. Examples are boards of directors, standing committees, cross-functional coordinating teams, project teams, and other ad hoc groups. The formal responsibility of such groups may range within their organization from coming to a specific decision on a particular matter, to monitoring certain results, to merely exchanging information so each member may better carry out his or her individual responsibilities.

Managerial groups that have responsibility for making decisions, or that must reach a consensus important to the results of the organization we shall refer to as "managerial decision-making groups." Their functioning is of such visibility and importance, and often so poor a use of managerial resources, that considerable attention is worthwhile in order to understand them and develop guidelines for improving their results.

It should be noted that our definition of managerial decision-making groups clearly includes those boards of directors, teams, and committees which are responsible for coming to a conclusion or choice on one or more issues, and which may also be responsible for implementing their decisions. The definition also includes groups charged with making a decision which becomes a recommendation for some other body or individual to use in making final decisions, or for others to implement. In these instances the group must interact in some fashion which takes them through one or more decision-making processes. We shall not include groups which meet, even if regularly, to exchange information or simply to inform each other or their chairman or organizational superior about something. The focus is on groups charged with sufficient responsibility to make the individual members seriously concerned and involved in results.

DECISION-MAKING GROUPS IN THE CONTEXT OF THE OVERVIEW MODEL

The essential aspects which distinguish managerial decision-making groups from others are that they have formal responsibility for reaching conclusions of relevance to organizational results and that by virtue of making decisions they engage in interaction in some form of problem-solving process. Both of these aspects relate to formal and identifiable organizational inputs or organizational tasks. Thus, the primary distinction between informal groups and decision-making groups is that the former have no explicit formal sanctioning. Rather than decision making in the usual sense, the primary task which emerges in informal groups is providing support and leverage for individual members to cope with pressures or proactively to achieve some political ends of value to one or more members. (See Figure 7-1 in Chapter 7.)

Of great importance to the functioning of managerial decision-making groups is the effect on them of influences from informal managerial groups, as discussed in Chapter 7. The perspectives of members toward the assignment and task in managerial decision-making groups are affected by these individuals' membership in informal managerial groups as well as by their individual characteristics and other inputs. In particular, the perspective which members bring to an assignment often leads them to bring "hidden agendas" of purpose deriving from their personality, from their informal group membership, or from emergent interpersonal relationships as well as from their formal organizational roles. The various hidden agendas thus become an input, along with formal task and assignment, to the decision-making group. The behavior of members in meetings and the results of meetings are affected by all these things.

Whether or not a decision-making group is successful in meeting its responsibilities will depend basically on two things. The first is the extent to which the group brings together in its membership the appropriate resources in relation to the hidden agendas they bring and in relation to the characteristics of the decisions to be made. An elaboration of characteristics requires that we describe further ways in which decisions may vary. This will be taken up below, where we discuss inherent uncertainty and inherent complexity.

The second variable for success is the quality of the process of decision making. That is, given an assignment of members and given a task, outcomes will depend in part on how well the group proceeds to do its job. Group decision making can be weakened when the resources are inadequate, such as there being inadequate inherent knowledge among members about the questions they face, when hidden agendas are so pervasive as to interfere with the work, or when even a relatively simple task is poorly defined and the decision-making process is poorly managed.

From a managerial point of view results are what count. In light of the potential barriers to success by a decision-making group, it is appropriate for those who would form such a group first to ask if that should be done at all. In other words, when should a decision be made by an individual and when by a group? Let us examine this question before elaborating further on the input and process aspects which affect group decision making.

INDIVIDUALS VERSUS GROUPS FOR DECISION MAKING

A great deal of research in the behavioral sciences has dealt with a comparison of individuals versus groups for decision making, and much of it has practical implications.

Early research on decision making tended to focus on differences between individuals and groups when each was engaged in relatively simple tasks. As one might expect, some studies suggested groups were superior and others, that individuals were superior. More recently, as a result of careful examination of these studies, and particularly as a result of more research and observation in *organizational* settings, it has been recognized that the broad question, "Which is better?" is an inappropriate question. Rather, we see that conditions of the nature of the decision, the nature of the group, and the process which the group uses all determine whether a group will be better or worse in terms of results than will an individual acting alone. As an experienced top manager once replied when asked whether groups or individuals were better, "Yes."

In their review of the literature, Kelley and Thibaut (1969) concluded that the primary condition determining whether group or individuals made better decisions was the nature of the decision. That is, controlled studies show groups to be better than individuals at making decisions which involve problems with multiple parts, better on average at problems which require few steps and in which any judgments or solutions can be verified, but less effective when a sequence of steps must be followed in a fixed order and when correctness is hard to verify. There are some useful guidelines here, although we should note that in terms of our overview model this review looks at only one of the inputs to managerial group decision making, the nature of the task. It is quite possible that the one-to-one connection between type of decision-making problem and quality of result would break down when the other aspects are brought to bear, as they are in any practical situation. Thus, whether a group would be effective on a complex decision (multiple parts) would depend in part on the experience and skills of those assigned to it; whether an individual would *ever* do better than a group would depend on how well the group process was managed by the discussion leader, and so on.

Maier (1967) has reviewed studies and specified conditions which he calls the assets and liabilities of groups compared to individuals. On the asset side, groups can bring a greater sum total of knowledge, more different approaches, better comprehension, and can generate among them better acceptance of a decision than can individuals alone. On the liability side, Maier concludes that group social pressure can inhibit quality of results, that a steamroller effect can take place, that an individual may dominate with the wrong view, and that the purpose for some in the group may indeed be to win an argument rather than solve the problem at hand. Certain other conditions become either assets or liabilities, depending, as Maier interprets the literature, on how well the leader manages the group process.

Process aspects include how disagreement is handled, whether or not the leader can manage to promote mutual interest instead of conflicting interest, whether the group is risk-prone or risk-averse, how much time is involved, and the question of whether those who change their views are the more or less capable participants. Overall, Maier's review concludes with an emphasis on the role of the leader as appropriately that of a facilitator and integrator of diverse arguments in the group, and that the leader should not exert a strong substantive input on the process.

Maier's review is useful so far as it goes, but dangerous in its final implication. The focus is on the process of discussion in groups, and the implications point to ways in which group discussions can be made more effective and better solutions reached depending on how the discussion leader does the job. On the other hand very little is said about the nature of the task as an input. The implicit assumption behind Maier's conclusion seems to be that these generalizations about process apply to all kinds of decision problems.

Clearly, for practical purposes a manager needs to take both task and process into account, and in this sense the reviews by Kelley and

Thibaut and by Maier together are useful. However, neither review, and virtually no controlled studies, have attempted to deal with both of these aspects, plus the variation of environmental pressure, plus the effects of organizational assignment, plus the effects of hidden agendas deriving from the perspectives of members who are also members of informal managerial groups engaged in a political process. These reviews of the literature are valuable to the practitioner in suggesting ideas, concepts, and techniques, but they must be seen as still only touching on and emphasizing parts of the whole complex reality which a manager faces in an organization.

FIELD STUDIES AND NORMATIVE APPROACHES TO MANAGERIAL DECISION MAKING

In an important book entitled *Decision Making*, Janis and Mann (1977) present another perspective that offers both an emphasis on one of our variables and some conclusions from research outside the laboratory as well as from traditional research. Their starting point is psychological. They see the individual decision maker as a cognitive information processor and as an emotional being with conflicts which inhibit purely rational processing. The Janis and Mann approach fits into our model in part by providing an overview theory of how individuals make decisions.

With respect to our concern here for group decision making, the approach by Janis and Mann suggests one or two useful guidelines. In their theory Janis and Mann point to the typical emotional problems for individual decision making as stress and the introduction of "preconscious bias." Whatever other advantages or disadvantages groups have as compared to individuals, we may note here that a well-managed group can create and mediate the personal stress felt by individual members, so that the level of anxiety is either raised to the point where most members recognize the process to be irrational, or it is soothed below the level of causing poor decision making. A group can serve an important role as a source of reality for one or more of its members who exhibit preconscious bias; the group can, under the appropriate process, serve as an anchor to reality. Finally, a group in an organization can provide *structure* to the decision-making process, an aspect often overlooked and underemphasized in research. Individuals acting alone often cannot provide adequate structure in terms of deadlines, review, and the like for themselves.

Based on earlier work by Janis, the Janis and Mann book also extends the theory into group decision making, with particular attention to the problem of "groupthink." This is the term coined by Janis to reflect the problem of decision-making groups in which members are more concerned with their satisfaction and achieving a comfortable *social* process as opposed to hard-headed decision making. Groupthink thus derives from individual member needs. In terms of our overview model, groupthink is a reflection of a certain emergent norms of a decision-making group. It reflects informal rules which say, in effect, "Don't rock the boat," and "Maintain harmony." In this attention to problems actually encountered by policy-making, high-level groups, Janis and Mann come closer than most other researchers to a recognition of the multiple complexities at work in decision-making groups in the organizational context.

A similar approach is to be found in Vroom and Yetton (1973). Based on field studies as well as controlled studies, these authors develop a descriptive theory of decision making and from it a set of normative guidelines for how managers should decide on the extent of use of groups versus themselves as individual decision makers. The significant contribution of this work is that it systematically takes into account many of the situational factors which we refer to as inputs in our overview model, including time pressure, many aspects of the nature of the decision-making task itself, and an assessment of group resources in comparison to organizational needs.

Critique of the research

On the whole, the literature is sparse which takes into account adequately the complex conditions and the process issues involved in managerial decision making. Indeed, the basic dichotomy of much of the research, on whether individuals or groups make better decisions, is something of a red herring. It misses the mark when it comes to important questions facing managers. Of greater relevance is the need to study the variables facing groups as decision-making bodies in the organizational context. More field study of actual managerial groups at work is needed, study of groups attempting to resolve complex and uncertain decisions when members bring to the table not only their formal roles, skills, and personalities but also their hidden agendas.

It is rare that a manager asks, "Should I or a group make this decision?" That question is most often not the manager's to make, but is constrained by dependence on or power over subordinates, or by the existence of formal structures or lack of structures and the prevailing expectations of the managerial culture. Rather, the manager is more often concerned with the question, "How can I improve the outcome of the decision-making process, given that in some instances it will be by me or another individual, and in many instances it will be by a group?" In other words, the manager is more often concerned with influencing the process, as for example, *how* a committee goes about its work, even where the committee may ideally be a less appropriate deliberative body than an individual.

To help with this practical need, let us return to the application of the overview model to situations of group decision making by expanding our concepts and by providing guidelines for the management of decision-making groups.

The nature of inputs to group decision making

In an earlier section we pointed to the relevance of informal group membership of managers as a factor affecting their perspective on group decision making, the hidden agendas factor. Certain other aspects of the general overview model should be highlighted to emphasize important aspects of the variables in the functioning of managerial groups. "Environment" is important because of the degree of urgency, criticality and contribution to uncertainty, and complexity surrounding the decision-making task of the group. An urgent decision will require great efficiency of group output; a critical decision will require greater effectiveness or quality. Both of these may increase the pressure on the group and the stress on members, thereby affecting the process of their interactions.

We now turn to a closer analysis of the task input for decision-making groups, namely the nature of the decisions themselves. Decisions facing managers may be characterized either by *type* or by certain *qualities*. Types of decisions are of less interest here. By types we mean such categories as strategic decisions, policy making, decisions which go into planning, decisions which require problem finding, and decisions which are primarily concerned with the implementation of the other types. In terms of the Anthony (1965) and Scott-Morton (1971) frameworks, in which decisions are categorized as operational, control, and strategic, corresponding roughly to the lower, middle, and upper levels of organizational hierarchies, our concern is with the upper levels, although we expand these to include decisions other than strictly strategic.

The common characteristic of these types of decisions is simply that they have some considerable impact on the organization. We are not concerned here with trivial decisions, even though they may be made by higher level managers.

Of greater importance for our purposes are three characteristics of decisions. These are uncertainty and complexity, discussed earlier in the chapter, and criticality. Uncertainty, it will be recalled, is the extent to which the outcome of a decision is difficult to predict in advance. Complexity is the extent to which a decision has a host of separate parts or requires a great deal of information or information from

widely different sources. As a general rule, complex decisions often can
be broken down into subparts which in themselves can be considered
decisions. Criticality refers to the degree of pressure or urgency which
the decision context provides.

These three inputs plus the nature of the assigned responsibility
constitute the situational or conditional factors governing the setting
within which managerial groups function.

The nature of results of group decision making

What does a decision-making group seek to *achieve*? How can
one measure or assess the outcomes of a decision-making group? To
answer this question we turn again to the overview model. Outcomes of
any process of organizational behavior should be thought of in terms of
efficiency, effectiveness, satisfaction of participants, the flexibility of
the unit in question to change, and the ability to acquire resources.

For managerial decision-making groups, clearly the most important
of these criteria is *effectiveness*. In this instance effectiveness means the
quality of the decisions made, that is, how well the decision takes into
account in an unbiased way all the facts, all the alternatives, and all
the implications of the situation. This emphasis follows closely that of
Janis and Mann.

Efficiency in managerial decision making, while it may be of secondary importance to effectiveness, is a criterion which offers an important
constraint. Efficiency here means the amount of output per manhour of
time consumed, and given the subjective measure of output, it is
clearly much more difficult to assess than for lower level groups or
units. Maier (1967) noted that there is often a tendency for problem-
solving groups (particularly, it would seem, in academic laboratory
experiments) to want to rush through the process and get it over with.
They seem to want to be too efficient and to downgrade the quality and
importance of the substance of the task they are engaged in. Most
managers seem to find that as often as not in practice the opposite is
true—meetings often drag on beyond the point of productive use of
time.

Groups of all kinds tend to have among their informal norms and
even their purpose for being the *satisfaction* of members. This is particularly true for informal managerial groups, where satisfaction is the
primary criterion by which members judge the outcome of group membership. To a lesser extent it is also a criterion for decision-making
groups. Clearly, without at least a certain minimum level of satisfaction by participants, a sense of harmony, there would be anomie or
grudging participation in meetings of the group. More significantly,
without some degree of enthusiasm, commitment, and satisfaction de-

riving from members' sense that they are accomplishing something in their collective deliberations, the kind of interaction and exchange of views needed for high-quality decisions would not be forthcoming. Perhaps more than anywhere else, there is a correlation between members' individual satisfaction and the effectiveness of the outcome.

But this does not necessarily apply if we include into satisfaction the sense of psychological well-being that comes from agreement. When a group values agreement over effectiveness, groupthink is the result. As Wilson (1978) has pointed out, a balance between an appropriate level of harmony, which leads participants to trust one another and exchange views in the interest of a common task, and too much harmony, where that becomes an end in itself, is clearly called for.

THE PROCESS OF GROUP DECISION MAKING

Given the three inputs and the ways of assessing outcomes, what lies between? Descriptively, what are the aspects of group process in managerial decision-making groups which can help us understand and manage them?

There are several variables which have been developed from observations of laboratory groups which will prove useful as ways for a manager to *observe* the *process* of decision-making groups. Summarizing several of these sources, including particularly Bales (1950), we present the following features of group process important for a manager to recognize:

1. The amount of *participation* in the discussion. This includes *who* participates and how wide is the participation. The range here can be from domination by an individual to even distribution to total silence.
2. The amount of *opinion giving* versus *opinion seeking*. Given a level of participation, another dimension is whether the exchange is give-and-take or not.
3. The extent to which there is *reflection of listening* going on, and whether in adjacent inputs to the discussion there is explicit or implicit recognition of points previously made.
4. The degree of *task* orientation in participation versus maintenance, tension relief, or whatever.
5. The *nonverbal* aspects of communications. These are the often subtle, nonverbal cues such as where people sit, their tone of voice, their body language, and so on.

Each of these aspects is an observable manifestation of group process. They do not in themselves carry any value connotations. Thus, it may be either a good thing or a bad thing for the ultimate quality of outcome of a group decision that there is dominance of participation by one member or virtual silence by all; whether sticking to the task or relieving the task with humor or whatever is a good thing may or may not, for a given period of time, affect the outcome favorably.

The relevance of these observable variables of group process is that they are the raw data which reflect the underlying nature of the emergent group made up of the decision makers themselves. That is, the group's norms and emergent purpose will be reflected in these observable process issues. For example, it is often quite easy even for an untrained observer to infer which member of a managerial decision-making group has the highest formal status in the organization. This individual is most commonly deferred to, may not be disagreed with, and more often that not will sit in a position of dominance (e.g., head of the table) and have the last word or the most influential contribution to the discussion.

Of particular importance to managerial groups is the question of norms that affect decision making. Thus, the process may reflect norms which encourage healthy disagreement, or they may be weak and allow for open conflict and emotional encounters. Wilson (1978), commenting on his review of the literature, has stated well a commonly held view that effective groups are those in which members debate and disagree on *ideas,* but not on personality. Maier (1967) makes the same point. Ideally, then, one would like to have groups be open and rational in debate, avoiding personalities. Right?

Perhaps. There are two problems with this, which really fall into the category of prescriptions and guidelines more than a descriptive format. First, as noted earlier, there are few important strategic decisions which do not require either the intense political involvement of participants for their effective resolution, or the intense involvement of the participants which commits the individual emotionally as well as intellectually to achieve implementation of the outcome. Second, it is our experience that managers who are career-oriented and involved are simply *unable* to divorce their ideas from themselves. The idealized group process, in which rational, unemotional debate occurs is at best a front for underlying emotional commitments, ups and downs by those whose ideas are accepted, built on, and received with enthusiasm or alternatively ignored, rejected, or destroyed. We shall return to the implications of this in the next section.

Meetings as forums for process

The convening of a managerial decision-making group in a meeting provides the forum within which process activity takes place. It is important to recognize the various types of meetings which can occur in organizations and the functions which they serve.

Jay (1976) has categorized types of meetings. They include the purely symbolic, the information giving, the information seeking (exchange of information), and the deliberative, consensus-seeking group decision-making meeting. Although the latter type most clearly concerns the discussion of managerial decision-making groups, it should be recognized that even for groups with explicit decision-making responsibility there may be meetings of the other types. The appropriate process and the appropriate leadership will depend, among other things, on the particular type of meeting which is being held.

A categorization of meeting types, such as this, is an important addition to what we have available from the research literature. In virtually every laboratory experiment the meeting has as its purpose or task, at least in the initial perception of the subjects, the conducting of the experiment itself. Other assigned tasks may be imposed, but they are almost always recognized by the participants as being of temporary duration. In organizations meetings have purposes, sometimes explicit and sometimes implicit, and they serve certain psychological and social functions which simply cannot be reproduced in their total complexity in a controlled experiment in the laboratory. These purposes and functions may seem alien to one unfamiliar with organizational reality. The subtleties often elude the practicing manager as well.

Purpose versus functions for meetings

An important purpose of meetings, particularly those of the information exchange type, is to promote integration among members representing different departments or coalitions. In general, the purpose of a meeting is that intent which the convener is aware of. It is, in general, the formal organizational charge or mission, broken down, as necessary, into the particular objective of the particular session. A *function,* however, may be quite different from a *purpose.* Functions are all the ends which are served, the implicit and personalized goals as well as the intended or explicit ends. Thus, a function may be to manifest the cohesiveness of the group of members—to serve to reinforce their commitment to the organization or their manager. A meeting may serve the function of expressing needed harmony even if it serves little or no explicit purpose.[1] It may be merely an opportunity to "show the flag." It may be a forum in which cultural and organizational norms are exercised, reinforced, tested, and changed. Seeger (1978) has

---

[1] This function of meetings is described in Zander (1977).

documented this in his research. It may serve to clear the air in a political conflict or to submerge it further.

Meetings are often crucial events in and of themselves, serving as turning points and climaxes of slow-burning political battles. More often than not, the full impact of interaction processes observable in a meeting is only realized by participants after the fact. It is only later that the full significance of what did or did not take place becomes apparent. This may well be because meetings are often the poorest places for the open expression of motives and intentions, given the relatively public nature of the process there and the necessarily nonexplicit nature of the expression of hidden agendas in political struggles. Conversely, commitments obtained from members in meetings are often short lived and not fulfilled. The sense of support and euphoria which can result from a process oriented toward harmony and agreement as a goal may elicit unthoughtful commitments which wilt as the pressures of day-to-day obligations and immediacy impose on the committed. All this easily contributes to the cynicism of many serious managers to the effectiveness and efficiency of meetings, committees, and managers who call for them.

At the same time, as we have suggested, meetings can serve certain important functions. In particular, if and when they are held in an ad hoc fashion, off the formal premises, and without the apparent trappings of formal sanction, meetings can be invaluable. In most organizations members have necessary roles to play, typically the formal required tasks they must perform. Where these call for the presentation of a "front," such as the role of bank teller, salesman, welfare counselor dealing with members of the public, or managers coping with an irrational boss, there is often a strong individual need for a forum for meeting with colleagues. Meetings at a party, at a bar after work, for poker once a month, all serve as "off-stage" opportunities for these people to express feelings and to form the informal managerial group. We learned recently of a practice in one company in England in which top management met monthly at 4:30 P.M. in the office to discuss their results. Invariably the meeting ran over the usual 5:30 P.M. end of the working day. Invariably, also, it was immediately reconvened at the local pub. There, the serious purposes of the earlier meeting gave way to the expression of opinions which for perfectly practical reasons could not be discussed openly in the office. The second meeting, in effect, served the functions of off-the-record commentary and reinforcement of important informal bonds among the management team.

Given the purposes and functions which meetings can serve, given the nature of the inputs hidden agendas and process of managerial decision-making groups, the questions which remain are what the manager can do to influence such groups to attain high-quality decisions with acceptable efficiency and satisfaction.

INFLUENCING DECISION-MAKING GROUPS

Once again, our first rule is "be aware." It behooves the manager who is leader or responsible member of a managerial decision-making group to take into account systematically all the aspects, concepts, and variables laid out up to now in this chapter. In this closing section we shall suggest how such an awareness may be used as part of the influencing of decision-making groups, and how a normative approach to the decision-making process itself can be useful.

In general, managers can manage the behavior of decision-making groups according to the three paths of influence described in Chapter 2. The first is direct influence. It is the face-to-face influence of individual members *apart from* the contact with them in meetings. The second, and of particular relevance here, is the management or leadership of the emergent group, the exercise of semidirect influence in the meeting which brings together fellow managers for some particular decision-making task. This involves the management of the interaction process, affecting the process features listed earlier in this chapter. The third is to manage by indirect influence, namely establishing the appropriate inputs. That is, to make determinations in advance of a meeting itself of who should attend, what the purpose and agenda should be, and what the particular decision-making task should be. The typical sequence will be the reverse of this order: first the exercise of indirect influence through input determination, then second the management of meetings themselves and/or the influence of individual members on a one-on-one basis.

Influencing inputs

What should a manager consider when deciding on the inputs to a decision-making process which may involve a managerial group? Based on the ideas in this chapter, we can suggest several sequential questions, given roughly in order of priority, and action guidelines based on answers to those questions.

First, the manager should consider the nature of the decision-making task itself. Relative to others, how critical, uncertain, and complex is it? What are the organizational resources available? To the extent the decision is high on any or all of these relative to the potential resources experience and decision-making capabilities at hand, an effort should be made to break down the task to subtasks which are smaller and more manageable decisions in themselves. This effort of adjusting or scaling the task is essentially one of buffering the decision-making group from some of the potentially overwhelming aspects of crucial, strategic, top-level decisions. Of course, the exercise is applicable for managers at other levels as well. It is, in effect, an exercise of individually *defining* the decision or problem to be solved.

The second structural or input question is to analyze the nature of the human resources to be employed. As indicated earlier, this is not merely a choice of whether an individual (possibly oneself) or a group should make the decision. In practice it is extremely rare that a single manager at any level has the luxury to decide how a problem will be solved or how a decision will be decided. There are several reasons for this. For one, critical, complex, and uncertain decisions do not come to the attention of one individual alone in a complex organization. They typically come from several departments or individuals simultaneously, or at the very least the symptoms of some problem are recognizable in various ways to different parts of the organization at the same time. All the constituencies and individuals, it will seem, must be given recognition that the problem or the symptoms have been identified and that "management is doing something." Another reason is that typically there are existing, well-established formal organizational structures and units whose roles and missions are to handle the decision brought to the fore. It is one of the alleged advantages of bureaucracy (in the Weberian sense) over particularistic entrepreneurship that there is a separation of important decisions from the potential idiosyncracies of individuals in favor of the checks and balances of role incumbents following constitutional procedures. It is rare that an individual manager, even if aware of an important problem before anyone else, is free to decide who will deal with that problem; more often than not the very nature of the problem and the organization dictate that it be shared with others.

If the liberty to decide who should be involved in a decision does exist, then the normative approach of Vroom and Yetton (1973) is a useful guide. They develop a decision tree in which the manager, having defined the problem, asks a series of diagnostic questions. The answer to each question leads down a path resulting in preferred decision processes for each path, particularly whether the decision should be made along a range from individual to group consultation. Their diagnostic questions deal with the importance of the quality of the decision, the availability of relevant information, the extent to which the problem is structured, the need for acceptance by subordinates of the result, and so on.

Influencing the group itself

The second basic means of influencing managerial group decision making, through semidirect influence, has two separate components. One is through effect on the informal managerial groups whose members may compose part or all of the membership in the decision-making group. We have covered this earlier in the chapter. The second is to affect the decision-making process itself through the management of meetings of which one is a part. We shall explore this in greater detail here.

The effective influence of meetings, particularly the running of meetings, requires—more than any other managerial role—an ability to maintain in mind at one time both an awareness of process variables and an awareness of substantive topics. The specifics of running a meeting should begin with an assessment of purpose. If the purpose is decision making, this should be defined in terms of what decision or issue is to be discussed or resolved. The next preparatory issue is, who should attend? From our earlier discussion it should be clear that this question will often be moot. Nevertheless, there will be opportunities to add or eliminate attendees, at the discretion of the chairman, even for established committees and boards. A final set of questions revolves around where and when the meeting should be held. This includes the seating arrangements, the timing in relation to other concerns attendees might have, and so on. Attention to these details can mean much to the success of a manager's efforts to influence the process of a meeting.

In the course of the meeting itself, the members and leader should attend to process without necessarily being explicit about process. There is, however, a normative process aspect which managers should be aware of and be explicit about. This is the sequential process of decision making itself. Seeger (1978) has summarized the literature on the steps in problem solving and developed a normative guide for the decision-making process. The steps proceed in the following order: problem definition, alternative generation, choice of solution, and implementation planning. Although there may be particular meetings whose purpose is not decision making or whose purpose may be limited to only one of these steps, the idea of having an agenda for the meeting process is invaluable.

Influencing individual group members

The final way in which decision making can be influenced is through individual, face-to-face contact with members. This approach may occur before any meetings or a particular meeting if leaders or managers believe they can expect a certain reaction. The exercise of canvassing the members of a group prior to a meeting, either mentally or literally, is most important and often ignored. Given that meetings are public forums, and given that many meetings are held in contexts of organizational climates and norms that do not permit total "openness," astute managers should do some thinking about hidden agendas or participants in advance, check out any hypotheses they may have on a face-to-face basis, and modify their formal agenda and style for running the meeting accordingly.

Given that a meeting has occurred, a manager has had an opportunity to observe individual members under some degree of pressure. On the basis of this, the manager should make determinations of what face-to-face discussions are needed. Quite apart from this, the typical social pressures of a meeting—the moderate stress which participants often feel in speaking out in a group—can be a most valuable source of data for the manager who has a responsibility for evaluating or helping others.

CONCLUSION

Unlike emergent managerial groups, decision-making groups have formal organizational sanction and some explicit task. Considerable research has been done on decision-making groups, particularly around the use of groups versus individuals, and some useful concepts for understanding them have emerged. Nevertheless, the manager needs to think in terms of his or her particular context and to think of the wide range of elements affecting groups in organizations rather than depend on single cause-and-effect conclusions from controlled research.

While managerial decision-making groups are formally sanctioned, the processes and dynamics which in part determine their effectiveness are subtle. Influencing such groups requires an understanding of the informal forces on members and of group process dynamics. Taking action to influence group decision making can include affecting inputs, the group itself, and the individual members separately.

QUESTIONS FOR STUDY AND DISCUSSION

1. Cite examples from your own experience of highly visible, but ineffective types of meetings? How were the effects of that inefficiency mitigated, or were its consequences apparent in poor organizational functioning?

2. Do you regard hidden agendas as contributory to or detrimental to the functioning of a decision-making group?

3. What are some of the similarities and some of the differences between informal managerial groups and decision-making groups?

4. If you are now a member of a recognized decision-making group in your organization, what is the purpose or decision on which you are now working? How effective is the process of meetings in working toward the goal?

   What specific steps could be taken by individuals to improve the process if improvement is needed?

5. Does the group to which you belong ever engage in a discussion of the process it is going through? If not, what forces act to prevent such a discussion?

   Do you think such a discussion would be helpful in leading to improvements in the group's effectiveness?

   How would you suggest that such discussions be initiated and conducted?

Case 8-1
Textile Corporation of America*

In 1963 the Textile Corporation of America (Texcorp) was formed from three family-owned companies: (1) Smith-Abbott Mills, centered in Fitchburg, Massachusetts, and directed by William Abbott; (2) North Carolina Mills, owned by the Ford family and headed by Robert Ford; (3) Carolina Cotton Company, a single large mill located in South Carolina and owned by John Rand. The three family companies had not been direct competitors. Smith-Abbott Mills produced high-grade spun rayon and wool blended fabric; North Carolina Mills specialized in fine cotton fabrics and staple synthetic fabrics; and the Carolina Cotton Company made high-quality cotton print cloth. By combining their firms' resources, Abbott, Ford, and Rand became owners of a major firm in the fine textiles industry, with sales in 1963 of $45 million.

Due to family loyalties and the strength of long-standing reporting relationships, Texcorp existed as a single company in name only. Few functions were integrated, although accounting for all three firms was done at the corporate office in New York City. Because his North Carolina Mills represented the largest portion of the Texcorp (1963 sales of $25 million), Robert Ford and his management team were able to dominate the company through 1966. William Abbott, the wealthy owner of Smith-Abbott Mills, avoided direct participation in Texcorp management. He kept an office in the New York headquarters, attended board meetings, and watched the Fitchburg operations, but much of his time was spent vacationing in Europe or playing golf. In 1967, Abbott decided to spend more time in New York City.

By 1967 it was clear that the fine cotton fabric market was declining in importance in the United States. In June of 1967, representatives of the National Chemical Company (NCC) were approached by Texcorp management at the suggestion of William Abbott. National Chemical was a multinational corporation with 1967 sales of over $2 billion. They had recently begun to diversify into nonchemical markets, and several Texcorp executives were personal friends of National executives. These informal relationships led to official discussions, and National Chemical purchased Texcorp in early 1968.

In the exchange of Texcorp stock for National Chemical stock, all of the directors of Texcorp became wealthy men. Texcorp's directors controlled 68 percent of the voting stock of the company when it was purchased by National Chemical. William Abbott became one of the largest individual shareholders of National Chemical common stock. Robert Ford, then 65 years old, agreed to step down as president of Texcorp and William Abbott became the chief executive. Ford, al-

---
* All names have been disguised.

though not entirely happy with the management arrangements, had considerable financial security in that his family's trust fund now owned over $10 million of National Chemical stock. Richard Hicks, the National Chemical vice president responsible for Texcorp, felt that Abbott would make a better chief executive than Ford, and encouraged the management transition. Abbott made several organizational changes himself at this time. Andrew Thompson, who had been the star salesman for Smith-Abbott Mills, was promoted to vice president of sales for Smith-Abbott Mills. Walter Hogan, a former plant manager for Smith-Abbott Mills, became vice president of manufacturing.

Texcorp's sales in 1967 had risen to $65 million. Profits had grown from 1963 through 1966, but had dipped somewhat in 1967 to $2 million. Exhibit 1 outlines the Texcorp organization in February of 1968, and Exhibit 2 presents the background of key personnel.

XHIBIT 1
ebruary 1968: Texcorp organization

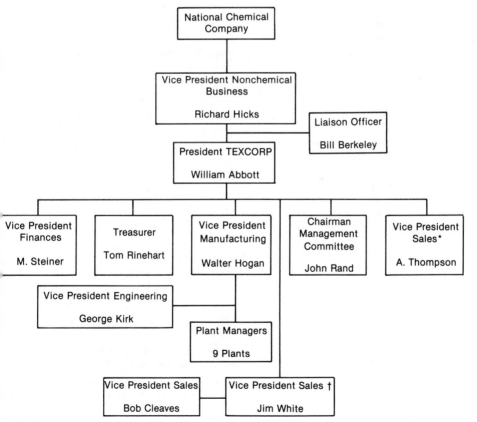

* Smith-Abbott plant.
† North Carolina Mills.

EXHIBIT 2
Personal background of Texcorp personnel

Name	Age	Background
William Abbott*	55	Former president of Smith-Abbott Mills, ex All-American football player from Princeton, independently wealthy.
Andrew Thompson	41	Former salesman for Smith-Abbott Mills, former professional golfer, long-time friend of William Abbott.
Walter Hogan*	62	Former plant manager of Smith-Abbott Mills, former football coach, long-time friend of William Abbott and Mr. Abbott's father (founder of Smith-Abbott Mills).
John Rand*	66	Former president of Carolina Cotton, Harvard College '25, independently wealthy.
Martin Steiner	42	Former chief financial officer for North Carolina Mills.
George Kirk	45	Hired in 1964, chief engineer for four Texcorp engineers, offices located in North Carolina.
Sam Jarvis*	54	Plant manager of Carolina Cotton plant, brother-in-law of John Rand.
Bob Hogan	36	Plant manager of Smith-Abbott Mills, son of Walter Hogan.
Jim White	55	Former sales manager of North Carolina Mills.
Bob Cleaves*	42	Former president of a small textile company bought out by Texcorp in 1964, independently wealthy, a bachelor.
Tom Rinehart*	63	Treasurer of Texcorp, former treasurer of North Carolina Mills.
Bill Davis	50	Plant manager of largest North Carolina Mills plant, appointed in 1965, son-in-law of John Rand.
Bill Berkeley	29	MBA from Berkeley, hired by National Chemical in 1967, worked for Hicks since December 1967.
Richard Hicks	50	Vice president of National Chemical, Harvard Business School class of '49, known as a "real professional" to other National Chemical executives.

* Indicates that an employment contract was in effect. (These contracts lasted through 1971 and guaranteed the men salaries ranging from $40,000 to $70,000 per year.)

JOHN MITCHELL, MBA

John Mitchell, 27, was married and had one child. He grew up in Darien, Connecticut, and was graduated from Harvard College in 1963. Mitchell had chosen Harvard because it was supposed to be a very liberal school. For the first two years he remained conservative, but during his junior and senior years he committed himself as a political liberal. He took courses in religion and psychology and briefly considered being a minister. After graduation he thought about entering law school or medical school, but his father wanted him to go to Harvard Business School (HBS). After receiving his MBA in 1965, he joined a Peace Corps project in the Far East, where he taught industrial psychology.

John Mitchell liked to think of himself as good at the "gamesmanship" of life. His interest in psychology led to a certain degree of introspection and he prided himself on his ability to describe the games people played. In high school, for example, Mitchell was often called an "apple polisher" because his school work seemed to follow the particular concerns of his various teachers. He was a straight-A student. In college, he hardly ever cut classes, and was a Dean's List student for four years. He was active in athletics, and was a starting fullback for the Harvard team. Mitchell even considered football a "psychological game." Commenting on his football experiences, he said:

> If the coach was in a mean mood, you growl and hit somebody . . . if not, you joke and try and have fun. Hell, the guys that were on the field to make the big plays not only *did* the right thing in practice, but *thought* and *said* the right thing too. . . . It's all a fantastically complicated game.

Mitchell earned a varsity letter each year in college.

Mitchell's experiences overseas strengthened his political "liberalism" (labeled "radicalism" by his mother). While at the Business School, he had participated in many lengthy discussions about the businessman's social responsibilities. John Mitchell was sometimes shocked by what he considered to be the narrow-mindedness of some of his classmates, and he often wondered if the business world could offer him the satisfactions he believed he needed in life.

His interest in psychology eventually led Mitchell to a one-year research project while at the Harvard Business School, and the co-authorship of a book on psychological aspects of motivation.

In 1968 Mitchell decided to return to the United States. He did not think he had the patience to be an effective teacher, although he had been very successful as a teacher in the Peace Corps. The business world in the United States in 1968 further challenged him because of the new emphasis being placed on social responsibility. Mitchell hoped

he could find a job that offered an outlet for his growing social conscience. Also, he was anxious to test himself in a real business organization: "I wanted to see if I could compete with my classmates from HBS.
But at the same time I love travel, love other cultures. But I kept wondering, if I were back in the States, would I be such a hot shot."

NATIONAL CHEMICAL COMPANY

Richard Hicks, the vice president of National Chemical and responsible for Texcorp, heard about Mitchell through family friends. Hicks
was in charge of National's nonchemical operations, and he wrote
Mitchell and asked him to come to National Chemical's offices in New
York to talk about the company's operations overseas. When they met,
Mitchell told Hicks that the chemical industry didn't really interest him,
because it was dominated by large corporations; however, after many
meetings and several offers, Mitchell agreed to go to work as assistant
to the president of Texcorp, William Abbott. Mitchell would be trained
for a year in the textile business and then go to a textile mill that
National was planning to buy overseas. The job sounded ideal to
Mitchell. He could test himself in the world of big business and also
indulge his interest in travel and living abroad. The Mitchells rented a
small house in Darien.

In July of 1968, Mitchell went to work at Texcorp, which was located
in an office building about ten blocks from the National Chemical
headquarters in New York. William Abbott had been told very little
about his new assistant, except that he was to train him for a year. Since
Mitchell knew nothing about the textile business, he asked to spend
two months in the mills—part of this time as a loom operator, which he
did, even though this was theoretically against union regulations.

Mitchell's initial impressions about Texcorp and Texcorp management were very favorable. Andrew Thompson, the vice president (VP)
in charge of textile products and the number 2 executive at Texcorp,
was a very outgoing and personable man, and Abbott told Mitchell to
see Thompson if there were any "problems" with his training. John
Mitchell spent most of his time at the large Smith-Abbott Mill in Fitchburg. Although the workers believed him to be a "spy from the chemical company" at first, they soon relaxed and Mitchell developed several
strong friendships. Since he was living in a motel in Fitchburg without
his family, he spent 12 to 14 hours a day at the mill and got to know the
personnel on both the day and the night shifts.

When he returned to New York in September, Mitchell found that
there was nothing planned for him to do. Although Abbott spoke to
him every day in his office for about 20 minutes in order to find out how
he was getting along, Mitchell felt that no one was really interested in
what he did. Consequently, he willingly accepted responsibility for

helping to collect and organize the financial figures for the first Texcorp five-year plan. (Systematic planning was one of the most well-developed management techniques at National Chemical.)

Mitchell was beginning to learn more about headquarters personnel at Texcorp. He observed that four offices, which he called "Executive Row," were large, spacious, and thickly carpeted, while the rest of the Texcorp offices were relatively modest. The four offices were occupied by William Abbott, Walter Hogan, John Rand, and Tom Rinehart. Mitchell was surprised to discover that Rand and Rinehart were rarely involved in the regular management meetings, and Hogan was not highly respected by many of the headquarters' personnel.

Although he got along well with all the Texcorp executives, Mitchell found that he had too little in common with them to spend much time socializing: "I was too young and unimportant. Also, I didn't play golf and I didn't drink. I had tomato juice at lunch while they were boozing it up."

Bill Berkeley, who was the "liaison man" assigned to Texcorp by Richard Hicks, became Mitchell's closest friend, since they were the same age approximately, and the only men at Texcorp under 40. Also, both Mitchell and Berkeley reported to Hicks:

> Bill Berkeley and I got along very well . . . . Berkeley spent half of every day over at Texcorp talking to Abbott or one of the financial VPs about liaison work. You know, fill this form in, the appropriations meeting is next month, etc.

Mitchell was distressed at the unsophisticated level of management he found at Texcorp, and he developed the habit of having long, one-sided conversations with his wife when he arrived home each evening:

> What a day! Discovered that I was the only—get this!—the only guy who could use a slide rule in Texcorp, except for Kirk . . . but he's an engineer . . . I don't know. It sure seems like some of those men waste a lot of time and stuff trying to butter-up Bill Abbott, and there's so little real *analysis*. Hell, no!! I'm not "buttering him up" with my slide rule! You ever tried doing 20 discounted cash flows without one!?!

As October wore on, John Mitchell began to feel frustrated and bored. One day he went around the Texcorp office asking executives if they had any jobs or projects he might help them with. He spent a day filing expense reports, and three days drawing graphs and charts showing loom utilization for the first half of 1968. He later told his wife:

> It's kind of dull right now. I didn't think it would be like this. What! Sure, I've talked to Andy. He doesn't know what to do with me. Let's face it . . . none of them really know what to do with me. First I was a "spy," you know. Now I'm a "bright kid with a lot of potential." I don't want to be underfoot all the time. You can only ask a guy for work so many times, then you just have to try and make work. What a drag.

And, in early November:

> Well, I finally talked to Andy today. Told him I was really going out of
> my mind. And I talked to Bob Cleaves. Anyway, they both told me I
> should lay it on the line to Abbott. "Talk to him at Oscar's," they said.
> [Oscar's was a large bar and restaurant often frequented by Texcorp
> executives.] I'm going to ask him for more responsibility. Hell, I've got
> absolutely zero now. He must know how I feel . . . but he's so damn
> silent. No one ever knows what's on his mind. . . . Except Andy, of
> course. Those two are like father and son.

Because William Abbott seemed constantly preoccupied and was
often out of the office, Mitchell was reluctant to speak to him about his
job. ("If I catch him wrong, he'll just see me as a complainer, or,
worse, an overly ambitious 'whiz kid,'" he explained to his wife.) Abbott ran Texcorp with the help of the two executives who had come
with him from Smith-Abbott Mills in Fitchburg, Andrew Thompson and
Walter Hogan. Thompson and Abbott were particularly close, and virtually all company decisions were made by these two men. Abbott had
also continued to direct Smith-Abbott Mills personally, and he and
Thompson spent five to eight days a month in Fitchburg. Finally, in
mid-December, Mitchell followed Thompson's advice and asked William Abbott if he could speak to him at Oscar's after work.

Mitchell discovered that his boss was much easier to talk to at Oscar's. Abbott liked to drink, and Mitchell found it relatively easy to ask
his boss for a line position with specific responsibilities. Abbott replied
that he would like to have a boy like Mitchell on his "team" and would
give him a position if he would pledge to stay "with him" for three
years. As the evening progressed, Mitchell observed that Abbott spoke
more and more about "loyalty" and the value of a man who would
"stick it out." Mitchell was reluctant to commit himself to any time
period, and at 10:30 P.M., when the two left Oscar's he remarked that he
would "certainly stick it out if things went well."

During the second week of November, Mitchell had spoken to
Richard Hicks. It was their first meeting since July, and Mitchell had
requested it because he had heard that the National Chemical Company's plans to purchase an overseas textile firm had "fallen through."
Richard Hicks' dynamic personality had been a large part of Mitchell's
decision to work at Texcorp and he enjoyed the 30-minute meeting with
the National Chemical vice president. However, he learned that plans
for expansion into overseas textiles had been delayed indefinitely. That
night he warned his wife:

> Don't pack those bags for Europe; we'll probably never need them.
> Yeah, the deal fell through . . . looks like it's Texcorp or nothing. . . .
> Anyway, the glamour has worn off a little; how about you? Good, if
> things go well, maybe we can rent a little bigger house next year.

This change in Mitchell's original career goals forced him to examine his present situation at Texcorp even more closely.

TEXCORP PERFORMANCE

For the next month, Mitchell continued to make work for himself. In order to keep completely busy, he fulfilled a long-time desire and signed on as a volunteer consultant for the New York Urban Coalition. Beginning in December, Mitchell spent at least two nights a week working late in New York City. He found the excitement and satisfaction of volunteer work made his late arrival home almost worthwhile. (Mitchell often skipped dinner and arrived home at midnight.) But in December, the November financial statements were released and the usual good humor in the Texcorp offices became strained. Sales had dropped sharply, and most of the plants were losing money:

> They're all waiting for some kind of axe to fall from Hicks. Man, were the figures rotten. One of our plants was showing a 22 percent loss before taxes! I don't know what National is going to do, but I hope they do it fast. What do you mean, *I* should do something?! Who am I? Anyway, I think there is a project I could do.

The disappointing financial statements brought to immediate response from the Chemical company. Texcorp managers, however, began to express their concern to Mitchell. Andrew Thompson and Walter Hogan pointed to the relatively stable performance of the Smith-Abbott plants, and at management meetings they emphasized the need to upgrade the plant efficiency at Carolina Cotton. Sam Jarvis, Carolina's plant manager, complained openly to Mitchell and other Texcorp executives that his product mix was unprofitable because several North Carolina Mills plants were now producing what he used to produce and he was never given the money he needed to buy needed new equipment. Bill Berkeley spent two or three days each week at the Texcorp executive offices. Berkeley and Mitchell often spoke about Texcorp organizational problems and the need for reform. Berkeley was often asked what, if anything, the Chemical company was going to do about Texcorp in light of the poor operating statistics, and his usual reply was one of assurance. "Calm down, fellas," Mitchell heard him say. "Just get out there and sell a little, and we'll do all right." Privately Berkeley admitted to Mitchell that he knew Hicks was concerned about the poor performance, but he didn't know if major policy changes were planned.

By the end of December, it was obvious that the year-end financial statements would also show sharp declines in sales and profitability. Although Andrew Thompson was beginning a two-week vacation in California and William Abbott was on a week's vacation in Florida, John

Mitchell decided to put together a marketing research study of Texcorp's two biggest plants. Rather than "clear" this study with the two absent executives, he approached the two plant managers involved and they responded enthusiastically to his proposed studies. For the next several weeks, Mitchell spent most of his time in Fitchburg and South Carolina (the location of the two plants he decided to study).

The poor performance reflected in the late 1968 financial reports prompted a minor Texcorp reorganization in December. Mr. Hicks moved to create operating divisions and attempted to formally alter the old family reporting and communications channels. After close consultation with William Abbott, he announced the formation of temporary committees to run three operating divisions. Each committee would have a chairman, and the chairmanship would rotate every quarter. It was understood that this was a short-term and temporary arrangement, and that permanent division managers would be appointed as soon as possible. Andrew Thompson was made chairman of the Consumer Products Division (primarily high grade spun rayon and wool blends), Jim White (former vice president of sales for the South Carolina Mills) was made chairman of the Industrial Products Division (find cottons and synthetic fabrics), and the chairmanship of the Specialty Products Division was left vacant. Exhibit 3 illustrates the new organization. This

EXHIBIT 3
Unofficial organization of Texcorp, December 1968

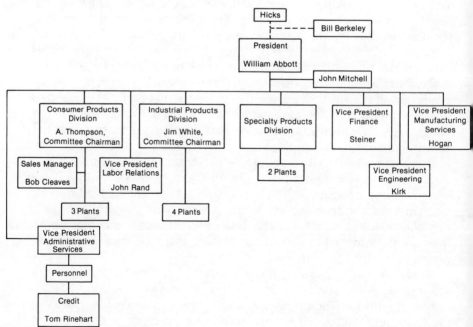

chart was drawn up by Bill Berkeley, but was never identified as "official." The presence of the "unofficial reorganization chart," however, was known and accepted by Texcorp executives.

Mitchell completed his first marketing study in mid-January. The study included an analysis of profitability by product line and by major customer, and was enthusiastically accepted by the plant manager. Mitchell sent a copy of his study to William Abbott but Abbott did not comment on it.

A REQUEST FOR PROMOTION

John Mitchell was growing increasingly impatient. He had developed a close relationship with Mary Fagan, the President's secretary, and the two often had coffee together in the cafeteria in the basement of the Texcorp office building. Mitchell found Mary a perceptive and intelligent girl, and soon he was discussing a wide range of company problems with her:

> You know, if it weren't for Mary, I think I'd go nuts in the office. Today we talked about Kirk. She agreed with me that he's a brilliant engineer . . . but really out of sight when it comes to company politics. You know, he calls Mary from his engineering offices [located in North Carolina] just to find out what kind of mood Abbott is in before calling him. And today he called me and asked who was meeting in the board room. He'd heard there was this big meeting and he wondered why he hadn't been invited.

The reorganization of Texcorp into divisions had not, in Mitchell's opinion, straightened out the most serious company problems. Lines of authority were still unclear. Old, informal relationships still prevailed over the new (and as yet "unofficial") lines of communication. Abbott and Thompson continued to make most of the decisions. And overall marketing and sales objectives were left undefined. Mitchell became more and more disgusted with his situation:

> I've decided that Texcorp reminds me of a country club. Abbott and Thompson are both top golfers. They must spend $300 a month taking customers, friends, etc., golfing. And when it comes time to make a few decisions, they do it like they might select an iron. You know, squint down the fairway, laugh a little, say "What the hell" and blast away. I'm convinced there are three or four of our top executives who ought to be retired . . . permanently . . . but Abbott could no more do that than he could give up his booze or his golf . . . Yeah, I am depressed. . . .

Prompted by his continued frustration and the company reorganization, Mitchell decided to write Andrew Thompson a letter asking for a new job. He anticipated that Thompson would show the letter to William Abbott. It is reproduced as Exhibit 4.

EXHIBIT 4
John Mitchell's letter to Andrew Thompson, dated January 13, 1969

Dear Andy,

I hope this note will help you understand my as yet unresolved anxieties concerning my future here in Texcorp. I am putting this in writing to save your time and to facilitate any further discussions. Let me try and describe my perspective.

First, I see a lot of work to be done at all levels of the organization. Much of this work is a matter of analysis (data collection, organization, setting priorities, etc.) Systems must be set up, studies made, programs established and monitored, etc.

Second, I see a limited number of people with the background and training to accomplish all of the analytical work that has to be done.

Third, I see myself and my own selfish goals. I have spent all of my lengthy (four-year) business career doing analytical staff work. I have developed a certain facility for this kind of work. But it no longer offers the challenge I desire. I want to assume more complete responsibilities. I want to be a boss. I want to be able to look back and say, "Look, I did that . . . that's my success." When I spoke to you earlier, I hoped you might have a line position for me in your division. I have been told—and I am forced to agree—that I lack the experience to be a line manager in sales or in manufacturing. Those are the only two lines at the divisional level.

Given what I see around me, I conclude that from the organization's point of view, I should be in a position where I could move freely about; conduct market studies in the divisions, assist engineering in plant relocation studies, help establish systems and procedures, etc. (As William would say, "For Chrissake, John, we have so much to do, let's just do it!") I would need some source and position of authority that everyone saw as "legitimate" so that cooperation would be maximized. I guess my present status and title of "assistant to the president" seems best suited to these organizational needs.

From a personal point of view, however, this role is less than ideal. William, I suspect, has never quite known what to do with me. I am always a little "in the way" or "under foot." My duties too often dissolve into those of a clerk-secretary-adding machine. I bear much responsibility for this, I will admit. I haven't tried to be "pushy" and I have avoided playing too many games with too many people. And I have paid a personal price: boredom. The frustration I can handle; the boredom slowly destroys me. All of this has been changing, but the deeper I get into the problems and the personalities, the less secure any "assistant to" position becomes. As your assistant, for example, a careful (and probably not very convincing) explanation would have to go out if I were to involve myself in the Industrial Products or Specialty Divisions. I guess it comes down to the fact that I don't think being anyone's assistant will offer me the kinds of challenges I desire. (Man, this is sounding more and more presumptuous and egotistical every minute.) Anyway—from my own standpoint, I would like to be in the position of vice president of administrative services. Here I would have the challenge of line responsibility and the opportunity to test myself. (Although I still wouldn't have the kind of "line" challenge and satisfaction you have when you sell a good fabric order, or a plant manager has when he reads the bottom line of his profit and loss statement.) In charge of administration I would still have both the time and the authority to conduct the needed analytical studies and services. I would be available to all departments—both informally and formally. In this position I would

Exhibit 4 (continued)

---

also be able to involve myself in those kinds of administrative tasks that do not require 20 years of experience in the textile business.

Before you laugh at my conceit, let me explain why I think it's a reasonable gamble from the organization's point of view. We all agreed some time ago that the job should be created. We knew that systems were needed and that a man was needed to supervise these tasks as well as purchasing and credit (neither of which involve close or imaginative supervision). Bill Berkeley can handle the job, and I've heard his name mentioned. But he has said "No" to both of us privately, and I doubt anyone will change his mind.

"NOW WAIT A MINUTE!! You really want me to say you can be VP of administrative services!?!" Yes, I'm only 27 (But, just think! I'll be 28 in June!) Yes, I just started shaving last year. Yes, only six months in textiles . . . only six months in this company. I realize William is the man to talk to in the end. It's his ball game. But with your understanding and support, my feelings, expectations, and anxieties can be more carefully presented to him. Anyway, I've got enough guts to think I can do a better job there than anyone else we've got. And I don't think it's the kind of position that a new man would be able to take over. I'd be the lowest-paid VP in the city, and that'll help our budgets.

I'd like to speak with you about this note and try to cover the 100 other questions that arise from my cocky, impertinent ambition before approaching William.

If and when you show this to William, remind him he once told me to stick around because "the way we are, there are plenty of opportunities to learn." Remind him he said that, and then ask him how he learned to catch a football.

John

Mitchell continued to work on his final marketing study. It was completed in February and focused on the declining profitability of the large Smith-Abbott Mill in Fitchburg. Using it as an excuse to talk to William Abbott, he tried to broach the subject of the unfilled position of administrative vice president. Abbott ignored Mitchell's casual inquiries, and at the end of February Mitchell's letter of January 13 still remained unanswered.

Well, scratch one effort. I guess they couldn't have made me any vice president. Who did I think I was . . . Oh well, it sounded good at the time. Here I am. A guy who's supposed to be an expert in human relations. And I'm tied up in knots by a bunch of dumb playboys! I can't figure it out. One day I think I know why Hicks hasn't done anything. I see a little spark of hope for Abbott. And the next day I hear that Abbott has gone and wasted more money on a project that has no chance of success. You should hear the other executives talk about him. They're all losing confidence. And, you know, he hasn't called me into his office in almost three weeks now. Hell, he used to give me little odd jobs every day.

On February 1, 1969, Bill Berkeley resigned from the National Chemical Company. The day he left, he and John Mitchell had a long luncheon and Berkeley talked about National Chemical and Richard Hicks:

> John, I've worked for that man longer than any of his previous assistants . . . and I still don't really know him. The "infighting" at National is intense as hell nowadays. The president resigned last year and they still haven't filled the position. Hicks knows he's in line. I'm sure the lousy 1968 Texcorp figures shook him up. Abbott keeps telling him "things will improve, things will improve," and I think he believes it! He won't listen to me. I've heard a lot of talk around the Chemical company about Hicks and some of the other vice presidents. There's the "pro-Hicks" and the "anti-Hicks" factions. . . .

Mitchell expressed his surprise at the extent of the office politics at National Chemical, but admitted that he knew Hicks must be under considerable pressure. Mitchell refrained from telling Berkeley that Berkeley could have prevented the "communications gap" between National Chemical and Texcorp by being more frank with his boss.

TEXCORP MANAGEMENT

Mitchell was also beginning to believe that everyone in Texcorp and National Chemical was guilty of "playing politics." Texcorp's plant managers operated with considerable independence. Martin Steiner, the vice president of finance, was the only home office executive who dealt with plant personnel on a continuing basis; yet, by January of 1969, he had been unable to implement a company-wide cost accounting system. The controller of Smith-Abbott Mills, for example, was very "secretive" with his cost information and Steiner received only token cooperation from him. On several occasions Steiner remarked to John Mitchell that "things were sure different when old Bob Ford was running the company."

In spite of Richard Hicks's attempts to restructure the Texcorp organization, the old company loyalties and factions continued to function. William Abbott, Walter Hogan, and Andrew Thompson directed the Smith-Abbott plants; Jim White and Martin Steiner spent most of their time dealing with the North Carolina Mills plants; and John Rand and Sam Jarvis concerned themselves with the Carolina Cotton plant. As the profitability of this latter plant declined, both Rand and Jarvis tried to "mind their own business" and avoided discussions with Texcorp executives of overall policies and problems.

Management meetings were held once a month in the Texcorp

Board Room. The members of the Management Committee were: William Abbott, Andrew Thompson, Walter Hogan, John Rand, Martin Steiner, George Kirk, Sam Jarvis, Bob Cleaves, and Richard Hicks. John Mitchell was invited to attend many of the meetings. His increasing concern over the company's viability and his interest in psychology prompted him to reflect upon the "patterns of communication" that emerged among the Texcorp executives.

When Hicks attended the meetings, a business-like atmosphere prevailed. The management meeting was almost formal, and the men seemed "on their toes." Many even took notes as the National Chemical vice president asked his pointed questions. However, Hicks was unable to attend all of the meetings. In his absence William Abbott would usually begin by smiling and saying, "Well, what'll we talk about today?" Mitchell noticed that these meetings often degenerated into rambling discussions of the performance of the three family companies. Members of the Management Committee were constantly being called to the phone to "put out a fire," and little seemed to get accomplished. Mitchell soon realized that it was an "unwritten rule" that nobody paid much attention to Management Committee meetings or decisions made there, for William Abbott consulted afterwards with Thompson or Hogan and decided upon the actions to be taken.

To John Mitchell, the most confusing aspect of the Texcorp management and communications system was the lack of objectivity. No matter what subject was raised—be it a question of buying a new loom or expanding a product line—everyone seemed to have a known and fixed position. Texcorp executives *expected* Andrew Thompson to fight for increased expenditures for blended wool fabric capacity, and everyone *expected* Sam Jarvis to say that cotton prints were the best long-term investment for the company, and Mitchell observed that they were never disappointed. Since the members of the Management Committee were already "on record" as holding certain opinions, discussions were usually routine and (Mitchell thought) uninteresting. New facts were seldom presented. The voluminous industry-wide marketing statistics published by the Textile Trade Association were never cited. Texcorp executives seemed to rely on their intuition and "gut feel" for the situation. The engineering studies of George Kirk were privately referred to as "worthless." Bob Cleaves and Martin Steiner confided to John Mitchell that on several occasions Kirk had changed his facts and figures to make the studies "come out the way Abbott wanted."

Mitchell tried to remain neutral as far as office politics were concerned, but this was often difficult:

With a climate so politically sticky—I never pulled punches or played politics. This got me into trouble. When someone said, "How's it going?"

I said, "Lousy." I was everyone's friend, and they (the execs) all wanted me for their assistant. All the division managers lacked management expertise.

Mitchell had tried to figure out why NCC was so reluctant to examine the situation at Texcorp. He thought one reason might be the fact that the presidency of NCC had been unfilled for several months and a successor had not yet been chosen:

> Hicks may be mixed up in the hassle over who gets to be president of NCC. He wants to sweep Texcorp under the rug because it's a bomb. They have lost at least $5 million in profits because of Texcorp, and part of this is company politics. Bill Abbott is one of the largest single stockholders in NCC and he also knows Bill Scott (board chairman of NCC). So Abbott is formidable.

What really shocked Mitchell, however, were the day-to-day politics at Texcorp:

> The number-one priority here is personalities. The prime commodity people fight for is Abbott's time. I'm shocked at the amount of time spent on personalities. From 80 to 85 percent of people's time is spent warming up somebody or cooling off somebody or on other nontask conversation.
>
> Another related commodity is information—facts about what's going on, who's talking to who, etc. But you can't get any data from the responsible people—the secretaries are the people to talk to if you want information. Everyone relies on rumor, and people here ask the secretaries to relate casual conversations they've overheard so they can figure out which way the wind is blowing. Mary Fagan even says that Abbott has asked her to spy on me!

Many people at Texcorp used Mitchell as a confidant, and Mitchell felt he had to keep a delicate balance of discretion and candor. For instance, Martin Steiner would complain to Mitchell that he desperately needed a new accountant and this complaint would serve as a smokescreen if Steiner's department got behind in its work. Mitchell felt that George Kirk, the head engineer, was almost paranoid about authority. If Abbott requested that Kirk see him in his office, Kirk would call Mitchell first to find out what Abbott wanted.

In February an incident occurred that John Mitchell found to be almost humorous. Three new looms had been installed in Bill Davis' (North Carolina Mills) plant, and William Abbott sent Walter Hogan south to "supervise the breaking-in period" at the plant. Bill Davis was not informed and was upset when Hogan walked into his plant and began asking questions. Davis placed quick calls to Jim White and John Rand protesting Hogan's presence, and finally called William Abbott. The irate plant manager said he could handle any "breaking in." Abbott explained that Hogan was just "inspecting" the new looms and said that George Kirk had suggested that Hogan be present when they started operations.

John Mitchell became involved in the controversy when he had lunch with Kirk the day following Hogan's arrival at Bill Davis' plant. Kirk was furious. He did not respect Walter Hogan and said he "didn't particularly care for Bill Davis" either. But he stated that he had never suggested that Hogan be sent to Davis' plant; "Now Jim White and Marty Steiner will speak to me. They think I sicked Hogan on Davis. You should talk to them, John, and tell them what really happened." Mitchell discovered from Mary Fagan that Kirk had, in fact, written a memo about the looms to Abbott. When questioned by Abbott, the chief engineer had evidently agreed that Hogan might "supervise the looms for a few weeks." A few days later, Mitchell mentioned the matter to Bill Berkeley. The young National Chemical representative pointed out that George Kirk seldom disagreed with anything William Abbott suggested. The entire incident seemed ridiculous to John Mitchell, but Berkeley pointed out that such "misunderstandings" were common at Texcorp.

A FINAL CONFRONTATION

Mitchell was becoming increasingly aware of his unique position in the Texcorp organization. More and more often he was asked to listen to the problems of various company executives. Bob Cleaves confided in him almost daily. Cleaves' responsibilities had been reduced when Texcorp was reorganized, and he constantly spoke of "retiring" or quitting. Walter Hogan was also expressing personal opinions to Mitchell. Hogan's new position as "manufacturing services manager" was a clear demotion. Hogan was 62 years old and admitted to Mitchell that he knew "his days were numbered." Martin Steiner and Jim White spoke to Mitchell in January about the financial and sales deficiencies they had observed at Texcorp. They encouraged Mitchell to "speak to someone at National Chemical" to see if Abbott could be replaced and new talent recruited. Mitchell responded by speaking to Bill Berkeley, but advised both Steiner and White that they should be the ones to approach Hicks:

> I don't know, the atmosphere is getting thick as glue around Texcorp nowadays. The company's going down hill. Abbott's spending more time on the links. Everyone comes to me with their problems. What am I supposed to do? Except Andy. . . . He and Abbott don't talk to me any more. I guess they know I think they're both doing a lousy job. But, hell, they're in charge. All guys like Cleaves and Jarvis and Steiner seem to be doing is bitching. . . .

During the months of February and March, Richard Hicks was out of New York City. This only added to John Mitchell's feelings of helplessness. He was now convinced, beyond doubt, that Texcorp was being badly mismanaged. His personal future seemed to depend on the National Chemical Company: when and if it would step in and replace Abbott and his management "cronies." On March 2d he spoke with William Abbott and told him he was "thinking of quitting." Abbott reacted very calmly and remarked that it was "too bad," but that it was his (Mitchell's) own decision:

> Hell, he just sat there. The bastard. Didn't even bat an eye. I gave him the chance to try and talk me out of it. It was half a bluff anyway. Man, now I have to find another job! Wait till Hicks hears this. He's going to wonder what's been going on while he was away.

The following day, Mitchell told Bob Cleaves what he had done. Cleaves reacted emotionally and told Mitchell he was a fool. "The future of Texcorp will rest with guys like you," he exclaimed. "You're throwing away a great opportunity. You know National Chemical will have to move in soon. And when they do, you will be the one who comes out on top!" Later on that day, William Abbott called Mitchell into his office and asked if he would "reconsider" his resignation. He said he could only reconsider if "major changes" were implemented at Texcorp, but Mitchell agreed to spell them out in writing. Abbott said he would read what Mitchell wrote and "we can talk when I get back from Augusta."

Mitchell proceeded to write a three-page description of what he saw wrong with Texcorp and what changes might be made. Excerpts from this letter to William Abbott are reproduced as Exhibit 5. When Abbott

EXHIBIT 5
Excerpts from Mitchell's letter to William Abbott, dated March 3, 1969

Mr. William A. Abbott
Augusta National Golf Club
Washington Road
Augusta, Georgia

William,

    I am sorry to bother your golf, but all of this is important to me and I wanted you to have time to think about it. I have not gone into personal requests. If this letter makes sense to you, we can speak about my future when you return to New York.

*   *   *   *   *

I. Prerequisites for success in textiles.
    1. Must have market specialization with a well-focused sales effort. This is the only way to avoid competition based on price alone.
    2. Must develop those services our key customers want (and will pay for).
    3. Must carefully control costs. Because of the competitive situation and the

EXHIBIT 5 (*continued*)

large capital investments involved, incremental profits derived from cost control are often the key to success.

II. Obstacles to Texcorp success in the market.

*   *   *   *   *

We lack almost all of the above prerequisites.

We are trying to serve too many markets . . . .

We are being forced to compete more and more on price alone . . . (cf. my Smith-Abbott study). Major product lines are declining in value and suffering heavy losses (cf. North Carolina Mills study).

We are unable or unwilling to specialize . . . our sales efforts are poorly directed . . . our cost controls are inadequate . . . where are our budgets?

III. Organizing to meet the market.

. . . must begin with the New York office.

Planning is critical . . . real planning and risk-taking depend on some very simple things: rapid, clear communication, getting the right people together to make the right decisions, collecting the right kind of data in the fastest amount of time, getting quick and decisive answers to questions that can be answered quickly.

The office of the president can set the whole "organization" in motion . . . . By demanding prompt decisions, by demanding facts (rather than feelings or opinions), and by demanding that standards be met, the office of the president can begin to make Texcorp one company.

And this is impossible unless the example at the top is consistent with what is being asked of the rest of the organization . . . . There are many decisions that I think can be made today . . . .

While doing this housecleaning and planning, talent must be recruited . . . .

IV. Some specific examples.

Bring talent into the central office

Redefine head office responsibilities. Much housecleaning is needed . . . . Have you reviewed Andy Thompson's budgets? His plans? If the office of the president can't answer yes to these questions . . . then why not?

Reorganize the Engineering Group . . . . Create budgets for all vital functions . . . change the layout of the head office . . . . Establish a uniform cost accounting system for all of the plants . . . create a system of sales management . . . without reports and communication, how can we expect focus and direction?

If you were to consult others in Texcorp, and if you could get honest responses, I am absolutely positive many other specific examples could be cited—examples of things that should *and can* be decided and implemented immediately. Your organization, William, will withhold information from you because they do not have confidence that the information will be used wisely.

*   *   *   *   *

In all honesty I must say that I really don't know if my leaving the company is a very good thing for Texcorp or a very bad thing. Because in the clutch, I guess none of the fancy degrees, and none of Harvard's "principles" count for much. And I've never been there in the clutch.

returned to New York, he asked Mitchell to have lunch with him at the Union League Club. During the lunch, it became clear to Mitchell that writing the letter was a mistake:

> He was really upset. I mean, he had the letter with him. And he would read for a while then say, "You're right." Then he'd read on. He said he agreed with everything I said. He didn't even argue! He didn't question anything I said. I know now it was a mistake. I've hurt him . . . he can't even read the words I wrote. If he *were* reading them, I know he would have disagreed with some of what I said.

After the lunch Abbott said he wanted to show the letter to Andrew Thompson. He said he would talk to Mitchell later that week.

John Mitchell was very discouraged. Word of his letter had spread around the Texcorp offices and he spent the next several days answering questions about what he had said. His efforts to evade questions only added to the tension in the office and gave the entire incident "mysterious" overtones. Without exception, Texcorp managers told Mitchell he was making a personal mistake to leave the company at this point in time, but they admired his "guts" and hoped his confrontation would force National Chemical into taking some action with respect to Abbott.

On March 11, Mitchell decided to speak to Hicks about Texcorp and what he had done. Hicks was in Washington, D.C., and Mitchell flew to the capital city and spoke with Hicks for two hours. Hicks was disturbed that Mitchell had acted so precipitously and rebuked him for not having come sooner. Mitchell showed him a copy of the letter he had written Abbott and told him that it was "impossible" for him to have come to Hicks before. "I felt I should quit first . . . before telling you all of what I know about what's going on at Texcorp. I guess it sounds hollow and self-righteous now, but it's how I feel." After Mitchell talked for a while about Texcorp's problems, Hicks asked him to write a more detailed analysis of the textile company's prospects for success. The National Chemical Company vice president cautioned Mitchell to be "cool" and reasonable in this report: "Tell me what my alternatives are; tell me how much it will cost to make the changes you think should be made; and tell me what the risks are."

For the next month Mitchell worked on his report for Richard Hicks. William Abbott did not ask to see him, and Mitchell decided not to renew their Union League Club luncheon discussion. On April 10, the 1969 first quarter results were published. They showed that Texcorp had lost over $1 million after taxes during the first three months. Texcorp executives now spoke openly of "moving to greener pastures" and the offices on Executive Row were usually empty. William Abbott took three and four day weekends; Walter Hogan, at Abbott's suggestion, spent all of his time at one of the large North Carolina Mills' plants in the South; Tom Rinehart seldom came into the office; and John Rand took a month's vacation.

John Mitchell, while researching and writing his report, was also actively searching for another job. He talked to his wife:

> This time I can forget about overseas work. How would you like to work in Denver? I've got a contact out there. No, I don't know if I'd stay at Texcorp no matter what Hicks does. You never know when action might be taken. A couple of other National vice presidents have been calling Steiner and asking for some financial data, so I guess the word is finally out that all is not well with their new acquisition. But I've waited too long already. The way I see it, it'll be a year before that company's alive again. Just not worth waiting around for. . . . What do you think?

On April 17, as Mitchell was putting the finishing touches on his report, Jim White stopped in his office. White announced that he had just spoken to Hicks and that he had tried to communicate to the National vice president some of the facts concerning "how bad things were at Texcorp." White smiled and said, "John, you just can't leave now. From what Hicks told me today, I'm sure we'll see big changes very soon. Really, this time I know it will happen. You've got to stay. We'll all be better off if you do!"

Case 8–2
Bay Markets Corporation (A)*

> *Any computer manager who's worth his salt wouldn't let that situation go unnoticed by top management. You've got a responsibility to do something!*

Ron Caldwell, head of Information Systems Operations of Bay Markets Corporation, faced the consultant of Peninsula Associates who was speaking to him. He looked around the conference room at the other Peninsula people with a nervous smile during the silence that followed the accusation. Everyone seemed to agree with the speaker.

Ron had not expected to be on the hot seat like this. On the foggy Friday in late February that he and Al Daniels had driven to Palo Alto from their offices in Oakland they had chatted about the problem of maintenance that was frustrating them both. They agreed that at best the consultants' presentation might give them some new insights. But

---
* All names have been disguised.

now Ron found himself confronted with a personal challenge by an associate of the consultants who had recently interviewed him, Al, and a few others in the Information Services group at Bay Markets Corporation. The challenge would give Ron a lot to think about over the weekend.

COMPANY BACKGROUND

Bay Markets Corporation was a supermarket and retail chain store company with sales well in excess of $500 million and headquartered in Oakland, California. The origins of the company went back to the 1940s when six independent grocery store owners in the San Francisco area joined together to create the "Calthrift" grocery company. In the early 1950s Calthrift established a policy of lowering gross margins to 14 percent, significantly less than the 22 percent prevalent in food retailing. The creation of low-margin, high-volume merchandising resulted in explosive growth in sales and the number of stores. The geographical distribution of Calthrift extended throughout the state, and into Oregon and Nevada.

By 1966 a group of Calthrift stores in the Bay area that accounted for nearly half of total sales of Calthrift broke away from the company and incorporated as Bay Markets. Sales and earnings for Bay Markets more than doubled from 1966 to 1972 (see Exhibit 1), reflecting the benefits of

EXHIBIT 1
Relative financial statistics (1966 = 100)

	End of October				End of January		
	1966	1967	1968	1969	1971	1972	1973
Sales	100	112	126	134	175	207	254
Earnings	100	152	192	140	178	220	093
Earnings per share—							
fully diluted	100	151	185	134	168	200	089

not only the low margin policy, but policies aimed at greater efficiency of operations. Bay Markets came to be known in the industry for its relatively high levels of sales per supermarket and sales per square foot.

In 1972 the company suffered a sharp earnings decline, largely as a result of increased price competition and increases in labor and other costs that affected the entire industry. Although the decline had a serious impact on earnings per share, top management had foreseen the difficulty and considered successful their efforts to reduce costs and expenses as much as possible during the year.

Bay Markets was organized into divisions by line of business. In addition to the chain of supermarkets of the Pricelo Division, which contributed 75 percent of 1971–72 sales, the company owned a chain of department stores and other smaller chains of stores including "home service" (do-it-yourself centers and catalogue centers). Divisions were highly decentralized with autonomous decision-making authority in virtually every aspect of their businesses.

DEVELOPMENT OF MIS

When Bay Markets broke away from Calthrift in 1966 it found itself faced with the need to develop quickly its own physical, operational, and managerial capabilities for buying, warehousing, and transporting goods to its stores, as well as providing other services such as EDP which had been provided centrally by Calthrift. Responsibility for these developments was given to Bernard Gold, one of the few managers at that time who was not a specialist in merchandising. In January 1968, Gold hired Stan Grant to help in the planning, organizing, and staffing for new facilities construction and operations. In October of 1968 Grant was made head of EDP by Gold, who saw the need to build up that function and to allow himself to concentrate on real estate. Under Grant was Harry Brown, an accountant turned systems analyst/ programmer, who had run EDP and had introduced important computer applications in the areas of accounting and payroll.

The period from 1968 to 1972 was one of steady development in the application of the computer as an aid to operations. One of the first applications was the grocery distribution system, which came on line in 1968. The system handled all aspects of ordering and distribution from the receipt of order from stores to the printing of labels for cases. Its features included cost-optimization of loading pallets and trucks and the reordering for warehouse replenishment. The system made it possible to turn inventory 28 times per year in the stores and 48 times in warehouses, a significant improvement over previous turnover. Orders received in the morning were on the way to stores between 4:00 P.M. and 6:00 A.M. Similar systems for frozen foods and nonfoods were added later. By mid-1972 there were 32 major separate applications systems in operation.

As one MIS manager described this period, "There was a tremendous emphasis to get things done, get applications on line, and get useful data to the users." The MIS budget for these years averaged nearly 0.4 percent of sales as compared to 0.27 percent for the industry as a whole. As more applications were developed there was a shift in the proportion of MIS budget expenditures away from development and toward operations. Operations represented less than 50 percent of the budget in 1969, and had climbed to 75 percent in 1972. According to Stan Grant the MIS department, known as Information Services at Bay Markets, achieved a considerable reputation for its rapid and innovative applications developments. Grant described the period as one in which the department was "on the cutting edge of applications," and pointed out that "the computer operation runs this business."

In 1970 the top management of Bay Markets hired the nationally known management consulting firm of Marshall Associates to evaluate its operating policies and procedures. In its report, which was generally highly favorable, Marshall mentioned as one of several minor criticisms the fact that the EDP budget as a percent of sales was above the industry average. In 1972 Stan Grant sponsored an examination of the organization and operations of Information Services by the local consulting firm of Peninsula Associates, which specialized in advising on the management of computer-based information systems. The study reported a "clean bill of health," with only some minor recommendations. The most significant of these was a recommendation to transfer some systems analysts to functional areas in the user divisions, in order to provide a better input of user needs when designing systems.

MIS IN 1972

The organization of Information Services in mid-1972 is given in Exhibit 2. As director, Stan Grant reported directly to the vice president of Distribution and Services, Carl Abel, whose other responsibilities included warehousing and transportation. The two largest units reporting to Grant were Systems Planning and Development (SPD) headed by Tom Johnson, and EDP, headed by Harry Brown.

Tom Johnson had 15 systems analysts reporting to him. Their responsibility was to receive requests from users and turn these into requests for new applications or for "maintenance" changes to existing applications systems. When a project was defined by an SPD analyst and approved in the appropriate divisional steering committee, it was turned over to Brown's area. It went first to Lopez's computer systems analysis group, consisting of ten computer analysts. There it was further elaborated, and computer and programming specifications were prepared. These became the guidelines for the actual writing of computer code by the programmers in Bob Mortenson's Application Programming Group, consisting of 30 programmers and two project leaders. If changes were required in a project, or if problems or delays arose at any point, it was expected that the person in each group in the development chain who had worked on the job would be contacted and would revise his part of the sequence as necessary. In other words,

EXHIBIT 2
Organization for Information Services, early 1972

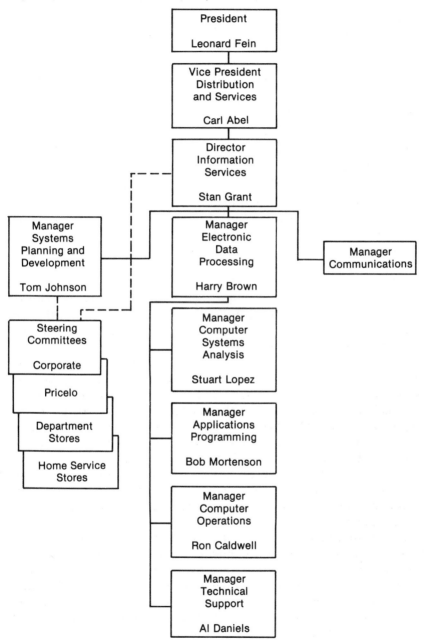

responsibility for applications or changes were passed from one functional group to the adjacent one in the sequence described.

Ron Caldwell's responsibilities included hardware operation, keypunching, and computer scheduling. Reports and other output from Operations went to users in all parts of the corporation. Much of this output, such as the daily grocery distribution runs, were critical to operating the business. The company leased a 360/50 running DOS/MFT and a 370/155 running OS/MFT. There were some 60 personnel in Operations, primarily keypunch operators and computer operators.

Al Daniels' responsibilities in Technical Support were to monitor developments in hardware and operating systems, make recommendations on new equipment or changes that might be required by a growth in CPU needs or that offered cost savings advantages over existing systems, support and maintain operatings systems, provide technical advice to other groups in Information Services and educate MIS personnel in the use of new systems. Working under Daniels were eight systems programmers and analysts.

Grant and Brown had been with Bay Markets longer than any of the other key managers, six and nine years, respectively. Grant was 54 and Brown 44. Tom Johnson was 42 and had been with the company 15 years. Lopez and Mortenson were each in their late 30s and with the company five to seven years. Brown considered them key to the continuing success of applications efforts. Al Daniels was 35 and had been with Bay Markets for a year.

Ron Caldwell, at 28, was the youngest of this group. He had been with the company and in his job for less than a year. During his short tenure, he had focused his efforts on the basics of his production unit, and had sought to streamline the various tasks his department was required to perform. Among the projects he had undertaken were a standardization of job flow procedures, an efficiency study of the keypunch operation, and the design of a multiple console hardware configuration. On the drawing board were a centralized user inquiry "hot line" and a three-day work week for computer operators. About 95 percent to 98 percent of the reports and output of Operations were being delivered to users on time.

Information Services charged users on a simple full charge-out basis for its work. Costs of development of applications and requested maintenance were charged out directly to the user involved. All other costs (such as equipment costs, operating personnel, technical support, general maintenance, etc.) were allocated to users on the basis of their usage share of computer time. In practice, an estimated hourly rate was calculated at the beginning of a quarter, with the actual determined at the close of the quarter when exact operating costs were accumulated.

THE REORGANIZATION

Early in 1972 the Marshall firm was asked to examine the MIS function of Bay Markets and make recommendations for any changes. Although some managers in Information Services felt that a more technically oriented firm should be hired, Marshall was selected by top management in part because they represented a combination of consulting experience in MIS and general management. In September the firm submitted its final report, including recommendations for a reorganization. The fees and expenses for the study totaled $94,000.

As background for their recommendations, the consultants noted that Bay Markets was nearing the end of an intensive five years of computer growth that had been painful but had achieved good payoffs from the computer. The task confronting the company now, according to the report, was to continue to achieve some high payoff projects in certain divisions, but also to concentrate on better control of the computer resource and to "clean up" the existing systems which had grown so rapidly. It was pointed out that the company continued to spend a high percentage of sales on computer budget compared to the food retail industry, but that these expenditures should fall into line in the next few years as other companies caught up and Bay Markets leveled off. No net increase in outlays for equipment or employees were seen for several years, and the consultants indicated that in some areas there should be reductions in the budget.

The major thrust of the recommendations were that Information Services be reorganized from the existing structure (Exhibit 2) to a new structure (Exhibit 3). The benefits of the reorganization and new policies and procedures to go with it were to be:

1. An improvement in selecting applications to work on.
2. A reduction in the time and cost of applications development.
3. An integration of the communications and data processing facilities in information services.
4. An upgrading of technological planning and research.

The report recommended that the senior vice president, Lew Fox, be assigned to head the new organization. Fox, a lawyer by training, had been head of the Legal Department and Store Development Department. Fox admitted to being unfamiliar with the technical aspects of MIS. His principal exposure to MIS had been to serve as a member of the corporate steering committee under the existing organization.

Stan Grant, as head of Information Services, would report to Fox. Harry Brown would report to Grant and become head of Information Systems Development, a group reduced in size from what had been

EXHIBIT 3
Organization for Management Services, late 1972

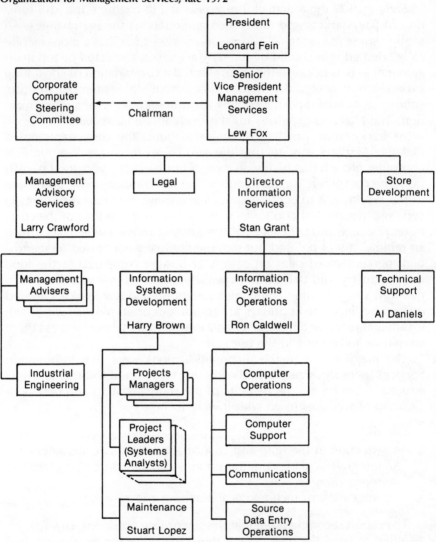

known as EDP under the old organization. Operations under Caldwell and Technical Support under Daniels would report directly to Grant.

The report established a new group, known as Management Advisory Services, which would report directly to Fox and would consist of systems analysts and business analysts closely tied to specific user divisions and groups. These people were to take on more of the user point of view, initiate projects for the project teams in Information Systems Development to work on and make it their business to understand the information needs of users to whom they were assigned on an ongoing basis. In his discussions with the consultants and top management, Stan Grant recommended Tom Johnson as head of this new group. However, the post went to Larry Crawford, a man in his 30s who had no previous MIS experience but had proven himself elsewhere in the company. Johnson went on to become a staff assistant to Leonard Fein, the president of Bay Markets.

The report indicated that attention to "maintenance," described as internal improvements of existing applications programs and data processing systems, was a high priority for the future. Nevertheless, little detail was given as to the exact means by which this was to be done. The report described the process of supplying information services in terms of three phases: (1) definition and selection of projects, (2) development and maintenance of systems to fit project requirements and processing of systems, and (3) testing, debugging, and implementing systems for users. It emphasized that the first and last phases should receive the most resources in the near future—that is, the initiation of high cost-beneficial projects from the existing backlog (some 60 projects made up the backlog) and the implementation of projects into user areas.

The report indicated that the new management advisors were to be the focal point for ideas of applications, including not only new projects but the upgrading of existing programs and ongoing maintenance. Having worked with users closely, MAS advisors were expected to represent user interests more forcefully in the development of new applications and changes in existing ones. On a given project, the MAS advisor was to develop a presentation for consideration by the new steering committee, chaired by Fox. Upon approval, the project would be turned over to one of the project managers under Brown. In contrast to the existing method of applications development the report described the process as "project management" or the "team approach," in which project leaders would head up a temporary team consisting of the MAS advisor and whatever other user, technical, or operations staff members were necessary.

In addition to carrying out projects suggested by the management advisors and approved by the steering committee, project managers were described as having the responsibility for keeping management advisors up to date on opportunities for making existing and future computer systems more effective and efficient, such as might be done through the integration of data bases.

Specific attention was given to the maintenance function in the reorganization structure by the creation of the "maintenance" group under

Stu Lopez in Information Systems Development. It was recommended that ten programmers and analysts man the function.

The report reiterated the existing role of the Technical Support group in keeping abreast of the latest technological advances in hardware and software, and recommending changes to the director of Information Services about improvements that should be made to the existing computer systems.

In addition to restructuring the organization, the report recommended increased formalization of control over the MIS function as a way of ensuring that user projects of the highest benefit to the company were worked on and that the function was run at the lowest possible cost.

The 1972 Marshall report was seen by management at Bay Markets as being a significant step toward increasing the role of users in MIS, and orienting the work done in the MIS function more toward user needs. As one manager described it, the aim was "to break the iron ring" of control over applications by Information Services that many felt had prevailed.

The report concluded with a two-page "implementation plan" that gave deadline dates for implementing the reorganization. The recommended reorganization was officially put into effect in November 1972, right on the schedule suggested by Marshall. Lew Fox called or met individually with all the managers directly affected, and followed this with a three-page memorandum that described the new organization and new responsibilities of the key managers.

THE MAINTENANCE ISSUE IN 1973

In February of 1973 Stan Grant called in the Peninsula consultants to examine the effectiveness and efficiency of Operations and its relationship with other departments in Information Services. Grant felt that there was growing pressure to obtain more CPU capacity, and that Caldwell was having an increasingly difficult time meeting the demands of users for on-time reports and output. The consultants interviewed Caldwell, Daniels, and Brown, as well as Grant.

As a major problem affecting his job, Caldwell noted that many of the systems running now were very inefficient, resulting in longer run times and operating near CPU capacity at the peak load time. This created a great deal of pressure on him and his subordinates and led to delays in the tight schedule on occasion. To make up for such delays, Caldwell sometimes found it necessary to cut back on the test run time scheduled for Brown and Daniels.

Despite his recognition of the efficiency problem, Caldwell was reluctant to insist on increasing capacity by the purchase of additional computer CPU. He had the strong feeling that the inefficiencies of the existing systems, including software and peripheral IO, were such that it might well be possible to avoid purchasing new CPU. However, he had neither the time nor resources himself to make a study of this. Instead, under the reorganization introduced as a result of the Marshall consulting project in 1972, Caldwell understood he was supposed to submit requests for specific maintenance improvements to Stu Lopez, who headed the maintenance group under Brown in Information Systems Development. At the same time, he recognized that the analysts and programmers working with Lopez might not be the best informed people to study the overall efficiency problem, which Caldwell saw as involving the question of additional CPU, the question of balancing hardware, and the question of operating systems software, as well as application program improvement.

Moreover, Caldwell suspected that his requests to Brown and Lopez were "put at the end of the list" of projects to be worked on. He pointed out that only 7 of the 29 people engaged in programming were budgeted for Lopez's maintenance group. This 25 percent commitment, he observed, compared to an average of 60 percent to 70 percent in other companies with a mature, user-oriented MIS function. In addition, he pointed out that far less than 25 percent of the budgeted manhours were actually spent on maintenance. Such work was considered "low status" by analysts and programmers, and did not get the pressure it deserved from the users themselves, who were generally more interested in new applications. Maintenance project teams were frequently "cannibalized" to get people to work on high prioroty applications projects.

When asked why this problem hadn't been discussed with the other managers of the MIS group, Caldwell replied that Grant hadn't called a meeting of Information Services managers in the previous four months. He expressed the opinion that a maintenance group should be assigned to him so that upgrading could take place as he determined it was required.

Taking a long-range view, Caldwell felt that if the immediate pressure could be relieved, so that the operation was not running so close to capacity and was improved in operating efficiency, the longer run problem still required a different solution. That is, he felt that the new Management Advisory Service Group, set up as a result of the Marshall recommendations and headed by Crawford, should take on the responsibility for educating the users to the need for ongoing maintenance and to the advisability of their paying charges for new programs developed for their use.

Caldwell concluded:

> It's at the time of project development for users that we need to get their
> commitment, verbal and monetary, to an ongoing use of resources for
> maintenance. They have to understand that maintenance is not some-
> thing that needs attention because their projects were done wrong, or
> because a program wears out in some way. It results from the inevitable
> changes in a program as it is used and modified over the years and also
> from the changes that occur in computer hardware and software which
> make old programs inefficient. They don't understand that now. . . .

The consultants next talked to Al Daniels, asking if he felt that substantial savings could be obtained from systems revisions as Caldwell
had suggested. Daniels responded that at any given time a major CPU
reconfiguration project on any major installation could yield up to 50
percent additional capacity. He added, however, that he and his group
were neither in a position to analyze maintenance proposals, nor did
they have the time to devote much attention to consideration of large-
scale application maintenance studies.

Harry Brown told the consultants that he totally agreed that maintenance expenditures were inadequate. He said that he had conferred
personally with Lew Fox on several occasions about the problem. He
explained that because he had formerly been head of Operations he
totally sympathized with the frustrations Ron Caldwell had described,
but in his present capacity his hands were completely tied. Brown
further stated that it was not his job to "grease the squeaky wheel," but
rather to evaluate user requests for development projects objectively
and to prioritize the funds allocated to his department as he deemed
appropriate. To him, computer operations was merely another user
competing for a limited development resource and that was how it
should continue to be.

Brown felt that the place for the maintenance group was right where
Marshall had placed it, in Information Systems Development. By having maintenance people under his jurisdiction, Brown felt the organization gained the flexibility of short-run changes in personnel, in that it
was possible to shift people easily to the most pressing and important
projects as necessary. He concurred that "maintenance" was a dirty
word among systems analysts and programmers, and pointed out that
he had recently changed the name of the group under Lopez to "Quality Assurance and Support." He had asked Lopez to be responsible not
only for maintenance but also for seeing that new applications and
specifications were fully documented and took advantage of efficiencies in the current operating systems. Brown suggested that the budget
for maintenance be broken down into two parts, one for "user related"
projects and the other for "efficiency" improvements. The efficiency
budget would be for projects initiated within Information Services.

In his discussion with the consultants Stan Grant focused on the question of obtaining additional CPU capacity by replacing the 360/50 with a 370/145 versus undertaking a major cleanup of systems, hardware, and applications programs. He felt this change would give additional capacity as well as provide greater realiability and compatibility with the 370/155. Moreover, he said he could arrange the lease agreements so that the switch could be effected with an insignificant increase in equipment expenditures. He felt that it would be a particularly bad time to undertake a major maintenance job.

To support the bad timing argument, Grant said that "the dust hasn't settled" from the Marshall reorganization, and that roles and relationships were still uncertain. As it stood, maintenance was under Brown, user relationships under Crawford, the problems of running inefficient programs fell to Caldwell, and it was Daniels' responsibility to build in efficiency with new hardware and software. Grant argued that a big new special project would require each of them to give up time from somewhere and to take special efforts to coordinate their work. He added that such a project would have to be paid for by someone. He noted that the charge-out system operated on the principle of users paying directly for as much work as possible, and that while some of the maintenance in a major project could be charged directly to particular users, the biggest costs would have to be overhead. Under the current corporate-wide budget crunch, Grant felt users would come bitching to Lew Fox if their billing rate went up as a result of this.

Grant believed users at Bay Markets didn't see the benefits of maintenance and system efficiency, but simply wanted their reports on time and new applications implemented "yesterday." With a new project the charge for it would go to the user immediately but the benefits in reliability or shorter run time would not be seen for months. Grant noted that a big project would necessitate having to pull some systems analysts off user projects and put them on the maintenance project which would be difficult to explain to a user who was waiting for his project to get done.

In commenting on his responsibility in this matter, Grant said he saw his job as gathering the necessary facts from each of his subordinates, making an analysis, and coming to a recommendation to present to Fox, rather than burdening Fox with technical details.

THE PENINSULA REPORT

On a Friday near the end of February the Peninsula consultants made a presentation of their findings to a colloquium of their colleagues and to the Bay Markets' clients. Because of a sudden important meeting at the corporation, only Ron Caldwell and Al Daniels were able to attend from Bay Markets. It was during the discussion, after hearing about the inefficiencies in the existing systems, that a Peninsula associate heatedly accused Ron Caldwell of being "not worth his salt" in letting the situation go unnoticed by top management.

On returning to his office the following Monday, Ron Caldwell picked up the phone and dialed Lew Fox.

Case 8–3
Bay Markets Corporation (B)*

On March 23, 1973, Lew Fox asked Stan Grant to remain after a staff meeting of MIS managers in Fox's office.

When they were alone, Fox began by telling Grant that he had lost confidence in him and could no longer feel that he could respect his judgment. He referred specifically to the question of the need for maintenance and the evidence of a lack of coordination among Grant's subordinates.

Fox said he recognized that Grant had many admirable skills, but that after very careful deliberation he had decided to dismiss him from the company.

Fox went on to explain that Grant should feel free to explain the cause of his dismissal as budgetary pressure, but that in fact the other reasons he had mentioned were the important ones.

Case 8–4
Bay Markets Corporation (C)*

As a result of his conversation with Ron Caldwell after Caldwell's visit to the Peninsula discussion in February 1973, Lew Fox had called a meeting of MIS managers at Bay Markets Corporation. Present were Fox, Stan Grant, Larry Crawford, Harry Brown, Ron Caldwell, and Al Daniels. (For background and organization chart, see Bay Markets Corporation (A).)

At the meeting Fox had called for a written report on the issue of central processing unit (CPU) capacity, with particular attention to the

---

* All names have been disguised.

feasibility of having a single CPU. He asked that all managers present take part in the study and that "dissents be aired."

It was approximately three weeks later, after discussion of the results of the study, that Fox fired Grant. Grant was relieved of his line responsibilities as director of Information Services, and of his leadership of a special, confidential project. He was to remain as a member of the team on the special project for two or three months.

This case presents the views of managers in Information Services regarding the single CPU project, the change in management, and the current state of and prospects for the MIS function.

THE SINGLE CPU PROJECT

The feasibility study had undertaken to answer two questions put by Fox: (1) Do we have latent capacity? and (2) What can we do to delay new hardware installation?

In the study, Caldwell and Daniels, who worked together on hardware and technical considerations, soon came to believe that not only could major additional CPU acquisition be deferred—perhaps for as much as two years—but that in fact the existing 360/50 could be dispensed with. The study revealed that computer channels were badly imbalanced and flooded with data that wasn't needed to accomplish the jobs being run. It was concluded that effective CPU capacity could be increased by 40 percent through improved balancing or "trimming" of hardware, upgrading the operating system to MVT to replace MFT, and the redesign and restructuring of applications programs and data bases to take advantage of these changes.

Caldwell and Daniels and the others reported their findings to each other and to Fox. After two weeks of the study, the team submitted a report recommending this reconfiguration and "clean up." This was followed by meetings in which the group discussed the pros and cons. In the meeting on March 23, Fox approved the project.

The 40 percent savings in capacity were expected to result from two different efforts. Thirty percent was expected from the hardware trimmings or "tuning" and the new operating system, with the responsibility for these falling to Al Daniels. Daniels would also be responsible for retraining operations personnel in the modified systems. The other 10 percent was to result from work by Harry Brown's Information Systems Group, which was to rework applications programs. In addition, Brown and Crawford were to communicate with users on efforts to ease the time pressure on Operations resulting from the tight daily schedule for delivery of reports and other output. It was calculated that these efforts, which constituted a five-month first phase of the project, would cost between $150,000 and $300,000, largely labor-hours of existing MIS personnel, and result in savings of $400,000 a year. Some 75 percent of these savings would result from elimination of the lease cost of the 360/50, and the remainder from the reduction in staff of eight or nine operators.

The casewriter was present at a meeting held on March 29th to discuss the single CPU project. The consensus seemed to be that the project made sense.

Stan Grant expressed his view that the users might object to the charge-out rate when it reflected the high overhead from the project.

Harry Brown pointed out that it might not have been possible to initiate such a project until the CPU capacity problem had arisen. He indicated that the size and scope of the project made it interesting and attractive to programmers who otherwise would prefer applications work. He believed that with the investment in the project and some ongoing allocations to maintenance after the project was completed the problem of future maintenance would be solved.

Ron Caldwell made the point that some steps needed to be taken to insure that maintenance was built in to future applications, after the project had cleaned up the current systems. At this point the following exchange took place:

Brown: *With this project we are really nearly there on maintenance . . .*

Caldwell: *"Nearly there?" How can you say we are "nearly there"? We aren't even into the project yet.*

Brown: *I mean we are investing a lot on this project, and once it's done we shouldn't have much trouble managing the maintenance thereafter. . . .*

Caldwell: *Yeah, but let's make sure we get to that point. What I'm saying is as an ongoing problem we haven't even been spending the 25 percent we budget for maintenance in your area, and some companies spend up to 90 percent.*

Brown: *Well, I think that is unrealistic. We should spend maybe 35 percent, but not 65 percent or 70 percent.*

Caldwell: *Like I said, we have to get the users educated to what maintenance is and why money spent on it is justifiable. . . .*

"We now have a 1973 view of the EDP management function," said Ron Caldwell after the meeting as he described to the casewriter the project and the way in which Fox had brought it about. As Caldwell put it, "the axe is over Daniels' head" for primary responsibility in the project, but "the really difficult part" would be the job falling to Crawford and Brown to make changes in user programs and to convince users of the need for less immediate output delivery. His own role would be monitoring the resource uses by Brown and Daniels as the project proceeded, by reviewing their reports and "making sure we're spending labor-hours we said we would" on the project.

For the long run, Caldwell said there was still the need for clarification of how maintenance problems would be handled on an ongoing basis. He suggested that one method might be to build in a maintenance charge at the beginning of a project. He added that he did not want responsibility for maintenance to come under his jurisdiction.

Caldwell closed by saying the project was "the first time we've had coordination among us." He added:

> There are natural conflicts among us, sure. Just the nature of our different jobs is enough to cause that. This project will put that organizational friction to the test. What's important is that we not try to do away with argument, but take these natural conflicts as a way of doing business and getting a better product.

LEW FOX'S VIEWS (MARCH 29)

Before leaving on March 29th the casewriter talked to Lew Fox about his job and his approach to managing Information Services.

Casewriter: *Would you tell me how you came to be in your current job?*

Fox: *I got a basic education in what was going on in the old Information Services when I was on the steering committee for corporate projects. Then when Marshall came in three years ago I worked a little with them. When they came in last year to work on reorganization they interviewed me and recommended that as the senior vice president I become head of Management Services. It was by a process of elimination: the president, the VP of distribution and services, and the corporate controller were all considered, but were too busy or presented a problem in terms of equitable distribution of services to users. So they offered it to me after some consideration of alternatives. I didn't resist.*

I should make it clear that I am not experienced or knowledgeable about MIS. Keep in mind that six months ago I was in charge of the legal department and the real estate department, plus a variety of ad hoc corporate responsibilities. I only knew enough about computers to sit in on a steering committee and that wasn't much.

I have been mostly educating myself. I spent four days at an IBM school, which was obliquely useful, and I plan to go to a few other computer management courses.

I sensed I would enjoy a broader involvement in line work. It has really proven to be a challenge and a thrill as I take on learning what is for me a whole new set of skills. At the same time, I remain as involved as ever in high level decisions and as a counsellor to the president.

Casewriter: *Would you describe the approach you are taking to manage Information Services?*

Fox: *Instead of talking abstractly, let me be concrete, and go back a bit. After a staff meeting last week I asked Stan Grant to stay over. I told him he was fired.*

I immediately called in Crawford, Brown, Caldwell, and Daniels and told them I had fired Grant. I knew the word would get around quickly, and I wanted to be the first to tell them rather than have them learn it from the rumor mill. On top of that, I wanted to make it clear that I did not intend to replace Grant, but that the three of them who had reported to him would now report directly to me. I wanted to let them know the slot has been eliminated, and that they shouldn't think I was examining them to see which one would fill it.

I gave them an "LBJ" speech. I said, "I need yo hep!" I said I had a technical knowledge gap, that I would depend on them to keep me informed, and that I would expect them to be able to translate what they knew into terms I could understand.

It became clear to me in that meeting that previously they had been under a lot of tension and had not been working together or meeting together. A lot didn't get done. For example, Caldwell might lose an hour of run time. Instead of getting together with Brown and Daniels to see who could best afford to give up the test time scheduled for him, the decision got made arbitrarily, so somebody was left mad. Brown, it turned out, had been particularly frustrated. At one time or another each must have thought the other was a fool.

I told them they would have to learn to ₋ettle their day-to-day problems without appealing to a higher court. I didn't want to be bothered with their daily problems. They would have to become a team for joint decision making. In addition, I told them we were starting regular Friday meetings where we would reveal our plans to each other and hash out any problems that arose from planning and schedules. For big decisions we will have five people who will help ask each other questions. For me, this is particularly important in Daniels' and Caldwell's areas—the highly technical areas. I will be depending on Crawford and Brown to help me ask the right questions. Although they are all at the same level now, they are not "equal." They have different skills and different expertise.

The organizational structure is not cast in stone. I'm still trying to settle the question of what the four should meet on and what should be pushed up to me. It's going to take a while to settle that. . . .

So, my approach now is to run without a Director of Information Services, and to run with as much sovereignty for subordinates and as much coordination as possible.

Casewriter: *The CPU reconfiguration question led to a man being fired and a big project being undertaken. What I wonder about is how do you intend to prevent this happening again? Do you have any assurances that it won't?*

Fox: *First, the reconfiguration question was just the most recent piece of data that led me to the decision to fire Grant. There are two devices to insure that it won't happen again. One is that these four men will be sharing information, exchanging information, and keeping informed on what each other is doing. . . .*

Casewriter: *Do you have some new reports?*

Fox: *No, I'm referring to the fact that each one will agree in our planning meetings about what the other will do, as for example on the allocation of manhours to the reconfiguration project, and the monthly and quarterly actuals report will let everybody know if the plan was followed.*

The second thing is the informal communications among the four.

VIEWS OF THE MANAGERS

Two weeks later the casewriter returned to discuss with each of the managers involved their separate views.

Ron Caldwell

As the casewriter waited in Caldwell's office he noticed the desk was cluttered, a sharp contrast to its cleared condition on the previous visit. When Caldwell entered he apologized for being late.

Caldwell: *One of the computers is down and I may have to get up off and on to see how things are coming. We will miss about 13 hours of run time by the time we get it up again, so several reports are going to be late today. There are 70 people out there waiting around to carry reports. The most important is grocery distribution. If it looks like we aren't going to get it fixed in a few hours we can go to the vaults and get our "moldulars." Modulars are output based on an average day of orders which we keep in the vault for an emergency.*

Casewriter: *So by using the modulars you can approximate the orders the stores place. Will it be close enough to what they wanted?*

Caldwell: *Well, they might lose some sales if we go to modulars and there are items on sale that have an abnormally high demand. But we should get it fixed soon. As for the people waiting around, they get about $5 an hour on the users' payroll, but they have to be paid whether they're waiting or .working. They could be put to some use, but so far the users don't seem to want to have them do anything but wait. I guess that's their problem.*

Casewriter: *Doesn't going to a single CPU make you more vulnerable to system breakdowns than having two?*

Caldwell: *We don't really have a full backup system with two computers now. Also, being down for 13 hours is highly unusual. We had trouble because IBM's diagnostic system didn't work. We took our two most critical runs to two different computers at other companies nearby, and damned if both of them didn't break down right after we got there! This kind of coincidence is very unusual.*

What we need to do is give ourselves more buffer time as a normal thing. We've got to get the users to accept the idea that they don't need their reports 15 minutes after they've been run. The user only sees his need for a report. Somehow we have failed to sell him on the idea that 100 percent reliability may cost more than it's worth to the corporation as a whole. The marginal cost of getting 100 percent reliability over getting 95 percent may be so great that it just isn't worth it. We've got better things to do with our money. But they don't see that. Nobody on the user side is taking a systems view of the thing, a corporate view.

At this point in the conversation Caldwell answered the telephone.

Caldwell: *Yeah, Paul, I know your output's late. We told you last night it was going to be late. . . . No, we can't. They've broken down, too. . . . I think it will be about four o'clock this afternoon. . . . No, I can't "guarantee" that. . . . Just as* soon as we can. . . . Well, there's just nothing I can do about it, as I've told you. . . . That's up to you. Hangs up.

There's an example of what I was saying. Accounts Payable in one of the divisions wants their checks. Their treasurer is putting pressure on them, telling them if they don't get checks out to some of their vendors this afternoon the vendors have threatened to cut off their credit . . .

Casewriter: Have the users been told about the single CPU project? Are they aware of how much more they will have to pay on their charge-out rate as a result of manpower being spent on work that isn't directly chargeable?

Caldwell: They are beginning to hear via the grapevine that we are investing in the project. I don't know why we haven't told them. Maybe we're lazy. It goes back to what I was saying about the need to educate them, though. What we really need to do is change the people in user areas, or change their thinking, so that they think like businessmen, taking all the costs into account, and not like merchandisers, just wanting to get stuff on the shelves.

It's a matter of corporate philosophy. So far all the corporation wants from EDP is that it be managed on a day-to-day basis, on a problem-by-problem basis. They have never set a direction for EDP, nor looked at our function as part of the whole. They don't seem to know how to use EDP. For example, we have no policy that I know of on developing an automated warehouse or a major point-of-sale system. What we do have is a clear guideline to spend as few dollars as possible during the current profit squeeze.

Casewriter: You are now reporting to te senior vice president, and you are two levels down from the president. Couldn't you take the initiative toward this kind of corporate approach to EDP?

Caldwell: You have to keep in mind that nothing below me has changed. Just six months ago I reported to Brown, who reported to Grant, who was two levels down. I could pay attention to directing people and handling problems as they came up. Until recently my thinking was oriented to helping Operations, not thinking about what services I should provide but how I could provide what we have more efficiently. Now I am in a position where I have responsibility for that broader view, and it is more a matter of negotiating with others to get those things done, rather than merely giving orders. But if my responsibilities are going to be increased it means I have to get my people to take on more responsibility for running things. That takes time. They're good, but they have to learn to pick it up.

Not only that, but take a look at this. Picks up a memo. I just got this new schedule from personnel of salary rates for the different grades. It's completely contrary to what Personnel had agreed to: they haven't added enough to the grades of my people to fit with the added responsibility I'm expecting them to take. I'm not going to accept this! I'll take this one all the way if I have to!

Casewriter: You mentioned that you now have more responsibility and opportunity to negotiate. Is that in any way due to differences between the way Grant manages and the way Fox manages?

Caldwell: Previously, the intermediate levels of the organization filtered information too much. What top management heard was what the people just below them wanted to be heard. It was impossible for them to get the full information on an inssue. When Grant recommended getting the 370/145 it wasn't in the form of alternatives. By contrast, when we looked into the single CPU project, Fox gave us the evaluation task in the form of questions. Our approach is a contingent one now. If it turns out in June that we need an additional CPU after all, we can do it. We are not committed to a black and white end result of no additional CPU. If we did that we would be taking the no-alternatives approach that Grant took.

Casewriter: *Isn't it unusual for a computer operations department to be reporting at so high a level? What are the implications?*

Caldwell: *For one thing, Fox needs a counterbalance to evaluate the situation in Technical Support and Operations. He ought to have a staff man to provide him with an appraisal of our views on the technical matters. What's happening right now is that the four of us Caldwell, Daniels, Brown, and Crawford provide a kind of balance within our level when we meet. We challenge each other. For example, Brown is very conservative on what I should have in Operations. He would have it pared down to the bone. Daniels would like me to have all kinds of computing power. But it would be very easy for Fox to be snowed if we ever banded together.*

Casewriter: *I understand the idea behind the present structure, with four people reporting to Fox, is that there should be a lot of group discussion and decision making. Is that workable?*

Caldwell: *It can work, but several things have got to happen. First, we have got to build up the people under us to take more of the load. Second, we have to better define what we take up as a group and what we leave to each of us to handle. For example, we ought to leave day-to-day problems out of group meetings and talk about things like company-wide technology, like divisions wanting to build their own EDP capability.*

Three is a potential problem of conflict among the four of us, but it doesn't exist as a problem right now. We have worked together before and we know what our roles and separate jurisdictions are on a day-to-day operating basis. We mediated our own problems before, and we have done so since the changes. I think Fox determined that we were a good mix before he decided to try this approach.

Casewriter: *You mentioned that Fox should have a staff person to counterbalance the technical people reporting to him. Wouldn't another approach be to fill the slot Grant was in?*

Caldwell: *I think filling that slot is a dead issue for about three years. We just don't need anybody there. We have a fixed equipment budget through January of 1975, so there will not be that much change in the nature of our resources. Also we are in a budget squeeze and there's $45,000 a year in savings. In a couple of years we can face decisions on where we go for the future, such as automated warehouse, point-of-sale systems, or whatever looks attractive at that time to get us out of the high labor cost bind we will be in. But at that time we can go out and hire an executive to fill the slot who has experience in whatever we're interested in. This means we are deciding not to be first with these systems—or rather we are recognizing the profit crunch as telling us we don't want to be first. Right now we have to retrench.*

In three years or so I wouldn't be surprised to see Fox become the president of this company. That's when they will need a new vice president for Information Services. At that point it may make sense for a Technical Support man to be a vice president, too. I doubt very seriously if I will be here. . . .

I think our organization is a little unusual right now, but I'm not sure we have seen the last of the changes just yet.

Al Daniels

Casewriter: What kinds of problems are you facing in the new organization and with the responsibilities of the single CPU project?

Daniels: A big problem I face is that I am understaffed. I am supposed to have nine people in my group, but I am down to four now. Stu Lopez from Brown's group is the project manager on the single CPU project, and because I am short of people I find myself in on the meetings. Right now I'm spending a lot of time interviewing people to fill my slots. I've lost three people in the last few months.

Casewriter: Any particular reason?

Daniels: Morale. Oh, in one case a guy had a big dollar increase offered by another company, and there have been some other reasons, but morale is pretty bad since the reorganization. I would estimate 90 percent of people below my level in Information Services had their résumés out after the reorganization last November.

Nobody knew Lew Fox. I finally asked him to talk to my people last week—they had a kind of "encounter" session. I understand they asked him what the next change was going to be. They don't think things have settled down yet.

Caldwell and Brown don't agree with me that there are morale problems below us.

The reorganization was expected back in November. Everybody knew a change was coming, but when it came it was very sudden and with no details. Fox told me over the phone what the new organization would look like, and said, "We'll talk about it." We never have. Then there was a three-page memo saying, "We are reorganizing, effective immediately" and describing the changes and new job descriptions. That was it. I can understand the emphasis Lew has in working out the new organization: first he spent time thinking about Brown's group, ISD, then he will get to Caldwell's. Meanwhile, I am having to implement changes in what we do in Technical Support on my own. It's disconcerting, sometimes. For example, I'm supposed to take care of educating Information Services, but I have no idea how important this is supposed to be.

Casewriter: What do you see as the differences in how Information Services is managed since Grant was dismissed?

Daniels: Grant worked one-on-one with his managers, or maybe would talk to two of us at a time on a particular problem where we had some expertise. He was more comfortable accumulating data himself. I can remember seeing him in the office of my systems programmers, and I wouldn't know what in hell he was there for. When he knew what he wanted he would advise or clear it with his boss. We never had a staff meeting. He wanted to make the decisions himself, then pass up the answer. Then, you have to remember, Grant was head of all this at a time *when we were still on the cutting edge of applications. Our primary purpose was to get data out to the users fast.*

Now we run into a decline in profits in the corporation. The attitude becomes, "the corporation can exist on the kind of information systems it now has, so let's restrict data processing expenditures and go after savings in hardware." So, we end up with the single CPU, which will save us $400,000 over a year and a half by doing some investment now.

It's too early to tell how Fox will manage. He's trying to be participative, getting the four of us together to pass information up to him and discuss things among ourselves. The four meet every Thursday, then again on Friday with Lew. He wasn't getting data from Grant. Grant was reluctant to give up the reins after the reorganization.

Lew is the kind of guy who wants to see all sides of an issue. He sees himself as a generalist, somebody who understands the users' point of view. And he comes right out and admits that he doesn't have EDP experience and doesn't know what's going to happen technically.

Casewriter: *How is the participative approach working?*

Daniels: *As I said, it's really too early to tell. With Fox as head and the four of us reporting to him there isn't one guy alone who can give him a technical decision. If you try to do that you have to battle the other three. So there has to be a lot of uncertainty, and a problem of backbiting that could crop up.*

For a while after the reorganization I think Brown hated like hell giving up Technical Support and Operations. Caldwell and I found it necessary to band together to break down the barriers that were created by Harry. That seems to be better now. I worked with Caldwell on the study for the single CPU project, and we seem to agree more often than not in staff meetings. But I have learned to watch myself with Caldwell. He's a guy who is in a hurry, and I wonder sometimes if he isn't likely to use people to get there. . . .

I'm taking an MBA course in night school, and the other night we were talking about different styles of management. The four of us really have different styles, ranging from authoritarian to participative. I would put Caldwell at the authoritarian end, next Brown, then Crawford, and me at the participative end. In a way, I guess each of us has a style that makes sense when you consider what we have to do with our groups. . . .

Casewriter: *So you think the new organization will work in time?*

Daniels: *What I'm wondering is how long the present structure will last. Fox seems to have taken over the management of the thing as an interim guy, who wants to get the user orientation into EDP. I think he is managing by committee right now waiting for the cream to rise, waiting for someone to show he can manage the other three. I think he wants to choose a filter, a buffer to head up the departments and report to him.*

Larry Crawford

Casewriter: *What kinds of problems are you having to deal with in the new job that was created by the Marshall reorganization?*

Crawford: I find that it is going to take me twice as long as the six months I first estimated just to establish my role with users and to stop and redirect existing projects that have been mismanaged. In MAS we have found all kinds of problems in applications projects that should never have been started the way they were.

The users need to be convinced to take responsibility, to stand up for their ideas and present their case to Information Services. That's the job I'm trying to get them to do. I have six people working for me. Four of them came out of the old SPD group under Tom Johnson, who reported to Stan Grant. These guys were used to resisting the users, and didn't like working with them to get at a problem.

When I took over Management Advisory Services there were something like 80 requests for maintenance projects that had been submitted by users to Information Services. Brown saw them all as low priority. When a user saw he couldn't get his request filled, it led to some interesting game playing. For one thing, a user would ask for a new application when what he was really after was just a minor change in an existing one. Or, he would put in multiple requests, many of which he didn't care about at all, as part of his negotiating strategy. Some users hired their own systems analysts.

Casewriter: What has been your experience in working with the other three managers who report with you to Fox now?

Crawford: Well, my contact has been almost eitirely with Brown, and I'm sure he sees me as on his back all the time. I'm having a very difficult time getting response to my requests for attention to projects. I find myself calling meetings with Brown and some of our people, and we'll get together and talk and seem to agree on something, then weeks will go by and nothing will happen. Or I will send Brown a memo about the need to set cost estimates for an application project–that's a very important thing we are supposed to do together. Time passes and I won't hear anything.

It's gotten to the point where I hesitate to call meetings, especially if they involve all three of the others, for fear I will seem presumptive.

Casewriter: Someone suggested that the team approach that Fox has instituted may be a way for him to observe who should be promoted to be in charge of Information Services under him.

Crawford: I don't know if that is true. I believe Fox has tried to make it clear that Grant's slot will not be filled.

But think about the situation if people do believe that. If the present structure doesn't work, Fox is going to have to do something different. If somebody thinks he has a shot at an open slot, it might very well be in his interest to see the current setup not work! It blows the mind!

I think Brown is in a funny position. Fox had depended on him to be his rudder in this team. Fox is the second most powerful man in this company, and he has accelerated the pace of the single CPU project, but he doesn't know the technical side. Since he fired Grant he has depended on Brown as the most experienced guy with technical knowledge. And he has gambled on Caldwell and Daniels. I think he learned from their work on the CPU project study that they knew the technical side of their jobs. Now he wants to see if they and the rest of us can work as a team. He's depending on Brown to help him understand *the technical side, since he could be easily snowed in that area. He's also counting on Brown to* adapt *to working with the rest of us as a team. That means he is depending on none of us trying to be a superstar in front of the others, and also for none of us to be dragging our feet. I got called down by Fox last week when I started talking to Brown in the staff meeting about why we hadn't made any progress together. Fox said I was being "too harsh."*

Casewriter: *How do you think the team might work better together?*

Crawford: *I don't really know. Maybe we need an "OD" [organizational development] session or something. The other day Brown called me and suggested we talk about why we weren't communicating very well. We got together and talked about the different way we approached things. I thought we really began to understand each other for the first time, but we haven't followed it up. . . .*

Harry Brown

As the casewriter began to interview Brown in his office, he explained that the case was intended to provide information related to the organizational and interpersonal aspects of recent events in Information Services.

Brown: *I will be glad to describe how we do things, but I don't delve in the political. My approach is to treat the job as a job and do the best I can. I don't really pay attention to the political side.*

Brown went on to explain the history of the MIS function at Bay Markets, the way in which the department operated before the reorganization, and the way it was designed to operate afterwards. (See Bay Markets Corporation (A) for a description of these points.) In talking about the single CPU project, Brown continued:

Brown: *I look at the single CPU project as a chance for us to regroup ourselves after five years of intensive growth effort in applications. Stu Lopez is the manager from my area, ISD, on the project. He has two systems analysts and seven programmers on it. Al Daniels has practically his whole staff on it. Caldwell will be retraining his operators when the time comes. Crawford will have the responsibility to reschedule and loosen up delivery times to help Operations get some breathing space in their schedule. So we are all involved in the project.*

After the five months of the first phase of the project is up, we will be continuing the effort. Lopez's group, which we are calling Quality Assurance and Support, will have three programmers and an analyst full time. One of their duties will be to continue to make sure the system is running efficiently, and also to take care of user requests for applications support.

Casewriter: *What will be needed for the team approach, with the four of you reporting to Fox, to work as a way of running Information Services?*

Brown: *Quite simply, for it to work we have to work as a team. It's a real democracy now, with everyone equal. We each have a responsibility to closely coordinate with the others. We used to have a "siphoning up" to the top, but no longer.*

It will take time to work out. We have got to be sensitive to establishing our new relationships. There is a need for mutual confidence, trust, and inputs from each other into our own areas. Al and Ronnie have a lot of new responsibilities they haven't had before. Crawford is a new man to us, with new people under him, so it will take time for him to adjust and develop working relationships with the rest of us. It will take time.

Casewriter: You have more people reporting to you than any of the other three. Has there been any morale problem as a result of all the changes?

Brown: No, no. . . .

Sometimes I wonder what I would be thinking if I were in the shoes of my two managers, Lopez and Mortenson. They are in their late 30s and have been with the company six or eight years. They have worked for me a long time, and I can tell you they are making very, very important contributions to this company. [Pauses.]

Casewriter: Do you mean there may be some problem for them about the fact that Daniels and Caldwell have been moved up relative to them?

Brown: Oh, no. There's no problem at all. Don't misunderstand me, these two are very loyal to the company. They haven't said anything to me that would make me think they weren't happy. I just wonder what's going on in their minds, sometimes. I don't know if Daniels and Caldwell have had a pay raise since the reorganization, but I know these two guys are about where they were before. . . .

You asked me before what it would take for the new organization to work. I guess what it will take is for the four people under Fox to be able to work together well. That's really what it boils down to.

Casewriter: Do you think—based on your knowledge of MIS organizations—that this one is a little unusual now?

Brown: In what way do you mean?

Casewriter: The fact that Operations, for instance, is reporting to the senior vice president.

Brown: Oh, I don't know. Is that strange? Do you think so? We've done a lot of innovative things in MIS at Bay Markets. Maybe by having Operations and Technical Support report alongside Systems Development to a senior vice president we are introducing in innovation for others to follow in organizing MIS.

Case 8–5
Bay Markets Corporation (D)*

At the close of his visit to Bay Markets in April 1973, the casewriter interviewed Stan Grant and Lew Fox.

Stan Grant

Grant and the casewriter had dinner in a small restaurant overlooking Berkeley and the Bay. Grant described his work in Bay Markets since he joined the company in 1968, noting particularly that his work had been primarily in planning for needed growth in EDP and other areas, establishing and running the necessary control systems, and filling the slots needed in the growing organization. He pointed out that he was proud of the work he had accomplished in MIS, and particularly that he had been able to build up an organization below him that was able to control and manage the MIS function with a minimum of interference or concern on his part. He pointed out that for the previous several months he had worked some 80 percent of his time on a special project that the company was conducting.

Grant: *I was hired by Gold, and now I am the last member of his team to go. In a way, I think what we were able to accomplish in MIS really amounted to me working myself out of a job. The department practically runs itself. We introduced 32 separate major applications systems over those years, and now we have a business in which the computer really runs the place. We were always successful in getting done what we had to do. We were deluged with visitors, too. We must have had something others wanted to see!*

Casewriter: *Would you describe the events from the time of the Marshall study last year, and how those events had anything to do with your being dismissed?*

Grant: *Yes. Some of this, of course, is with the benefit of hindsight. I think I can describe what has happened in terms of four emotional shocks since just before Marshall was brought in.*

The first shock was when Mr. Fein invited Marshall to come in for the study in 1972, after asking several of us to comment on the choice of a consultant. I looked over their experience in EDP counsulting, and I felt another firm could have done a better job, particularly one we knew had more technical capability. I was overruled. I was pushed to a particular consultant.

Looking back on it, I think what has happened since then really reflects a difference in philosophy between me and top management. There was an anticipation of a decline in earnings in 1972. This is a fairly closely held corporation. A decision was made to tighten belts, to control costs, and to go after savings in visible expenses. Lew Fox represents that approach. This is in direct conflict with

---

* All names have been disguised.

Stan Grant. I believe you treat the business like a going concern, and do not pass up important long-term investments for short-term gain. I think that difference in philosophy was there even before Marshall came in.

The second shock was when Marshall outlined their proposed reorganization, with a new function not reporting to me, and with Lew Fox as head of the function.

The third thing that made me begin to wonder happened when Marshall was contemplating who should take over the job of head of the new MAS function they were setting up. They asked me, and I recommended Tom Johnson. Again, I was overruled when they went outside the department and chose a man who had no previous EDP experience. Part of that, though, was because Johnson was asking a lot of money.

Finally, I found it very hard to communicate with Fox, very hard to get to see him. He was out sick in early January, and when he came back, I had no chance to talk to him. Rather, he wanted all the three who reported to me to be there, along with Crawford. When a question would come up, I think most of them were confused by being there. We started these weekly meetings the third week of January.

Casewriter: What's your view of the single CPU project?

Grant: In recommending that we add a 370/145, I was trying to look ahead to the growth in user demand on computer capacity. I think it is very questionable whether growing user applications won't catch up with capacity before it is planned to expand again. In addition I felt we should not reduce development expenditures. The project will result in that, since existing or potential user projects will have to be cannibalized. I felt we should make the kinds of improvements in efficiency more gradually, such as by implementing them along with each new project.

So, I wonder if efficiency improvements of the magnitude that are being undertaken are worth it, especially since it could be done with users paying directly and over time instead of with a higher overhead.

Casewriter: Couldn't the charge-out system be changed?

Grant: Changing it now would be a smoke screen. The project is an out-and-out taking advantage of the users, in my opinion.

Casewriter: So you feel that with a single CPU, even with increased user capacity, there is likely to be a problem?

Grant: I think there might very well be.

Casewriter: Would you go so far as to predict when?

Grant: The second or third week of next September. That would be after Labor Day vacation, when people have returned to the Bay area, and buying reaches its peak. The load on EDP will be highest then.

Casewriter: What's the job situation for MIS managers at this time?

Grant: Oh, it's very good. I have several contacts already, and I've just begun to send my resume out. I'm 55 now, earning in the high 30s, but the market looks good. I know that 10 or 12 others in Information Services have their resumes out right now.

I look forward to a change. I would most like to be the director of the staff of an MIS operation where the computer is recognized for what it can be, where the data base is established and there is a recognition of the potential from a well-organized and well-managed data base.

I'm not at all bitter. I'm disapponted about what's happened, but not bitter. I think I have to blame myself for not publicizing my accomplishments more. People might have looked at our shop and thought because we didn't look busy we were overstaffed. Maybe we were. Maybe that's why I had to leave. I guess time will tell. The computer organization at Bay Markets always succeeded in what it was asked to do. I know I'm not good at public relations. In a way I think Stan Grant was taken for granted.

Somebody ought to go into the business of providing public relations agents for MIS managers!

Lew Fox

Casewriter: Would you describe what led to your decision to fire Grant?

Fox: The story began back in December. I had been in this job a little over a month. Grant came to me and said, "We need to replace the 360/50 with a 370/145." I said, "Why?", and he answered that we were at capacity and that Ron Caldwell was having delays at peak load time, having to defer test jobs by Brown and Daniels just to get the operations done. He told me Caldwell would quit if we didn't get a bigger machine.

Well, I said to him that I seemed to remember that in the Marshall report they had said we wouldn't need to add capacity until 1975. He said, "No, they didn't."

That night I went through the Marshall report. I found it, all right. I confronted him with it and he said, "The facts have changed. For one thing, they did not really anticipate our loads correctly. We have to buy the new machine." I told him I would think about it.

I was out sick for three weeks in January. The first morning I was well enough to work, as I was driving in, it struck me that up to that time I had been dealing with Grant and his subordinates like I was their lawyer and they were my clients. I knew I had to learn the facts of their positions, but there is a subtle psychology to becoming your clients' advocate in facing top management and users. That might be a good thing sometimes, but I was put in this job partly because I was expected to bring the user point of view into the computer operation. I decided I had to be more of a politician, you might say, and not be drawn into the vortex of affiliation with the MIS side.

Anyway, toward the end of February Caldwell called me. He said we ought to look into a single CPU. He also told me there hadn't been a staff meeting of Grant's people for four months. I told Grant I wanted to have a staff meeting with him and his three people. I walked in with one question: "Would it be possible for us to keep our existing CPU?" They went round and round about it all morning. At lunch I left. I said to myself, "I have got to see each one of them separately."

Using one excuse or another, I spoke to each of them. The upshot of it was we did the CPU study, which resulted in a plan for reconfiguration that will let us sell the 360/50 without buying more capacity. It will save us $400,000 a year, and cost us between $150,000 and $300,000 over the next six months. With that kind of return it is indubitably a good thing for the corporation as a whole.

As we were coming to a conclusion on a single CPU project I spent an agonizing week thinking about Grant. He had tried to block it, but his dissents had been answered, it seemed to me. In light of all that had gone on, I decided he had to go.

Casewriter: How do you look on that decision now?

Fox: In retrospect, I see even more clearly how the problems we were having seemed to get back to poor management of Information Services.

Maybe I'm just rationalizing, but I'm comfortable with letting Grant go. I remember sitting in on Steering Committee meetings and feeling that we were doing badly, but I had no power and not enough knowledge to do anything about it or to suggest how to do it better. When we created Management Advisory Services we could have chosen a director for it who had been under Grant before, but we saw the clear necessity for a new man there. I remember that in their first round of recommendations, rough draft stuff, the head of the Marshall team had confided to Fein and me that they were thinking of recommending that we not fill the position of director in the new organization. Fein and I decided "no" to that. We thought having Grant in there would mean less of my time would be required.

Also, I have to admit, I was damned scared by the unknown of what it would be like to run that department by myself. I would never have believed then that I could know what I know now about the function and about what was going on there.

It has become clear to me that there was dangerously little coordination and communication. For example, Information Systems Development—and before the reorganization what was called Systems Planning and Development, the group responsible for developing and implementing applications, never knew what equipment was coming. An example was the impact of MVT and changes in partition width (changes in the operating system of the computer)–these had a serious effect on program development, but there was very little education for the systems analysts and programmers. As I see it, the way in which Information Services was managed was a serious part of that problem.

When I was agonizing over the decision to fire Grant, I could have accumulated a lot of evidence to back it up. I considered delivering a coherent indictment to him. But in view of his age and experience, I saw no reason for it. I fired a young lawyer once, and in that case I took a lot of time to explain what went wrong and how he could improve.

But there was no way I could put it to Grant in detail so that he wouldn't feel screwed. So my meeting with him was very short. I explained the reasons, but told him he was free to tell the world it was a budetary matter. That was something he could believe if he wanted to, and the world could believe. There was more data there that I could have used. . . .

When I first took over Information Services I believed in Grant's intellectual honesty. But on things like his recommendation for the new computer, and on *his response to my asking about improvement in the charge-out system, I soon lost faith in that honesty.*

We haven't looked at a single applications system under development without finding problems with it. The charge-out system is masking relevant data. One of our divisions wanted to sever the relationship with MIS.

The question is, are these normal problems, or has five years of mismanagement left an infection? It may be hard to compare our use of MIS with others. We have introduced a philosophy of systematizing in a retailing business that is highly intuitive. It's not even like a big department store, with a tight control over inventory. We were volume oriented and not tightly controlled. We had to be able to move products quickly and cut prices in a day. This may explain what began to happen in the way of misunderstanding and the Pinter-like missing of communications between users and MIS.

Casewriter: *There seem to be some uncertainties in the minds of the four as to how the team approach is supposed to work. How are you dealing with that?*

Fox: *I don't have a coherent program.*

When I started out after Grant was fired, I only knew Brown well. I had known him for six or seven years and I knew what he could do. I had to build up my personal credibility with Daniels and Caldwell and with Grant gone I wanted to free them up to tell me the truth. I felt Grant had got in the way of my hearing that. As one manager said to me, "Grant is an advocate of the 'sole possessor of wisdom' approach."

I told them I wanted them to talk to one another, that they should consider themselves in a continuous unadjourned meeting. That seems to have led to some misinterpretations. Crawford interpreted it to mean, "We don't take a step unless we agree among ourselves." Brown felt he reported to me, and that it was silly to require a consensus on most matters. An example was Brown designating Lopez to run the ISD portion of the single CPU project. Crawford saw it as a proposal that Lopez do that, something to be approved by the group.

We tried to formulate some rules, but we didn't seem to make much progress, so I said, "Let's stop." We've left it incoherent.

I have an important need in all of this to get counsel on the advice I get from Daniels and Caldwell. Furthermore, I think of my needs in this as the same as the company's needs. I see the committee approach as providing me with that counsel.

But this approach doesn't mean we don't get explicit about some things. For example, I asked each man to write plans for his area of responsibility. Brown had his but it needs updating. I'm having a hell of a time getting them. I can't even seem to get a PERT chart for the single CPU project! For that matter [laughing] I don't know if I need a PERT chart. . . . Do I need a GANTT chart? Do I need a list?

Casewriter: *What particular tasks are on your mind as you look at MIS?*

Fox: *Where to begin? They seem innumerable. There's a question of how to cut it—substance or procedure.*

We had a meeting on training. I naively believed I could ask my managers for a personnel development program. I discovered there was simply no appreciation among them for that.

The charge-out system is suspect. It's important. I wonder if I should hand it to one of the four to work on.

I have not activated the Management Steering Committee yet. I have to decide what the role of that will be.

There are flocks of problems in the MAS-ISD interface.

As I think about these, quite honestly, it makes me wonder if I made a mistake in taking this job. [Smiles] At the very least, I realize that I didn't anticipate what life would be like without Stan Grant. . . .

There is a centralization-decentralization question. We have two new divisions that want to expand their data processing capability, and it raises the question of what responsibility there should be for Daniels and Caldwell. This is a hard issue. I don't believe the time is right to raise this with my four subordinates. There is a whole range of problems over teleprocessing and remote data entry, not to mention CRTs on executives' desks.

Then we have to look at point-of-sale systems. They are already being introduced in department stores and are coming soon in supermarkets. It will make possible unprecedented control over inventories, shrink, and productivity. It is truly revolutionary. The questions we face are, "Should we be first?" and "If not, how late should we be?"

Underlying all these kinds of issues is a question of how I should use my time. This could become a huge burden. I found out that Grant had been doing all the budgeting, forecasting, and retrospective billing. I was tempted to take it on myself. It was as though I was being drawn into it. But last week I ordained that each of the four should do it for his areas. It adds to each of their responsibilities.

Part **IV**

Managing interpersonal relationships

A topic worthy of a book in itself is that of Part IV, interpersonal relationships. Like earlier parts, this one is a combination of concepts and guidelines for action. More than the previous parts, however, there is a focus on what makes up "perspective" in the overview model. Moreover, in this part the reader must be more subjectively involved if effective learning for his or her own action is to occur. One must exercise imagination and empathy in order to learn how to use the ideas effectively.

Most of the cases in Part IV are characterized by their presenting insight on one or two individuals' perspectives in an interpersonal relationship. These are named after one of the protagonists: John Brownell (Cases 9–1 to 9–3), Jan Vanvoort (Case 9–4), and Douglas Ashton (Case 9–5). Great Eastern National Bank (Case 9–6) is an opportunity to analyze perspectives in a particularly important interpersonal encounter—performance appraisal discussion. Sturdivant Electric Corporation (Case 9–7) depicts a bitter interpersonal conflict which raises the need for explicit action by a manager.

Chapter 9

UNDERSTANDING AND MANAGING COMMUNICATIONS AND CONFLICT IN INTERPERSONAL RELATIONSHIPS[1]

By John J. Gabarro and Cyrus F. Gibson

The range and number of people with whom a manager is in relationship varies widely depending on the nature of the manager's job. Typically, the people a manager works with include subordinates and important peers whose input, support, and cooperation is vital to the manager's effort. They also include the manager's own boss and other important seniors who provide advice and support and help determine career promotions and other job rewards. Even a portfolio manager in a financial institution who is likely to have few, if any, direct subordinates must rely heavily on analysts, researchers, and outside contacts to perform effectively.

The value of interpersonal effectiveness and good communication in two-person emergent relationships seems fairly apparent. We shall see it as fundamental to certain kinds of conflict resolution. Not so obvious, however, is what a manager can do to develop and maintain effective interpersonal relationships. Some of the factors which determine the effectiveness of the relationships between individuals have already been discussed in this book. We have talked about the larger context within which emergent relationships develop, such as the nature of

---

[1] This chapter is a revision of material which appeared as chapter 4 in *Interpersonal Behavior: Communication and Understanding in Relationships,* by Anthony G. Athos and John J. Gabarro. Englewood Cliffs, New Jersey: Prentice-Hall, Inc., 1978.

organization structure, the history of departmental relationships with
the rest of the organization, and the "fit" of organization structure,
organization task, and the expectations of whole groups of people. Generally, we would expect that the better the fit among the contextual
variables, the better will be the quality of communications, the lower
the amount of conflict, and the more effective the interpersonal relationships.

Although one-on-one relations exist within the context of the larger
organization, the dynamics and problems of two-person relationships
depend very much on factors of an individual and personal nature. In
particular, aspects of people's personalities and perspectives are important in two-person relations. In this chapter we focus explicitly on the
problems of interpersonal behavior as they exist in two-person relationships.

In Figure 9–1 we show the elements of our overview model which
will be discussed in this chapter to help us understand conflict and

FIGURE 9–1
Two-person relationships in the overview model

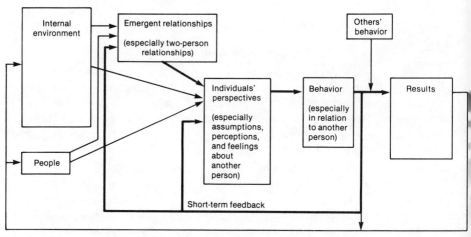

communications in interpersonal relationships. The emphasis is on
two-person emergent relationships.

At any time, the relationship between people may be characterized
as being either in conflict or trusting, and either developing or stable.
The perceptions of the relationship, combined with factors from the
individual's personality and the organization's internal environment,
determines the individual's perspective on the relationship. In other
words, just as with respect to any other particular issue in the work
environment, a person's assumptions, perceptions, and feelings about

another person are structured or formed by these elements. Early in a relationship, in the absence of interaction, one's perspective will be shaped more by first impressions, formal authority relationships, and one's own personal likes and dislikes. As the two people interact, the perspective and behavior of each toward the other will be affected increasingly, although not entirely, by the events or phenomena which occur between them. We shall concentrate here particularly on this process of relationship development, occurring by virtue of the "short-term feedback" loop in Figure 9–1.

CONFLICT AND COMMUNICATIONS PROBLEMS

Sources of conflict

Almost everyone has experienced interpersonal conflicts and misunderstandings in both their personal and professional lives. So pervasive is this phenomena that it takes up a disproportionately large amount of space in the literature written for and by managers. Indeed, the expression "communication problem" is now used so commonly that it is often applied to just about any problem that exists between two people, whether or not a problem in communication actually exists. Not all interpersonal problems or conflicts are communications problems. Two managers may have difficulty working with each other for many different reasons. They may understand each other extremely well but one of them may not behave as the other wishes. Take for example the following three possibilities:

Political in-fighting and power struggles Two people may not really want to reach an understanding because each wants the other to lose for political or other reasons. Each might understand the other's intentions and needs quite well. The real agenda in such a situation lies in increasing one's own power and resources at the expense of the other. We covered much of this in Chapter 7.

Personality conflicts For reasons of a psychodynamic and unconscious nature two people may have a propensity to dislike each other's personal styles, personality predispositions, or personal techniques. Again each person may understand what the other wants, but they still have difficulty working together.

Conflicting goals Two people may have goals, personal or organizational, which are so conflicting that it makes it difficult for them to collaborate. This may not be because the individual involved does not understand the other's position, or has failed to communicate the other's needs. Indeed, they may understand and communicate very well; it is just that they do not like what the other does, says, or wants.

Many examples could be given of interpersonal conflicts which are not, strictly speaking, problems of communication. The problems listed above involve influence, trust, and competition. However, many, if not most, of the interpersonal difficulties which managers face actually do involve problems in communicating or in understanding another person's point of view. It is these "phenomenological" issues which we will focus on here.

Effective communication and good communication

The following distinction between "effective communication" and "good communication" will be useful to our basic understanding. It is taken from Tagiuri (1972).

The major common concern is with effective communication. And it is a suitable concern for people in management and administration who are constantly trying to use communication to obtain specific results. When a communication does obtain the intended outcomes, it can be properly called effective. But effective communication requires in most instances good communication, which means that party B has understood a concept that party A wishes to convey to B.

Good communication is a prerequisite but does not ensure effective communication. If A said to B, "Jump out the fourth-floor window," B would probably not do it unless there were a fire and no other escape alternatives. Yet if we can assume that B has understood A perfectly well, this communication was good without effective communication, for the latter includes aspects of behavior such as persuasion, motivation, power, coercion, and the like, which need not be considered as part of the pure communication process itself.

In practice it is not easy to separate the communication process itself from the other processes involved in effective communication. But the communicator should be alert to this distinction.

One-way and two-way communications

In addition to the quality of communication, namely whether it is bad, good, or effective, it is useful in analyzing communications to consider the type: either one way or two way. When A speaks or writes or transmits information through some symbolic means to B, the transmission may be in one direction only or it may be part of a continuing transaction (Figure 9–2).

In general, either type of communication may be good or effective. The big advantage of one-way over two-way communication is its efficiency: A yells to B, "FIRE!" or "Push the 'stop' button!" and neither one takes the time to discuss the matter. When the message is more complex, in the sense that B's perspective may not be conditioned to understand or to accept the message, then two-way communications

FIGURE 9–2

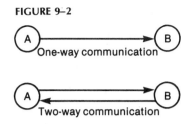

are better. Most explicit communications are intended by the sender either to *inform* or to *influence* the behavior of the receiver. Communications is the essential means for exercising direct influence, as discussed in Chapter 2, in which one person attempts to change the behavior of one other. For important matters, where there is time to do so and possibility of misunderstanding or insufficient power of A over B to exercise desired influence, then a two-way dialogue of checking the message is preferred to a one-way statement.

But why are communications ever misunderstood? Basically, we shall answer this in terms of the perspectives of the sender and the receiver. There are several ways in which the perspective of each can affect the message of a communication. These are illustrated in Figure 9–3. What person A *intends* to send may not be what is *actually* sent;

FIGURE 9–3
Effects of perspective on message in a simple communication

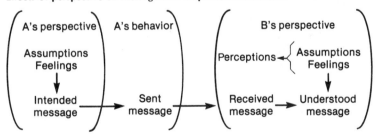

what B *receives* may be something else, and what B interprets and understands may be yet again different.

If effective communication depends at least in part on good communication, and if perspectives affect messages, it is worth considering what gets in the way of good communication and causes misunderstandings. In doing this, we will use the concepts of assumptions, perceptions, and feelings.

Assumptions, perceptions, and feelings in communications

These concepts were explained briefly in Chapter 1. Let us repeat the definitions here in the context of two-person communications.[2] By *assumptions* we mean the attitudes and beliefs that a person has relevant to any given topic. A person may or may not be consciously aware of all of his or her assumptions. Frequently, one's assumptions lead to expectations of how things "ought" to be in a given situation. By *perceptions* we mean what the person actually sees, hears, or otherwise perceives as taking place in a given situation (as compared to what he might think ought to be occurring). By *feelings* we mean the emotive and affective responses of a person to a given situation. In the simplest terms, feelings are the emotions a person feels which are triggered by what he or she sees taking place. These concepts of assumptions, perceptions, and feelings comprise a person's immediate perspective on the situation. In particular, we are illustrating their use here as affecting interpretation of messages and behavior in interpersonal relationships.

AN ILLUSTRATIVE CASE

To begin the process of using these concepts in understanding problems of communication, we will carefully examine a set of interactions which took place between two people in a work situation. Although the setting and names have been changed, the important elements of the story remain the same. Their relationship was not an intimate one, but nonetheless an important one in each of their lives. As you read about what took place in this situation, imagine that it is not "just a case," but your company, or one in which you might be employed. Imagine that you are well aquainted with both men concerned, that you like them both, and that you care about the outcome. Your capacity to *imagine,* which is crucial in developing empathetic understanding, *is* important to exercise as you read this vignette. Just reading the note without practicing imagining will not be of as much use to you. It takes practice to develop skills.

An opportunity

Tom Ellery was vice president of sales and Steve Watson was a regional sales manager in charge of four district managers. Steve reported to one of Tom's area managers. Tom had followed Steve's career with interest and considered him one of the best sales managers in the company. It was not surprising, then, that Steve's name came immedi-

---

[2] The use of assumptions, perceptions, and feelings as concepts for explaining interpersonal communications is fully developed in Turner and Lombard (1969).

ately to mind when Tom received a memo from the marketing vice president asking for recommendations for someone to take over the Marketing Services Department.

Marketing Services employed about 400 people and provided promotional support and special services to the Sales Division. In terms of salary grade, the position was one level higher than regional sales manager so it would offer Steve a promotion. Tom felt Steve was the ideal candidate for the job for several reasons. First, people in both Marketing and Sales divisions felt Marketing Services had become unresponsive to Sales Division needs. The department was now more of a bottleneck than a service, and Steve's extensive experience as a sales manager would give him a clear idea of what kind of support the department ought to be giving.

Second, the department had begun to suffer from an image problem which Steve's transfer could do much to correct. Marketing Services had developed a reputation of being a place where people were assigned when they ceased to be effective in product management or in field sales. Putting an acknowledged comer like Steve in charge of the department would go far in dispelling that image. The position would also provide Steve with an opportunity for wider corporate exposure and one in which he could influence total company marketing and sales efforts.

After consulting with the marketing vice president, Tom sent Steve a copy of the original memo with the added note—"Are you interested—I think you're the best person for the job. Come by and let's talk about it." Tom was pleased that his own division was finally strong enough to allow him the flexibility to offer one of his best men to another division. It had taken three years of systematically identifying weak spots and moving strong new people like Steve into them to provide this luxury, and he planned to make the most of it.

> Pause for a moment before you read on and consider what *assumptions* Steve *might* make on receiving the memo, and what his feelings were likely to be. Note them briefly on a separate piece of paper.

A few days later, Steve came by to discuss the memo. Tom was surprised to find Steve both uninterested in the transfer, and a little curt and ill at ease as well. Steven began by saying he didn't think he had the background to do the job and that he still had a lot to do in the region before he felt he could move on to another job. Sensing that Steve might be a little anxious about moving into the Marketing Division, Tom went into more detail on the reasons why he thought Steve could handle the job and do it well. Steve remained unconvinced, however, and as a last resort Tom suggested that Steve talk with the marketing vice president about it before finally deciding. Tom could not help feeling a little annoyed at the end of the conversation, and found himself questioning his original judgments about Steve's flexibility and adaptability.

Pause for a moment more and consider what inferences and assumptions Tom is making about Steve's response, and why they lead to feelings of annoyance.

To Tom's continued disappointment, Steve's talk with the marketing vice president failed to change his mind, and Tom began to feel his relationship with Steve become strained. Soon afterward Tom noticed Steve was avoiding him in the company cafeteria and seemed especially silent in his presence. About a month later, Tom received a call from Steve's area manager saying that Steve had resigned to take a position with a competitor.

Consider what perceptions and assumptions could lie behind Steve's action? How do you sense Steve feels in taking such an action?

Tom later learned from a mutual friend that Steve had left because he had concluded that his career with the company was finished when Tom offered him the Marketing Services job.

Did you deduce this from what went before? How do you sense Tom felt when he heard this news?

A case of misunderstanding

A misunderstanding had taken place, the roots of which we cannot begin to understand without getting a better sense of what Steve was experiencing before and during his dealings with Tom. To begin with, Steve had no serious intention of moving to another company until after the memo from Tom arrived. On the contrary, he was very satisfied with his career in the company, had enjoyed his work, and had received two promotions within three years. Why then, did his interpretation of the transfer differ so much from Tom's intention?

While Tom saw the transfer as a recognition of Steve's performance, Steve saw it as a sign that his past performance was not good enough. Steve had reasons on which to base this supposition. As long as Tom had been in charge of sales he had never transferred an *effective* sales manager out of the division—only ineffective managers. Steve, like other sales managers, was very much aware of Tom's practice of identifying weak areas and bringing new life to them in the form of new managers. Indeed, he had been a major benefactor of this policy, and was one of the people who had advanced rapidly as a result. But now he wondered if it was his turn to be replaced as a regional sales manager. He had accepted his promotions and Tom's praise as clear signs of approval but now wondered if Tom had been less satisfied than he had seemed. The thought that this might have been the case especially angered him because neither Tom nor his area manager had given Steve any indication they were unhappy with his results.

The more Steve thought about the situation, the more suspicious and angry he became. If they wanted to get him out of the way, he could not think of a better place to send him than Marketing Services. Hadn't he joked with other sales managers about it being the burial ground for old product managers?

Steve's talk with Tom failed to dispel any of these suspicions. All Steve heard were Tom's attempts to sell him on the Marketing Services and Tom's obvious annoyance when he refused the transfer. The whole series of events left him so suspicious and uncertain of his status that he decided to leave the company.

Understanding the misunderstanding

The reasons for the misunderstanding can be better understood when we look at each person's assumptions, perceptions, and feelings before the talk between Steve and Tom and as they developed after their conversation.

What Tom assumed, perceived, and felt (Figure 9–4) Tom's initial assumption was that he ought to recommend an outstanding man with sales experience for the job. He decided to recommend Steve based on his perceptions of Steve's past effectiveness. He further assumed Steve ought to see the transfer as an opportunity for further advancement and as a recognition of his past achievements. Given these assumptions it was not surprising that he also assumed Steve ought to be pleased and interested in the transfer. When Tom perceived Steve reacting negatively to the offer, he felt surprised because Steve's behavior was inconsistent with his expectations. When Steve also failed to respond to his arguments for taking the transfer, he felt annoyed, and ended up questioning his original assumptions about Steve's flexibility and adaptability. Very possibly Steve's behavior may have also threatened some of Tom's assumptions about his own ability as a manager and judge of people. Tom's annoyance no doubt reflected itself in his nonverbal behavior with Steve.

What Steve assumed, perceived, and felt (Figure 9–5) Steve's assumptions (based on past perceptions) were that "effective" sales managers do not get transferred out of the Sales Division and that Marketing Services was an assignment for people the company wanted out of the way. Both of these assumptions/perceptions were based on observations of what had taken place in the past, and provided the basis for his concluding that the transfer was a sign of Tom's dissatisfaction with his

FIGURE 9–4
Development of Tom's perspective and behavior

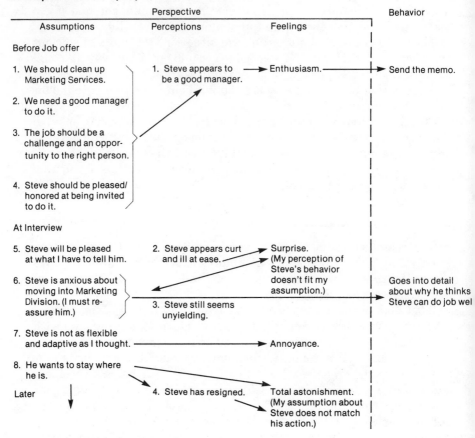

past performance. But this conclusion was inconsistent with his own assumption about himself, "I am a good manager," and his perceptions of the feedback Tom and his boss had given him earlier. This conflict between his own assumptions and what he saw as the meaning of the transfer led him to feel surprise, anxiety, and threat.

Tom's behavior in the meeting (from Steve's point of view) gave Steve little reason to change his new assumptions; rather it gave him a further basis to reinforce them. Tom tried to "sell" the transfer and appeared annoyed when Steve was not interested—behavior which could reasonably be expected from a man who wanted him out of the division. This led Steve to conclude that he no longer had a future in sales, and he resigned in anger to take another job.

Before thinking about how the problem could have been avoided, try

FIGURE 9–5

Development of Steve's perspective and behavior

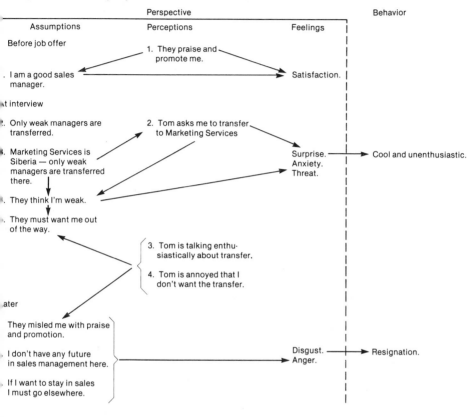

to develop an empathic understanding of how each person was experiencing his feelings and perceptions in the relationship and how this influenced their behavior in relation to each other.

You may wonder how such a misunderstanding could possibly have occurred between two reasonably bright and probably sensitive people. Why didn't Tom explain his intentions better or anticipate how Steve's assumptions may have differed from his own? How could Steve so seriously misinterpret the offer? Admittedly, these were some of the same questions that came to my mind on first hearing about the situation. But these questions are reactions from *our* point of view about what took place. They deny the actuality of what each person must have experienced for the situation to develop the way it did.

Try to imagine for a moment how each person might have experienced the situation. Imagine Tom's sense of surprise when Steve refused an offer which seemed to him a compliment and an opportunity;

how it must have conflicted with his expectations of himself as well as
Steve; how this surprise slowly turned to annoyance and possibly anger
as he experienced what he saw as irrational behavior on Steve's part.
Consider the strength of Steve's feelings in terms of the extent to which
his self-concept of being an effective sales manager was in jeopardy, his
expectations about his future, his sense of identity in the organization,
and his ability to master a complex situation effectively; and how all
were being challenged by his perceptions and assumptions about Tom's
view of him.

Facilitating understanding in two-person relationships

Having glimpsed how each of the two people experienced the situation, it becomes easier to understand the misunderstanding. The actual
situation as it was experienced by Tom and Steve was no doubt a great
deal more subtle and complicated than this simple description implies.
For example, our understanding of what happened would no doubt be
sharper if we knew more about the personal histories of the two men,
their sources of identification, the expectations they had of their careers
and broader lives, and the ways in which they achieved mastery and
gained acceptance in their lives.

However, even with the little information we have about the episode, we know a great deal more than either man knew at the time
about some of the important *differences* in the way each was experiencing it. We have had the advantage of seeing some of the points of view
and assumptions of *both* men, an advantage which unfortunately
neither of them had until it was too late. The ability to recognize when
important and disabling differences exist in assumptions, perceptions,
and feelings is a skill which people seldom cultivate in their relationships with others. It is easy to do when the data is laid out as it is in a
case, a film, or a story, or when it is "out there." But what do you do
when you are one of the people in the relationship? Even more importantly, what do you do when you are part of the problem, as Tom and
Steve were? What do you do when your own assumptions structure
your perceptions and create feelings that prevent you from hearing or
seeing how the other person's views and feelings differ from you own?

The simple, although not necessarily easy, answer to this question is
to try to increase your awareness of what the other person is experiencing, of what his important assumptions, perceptions, and feelings are.

Assumptions about communication which impede understanding

Much of the misunderstanding between Steve and Tom stemmed
from their different sets of assumptions. Many of these assumptions

were about the other's intentions and the specifics of *what* they were talking about, that is, the transfer—what it symbolized and what its implications were. In a sense, these were assumptions about the content of what they were communicating to each other. To a great extent, all of us constantly make such assumptions in our relations with others. It could be argued that such content assumptions enable us to operate in a world in which we can never know in any total sense what the other person is experiencing, or how his specific meanings may vary from our own.

However, we also make assumptions of a somewhat different kind—assumptions about the *process* of communication itself. These are assumptions about what is taking place when two people talk to each other, rather than the specifics of what is being talked about. These process assumptions can be much greater barriers to communication than content assumptions because they keep us from discovering that our content assumptions may differ. For this reason they can be especially dangerous. For example, consider the following process assumptions we often make in day-to-day communications with others:

□ That the other person perceives the situation the way we do.

□ That the other person is making the same inferences and assumptions we are.

□ That what is taking place should be logical from our point of view.

□ That the other person is experiencing or ought to experience the same feelings about the situation as we do.

□ That the communication process in a given situation has little or no relation to other events in the situation, or to past history.

□ That the other person's understanding of the situation ought to be based on logic rather than feelings.

Most of these assumptions about the process of what was going on were implicit in Tom's behavior. These process assumptions were much more critical in impeding his understanding of how Steve experienced the situation than were the set of content assumptions in Figure 9–1, because these process assumptions kept him from discovering how different his content assumptions were from Steve's.

The tendency to evaluate and judge

One of the reasons why both content and process assumptions impede understanding is that we tend to act on these assumptions, and by so doing we pass judgments on what we think others are saying without ever getting to hear the other person's underlying assumptions.

Carl Rogers, a therapist who has spent much of his career studying the process of increasing understanding and communication, has postulated that "the major barrier to mutual interpersonal communications is our very natural tendency to judge, to evaluate to approve (or disapprove)" of what the other person is saying. We approve when our perceptions of the other person's behavior fit our assumptions about how he or she should behave. We disapprove when they do not fit.

It is interesting to note that both Tom and Steve were most judgmental when they were experiencing strong emotions, and this is where the rub is. It is most difficult to listen nonevaluatively and refrain from passing judgment when feelings are strongest. This is especially the case when what we think the other person is saying threatens us, because our defenses against anxiety are highest at those times. It is only by listening nonevaluatively that we can hear enough from the other person's frame of reference to begin to understand this person's assumptions, perceptions, and feelings.

If, for example, Tom had been able to suspend his judgments and inferences about why Steve was being reluctant and inquire about Steve's lack of enthusiasm for the job, the misunderstanding might have ended there. If Steve had been able to suspend judgment on Tom's intentions long enough to hear him out, he may have discovered that Tom's intentions were quite different from what he assumed they were. The difficulty, of course, is to be aware that our own *feelings* are signaling us that we are not really hearing the other person and to shift our emphasis from focusing just on our own reactions to focusing on the other person's concerns as well. That frequently helps us to begin to listen less evaluatively.

This nonevaluative stance is a precondition to understanding another person from his or her point of view and for imagining what that person's reality must be like. This does not necessarily mean that your view must agree with the other person's view of the situation, but it does mean suspending judgments in order to appreciate the other's point of view. We hope we have demonstrated in this chapter both respectful curiosity and some analytical skill. But empathetic insight is what each person has to add for himself or herself. Only you can put yourself into the shoes, first, of Tom and then of Steve. As tedious as it may be to practice, it is the only way to develop a skill so that it becomes intuitive.

Sit back for a moment, and feel your way through Tom's experience:

☐ His initial enthusiasm for Steve's transfer.

☐ His hopes for the Marketing Services group.

☐ His surprise and disappointment at Steve's lack of enthusiasm and curtness.

☐ His sense of need to reassure Steve about his ability.

☐ His irritation when Steve remained unresponsive.

☐ His disappointment when Steve's interview with the marketing vice president failed to influence Steve's decision.

☐ His gradual estrangement from Steve around the company.

☐ His final astonishment when Steve resigned.

Now put yourself into Steve's shoes and follow the same process. Try to recreate within yourself a sense of the flow of Steve's feelings, beginning with his sense of pride and confidence in his performance as an effective manager. Try to imagine the sequence of his feelings so that you begin to share some sense of what this experience meant to him. Then, if you can, try to use this approach in a relationship that you are currently involved in which is important to you.

CONCLUSION

To anticipate and deal with problems of communication, four things are necessary. First, a manager must develop a sense of awareness of what the other person is experiencing, as well as an awareness that difficulties in communication arise more often than we would assume. (This is a matter of attitude.)

Second, a manager needs a conceptual understanding of how and why people are apt to see the same thing differently. (This requires finding a useful framework.) The simple notions of assumptions, perceptions, and feelings and how they might differ for two people, and their impact of these differences on behavior can be very useful in gaining this understanding.

Third, a manager who is responsible for acting must in many cases abandon a nonevaluative stand and make a judgment. This may very well lead to action perceived as *not* in the interest of some other people, at least from their point of view. It may take a great deal of courage to do this. (A matter of attitude.)

Fourth, a manager needs a way of examining and acting upon what is taking place in the process of communication. This requires an understanding of some of the process assumptions that get in the way of good communication and understanding. It is the implementation of direct influence action, and it is analogous to the implementation of organizational change, discussed in Chapter 5. (This is a matter of both attitude and behavior.)

Tagiuri suggests the following strategies and attitudes as useful guides in preventing and anticipating communication problems:

1. Suspend judgment of right versus wrong—at least temporarily until you have understood the other person's point of view (attitude and behavior).

2. Assume legitimacy of others' view (attitude).
3. Try to see the situation from the other's point of view (behavior).
4. Define terms (behavior).
5. Deal as much as possible with facts rather than with interpretations or inferences.
6. Take the other person's and your own emotions and feelings into account as being important and, if appropriate, recognize them (behavior).
7. Reopen communication (balance between telling and listening) (behavior).
8. Restate issues as the other party sees them (feedback to the other person).
9. Attend to and stimulate feedback in terms of consequences of the communication.

QUESTIONS FOR STUDY AND DISCUSSION

1. How realistic do you find the events which occurred between Tom and Steve as described in this chapter? What might each of them have done and at what point in order to avoid the misunderstanding and unfortunate final consequence? Why do you think these actions were not taken by Tom or by Steve?

2. Think of a situation of misunderstanding in which you participated or which you are familiar. How could the misunderstanding have been avoided?

3. Name one other individual who is important to you in your work or personal life. Under three columns headed, respectively, assumptions, perceptions, and feelings, make a list of those aspects in your perspective toward the other person. Now, do the same as best you can for the other person toward you.

   In what ways do the assumptions of each of you stand in need of correction? What are the barriers to communications between you which would result in these corrections? What gateways or opportunities can you imagine which could lead to communications or other means of changing the incorrect assumptions?

   If the other is a member of your work organization, what means of influence by individuals other than yourself on either of you could help to remove the incorrect assumptions?

4. Write a brief paragraph describing your own perspective toward each of the following: (a) your career and (b) your work organization.

   Go back through these descriptions and identify the aspects which represent assumptions, perceptions, and feelings on your part. To what extent is there need for improvement of your perspective in order to achieve your personal job-related, long-term goals?

   Develop a step-by-step personal plan of action for achieving the change in your perspective which can lead to behavior on your part that will provide greater assurance of achieving your goals.

Case 9–1
John Brownell (A)*

In late May of 1972 John Brownell, a first-year student at the Harvard Business School (HBS), was concerned that he might lose a summer job he had lined up some months earlier. John's recent conversations with George Gardner, his prospective employer, had left him more and more convinced that there was a serious problem of communication between them. He felt that Gardner might decide to drop him before he was due to start work in two weeks.

As John thought about what had happened and what he should do, he reminded himself of how valuable the job could be for his career interest in personal finance. Gardner was the sole owner of a thriving consulting operation specializing in advising individuals, especially doctors, on pension plans, investments, and other financial matters. John felt particularly anxious about the uncertainty at this late time because of the tight summer job market and the fact that he needed a job near Boston. His wife had a well-paying job that she liked, they held a lease on an apartment through the summer, and they had a one-year-old child. John had gone into debt to come to the Business School, and was counting on a reasonable summer income.

John had begun looking for a job over Christmas vacation, when he searched through the student reports on summer jobs in the Placement Office. He confined his search to financially-oriented jobs in the Boston area, and sent a letter and a copy of his résumé (Exhibit 1) to 30 or 40 such employers. By the second week in Feburary John had received back four positive-sounding replies and only one negative. Talking to the casewriter in May of 1972, John described his reaction to the response to his mailing:

> It was amazing. I thought I was really pretty hot stuff initially. But I guess I was just seeing a pattern. If people are going to respond positively, they'll respond immediately, and if not, they'll just let you hang, and probably send you a "no" letter later on.
>
> Anyway, the 4 positives out of 5 soon became 4 out of 20. I think out of the 30 or so letters, I finally got back 7 or 8 positive responses. Now, this wasn't too bad, compared to my classmates. I checked around, checked the averages, and that was probably a little better than average. People were sending out 20 or 30 letters and getting *one* interview, if they were lucky. I got two interviews in February.
>
> So I felt pretty good then. Your résumé is a fairly standard thing, and everybody from here is sending out pretty similar material. The thing that made me a little different was my major in Actuarial Science. I attribute a lot of my success to that.

---

* All names have been disguised.

EXHIBIT 1

RÉSUMÉ OF JOHN P. BROWNELL

5211 Stearns Hill Road
Waltham, Mass. 02154
Phone: (617) 891-7132

Home Address:
111–7th Greenacres
Cleveland, Ohio
Phone: (216) 961-9820

Married   5 ft. 7 in.   150 pounds   excellent health

job objective	Summer employment in the areas of finance, consulting, or marketing.
education 1971–1973	HARVARD GRADUATE SCHOOL OF BUSINESS ADMINISTRATION Candidate for the degree of Master in Business Administration in June 1973. Following general management curriculum in first year. Second-year emphasis to be directed toward finance and marketing. Member of Finance, Marketing, and International Business Clubs. Participant in intramural athletics.
1962–1967	UNIVERSITY OF WISCONSIN Received Bachelor of Business Administration in Actuarial Science. President of Sigma Phi Epsilon Social Fraternity. Rush Chairman, Inter-Fraternity Council. Company Commander in Naval ROTC. Member of Scabbard and Blade military honorary. Participant in intramural athletics.
summerwork 1963–1966	U.S. NAVY Served as a midshipman aboard various Naval vessels fulfilling the summer requirements of Naval ROTC scholarship.
military 1967–1971	U.S. NAVY, Lieutenant, USNR Served 4½ years as a Naval Flight Officer. Flight duties included over 1,000 flight hours and 200 carrier landings as jet navigator. Worked in areas of operations, electronics, and training. Spent last 1½ years as department head (Training Officer) of fleet replacement squadron. Deployed to Western Pacific for 14 months. Awards include Air Medals (2), Navy Unit Commendation, Meritorious Unit Commendation, and Vietnamese Air Gallantry Cross. Received final Top Secret clearance based on background investigation completed September 1968.
personal background	Brought up and attended public schools in Cleveland, Ohio. Traveled extensively in the Orient and have visited 49 U.S. states. Interests include sports, music, reading, and bridge.
references	Personal references available on request.

Anyway, I've still got a stack of résumés. After what's happened the last few weeks, I carry them around just in case I meet somebody on the street who looks like he might need an MBA for the summer!

One of the first responses John received was from George Gardner, who called at ten o'clock one Tuesday night in February and invited John for an interview the following Friday afternoon. In the interim John re-read the summer report by Tom Sanderson, the second-year HBS student who had worked for George the year before, and decided to call Sanderson for more information.

On the phone, Sanderson reiterated the enthusiasm for the job that was in his summer report. He described George as "very dynamic, very intelligent, very hard working." He told John, "You probably couldn't ask for a better job as far as experience goes. You could learn a helluva lot from him." In response to John's questions about pay, Tom said he got a take-home of $800 per month, equivalent to about $1,000 gross.

From what he had heard, John was very interested in the job. He thought carefully about how to approach the interview with George Gardner. This would be the first serious job interview he had ever had, having gone directly into the Navy after college and directly to HBS after the Navy.

The advice I got from others was not to try to fool anybody about my qualifications, and to just be myself. I chose to follow the path of complete honesty.

John went on to describe the interview with Gardner:

The office is in Cambridge, in a very nice neighborhood. It's a very small office. He's got one outer reception office and two inner offices, one of which is his and one of which has a desk but is empty except it is full of records and stuff.

The man seemed very personable and easy to talk to, and I thought we hit it off very well. He was very much interested in my actuarial degree, and he asked me several questions about my skills in that area, such as, "If I were to sit down and draw up a pension problem could you do it?" I didn't want to mislead him at all, so I said, "Well, the experience and the background that I have is academic; it was all six or seven years ago. But, yes, I believe I could do it if I was given time to do research and recall what I learned."

He went on to say that he had had a bad experience with the HBS guy he had hired the previous summer, which made me perk up my ears. That was Tom Sanderson. George said the guy had been very capable, but that it took all summer for him to get trained, and that when he walked out the door at the end of August he hadn't done anything all summer to pay off his investment in him. He said that as a result of that he would require his employee this year to come in before the summer began and train a little.

The only mention of salary in the interview was when he asked me if I had talked to Sanderson. I said I had and he said, "Well, the salary will be the same for this summer." He didn't mention a specific figure. I said, "Fine." That was fine with me. The salary was not really much of a consideration at this point in time.

Toward the end he said, "I'll be very honest with you. I'm considering four or five other people and I want to talk to them over the weekend and next week. So I'll get back to you within a week." I thought that was fair.

I left there really enthused, very happy. I told my wife that this really looks like an excellent opportunity, and I would like to work for this guy. I thought I had made a good impression, but I realized there was some competition for the job.

John did not hear from George for the next two and a half weeks. During that time he had three more interviews with other firms. One of these was another pension firm, quite a bit larger than Gardner's. John learned from a second-year student who had worked there the previous summer that they paid very little. On his second interview with Paul Anvil, the head of the firm, the question of salary came up. John explained,

They were talking very little money. I told Anvil I had specific skills to sell, and if they weren't willing to pay at least what I consider the going price, then I just was not interested. So we broke it off back in February.

John also interviewed with two very large firms that he understood were interviewing hundreds of MBAs for only one or two summer positions. Neither of these led to a job offer.

After two and a half weeks waiting to hear from George, John called him. George said he had narrowed his candidates down to John and one other person. He said he was considering both of them, that the other would be excellent out of the office selling with him, and that John would be excellent in the office doing analyses. He added that he had a meeting later that week that might lead to an association with another firm, and if that worked out he might be able to hire both of them. "I really have to decide what is best for me this summer," he said. "Give me a call this time next week."

John called a week later. George told him his father had died and he hadn't had the meeting with the other firm. He said he hadn't thought about the summer job situation any more, and told John to call him again the following week.

Again, John called. This was the first week in March. George said, "Come in Saturday at ten o'clock." John said he would be there. He described the situation as follows:

I thought to myself, "Do I have the job?" I didn't really know. Maybe he just wants to look me over again and compare me to the other guy, since we have only met once. Maybe he wants to tell me in person he can't use me. Maybe he's made up his mind and wants me to get started with some training.

Saturday came and I went in. During the first half hour of discussion he never came out and said why he wanted to see me, but he was talking about things that were going to happen in his business over the coming months, things he would want me to do before the summer, and so on. So I got the feeling I was the man to be hired.

Finally, after a half hour I came right out and said, "Am I to assume from our conversation that I am hired?" He said, "Yes, you are." That was the first definite thing he had said about my employment.

After that we talked for about another hour. He gave me a lot of stuff to read. I told him I had exams coming up in the middle of March, then we had spring vacation and I was going to Ohio to see my parents. He said, "Fine. Take this reading material and see what you can do. I know with exams you will be pretty busy. Read what you can and give me a call."

He also gave me a pension problem to do, relating to a doctor who was a client of his who wanted to put money away for retirement several years later. He said he was going to meet with the man in a few days, but that my figures weren't necessary immediately because obviously he was going to work it out himself. He gave me the figures off the top of his head, didn't read anything out of his file. I said, "Great, OK, I'll work on it."

During the conversation I asked him if I would be compensated for the time I worked before the summer. He said, in effect, that he had been so badly burned the summer before that he hadn't planned to pay me for the time, but then he said, "If things work out, you'll be well taken care of."

I said to myself, "Well OK, this guy is going to take care of me, and I don't mind putting in a few hours for him." So I let it go at that.

The meeting was extremely pleasant, like the first one.

THE JOB IN JEOPARDY

The evening after the second interview John started working on the pension problem George had given him. It seemed to him to be a straight-forward annuity problem, but George had not given him insurance rates which would be a necessary input to solve the problem. He called George the next day.

I told him I really thought I needed those rates. He said, "No, you don't," and then he launched into gyrations about how I was to do the problem. It really surprised me. He came on very strong, very insistent. He made it sound like it was pretty simple, like something I should know.

You know, this was the first time I saw another part of his personality. Up to this point he had always been extremely pleasant whenever I had seen him or talked to him. But this time he was just telling me what to do, and making me feel stupid.

In retrospect, this guy really has two parts to his personality. He is a great salesman. It's amazing how he can sell himself to clients. The way he works is to get their confidence. He sells himself first, then he sells other things. I'm sure he also has a lot of knowledge, but what I'm saying is he's not an expert by any means.

Anyway, I thought I understood what he was saying, so I said, "OK." I didn't really think he was right, but I thought if that's the way he says to do it, fine.

I told him I had exams coming up before vacation, so he said, "All right, call me after your vacation and we'll talk about it."

Before I went on vacation, of course, I tried to check up on the right way to do the problem. I went to Baker Library, got out some pension books, and satisfied myself that my initial approach was right. But I decided to work on the problem his way.

That was the last I talked to him until after vacation.

When John and his family returned from visiting his parents in Ohio during spring vacation there was a letter from the Navy waiting for him. Even before he had begun his summer job search in December, John had applied for summer active duty in Newport. The work would pay around $2,000 a month, but he had felt all along that he wanted business experience rather than a continuation of his military experience. He had applied because he wanted "an ace in the hole" in case no summer job came through by the time the Navy decided on his application. The letter from the Navy told him he was accepted for the summer active duty, and that he had to respond within a few days as to his decision on the offer.

In the first week of April, John called the Navy office in Newport and told them he had other job commitments and would not be working for them.

John tried to reach George on five successive days right after vacation, leaving messages with his secretary to have George call him at home. Another ten days went by and John called again. George told him he had tried to reach him a couple of times but the line was busy. John thought this was "a lot of baloney," and figured George must have been busy with clients' tax returns. They agreed to meet in George's office on a Wednesday afternoon. John described the meeting as follows:

When I showed up at 2:30 P.M., the time of the appointment, the place was locked up tighter than a drum. At five to three he shows up, walking fast. I could tell he was rushed, and not in a good mood.

We sit down and he says, "Show me what you have." So I pull out the problem, he glances at it and says, "Nope!" Then he starts going round and round about why the problem isn't right. I didn't understand what he was trying to tell me. I thought I had understood what he wanted. I kept prodding him with questions, trying to find out the procedure he wanted to use, but I couldn't seem to get a straight answer, or nothing I could fit in with what he said before.

All of this made me think for the first time that he was not really communicating with me in our relationship. I was trying to draw information out of him and he wasn't responding.

So, we had a very bad afternoon. He blows up at me. I can remember his words exactly: "Look, John, I am under the gun to produce for my clients, and frankly you are under the gun to produce for me." He was deliberately trying to apply pressure.

We talked a little bit about the readings he had given me. I told him I had done what I could, but that I hadn't done all of it because of the time constraints I was working under.

Finally, he thought he communicated the way he wanted the problem done, and I said I would go home and do it.

That night John caught the flu. He cut classes the next day and worked for four hours on the problem. The next day he called George during lunch.

I said, "This is the answer I have come up with." He said, "I have come up with twice that amount." I said, "Mr. Gardner, there is just no way that could be true, because of the fact that if you put in twice the amount I get you're excluding any interest that might be earned on the pension for the next 12 years. When you multiply the amount you say by 12 years you come up with what the man needs at age 65. So, that just couldn't be right!"

So needless to say, we started going round and round again. He was not happy. He said I should come in a week from that coming Monday.

That afternoon I picked up my wife after work and told her I had talked to George. I said, "You know something? I think my summer job is in jeopardy." She laughed about that. She didn't think that could really be accurate.

This was in April. That was the first time that we really went at each other . . . . Let's put it this way, he went at me. I was, I guess, fairly timid at the time, and I didn't confront him at all. I was "yes-sir"-ing him to death, because I was a little scared of the whole job situation. I had never come in contact with it before. The only organization I had worked for was pretty structured. They told you when to go to the bathroom. You had some leeway, but not much. I didn't really know what to expect in this business, so I was fairly subservient to him.

I was calling him "Mr. Gardner" at that point. A little later I started calling him George. Not on his initiation, either. I think he liked the "Mister," I really do.

Maybe it was when I started calling him George that things began to get bad. I don't know. But I really felt after that phone conversation that things were bad. And that was the first indication I had. That was how bad the conversation went.

> At that point in time I guess I had the feeling he was right about the problem, and maybe I'm just dumb. I thought that maybe I really don't have the ability to hack it in this kind of a job.

Before their next meeting, which was during the first days of May, John thoroughly researched the problem. He checked two books out of the library and did a lot of reading on pensions and annuity calculations. It all seemed to confirm his initial approach. He talked to several people, but none could understand a way of approaching the problem that was different from the first one he had taken.

> I just didn't know how to approach the Monday meeting. I went in, and right off the bat he starts yelling at me, telling me he is right. I was still very timid. I think we finally resolved what he was trying to get at. Basically, what he was saying was exactly what I had said back at the very beginning, that you need to know how much this annuity is going to cost at age 65. It was not what he had described to me as another method, based on the mortality of the man. So, my initial approach to the problem was absolutely right. We had spent the last two months going round and round.
>
> In the course of this, he kept saying, "With your background, you should be able to do this," and I kept telling him, "Well, my background is only such and such, and I have never distorted my background. I've tried to tell you exactly what I can and cannot do." That didn't seem to make any difference to him.
>
> So, he's saying my background should have prepared me to do these problems without asking him question one. I'm beginning to see now that he didn't *want* me to ask him any questions! He was instilling a fear in me not to even ask him anything.
>
> I think we finally got it resolved that I was correct to begin with. But, you know, he wouldn't admit this. In fact, he wouldn't even admit the fact that I had approached the problem this way in the first place.
>
> Anyway, he said finally, "OK, let's forget about this. Here's another problem I want you to do. It has an incorporation part and a pension part. I'm meeting this guy at the end of the week. Call me before then with some numbers, and maybe I'll use them."
>
> So, I at least got a feeling I was making some progress with him. The first problem had been, "call me with some numbers and I'll check you." Now this one was, "call me with some numbers and I'll use them."

John took the new problem, worked it through to his satisfaction, and called George on Wednesday. They discussed the incorporation part of the problem first, and John learned George had also done the problem, and that they agreed completely on the incorporation part.

> Then I told what I had for the pension part. He started yelling and screaming over the phone, saying, "No, you're not right." I said, "OK." Then he told me I should come in on Saturday to really go over this problem. He said we should really hash this one out. I said I would.

That night John felt very agitated, and more concerned about his job than ever before. He described his thoughts:

> I started thinking, "Maybe it's not my ability. Maybe this guy just doesn't want to have *anybody* working for him this summer, because he's going to have to pay out $3,000, and it's all coming out of his pocket. He has attacked my ability from all different angles, and not once acknowledged anything useful I've said or that I tried to do things in the right manner. He is having second thoughts about hiring anybody, and the way he approaches it is to play psychological games with me."
>
> The more I thought about it the more aggravated I got. There it was, the middle of May. I couldn't imagine I would have much chance getting another job.
>
> I called him the next day. I think this was the first time I called him George. I just said, "George, things are not working out. We're just not getting along. And I think we really need to get them squared away before the summer begins."
>
> Then he said, "I had the same feeling. You're not showing me what I expected of you. With your background you should have been able to come in here and really take over my office without me giving you a bit of help. You haven't come in here that much."
>
> This was when I started to answer him back. I told him I would not accept responsibility for that. I said I had leveled with him about my background, and besides, we had both been busy and had trouble meshing our schedules.
>
> He said, "Every time you've been in here you have wanted to leave," and I told him, "I don't know how you have gotten that impression. I have never said I wanted to leave. If you have gotten that impression, it is only because our meetings have been unproductive."
>
> So, we went on like that for a while, and it ended up with our agreeing that I would come in right after classes Monday so we could get the whole thing ironed out.

DEVELOPING A NEW APPROACH

When John hung up, his first thought was that it was time to talk to Tom Sanderson again. He called Tom and told him things didn't seem to be working out, and started to relay some of the things that had happened. Tom suggested they meet the next day between classes.

When they met, Tom told John:

> Geeze, that's how George is. You really described him well. George is a hard man to work for. He and I had two or three battles last summer. In fact, George went through three secretaries last summer because he has this communication problem where he doesn't tell people what he wants them to do, but he expects them to do it anyway. He thinks people should do things by osmosis. With the secretaries, he would expect them

to do something he had not told them about, and when they hadn't, he would say, "OK, go look for other employment."

George is the kind of guy who wants you to work 50 or 60 hours a week. He wants you to put your absolute all into his business, even though you are only going to be there three months. And he is not willing to give you any reward other than the paycheck. He is very short on praise. I don't remember him ever praising me the entire summer last year.

Another aspect to George is he makes every minute of his time count. He bills his clients for time down to the minute. He even keeps a log of phone calls, and charges them for that time. They seem to think it's worth it.

John told Tom he thought his job was in jeopardy, but Tom told him not to worry, that if George was anything he was honorable and ethical. "If he told you you have a job, then you have it for the whole summer," Tom said. Then Tom reiterated what he had said earlier, that George was very dynamic and intelligent, and that you could learn a lot from him if you could get along with his way of thinking.

John noticed that Tom seemed to be feeling guilty about John's trouble with George. At one point John said, "Tom, you really shitted me about this guy when I first talked to you." Tom said he was sorry he hadn't expressed it, but that John should not worry at all about losing the job.

Tom had brought to their meeting a folder containing some of the work he had done for George the previous summer. John looked through it, and at the time felt it was not of very high quality or difficulty. John recalled what George had said about being "burned," and it occurred to him that Tom may have been led into a job that he wasn't really qualified for, because the two of them had not fully understood what was required.

John described his thoughts after the meeting with Tom as leading him to a clearer understanding of what was needed:

> I said to myself, "This man is looking for commitment. I can understand why. It's his business and he wants people to be as enthusiastic about their work with him as he is."
>
> I thought, maybe I haven't shown a commitment. Then I remembered part of my last conversation with George. I had asked him if he could give me an approximation of the hours I would be working during the summer. I remembered he got a funny look on his face, and I couldn't figure out why, especially because I had explained to him fully the reason I asked. I told him my wife worked and we had to hire a babysitter for our baby, and we have only one car. You can't depend on public transportation, so you have to tell the babysitter the time you are going to pick up the child. I had explained that to George, but he still got this funny look

on his face. He answered something like, "We start between nine and ten and we end when we're done."

Now that Tom had told me what he had I said to myself, "Boy, did I ask a bad question!" I probably had hit a very, very tender spot with this man because it looked like I was trying to say, "When the clock strikes five, I'm leaving." This man doesn't operate that way.

So I decided I would go in to see him Monday and really make it clear that I am committed to working hard this summer, and it doesn't bother me. Working hard will be good for me.

I talked it over with my wife that weekend. I told her the first thing we had to do is get a second car if I have this job. The worst thing that can happen is we spend a couple of hundred dollars for an old clunker to get me to and from work for the summer.

The other thing I decided was to tell him on Monday about all the other jobs I've turned down, especially that attractive job with the Navy. That ought to signal that I was committed to working for him.

So, that was my strategy. I felt like I had a good fix on the key to this thing.

THE MONDAY MEETING

John left about halfway through his last class of the day on Monday to make his appointment with George. When he walked in he said, "OK, can I start, and get a few things off my chest?" George said, "Go ahead." John described the meeting as follows:

I hit him with the fact that I was committed to the job, that I had turned down the Navy job, that I was going to buy a car, and that I was sorry I had asked about the hours because it was obviously a bad question and that I wasn't motivated by working shorter hours. I talked for 15 minutes.

At the end of that, George said to me, "John, to tell you the truth, I had intended on severing our relationship before you walked in here."

Boy, that hit me like a bomb. Even though I had thought the job was in jeopardy a month before, and had told my wife and Tom that, it still hit me like a bomb. You never really want to admit something like that could possibly happen in this sort of situation.

Then he went on. "But since you have come in here and talked this way, I am going to give you another chance." Then he kept talking, implying really, that he really wanted a guy to show initiative, to show that he was an entrepreneur. He said he had wanted a guy to come in before the summer and rubble through the office and work on his own.

Finally I couldn't hold it any longer. I said, "For Christsake, George, why didn't you tell me that? If you had told me you were looking for a guy to be on his own and do things, I would have. I've been in here several times, and every time you've given me no guidance whatsoever. Maybe it's a lack of ability on my part, but I really don't see it that way."

While I was talking I noticed he showed signs of being very aggravated, and he was holding his stomach so it looked like he might have ulcers or something. I could tell he was definitely getting up tight.

Then he said, "OK, we've got two weeks before the summer. Let's see what we can do. Two weeks from now, if you haven't produced, that's it.

I didn't know how to react. He was implying I should come in and do as much as I could, even nights or Saturdays, within the next two weeks, all just to show that I had initiative and was willing to work. Not only that, but the thought crossed my mind that we had several more days of classes, then I had to spend several days on a final exam and paper.

I was quite upset. I was mad. I was very mad at the time. But I said, "Hold yourself. This is probably not the time, without gathering your thoughts, to really lay into this guy." I guess I sort of maintained the subservient position again.

So he gave me some files to look at, and when I left I said, "Well, right now I plan on being in every day for the next two weeks. So, I'll see you tomorrow."

I went home, and the more I thought about it the madder I got. What this guy was doing, basically, was trying to strip me of any pride I had. He really was. He was trying to blame the whole thing on my ability. I didn't think that was it at this point. He had me believing it for a while, but this just wasn't the case.

I told my wife, "I don't know what we are going to do about this." We started talking about other possibilities for a job. . . .

I went to school the next day with a suit on, with the thought of going to his office to work after classes. But the more I thought and the more I talked to some of my classmates about it the more I said, "There is just no way I am going to go in there this afternoon. As soon as I go in there that guy has got me exactly where he wants me, and there is no way I can think of to escape once I have made that move. I could go in there and work for two weeks and still end up without a job."

Before his afternoon class John called the Navy office in Newport to see if he could be reinstated in the summer position. The answer was no. As John put it, "That was what I expected, but I thought that maybe there was a 5 percent chance I could get back in. That would have been great, because then I could go in and tell that _____ to go to hell. That's about what I wanted to do at that point."

John also called Paul Anvil, the man in the larger pension firm with whom he had met twice in February. Anvil said the position had been offered to someone who had promised to tell him within ten days. If he turned them down, Anvil said John could have the job.

Then he went by the Placement Office, where he found several interesting leads for summer jobs. One was from a Boston bank. Another was an opportunity to run a summer camp in North Carolina. This appealed to John because he could take his family along, all living expenses were paid and he could net around $2,000 for the summer. He called the local number given on the announcement. It was a

second-year student who said the job had not been filled and suggested they get together the next day.

John described his thoughts as he sat in his last class of the day:

> Maybe things aren't so bad. Here I've spent less than one day looking
> and there are two live prospects for other jobs. Maybe this guy doesn't
> have me over a barrel after all!
>
> I wondered what I should do.

Case 9–2
John Brownell (B)*

John left class 20 minutes early and went to the pay phone in the
Coop to call George Gardner. He described the conversation as follows:

> I didn't let him get the upper hand. I hardly let him get a word in
> edgewise.
>
> The first thing I said was, "I cannot work under your ground rules. I
> cannot come in there for two weeks and have you tell me I don't have the
> job. I have got to know now. That's all there is to it. There is no way in hell
> I'm going to find a job then, and only a slim chance I can find one now.
> But whatever the chance, I can't be spending every afternoon in your
> office and lose the time of looking for a job."
>
> He did talk a little at the beginning of the conversation. It sounded like
> the job relationship was severed. There was no way that even if we came
> to an understanding we could spend the summer together. I was really
> mad.
>
> I told him he was not willing to bear any of the training costs, because
> he could give me the heave-ho and not pay me a cent. I said, "It's just not
> done that way. It's unethical." I also told him he was naive to think
> somebody could just come in and take over and do the work his way
> immediately, without even being able to ask a question.
>
> When we were talking about training costs he asked me how many
> hours I had worked. I told him approximately 20. He said, "I'll send you a
> check for those hours." I said, "That's good, because I would have sent
> you a bill."
>
> I told him he was leaving me completely out in the cold. The summer
> job was very important to me, because if I didn't get one I would have to
> go deeper in debt to get through the Business School. On his side, I told
> him it really didn't mean that much because his profession and his work

---

* All names have been disguised.

would just go on. He wouldn't suffer except for having to put up with me telling him what a _____ he was.

After 30 or 45 minutes of me dominating it there was a pause in the conversation. Then he said, "OK. Maybe you're right. I guess there has been a lack of communication, and I will accept full responsibility for it."

I thought, "Geeze, this is the first time in our entire relationship this guy has given an inch!" I think what was happening here was that he was seeing that things weren't exactly as he had seen them. I think he was shocked by how strong I was coming on. I think I was telling him things that he really didn't want to hear. It was breaking down the whole image of the situation he had built up.

It ended up with his asking me how much time I had for the next week. I told him I still had a big end-of-the-year project, and I didn't know how much time I would have available. So he said, "OK, let's forget about this week." Why he said that I still don't know. I think he basically wanted a vacation from the whole affair, just wanted to stay away from it for a few days. I think that was pretty smart. If I had come in that day or the next day we could have just continued the whole conflict.

So, we agreed I would come in a few days later. I figured, "If I'm not going to get this job, at least I can get as much as possible out of this guy for hourly work."

Two days later John was turned down for the North Carolina camp job, the reason being that the employers were concerned that his child was too young.

When John went to Gardner's office the next time Gardner was not in, but had left some work for him to do. Gardner appeared after an hour or so. John described what happened:

He comes in with a client and sees me in the side office. Well, he walks over to me, shakes my hand, and with a big smile says, "Hi, John, how are you? I'm really sorry I wasn't here when you came in. I hope you got my message about the work."

It was unbelievable. He was so personable. He asked me what I was doing. I told him, and he said, "That's fine. That's exactly what I wanted you to do. That's great."

He asked me when I planned to come in again. I told him the day after next, and he said, "That's great. How would you like to go out with me and look at a couple of houses a client is thinking of buying?" I said, "That's great."

Well, it was just yesterday that we went out to the houses. Everything was pleasant. He showed me what to look for in buying a house for rental. I think basically he knows as little about real estate as I do. He even bought me lunch, which is really something, because it is the first money he's spent on me. We had had a little section party after our last class, and I had had a few Bloody Marys. I was feeling good. We had a good conversation. He was very honest about the business, and talked about what he wanted to do with it.

He told me he was firing his secretary. That was very interesting, because before he came in the other day she told me she was quitting. I thought to myself, "That's two conflicting stories. I think this is another part of his personality: nobody quits him. Nobody could quit him, because to him it is such a tremendous opportunity for anybody to work for him."

So, anyway, as far as I can see things are all set for the summer. I start full time next Monday. What will happen from here I really don't know. I'm going to give it my all. I think I can play his game. I think I can show him I'm capable enough to do the work he wants me to do. As long as I keep it on those terms I have a future at this job. It can be a great job if I do keep it up during the summer. I still have a couple of things that are other possibilities, and if something else comes along, I'll make a choice then. But as far as I'm concerned, I'm employed with him until further notice, and I hope further notice doesn't come until August 31st.

Case 9–3
John Brownell (C)*

George Gardner's thoughts on HBS students[1]

I've always had a fairly high respect for the Harvard Business School education, but the more I come in contact with HBS students, the more I doubt the validity of my own opinion.

The one characteristic of the HBS student I find most appealing is his confidence in his abilities. This quality has been evident in all four HBS students under my employ in the past. What bothers me, however, is that in my experience this confidence is not backed up by ability. It almost seems as if HBS breeds an attitude of self-assurance in people which cannot be met by performance.

For all their apparent self-confidence, I have not found HBS students to be particularly forceful or able to take the initiative in working with me. Anybody who runs a small firm like this is terribly busy and really on the job or thinking about it 24 hours a day. I can be pretty impatient and abrasive, but it means a lot to me if a person can take hold of a problem without spending a lot of time, or can even go find the problems without my having to explain everything to them.

One other thing about HBS that really makes me mad is the fact that

---

* All names have been disguished.

[1] Note: These views of Gardner were written by John Brownell at the end of his summer job and are based on conversations between the two and Brownell's assessment of Gardner's opinions.

the school has sold itself to the business world and as a result HBS summer students and graduates demand and are able to receive starting compensation levels which I am sure are far greater than their worth. I have worked hard for everything I have, and it irritates me to see someone get something for nothing.

My first contact with HBS students was four years ago. Joe Brown worked for me during the summer of 1969, when my firm was in its infancy. I hired Joe and subsequent HBS students because I felt if the firm were to expand it would need talented people that could be lured in by a promise of equity participation. I was very impressed with Joe's performance that summer. He and a classmate of his came to me in September and said they wanted to do their research report on my firm. I was delighted. I felt that with two intelligent HBS students doing an in-depth report on the firm, they could come up with recommendations I needed but didn't have time to do to provide future direction.

In the process of writing the report the two said they had become interested in the firm and would like to join the business following graduation to implement their ideas. Spring recruiting season came and both Steve and Joe were lured away to big companies able to pay large salaries. There I was, holding the ball. I decided to implement their ideas on my own.

Looking back, I can now say that that was the biggest mistake I've made in my business. The program they proposed set me back three years. It involved lowering my fee structure. We are presently at the fee level we were at before the change. The problem was the volume did not increase enough to make up for the lost contribution.

During the summer of 1971 the firm's business showed improvement so I decided to hire another HBS student, Tom Sanderson. It took three months to train Tom and when he walked out the door in September he never returned. As a result I never got any return on my investment in him. Tom basically was useless—a very slow learner.

I swore I wouldn't hire another HBS student, but prior to last summer (1972) I received a résumé from John Brownell, a man with a degree in Actuarial Science. With that background I felt little or no training would be necessary. This is the reason I hired him. John and I made an agreement when I hired him that he would come in between March and June to learn as much as he could before the summer began.

I was quite pleased with this arrangement. It would have been great if it had worked. John proved to be extremely lazy during this period. He showed very little initiative toward the job. I almost fired him before the summer began, but my conscience wouldn't let me.

John worked hard during the summer, so in that respect I was wrong. However he did abandon the company when the summer was over so it was the same old story again: An HBS student taking the valuable experience gained in my firm elsewhere.

Case 9–4
Jan Vanvoort*

Jack Armfield resolved that he simply had to talk to Jan Vanvoort, and that there was no time like the present. Armfield had just finished talking on the phone to the president of the Benelux subsidiary of their company, Electric Appliances. Although he did not report to the man, Armfield depended on the Benelux people for office space and some personnel services in Rotterdam, where both of them were located.

The Benelux president had made it clear what he was concerned about:

> Jack, my personnel manager complained again to me about Jan Vanvoort. Apparently, Jan continued to refer job applicants to our personnel department, even though he knows we are under a hiring-stop policy.
>
> I understand Jan has a lot of personal obligations, but the dirty job of telling people we can't hire them falls to us. A lot of them seem to have the impression that all they had to do was give us their name and we would put them on the payroll. With the year-end crush of putting together statistics for the government, my personnel people are already overburdened. And there's another thing. This morning I was walking through the cafeteria and saw Jan talking to the two main union negotiators. The negotiations for the new contract are at a very delicate stage right now. For all I know Jan was talking about tomorrow's soccer game, given how crazy these Dutch are about it!
>
> But, Jack, I would really prefer that since Jan is working for you in the Components Marketing Group and no longer for us in Benelux, he just had no contact with the union people anymore. I wish you could see what you could do for me . . . .

Jack had promised to do what he could.

As he had hung up the phone, Jack mused that he now had two unpleasant messages for Jan. For several days he had postponed telling Jan that right after New Year's he wanted him to take a four-week trip to the Middle East, and that he would not be able to come home over the middle weekend. For the ten months Jan had worked for Jack, since February 1976, they had had a kind of implicit gentleman's agreement that Jan's trips would not extend over two consecutive weeks. Jack had not enforced the company rules on economizing on travel cost in Jan's case. After all, Jack had reasoned, the man was 58, had been with Electric Appliances for 30 years and had never had to travel much outside his native Holland. Moreover, Jack knew well that Jan considered his family very important to him.

---

* All names have been disguised.

Just that Monday, however, Jack had received a memo from his boss, the general director for Europe and the Middle East, to the effect that the rules on travel and expenses should be strictly enforced. The cost savings campaign was referred to as the reason for the reminder. In Jan's case that meant an end to the not more than two weeks away travel. Jack had already reminded each of his other four sales managers to stick to the policy, and he felt he could not make an exception for Jan.

It was 4:00 P.M. on Friday, but Jack decided it was as good a time as any to talk to Jan. He would not have much time next week, as the director of personnel of the entire International Division would be flying in from headquarters in White Plains, and Jack would be tied up with him.

Jan's secretary answered his phone, and told Jack, "Mr. Vanvoort had to leave a little early today. I believe he is attending the party at the home of the Mayor of Rotterdam."

Jack felt annoyed but slightly amused by the irony of it. Here he was, an American, about to reprimand a member of a prominent Dutch family. It seemed a small matter compared to making his new organization succeed. Then again, Vanvoort had many friends in Electric Appliances, in White Plains as well as in Europe, and Jack himself felt personally close to the man. "Perhaps it would be better to talk to him next week, anyway," Jack thought. "I can make sure I do it right."

JACK ARMFIELD

Jack Armfield was 40, the son of an automobile mechanic in Atlanta, Georgia, where he grew up. After high school he attended Georgia Tech on a football scholarship, and obtained his bachelor's degree in electrical engineering in 1959. One year later, at 24, he had joined Electric Appliances.

Jack's first job had been as a field service representative with the Components Division in Georgia. He had held this job for four years and was promoted to sales representative for Metropolitan Boston in 1964. From there on he had risen rather fast in the Components Division's management. In 1966 he moved up to district manager for the State of Massachusetts. Electric Appliances' sales and profit within his territory improved. In 1970 he was appointed zone manager for the whole of California and in 1972 he was promoted to staff assistant to the general manager of the Components Division in White Plains. He had been quite excited about this at the time, because it was well known within the company that this position usually served as a preparation and springboard to further important assignments.

He had not expected to wait for very long. The offer he got, however, was quite unexpected. One year later, in 1973, he was asked to head the European Components Marketing Group (ECMG). Not only did this mean that for the first time he would have to work in a foreign country, there was the additional challenge that the ECMG was new and part of a major reorganization within the International Division.

Jack knew that his further career opportunities would be a function of how well he would pull off the reorganization and make it pay in terms of increased market share for Electric Appliances Components. That would largely depend on how well he could work with each of his new group of subordinates, mostly experienced managers, each of whom had previously worked for one of Electric Appliances' European subsidiaries.

ELECTRIC APPLIANCES CORPORATION IN EUROPE

Electric Appliances Corporation was one of the largest manufacturers of household appliances in the world. Its product range included washers and dryers, stoves, ovens, refrigerators, air-conditioning units, etc. Although in 1976 70 percent of the business of the corporation was still domestic, 30 percent of manufacturing and sales was accounted for by the International Division, mainly in Western Europe. That percentage was expected to increase over the coming years.

Electric Appliances began operations in Europe through an export division shortly before World War I. Later, two European appliance companies had been acquired: Forza in Italy and Champion in England. These two "source plants" continued to develop, produce, and sell their own products under their own trade names. Just before and after World War II Electric Appliances built several assembly plants for the larger appliances made in the United States and by Forza and Champion like refrigerators, dishwashers, and commercial hotel and restaurant appliances, and also a plant in England for making accessories, components, and parts under the same Supreme. Despite the fact that all these facilities were wholly owned, the public was not generally aware until the late 1960s that Forza, Champion, and Supreme were owned by an American corporation.

Until the major reorganization in 1973 the International Division of Electric Appliances in Europe had been geographically decentralized (see Exhibit 1). In those countries where there were manufacturing and assembly facilities the sales of all company products were handled through the sales departments of the subsidiaries which ran these facilities. The rest of Europe was covered by eight distinct marketing subsidiaries which had been established to import and sell the complete line of products. Each of these subsidiary companies was headed

EXHIBIT 1
Partial organization chart of Electric Appliances—Europe before 1973 reorganization

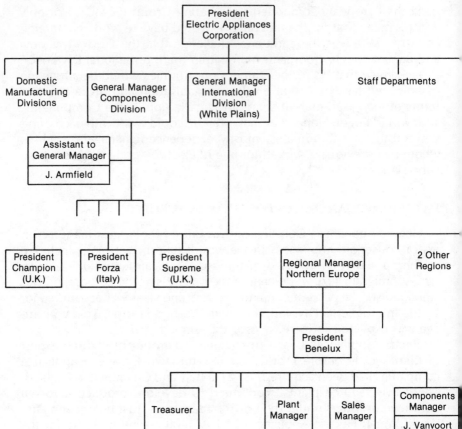

by a president, and each had an Advisory Board of Directors consisting typically of some of its own managers and a few prominent businessmen. These presidents reported either directly to the International Division headquarters in White Plains or through three regional managers for the marketing subsidiaries.

The 1973 reorganization, referred to as a move toward a matrix organization, reduced the amount of geographical decentralization and increased the emphasis on product lines (Exhibit 2). This meant, for example, that the plant managers of assembly plants would report to the works managers of Champion and Forza on such matters as scheduling, production levels, product mix to be assembled, etc. Also, all sales

EXHIBIT 2
Partial organization chart of Electric Appliances—Europe immediately after 1973 reorganization

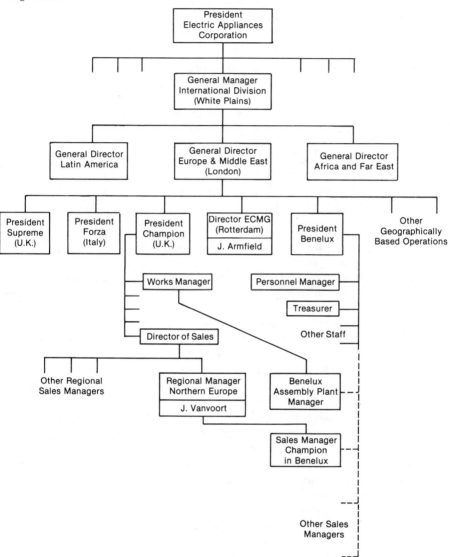

managers in the subsidiaries would report to the sales directors of Forza and Champion on all marketing and sales related issues. Plant and sales managers kept reporting to their respective local presidents on issues related to personnel, public and government relations, control, and other staff functions. The presidents of the nonmanufacturing operations now headed what came to be called "assist units" to the two source plants. To the outside (i.e., the general public and local government or union officials) no change appeared to have taken place, as the company did not change the legal identity of its subsidiaries.

The intricacies of these reporting relationships were illustrated by an example given by the personnel director for the Benelux subsidiary:

> You see, we assemble here both Champion and Forza products. Every two years we negotiate a contract with the Dutch unions. Our workers are on the payroll of Electric Appliances Benelux, not on Forza's or Champion's. Assume now that at the time of negotiations Forza is doing extremely well and can hardly keep up with demand, whereas Champion is experiencing a slump with large unsold stocks built up. We can then easily imagine that Forza's management will put the plant manager and myself under pressure to be lenient on union demands, while we would experience the reverse pressure from Champion. I think we will be in for a lot of compromising!

The corporation's top management had given two reasons for the reorganization. The first one was to rationalize and consolidate operations judged to have been too redundant throughout Europe. It was felt that staff effort and operations management time could be saved if, for example, a European marketing strategy for each product line were developed, instead of having each subsidiary develop its own. Top management reasoned that while the localized approach might have made sense in the past it now appeared to make far less, given the existence of the European Common Market. They also felt that the new organization would help in promoting the sales of Champion products on Forza territory and vice versa. The two source plants had traditionally put most of their sales efforts into their home markets and had shown little interest in export. Making the director of sales in each source plant responsible for sales throughout Europe and the Middle East would, it was thought, stimulate that interest. This first reason was closely linked to the second one. Electric Appliances had long been described as an American Company with a number of foreign operations. It was a corporate objective to change the image of the company to a multinational one. Before, most top positions in each operation, such as president, treasurer, etc., had traditionally been filled with U.S. citizens. The company was now striving to appoint more Europeans in key positions.

EUROPEAN COMPONENTS MARKETING GROUP (ECMG)

At the time of the reorganization ECMG had been established to market electrical accessories and spare parts. These included four different kinds: the Champion and Forza parts, the products from Supreme, and accessories and components imported from several subsidiaries of Electric Appliances in the United States. This plan had met with severe opposition from the two European source plants, Forza and Champion, and it had been finally decided in White Plains that ECMG would only handle the Supreme and the U.S. component lines, leaving Forza and Champion to market their own components as they had in the past. Thus, the ECMG mission was to import and market electrical accessories, components, and parts from Supreme and the U.S. subsidiaries, using either Electric Appliances' existing subsidiaries or other channels of distribution. It was also decided that ECMG, which Jack Armfield was to head, would not be based at the new headquarters of Electric Appliances-Europe, in London, but rather in Rotterdam. The logic was simple. For the last 20 years Rotterdam had hosted Electric Appliances' largest accessories and components warehouse in Europe. This decision put Jack Armfield in a somewhat unique position. Although he enjoyed considerably higher status than the president of the Benelux subsidiary, he was in some respects dependent on him. His clerical staff and warehouse workers, for example, would be hired through the local personnel department and although billed to his group they would be on Benelux's payroll. He also had to "report" to him for office space, telephone and telex connections, etc.

Exhibit 3 shows the partial organization chart for ECMG under Jack Armfield.

JAN VANVOORT

Jan Vanvoort reported to Armfield as ECMG's general sales manager for Supreme components, a position he had held for ten months. Jack had met Jan almost immediately after he arrived in Rotterdam to take up his assignment early in 1974. At that time Jan had just changed from his job as components manager for the Benelux operation to the regional sales manager, Northern Europe for Champion products, a position under the new organization, with responsibilities covering Benelux, Scandinavia, and Finland (see Exhibit 2). As such, Jan became one of the first European nationals to take up a position at a level involving responsibility for a territory larger than one's native country. Given the territory for which he was responsible Jan had kept his office in Rotterdam. He also continued to serve as a member of the Board of Directors for Electric Appliances Benelux, a position to which he had been appointed in 1969.

EXHIBIT 3
Partial organization chart—European Components Marketing Group (December 1976)

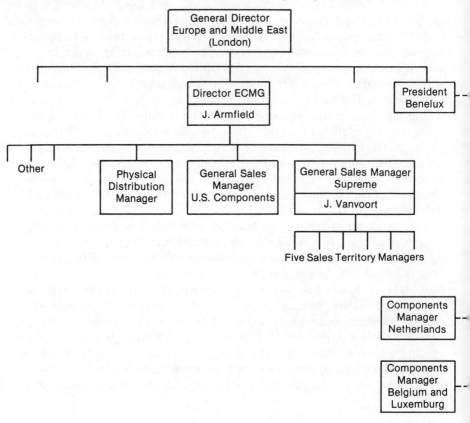

Jack Armfield remembered that upon his arrival Jan had been very helpful. He had assisted him in looking for a house, had his wife take Dorothy to the better shopping centers, and suggested the language lab, run by an old family friend, which the Armfields used to learn Dutch.

About six weeks after his arrival Jack and Dorothy attended a cocktail party given by Vanvoort in honor of his sister, who had just been reappointed as legal counsel for a committee of the Dutch parliament. Jan told him that this would be a good opportunity to meet prominent businessmen and city and government officials. Jack remembered the informal stylishness and sophistication of the whole affair. Jan had personally ushered them around to most of the guests, which included several members of parliament belonging to the Christian Democratic party, the chairman of the Port Authority for Rotterdam, several heads and owners of Dutch companies, and two of Jan's brothers: Henk, a Protestant theologian who was on vacation after a two-year trip throughout the world as a consultant on reform for the World Council of Churches, and Hans, the managing director of the Vanvoorts' family business. Five of Jan's ten children were also present. Jack had briefly talked to Jan's two elder sons, one a social sciences professor and one a lung specialist. The oldest daughter was a geologist, on vacation from Iran. The other two girls were a professional nurse and a physical therapist. Two other of Jan's daughters were in nurses' training.

Later in the evening Jan had drawn Jack into a circle of business executives. Jack remembered Jan being quite adamant about business responsibility:

> I always believed in the principle that as an executive for Electric Appliances I should be socially engaged, because if we want to have the name of Electric Appliances respected we must take time for our community, which is part of the public relations assignment which every manager has. For my part personally I definitely have always been extremely engaged in social work, in church and also in education, because I think the better people are educated the better chances we have to develop our country.

Jack and Dorothy had been most impressed by the party.

Jan Vanvoort belonged to one of the Netherlands most well-known families. Jan's father had built up the family colonial products business he had inherited from his father. He was also very active in the Christian Democratic party. Before World War II he had served several terms as a city council member in Rotterdam and in 1946, after he had turned over the management of his business to Hans, he won a seat in the Dutch parliament which he occupied until his death in 1960. Jack learned that there existed a special relationship between Electric Appliances and the Vanvoort family. In 1937, as a city council member, Jan's father had been very instrumental in getting the company to build its first overseas assembly plant in Rotterdam on land leased on very favorable terms by the Port Authority. At the outbreak of World War II, when the Vanvoorts had fled to the United States, executives of Electric Appliances in Rotterdam had helped them get the necessary visas and expedite their evacuation. On arriving in the United States the family was welcomed by the general manager of the International Division and assisted by the company in finding housing and getting the children enrolled in colleges. Jan entered a U.S. college, but answered an appeal by the Dutch government in exile and joined the Dutch armed forces in Canada. After training as a commando he became an infantry officer and participated in the Allied landing in Normandy. After the war Jan had an opportunity to pursue a career in the Dutch army, but turned it down because much of the family wealth had been lost and he felt he could not afford the low pay if he wanted to give his wife, the daughter of the Christian Democratic party's chairman, an adequate standard of living.

Quite naturally Jan applied for a job with the Benelux subsidiary of Electric Appliances. In May 1946 he was hired as a district manager in the sales department. In 1949 he was selected for a two-year training program at the International Division's headquarters in White Plains. There he was trained in the various departments: sales of finished products and components, supply, and particularly government and public relations. As far as Jan could gather the intent was that he enter the public relations field upon his return to the Netherlands, which interested him greatly. When he came back in 1951 he learned that when he had been selected his immediate superior had not been consulted and in fact had objected to the training. As Jan remembered it:

> He considered my selection as being a favor and not based on my ability. When I came back that man had become a director for Electric Appliances Benelux and he refused to take me back in the sales department. Also, in view of my father's business and political reknown he thought that I could never be neutral enough to become the governmental and public relations spokesman for the company.
>
> I was transferred to the supply department of Benelux in charge of exports to Morocco and Turkey. After one year of this, Mr. Davis, an American who was the general manager of the International Division, told me he did not think this job important enough for somebody who had spent two years training in the United States, and made it clear to management that either they fire me or give me a job where the training would pay off.
>
> I was then assigned to become the assistant supply manager. The job was presented as a tough one and I was given one year to prove myself. I got a very particular introduction to the three immediate subordinates of the supply manager. The traffic manager was told that I was the assistant *to* the supply manager, but that I would not interfere with traffic because that was much too specialized. And the same happened with purchasing and ordering managers!
>
> So there was not much of the job left. After one year, in 1954, I demanded an interview with the president of Benelux and made it quite clear that on this basis I could not be judged and I wanted to have a fair chance and challenge.
>
> This challenge was offered and I became components supply manager reporting to the components manager. Much later the treasurer told me that he had made a bet that I would be a total failure. He had to pay!
>
> The circumstances under which I took my job were difficult. My predecessor had been a weak manager and I had the choice either to continue the old road or take a creative approach. Also, components supply was then being put on EDP. Nobody knew anything about it, and by

selecting that road I could easily be the leader and immediately know as much as any of the old-timers. But the challenge was that I had to lay off 8 people out of 50 within six months. In our country this is not an easy assignment. After three months I made a list based on performance and career prospects and not on seniority. These people were laid off, and none of the names was ever challenged by management or by the unions.

During the time Jan was components supply manager the performance of the department improved considerably. Also while in this job Jan was selected to be the tour leader for Electric Appliances' president on his first trip to Europe. As an aide-de-camp he took care of all the plans and arrangements for a big group visiting all the company's operations in Europe.

In 1963 Jan was transferred to the sales department as staff manager. Four years later he became sales manager for both Forza and Champion products for the Netherlands. In 1968 he was appointed components manager for Electric Appliances Benelux (see Exhibit 1) and in 1969 became on of the directors of the Benelux subsidiary. As components manager Jan was responsible for all sales and supply of Forza, Champion, Supreme, and U.S. accessories and components in Rotterdam. This warehouse served the whole of Europe and the Middle East.

When the 1973 reorganization came Jan was contacted by the president of Champion to become the regional sales manager for Northern Europe including Benelux, Scandinavia, and Finland (see Exhibit 2). As such he would report to the director of sales in the United Kingdom but on a dotted line to the president of Electric Appliances Benelux. Mr. Cormick, the president of Champion, had on three occasions been Jan's boss, and Jan did not hesitate to accept the job.

Champion has always been known as the weak brother in the company. I would never have taken that assignment if it wasn't because of Mr. Cormic, the man who was trying to straighten Champion out. He instilled me with a lot of confidence; he is really a leader and if ever there was a time we could bring Champion in line, it could only be done under him. I was willing to accept that challenge and give him my full support, so that he might succeed in his very difficult, nearly impossible assignment.

For Jan, as for many other European executives, the 1973 reorganization meant quite a change. The enthusiasm for it among them was less than it was at headquarters in White Plains. Many local managers expressed the feeling that the multinationalization would not go as smoothly as it was imagined on the other side of the ocean. Although over the years pressures had built up to appoint Europeans to top positions in their countries, it had on the whole been generally accepted by Europeans that the key jobs would be filled by U.S. citizens. After all, Electric Appliances was an American company. The prospect of now having in a key position in one's country some *other* foreigner was not unanimously welcomed. As one Dutch executive commented:

> Working for an American boss is not always that easy. But we accept it and get used to it. I do not know however how I would react if tomorrow my new boss would be German!"

Doubts were also expressed about the workings of the new matrix organization. Although major decisions would now be made at the source plants or by ECMG, it would still require the approval of local presidents to carry them out. This was considered an elaborate and time-consuming approach. In addition some felt that the attitude changes required would not be easily made.

Jan was not reticent in describing to friends and colleagues how he experienced the change:

> For me it meant a complete change away from making Electric Appliances strong at the national level and toward strengthening the source plants in other nations. Within the new set-up, working for Champion in several countries, I found myself operating more as a consultant and adviser than as a decision maker. I was used to running a department with 275 people and lots of decisions to make. In my new job my staff consisted of only six subordinates. The biggest problem I had was to get known in the source plant as an authority. For many Champion executives in the United Kingdom, who were not all that interested in exports, I seemed to bother them on what were for them minor things. I felt like an appendix in Rotterdam with no direct influence on the future of the company. It took me six months to find out that I could influence things and accomplish objectives and get Champion interested in exports toward the rest of Europe. In my new assignment I drifted away from Electric Appliances Benelux. I started to feel like a stranger. After 30 years of hoping to become a leader with the local subsidiary I felt I had become anonymous, lost in the mass of managers. It affected my personal life as well. From being most of the time at home, I had to learn to live out of a suitcase. Fortunately, my wife accepted the hardship rather willingly. She realized that if one wants to move ahead, one must be willing to make some sacrifices.

Late in 1975 the Champion expansion plans proved bigger than the money available for them. Mr. Cormick had to reduce his organization to be more in line with the volume of business and cut down on his expensive management staff. He knew that Jack Armfield, the new director of ECMG, was still looking for somebody to handle the sales of Supreme components in his territory, which was Europe and the Middle East. He asked Jan whether he would be willing to consider this job. Jan felt qualified for it because of his previous experience with components and was interested "because Mr. Cormick made it quite clear that he had to reduce his European organization to a skeleton and could not afford the burden of the expense of the high level of management he initially wanted." Shortly after that Mr. Cormick had recommended Jan to Jack Armfield, who, knowing Jan and being impressed with his experience, offered him the job early in 1976. Among his friends Jan spoke about his new job in the following way:

Well, it is another challenge. Coming from Champion sales to Supreme components sales is like going one echelon down. Finished product sales always gets priority in the company. So, I have to fight to get attention. But I like Jack Armfield. I have no regret to work for him. His age does not matter. He is a good leader, objective, communicates well, and as long as I keep him knowledgeable about what I am doing he lets me run my own organization. You see, I am enthusiastic by nature.

As for the future, I have still some ambitions left. I am personally convinced that Electric Appliances will have to come to yet another new reorganization with more room for decision making by national management. I think that multinational companies should be cautious not to give the impression that decisions having direct effect on people are made outside of their national company. These decisions can be advised, suggested, guided, or oriented by top management, but for the public we should always leave the impression that we are a national company. Europe, unfortunately, by its historical past, is very nationalistically oriented and not too many people are internationally trained. I think the problems of the current reorganization are going to teach Electric Appliances this lesson.

I do not want to move out of Rotterdam. When I was in the States in 1950 I asked Mr. Davis whether I should obtain the American nationality and become an international manager. He advised me they were looking for local people and that I should stay in Holland. Now at the age of 58 I do not think that I can become a gypsy. I would rather travel from my home-base and not move my family. That would be very difficult for my wife and for the children. In particular I would have to change the education and language of my youngest children.

Being well-known creates certain obligations toward the family and country. I was taught at home that we had to serve people and that we should not expect things for free. We had to work and be socially engaged, loving other people, be interested in community affairs. The problem in Europe is that if one is privileged to belong to a well-known family it is difficult to be judged on one's own merits. Of course there is an influence, but it is like having a better general education. That, too, is more difficult to acquire if one is the son of a workman. It gives you an edge, but other people are always suspicious that one is trying to take advantage of one's privileged position. Having relations in government circles is a two-way street. My contacts, which facilitate some things, expect me to do the same. It has never led me to hire anybody for the company who would not have been hired without me. I have never done

favors. In fact I always went out of my way not to give special consideration to people of the same political or religious convictions as I. Indeed, I
guess I went overboard sometimes to avoid the accusation.

I have always been available to the company to provide contacts, but
Electric Appliances never took advantage of it. They never capitalized on
me. Politicians have often expressed surprise that I did not get more
involved. I regret that the company did not use me more. I think it is
because they feel they would be choosing a political color. I think this is
wrong.

For the last three and a half years, since the reorganization, Electric
Appliances Benelux does not consult or involve me. If I were not a director they would no longer consider me as part of Benelux. I regret
this. . . .

On the Monday morning following his decision to talk to Jan Vanvoort, Jack Armfield's first appointment was with Mr. Baker, the director of personnel for the International Division from White Plains. Jack
asked how his trip had been, and Baker replied:

Oh, everything went fine until I got to Amsterdam Airport. Upon my
arrival I was paged and told that the driver of the company car supposed
to pick me up had called and asked me to hire a limousine because the
car had broken down. I was fortunate though. As I walked to the exit I
ran into Jan Vanvoort, who had just seen two of his younger children off
for a trip to their sister in Iran. Of course Jan offered me a drive and
invited me for dinner at his place. It was good to see him again. Ever since
he was in White Plains—that must have been almost 30 years ago—we
have maintained contact. Over dinner he gave me his views on how our
reorganization is working out. You know, I think he made a few good
points, Jack . . . .

Jack Armfield wondered what Jan had told the personnel director.
The thought also crossed his mind that he might well take this opportunity to ask for some advice on how to handle Jan. Baker had extensive
experience in dealing with international personnel and apparently
knew Jan rather well.

Case 9–5
Douglas Ashton*

It was late in March 1975 and Douglas Ashton stared out of his room at the snowy Cambridge landscape. He couldn't concentrate on reading the case in front of him. Earlier that evening, when he had put through a long distance call to his wife back in Nirania, she had read him an ad from the real estate section of *The Nirania Banner-Times*. Victor Lobo was selling his house. This could mean only that Lobo expected to be named vice president of operations of Inland Copper Company and move into the house that came with the position. Mrs. Ashton also told Douglas that the rumor was around that Lobo was to get the job. At an informal meeting shortly before Ashton left Nirania to attend the Program for Management Development (PMD), a 13-week executive program at the Harvard Business School, Mike Blake, group vice president, Overseas Division of Inland Copper's parent, American Copper Company, had strongly hinted to Ashton that *he* would be named to the position of vice president of operations. Blake had also said at that time that the new vice president of operations could expect to become vice president and general manager of Inland Copper within five years. Ashton was puzzled and at a loss about what to do.

INLAND COPPER AND NIRANIA

Inland Copper Company (ICCo) was a subsidiary of American Copper Company (AmCCo) (see Exhibit 1). Its operations were devoted exclusively to mining copper ore prior to shipment to the United States where it was refined. Inland Copper provided 80 percent of American Copper Company's raw materials requirement. Most senior management positions were held by U.S. expatriates.

Nirania was the world's second largest producer of copper ore, and in turn, copper ore was the country's most important natural resource. American Copper had been mining Niranian ore for 30 years. It was one of five large U.S. copper companies with mines in the country. Nirania, a country about the size of the state of Vermont, had a population of 3 million, almost exclusively black. It had been a crown colony until independence in the early 60s. It was now governed by an elected Parliament and had a two-party system: the Conservatives and the Progressives. The importance of copper ore as a major natural resource had become very clear to both parties, and as the country's own economy reeled under the impact of OPEC price increases in 1973 and 1974,

---

* All names have been disguised.

EXHIBIT 1
American Copper Company partial organization chart, March 1975

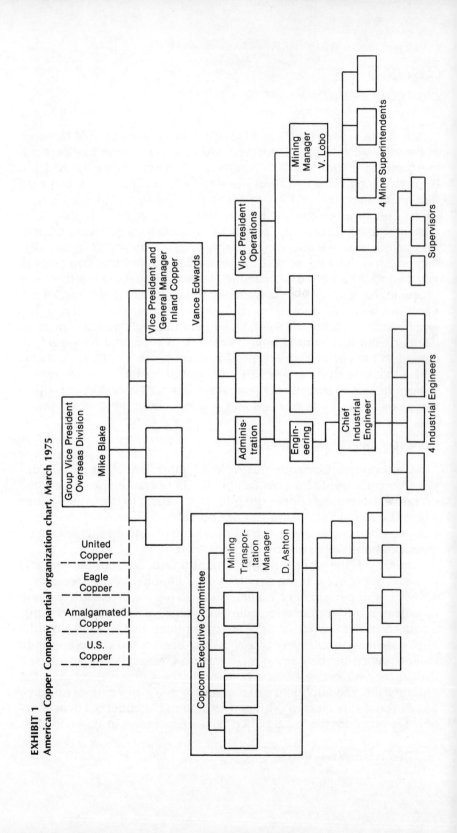

the country's leaders began to recognize the potential leverage inherent in Nirania's position as a major supplier of copper ore to the American market.

Ashton and Lobo

Douglas Ashton had joined ICCo after graduating from college in California with a degree in metallurgy. Few Niranians returned home after completing their education, and there was a chronic shortage of qualified managers, so Ashton had his pick of positions among the various multinational companies with subsidiaries in Nirania. He had chosen to join ICCo in the industrial engineering unit because he considered a staff position of this type the quickest way to learn about the organization and its problems. Within five years Ashton was appointed to his first management position, mine superintendent, and at 27 was the youngest national in ICCo management. Four years later, bypassing both national and expatriate senior managers, Ashton was named manager of mining and transportation services at Copcom, a large new mine and refining plant run as a partnership by all of the five American copper companies doing mining in Nirania. Two years later, Ashton was told that he was to attend the PMD program at Harvard.

Victor Lobo, mining manager at Inland Copper, was among the highest placed Niranians in the company. At 40, he had been with the company nearly 20 years, most of this time having been spent in mining operations. Ashton knew Lobo well. As mine superintendent he had reported directly to Lobo. Ashton felt that he had learned a great deal about mining from Lobo and was impressed with his keen mind. Working with Lobo, Ashton had learned much about the company itself, for Lobo had an uncanny ability to second-guess his superiors. His way of doing things invariably had the approval of Vance Edwards, Inland Copper's general manager. In September 1974, Lobo had returned from a year of training at AmCCo's refining plants and headquarters in the United States.

As he sat in his room at Harvard, Ashton knew his concern about Lobo's apparently expecting to get the position of vice president of operations of ICCo, which he himself expected, was heightened by the situation at Copcom. Copcom was run by an executive committee of representatives from each of the five parent companies (Exhibit 1). Since the creation of Copcom in 1969, American Copper had been the "managing partner" and had filled most of the senior management positions from its ranks and from Inland Copper. Now, in early 1975, the managing partner responsibility was being turned over to Eagle Copper, another of the parent partners in the Copcom venture. It was widely expected that Eagle would replace the managers at Ashton's level with its own people within the first three months of 1975.

RETHINKING THE PAST

Tonight, Ashton found himself thinking about Lobo and reflecting on his own career at ICCo. A number of incidents stood out in his mind . . .

After 18 months in industrial engineering (IE), his first job at ICCo, Ashton was appointed to his first line position, mine superintendent. Within two years, told that he had "a poor safety record," Ashton was reassigned to IE. Tonight as he recalled this first line assignment, he did not think that the number of accidents had been unusually high. Instead he remembered the frequent work stoppages in his section and quarrels he had had with the then mining manager over technical problems in the mine. It seemed clear enough now that these had been the real reasons behind his transfer.

Back at IE less than a year, Ashton was told to return to the mine. ICCo was opening up a new section of the mine and needed an additional mine superintendent. Before accepting the promotion, Ashton requested an appointment with Vance Edwards, ICCo's general manager. Edwards was 63 and had been with Inland Copper since it was formed. Asked why he was being promoted, Edwards told Ashton, "I think you're ready, and you'll do a good job." Ashton had replied, "You know, Mr. Edwards—Vance—I look around me and I don't see any young managers being developed. I see a lot of men who've been with ICCo for years, and I don't see anybody being trained to take their place. I think you're stuck now. You need another superintendent, and I'm all you've got if you don't want to use a senior person. I'll go, but you'll have to give me a raise."

Edwards had dismissed him with a curt, "Go to hell!" The next day Ashton had read an announcement that Victor Lobo had been named mine superintendent and not mine manager, the higher position to which he had previously been named. Two months later the retirement of the operations manager created a critical shortage at the mine. The mine manager was promoted to operations manager, and Victor Lobo was promoted to mine manager. Ashton was again told of his reassignment. This time he accepted without complaint. By way of congratulations, Edwards said to Ashton: "Go up there and do a good job and I'll take care of you." No salary increase was promised, but within weeks of starting in the new position, Ashton got a significant raise.

This second line assignment went more smoothly for Ashton. He believed that his success was due to his deliberate adoption of a management style emphasizing flexibility, communication, and participatory decision making. He believed that these lessons could be applied elsewhere, so he drafted a position paper suggesting that ICCo consider adopting a less rigid management approach. He forwarded it to Edwards for comment, and was puzzled when it was never returned or discussed.

ASHTON GOES TO COPCOM

Ashton had first heard ICCo personnel discussing Copcom and its operating problems when he was a staff engineer in IE. Copcom had been opened in 1969 and was the first attempt to refine as well as mine copper in Nirania. It was run by an executive committee of representatives from each of the five parent companies (Exhibit 1). American Copper, as managing partner, had primary operating responsibility. In 1973, Copcom was experiencing serious operating problems, including frequent work stoppages in the mine. A new manager of mining and transportation was soon to be named. He was expected to come from among senior managers already at Copcom, and certain expatriates believed the position to be rightfully theirs, or that a minimum it would go to an expatriate.

There was no sure way of knowing who would be appointed to the position. However, there was increasing pressure on multinational companies in Nirania to develop local talent. Recently, the Niranian Parliament had voted to require that all expatriates have work permits. These were to be given only if the company could prove that no Niranian could fill a specific position. Ashton learned later that Mike Blake, who at age 47 had only recently been appointed head of American Copper's Overseas Division, had wanted a Niranian for manager of mining and transportation. When Blake asked Edwards' advice on whom to choose, Edwards had recommended Lobo. Commenting on Ashton, Edwards had told Blake that he was "too immature."

Ashton was somewhat surprised when he was named to the position. He met with Blake shortly after learning of his promotion, and Blake made it very clear that he intended to let Ashton make his own decisions on how to run the operation. The three-week interval before he assumed his new responsibilities gave Ashton a chance to consider the situation and decide on a number of possible changes.

Ashton was personally determined to challenge what he perceived as a typically expatriate notion that Niranians were ineffectual managers, and he sensed that this would be his opportunity to do so. Moreover, his brother-in-law, an active member of the Progressive party, had mentioned that the Progressives were thinking of drafting legislation to make worker participation in management compulsory. Ashton considered this idea far too radical, but saw that some attempt to increase worker's participation in decision making would help ease the tension between union and management at Copcom, and perhaps even forestall the problems that Parliamentary discussion of worker ownership would cause with the miners.

Ashton's first official act as manager of mining and transportation was to request the removal of the three expatriates who would have reported to him. He replaced them with Niranians. Ashton met with his subordinates frequently, sharing information and asking their opinion on problems in the mine. Victor Lobo had resented unsolicited advice when Ashton reported to him at ICCo, so Ashton made it a point to show his disapproval clearly when his own staff responded to his suggestion with an attitude of "Yes, sir, you're the boss." Thinking again of Lobo, Ashton felt that he could not successfully emulate Lobo's hardline approach to the miners without further exacerbating the tense labor situation in the mine. Instead, he initiated monthly meetings with each of the five sections of mine workers, keeping Blake informed of his plans. At the first of these meetings, workers requested information about production schedules, potential layoffs, the financial health of Copcom's parent companies, and the state of the copper industry in general. Ashton found that they had useful suggestions about mine procedures, equipment purchases, etc. Ashton soon formalized these "rap sessions" and established a Safety Committee and a Mine Operations Study Committee drawn from management and labor. Labor relations improved markedly; in the next year there were only two work stoppages in the mine. His brother-in-law commented dryly, "Copcom is lucky to have found a 'roast breadfruit' (black on the outside, white on the inside) like you."

Many of Copcom's managers lived in a plush suburb west of the capital. Ashton and his family lived there also, and Ashton played bridge weekly with Blake, Tom Yash, and Ron Meeger, who, like Ashton, sat on Copcom's Executive Committee. Since Ashton was the only Niranian on the committee, these informal evenings generally served as an opportunity to discuss Niranian politics, which were becoming ever more complicated, and for Ashton to express his views on sensitive issues without confronting the committee as a whole.

In May 1974, Nirania's Prime Minister announced a 500 percent increase in the royalty on raw copper ore, and reportedly would demand that these payments be tied directly to the price of finished copper in the world market. That evening Ashton heard animated voices as he approached Meeger's house for bridge, but the expatriates fell silent as he stepped onto the veranda. As they settled down to their bridge, Ashton, himself, began to discuss the new tax. The table was quiet. The silence was finally broken by Meeger's bid, "one no trump."

Early in June 1974, the five companies with mines in Nirania requested that the World Bank's International Center for Settlement of Investment Disputes arbitrate their dispute with the Niranian government. At the June Executive Committee meeting of Copcom, Ashton asked Blake for the latest developments. As Blake began to reply, avoiding Ashton's eyes, Yash interrupted, "I don't think my company would want this discussed here." The others quickly agreed.

THE WORK PERMITS ISSUE

During 1974 Nirania modified its policy on work permits, making training programs to prepare nationals to replace expatriate managers a prerequisite for issuing the permits. Ashton knew that Mike Blake had drafted specific guidelines for a program of on-the-job training and one-on-one development of nationals on the staff. Since several Niranians had been promoted to management positions recently, he thought the program was working well. When the government refused to renew the permits of several key Copcom managers, Ashton, as senior Niranian manager, decided to approach the other Niranians at Copcom with the suggestion that they write a letter to the Ministry of Mining supporting Copcom's program and favoring renewal of the work permits of the expatriates. He called a meeting of Niranian managers and superintendents for a Tuesday afternoon.

The plant manager was gone and Blake was out of town. That morning Ashton told two of the expatriate managers about the meeting he's scheduled. At the meeting the Niranians refused to contact the Ministry. Their spokesman, young Ned Dickens, said, "We don't have a training program, and if we did, it wouldn't be any good. If these expatriates had any talent, they'd have responsible positions back home." Ashton told them that the Executive Committee had developed an appropriate training program and the nationals finally agreed that they might reconsider their position if Ashton could demonstrate that steps were being taken to activate such a program.

On Wednesday, Ashton went to Jamestown to meet personally with the Minister of Mining to discuss the work permits. He returned to find a meeting of the Executive Committee in progress. When he joined them, the expatriates accused Ashton of conspiring against them with their subordinates. A startled Ashton replied, "Don't you trust me enough to know I'd never do anything to hurt Copcom or you?" The two expatriate managers had said nothing of his Tuesday morning call. With Blake's help, he finally persuaded the group to meet with their subordinates to discuss the specifics of the development program.

Ashton considered the problem closed and scheduled another meeting with the Niranians to draft the letter. Much to his surprise, the group still refused—reporting that their expatriate supervisors had not yet discussed training and development with them. Ashton referred the matter to Blake who approached each expatriate individually to emphasize the importance of discussing the management development program with the Niranians. At a third meeting the Niranians complained to Ashton about what they perceived as gaps in the development plans; criticizing their supervisors and, more generally, Copcom's treatment of Niranians. When Blake joined the group they fell silent. Furious with his countrymen, Ashton told the group that they were to discuss their problems in front of Blake or, as far as he was concerned, forget about them. The discussion that followed seemed to clear the air, finally, and the Niranians composed a letter to the Ministry. The work permits were renewed.

OFF TO HARVARD

In October 1974, Ashton learned that he was to attend Harvard's February 1975 PMD program. In November, AmCCo announced Blake's promotion to executive vice president and his reassignment to AmCCo's U.S. headquarters effective January 1, 1975. Ashton met with Blake several times before Blake left for Christmas in the United States. At one of the last of their meetings, Ashton asked Blake what he thought of the PMD program. "I went myself and I remember it as a lot of hard work," Blake commented, "but after I got back, the promotions started coming fast and furiously. Doug, I think this is a really good opportunity for you, take advantage of it. I have a lot of confidence in you, and I expect that one of my last acts before leaving Nirania will be to recommend your promotion to vice president of operations at Inland Copper."

The Niranian political situation worsened steadily. In January the government again increased the royalties on copper ore. The newspapers spoke of equity participation or possible nationalization of the mines. The Ministry of Mines regularly requested that Ashton provide information on mine operation. Ashton found himself frequently defending the company's need to operate without Ministry interference. Blake had known of Ashton's frequent contact with the Ministry, but not everyone at Copcom could be expected to know and trust Ashton. Ashton began to think of 14 weeks at Harvard as a welcome relief.

Shortly before February 1975, John Wailes, an undersecretary at the Niranian Ministry of Mines, and an old schoolmate of Ashton, visited Ashton at Copcom. After chatting about family and mutual friends, Wailes asked about the Harvard program and wished Ashton luck. As he was about to leave he said: "You have heard that our government and the three other member nations of the International Copper Association plan to go ahead with a joint venture to produce refined copper in Zaire.

"Well—yes," replied Ashton.

"Work real hard at Harvard," said Wailes.

Case 9–6
Great Eastern National Bank*

In June of 1976 Jay Burkhardt, senior vice president responsible for branch administration in Great Eastern National Bank, was concerned about his performance appraisal program for branch managers.

On Burkhardt's desk were the completed performance appraisal forms for 2 of the 21 branch managers in his organization. These completed forms had just been turned in to Burkhardt by the two regional branch administrators who reported to him, Bill McNally and Walter Morley, after each of their appraisals of one of the branch managers under their jurisdiction. The form itself was a new one, and these were the first uses of it. McNally and Morley had also given Burkhardt a thorough verbal description of the interviews. (The performance appraisal form is Exhibit 1, and edited transcripts of the two interviews are Appendix A and Appendix B.)

Burkhardt knew that he could make virtually any changes he wished in the form and procedures for branch manager performance appraisal. He considered performance appraisal a key to the development of branch managers, and he knew in turn that top management of the bank was expecting an increasing proportion of total business and profits to be generated from the branch or "retail" side of the business. Burkhardt's objective was to have a performance appraisal system which would, in conjunction with other management controls and incentives, do the following things:

1. Provide a forum for useful feedback on performance and for effective two-way communications flow between appraiser and branch manager.
2. Help to develop the branch managers to be more innovative, resourceful, and receptive to changes in products and automation procedures which would be coming.
3. Encourage branch managers to be more aggressive in increasing profitable business.

THE BANK'S BUSINESS SITUATION

Great Eastern National had been established early in the 19th century and had thrived and declined with the ups and downs of the national and local economy. It was located in the city of Bridgeton, in a New England state, and with its branches covered an area with a total

---

* All names have been disguised.

EXHIBIT 1

PERFORMANCE APPRAISAL

Officers and Staff Supervisory Personnel

NAME	DEPARTMENT	LAST INCREASE		Job Grade	PRESENT SALARY	RECOMMEN-DATION (annual)	NEW SALARY
		Amount	Date				
POSITION	TITLE						

PROFESSIONAL KNOWLEDGE: Depth and breadth of understanding of basic principles, disciplines, fundamentals, techniques, and procedures necessary in his/her particular field of professional activity or specialization.

☐ Has thorough and authoritative knowledge of his/her field, with an excellent grasp of new developments.

☐ Has full working knowledge of his/her field, and is well-informed on most new developments.

☐ Has acceptable knowledge of the basic fundamentals in his/her field to accomplish the job, and keeps current with some of the major new developments.

☐ Performance is hampered by limited knowledge of basic fundamentals in his/her field or failure to keep informed of new developments.

COMMENTS: _____

_____

ANALYTICAL ABILITY AND JUDGMENT: Capacity to secure all essential facts and opinions and to arrive at sound conclusion based on objective reasoning and evaluation of their inter-relationship.

☐ Has exceptional ability to obtain all pertinent facts of complex and broad problems, to analyze them in a manner which consistently produces outstanding, imaginative conclusions.

☐ Can be relied upon to obtain the essential and more readily identifiable facts of most nonroutine problems, and generally arrives at practical and valid conclusions.

☐ Occasionally overlooks significant facts in arriving at conclusions, but is capable of solving most routine problems.

☐ Tends to reach conclusions without obtaining pertinent facts to support his/her position, or lacks ability to sufficiently analyze facts when available, resulting in erroneous or unsupportable decisions.

COMMENTS: _____

_____

INITIATIVE: Ability to proceed independently, without specific instructions, and in a self-reliant manner within the scope of his/her work and level of responsibility.

☐ Is very resourceful in initiating positive action on new ideas without relying on specific instructions.

☐ Takes positive action on own initiative in carrying out all but the most difficult assignments.

☐ Usually acts on own initiative in the daily contact of the job, but requires direction in nonroutine, complex matters.

☐ Seldom acts on own, usually waiting for specific instructions and direction to carry out assigned duties.

COMMENTS: _____

_____

PRODUCTIVITY: Quality and quantity of the employee's contribution, and the consistency in producing accurate, thorough and dependable results.

☐ Very conscientious and can be relied upon to produce consistently a large volume of high-quality work.

☐ Generally produces a large volume of high-quality work on most assignments requiring unusual accuracy and sense of responsibility.

☐ Usually dependable and meets acceptable standards for quality and quantity but seldom exceeds basic requirements of the job.

☐ Cannot be depended upon to meet job requirements for quantity and/or quality of work without frequent follow-up.

COMMENTS: _____

_____

EXHIBIT 1 (*continued*)

SELF-EXPRESSION: Ability to organize, express and communicate ideas and to present oral and/or written recommendations in a manner which effectively conveys understanding and gains acceptance and approval.

☐ Skilled in communicating well-organized ideas in nearly all situations, strongly influencing favorable consideration of his/her recommendations.

☐ Acceptance of his/her ideas and recommendations is generally facilitated by good oral and written communication.

☐ Ability to communicate ideas is adequate for most daily situations in which organization and expression of complex ideas or detail is not essential.

☐ Acceptance of ideas or recommendations is hampered by inability to communicate effectively.

COMMENTS: _____

_____

LEADERSHIP: Ability to achieve goals and objectives through effective planning, organizing and controlling the combined efforts of his/her group.

☐ His/her fine leadership qualities generate cooperation and consistently high morale in the group.

☐ An effective leader who usually inspires the group toward good teamwork and morale in meeting objectives and goals.

☐ Only moderately successful in getting group results.

☐ Occasional friction, dissention, and/or low morale, resulting from ineffective leadership, hamper productivity of the group.

COMMENTS: _____

_____

ABILITY TO DEVELOP PEOPLE: Effectiveness in guiding and training those under his/her direction to improve their overall performance and increase their potential for advancement.

☐ His/her dedication and effectiveness in guiding, training and developing people contribute substantially to the overall improvement and promotability of his/her employees.

☐ Generally helps his/her people to improve themselves by advising, counselling or coaching them for acditional responsibility and advancement.

☐ Shows limited inclination or effectiveness in helping his/her people to improve and develop.

☐ Shows unwillingness and/or inability to assume responsibility to develop and improve his/her people.

COMMENTS: _____

_____

_____

1. A. - What do you consider your outstanding work characteristic?

_____

_____

B. - What do you think is your weakest work characteristic?

_____

_____

_____

Employee's signature_____

EXHIBIT 1 (*continued*)

PERFORMANCE APPRAISAL DISCUSSION REPORT

Informal discussion of the Employee Performance Appraisal between the employee and immediate supervisor is essential to successful personnel development.

The following guidelines will assist in keeping the discussion factual in interpreting judgments and recommendations objectively, and in adapting the performance interview to the needs of the individual:

Encourage the employee to analyze his/her own strength and weaknesses. Use specific illustrations and actual examples to highlight outstanding strengths and significant weaknesses. Be as thorough and helpful with the outstanding employee as with the employee who has clear-cut problems in performance. Discuss with the employee specific and realistic objectives and self-improvement plans for the future. Emphasize performance rather than personality, and improvement rather than shortcomings, so that the employee can more easily understand and accept the appraisal.

SUMMARY OF PERFORMANCE: The overall manner in which the employee carries out assigned duties and responsibilities, taking into consideration judgments made about specific traits.

☐ OUTSTANDING. Employee's overall performance is consistently excellent, approaching the highest level that could be expected on the job.

☐ VERY GOOD. Employee's overall performance substantially exceeds normal job requirements and is fully adequate in all respects.

☐ GOOD. Employee's overall performance meets job requirements, with weaknesses in certain areas clearly outweighed by strength in other characteristics.

☐ MARGINAL. Employee's overall performance is marginal because a major weakness in one or more characteristics is not compensated by strength in others.

☐ INADEQUATE. Employee's overall performance is deficient enough to justify release or demotion unless immediate improvement takes place.

What is employee's outstanding work characteristic?_____

_____

_____

What is employee's weakest work characteristic? _____

_____

_____

POTENTIAL:

(Present your objective opinion and analysis of potential for advancement, indicating possible alternative avenues. Consider past performance, capacity, and willingness to handle greater responsibilities, cooperation with associates, personal goals, emotional stability, intellectual capacity, and other pertinent personal circumstances. If promotable, estimate when ready for next advancement and indicate what is being done to broaden capacity.)

_____

_____

_____

_____

_____

_____

_____

_____

_____

EXHIBIT 1 (*concluded*)

Appraisal made by:

_____   _____   _____
              Signature   Title   Date

SUPERVISOR'S RECOMMENDATION

Salary increase _____   Promotion_____

Remarks: _____
_____

MANAGEMENT DECISION

Salary increase_____ New salary _____ Promotion _____

Remarks_____
_____

Comments after interview: (by supervisor) _____

COMMENTS: _____
_____
_____
_____

population of some 750,000. Bank assets in 1975 were approximately $500 million, making it by far the largest bank with home headquarters in Bridgeton. Four other banks in the state were larger.

Great Eastern had always been an innovative bank, and for many years since 1950 had grown at a rate greater than the growth of population and economic activity of the area. In the early 1970s, however, a number of economic, social, and competitive changes had taken place which adversely affected Great Eastern and imposed a need for new reactions to the business.

For one thing, state banking laws had been changed to permit large banks headquartered in the capital city of the state to open branches throughout the state. This had begun in 1970. By 1976 three large banks which had not existed in Bridgeton before had 12 branches in the area.

Another factor had been the increasing sophistication of Great Eastern's corporate customers, who steadily reduced the average levels of their cash balances with Great Eastern. As a result, the bank had to work ever harder to maintain demand deposits from those sources at levels required for continued growth of the loan portfolio.

Finally, Great Eastern's commercial and retail customers had suffered as much as any due to the economic recession of the early 70s. Much of the industry in the area had obsolete plants and equipment, wage rates were higher than the national averages, and state and local taxes and costs of services were serious burdens to businesses and households.

As a result of these forces Great Eastern's market share of the commercial business in its area was estimated to have dropped from over 50 percent in 1970 to less than 40 percent in 1975. Net profit per share, after rising at an average rate of 6 percent a year through the 1960s, had leveled off in the early 1970s and declined slightly in 1974 and 1975.

Top management of Great Eastern had taken a number of steps to deal with these adverse forces. More attention was placed on the retail market, that is, customers typically reached through the branches. The bank introduced a number of new products and services backed by advertising to increase that aspect of the business. An aggressive policy of acquisition and new branch construction was initiated, leading to growth in the number of branches from 14 in 1972 to 21 in 1975. By 1975 the proportion of Great Eastern's total business attributed to retail banking stood at about 60 percent, compared to 40 percent in 1970.

In 1974 Great Eastern began merger negotiations with Yankee National Bank, a $300 million bank in a metropolitan and suburban area adjacent to Bridgeton. The merger would increase the asset base and customer potential for both banks and make them more competitive with the larger state banks. In 1975 the Justice Department stepped in and challenged the merger under the antitrust laws. At that point it had been decided by top management that during the legal proceedings

Great Eastern should not open any additional branch banks. Thus, in June of 1976 the number of branches had stood at 21 for over a year. Burkhardt did not expect any new branches to be opened within the coming year.

THE BRANCH MANAGER'S JOB

The branch manager's job was considered one of the most varied and high-pressured jobs in the bank. He was responsible for the physical facility, had to oversee and motivate personnel, was expected to maintain contact with customers in the branch and develop new business through outside contacts, and was expected to respond to requests for reports and inquiries from the head office. To conduct this work the manager was in frequent direct communication with officers in one division or another at the head office, including personnel, credit, comptroller, and EDP operations as well as with the manager's own superior, one of the regional branch administrators (either McNally or Morley) for approval of loans above the authorized limit and for counseling in any area of concern. (See organization chart, Exhibit 2.)

EXHIBIT 2
Organization chart—Great Eastern National Bank

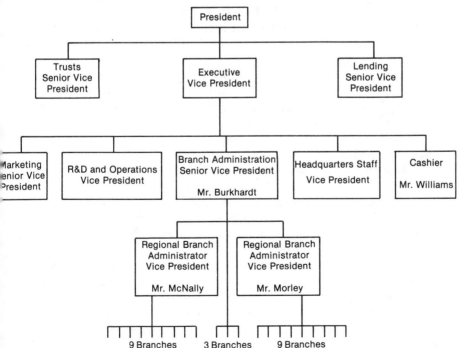

Great Eastern had just recently increased the loan limit of branch managers and changed the procedures for most loan approvals. Unsecured loans up to $30,000 and secured loans up to $250,000 could be approved by the branch manager alone. Moreover, approval for most loans above this amount could be obtained by the branch manager from the regional branch administrator, rather than from loan counsellors in the credit department. These changes, which had been fought for by Burkhardt for several years, were widely welcomed by branch managers.

Management of branches in the inner city of Bridgeton presented particular problems of managing personnel and maintaining good customer relations. Many white branch managers had, over the last few years, asked to be transferred from branches in these areas. Although every one of the five branches in this area had an assistant branch manager who was black, only one of the branch managers was black. Since 1973 there had been four black branch managers, but three of them had left the bank for better opportunities elsewhere. Burkhardt and his two assistants had often discussed the question of how long to leave a white branch manager in one of the inner city jobs, given the greater pressure this manager was assumed to be under. They had not come to any definitive conclusions. They recognized that problems of managing branch personnel were generally greater for white branch managers in those locations, but did not know how to factor this into a comparison of managers' performance across branches.

In general, Burkhardt knew the pace of changes in product innovation and automation affecting the branch system would accelerate over the next two to three years. Great Eastern had to meet and exceed competition from branches of the larger banks which had moved into its area and from savings banks, which were just beginning to offer checking account products, and it had to continue to reduce operating costs and increase the convenience to customers through major investments in automation. Only three or four of the current branch managers had any familiarity with such equipment.

A branch manager was judged in part on how well the branch performed as a profit center. There were great difficulties, however, in allocating expenses to branches, in determining what expenses were controllable by the branch manager, and in compensating for widespread differences in the business potential for different branch areas. Although Burkhardt did receive quarterly reports on branch profit and loss, he was reluctant to use these in their present form as a tool for evaluation. Without question the vast majority of line items on the branch profit and loss were beyond the control of the branch manager.

Burkhardt and the comptroller received detailed quarterly reports of direct branch expenses. These too were considered of limited use for evaluation purposes because even directly chargeable expenses were relatively fixed. Labor, for example, was fixed by the number of staff assigned to the branch. Work measurement was thought not to be effective for assessing most branch jobs because work load depended upon when the public entered the branch. Tellers, for instance, worked at a peak rate only one or two hours a day. Beyond that business was usually quite variable. Tellers required extensive training, and it had not been thought feasible to try to hire tellers on an hourly basis.

The daily Proof Report, which listed each branch's intake and dispersal of cash by each teller, came to Burkhardt every morning. Any overages or shortages were prominently noted. The report was also sent to the comptroller, the cashier, the executive vice president, and the president. While excessive shortages or overages could cause some concern to top management and branch managers alike, the Proof Report was not useful for evaluation of managerial performance beyond considerations of training or fiduciary responsibility.

Burkhardt and his two regional administrators, McNally and Morley had from time to time discussed the possibility of introducing a "management by objectives" approach for branches. This might include the setting of specific performance targets each year, such as a percentage increase in installment loan volume, percentage increase in number of new checking accounts, and so on. At the end of each year managers would be appraised largely on how well these targets were met. The difficulties of this approach included the uncertainty of each branch's effective trading area and what was likely to happen in its area that would realistically affect its business. This approach had not been carried beyond the idea state, however, due to the pressure of other matters and the lack of expertise in the bank in designing such a system.

McNally and Morley made calls at each branch under their jurisdiction on average about once every two weeks. The purpose was both to offer assistance to the managers and to check up on how they were doing. More often than not these visits were in response to some crisis. While these visits provided a wealth of information about branch activity, personnel, and market problems, and a manager's capacity to cope with the job, they provided very little information of a quantifiable nature. Nevertheless, Burkhardt knew that McNally and Morley were in an excellent position to influence the performance and development of branch managers.

THE NEW PERFORMANCE APPRAISAL PROCESS

The new forms for performance appraisal (Exhibit 1) had been developed by the Personnel Department of Great Eastern at the urging of

Burkhardt. One week prior to the appraisal interview a copy of the form was given to branch managers, who were instructed to fill it out on themselves. At the interview, it was intended that the regional administrator and the branch manager would come to agreement on which box to check under each category. The agreed-upon ratings and the comments on both forms were then to be submitted to Burkhardt and then to the vice president of personnel. This procedure was to be followed once a year.

This was the procedure which had been followed in the interviews for which Burkhardt now had the completed forms. One was for McNally's appraisal of John Seibert (Appendix A), and the other for Morley's appraisal of George Maloney (Appendix B).

The new form and procedures for branch manager performance appraisal represented several changes from the previous system. The new form was similar in the names of factors being assessed ("professional knowledge," "analytical ability and judgment," and so on; see Exhibit 1). Also similar was the procedure whereby appraiser and appraisee filled out the old form prior to the interview. However, the new form offered a choice of simply four boxes for ratings under each factor, and there was no numerical calculation required. In the old form, each factor was given a "job standard" numerical rating between 1 and 6, and then each person being evaluated was given his or her rating for the year on each factor. For the branch manager job, the most common "job standard" ratings had been 2s and 3s. A "6" standard was reserved for officers at the senior vice president level and above.

As a result of a performance appraisal interview under the old system, after all the factors had been rated and agreed upon, a summary ratio was computed by adding the ratings given to the person and dividing that by the total of the job standard ratings. This ratio of "performance" to "standard" had then been used in conjunction with the comments to determine promotions and annual salary increases.

Burkhardt had felt that this old system was good in that it encouraged a face-to-face discussion between boss and subordinate. However, he and others had become concerned with the trend toward higher and higher numerical ratios for branch managers. As the president had remarked at one salary review meeting, "All these branch managers should be in Rome with the Pope!" This situation had made it difficult to discriminate among branch managers as to which should receive higher and lower merit increases.

Moreover, Burkhardt was uncomfortable with the emphasis on numbers connected with the old form and procedure, particularly when those numbers could be directly associated by the employee with salary increases. Burkhardt felt it was not a good policy to link directly quantitative evaluation with dollar amount or percentage amount of salary increase.

The new form was an attempt to correct these problems in the old form while retaining the good features of the performance appraisal process. In the new form (Exhibit 1) there were no job standard ratings and no summary ratios.

It was hoped that the appraisal discussion between regional administrator and branch manager would be a frank and rational exchange which would both lead to mutually acceptable agreement between them on the branch manager's performance and encourage motivation and development for the coming year.

APPENDIX A

Bill McNally—John Seibert performance appraisal interview

Appraiser: Bill McNally, Regional Vice President.

Appraised: John Seibert, Vice President and Manager, West Corridor

Place: Seibert's office at the West Corridor Branch

Date: June 5, 1976; 11:00 A.M.

Bill: *John, I have indicated on a couple of items—although there is no room for it—a plus or a minus if we felt there was some leeway, a possibility that maybe you rated one and I rated the other.*

Under "professional knowledge" which indicated the depth and breadth of the understanding of the basic principles, disciplines, and fundamental techniques and procedures necessary in this particular field or professional field of activity or specialization." In other words—it means how long you've been in the business and how much do you know about it—what did you rate yourself?

John: *I put down the second box—"has full working knowledge of this field and well informed on most new developments."*

Bill: *I marked that, too, John. I feel that you, with your depth of experience, and I wrote out your years of experience in branch operations. . . .*

John: *For comments I put: "I've worked in several departments and know banking by experience, exposed to all phases of banking."*

Bill: *I agree with you, John, the first one there "has thorough and authoritative knowledge of his/her field with an excellent grasp of new developments". . . .*

John: *I don't get involved in new developments. My exposure, I think, isn't in that field.*

Bill: *There isn't that much new, other than your aggressiveness for new accounts and things of this nature, but as far as policy decisions. . . .*

"Analytical ability and judgment: Capacity to secure all essential facts and opinions and to arrive at sound conclusions based on objective reasoning and evaluations of their inter-relationship."

John: OK, I put down the second box, again. "Can be relied upon to obtain the essential and more readily identifiable facts of most nonroutine problems, and generally arrives at a practical and valid conclusions."

This is true, but there are two different things (going against me); and for comments I put: "I don't like paper work, I really don't, or reports, but I've become bogged down in details and sometimes it slows my productivity."

Bill: I think you're conscientious in your reports.

John: I know that but. . . .

Bill: It's again tying in maybe with production, my appraisal—you try to do too much.

John: No, the customers come first. That's my problem. I let my work go and just to make sure the customers are happy and no complaints—and that the public relations is fine. This is my biggest problem, I think. I worry too much about customers.

Bill: It's a large shop here; two assistants, two secretaries, and we try to find a trainee—floater; to match the nature of the individuals. One person has had physical problems. The other person—the number 1 assistant, in all fairness and honesty to the individuals, did not have the exposure. It's a type of situation where the majority of the people go to the manager with their problems, and it's a hard thing to change or to delegate, based on my experience.

John: Well, the biggest problem is, you know, having been in this branch before, and this is the way I rate this branch; as a retail bank—branch really.

You get to know the people. I live in the community. I work in the community. I've been here for a good many years. Also, since I was an assistant, I sat out and I got to know people. My biggest problem—it's hard,—is that when somebody comes in, because I've waited on them all these years, and they want an installment loan, really I should turn them over to someone else, but I feel: "Gee, if I went to a store and I have the same salesman all the time, and I go to him and he says, 'Well, yeah, go to someone else,' I'd feel, Well, aren't I good enough?"; you know.

Bill: Many times it's the old lady who says, "I want to see Mr. Seibert. . . ."

John: We all do.

Bill: "Oh, no, I'll wait," she says, and by the time she gets into the office, all she wants is to stop payment on a check or, "Would you please look my checkbook balance over?" It's something that a clerk could do.

John: It's hard, as I say, because they are repeats and you get to know them. You live with them. Your problems are their problems. Their problems are yours.

We'll put 2+.

Bill: I'll agree to that, John because I think part of number one certainly figures; and I think you are shouldering as great a productive volume as any manager in the system.

John: I think I am.

Bill: Even though, you would look at the other side somebody would say, "Well, if he's doing that much, he should delegate this authority down the line." But you have to take in other factors, you have to take the individual you're going to *delegate it to, you've got to take the nature of the traffic—the people, as you have pointed out.*

Banking today, particularly in the medium-size and small banks, is in such a squeeze that you have to battle as much for retention as you do for new business, even harder, and so often that little personal approach will keep the person coming to you, which you do so excellently, as against the cold shoulder, saying: "Oh, well, wait out front."

* * * * *

Bill: *"Self-expression." "The ability to organize, express, and communicate ideas, present oral and/or written recommendations."*

John: *I went down to the third one. "Ability to communicate ideas as adequate to most daily situations in which organization and expression of complex ideas," etc.*

Bill: *Why did you rate number 3?*

John: *Why did I rate three? Because I am weak in this field. I've never been a salesman or speaker, and at times I have difficulty expressing myself.*

Bill: *I rated number 2 because, well, let's read it. "Acceptance of his ideas and recommendations is generally facilitated by good oral and written communication."*

True, I think you and I are pretty much from the same cloth. We know what we want to say, but sometimes it's difficult to express it. I don't think either one of us would carry the handle of super salesman, but I just think that your ability is more than adequate.

John: *Well, yes. I agree to that.*

Bill: *And here you're saying that—you indicate number 3 "ability to communicate is adequate for most daily situations." Between you and me, expression—goes along with communications—I still feel that I know what you're doing and if you have problems, you relate them to me and to management. You're able to express yourself adequately.*

John: *In other words, I'm not a memo writer.*

Bill: *That doesn't matter. We've got people on the second floor in the main office who will write volumes and volumes, and you could condense what they're trying to say into maybe one sentence.*

John: *Even if people come in—I don't sit around to chat.*

Bill: *And many times, too, particularly in this rat race that you have here, you don't have the time to immediately sit down. It's very nice if you can program your work like they can do in some departments, and in some branches where, "This is what I'm going to do today—bing, bing, bing."*

John: *Well, you can't, no.*

Bill: *You can start out that way at 8:00 and at 8:05. . . .*

John: *You're here at 8:00 and, as you say, you never know what the phone call is; who is going to be out or who is going to be in, or what customer is going to have a problem.*

Bill: *This used to be my—I'm not that much involved any more—but my biggest* *weakness was written communication. We're responsible for writing up commercial loans, giving the details, etc., on the loan. On every loan there should be a vital file in the credit department, and the volume gets to the point, some days, and some days it carries on into weeks, and before you know it, into months — by the time it is 5:30 or 6:00 at night, you're like this. You say: "Well, I'll do it tomorrow." And tomorrow it's the same rat race all over again.*

I feel, John, I'd like to have you consider a 2; it's to your advantage; I think it's merited that you express yourself all right. You and I, I don't think we're expert after-dinner speakers.

John: *We'll never sell the Brooklyn Bridge.*

Bill: *But I think we get our message across.*

"Leadership: ability to achieve goals or objectives through effective planning, organizing and controlling the combined efforts of his/her group."

John: *I put number 2.*

Bill: *Do you have any comment on it?*

John: *The only thing is—I put down—maybe I'm not building myself up, which I never do. And I'm too softhearted, think too much of people's feelings. I have to be more forceful, I think.*

Bill: *Yes, I agree.*

Effectively, as I graded you with this, too—you do an effective job on it, and I think that you are too sensitive—as I was in your spot—to your employees, to a point where—you try to bend over backwards for people, but sometimes if you took a little harder line, you're more respected for it, because many times you lean over for somebody but there is always somebody in the wings who is going to take a potshot at you, or to take advantage of you. . . .

John: *It always happens.*

Bill: *I think that you're, as I used to tell my gang, the old cliche; I see my employees more than I see my wife. You live with them, and if you can't live together on a friendly relationship. . . .*

John: *I think that sometimes your feelings are that if you do these things they will really come back and help you out, too. Sometimes some of them do, some of them don't. Some will take advantage anyway. They feel, if you bend over backwards for a little while, they will develop more work for you.*

Bill: *Isn't it the case though that when you do this, historically, something else comes up which is on a negative or defensive side.*

John: *It always happens.*

Bill: *The individual will never remember what you did for him. "You did it for Susie—now I need something else."*

John: *This happens time and time again. You try to arrange the vacation schedules so everyone gets what he wants. You work for a whole year, and you would like to go with your husband—or your wife's vacation times. We try to please them all, and sometimes you have two out when you should really only have one out, and you say, "Well, it's the middle of the month, it won't be that busy." You let two go, and it will never fail—someone else will be out sick or something will happen and you will call up for help and they say, "How come you have two out for vacation, then?" So you try to struggle along with what you have.*

Bill: *You try to take the approach that if people are happy with what they are doing, they perform better.*

John: *That's right, yuh.*

Bill: *It seems today, by the attitude of—I don't say this from an old bitchy standpoint; the younger generation doesn't have a sense of loyalty.*

You interview people for employment—the first thing and all they want to know is, "How much money do I get, how many days off do I get, what are my fringes?" You do a little favor for them. You feel it is a favor. They feel it is something that is supposed to be done for them.

It seems to me they don't have any sense of loyalty for the organization. If they have a sniffle, they call in sick. Many times you learn you were run through the wringer, but you felt you owed it to the company, they are paying your bread and butter.

John: *In the same line, people say: "Well, if you would pay the tellers a decent wage, they would do more for you, you could motivate them better." I disagree, because I think that you gave them all the money. . . .*

Bill: *Well, where do you start?*

John: *They still won't be motivated, and they still just plod along. There is no feeling of being a part, or of pride in their work any more. I go over there and I blow my stack with the teller. You pick up a bundle of money and it's not all in one. We learned to face your money the same way. I went over there and got a bundle of money the other day and I would be ashamed to give it out, but they don't care. You talk to them and they'll do it for a week, and they're right back again.*

Bill: *And you see, the turnover factor, as personnel points out.*

John: *I think it is getting better.*

Bill: *Better than 50 percent of the staff turns over in the first three years, so you don't get too many career people with 29–30 years of service like you or me. If you do, you've got some good loyal employees, but historically, the ratio of the first year, I guess, of the younger people would be 33 percent.*

John: *You might appease them for a month or two or six months, but then we get right back to the same.*

Bill: *But you see, over the past 20 years, jobs have been so easy to come by— up to the last three years—there has been a little change in some thinking— "Heck, if you don't give me my raise or, my day off, I'll quit and go somewhere else."*

When you get into categories such as tellers, bookkeepers, and proof operators, the way the economy is structured, they're better off not working; they can go out and collect their unemployment. Now they get food stamps, so that they get a discount on prices, so that a person who starts out at $90–$95 a week, by the time they net out, they're better off being out of work.

You're continually on the defensive. When jobs are tight, you could say, "This is it. If you don't like, I take a firm stand." You're coddling people—and I say, "Won't you please do this or please do that" because what is coming along behind it isn't any better.

John: *There is an awful lot of money in training. You have them six months and you lose them. It's wasteful—money down the drain!*

Bill: *So a number 2, John. I think we agree on that one?*

John: *Yep.*

Bill: *"Ability to develop people." "Effectiveness in guiding and training those under his/her direction to improve their overall performance and increase their potential for advancement."*

John: *I put number 1 "dedication and effectiveness in guiding, training and developing people contributes substantially to. . . .*

Bill: *I put number 2 "generally helps his/her people to improve themselves by advising, counselling or coaching them for additional responsibilities and advancement." "Dedication"—there is no question. I'm underlining that.*

John: *I did have number 2 at first. Then I changed it—I don't know why.*

Bill: *My only feeling here is in the "guiding" yes, but the actual training?*

John: *No, that's right, I don't train.*

Bill: *Other than your assistants.*

John: *I would agree to a number 2, but let's put a plus on it, I did have 2 at first.*

Bill: *You've got under your command here 18–20 people as a total, which is one of our largest branches.*

John: *We've had people on the platform come and go. We've trained them, sent them on their way. I also put under comments—I never hold anyone back because of his/her need here. That's one thing I don't do. If they have an opportunity to advance, I say: "Look, I wouldn't wany anyone to hold me back. I feel this way." On the other hand, I'll help those who want to learn. If they don't have any initiative, to heck with them. I won't waste the time. Most of the trainees can be appraised pretty well; the fellow who has initiative and is ambitious wants to learn more, and the other fellow who sits back and waits for you to take something and say: "Here, please do this."*

Bill: *"Generally helps his/her people to improve themselves by advising, counselling and coaching." There's one word on some of these. If you play heavily on one word, you can almost hang your hat on it. Or you could say: "Dedication and effectiveness in developing and training people."*

John: *Well, let's leave it at number 2, Bill.*

Bill: *Let's take a stab at your strongest and your weakest points.*

[Laugh]

John: *I didn't go into very much detail. Outstanding work characteristic, I would say, "Knowledge of the banking field and desire to help customers."*

Bill: *I think that we discussed this a little earlier, and I put for your outstanding trait, your personality and your ability to carry a heavy work load. The weakest point I put, "At times too lenient with personnel." I think we discussed this.*

John: *Yeah. I guess what I put really isn't a "characteristic." "Don't complete paper work that requires details."*

Bill: *Very good. I hope to get back before the week is out.*

John: *Now, what are you going to do, type everything on here?*

Bill: *Yes, you've written them—so leave them as they are. I'll come back down and we'll sign each one in our presence, and then we'll submit it with the recommendation to personnel.*

APPENDIX B

Walt Morley–George Maloney performance appraisal interview

Appraiser: Walt Morley, Regional Vice President

Appraised: George Maloney, Brance Office and Manager Brandon Center Branch (Main St., Brandon)

Place: Morley's office, Brandon Shopping Center Branch

Date: June 6, 1976; 9:00 A.M.

Walt: *George, as you know, this is a new sheet and I'm sure there could be a little difference of opinion as we go through. What I would like to do is say to you how I have rated you initially, and what my comments are, and then if you would express what you have develop on that basis.*

* * * * *

Walt: *As far as your "professional knowledge" is concerned, I checked off the second block, and that states that you have a full working knowledge of your field, and are well informed on most new developments. My personal feeling is that that fits you pretty closely. As far as my comments go, I thick that you have worked in several departments in the bank, and that you are presently at Williams College in the School of Banking, and that your managership of the past year has no doubt added to your overall knowledge.*

George: *All right, I have also the second box. I've put a little plus next to it.*
    My thinking is . . . because of the extensive banking background, and in the branch—it being a class I or a smaller type branch—not that I am overqualified for the branch, but my background in the commercial end of banking of the operations end is probably somewhat better then that of some of my co-workers in the smaller branches.
    I feel . . . I know, in talking to people, I have a better, say, depth in the workings in the main office above the third floor—probably than most of us, but. . . .

Walt: *OK. Quickly, can you give me a rundown of the department's you've been in?*
[Describes his career history at the bank.]

* * * * *

Walt: *I don't know. You know, that second box, in itself, "has full working knowledge of his/her field" and to me that's a pretty strong statement within itself. . . .*

George: *All right. . . .*

* * * * *

Walt: *When you get up into the first box, it says: "thorough and authoritative knowledge of his/her field, with an excellent grasp of new developments," now you are really getting up into the high management area. . . .*

George: *Yeah, ...*

Walt: *So much of a manager's position and job is pretty cut and dried. You can't go grabbing here and there. There are certain times at certain meetings that we attend where we can throw out ideas, suggestions, and so forth, but the majority of the work within the branch is pretty cut and dried and has been like this.*

George: *OK. Not to belabor the point, and not particularly on this item, but my understanding of this is that I am being appraised and what not on my own job grade. So as far as upper management and what not or the president's job, no, I'm not marking that. In other places through here, and we might come up against this again, I'm not at all saying that I am the equivalent of a branch III or something in any of these categories, but in the particular situation I am in now, being graded for this, I. . . .*

Walt: *Well, that's right. That was a complaint under the old form.*

George: *They mentioned before that you shouldn't be a 5 because only the president is a 5. Well, not so. Not that I'm not looking for that job, but I don't feel that I'm there yet. OK.*

Walt: *So we're settled on that.*
Your "analytical ability." Once again I checked the second box. "Can be relied upon to obtain the essential and more readily identifiable facts of most nonroutine problems and generally arrives at practical and valid conclusions." Under the "Comments" I put: "Loan record shows that he analyzes facts properly and makes good judgments. This carried over into other areas of his branch management."

George: *Well, that's something . . . I checked the same one. In a lot of these there is such a big gap between the first, second, and third spot that you can't come out differently. . . .*

*   *   *   *   *

Walt: *OK, under "initiative" I checked the second box. "Takes positive action on own initiative in carrying out all but the most difficult assignments." Under "comments" I stated: "Works in a small branch where initiative is important. Branch runs smoothly with work always done on time."*
You have nobody watching over you except me and I get in once every couple of weeks. Therefore you have to take initiative.

George: *Now you will find that I will use you as a sounding board, because I don't have an assistant manager to throw ideas at, to pick out loopholes.*
I checked the second box, put a small plus, too. The only thing in the statement itself, now I won't say that I go up to the top one, but on this it says: "all but the most difficult assignments"—I don't know how that is applicable. You're saying the individual has this ability but at the same time, only in a limited. . . .

Walt: *Not necessarily limited, but up to a certain point. . . .*

George: *What would you consider "difficult," whether it be mine or someone else's work? I couldn't see where it was applicable, so I hedged on it a little bit*

Walt: *Well, as you have more and more people come in to you, especially in the commercial loan area, which they haven't been doing up at Brant, this could be an area where, due to your past experience, you might not have the tools to talk completely intelligently with a loan customer or to be able to give him the right* advice or come up with the right answers, and you might call on me or Fritz for assistance at that point.

Just to change the subject for a second, I can see putting a plus in front of there, and I think what sold me was the comment that you don't even have an assistant to hash things over with. This really is too bad because I think this is one of the nice things in a larger branch.

George: Yeah, I kinda miss that. . . . Not so much asking, "What's your opinion on this," although some of that too, but you know, you would go over and say, "This has happened and this is what I wanted to do," and you only think of one way, and you would like to explore different avenues, but none hit you at the time.

Walt: Just because of that I think that is an important point. We'll "plus" that.

OK. "Productivity." I have checked the second box. This seems to be the thing to do. States: "Generally produces a large volume of high-quality work on most assignments requiring unusual accuracy and sense of responsibility." Your loan volume is not large, but the work that goes on in the branch, primarily through the teller area, is high volume.

George: It's picking up.

Walt: It's a busy little operation, and you're overseeing it, and as far as the other work that falls on your shoulders, problems and customers, and the loaning activity, opening new accounts and all, that's continuing to move upward, and while that particular end of your job does not have large volume, it still requires high-quality work and has to be accurate. You do have to show a sense of responsibility.

George: OK, I also picked that box, my comment was, that, "I feel the work produced by the branch's personnel and myself is of highest quality." This branch is not conducive to large volumes of work.

Walt: OK. "Self-expression": This is one where I've put a check in the third box, but with a plus, and that reads: "Ability to communicate ideas is adequate for most daily situations in which organization and expression of complex ideas or detail is not essential." Under my comments I put: "Most communication is oral in form, and there is no problem here." Now, the reason I checked the third box, George, is primarily because in your particular operation it runs pretty much from day-to-day with very little change in routine and very rarely a problem. Therefore, the need for you to communicate with me or others in the bank I think is rather limited, whether it be oral communication or written communication. So I'm not really putting you down because of . . .

George: You say the need isn't there. . . .

Walt: . . . your ability to express yourself adequately, but because the need is not in your present operation, and therefore, there hasn't been that much reading from it. I'm sure that you could do the job if it was required and necessary, but at this point and with this particular operation, I don't think it is. That's why I put a plus. I really didn't want . . . and my comments pointed out that there really is no problem here, either.

George: As I read the statement: "Ability to organize, express and communicate ideas and to present oral and/or written recommendations in a manner which *effectively conveys understanding and gains approval"—so that's and/or written/oral. We have very little written communication at any point. Everything is either telephone or in person. As far as asking about the ability for one to do this, its not so much the content or how often it happens.*

As far as the ability to organize, communicate ideas, and to gain approval and acceptance within my own branch, I think this has happened within the year. I think that there were a lot of things that had been on the books for six years, a lot of thoughts that were passed on from the previous two managers that were ingrained in the help up there, and I felt it was up to me to, in some instances, break these down, change them. There were new ideas, new ways of doing things, new systems; not all my own thinking, but there is a normal resistance to a new manager or a new idea, and I felt that I handled it well; that my ideas or my changes have gone through there without animosity of any sort, without anybody, as far as I know, being hurt by it. I feel that they accept this. They accepted my ideas and recommendations. I felt that this was done through good oral communications.

Walt: *OK. So you put most of your cards in the area of your expression of the job and the way it should be done down to your employees, more so than up to me. I'll have to admit when I was looking at that particular facet of this review, I was not looking at your relationship with your employees. I felt that came under the next category—"Leadership" or the ability to develop. . . .*

George: *OK. Then you're takling about the ability to. . . .*

Walt: *Your expression was more along the line of your trying to convince me or other department heads that you were in communication with on a daily basis, when necessary. You are able to get your point across to them whether it be written or oral to win your point, rather than bringing it down to your employees.*

George: *I'm looking at the word ability as opposed to need. The only way I have to show this ability at this level is for —you know—there is not that much communication above me—I don't get skilled in it because it doesn't happen, but there is the ability. I would think it would be somewhat demonstrated in the fact that it happens on that particular level.*

Walt: *I take it that you checked the second box. Right?*

George: *Yes.*

Walt: *And that reads: "Acceptance of his/her ideas and recommendations is generally facilitated by good oral and written. . . .*

You know, in the course of a year, I don't think I really have had that much communication regarding problems or ideas, but there is no question, especially in view of the prior managers at that branch, no question but that there's been a great deal of self-expression on your part toward the employees in order to get them to accept your ideas and recommendations. So this is an area where it's shaded—depends on which way you're going to be looking at it.

George: *Looking at it from your point I can also see why you went the way you did, and I feel I can give it a second box with a minus, which is somewhere in the middle. As I said, I didn't look at it from your viewpoint entirely, although for this purpose I wasn't looking at it from anybody else's viewpoint but my own because it was for my own viewpoint that I'm doing it. At the same time, you were looking at it from a different angle too, maybe. . . .*

Walt: *I would say then—let's put a check in the second box, no minus, because I put a plus anyhow, so we're not too far off.*

But, if I were to review you next year, don't be surprised if I ended up doing what I've done this year—checking that third box with a plus, because I think during the past year you should have had your primarily oral communication with your employees, expressed yourself in such a way as to have won them over to your way of thinking, your idea of how to do things.

It's done and over with and the branch is now running on the level that you want it to on that basis. I don't think that you will necessarily be able to use that as a wedge in another year.

If you're still at that same station, I question whether item two would fit at that particular point, really because I just don't think there is that much opportunity at Brandon Center for you to present oral or written communications to others above you or at the main office in order to gain acceptance of your ideas. And yet I think the third box states right there, the word "ability"—the first word— "Ability to communicate ideas is adequate for most daily situations"—but I'll go along as far as that second box is concerned.

George: *All right, taking it out of context and breaking it down—I'm not, again, belaboring the point because there is not a great deal of difference between the mark that you had and the one that I had. If, during the course of the year, one idea presented itself, and if through good oral and written communication with whomever—and we'll say, the chief loan officer, I made my point and gained acceptance, and that was the only occasion that we'll say I opened my mouth. That would show an ability for it—this is what I'm getting at—not opportunity. . . .*

Walt: *You wouldn't have to be doing it once a week or once a month or anything like that —you've got a point there.*
All right?

George: *Fine.*

Walt: *OK, under "leadership." I have the second box checked, but I've got a very, very small minus in front of it, and it states: "An effective leader who usually inspires the group toward good teamwork and morale in meeting objectives and goals." I have, under comments, put that I feel you "could work a little closer with your personnel and that this in turn would help to improve morale."*

Now, as far as your operating is concerned, I think you had a tough job up there when you took over from Ross. He was a big happy-go-lucky fellow, lackadaisical attitude, and never wanted to say anything to upset people or do anything to upset people.

You then come on the scene and you're the type that would like to see things done at the proper time, and in the proper manner. You're therefore going to be more demanding on the help, staff, and I think you have been, and I think that for the most part you have won them over. I think that they now understand that your way of doing things is better than Ross's, because there are probably fewer problems and less discontent from customers as well as other departments of the bank. And because the jobs are going along on schedule and in proper form.

I still have the feeling, though, that you place yourself quite a bit above the staff. And, in so doing, you're not working quite as closely with them as I think you should *be. I think that this, in turn, while the morale is good, I think it could be a little bit better.*

George: *Then you feel somewhat that there is a morale problem?*

Walt: *No, not one that's upsetting anyone, George. I haven't had them come forth and tell me that there is a morale problem, that they are dissatisfied with you or anything like that; nothing close to it. I do feel that the morale has improved, although I think that they thought originally that it was good to begin with under Ross, but I think that once they started doing things under your line of thought, that they backed off and realized, "Hey, things are better now than they used to be," and this in turn did push their morale up, but I still think it could go a little bit higher.*

I think they are satisfied, but they were satisfied before.

George: *OK.*

Walt: *To a degree. They used to get—Mary, especially, would occasionally get upset with Ross because he just let things go. . . .*

George: *Coming in there, one of the biggest obstacles to overcome was the fact not that I feel that I am better than them, I don't deny that there might be a little aloofness now between myself and the employees, but only because he became so ingrained, as did Joe, because it was so slow up there, there was very little to do other than socialize, to keep one's sanity. . . .*

Walt: *That's right, especially when Joe was there.*

George: *When anything new came through, and we only worked together, Ross and myself, maybe a month, a month and a half, but whenever he did bring anything up, because there was no difference between the employee and himself, they would not take it as, I won't say as an order because that's too strong, but not accept it as something being a directive from the main office.*

So, I feel now when I say, "We have this memorandum, and we're going to start it Monday," they don't automatically start by telling me what is wrong with it. They accept it. They'll do it.

I feel, to a certain extent, there's got to be a little—this is my own feeling— personnel-wise that there should be a gap, not a big gap—I don't want to be a god, and I don't want to be a leader, I don't have to lord it over anybody, not at all.

But to have them accept ideas without rebuff or without criticism initially, I think you have got to have this little break, otherwise they don't pay attention. They have the ability to try to take advantage of the situation because of this friendship. It's a tough thing to be a good friend and a boss.

Walt: *Just to give you a bit of my philosophy. When I was a branch manager what I used to try to impress upon the employees was, yes, I was the boss, but I'm also reasonable. We're all human beings working together eight hours a day, so let's make it as pleasant as we can all the time.*

I didn't like coffee, but I started taking coffee breaks, only to be out there where you could let your hair down in the coffee room. I tried to go out at different times so I could meet different people and they could all get a chance to know me better and I could get to know them better.

Whenever I did come forth with a new plan, a new idea, or a new way of doing things, I tried to, rather than just hand them a memorandum or call a meeting and say, "Well, starting tomorrow you're going to do thus and so in this manner," and then leave it, I would try to impress them: "Look I know what this is all about and I know you do, too, and while you might think that the present way of doing things is fine, why rock the boat? We've been asked to do it in this new manner, so let's give it a try. If everything works out, fine. If it doesn't, let me know. Let's talk it over further. Maybe we can get the main office or whatever department is involved to change back to the old system or make adjustments."

So, what I tried to get across to them was that I have been around long enough to have gone through most situations, so I'm not asking you to do something that I would not be willing to do myself or that I haven't done myself. And I think the employees appreciated this mannerism. And yet, they knew me well enough so that when I told them to do something they knew damn well that they had better do it, because if I learned at a later date that they hadn't done it or weren't doing it properly they were going to be reprimanded for it. And I don't normally wait until review to reprimand somebody. I do it when the situation is fresh and current and really is the proper time.

So I think you can get pretty close to your employees and still gain their respect as long as you're fair in your dealings with them, don't play favorites, and things of this sort.

So, it doesn't surprise me—some of the comments you came out with, because it kind of solidifies what my own thinking was, that you have tried to put yourself a little bit above them and it has shown very clearly, I think. And, I can certainly understand why you have done it but I think that you could come down off that perch a little bit and yet not hurt yourself in any way. If you let them start to run all over you, then you've lost. Or if you're not fair in your dealings with them at all times, or if you play favorites, then you've lost too. I think as long as they understand that you are going to treat each one of them as you yourself would like to be treated, they're not going to make a fuss.

George: Look, I'll accept this and I'll accept it with a minus, I say grudgingly, but only so that if we should do this again next year in the same position—I can get a barometer on your feelings.

Walt: Someplace you've got to have a place to improve or you're just standing still! The last one is "ability to develop people." I've checked the second box. "Generally helps his/her people to improve themselves by advising, counselling or coaching them for additional responsibility or advancement." This is almost what I said a few moments ago, and there is a tie-in between these last three. "Knows how to do all jobs of those working under him. Therefore, is able to advise and counsel them in such a manner that they will develop and improve."

George: OK. I also went with the second one.

Walt: OK. What do you consider your "outstanding characteristic?"

George: That's tough. It took me a week to figure out what is meant by "work characteristic." But I put down "dependability."

I feel that I can be relied on to perform competently within my sphere of influence, and am capable of handling most personnel and branch problems without assistance.

"B. What do you think is your weakest work characteristic?"

Again—that's another one. I'd like to put down "none—let's chew on it for a while." But I think the one that bothers me that I see cropping up in myself, mainly, is impatience. At times there is an inability to remain interested in uninteresting, unimportant, or routine matters, and this seems to be cropping up with this branch because it is, and has a slowness. Routine things like every day taking in an approval sheet, marking it, and sending it in. I'm sure it serves a purpose up there, but it is very routine. You get impatient.

Walt: You do it grudgingly. . . .

George: I don't begrudge it, it's just a pain in the neck to do it. And, again, because I have the time to think about it, some of this builds up, so it's impatience. By now I had hoped to be president, that didn't work out, so you're impatient. I think that impatience is probably something that everybody puts up with to a certain degree depending on what they see for themselves.

Walt: OK. On my report I have something a little different. I have a summary of your overall performance in which I can rate you as "outstanding," "very good," "good," "marginal," or "inadequate." I rated you in the second block which is "very good." "Employee's overall performance substantially exceeds normal job requirements and is fully adequate in all respects," and I really feel that this fits you, George.

Now, as far as your outstanding work characteristic is concerned, I felt that you have a good background in banking which makes you suited for your present position as a branch manager. Having worked in so many departments in the past, you've developed a wealth of knowledge which is going to be very helpful to you in your job and in jobs of the future.

Now as for your weakest characteristic, I put down that I felt you could be more outward-going and friendly with customers, especially those that you don't really know, and I don't mean necessarily customers that you are dealing with at the desk. I think that you conduct yourself properly at that time, but I think that you have the tendency, like many others I've known in the bank, today and in the past, who get so deeply engrossed in what you're thinking or doing so that you really don't notice this blank face walking by you to the point where you recognize it by, "Hi, how are you?" or give a wave even if you are tied up with customers.

And I've had this come back to me recently from the outside, and I've tried to point out to these people, that, look, he's got something on his mind at that particular point in time or I'm sure he would recognize you. But I'm not sure of this. I'm not sitting up there that long that I can personally see how you conduct yourself, but you're right out in the lobby there right at the front door, and I think you've got a real friendly branch up there. People like to go in there. This is great, this is what we like to see, but I think that you should be a little bit more aware that, you know, somebody is walking out the door, and somebody is coming in the door, and even if you just give them a "hi" sign, or something.

I know Paul Jones pointed this out two or three times in the past two or three years, when we've been in different discussions down at the main office. One thing that he noticed more than anything else when he worked with me for two weeks under the orientation program many years ago at East Corridor, was that no matter how busy I was, either with a customer or on the phone, if I happened to look at somebody coming in or out of the lobby whom I knew, I would either give him the "hi" sign or say "hello" to him. He said, "In most cases if you were able to speak to them, you called them by their first name. Walt, to me this is just fantastic. Really appreciated it back in those days." It was his first year in the bank.

So, that's the only area where I feel, along with the other area where I think you can come down a little bit as far as your relationship with your employees is concerned and still not lose their respect toward you as their boss.

George: That is something to work on. To back up what you have said, it is not unkown to me. My own feeling is that I'm more introverted than extroverted.

Walt: OK. One last thing. Under "potential." I've put down here that I feel that at any time you could handle a branch of a larger volume, especially in a growing area. I think that it was pointed out to you when you came out here that it was a good opportunity for you to get your feet wet in branch management.

I think that one of these days, without any question, when we sit down and play the old game of checkers, you may very well be involved. I am sure that you could take over a branch with more volume.

So overall, George, I would just like to say that it has been enjoyable working closely with you in the past year and I think overall you have come up very well in this appraisal, and there is nothing to be ashamed of, and if you'll just give thought to a couple of areas that we did discuss where a slight improvement I think would be beneficial, all the better. You want to comment on it?

George: I think that the fact that the farthest we were away was a plus or a minus is indicative . . . I feel this way because I haven't, in any of these categories, had anything in the way of complaints or calling downs. We communicate, although we don't see each other that often, our ideas and whatnot. I would rather know about it by month than wait till the end of the year to find out that I think I'm a "1" and you think I'm a "4" in any of these categories.

Walt: This is the basis I work under.

George: A couple of things that probably are cited for I could belabor for different reasons, but I think both of them go to a certain amount of personality that I have worked on or do work on or feel that I work on.

The other thing—as far as the saying "hello" to people. In that position, because there is nothing else to look at on their way out, they are looking at me. I've thought of moving the desk, but that has its disadvantages, too. If the desk were in the back, this problem wouldn't show up—the problem wouldn't be there as much.

Walt: Look, we have a senior vice president who'll walk right by you and not give you the time of day, because he is so deeply engrossed in what he's thinking of at that moment.

George: I don't slight people. . . .

Walt: We had an auditor years ago, John Post, who walked through the bank lobby every morning and I'd walk by him. He and I were very good friends. He wouldn't say "good morning" because he had a piece of paper and he was studying that and he had something on his mind. So you know, this is human nature in a lot of people. It's just something to work on.

George: *No problems . . . that can't be resolved. Do you want me to sign one or sign mine?*

Walt: *Yeah, if you would sign yours . . . sign both of them because I've signed this one.*

*   *   *   *   *

George: [As Walt is leaving.] *I think something—I won't say is* lacking *in this form—but something in an area where you like to get marks or where you like to achieve grades or something. The previous form, after all the marks were in, would graded and you would get so many points for each box, and you had a level you were supposed to attain, and any points over that would mean you were better or way better, or whatever it came up to. But this had no bearing on the dollar amount of your raise, so to speak, although if you were deficient in this area, it would. Or, if you were above, it would. Achieving a certain level didn't guarantee you a certain raise.*

This isn't my problem, particularly; I think its everybody's. You'd like to be able to say, "Well, if I really strike that thing, really hit it right, and I get very good marks for my job in that category, then I will come out with a $3,000 raise." But that doesn't happen here. . . .

Walt: *Especially in these times, as we were discussing.*

Case 9–7
*Sturdivant Electric Corporation**

Personnel of the Sturdivant Electric Company were entering the stage of running final acceptance tests on a special purpose computer they had subcontracted to supply to the armed services. One of the stipulations in the contract for the computer was a demonstration by the supplier that it would function correctly and reliably under test conditions. The special operating system of the computer was prepared by Sturdivant Electric's chief programmer, Al Abrams. Several days prior to the beginning of these tests Abrams submitted his work to his immediate superior, Bill Eden, who was computer project engineer (see Exhibit 1). Eden was to review the design of the operating system and compare it to the specifications. It was not intended that Eden check the correctness of the operating system itself, since forthcoming operational tests would accomplish that check.

In the course of his check, Eden found that Abrams had taken some liberties in one of the terms of the specification, and had told Abrams

---

* All names have been disguised.

EXHIBIT 1
Abbreviated organization chart of the Missile Control Department

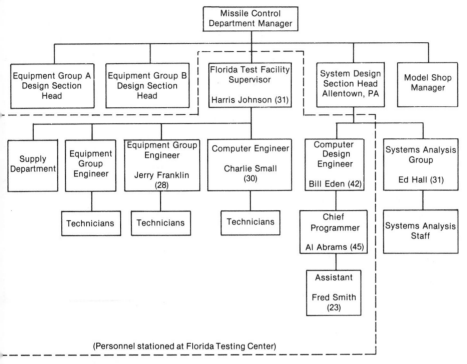

(Personnel stationed at Florida Testing Center)

to reverse the changes. Abrams had become enraged. He shouted that Eden was not capable of passing judgment on his work. Abrams had stormed out of the computer room, bellowing and cursing, and had bumped into Harris Johnson, the Sturdivant test facility supervisor, in the hallway. Johnson had tried to cool Abrams down, but Abrams had pushed past, claiming he would leave his security pass at the gate as a sign of his permanent departure.

Johnson knew that Eden and Abrams had had difficulties before, and that the project, nearing completion, was in a particularly sensitive stage of development. Realizing that he did not have direct line authority over Abrams within Sturdivant, Johnson needed to decide quickly what his next step should be.

COMPANY BACKGROUND AND THE ORGANIZATION OF THE FLORIDA TEST FACILITY

Sturdivant Electric was a large manufacturer of electrical equipment for industry, the armed services, and the consumer. Their industrial electronics division specialized in radar and all types of communications equipment. One of the subdivisions of this operation was engaged in the development of missile guidance equipment. This group had a field test facility at the U.S. Government's Special Weapons Test Center in Florida. The purpose of the facility, which had been under construction and partial operation for 14 months, was to conduct performance tests on missile guidance systems.

Although located on a military base, the test facility operated as an independent entity insofar as the direction of its activities were concerned. It relied on military personnel and supply for support only. For instance, the buildings were within a classified area guarded by military police, but the company retained responsibility for security of the project and could give or withhold permission for entrance to the test compound. When shipments had to be unloaded it was done under the direction of the company, but with thehelp of military personnel and equipment. The military also supplied certain types of vehicles which were driven by Sturdivant employees unless some specialized skill was required. In general, the arrangement was intended to allow the armed forces to provide services and facilities required by Sturdivant and the various other contractors with test facilities on the base, and thus to avoid unnecessary duplication.

Organizationally, the Sturdivant Electric test facility supervisor reported directly to the manager of the Missile Control Department at corporate headquarters in Allentown, Pennsylvania. Harris Johnson had been placed in charge of the Florida center when it was first set up and took with him from Allentown several key people who would form the nucleus of the field organization (Exhibit 1).

In addition to the transplanted Pennsylvania personnel, Sturdivant employed several technicians and others from the local area. These people lived either in their own homes or in apartments nearby. The workday for the test facility staff, which numbered approximately 15, began at 7:00 A.M. with a coffee break at 8:00 A.M. when the post exchange coffee wagon made a stop at their building. The lunch period extended from 11:15 until 11:45 but, because of the nature of their work, the personnel took the half hour when it was convenient rather than observing a strict schedule. The staff members were very congenial and enjoyed many outside activities together such as beach parties, fishing trips, etc. The workday ended at 3:30 P.M. except when overtime was scheduled.

The bulk of the missile control equipment was built by the company in its Allentown plants and then shipped to Florida. In order to assist in the start-up process, assistants had been sent from Allentown on a temporary basis. These people reported to Johnson for administrative purposes while in Florida, although any technical direction specifically relating to their equipment grouping came from their respective supervisors at headquarters.

Several members of Sturdivant's computer group had also been assigned temporarily to the Florida facilty. Of this group, Bill Eden, the chief computer engineer, Al Abrams, the chief programmer, and Fred Smith, assistant, had stayed with the project on a full-time basis, while other temporary personnel rarely stayed more than a week at a time. These three men and their families occupied adjoining two-room motel apartments at a tourist court not far from the military base.

Although their wives saw each other daily and their children played together, the families did not share many common social activities. The apartments consisted of one bedroom, a large living room which made up into a bedroom, a combination kitchen and dining area which opened off the living room, and a bath. The motel was located on the ocean and, while reasonably comfortable, did not constitute luxurious accommodations by any means. Transportation to and from work was generally by company car, although because of the extended period of time they would be there, all three families had brought their own cars to Florida.

THE COMPUTER

A central component of the test facility was a digital computer. Although Sturdivant had prepared the performance specifications for the computer, it was the only major piece of equipment not designed and built by the company. When the subcontractor delivered the machine to the test facility, its installation and software development remained to be done. Consequently a group of technicians from the subcontractor accompanied the computer to help the Sturdivant staff bring it up to operation. Eden, Abrams, and Smith had all spent a good deal of time in the design and production stages of the computer project back and forth between Sturdivant headquarters in Allentown and the subcontractor's headquarters in Concord, Massachusetts, so they were familiar with the problems involved. Sturdivant's contract with the government stipulated that the supplier demonstrate that the computer would perform correctly and reliably. This demonstration was to be the acceptance tests, based on the performance specifications.

Sturdivant Electric's chief programmer, Al Abrams, had been working on the operating system of the computer under the supervision of Bill Eden, computer project engineer.

The fact that there were still many unresolved problems in the computer when it was delivered made the workday rather hectic. The computer contractor's personnel had first priority in working on the machine since they were vitally interested in completing their field work as rapidly as possible. Their headquarters' interest in completing their contract along with the ever-mounting costs associated with the installation and check-out operation provided a sense of pressure on the daily work.

Bill Eden's purpose in Florida was to represent Sturdivant on installation questions with the computer contractor, make preparations for the acceptance tests of the machine, and generally to keep track of progress on the operating system. He did not have a great deal to keep him busy. His workday soon settled down and became rather routine. A great deal of the time he merely stood by in the computer room observing the work being done by the contractor's personnel. He was always willing to take on special jobs suggested by Johnson from time to time and relished the opportunity to do something tangible. Fred Smith was kept busy running detailed computations for Abrams.

In addition to the pressure created by the push to debug the computer quickly, further tension was produced by the necessity for Abrams to begin checking out on the computer portions of the system which he was developing. It was necessary for Sturdivant to have a finished operating system before the computer could be put through exhaustive acceptance tests, yet the testing of the system required operational machine time. This made it mandatory to utilize any time when the contractor's employees were not performing development work which interfered with machine operation. Much of this "available" time was lost, however, because Abrams was unable to interrupt abruptly his efforts on one phase of the system to place other parts of it, which he may have mapped out several weeks earlier, in the machine, run them, and evaluate the results.

The stresses inherent in this working arrangement were manifest in an incident that took place earlier in the computer installation and development process.

One day following lunch Abrams walked into Johnson's office with a look of disgust on his face.

Abrams: *I'm sorry, Harris, I just can't take it any longer. I've talked it over with my wife and she agrees that my health is more important. I want to resign, effective immediately. I've never had to take the kind of guff that I'm getting around here.*

[At this point, Bill Eden, obviously disturbed, walked into the office.]

Abrams: *I don't know what this guy [pointing to Eden] expects of me. I've never taken the kind of treatment he's been giving off of anyone—even during the recession when jobs were tough to find. He hounds me all day long. I just can't be driven and I can't be paced by that machine.*

Eden: *Al, you know I do no such thing. I try to be as considerate of you as I possibly can. We've got a job to be done, and you've got to work on the machine when it's free.*

Abrams: *I don't work that way! When I get on a train of thought at my desk, I've got to follow it through. When you interrupt me I lose the train and it means I have to repeat the entire mental process that led up to it. I just can't stop in the middle of a sequence and run back to that damn computer just because it's free for a couple of minutes. I've been on a milk and crackers diet for the past two weeks because my ulcers are acting up again and it's all because of this work. You're driving me crazy.*

Eden: *That's not so. Al, you know darn well that I try not to aggravate you. You're so doggone touchy, it's pitiful.*

Johnson: *Hold on now! It's not going to do either of you any good to get hot under the collar. Let's try to get at the root of the trouble without all the fuss.*

Abrams: *Just take today, for instance. You call me down to the machine this morning because it's going to be free for an hour. What happens? The damn thing isn't working and all my efforts were wasted. It took me two hours to retrace the steps up to the point at which you interrupted me.*

Eden: *It wasn't the machine, Al, your system had a mistake in it. The machine is okay.*

Abrams: *That's not so! You know damn well the computer was consistently failing to meet the maintenance routine density test limits for disk storage. How in the hell do you expect me to test part of my program with an unreliable disk?*

Eden: *The program checks you were making didn't involve the disk.*

Abrams: *How the hell do you know what I was checking?*

Johnson: *All right, come on back to earth!*

Abrams: *This business had me so upset this morning that I called my wife and asked her to meet me at the PX right away so we could discuss it in private. I left here on the 11:00 A.M. bus. We decided that it just wasn't worth it. My health is more important than this job. I know I'm not doing myself any good professionally by quitting, but it's the only answer. And that's not all; I got back here at 12:00 and the first crack out of the box this guy says, "Where the hell have you been?" in a nasty tone of voice.*

Eden: *I did not use a nasty tone of voice! You'd been gone for an hour and a half and you didn't even have the courtesy to tell me when you left or where you were going!*

Abrams: *It was none of your damn business! I don't have to tell you every time I want to walk away from my desk. And for your information I told Mary when I left and when I'd be back.*[1]

Johnson: *How about it, Bill, did you check with Mary? You know she keeps pretty good track of us.*

Eden: *No.*

Abrams: *Harris, I didn't have any trouble working in this group until Bill took over from McAlpin. Mac and I got along fine. And I don't want to put the company in an embarrassing spot by walking off before the system is complete. But I've got to think of myself.*

---

[1] Mary is the office stenographer.

The conversation continued along these lines for another half hour. Eden walked out after a while, and Johnson and Abrams discussed in detail some of the factors behind the blowup. It became evident that Abrams had been stewing over the interruptions to his work at the desk for several weeks. A previous incident that had occurred in Allentown was also rehashed. At that time Abrams had mistakenly interpreted Eden's request for the name of one of the computer contractor's programmers as an indication that the company was trying to hire a replacement for him and that he was going to be fired. Eden simply asked the question and gave no explanation. After Abrams had thought about it for an hour or so he had become so incensed that he had marched into the manager's office, broke up a meeting, and asked if they wanted him to quit.

When Abrams related this to Johnson in Florida, Johnson assured him that, "the company did not operate in that fashion", and that if they were ever dissatisfied with his work, that fact would be discussed completely with him.

The conversation drew to a close with an agreement that Abrams would continue to work on the program until it was finished. Johnson promised to try to arrange a transfer to another department as soon as it was complete and also to attempt to find a solution to his difficulties with Eden.

Then Johnson called Eden back into his office.

Johnson: *Bill, Al has agreed to finish up on the operating system. I hope you two will try to keep in mind the other fellow's feelings and try to be a little more tolerant and considerate. You know Al is doing the sort of work that involves uninterrupted concentration, so make sure that the free machine time is really worth breaking in for.*

And, Al, you know that Bill's chief concern is the schedule and that he is afraid that we won't meet it. Understand that when he becomes apprehensive over your progress he is not being critical but just wants to know where we stand.

One thing more, I want it understood that neither of you has prejudiced his position by what has been said here today. You have honest differences and we'll try to resolve them, but we'll need the cooperation of each of you.

[With this, Abrams left, but Eden stayed behind.]

Eden: *You know, Harris, I bend over backwards with that guy. I'm just as nice as I can possibly be. I never go near him unless it's absolutely necessary. I leave him completely free for the program and screen out all of the little detailed matters. But he's so darn suspicious of everything you do. Why, one day in Allentown the boss asked me to check on the name of a programmer. The Concord crowd owed us some instruction time under the terms of the contract and since the fellow in question was familiar with our machine, the boss felt we might collect the time by sending some work up there. All I did was to ask Al for his name, nothing more, and darned if he didn't think we were going behind his back and trying to hire someone to take his place. After he blew up and learned the whole* *story he changed his tune to the effect that he wasn't being consulted on such matters as he should be.*

The chief computer engineer

Bill Eden, age 42, had graduated from college following the Korean War, during which he had served as a first-class petty officer in the U.S. Navy. He was fortunate in not being required to take the labs associated with his major field, electrical engineering, at a large midwestern university, because his full-time, 40-hour per week job, was in the university's research laboratory.

In spite of the tremendous work load he managed to complete the requirements for a bachelor's degree in three years. His wife, whom he met and married while they were in the Navy, also obtained her degree. Following graduation Bill continued on as an engineer in the research laboratory, working on basic development work for the defense effort. A year later he accepted a position with a large West Coast aircraft manufacturer where he was placed in charge of a group preparing technical manuals. He left their employ in 1967 to accept a position with Sturdivant Electric Corporation as project engineer in the systems section. Bill had been dissatisfied with his prior job, in part because of a golfing friendship that had developed between one of his subordinates and his boss. The subordinate's professional loyalty appeared to be open to question and Bill felt that he used the golf course to further his own cause.

With Sturdivant, Eden did an excellent job of coordinating the many system functions assigned to him. Prior to his coming, the entire design department had grown very rapidly. This, coupled with the new personnel's lack of familiarity with system concepts and requirements, the steady progress in design of the many hardware components of the system, and the pressure of early design and dates, had created impetus for assigning the detailed coordinating responsibility to one person who could work with all of the design sections and gather, sort, analyze, and evaluate data and design considerations. With the help of two assistant engineers, Eden accomplished the desired results. He continued in this capacity until the promotion of the former computer project engineer created the vacancy into which he moved.

The chief programmer

Al Abrams was 45 years old and had worked in three distinct fields: accounting, teaching, and engineering. His undergraduate college training had prepared him primarily for teaching but his interest in mathematics led him into graduate work preparatory for a master's degree in that field. His quest for further knowledge carried Al into electronics and he completed in excess of 150 semester hours of undergraduate and graduate study in radio engineering.

He began his business career in the tax department of New York State, but left it after two years to take a position as test planning engineer for Northern Electronics, Inc. While there he also began teaching electronics for the Army Air Force. Following this he ventured back to accounting and served for a year as agent in charge for an Internal Revenue Service office making examinations of the tax returns of individuals, corporations, estates, and trusts. During this period he also began teaching freshman and sophomore engineering physics at a New York college and continued there for seven years. Concurrently he operated his own business, preparing financial statements and tax returns, which he continued until mid-1966. During an eight-month period he also tried various positions with four different companies in which he reviewed tax reports, gave advice on items that might invite examination by the IRS, audited books, and prepared financial statements. In late 1968 he accepted a position as a circuit and applications engineer with Erie Tube Corporation and remained with them until he came to work for Sturdivant in April 1970.

Upon coming to Sturdivant Abrams was assigned to the missile control project where he assisted in the preparation of the purchasing specification for the computer. During the time lag while the contractor was beginning production of the machine, he assisted the analysis group at headquarters on the solution of mathematical problems. Following this he was sent to the computer contractor's plant in Concord where he attended their school for programmers as well as filling a minor capacity in the coordination of the equipment manufacture. It was during this period that he also began work on programming the actual operating system to be used in Florida. It was also during this period that the original Sturdivant computer project engineer, McAlpin, was promoted and Eden was assigned the technical responsibility for the computer.

Abrams had spent two months at the computer contractor's school for technical programming. During this period he learned the logic of the computer he was to work with, that is, the characteristics of the various sections of the machine, how they functioned in relation to one another, the forms in which data was placed in and taken from the machine, the speeds with which computations could be handled, and many other factors which provided him with the basic tools needed to develop the operating system.

From there on the work of development was up to the ingenuity of the programmer. This task required a high degree of proficiency in math and the type of mind that could, in an orderly, systematic fashion, juggle a vast number of factors, trying first one arrangement and then another, until the desired result was obtained. Generally, provision had to be made to store bits of information in the memory sections of the machine since the value was to be used later in a subsequent step. Particular attention had to be given to the amount of time taken to perform each operation since the problem was being solved in "real time," that is, the time required for the performance became an integral part of the problem and affected the final answer. Because of the close interlocking relationship between computation time and sequence of operations it was possible to have several days' work proved worthless because of an incongruity which suddenly appeared. When a particular element of the operating system was completed, it was then pieced with a number of other elements to form a larger part of the entire sequence, in effect pyramiding the complications that could arise from incompatibility. Each element was a building block and it was not uncommon to find misfits, hence many painful and time-consuming repeats. In absolute magnitude the job had hundreds of separate and distinct operations. Abrams was the only member of the Sturdivant computer staff who had been through the entire training program at the computer manufacturer's school, although Eden and Smith had been exposed to portions of it.

AN EARLIER ENCOUNTER

When Johnson had occasion to leave the office for several days he made it a practice to designate one member of the permanent staff as being responsible for the operation of the test facility. On one such occasion Jerry Franklin, who generally filled this spot, was playing bridge with several other members of the staff, as was the lunchtime custom. As the group was completing the final hand, Bill Eden walked over to the group, who were sitting around a desk which served as their card table, and observed for a minute or two. He cleared his throat a couple of times and finally said, "Don't you fellows think it is about time that you all got back to work?"

When the group did break up Eden followed Abrams over to his desk.

Eden: *Say, Al, I'd like to get a progress report from you. Would you let me have the parts of the system you have completed?*

Abram's reply was to the effect that none of the work was in such a form that it would mean anything to Eden. He maintained that he had a series of notes in his file which contained the rough outline of the system and some finalized elements. He stressed that, in their present form, they would be valueless to Eden and were more likely subject to change in any event. Eden was nevertheless insistent. The level of their voices rose. After several heated exchanges in which charge and countercharge were hurled, Eden stalked off.

When Johnson returned the following day Eden stopped in to see him.

Eden: *If you've got a minute there's something I'd like to discuss with you.*

Johnson: *Sure thing, pull up a chair.*

Eden: *Well, I had another run-in with Al the other day and, frankly, I'm worried. He just will not give me anything concrete in the way of a progress report. He maintains that he is making satisfactory progress and will tell me if he feels he is getting behind.*

You will recall that when he made his original estimate of how long it would take him to do the job, I made a point of letting everyone know that I didn't agree that he had allowed sufficient time. Now with his reluctance to let me see what he has done, I'm more convinced than ever that we will not finish on time and that he is hiding the fact. Every time I try to find out where we stand he gets temperamental on me. And if there's anything I can't stand it's a prima donna! When he finds that time has run out he'll probably up and quit on us.

Johnson: *Ouch! That's all we'd need! I hope you are misjudging Al.*

Eden: *I hope so, too, but the fact remains that I have no means of measuring this progress and have only his word for assurance that we are on schedule. You know the blood will be on my hands if we miss our dates. I'm plenty worried.*

Johnson: *Well, for peace of mind, if nothing more, we have to determine the status of the operating system. After all, our schedule for the entire test facility is based to a large extent on Al's end date. If you had his file on the system could you do a sufficiently comprehensive analysis of the contents to establish our position?*

Eden: *Possibly, but I doubt it. Ed Hall up in Allentown would be in a much better position to do it since he has had a great deal of general operating system experience. But I know if you call in Hall for that purpose it'll make Al mad.*

Johnson: *You're certainly right about that! However, if Hall would come down for a visit on a related matter, the progress report might be obtained as a by-product. With his work on system simulations, there should be plenty of common ground on which the two of them can get together.*

Eden: *That's a thought.*

Johnson: *Suppose I discuss the matter with the boss and see what we can cook up.*

A visit with Hall was arranged. As a result of some rescheduling at headquarters, it was convenient to shift some work associated with the Florida testing to Allentown. Abrams had originally planned to do this work after completing the main operating system. The stated purpose of Hall's visit was to coordinate the transfer of this small block of work. After making the arrangements, Johnson called Abrams into his office and informed him of the plan and the reasons. Abrams thought it was a good idea and promised to help in any way possible. After the visit, Hall assured everyone that Abrams appeared to be making satisfactory progress and that for the present, at least, he had every chance of meeting the schedule.

THE OVERTIME INCIDENT

On a Friday, several weeks following the work status controversy, Abrams stopped Johnson in the lab.

Abrams: *Say, Harris, Bill wants Smith and me to work tomorrow and I don't see the need for it. I'm keeping up with the schedule I've set for myself and until I get behind I see no reason for putting in overtime. Besides, I'd like to spend some time with my family.*

Johnson: *Can't say I blame you for that. Why does Bill feel that it is necessary?*

Abrams: *He just said that we should make use of every available minute now as a cushion against missing our schedule. I'm being very careful to be sure I maintain a progress rate consistent with our dates and I feel that overtime now is a needless imposition. If I find myself falling behind in any week, I'll certainly tell you and request overtime.*

Johnson: *From what you've told me I've got to agree with you. Suppose I talk it over with Bill and see what he has in mind.*

Abrams: *Okay.*

On his way back to the office, Johnson stopped by Bill Eden's desk and asked him about the overtime situation.

Eden: *Two fellows from Concord who are experts on the disk section are leaving for home on Sunday. So far this week we haven't gotten in more than two hours of actual operating time on the machine and I figured that if we worked Saturday we could get in a solid eight hours with these boys standing by in case of trouble. In fact, they suggested that we do it so that they could be sure that the reliability of that section of the computer was up to par. Besides, it won't do any harm to get in all of the time we can now. I know Al is sore about it because he had planned to take off for Miami with his family tonight to spend the weekend with relatives.*

Johnson agreed that they should work Saturday under the circumstances and walked back to the computer room to find Abrams. When Johnson related Eden's full story, Abrams quickly agreed to work. His closing remark was, "If Bill had only said something about the fellows leaving for Concord there wouldn't have been any argument in the first place."

JOHNSON'S CURRENT PROBLEM

As Sturdivant moved into the stage of testing of the computer, Bill Eden reviewed Al Abrams' work. Abrams had finished the operating system a few days earlier and had submitted it to Eden.

In the course of his review, Eden found that Abrams' design of the operating system differed from the approved government specifications. When asked about it, Abrams replied that he was aware of the discrepancy but that it would make no difference in the end result. Eden discussed the matter with Charlie Small, another computer engineer for Sturdivant, and they agreed that the program was not acceptable as presented. When Abrams met with Eden and Small, Eden told him to correct the discrepancy. Abrams became enraged and made some caustic comments about their ability to pass judgment on his work. His closing comments were:

Abrams: *I'm not going to have my work checked by everyone! I've been working on this system a long time and I'm the only one who can say whether or not it is okay! You guys have made my life miserable from the start! You sneak around behind my back and pull all sorts of stunts. I deserve to know what's going on around here. Eden, you've driven me like a common laborer since you were assigned to this job. You've never given me any help—I've been all alone on this job. I don't know what to expect next! As far as I'm concerned this is the finish. I quit!*

With that he stormed out of the computer room. Johnson, who had heard the last part of the conversation, caught up with him at the outer exit. Abrams tried to turn in his security pass.

Johnson: *I won't take your pass now. Take a minute to relax and calm down.*

Abrams: *Damn it! Take it!*

Johnson: *No! Go on home and cool down. If you still want to quit in the morning, I'll accept your pass then.*

Abrams: *I don't want to be mollified! I don't want to cool down! If you won't take my pass, I'll leave it with the guard at the gate!*

Once again, Johnson was faced with the problem of how to handle an administrative situation over which he had no direct line responsibility. Abrams and Eden worked for the systems section head, and although Johnson had kept him informed on all developments in Florida, the geographical separation seemed to Johnson to make him the one who had to cope with the problem on the spot. There was always a question as to what lengths he could go in handling the matter because of his inability to make any commitments which would be binding on the section head.

Part **V**

Managing for motivation

In Part V, which consists of one chapter of text, we combine a discussion of conclusions based on research into work motivation and management style with a discussion aimed at stimulating the reader to reflect on his or her own style.

The approach in the chapter will first deal with the question, "What motivates people?" We shall look particularly at the "path-goal theory" of motivation and see how it fits into our overview model. Second, we shall examine some of the rewards which people may value, and discuss the perspective toward rewards which people hold and which others hold about them. Third, we shall address the question, "How can I motivate people?" paying particular attention to management style. The final section of the chapter is a discussion of three broad types of organizational roles for people with responsibility for results. The roles are administering, managing, and leading.

The cases at the end of Part V focus on two managers with different styles. A full understanding of the Nuclear Tube Assembly Room (Cases 10–1 and 10–2) requires knowledge of the emergent group phenomenon, covered in Chapter 6. Case 10–3, Product Management at United Brands, and Case 10–4, David Alpert (A), describe a dynamic job and show one person's style in fulfilling it. David Alpert (B) (Case 10–5) provides information on that person's background and philosophy.

Chapter 10

MOTIVATION, MANAGEMENT STYLE, AND LEADERSHIP

Leadership is getting people to do what they don't want to do, and liking it.

Harry Truman

Managers often ask two questions about the motivation of employees: "What motivates people?" and "How can I motivate people?" Implicit in the first question is the notion that motivation derives from the person, or is a state that originates within that person. In the second question the emphasis is placed on what the manager can do to elicit motivation.

In one sense the first question is broader than and includes the second question. By asking about the source of motivation one is asking for an understanding or explanation of what is known psychologically about the tendency of people to expend their energies. By asking how to motivate others, a manager is assuming (*a*) that one can affect another's behavior and (*b*) that one's effect can override other effects on another's behavior.

Our overall purpose in this chapter is to answer these questions, to help the manager understand motivation and act to elicit it. In doing this we shall deal with the meaning of motivation, the practical usefulness of the concept of motivation, the nature of what motivates people, a way of thinking about what motivates people, and some guides for behavior by a manager which can lead to motivated employees.

WHAT MOTIVATES PEOPLE?

The more analytically oriented question regarding motivation is the basic one of what leads to a person being motivated. To understand and answer this question requires that we first define and explain motivation. We shall do this in terms of our overview model and the ideas introduced in the preceding chapters. Beyond that, we shall discuss theories of motivation and what they imply for practical affairs.

Motivation in the overview model

From a managerial viewpoint, and using our overview model as a guide, where does "motivation" fit in, and what causes it?

A manager's interest in motivation, either someone else's or his or her own motivation, comes about because of an interest in some *result*. The result may be a strictly work-related matter, such as whether a particular order will be filled or a diagnosis of why sales fell below budget. It may also be a concern for other organizational outcomes, such as the satisfaction and well-being of employees, or a concern about turnover, or it may be a personal concern, such as one's own reputation as a manager.

These concerns over results should lead to a number of other questions, as described in Chapter 1, pertaining to work behavior and perspective: what *behavior,* and by whom, is the cause of or potential cause of the results in question? And then: what is the *perspective* of the individual or individuals whose behavior has been pinpointed? It is here, as part of the diagnosis of perspective, that the concept of motivation fits into our model.

Motivation may be defined as the state of an individual's perspective which represents the strength of his or her propensity to exert effort toward some particular behavior. From this general definition one may easily think of motivation as applying only to work behavior, but it is important to think of motivation more broadly to help us remember that people behave, even at work, as a result of *multiple* interests and motivations and toward ends other than work results alone.

For example, let us say a computer programmer has missed an important deadline for completing a particular program. Does this evidence mean the programmer's motivation is low? Obviously, it does not necessarily mean this. It *may* be that the person is generally poorly motivated at this time, for reasons such as health or personal anxieties. On the other hand, the person may be working very hard, and be highly motivated toward programming work, but may be so involved in the intrinsic rewards of that kind of work that the need for meeting the deadline has become less important in his or her perspective. There are still other possible explanations for the missed deadline. What are they?

The point of this illustration is that in diagnosing a state of work motivation a manager is dealing with an invisible world, the perspective of the person. As such, the manager must use evidence of behavior (past and present) to *infer* what that person's perspective is. In order to be useful for action, this inference-drawing or model-building process must recognize the total competing motivations in the other's perspective.

As suggested in Chapter 1 and in the above illustration about the computer programmer's missed deadline, a diagnosis stimulated by a concern for results may or may not terminate with the conclusion that an individual's work motivation is the problem. Rather, in carrying out the diagnosis, once some tentative analysis of perspective has been formulated, the diagnosis proceeds back further in the overview model to include the emergent group and inputs of the inner environment, outer environment, and the makeup of the individual people themselves as these elements may affect perspective. Note, for example, that the problem with the missed deadline may have been inadequate project management, direction, and incentives toward the result of on-time delivery, and not the work motivation of the programmer. In other words, more careful direction and *channeling* of the motivation by virtue of clearer organizational inputs may have been the problem.

But let us focus here on problems of individual motivation. Assume that a manager has pinpointed the problem as the level of work motivation of one or more employees. What further analysis is needed in order to take action to exercise influence in order to raise the level of work motivation?

The path-goal theory of motivation

Some of the tools necessary for further diagnosis were provided in Chapter 9. There, we learned that perspective can be analyzed by inferring what assumptions, perceptions, and feelings an individual apparently holds. These same concepts may be applied to motivation. More particularly, one stream of research has developed the "path-goal theory" of motivation (House and Mitchell, 1974). The concepts of this theory represent more specific notions of assumptions, perceptions, and feelings as they apply to motivation.

The path-goal theory of motivation may be summarized as a formula:

$$M = V \times E$$

where M is an individual's motivation to *behave* in a certain way; V is the value a person holds for a reward or outcome which may come as the result of the behavior (his or her *assumption* or belief about the reward); and E is the expectancy (a combination of *assumption* and *perception*) that the reward will be achieved if the behavior is carried out. The expectancy part of this formula for motivation can be thought of as the probability that the person implicitly places on the event that the reward in question will be forthcoming.

Thus, according to the path-goal formula, high motivation depends both on a person holding a potential reward or outcome high in his or her beliefs and on believing the reward will be forthcoming.

An individual's perspective of perceptions and assumptions regarding the value of certain rewards as outcomes for himself or herself and the expectancy of those rewards being forthcoming are a function of two things. First, they are a function of the individual's personal value system, or the *goals* which he or she values. In terms of our overview model, this comes in part from the personal inputs to perspective. Second, they are a function of the situation or context in which the person finds himself or herself, or the potential *path* to the goal. This is represented by the inputs from the inner environment, including what rewards are available in the compensation system, from other people, and from within the individual, and how well the availability and linkage of these rewards are communicated, particularly by the management style of the boss. This discussion of motivation and the path-goal theory in terms of the overview model is illustrated in Figure 10–1.

Let us look at each of the major components of the path-goal theory in turn. In the next part of this chapter we examine some of the possible rewards which people may value. Following that we examine what managers may do to affect expectancies by improving the paths toward goals and by taking action to enhance the values people place on particular rewards. That discussion will center on management style and a consideration of leadership.

REWARDS PEOPLE STRIVE FOR

In practical terms what are the objects, things, or feelings which people value as rewards for their work effort? In other words, what do they strive for in their work?

Historically and psychologically there are several answers to this. Schein (1970) has outlined these in a description of "management assumptions" about people. There are three primary sets of assumptions, each of which includes assumptions about what rewards will motivate others, and then a fourth set which is conceptually and philosophically different from the first three. Let us approach the answer to "what

FIGURE 10–1
Motivation in the overview model

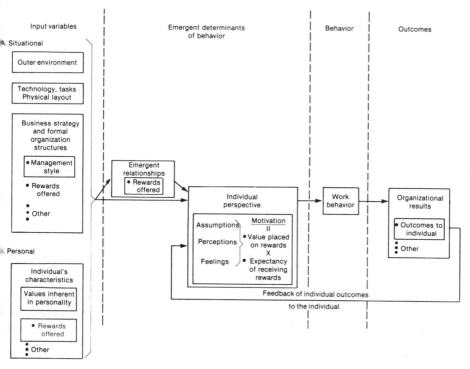

motivates people?" by a paraphasing of Schein's sets of managerial assumptions about people.

Assumption Set I: People are motivated by material rewards

The first set of assumptions is basically that people are motivated to work by the expectation of material or economic rewards. People are viewed as essentially rational in their behavior, in that they will respond with more work effort if there is promise of greater pay. Other potential influences on perspective, such as peer group pressure, praise, or a need for control and mastery over their work, are seen as secondary and unimportant compared to people's needs to maximize material gain.

These basic assumptions about what motivates lead to other managerial assumptions and to policies and normative styles for managerial behavior toward employees. For one, the notion that people respond only to material rewards and in proportion to the amount of such rewards has as its complement the proposition that *unless* the rewards of pay are offered, people will *not* work. Thus, people are viewed as inherently lazy, like machines which must be fueled by pay and which will do productive work only under those conditions. Similarly, employees must be carefully programmed and guided; they are seen in this set of assumptions to prefer the known to the unknown and to resist any change in familiar patterns.

The implications for organizational and managerial practices of these rational-economic assumptions are straightforward. Assuming people are motivated primarily by rational-economic factors, organizations must be designed to deal with those essentially unimaginative, noncreative perspectives of employees. This means a tops-down, bureaucratic structure, supplemented with extensive rules to cover every conceivable contingency. Elaborate incentive schemes, including a high percentage of bonus based on performance, are called for.

The type of management style, or the pattern of behavior for a manager, which would elicit motivation from an employee who valued these rewards would be a directive, authoritarian style in which the manager closely plans, directs, and controls the work of subordinates.

The rational-economic set of assumptions underlies the writing of Frederick Taylor in his book, *The Principles of Scientific Management* (1923). These assumptions and their implications for management have been called scientific management or machine theory. In Likert's (1967) four "systems," these assumptions correspond to System I, in which management exhibits low confidence and low trust in subordinates. McGregor (1960) termed these "Theory X"; Blake and Mouton (1964) would place a manager whose behavior reflected these assumptions at the "9,1" point on their "managerial grid," that is, very high on concern for production or task accomplishment and very low on concern for people. In terms of the transactional analysis approach to understanding communications (see Harris, 1969), in which the two parties to any communication may be speaking from and to one of three ego states—Parent, Adult, and Child—managers here would communicate from their "Parent" state to the employee's "Child."

Although some of the authors mentioned above present their characterization of the rational-economic assumptions in a purely descriptive way, most of them use these assumptions only as a straw man. The writers go on to describe assumptions that are more humanistic. Certainly in the bald statement of these assumptions it is easy to see their oversimplication of motivation. In this day and age, most managers would deny their own belief in this rational-economic approach to thinking about motivation of employees.

Or would they? *Do* they?

Most practicing managers quickly recognize the limitations and oversimplifications of the rational-economic assumptions. At the same time, the experienced manager (and many inexperienced young managers trained in the modern equivalents of scientific management) in fact *behave* as though these were their assumptions about motivations. And, in many instances, these managers get results. That is, employees do sometimes respond to strictly economic incentives, show no interest in new and higher levels of responsibility, seek direction and control, and resist any innovation or change.

Despite a great deal of research, not to mention common sense and insight, which suggest that people do not exclusively seek economic rewards, any full explanation of what motivates people must allow for the continuing partial validity of the rational-economic assumptions as reasonable explanations of what occurs in practice. We shall return to this later.

Assumption Set II: People are motivated by social rewards

The basic assumption here is that people are essentially social animals and as such are motivated by their need for human relationships. If people are demotivated or antimanagement, these assumptions suggest it is because they have not been communicated with, have not been listened to and provided the opportunity for human contact, or that some other relationships, such as may be provided by an effective union or a strong emergent group within the organization, are fulfilling the basic need for relationships. The assumption is that people with social support and encouragement can adapt to change and be creative in developing new solutions to problems. It follows that management's role is to structure the work environment so that social contact is possible. Examples would be to structure work so that it can be done by groups, to provide supportive human contact between superiors and subordinates, and to establish open-door policies, counseling services, and the like.

The landmark research underlying the social rewards school is Roethlisberger and Dickson's *Management and the Worker* (1939). Another name given to this field of thought is the "human relations" school. It is very closely aligned with the style which Blake and Mouton (1964) refer to as "1,9" on the managerial grid, that is, a manager very high on concern for people and very low on concern for production or task. In terms of transactional analysis (Harris, 1969), the role of the manager implied by this may be thought of as "Child to Child" as the manager is primarily concerned with the feelings and emotional state of the employee.

The social rewards assumptions imply a management style that is, in many ways, diametrically opposed to that implied by the economic rewards assumptions. The latter relegates people in organizations to the status of machines and places emphasis on getting the job done, while assuming people will be satisfied with pay. The former emphasizes the human element as most important and assumes that a happy worker is a productive worker. The dichotomy between these two basic types of management style has deep roots. The rational-economic person emphasis is on production, task, things, clarity and predictability, and the sacrifice of the human element to larger institutional goals. The social person emphasis is on people and human relationships, on the importance of meaning in terms of the relative point of view of the individual, and flexibility of organization to human needs. The two basic dimensions of task-oriented behavior and relationships-oriented behavior are the underlying emphasis of each distinct style. These dimensions have been recognized in a number of authors' research and advice. For example, these same dimensions were shown empirically to be the underlying, essentially orthogonal factors in the Ohio State leadership studies.[1]

Despite its oversimplifications and obvious limitations, management style based on the social motivation assumptions is, like that based on the rational-economic assumptions, alive and well. Sometimes it works, not only in leading to satisfied employees but also in getting other results. Then again, sometimes it doesn't. The inadequacies of both these approaches suggest the need to look further for *the* valid underlying set of assumptions and a management style which exhibits them in leadership behavior.

Assumption Set III: People are motivated by intrinsic rewards

The third set of assumptions is labeled by Schein (1970) "self-actualizing man." The basic assumption is that the most important motivating force is a need to achieve feelings of mastery in activities and the full realization of one's potential. The assumptions continue that if the work environment does not provide the appropriate challenges and opportunities, people can lose interest and be demotivated. It follows from this that individuals will welcome change if it promises to enrich their experiences and give them additional opportunities for self-fulfillment. Management's role, then, is to structure work and relationships to provide challenge and opportunity for learning and to encourage the participation of subordinates in decisions which affect

---

[1] For a review of these studies, see Korman (1966, pp. 349–61).

them. The classical management-by-objectives approach, in which superior and subordinate jointly set objectives and the subordinate is given wide leeway in deciding how to reach these objectives, is a direct offshoot of this set of assumptions.

The self-actualization assumptions correspond to McGregor's (1960) Theory Y, to Likert's (1967) System IV, Blake and Mouton's (1964) "9,9" style and to communications that are "Adult to Adult" in the terminology of transactional analysis (Harris, 1969). In *The Human Side of Enterprise,* McGregor (1960) pointed out that earlier "theories" about motivation were not so much wrong as they were dated. People may have been motivated primarily by money and the need for material comforts in our society at the turn of the century, but he argues that this is no longer the case. Maslow's (1954) "need hierarchy" applies to the three sets of assumptions. The lowest order needs are those for food, shelter, and the basics of subsistence, that is, for at least some minimum level of material necessities. Once these are attained, their function as a motivator gives way to *social* needs. When those are satisfied the higher order needs for *ego* gratification and *self-actualization* become salient and motivating. Thus, as individuals and societies mature, argue Maslow (1954) and McGregor (1960), they eventually come to be motivated by the highest order of needs. Herzberg (1966) also points out that rewards aimed at satisfying economic and social needs are really not motivators for employees, but what he calls "satisfiers" or "hygiene factors." They are *extrinsic* in nature, whereas true motivation comes from within the person and is *intrinsic* in nature. Conditions which can release intrinsic motivation include restructured jobs, promotions, and granting autonomy and control to an employee over his or her own work.

Like the earlier sets of assumptions, self-actualization has its adherents in organizations and manifestations in styles of managers. Sometimes people are very responsive to settings which permit and encourage self-actualization. But sometimes they are not.

Thus, we have reviewed three common sets of assumptions about what people value as rewards for work behavior. In each set we have referred to how the set fits with the writing of theorists in human motivation. We have also noted how each set, if held by a manager with respect to subordinates, leads to a different management style and to different organization structures and policies for getting results.

In presenting each set of assumptions of valued rewards we have stressed that in practice there are occasions when people are motivated by the granting of these rewards and occasions when they are not. In light of the path-goal theory, how can this be explained? The reader should pause and come up with an answer to this before proceeding.

The complexity of people

No *single* set of assumptions about a single type of reward will predict what will motivate everyone or even the same person all the time. By looking at the motivation formula from the path-goal theory, $M = V \times E$, the reasons for this become clear. First of all, people differ in what they value, and what they value may change over time. In a way, each individual has his or her own $M = V \times E$ formula. A person who has fallen heir to a fortune or won the grand prize in a lottery would probably have little motivation to work on an incentive pay basis. More realistically, while financial rewards can never be entirely dismissed from most people's valued goals, it should be recognized that money may be important up to some minimum threshold, but not thereafter. Moreover, money is often valued as a symbolic indicator and a measure of ego and self-worth rather than exclusively as a means to further material gain. Thus, money may be valued or not, even by a well-paid employee, depending on its meaning and the special circumstances in his or her life at a given time.

Furthermore, people may have certain long-term valued goals but different short-term ones. Thus, a young professional considering new jobs may wisely give up the highest paying job for one which will provide greater learning opportunity in the short run, or an older employee may forego some income for the assurance of a secure job.

These and many other examples simply point out that people value different things and that people are too *complex* to be categorized as valuing only one type of work reward. In his discussion of the sets of assumptions about what motivates people, Schein (1970) refers to a fourth set of assumptions about "complex man" as those recognizing this complexity. Recognizing that people are complex, that their valued rewards vary, is the first rule for the manager who would motivate others. As we have suggested, the diagnostic process can follow the guides of the overview model, and when motivation is the problem, the path-goal theory can suggest steps to managerial action.

Path-goal theory suggests another difficulty with a straightforward application of what people value as leading directly to motivation. That is, even if a person did value highly a particular reward, say social relationships with respected others, the situation of the work may not be perceived by the individual as leading to that reward. In other words, his or her expectation of achieving the reward may be too low for its presence to create a high level of work motivation.

On the whole, then, what motivates people is in part a function of what they bring to the work place as assumptions about valued rewards. Porter (1973) has provided a useful list of the kinds of rewards which can be valued by employees and which can be provided by organizations. His list of rewards and their typi-

FIGURE 10–2
Types and sources of organizational rewards

	Source*			
Reward type	Organi-zation	Emergent group	Superior	Individual self
I. Financial				
1. Wages	X			
2. Fringe benefits	X			
II. Interpersonal				
3. Status	X	X	X	
4. Recognition	X	X	X	
5. Friendship......................		X	X	
III. Intrinsic to work				
6. Completion	(X)		(X)	X
7. Achievement	(X)		(X)	X
8. Energy expenditure	(X)		(X)	X
IV. Development				
9. Skill acquisition			(X)	X
10. Personal growth..................	(X)		(X)	X

* X = Direct source; (X) = Indirect source.
Source: Adapted from Porter (1973).

cal organizational sources is given in Figure 10–2. Note that the categories of reward types are approximately the same as Schein's (1970) three categories of assumptions of valued rewards, with Porter adding a fourth, "development", which may be thought of as an outgrowth of intrinsic or self-fulfillment rewards.

Up to now, the emphasis in this chapter has been on what motivates people in terms of a way of conceptualizing motivation in the context of the overview model and in terms of the path-goal theory, and with emphasis on what assumptions or values people hold about different rewards. We have laid a basis for managerial understanding of motivation. Now let us elaborate on action managers can take to facilitate motivation.

HOW CAN I MOTIVATE PEOPLE?

A common answer to the question, "How can I motivate other people?" is "You can't. Motivation only comes from within the other person."

To some extent this is true. As we have seen, motivation is a state of a person's perspective. As such, it lies within that person and is a function of the particular assumptions and perceptions which determine that person's valued rewards and expectancies of achieving those rewards.

However, a manager most definitely can affect the level of motivation of another. He or she can work to provide the appropriate reward and can work on the values and expectancies of employees. In general, this is done through exercising one or all three of the forms of influence toward others described in Chapter 2: indirect influence, semidirect influence, and direct influence.

Specific actions to motivate others

As has been the case throughout this book, in prescribing action we urge first of all a thorough understanding. Here, this means a diagnosis of the problem in the context of the overview model, and if the issue or problem is individual motivation, an understanding of perspective in terms of what the individual values and what his or her expectations are. Managerial action, in general, can then take four forms:

1. Provide more of the valued rewards to the person.
2. Change the values of the person toward the rewards which are available.
3. Improve the person's *perception* of the behavior-reward linkage.
4. Improve the *reality* of the behavior-reward linkage.

The first two of these deal with actions which affect the *goals* which people value as outcomes for their work; the latter two deal with their expectation of whether the *paths* available to them will lead to those rewards. Let us see how each of the three forms of influence may be used to achieve one or more of these four forms of action.

With respect to individual motivation, and in the context of the path-goal theory, managerial action which constitutes indirect influence is aimed at arranging the appropriate strategies, structures, and policies to encourage and support motivated people to achieve organizational goals. This includes, for example, establishing incentive and reward systems which will be valued by employees. Indirect influence also includes selecting and employing people who have necessary skills and who value the kinds of rewards available in the organization. Finally, indirect influence includes developing in oneself and others the managerial skills, particularly the management style or pattern of behavior in dealing with subordinates, which will have the effect of creating higher motivation. We shall say more about the selection and development of management style for an *individual* manager below, for it is an element of organizational input for indirect influence and face-to-face direct influence as well.

Semidirect influence, it will be recalled, is exercised when a manager acts to affect an individual through his or her social relationships at work. The emergent group has a strong effect on what its members value and what their expectations are with respect to the outcomes from behavior. A good example of this is the case of Data Terminals Corporation (Solomon, 1979). In 1977 and 1978 the president, Robert Collings, offered all his employees free vacation trips, one year to Disneyland and the next year to Italy, if company sales and earnings doubled each year. They made it both years. Apparently, this group reward not only appealed to what most employees valued, but served as a highly visible symbol of the need for intracompany cooperation as well.

Direct influence on an individual involves communications and a personal, face-to-face relationship. A manager who attempts to increase the level of motivation through direct influence is typically trying to do the second and third actions mentioned above with respect to that person's values and expectations. Thus, the manager may work overtime to convince an employee to value more highly the rewards already existing and available in the organization. This may be particularly difficult in times of major social change, as occurred at least temporarily in the United States during the late 1960s. At that time, young employees were not particularly attracted to the long-term rewards which could result from loyalty to organizations, such as promotion and higher pay.

The other form of action for direct influence is to improve the employee's perception of the linkage between behavior and reward. This might involve, for example, personal conversations about what can result from certain levels of performance, such as promotion, bonus, or greater responsibility.

As important as *what* to do to motivate others is the question of *how* to do it. We turn now to a closer look at the manager's behavior required to motivate others. To do this, we discuss management style and leadership.

In working relationships with others, and particularly in direct influence in motivating others, a manager exhibits one or more characteristic styles of behavior. We may define management style as the pattern of a manager's behavior in working relationships with others over time. This definition is relatively loose, being more a concept than a precise variable. In order to be more precise, we need to set up one or more categories of behavioral characteristics.

MANAGEMENT STYLE

Management style and the assumption sets

As indicated earlier in our discussion of sets of assumptions which people may hold about valued rewards, there is a logical management style associated with each one. These styles are, first, a highly directive, task-oriented, controlling, authoritarian style, which may be appropriate where employees for one reason or another see their work only as a means to economic rewards. A second style is a supportive, people-oriented, humanistic style, which may be appropriate for employees who value social rewards. A third is a participative, mutual goal-setting style in which the manager works with subordinates who value autonomy and are rewarded by self-fulfillment.

In a way, then, we say that a manager who holds one of the three basic sets of assumptions about what motivates others should exhibit a style which is consistent with those assumptions in order to provide the appropriate means to exercise direct influence. In other words, managers need to understand what rewards subordinates value, and behave in a pattern which will fit with that understanding as one part of providing a consistent environment for the employee.

The manager who believes, as part of his or her perspective, that people are complex is in a conceptual sense going above and beyond the three operational sets of assumptions about valued rewards. The "complex person" assumptions imply that a manager will have no fixed, a priori beliefs about what motivates people in general or what style to employ in all situations. Rather, the manager will attempt to understand the particular subordinates, the particular situation, and ideally, select a style to fit the situation. Thus, recognizing that people are complex and that a diagnosis with a tool such as the path-goal theory must be performed before employing a style, the manager cannot have one particular style for all situations. Rather, the manager must be able to *choose* an appropriate style for a situation and then to *change* that style if necessary. A classic article describing this concept is by Tannenbaum and Schmidt (1973). One may call this approach a "contingent" management style, but it is important to note that it refers to the process of diagnosis and choice of managerial behavior rather than to the pattern of behavior itself.

This discussion is summarized in an adaptation of our overview model, Figure 10–3. In that figure, the elements of the model are described as they pertain to the perspective and behavior of an individual manager. Note that this is in contrast to Figure 10–1, presented earlier, in which the overview model pertained to the perspective and behavior of individual subordinate and was used to focus on the motivation of employees. In Figure 10–1 management style was an *input* affecting employee motivation. In Figure 10–3, management style is in the *behavior* column. The reader should think through how the two diagrams are related.

Human complexity and contingent style: The implications

Imagine that there is a manager of manufacturing who holds the "complex man" assumptions has diagnosed that two units under his or

FIGURE 10–3
Management style as a managerial characteristic

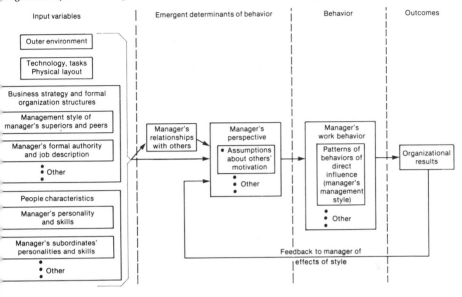

her supervision require very different management styles. He or she has the opportunity to replace both the managers or to manage both units personally. One unit is a production shop with highly routine, labor-intensive fabrication processes. Shop employees are represented by the local of a strong national union known for its militancy and emphasis on wage and fringe benefit demands in negotiations. Virtually every aspect of management-labor relationships is spelled out in the union contract. The other unit is an engineering group which is responsible for developing tools and dies for the production shop. Compared to the shop, the group has a wide span of control, its work requires a high degree of skill, and there is no union.

The manager determines that the shop needs a style that is very task and formal-control oriented. It needs a manager who can deal firmly with the frequent grievances. In engineering there is a need for a more people-oriented manager, one who will get to know the engineers and provide a supportive climate in which they can work to their own high standards of quality.

If the manager chooses to place a subordinate in charge of each unit, he or she would be applying the contingency approach by trying to select managers who will exhibit very different management styles as inputs to their organizations. The manager is engaging in an exercise of partial organization design: the establishment of a structure of input variables that will provide a fit. The immediate problem becomes one of selection. What criteria and models can be used to predict that the new managers will exhibit the appropriate leadership patterns? This problem of course arises whenever a personnel selection decision is made: management must make a trade-off between bringing in someone, say from outside, or promoting from within. A person brought in may have a clearly proven ability to run an operation, but the manager may have to pay more and may run up against difficulties in the morale of those below who were passed over. On the other hand, promoting from within alleviates some of these difficulties but runs the risk of the Peter principle: Will someone competent at one level also be competent at a higher one where the situation is different?

But this particular option also raises the issue of how the manager will work with each subordinate manager. Given that their styles to them are *not* to be contingent, but uniformly task oriented in one instance and relationships oriented in the other, their boss will need to deal with them differently to some extent. Thus, his or her own style will need to be contingent. This is particularly true if these managers are relatively inexperienced and need on-the-job development themselves. Under the first option the manager is applying contingency in choosing different subordinate managers and different input management styles to exercise direct influence in different situations. In addition, the manager may be faced with the need to be contingent or adaptive in behavior toward each new subordinate; that is, contingent in management style in exercising direct influence.

The manager who chooses to manage the two units personally must be contingent or adaptive with the larger organizations. In this instance the manager's behavior will be more visible; he or she will be identified as "the boss" by the people in each unit. The difficulties that can arise from having to be adaptive are more severe when there is no buffer.

In essence, by following the process of diagnosis implied by "complex man" assumptions and the contingent management style, the manager faces one or more of several challenges which would not arise in a noncontingent situation. These are:

1. The challenge of being explicit and systematic in thinking. This requires a vocabulary for expressing management style options, organizational inputs and human behavior, and a skill at inferring, hypothesizing future events, and imagining outcomes.
2. The challenge of dealing differently with different *individual* subordinates. This is an issue largely of how best to handle face-to-face communications.
3. The challenge of dealing differently with different *units*. This is mainly an issue of how best to influence the perspectives of two different groups of people.

Dealing with the challenges of contingent style

One guideline for the manager who has to deal differently with different subordinates is to make the differences in expectations known to them. A relatively explicit statement to each subordinate, aimed at sharing with them the reality that different standards, measures, and styles are being applied, can go a long way toward alleviating the potential perception that the boss is inconsistent. Such explicitness requires a degree of personal relationship and trust that is very difficult to attain in managing whole units. The differences can be maintained to some extent if the organizational units themselves are highly differentiated and require relatively little integration. Physical separation of the work places can contribute to this. The manager is then tailoring his or her own style to groups who indeed perceive themselves as different. If a great deal of integration of the work of the units is required, and might be accomplished by mutual interaction among employees at several levels, yet the basic high differentiation is also required, the creation of a separate organizational group or special procedures to accomplish the integration can help to make possible the exercise of different styles.

How well these challenges are met by managers will depend not only on their abilities to rationally understand the situation, but also on their own skills and personalities. Note that in Figure 10–3 the input "people characteristics" has been detailed to show the importance of these variables in managers' own makeups.

A manager may improve personal skills at understanding, diagnosing, and planning action to motivate others and adapt a style. Most of this chapter is aimed at just this kind of skill development, with the path-goal theory being a key tool to help operationalize the concepts of the complex person and the contingent management style. Management training which adds to this an experience of practicing new behaviors, such as active participation in a good case discussion or role-play exercises, can enhance and make personally useful the intellectual skills. Particularly valuable is training which builds on experience and which helps the manager articulate and store in his or her perspective assumptions that may have been latent and exhibited largely through intuitive behavior previously.

Nevertheless, we should recognize that aspects of the manager's personality set limits on what can be learned in most management development programs and on how much style can be adjusted. A manager's innate ability to conceptualize is often not as great as the ability to think concretely about "people problems." Thus, the process of expanding or changing one's style requires on-the-job practice and often support and "coaching" from others as well as conceptual and classroom learning.

A manager's own motivational pattern determines whether he or she can be comfortable using different managerial styles. If the manager's need for power (McClelland, 1975) is relatively high and channeled toward achieving institutional goals rather than personal dominance, then a basic personal requirement is met. Such managers exhibit a zest and interest in people problems. Managers whose required style is people oriented may have a high need for affiliation, and those who must lead by personal example, a high need for achievement.

Perhaps the most important personal requirement for any manager is a firm sense of self, an established although potentially growing *identity*. For the general manager, who by definition needs to deal in adaptive ways with different subordinates and units, something additional is required. Such a manager *must* be able to act in different situations, in effect to play different roles, to be a "gamesman" (Maccoby, 1976). Being able to maintain a firm identity and at the same time conduct oneself effectively in different roles without losing that identity requires distinguishing behavioral patterns from the "true" self. In short, the manager who would motivate others must exercise influence on the situation, through indirect and semidirect influence, and on individuals through direct influence. Moreover, he or she must exert influence on himself or herself. Issues of managerial motivation, self-influence, and identity under conditions calling for a gamesman will be discussed in Chapters 11 and 12.

LEADERSHIP

Let us review the action implications of this chapter by placing them in the broader context of influence types and by introducing some particular definitions of managerial roles. The three roles we shall use are *administering, managing,* and *leading.* For our purposes, *administering* refers to a managerial role which requires limited efforts to influence others. The administrator is one who essentially carries out existing structure and procedure, who performs the necessary function of maintaining and supporting structure and relationships. Such a role includes nonmanagerial jobs as well. Examples are work by people who have responsibility for self-contained tasks (such as clerical workers), by people who apply a high degree of expertise to problems (such as legal experts, researchers, professionals, and independent staff specialists of all kinds), and by people in managerial positions who basically monitor or enhance the work of subordinates (such as heads of bureaus engaged in tasks which do not require organizational changes or behavioral changes for results to be achieved). It should be clear that the administrator role is absolutely vital for organizational results, and it may require substantive knowledge based on extensive education and experience. At the same time, it is just one of the three important roles most organizations need to have fulfilled to achieve long-term results.

Managing is the role to which this book is primarily dedicated. It involves attaining power and influencing people through one or more of the three paths described in Chapter 2: indirect, semidirect, and direct. Forms of indirect influence include making changes in administrative structures, such as organization structures and policies, strategies, business plans, and the like. The acid test of the success of indirect influence is the achievement of behavioral changes among people and the consequent enhancement of organizational results. Thus, even the design of structural change, which in itself is largely an administrative function, requires an ability to understand and implement behavioral change in others, which makes it a part of the managerial role.

The managerial role is most purely manifested in semidirect and direct influence, where face-to-face interaction between the manager and groups or individuals is a part of the influence action. As we have reiterated throughout the book, success at these types of influence requires both an understanding of the causes of behavior and results and an ability to carry out action.

The key characteristic of the managing role is that it involves exercising influence, and for the most part the key assumption we have made about managing is that the manager can affect results by knowledgeable and judicious use of the concepts and actions described in this book. In short, we have emphasized the rational. To be sure, in Chapter 3 we placed, in a sense, a limit on how much a manager might expect to achieve in light of natural processes and forces, but we proceeded to deal with what most managers can *learn* to do better to affect results.

In our discussion earlier in this chapter of direct influence aimed at achieving others' motivation through a change in the *value* they place on certain rewards, we were in fact pushing the limits of what a manager can learn to do. It is the changing of others' values which gets us into the leadership role.

We define *leading* as that aspect of one's behavior which results in changing other's values. *Leadership* is a form of direct influence which we wish to distinguish from managing because its success in an organizational context is dependent on deep psychological aspects of the leader and the led. As Hollander and Julian (1969) point out, this has not been well studied. Successful leadership requires more than intellectual diagnosis and action, although these may be a part of a leader's strategy. What it requires, in many instances, is charisma by the leader and identification by the led; characteristics which may or may not be developed and achieved by a manager through hard thinking and hard work. Many leaders, perhaps the most powerful and influential by this definition, are born and reared with certain necessary characteristics, such as strong or charismatic physical and emotional attributes.

Few managers can transcend to become leaders, but organizations may need leadership in this sense only infrequently. Leadership is a matter of degree. Just as some administrators can exercise managerial roles, so can some managers exercise leadership. The reality is that there are limits on the managerial role, on influencing people strictly through learned skills, actions, and techniques. Where those learned abilities leave off, leadership begins. Leadership ability evolves more than it is learned, involves wisdom as much as intellect, and must fit the environment of the organization and the culture to be effective.

CONCLUSION

In this chapter we have completed the description of conceptual tools which fit into the overview model, and we have completed the prescriptive action step alternatives which go with each element in the model. In particular, we have elaborated in this chapter on direct influence to achieve motivation of others, and have defined the roles of administering, managing, and leading in terms of the extent to which each role requires its incumbent to exercise influence.

QUESTIONS FOR STUDY AND DISCUSSION

1. Using the concepts in the path-goal theory of motivation, describe the motivation of a person with whom you work. What particular rewards does the individual value?

   What can you infer is the individual's expectation of achieving those rewards within a reasonable time frame?

   What forms of influence by you or others in the organization could be exercised to improve the individual's motivation?

2. Go through the same exercise using the path-goal theory in assessing your own motivation toward your work. To what extent do you now value most intrinsic versus extrinsic rewards?

   Was this any different for you five years ago? Do you think it will be any different in ten years? 20 years?

   Based on this exercise what can you conclude is the appropriate management style for someone to use in working with you?

Case 10–1
The Nuclear Tube Assembly Room (A)*

The nuclear tube assembly room was a production unit of the American Radiatronics Corporation, one of the leading producers and an early pioneer in the nuclear electronics industry. The company manufactured a line of nuclear instruments and other electronic devices for nuclear applications. The company's regular line of electronic tubes was assembled, tested, and prepared for shipment in the nuclear tube assembly room. Ralph Langley, general foreman of the process department, described the tube room group as the most successful and, from certain standpoints, the most interesting of the several units in his department. Exhibit 1 is an organization chart.

EXHIBIT 1
Partial organization chart of American Radiatronics Corporation

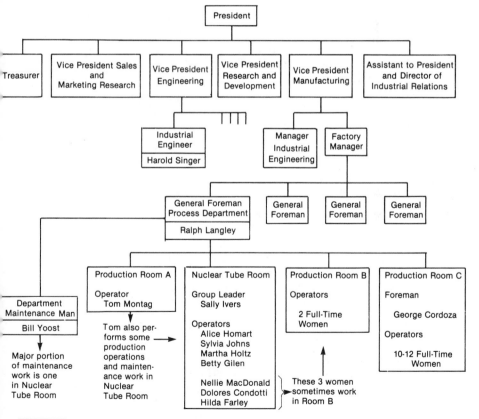

* All names have been disguised.

Prior to Langley's assuming the leadership of the department, some 24 months earlier, the women in the room had acquired the reputation of being agitators, hotheads, and persistent troublemakers. Production was down, costs had gotten out of hand, and deliveries had become very unpredictable. Some thought had been given to eliminating the entire operation. A report, prepared by the director of industrial relations at the time, that described the existing problem is presented in Exhibit 2.

Some data on labor efficiency during the subsequent 24 months are presented in Exhibit 3. During the most recent three-month period the tube room's direct and allocated monthly costs had averaged $36,750,[1] while the actual sales value of the room's monthly production for the same three months averaged $106,600. A recent special management report presented some additional figures of interest. Between January of the previous year and March of the current year, the group had shown a 53 percent improvement in the dollar output of product per labor-hour of work, direct labor efficiency had increased approximately 24 percent, and there had been about 11 percent to 12 percent improvement in the raw material utilization on tubes produced. During this same period they operated at 81 percent of their expense budget. In other words, they had used some $11,000 less on miscellaneous expenses than had been budgeted for such items. During this time period the hourly wages of the women working in the room had risen from an average of $3.45 to $4.15 per hour. In summary, the profit position for tube manufacturing operations as a whole was now one of the best in the company, where previously the activity had been operating at a loss. This record of progress had been widely recognized throughout the company.

In commenting about the group, Langley said,

> The unique aspect of this performance was that it has been accomplished by the group itself—not so much by any tangible thing that I or management has done. These people, previously considered a problem group, are now performing in an efficient and profitable way. They have a very active interest in seeing, not only their group, but the company as a whole, progress and make profits. It seems to me that this is quite an impressive thing for them to have accomplished by their own efforts.

Before conducting the observations and interviews reported on in this case, the casewriter talked to Frank Halbert, president of American Radiatronics. In approving the study, Halbert said, in part, "I hope you find what you are looking for. It would be tremendously important for the whole economy to bust through this 'least work for the most pay'

---

[1] Indirect costs were allocated to the department at the rate of 425 percent of direct labor dollars.

EXHIBIT 2
Industrial relations director's report

MEMORANDUM

Re: Process Department—Nuclear Tube Operation   July 10*

To: T. Bishop,† R. Langley

From: S. K. Lowe‡

I. **Summary**
    A brief summary of history, data from supervisors (various levels), employees, and exit interviews would indicate the following:

    A. This section has always had a reputation for being a "problem department." It is less well organized than other sections (work flow,
        safety, basic processes, equipment, housekeeping, etc.). Group behavior gives evidence of intense frustration, personal differences,
        rumor-mongering, and concern over operations. Misunderstandings
        regarding wages have been reflected by new employees; discouragement about "getting ahead" is reflected by them after a few short
        weeks of work, after talking with the older employees in the department.

    B. Productionwise the section has had a history of not meeting delivery
        dates or production quotas—with a high rate of product rejects.

II. **Analysis**
    From examination it would seem that problems may result from the following:

    A. *Operations—basic product difficulty*
        The products (fairly diverse and delicate) have not been "beaten
        down." Quality is dependent upon process, thus requiring a different
        kind of standardizing. Certain tube reactions are still technically unexplained. Is it a problem of basic design?

    B. *Instability of product*
        Product results, therefore, have been unstable and/or unpredictable.

    C. *Work flow*
        Organization of the work flow, methods used and work steps do not
        appear as well defined as other operations, largely due, it would
        seem, to basic unresolved technical problems.

    D. *Work standards and conditions*
        Standards of cleanliness, observing eating, smoking, etc., restrictions
        (directly affecting operations) have not been rigidly observed.

    E. *Equipment*
        Equipment failure and repair have, until recently, been a subject of
        complaint.

EXHIBIT 2 (*continued*)

> F. *Coordination*
> There is evidence of need for better liaison with sales, scheduling, planning, and meeting promise dates.
>
> **III. Attitudes**
> A. *Top management*
> With a myriad of pressures (merger, new plant, move, etc.) perhaps this small department did not have adequate recognition of its fundamental technical dilemmas, or it did not know how to deal with the basic technical problems—thus unraveling the other tangled department threads. Perhaps in the pressure of bigger problems, it received a step-child treatment.
>
> B. *Supervisors*
> To most management personnel concerned with its operation the nuclear tube section was not only a headache, but a bewilderment. Had they been able to solve the basic technical difficulties, it would not have operated on a crisis basis, nor reflected the high degree of frustration which characterized their attitudes.
> For the supervision level nearest the employees the same pattern has existed over a period of time—inability to organize due to basic technical product difficulties, poor equipment, little attention or inadequate understanding *and solution* of basic technical problems.
>
> C. *Employees*
> Employees reflect a high degree of frustration and worry for several reasons. They tend naturally to reflect the attitudes of their supervision. As a work group, they are older than average, tending to seek satisfaction from a well-ordered operation. This by reason of product process has not existed.
> Employees are hourly and used, from past employment, to more routine, less variable operations. They do not understand the *still experimental* technical "debugging" factors which must be resolved before operations run smoothly. It is not yet a traditional *production* department although we tab it thus; it is still in certain developmental stages.
> Employees are distinctly upset by variations in tube results—not knowing "reasons why," feeling they should be getting more consistent results.The high number of rejects on items produced is hardly a source of job satisfaction *unless recognized* and *understood* as part of the stage of product development.
> Employees may be confused by the variety and types of things on which they work—upset by poor scheduling, crisis upon crisis, coupled with hazy work steps or unanalyzed process.

* Ralph Langley took over the Nuclear Tube Room Department on June 15.
† Factory manager.
‡ Director of industrial relations.

IBIT 3
:lear Tube Room labor efficiency* three-month moving average†

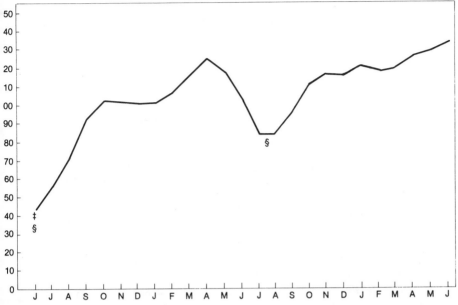

* Standard hours produced ÷ Hours on rated jobs (approximately 90 percent of time is spent on rated jobs).
† All percentages are calculated on new standards.
‡ Prior to this period labor efficiency figures are not available. However the best estimates attainable indicate that
:iencies were averaging between 40 percent and 50 percent of standard.
§ Somewhat lower labor efficiencies are expected during the hot summer months than during the remainder of the
ar.

idea workers in this country have." Later he said, "Do you really think
there is any substitute for fear as a motivator? I doubt it. All of these
fringe benefits and things won't do it; we've certainly learned that."

About Ralph Langley and operations in the tube room, Halbert
commented,

> I don't want to downgrade Ralph Langley or anything like that—I think
> he has been extremely successful in what he is doing—but it should be
> kept in mind that that tube room is not such a tough place to handle. We
> have some real trouble spots in other parts of the company. The tube
> room, after all, because of the kind of work done there, lends itself to the
> women seeing the connection between what they do and the final prod-
> uct. The work has challenge; it's interesting. There are opportunities
> there for satisfaction in the work itself that you couldn't begin to find in
> these other places.

BACKGROUND FACTS ABOUT THE COMPANY
AND ITS PRODUCTS

The history of American Radiatronics epitomized the pattern of development followed by many young companies that had taken part in the nuclear electronics boom after World War II. Starting in a small garage workshop on a back street in Baltimore, the company had been founded approximately ten years earlier by two young scientists convinced of the coming industrial applications for nuclear processes and instrumentation. Following an early period of rapid growth and a later series of mergers, the company had prospered and finally stabilized at a level of sales around $20 million annually. It remained at this volume for several years. In most recent years the company had been experiencing increasing competition from other young companies that had also grown to formidable strength of size and resources, and from older electronics firms that had more recently decided to enter the nuclear field. The later history of the company was marked also by a number of shifts in the top management structure. The present management team had been installed approximately two years earlier.

The Baltimore plant contained the main factory and home office headquarters for the company. Located in an industrial park area on Baltimore's outskirts, the plant employed approximately 600 people, most of whom commuted to work from Baltimore and its outlying suburbs. The plant had been moved to its present site two years previously from a former downtown location. A new building had been erected at that time. The structure had been designed to incorporate into its features the latest conceptions in industrial architecture and general public appearance. Well over half the company's sales volume was derived from the Baltimore plant's operations.

The nuclear tube assembly room

The nuclear tube assembly room was one of several production units in the plant's process department. Under Langley's direction, the department produced a variety of equipment parts, some of which went into larger equipment units manufactured by the company, while others were sold directly to customers. Besides the nuclear tube assembly room, there were three other production units in the department, each housed in an adjacent separate room. The products and manufacturing processes for each of the production units was such that the work of one group was not linked to that of the others.

The nuclear tube assembly room produced all of the company's regular line of electronic tubes. These products varied considerably in size, shape, design, and materials. In appearance they ranged from delicate glass vials three or four inches in length to massive steel chambers with bolted covers. Some were all-glass construction; still others consisted of all-metal assemblies, with numerous variations in the thickness and kind of metals employed. In all, approximately 25 different types of tubes were manufactured on a regular production basis, although not all styles were in production at the same time. A normal production month would call for eight to ten separate tube styles to be produced in quantities varying between 300 and 500 per style. A number of miscellaneous small jobs consisting of repair, modifications, or experimental mock-up of regular and/or experimental tubes were also assigned to the room each month. Out of the total number of tube types produced, four major tube styles accounted for approximately 80 percent to 84 percent of the dollar value of the room's output.

The production process

The production process varied with each style of tube, depending upon the materials employed, the mechanical design of the tube, and the particular electronic properties called for by its function. The precise relationship between a given tube's design and its performance was not always clearly known. Certain tube designs were developed over the years by trial-and-error methods while others were developed from known formulations and in accordance with standard design procedures. For this reason there was always an element of change in the air concerning details of the manufacturing process. For each tube a set of written standard operating procedures had been developed by the company engineers to describe each assembly operation required. From the viewpoint of production personnel, however, the history of modification and innovation that surrounded the evolution of many tube designs and production methods implied that the process of developing ultimate designs was not yet at an end.

Most of the operations performed in the assembly process were of a handwork nature, in which a variety of jigs, small implements, heating torches, and special-purpose machines were employed. Customarily the work was performed on a batch of parts at a time until a sufficient inventory of parts had been accumulated to allow a number of tubes to be assembled in one operation.

The work of the tube room was roughly divided into (1) glass works, which consisted of making tube shells and internal glass parts; (2) metal work, wherein internal metal springs, wires, grids, leads, etc. were made and prepared for use; (3) tube assembly, at which time the entire tube was put together; (4) vacuum testing and exhausting, where tubes were lead-tested, exhausted, and filled with special gases; and (5) electronic testing, where tubes were tested as functioning units. After final testing, tubes were labeled, recorded according to individual serial numbers, and packaged for shipment or inventory storage. At all stages of production assembly tubes were given visual and electrical tests to minimize defective parts or subassemblies finding their way to final assembly. All testing and quality control measures were performed by the production workers themselves, including the final test before packaging.

THE PRODUCTION WORKERS

The major part of the production work in the tube room was performed by eight women, one of whom, Sally Ivers, served as group leader. Each worker performed several kinds of operations, although each had, at the same time, one or more operations which she regarded as her particular specialty. These special jobs which were part of the regular production process had emerged over time as the most suitable work for a woman to do in view of her skills, her preferences, and the needs of the department. They were the most frequently recurring operations performed, accounting for roughly 50 percent or more of each woman's time, and were the chief identifying characteristic of her job. In all, an almost infinite variety of combinations of worker and job were practiced in the room. It was not uncommon for several women, each at different times, and occasionally at the same time, to perform the same operations. Not even the special jobs were necessarily exclusive, as usually at least two women had the special skills required to do a given job, and in the case of absences or emergencies, one would take over for the other.

The tube room production staff was augmented by two men. Bill Yoost served as maintenance man for the whole department. The other, Tom Montag, worked in the tube room part time assisting in various of the production operations. He did this when not busy in Room A, his normal work assignment, a single-person operation which did not keep him busy full time.

Some additional personal and job information about these people and the department general foreman, Ralph Langley, are given in Exhibit 4.

Pay rates and employee evaluation

As shown in Exhibit 4, the employees of the tube room were paid on an hourly basis. Pay grades were established for each job classification by the industrial relations department according to an evaluation of the amount of skill and knowledge required of a worker in the job. Within each pay grade there was an established range through which the

EXHIBIT 4
Job and personal information—tube room personnel

Name	Job classification	Hourly pay	Age	Seniority with company (years)	Seniority in tube room (years)	Education	Ethnicity	Marital status
Ralph Langley...........	Department general foreman	not available	41	3	2	MS in physics	Yankee	M
Bill Yoost	Maintenance mechanic	$5.06	39	3	2	High school and trade school	Yankee	M
Sally Ivers...........	Group leader	5.00	43	12	12	High school	Yankee	S
Alice Homart...........	Production worker AA	4.70	53	3	3	High school	Yankee	W
Nellie MacDonald	Production worker A	4.25	46	5	5	College 1 year	Yankee	M
Hilda Farley	Production worker A.	4.15	46	11	1	Grammar school	Irish	S
Martha Holtz...........	Production worker A.	4.05	56	6	4	9 years in Germany	German	M
Betty Gilen	Production worker A.	4.00	42	4	4	High school and art school (3 years)	Yankee	W
Sylvia Johns...........	Production worker A	3.95	42	1	1	Junior high school	Belgian	W
Tom Montag	Production worker B	3.75	26	0.5	0.5	High school	French	M
Dolores Condotti	Production worker B.	3.70	31	3	3	Junior high school	Lithuanian	M

hourly wage rate could progress. An employee's progression within the range was determined by periodic merit reviews. At intervals of four months, each employee was rated by his department general foreman on evaluation forms designed to reveal his strengths and weaknesses. These evaluation forms were forwarded to the industrial relations department where eligibility for pay increases was determined. The industrial relations department processed the wage increase if one were warranted and returned the completed evaluation form to the general foreman, who discussed the ratings and increases with the employee.

The tube room workers were not unionized, although certain other manufacturing groups in the company had been organized some years previously by a large international trade union.

Work standards and output records

Approximately 95 percent of the tube assembly operations performed by the women had been figured into standard hours by the company's industrial engineers. These standard hours were used in costing out direct labor costs for tube manufacturing operations by the accounting department, and they served as a standard of efficiency against which the room's actual performance was measured. Tube production for the total group was determined weekly when a physical inventory was taken of all finished and in-process tubes. Thus, labor invested in defective or destroyed tube parts or assemblies was "lost" to the group in figuring its net labor efficiencies. Monthly summaries of weekly efficiency figures were submitted to higher management for examination and review. Exhibit 3 presents these monthly efficiency figures for the previous 24 months.

All the labor efficiency figures in Exhibit 3 were based on revised standards put into effect three months prior to the writing of the case. The former standards, which had been set against the group's historical performance some years previously, had become inadequate in relation to the level of output then being achieved by the group. Consequently, Langley had initiated a review of all standards, "tube by tube, operation by operation," revising the allowed hours downward between 23 percent and 59 percent on individual tubes to an average 34 percent decrease on major tube types.

When Langley first took over supervision of the tube room group, the work force had consisted of 14 production workers. In the ensuing six months improvements in the group's performance created a surplus of labor which, because of a relatively stable volume of operations, required a series of layoffs to be made. It was during this period that the original force was reduced to the present eight. The layoffs were made in two steps with the women selected for layoff primarily on the basis of seniority with some secondary attention to the variety of work the women could do, and the quantity and quality of their work. Langley commented, "Those that stayed seemed to take it all right, even though none of them knew for sure whether she would be staying or not. They understood. One woman in the group I fired outright because of her attitude. She just couldn't and wouldn't fit in with the others. We had had a long history of trouble with her."

During the 24 months since Langley took over the department there had been no major changes in the production facilities, manufacturing methods, or basic tube types in production. Much of the equipment in use was regarded to be of antiquated and inefficient design. The improvements in group performance were attributed primarily to improvements in labor efficiency and informal production method innovations. Some minor alterations in tube design had been made by the company's scientific personnel, and a number of such changes had been initiated by members of the work group themselves, but as these changes were made their labor-saving effects had been largely incorporated into revised work standards.

HOW THE TUBE ROOM GROUP OPERATED

The most immediate and apparent feature of the room was its physical layout and the location of various work positions within it. The room itself was a large, grey, concrete-floored enclosure approximately 60 feet long by 50 feet across. Closely assembled rows of tables, workbenches, production machines, and test stands filled its central portions while an ordered assortment of miscellaneous cabinets, shelves, benches, and additional production equipment banked its wall areas. A row of windows looked into production room C, immediately adjacent. A single door provided access and egress for the room.

Movement throughout the room was frequent and widespread, and the occasions were very seldom in which at least one or two people were not in motion. The changing of settled work positions was likely to occur at any time during a day. Bantering, horseplay, and visiting were frequent occurrences; and at times, periods of total inactivity, such as when a woman appeared to be daydreaming or silently contemplating her work, were observed. The pattern of activity did not appear to vary with the comings and goings of Sally Ivers, Langley, or any of the other supervisory personnel.

Exhibit 5 summarizes the participation by individual workers in various nonwork activities. These activities were well established and they occurred regularly. For the most part they had been in existence for two

EXHIBIT 5
Participation in various nonwork activities

	Coffee break (Alice)	Lunch table	Walks	Poor box	Pool	Card game	Coffee break (Sally)
Martha Holtz	x			x			
Sylvia Johns	x	x		x	x		
Betty Gilen	x	x		x	x	x	
Alice Homart	x	x		x	x	x	
Nellie MacDonald	x	x	x	x	x		
Sally Ivers		x	x	x	x		x
Tom Montag				x	x	x	x
Bill Yoost				x	x	x	x
Dolores Condotti				x	x		x
Hilda Farley				x	x		x

years or more, dating back to the premove days at the old downtown Baltimore location. Although not participated in uniformly, they were well known to all.

Briefly, these activities were:

Coffee breaks: Coffee breaks were allowed twice a day, at 10 o'clock in the morning and 3 o'clock in the afternoon. The official company position was that 10-minute breaks were allowed twice a day at the work position.[2] However, because of heat generated by certain machines, tube room workers often gathered elsewhere in cooler locations. The total group invariably broke up into two smaller groups at coffee time—one group gathering around Sally Ivers at her workbench desk, and the other at the rear of the room near Alice Homart's customary work station (incidentally, one of the warmest areas in the room). The separate membership of these groups is given in Exhibit 5.

Lunch table: Several women regularly ate lunch together at a certain table in the company cafeteria. Although they did not need or use the whole table, the unoccupied places were never filled by other company personnel. The table usually filled, however, immediately after they left it.

Card game: These people met back in the tube room for a 10- to 15-minute card game before returning to work. The game was always played at Alice Homart's work station.

---

[2] In practice these breaks were observed to vary in length.

EXHIBIT 6

Question 1:	In all of American Radiatronics, whom would you say your best friend or friends are?	
Question 2:	If you were assigned to work in a room with only one other person at American Radiatronics, whom would you select?	
Question 3:	If you were assigned to work in a room with only one other person at American Radiatronics, whom would you wish to exclude?	

Respondent	*Answer to Question 1 (friends)*	*Answer to Question 2 (chosen work partner)*	*Answer to Question 3 (rejected work partners)*
Sally Ivers	Dolores Condotti Nellie MacDonald	Alice Homart	Hilda Farley Nellie MacDonald
Alice Homart	Sally Ivers	Sally Ivers	Nellie MacDonald Martha Holtz
Nellie MacDonald	Alice Homart Betty Gilen Sally Ivers	Alice Homart	Martha Holtz
Hilda Farley	Production worker outside this department	Woman in room B	No one
Martha Holtz	No one	Sally Ivers	No one
Betty Gilen	Company nurse Nellie MacDonald Alice Homart	Sally Ivers	Dolores Condotti
Sylvia Johns	No one	Martha Holtz	Nellie MacDonald Alice Homart
Dolores Condotti	George Cordoza Sally Ivers	Sally Ivers	Woman in Department B

Walks: Whenever the weather permitted, Sally Ivers and Nellie Mac-
Donald took a stroll around the perimeter of the plant site and
occasionally into the woods nearby. They had been known to persist in these walks even in a drizzle or light snow.

The pool: This consisted of a weekly drawing for high and low stakes of
a pool made up of 50-cent contributions from active members.
Names on discs were drawn from a tin can reserved for the purpose, with the high winner taking $5, and the low, the balance.
Membership in this activity included a few people from outside the
tube room. At one time the number of participants had been much
larger, including all the production workers from Room C. They
had entered the pool after asking to join it. When they came in,
three tube room girls had dropped out—Alice Homart, Nellie
MacDonald, and Martha Holtz (who at that time had been active).
When Room C later started its own pool, Alice and Nellie returned
to their pool, saying, "As long as it stays in this department we'll
come back in." Martha Holtz never returned.

The "poorbox": This referred to a weekly 25-cent collection—sometimes
raised to 50 cents when the kitty was low—used to finance special
events such as going away presents, wedding gifts, sickness and
death remembrances, etc. A limited number of extradepartmental
events could qualify, but usually the poorbox was reserved for tube
room workers. Sally Ivers administered the funds; everyone
joined in.

In addition to making these observations, the casewriter had asked
each member of the working group three questions involving certain of
their sentiments toward one another. The questions and the responses
are presented in Exhibit 6.

WORK ASSIGNMENTS AND SUPERVISORY PRACTICES

In performing their work, the women customarily obtained their
working instructions from Sally Ivers first thing in the morning. Sally
would move from one to another checking preparations, answering
questions, and discussing the day's work schedule. At times, this
instruction-giving would occur during the workday as a woman finished the batch of work she had been on. Often the exchange would be
phrased as an "Okay if I go to so and so now?" and "Sure." Or if more
detailed instructions were required, Sally and the other woman would
go over to the appropriate work stations and discuss the detail together. On a number of occasions, changes in work position or kind of
work being performed took place without any apparent prior consultation with Sally.

One of the most concrete features of work scheduling practices in the tube room was a monthly production schedule delivered to the group by the company's production planning department just before the first of each month. Ralph Langley commented about this production and how he and Sally Ivers used it in scheduling work:

Ralph Langley: *When the production sheet comes in to us, Sally and I look it over. The production planning people can make a mistake like anyone else. Sometimes the company has so many tubes of one kind in stock that I just know they couldn't have wanted as many as the schedule calls for, so I will second-guess them. I keep an eye on the main company inventory, you know; it's in the room right over there down the hall. All I have to do is walk in and look around and I can see how many of what kind of tubes are in stock. Often I happen to know how the sales are running on particular tubes. People from the sales department come down and ask questions about things—questions about tubes, how much they cost, whether we are having any particular difficulty with them. In fact, I have often spoken directly with customers. Of course, I am not supposed to do that, but they will often refer a customer to me to talk about a particular tube, and in this way I have a feeling of how the sales of different kinds of tubes are going.*

With this information about sales, inventory, stock situation, and the general work load I am able to make some pretty fair guesses about the figures that production planning has set up—that is, whether we should follow their figures or adjust them slightly. Sometimes we miss, but usually our estimates of what the best schedule should be are good. In fact, it has happened more than once that the people from production planning have come to me and asked for my opinion on how many tubes I think they should put on the production planning sheet.

One of the production women, Betty Gilen, spoke about the production schedule in the following manner:

Betty Gilen: *You'll see satisfaction written all over everyone's face the last working day of the production month when we've met schedule. You'll see them the last days before the end of the month walking to the production record over there, checking that, then checking the production schedule again on Sally's desk. It's amazing the change that begins to come over people when they move into the last part of the month and see we're going to have to step it up in order to make our quota. Everyone works a little harder, everyone tries to get her part of the work out of the way a little faster and on to the next person. This is what makes this department work together so well. Everyone, and I would say there's not a single exception to this, is willing to cooperate, and we all feel the same way about meeting schedule. Now this is provided that no one is pushing us. We meet our own schedules and no one breathes down our backs. We do it ourselves.*

ATTITUDES TOWARD THE WORK

The casewriter held a number of conversations with other women also about their work and how they felt about it.

Martha Holtz: *I like my job. It's a good job as far as jobs go. Right now I'm doing mostly coating. I have done ceramic lining for Alice Homart over there, and fire polishing, and toward the end of the month I even do testing. I can do a lot of jobs.*

I make the anodes for these tubes. We used to make them out of stainless steel, but now we always make them out of platinum. You know, that was funny. About six months ago, while we were still making them out of stainless steel, I made a mistake and made a whole batch of platinum. When I finished, I told Sally Ivers about it. She said, "That's all right, Martha, let's test them out this way and see how they are." They tested out perfectly, so she told Ralph Langley about it, and the next time I made anodes for that tube, Sally told me to make them out of platinum again because they had tested out so well. Always before, we had trouble testing out a whole batch of them without having some bad ones, and, you know, since we've been making them out of platinum, we have had hardly any bad ones at all. And to think, just because I'd made a mistake.

*   *   *   *   *

Alice Homart: [Referring to some tube stem assemblies she was reworking from a batch made a few days earlier] *We've been having a lot of trouble with leaking stems lately, and we're trying to figure out where the trouble is by studying these stems from rejected tubes. I'm spending quite a bit of time right now trying to find the trouble, so that we can get the production rate back up again.*

Casewriter: *Does anyone ever say anything to you when you get behind on production?*

Alice Homart: *You bet they do. We hear about it all right, and believe me, we hear about these leaky tubes, too. Nellie MacDonald shoots them right back at us when they don't make her leak test. That's what we're here for. No one stands over our shoulder counting what we do, but we know how many finished tubes we make and how many the production schedule calls for. Besides it's always nicer when things are going along without any trouble. You know we're not supposed to do this* [indicating the defective stem she was examining], *this is not our job. We're just production workers. We're not supposed to know the technical parts of this kind of work. The only thing is—there's no one else at the plant here who knows much more about this kind of work than we do. There's just us here in the room, so I guess it's up to Sylvia Johns and myself to figure out what goes wrong when we have trouble. Ralph Langley can help us sometimes, but he can't do everything. Besides, we're closer to the work.*

*   *   *   *   *

Sylvia Johns: *I'm a glass blower. I learned the business from my husband in Philadelphia, where we operated a neon sign glass company for 25 years before he died. I had to go back to work after he died, and that's why I'm here. I like my work here. It's a good job, but it wasn't easy for me to find the kind of work I like to do after my husband died. Actually, glass blowing is all I do here, and it's what I prefer doing, too. I never work much on tube assembly, although I guess I would if I had to. Glass work is really my line. After 25 years I know it. My husband taught me well before he died.*

*   *   *   *   *

Casewriter: [Standing beside Betty Gilen at her customary workbench] *Could you tell me the name of this place here where you seem to be working most often?*

Betty Gilen: *You could call this the heavy metal tube station. You see, I make all of the heavy tubes in here, and I guess I'm a sort of a specialist in it. But we're not making very many at the rate we're going now. Somebody goofed. These covers are made here in the machine shop, and the containers are made by a vendor, and you can see that the cover doesn't position right on the container, and that won't pass inspection.*

Casewriter: *Does this delay affect you personally?*

Betty Gilen: *Personally is right. It's driving me crazy. This is a big order, and we're way behind on it. We won't get them done—can't work on them at all. This means I haven't got anything to do, and I've got to hunt jobs. This day is 16 hours long for me these days. I like to keep busy.*

Casewriter: *Where else do you sometimes work?*

Betty Gilen: *Oh, you'll find me over at the glass machine; you'll find me at the wash basin and you've probably seen me quite a bit over at the pump stand there. You see, I do all the glass welding, connecting tubes to the vacuum outlets. It's not that it takes any kind of particular genius to do it but I'm kind of familiar with that type of work. As I say I do all kinds of things. If you want to see where I'm working you'd better look fast because I won't be there long.*

Employee attitudes toward each other

Here is how several of the women talked and behaved with respect to their relations with one another:

Alice Homart: [In response to a question about why there were two separate coffee groups] *Why, I never thought about that until you mentioned it now. We've always had the two groups, but it doesn't mean anything. We're all friendly with one another. Why we were the same way before we were in Baltimore, except for Sylvia, who's only worked here one year. I can't imagine it being different.*

Casewriter: *How do you decide when to start and stop?*

Alice Homart: *Ralph Langley says it's up to us how long we take just so we get our work out. So we don't go by the company rule. Sometimes we take 20 minutes, and sometimes quite a bit less. At the end of the month, if we're rushed, we'll cut it pretty short, but no one ever says anything to us. We just gauge it by how busy we are.*

*   *   *   *   *

Casewriter: [Addressing Betty Gilen one day at her workbench] *Are there any topics of conversation or things to talk about that you tend to avoid with one another as you visit, say, during coffee breaks, at lunch, or even during work?*

Betty Gilen: *No, I don't think so. We'll talk about our work schedule, things that happened at home, weekends, just about anything. Politics can get pretty hot, and we have had a few scrapes in the past, so we leave that one alone entirely now. I guess there is another thing too, in a general sort of way. If anyone is particularly bothered about anything we will avoid that subject, whatever it is* *that they're bothered about. We don't want to hurt anyone or make them feel bad by rubbing salt in wounds. This is especially so if it is something connected with our work here. If there is something going on that someone is particularly upset about we'll avoid talking about it as long as it is happening. Later we will talk about it and laugh over it, but not at the time. We can't afford to hurt anyone. We get along by cooperating and being friendly with one another.*

A WORK INCIDENT

One day, as the casewriter was working at his observation desk, he heard a loud pop and the sound of breaking glass. Looking up he saw Betty Gilen standing at the finished tubes inventory cabinet, with the door open, and a tray of finished tubes in her hand. At her feet were the remains of a broken tube (retail value, about $45). Sally Ivers was standing about eight feet away, working at a bench with her back to Betty. Nellie MacDonald was at her pump stand about the same distance away. Sally did not look up, but continued steadily with her work. The noise was very audible and its point of origin was also quite clear.

Nellie, from her pump stand, looked over to Betty, shook her head slowly from side to side and said, "Tsk, tsk, tsk," then made a comment having something to do with what had caused the tube to fall out of the cabinet. Betty's elbow and tray were resting close to the shelf from which the broken tube had obviously fallen. Betty corrected her position, and at the same time looked forlornly at the smashed tube. Nellie walked over to the other side of the room, obtained a broom and dustpan and swept up the mess. Betty proceeded to the electronic test stand with the tray of tubes. It would have been very easy for Betty to put the tray down and clean up the broken glass herself. Throughout the incident, neither Betty nor Nellie glanced in Sally's direction, nor did Sally change the pace of her work or look up.

RALPH LANGLEY'S BEHAVIOR

Langley had developed relationships with the group in a way which allowed him to retain a high degree of involvement in the affairs of the room without extensive personal presence on his part. He would make a tour of the room each morning near the beginning of the workday speaking briefly with nearly every one (although usually in different order from day to day) and taking part in various technical discussions. From then on, he would reappear at fairly regular intervals, two or three times during the day or when some kind of unusual work event occurred.

During his periods of absence from the room he visited the other rooms of his department, attended conferences and other scheduled meetings, paid informal visits to members of other departments in the company, or, as was more customary for extended periods of time, retired to his desk in one corner of Room B next door to the tube room. It was to this desk that members of the tube room group would come when they had a question or a problem. Any one of the women or two men from the tube room were equally likely to visit Langley at his desk, and unless the situations prompting the visit were unusually complicated or pressing, he would respond with a few words of explanation, approval, or a promise to "do something about it." During a two-day period in which Langley once happened to spend nearly all his time at his desk, these visits averaged about six or seven per day. His characteristic demeanor during interactions with subordinates was grave and intently serious, although his face would often break into fleeting smiles. Seldom effusive, he nevertheless usually managed to convey by his bearing and conversation an impression of friendliness and personal interest and of confidence in addressing problems.

Comments of the women about Langley

Sally Ivers: *If anything does go wrong around here we first of all try to find out what the trouble is ourselves and if that doesn't work we go to get Ralph. Ralph always helps us out. Ralph always knows the answers.*

*   *   *   *   *

Betty Gilen: *Ralph is fair, and he knows what he is doing.*

*   *   *   *   *

Martha Holtz: [In connection with a rumor that Ralph Langley was being considered for promotion to do a bigger job.] *Ralph, he's the best. I don't know what we would do without him. He is always so fair, treats us all alike. We're very proud of Ralph. We would miss him terribly if he left.*

*   *   *   *   *

Nellie MacDonald: *If Ralph were promoted, we all would be very pleased for him. He deserves it, and it's time he went on to bigger things. But as for me, it would mean I'd lost my purpose for working. That guy made our work something it had never been before. I would never be able to feel the same way about George.* [George Cortoza, foreman in Production Room C, was rumored to be Ralph's replacement.] *George is all right. He's pleasant, and he's a nice guy, but I have a respect for Ralph I'd never be able to develop for George. And it's not only respect I feel for Ralph. Ralph is my friend. I look forward to work every morning. We're a zany bunch—real screwballs—you couldn't find a bunch of people anywhere with more different personalities than we have. You've seen the way we horse around, the stunts we pull, and we don't feel the least bit embarrassed*

*about it. We can get away with anything, but when it comes to our work, there's
no one better than we are either. Now this is just a small department here, and
I'm not over anyone, but I feel important. I feel there's a purpose in my life. I'm
responsible for the pump stand and it's a critical part of the operation in there. It's
a part of me and I'm part of it. I worry about how it's going. I'm checking it over
all the time, and I'm turning out a lot of work on it.*

*But you see, it's not only the pump stand. It's how Ralph and people like him
can make you feel about it. I know I'm not very bright and it doesn't take much
for anyone to make me feel really stupid, but Ralph has never done that. He's
always made me feel that I've got ideas that are useful. Now, I know my
knowledge about the pump stand is very limited, and I lean a great deal on Ralph
to help me out of scrapes, but you know, everytime I talk over a problem with
him I feel as though I'm learning something. And I am learning!*

*Right now we've run into a problem on the pump stand. There's something
wrong in the exhaust manifold system. We're not getting the tubes clean enough.
Sally and I have gone over and over the system and we don't know what it is. We
will wait for Ralph until he has time, and we know eventually he will help us out.
Sure, we've got an engineer assigned to the department who is supposed to take
care of these problems for us. We're not supposed to; we're just production girls,
not supposed to know anything. And, brother, is the engineer convinced of that!
I'd walk out of the plant before I'd turn to him for help on my pump. He doesn't
really know much about them, and with what little he does know, he makes you
feel so darn stupid in such a short time, you could scream. We don't need him in
here and don't want him. Ralph, on the other hand, has a way of using his
knowledge to help a person build up her own knowledge. He gives it to you—he
doesn't use it on you. That's how I feel about Ralph as a friend and as the best
boss I've ever had.*

RALPH LANGLEY

The casewriter talked to Ralph Langley on a number of occasions
about Langley's perceptions of his job and his concepts of himself as a
manager. Following are excerpts from some of these conversations.

Excerpt 1   Langley on his relations with the tube room production
employees.

Ralph Langley: [Speaking about what had been responsible for the marked improvement in the group's performance over the past two years.] *I would say it was
mostly a matter of treating the women in there the way they wanted to be treated
and needed to be treated in order to feel as though they were part of American
Radiatronics.*

*When I took over the department, one of the first things I told them was to
forget about standards, to figuratively throw the standards out, pretend they
didn't even exist—to just do the best job they knew how. I told them I felt they
were working for American Radiatronics and not for me, that my job was to help
them and not tell them what to do, and that they were strictly on their own as far
as getting out production, scheduling their work, pacing themselves, watching*

their own waste, and so on. If they got into trouble they could ask me for help, and I would give it to them. Above all, I told them, we were going to be interested in making a better tube and learning how to do our job better at all times. They didn't believe me at first. Some of them gave me a really rough time, but gradually they learned I meant what I said and things began to improve.

I have no supervisor in the room. Sally is group leader for the others, but each person in the room is responsible for her own operation. I'm always careful and insistent that they're given credit for everything they do. If she gets into trouble, or if she has a question, she's free to come to me directly. I then work out her problems with her personally. When I'm presented with a problem, such as an order for extra work from one of the other departments, I'm able to just turn it over to one of the women, and it gets done.

I go in to them every now and then, just now and then, to keep an eye on things and to stay in touch. I check the production record to see how things are going, and I always speak to the women. I try to be careful, whenever I come into the room to see that I always talk to a different person first each time. This way each one feels she is getting her fair share of attention. I talk with them about whatever is of interest to them. If it is about their families, fine—if it is about work, fine.

I keep no secrets from the women. They know as much about this operation and about what is going on in the top offices as I do. I'm honest with them and I ask that they be honest with me. This has paid off, too, because none of the women is afraid to admit her mistakes and they're always anxious to learn how to do something better. Of course, I may be exaggerating this a little bit. I have noticed here lately that there is almost a tinge of neuroticism in the way several of the group have become so concerned about production and quality. It causes a little stir now and then.

Excerpt 2   Langley on motivation.

Ralph Langley: A person spends the majority of his waking hours on the job. It seems to me that the job should be important, that the job should represent the source of greatest satisfactions that a person experiences. To feel that satisfactions should be obtained only off the job is not realistic. People get drunk, or go to shows, but that doesn't always lead to the kinds of satisfaction that they really need. People need to feel important, to feel as though life is worthwhile, and to feel as though they're accomplishing something. These needs can be satisfied on the job, but it doesn't just happen by accident. You have to work at it.

One of my firmest beliefs is that the trouble with most managers is the way they think about their people. They see the company as the center of everything—and they're really thinking about themselves when they think about the company. They then see workers as something clustering around this central company or management—that is, they're only there to serve management's interests, to work for management. But these people, these workers, are the same as you and I, and they are the same as management.

The boss that uses workers to build his or her own ego, to satisfy his or her sense of power and prestige, is not doing right by the workers. They'll act just the way he or she treats them. As long as the worker is seen as something to be used *by the company, he or she will resent it and give no more than he or she has to. But if the worker can be motivated, I'm convinced that any worker has a potential of productivity that's greatly in excess of anything that he or she usually gives.*

Excerpt 3 Langley on controlling subordinates' choice of task.

Ralph Langley: *There is the kind of work you get out of people when they are doing what is prescribed for them to do and then there is the bonus you get when they are doing what they want to do. I want Bill and Tom to figure out for themselves what they want to do, what they are happiest at, and let them do it as much as I can. That is my way of thinking.*

Take Tom for instance. Prior to Tom's going into Room A, which was about a year to a year and one-half ago, 65 to 70 units a month of the work in there was considered to be a good production record. The man in there before Tom did manage to get it up to about 100 units a month. When Tom took over he managed to get up to 110 units per month quite quickly without trying too hard. So I just left him alone, raised the standard up to that, and he kept pushing it ahead. Now we are doing more work than ever in there—he has hit as much as 160 to 180 units a month and yet frequently he is able to come in here and put in the equivalent of a full day's work in the tube room. That is what I mean by the bonus you get for letting people do the kind of work they want to do.

Tom is doing more than what was a full day's work in Room A previously, and at the same time he is doing a lot in here besides. He wanted to do this so he just figured out how he could get things done in there quicker in order to spend more time in here. I want him to find out what he likes to do best. Right now I am kind of pushing him to take on the pump stand work, which he is doing besides picking up a lot of various maintenance work. No one knows at this time what he will end up liking best, but he is free to go in either direction without my telling him which one to take on. If it develops that he prefers the maintenance equipment kind of work I'll ease off on the pump stand encouragement, and let Nellie MacDonald take on more of that. It's up to Tom.

One thing, and this is important. I'm not trying to handle Tom. Tom isn't trying to work harder, and I don't think I could make him work harder. The reason he is doing as well as he is is because he hasn't been thinking in terms of getting more work done; he has been thinking about learning and about getting ahead. I know he would think I was taking advantage of him if all he heard from me was getting more work out. For instance, if instead of feeling the way I do I felt that Tom wasn't getting enough work done out there in Room A, I wouldn't push him. I would leave him alone to find his way. As it is now, he moves in, he learns more, he takes on more and more responsibility. This is the way you grow. I changed his grade when I opened the door for him to go into the tube room. I jumped him up two grades. When I see he can take on more work yet I'll jump him again.

Excerpt 4 Langley on the use of work standards and budgets.

Ralph Langley: *I believe in work standards as a yardstick of measurement that has no inherent validity of its own but does have a practical value. To me, the function of the standards is to serve as a guidepost on the side of the road to tell us where* we are today in relation to where we were yesterday and where we think we can go tomorrow. They provide management a means of determining in advance what they can sell their product for while being competitive and profitable.

It isn't the standard that should determine how people work or pace themselves; instead the energy, drive, and interest they put in their work should be determined by how they feel about their work. I've indoctrinated my people to use standards just as a guide.

I tell my people, "You should be taking your incentive from yourselves." But I also emphasize to them that it is of vital interest to the company and therefore to themselves that they make the operation as profitable as possible because they, the workers, are just as meaningfully the company as management or the stockholders are, and in many ways even more so. I drive into them that one of the important satisfactions available to them is being engaged in a successful profitable activity. "After all," I tell them, "work is a way of life," and we've got to be getting something out of it as people. One of these things that can be important is the knowledge that we are connected with a successful operation that we helped make that way.

I have a budget, but I don't use my budget to control my people. Rather, I use it as something which they themselves can get satisfaction out of. For instance, we have cut our operating expenses way down since I took over, but I didn't do it, my people did it.

Our department maintenance man, Bill Yoost, administers our supplies expense budget himself. He does all his own ordering and he does it in accordance with the amount of money that he has available in his budget. These are supplies that are not used only by himself but by the girls in the department as well. Since they all know that it's up to them to control their expenses, they do it. If someone from another department comes and tries to borrow something which they know has been charged against their budget, they simply won't allow it. They'll say, "No, you'll run our expense budget over. You'll have to get it somewhere else."

I go over the budget with Bill once a month, whenever it comes out. We talk about it. From then on it's up to him. I keep an eye on it every now and then just to see that he isn't running too far out on a limb, and if I see something wrong, I'll ask him about it. But if he tells me that he's making out all right, I let him go.

Excerpt 5 Langley on required features of his department's organization.

Ralph Langley: *There are three things I'm very firm on in the department. One of them is the production schedule. That's sacred! That is a must. Under all circumstances we must produce the schedule.*

Casewriter: *Is this because your superiors have imposed the schedule on you that same way too?*

Ralph Langley: *No, it's because I want it that way. This is what we're in business for. We want to get goods out the door. The way we go about doing that will, of course, make a difference in how successfully we accomplish the things not directly connected with production that are also real and important. But we want to keep the record straight. There is no wavering or compromise on the schedule. That will not be tolerated and everyone knows it.*

Second are the employee evaluation sheets. These sheets are absolutely required by management and I can't get around them. I don't like them; I think
they can do more harm than good at times, but they are there and I have to go
along with them.

The third thing is that I expect my people in this department to get along with
one another. I say to them, "You must adjust to and with the group—become a
part of it. At the least, you must have a willingness to try to do this." I think they
all know this, I've told them so directly and I've talked about and around it
repeatedly on every occasion I could. This doesn't mean I forbid people to have
personal differences. That would be stupid. But I do require that they overcome
whatever personal differences they might have to the extent of being able to
function cooperatively with one another. Two years ago, I had to get rid of a
woman who just had to fight with everyone she worked with. I tried my best to
help her, but it did no good. So I fired her, and everyone knew why, too.

Excerpt 6   Langley on relations between groups at American Radia-
tronics.

Ralph Langley: *Ryerson from the research department wants to use Sally on some
special work he needs to have done in the electronics lab. He likes to have her
do it because it's very delicate work and no one can do it as well as she can. I
told him I'd speak to Sally and that he should check back later to talk to her
himself. You know, we do this sort of thing back and forth all the time. We help
them out and they help us out and there's a good relationship all around, but
good relations have to be built. They don't just happen.*

*I started out in just small ways doing things for them, and as we began to
build mutual trust and confidence, they started doing little things for us. Gradually, these exchanges got bigger. I once spent close to four weeks almost full time
helping them out on some equipment setup they were working on. There were
four of us, three of them and myself. We formed a team, made our own designs,
then put it together. It worked out very well.*

*Their glass blower comes up here and does all our glass system repair work
for us. If we ever need any stopcocks or other parts in a hurry we just ask for them
and get them without any questions. Now if any other department should try to
do this, they would be out of them. There has never been a piece of paper passed
between us. They've never asked us to sign for anything or keep records. We
don't distinguish between ourselves as far as things we can do together or for one
another are concerned. It's a good feeling.*

*This is an important problem at American Radiatronics—how to build rela-
tionships between different groups. Right now relations are generally pretty poor:
foremen fighting with one another, saying this man is holding me up because he
isn't getting the right parts to me or that man is holding me up for any one of a
dozen reasons they will have. They say they're overloaded. They just can't get
the work out with the manpower and equipment they've got. The schedule is too
tight, parts are too slow. I just don't think this is true. I think there is plenty of
manpower here and the productive capacity of each department is at least twice
what they're getting out of them now. I think these problems are in the men
themselves and in their relations with one another. They don't trust one another.*

*They're fighting instead of cooperating; protecting themselves rather than work-
ing freely and confidently. It's around this problem, in little ways, that I'd like to
do more. I'd like to begin to turn the tide if I could some way.*

Another view of the nuclear tube room

The casewriter interviewed Harold Singer, an engineer from the
company's industrial engineering department who was familiar with
the nuclear tube room. Mr. Singer and his colleagues served as central
staff specialists for various operating departments and also worked on
product development, production process planning, and technical aspects of long-range business planning. Excerpts from the interview are
given below:

Harold Singer: *I really can't understand how this operation makes money. The products are primitive in design, no changes have been made in years, and there's no
engineering control of any kind. Everything is run on a casual hit or miss basis. It
shouldn't make money, but somehow it does . . . .*

*Dollarwise they're doing a pretty good job in here, as far as it goes, but
they've got one overriding weakness in the way they are presently set up. Do you
realize the people do all their own testing in here? The same people that make
the tubes test them. It just isn't logical. It's against human nature. You can't trust
the same people who make something to also test it. It's not healthy. They'll
always try to protect themselves. This group of test equipment over here should
be operated by a distinctly separate group of people completely removed from
the production and under different supervision.*

*We've got plans in the works for taking on this place and really making it
over. And when we do we'll see to it that the testing operations are carried on in
a separate department. We'll really whip this operation into shape . . . .*

*There's a tremendous potential in this kind of activity, but it's never been
exploited. We've got designs on the board right now that would revolutionize the
way of doing things around here if we could get them going. I'd like to make this
a model showplace for the company. Right now it's the worst in the company.
Look at all this dirt around and the disorganization . . . .*

*This place has never been under engineering control. That's the trouble with
it. The products and processes here now are what they've traditionally been from
almost the start. Most of the product design changes that have been made have
been developed and put into practice by the production people themselves.
That's not good. Too much can creep into an organization that way that isn't
good for it. They design their own products, they alter and maintain their own
production equipment and processes, and they are free to go off in all different
directions at once. The first thing we would do if we could get hold of this room
would be to put every operation under close engineering surveillance. The
whole setup needs to be revamped and overhauled from one end to the other.
We'll do it too. You won't recognize it two years from now.*

*Some of the new products we have in mind will call for a level of sophistica-
tion in production methods, equipment design, and cleanliness that'll make this*

look sick. You've seen pictures of how some of these production departments look in other companies—cleanliness precautions that make them look like operating rooms, temperature and humidity controls, all white painted walls and equipment. That's what we'll have here. Personnel is right now looking into available sources of production workers for us, and when we start getting them in here and training them properly and install modern production methods with the true mass production setup then you'll see what this department can do . . . .

I'd like to think time zero for this department's operations in this company's history will start three months from now. We've got all the preliminary design work and process system concepts worked out already, and in about three months we'll begin to pick up some real speed. Two years from now you won't know the place. In contrast, everything that will have gone on before will be nothing. Take a good look around at what you see in here right now, you'll never see it again. Before long it will be like looking back at the covered wagon era.

Case 10–2
The Nuclear Tube Assembly Room (B)*

One Monday morning, the casewriter first heard about the problem of leaking stems in the nuclear tube assembly room at American Radiatronics.[1] As events subsequently unfolded, the leaky stem problem and the way it was handled provided a useful example of the dynamics of the tube assembly room group.

The casewriter learned of the problem from Alice Homart, who commented, "We sure have been having a lot of this stem trouble lately. We've got to figure out what the problem is. It's a headache."

The next day, Nellie MacDonald was explaining the leak test she was giving tubes on the test stand. She said,

> You see, I test them here on the leak detector by first exhausting the air then passing this little jet of helium gas past the anode and cathode connections in the stem, and if there's a leak it will show up on this dial reading. I collect the bad ones and send them back to Alice. We've had a string of bad stems now for three months, and we can't seem to figure out what the trouble is. It's hurting our dollar volume badly.

Later in the same day, Sally Ivers, the group leader, commented about the problem.

> Our rate of leaking tubes went from around 5 percent up to 25 percent or 30 percent of tubes made. This is what I would call a real problem.

---

* All names have been disguised.
[1] See the Nuclear Tube Assembly Room (A).

We've tried ever since we discovered it to correct for it but no luck so far. Ralph Langley has been in on it all along but it kind of has him stumped too. We once thought we had the answer. Martha [Holtz] was being too rough on the leads when she filed them before putting tubes on. I talked to her about it and the next batch came out okay, but then the rate went up again.

Casewriter: *Is there anything you're doing right now on the problem?*

Sally Ivers: *Yes, we think the trouble might be in the glass we've been using for the beading sleeve around the cathode lead. The glass manufacturer's catalog says we should be using the three-mill sleeve for a good seal, but we've decided to try a two-mill sleeve to see if that will give us less bubbling. We have a batch of the new stems in the annealing oven right now and we'll inspect them, seal them to tube walls, and leak test them tomorrow. Maybe that will like the problem. If it doesn't we'll have to try something else.*

Alice Homart was at her workbench reworking some stems that had appeared to be defective by visual inspection. She commented:

Alice Homart: *I'm working these over because we've been having so many bad stems lately that if I don't try to salvage the work we already have in these, our shrinkage rate is going to shoot sky high. Our trouble is little bubbly cracks. I just got these back from Martha. She had been filing the nickel blocks on the leads. It doesn't take much pressure on the lead to open up cracks down inside here.*

You know everyone looks to me to lick this problem. It's a glass problem, and I'm involved pretty much in the glass work. It's driving me crazy. Sylvia [Johns] and I keep going over and over our work trying to find something wrong but we're doing it just the same way we always did.

I think our real problem is the leads we use. If a lead isn't perfectly clean we'll get outgassing from it when the annealing heat is put on and that's the start of cracking. We buy the leads from outside but the cleaning is done here in the hydrogen furnace. Bill [Yoost] does that. I don't think he's doing it right. He's not leaving them in long enough or the furnace atmosphere isn't clean enough or something. This leak business is a real headache. I just won't feel comfortable until we solve it.

The next morning the casewriter asked Ralph Langley about the problem:

Ralph Langley: *I've been involved in the stem problem from the beginning, but it's a problem the department's going to have to work out. They keep me informed, and I talk it over with them, give them my ideas when I have any. Glass work is a technology of its own. You've got to be familiar with it from many years' experience and involvement in working with it. Alice and Sylvia have that knowledge, they see it as their problem, and it is. They'll work it out eventually.*

I've made it known to my bosses that we're having trouble with leaky stems. I always try to forewarn the management about these problems even before they become obvious problems so that they will know what to expect of us. That way, pressure doesn't build up on the department for not coming through with what had been expected of them.

A big part of the problem is that stem machine over there. That's a real pile of junk but we really can't justify replacing it with a new one on an economic basis because we just don't make that many tubes. The girls know these facts and they're willing to live with the old one and just be extra careful with it. They'd still like to solve the problem, however, and they're doing everything in their power to get around it in some other way.

As the casewriter left Langley's desk area and returned to the tube room, he observed Sally Ivers typing tube labels on her typewriter when Alice Homart walked up carrying the test batch of completed tube stems.

Alice Homart: *Sally, there isn't a single good one in the bunch here. We've just gotten them back from Martha.*

Sally Ivers: *Yes, I see what you mean. They're cracked right down here at the base. Martha didn't file these, did she?*

Alice Homart: *Oh yes, she did! I saw her, she said she couldn't get the wire to stick to the cathode so she filed them down to clean them.*

Ralph Langley: [Who had just walked into the room] *Well, how'd they turn out?*

Alice Homart: *Every one of them cracked. Not a good one in the bunch, Ralph.*

Sally Ivers: *Martha filed the cathodes. She couldn't get the wire to stick so she filed them all down.*

Ralph Langley: *Oh, oh. There goes our test.*

Alice Homart: [walking away] *Well, at least I'm glad it's off my shoulders now.*

Sally Ivers: *It's really my fault, Ralph. I guess I just didn't make it clear to Martha that she was not supposed to file the wire under any circumstances. I just told her to make them up the same way she made up the "sixes."* [Sixes referred to another tube stem customarily made up the same way the test batch was to have been made up.] *I guess she couldn't make them stick in spot welding so instead of cleaning them electronically with sodium hydroxide she filed them.*

Alice Homart: *But now we know where the trouble is anyway. These were all perfect when we checked them this morning and this is the only operation performed on them since.*

Ralph Langley: [Quietly and without evident display of emotion] *Yes, that's right. Well, we'll just make up a new batch.*

Sally Ivers: *And we'll be sure Martha understands how to clean them without filing.*

Ralph Langley: *Okay* [walks away].

Alice Homart went to her end of the room and Sally Ivers returned to her typing. Shortly thereafter the casewriter started a conversation with Alice Homart.

Casewriter: *Does this mean you're all pretty sure now the cracking occurs as a result of filing the cathodes?*

Alice Homart: *Yes, I'm afraid it does. We all three inspected these stems this morning and now you can see what they're like.*

Casewriter: *Did you see Martha filing the stems?*

Alice Homart: *Sure I did, and she told me too that she was going to do it, that she couldn't get the springs to stick. But it's not my job to do anything about that. I'm just here to do my work and not interfere with anybody else doing their work.*

Casewriter: *Were you tempted to say anything to her?*

Alice Homart: *And have her blow up in my face? Oh no! I've been through that before. There are some people you can't tell anything to. Most of us make our mistakes and then admit them, but not Martha. We all saw what she was doing. Nellie and Betty [Gilen] were standing right over there, too, as she tried to spot-weld the prongs, couldn't, and said she was going to file them. They didn't say anything either. Some people are perfect, they don't make mistakes. The rest of us just have to suffer along with it. But at least it puts me in the clear.*

You're really seeing us at our worst now. It's too bad you couldn't have been here when things were going along smoothly. Then you could have seen how we really operate. Usually we don't have any problems like this.

Shortly after this conversation with Alice Homart, the casewriter noticed Ralph Langley talking with Martha Holtz. Later in the day he asked Ralph what took place in that conversation.

Ralph Langley: *I had an idea that she might need a little bolstering up so I stopped by and asked "How's it going?" the same question I always ask people when I stop to talk with them. She was looking real glum. I grinned and said: "Oh, come on now, don't be like that," as though I were telling her in a kidding way, "don't be a bad girl now." She said, "They're trying to blame me for those bad tubes." I said, "No one's blaming you, Martha. We've got a problem and we're trying so hard to find it, we're apt to feel a little guilty about it, all of us. We're just a little touchy."*

Then I explained to her the various technical parts of the problem, and how important it was that everything be examined closely. Then she said, "They didn't tell me that these were supposed to be done the same way as the sixes." I replied "I know, Sally told me that she forgot to tell you, so as far as I'm concerned, the first one didn't work out and we'll make some more. The important thing is that we get the answer." I then switched the conversation over to the weekend fishing she and her husband had been doing. We visited for a while, then I left.

When the casewriter came into the tube room several days later, he found all work at a standstill. Nellie and Betty rushed up to him to say that Ralph had asked Sally to call Alice, Sylvia, and Martha into his office for a conference.

Betty Gilen: *Oh boy, it's finally out in the open and am I ever glad. We have never had anything like this before. In five years we have never had this kind of dissension, conflict, backstabbing, accusing back and forth. We know who it is. It's not fair, but we are prejudiced. We never had a single solitary bit of this kind of trouble until she came.*

Nellie MacDonald: [Interrupting] *If she thinks we are not good enough for her here, why doesn't she go back to where she came from? Do you know what she once said to Alice? She said, "I am not used to such a queer bunch of people." Imagine! We didn't ask her to come here!*

Casewriter: *Who are you talking about?*

Betty Gilen: *Sylvia Johns. As far as she is concerned everything she does is perfect. Where she came from is perfect, her friends, the people she used to associate with were perfect. The rest of us admit it when we are wrong. We don't mind making mistakes. We know that every time we do, we learn something, and that is how we handle our problems.*

Nellie MacDonald: *Another thing, have you noticed how she and that David of hers are always huddled together, always conniving, always going behind our backs?[2] They think they know more than all of us about glass work. Why, Alice knows more in her little finger than those two will ever know. What does she have to keep bringing him into our problems for? He's not one of us.*

I saw him walking out of here the other day with a box of stems sort of hidden under his arms. And then to find out later that he had been working on our stuff. Right now he has some of my tubes that I've already vacuum tested down there testing them again. My tubes, imagine. If I hadn't tested those tubes right, I don't want to find out from him, I want to find out from Ralph or Sally. He's not from our department.

Betty Gilen: *Nellie's absolutely right. We solve our own problems first. If we can't, we get Sally in on it, and then Ralph if we need him, and if Ralph can't handle it we turn it over to engineering and get regular proper company personnel to help us out. We don't want to find out from an outsider that we've been doing something wrong even before we've worked it through ourselves.*

You know Sylvia is not the only one that never makes mistakes. Martha is the same way. Just can't ever acknowledge she has done anything less than perfect. That is why Alice is caught in the middle. How do you work with people like that? This is really the problem. Since it's the three of them who take care of the glass work, it affects all of us. I'm glad it's out in the open now. Maybe we can do something about it.

Just then Martha Holtz came walking hurriedly back into the room and went immediately over to the sink at the other end of the room to attend to something in it. Betty Gilen left to go over to talk with Martha. Just about this time, Sylvia Johns returned with what appeared as a very set, tense look on her face, and walked directly over to her sealing machine where she began to perform some puttering-type operations with the work set up on it. It was then time for lunch, and the group began to go out. No one spoke to Sylvia.

After lunch the casewriter talked with Martha and asked her what was going on.

---

[2] David Johns, the son of Sylvia Johns, worked as an expert on glass in another department of the company. Ralph Langley occasionally called on him for technical advice.

Martha Holtz: *Oh, you know this problem about leaking stems we have been hav-*
ing. Well, it finally came out in the open.

Martha then went on to describe events that transpired in the meeting in Ralph Langley's office that morning. She said she had told them
of her complaints about the condition of the stem machine and about
the "underhanded" accusations Alice had been making and the general
unpleasantness of recent weeks.

Martha Holtz: *Then Ralph asked me if I would be willing to forget all that happened*
and start from the beginning again as though nothing had ever happened before.
I said sure I would and Sylvia said she would too. But Alice said no, she couldn't.
I had to see to these leads I had washing in the sink here, so I left just after that.

    I am glad it is out in the open. I couldn't have stood it much more. Always
being accused of doing something wrong, never knowing what someone is
saying behind my back. All I want is a job and to draw a day's or a week's pay.
I'm easily satisfied.

Following this talk with Martha, the casewriter joined Alice Homart
who had just returned from having a late lunch. She and Ralph Langley
had stayed on in his office talking after Martha and Sylvia had left and
then later had had lunch together.

Alice Homart: *This is the end as far as I am concerned. I hate to leave Ralph in the*
lurch, but I can't see taking any more of this. If that is what they think of me, if
that is the way they are talking about me, I don't see how I can stay around here.
Maybe they're right. Maybe I have been doing all those things they accuse me of.
I don't know. They said I was going behind their backs complaining to Ralph and
Sally about them, trying to get them in trouble, lying about them, accusing them
of doing things wrong that I had really done wrong myself. I was only doing my
job. I'm responsible for the glass work here. We've had a problem, and I was
trying to find the answer.

    For weeks now it has been building up. Everyone is so perfect, neither one of
them even willing to concede to the possibility that the trouble might be in
something they were doing. If Sylvia is so damned perfect what did she come
here for!

    For 11 months now I've been trying to help her, trying to show her how we do
things. And this is what I get for it. When she first came here she didn't have a
single friend. I belong to the Eagles Club Women's Auxiliary. We're a nice bunch
of people there. I'm a widow and so was Sylvia. So I started taking her to our
dinners and dances. I got her dates. I took her in as a friend. This is what I meant
the other day when you asked me who my friends were and I said, "It doesn't
pay to be too friendly with anyone at work." I introduced her to one man who
became very much interested in her. And I really tried to help that romance
along. Then she got into troubles with him, wouldn't speak to him. Then the first
thing I knew Sylvia was accusing me of being responsible for their not getting
along. Ever since then we began to have a strain between us. Nothing I would do
at work here was right. She would be suspicious of every little thing I did, saying I
was making trouble for her.

She thinks she knows everything there is to know about glass blowing. No one does. And that David of hers. Every time I turn around he is sneaking behind my back checking my work. Accusing me of doing this wrong or that wrong. She takes it upon herself to set her own son up as an expert to judge our work and tell us what we have been doing wrong.

Sylvia and I have to work closely together. We divide up the work. Sylvia is a good enough worker all right. She knows her glass, but how can you work and get along with people when people don't trust you? Like the way this all started last night. I went over to Sally with a tray of stems. I said I was not accusing anybody of anything but can I make up a tray of stems myself just to see how a batch I made up would work out. Sally said to go ahead. All of this time Sylvia was watching us like a hawk. When I started to work, she turned around, looked at what I was doing, got up, and stormed over to Sally. I could see her hollering to her, waving her arms all excited, and telling her Lord knows what about me. That is why Ralph called the meeting for today.

Nothing is settled. We're right back where we started. Ralph asked Martha and Sylvia if they would be willing to forget everything that had happened. They both said they would. But you know they were just saying it. Nothing had really changed. Ralph asked me if I would do the same. I said, "No, Ralph, I can't, it has gone too far. I'm handing in my resignation. I would like to leave at the end of the month." Ralph was very upset about this, and I guess I was crying pretty bad. I don't want to leave the company. I like it here. I have always gotten along well with everyone until this started. I'd probably have a hard time finding as good a job as this one, but life is too short. No job is worth what I have been through.

I have a lot of friends here I am pretty sure they would rather I didn't leave. I hate to leave the department in the lurch because good glass blowers are hard to find. It would hurt the department I know if I'd leave them now. I think I'll be able to make out all right here until I leave. At least we know where we stand. I know just how I will act with Sylvia from now on. I will speak to her and be pleasant but it will only be on work matters. I think as long as we keep it that way we'll get by. I don't mind telling you that it has been pretty awful. I felt all tightened up inside, and whatever it was wouldn't let go. It's really quite amazing that I could feel as much better as I do now.

Shortly after this conversation, the casewriter talked to Sylvia Johns during her afternoon coffee break.

Sylvia Johns: *Every time we've had leaking stems, Alice has said, "Maybe you're doing this wrong; maybe you're doing that wrong." And every time she goes to Sally or Ralph to tell them what I'm doing that's not right. I can't stand it any more. I have been doing everything I could to help find out what causes those stems to leak. David has been working a long time with me on that, too. He knows more about glass than Alice or I do together, and all they do is criticize David and me for trying to do what is right. This is not the way to solve a problem. Each of us should be willing to consider what it is we're doing that might be wrong.*

She's all the time talking about solving our problems, working out our difficulties together, and then running to Sally each time she thought she had something on me. First it was Martha that was breaking the glass when she filed the leads. Then it was Bill, not cleaning the leads well enough in the furnace, and then last night I saw what she did—she took a tray of my stems to Sally and showed her how they are all bad and then she came back to her place and started making stems herself. Making the stems is my job. She had been trying to blame me all along, but she couldn't. So she would blame this person, then that person, and finally she thought she could show where it was me.

When I saw her talk to Sally and then start making stems herself, I went up to Sally and I said, "Has Alice been blaming me for those stems?" Sally said, "No, she wasn't blaming you. She just wanted to try making some herself." But why should she try making stems herself if it wasn't to prove it on me? So I said to Sally, "This is the end. I won't work this way any more." Sally didn't say anything, but she knew what I meant. That is why Ralph called the meeting; because I talked to him myself later in the day, and then I saw him and Sally talking together.

In the meeting, Alice started talking, oh so sweet, about how she was trying her best to solve the problem, but no one would cooperate with her and check their own work. That's when I knew I had to say something. We're not supposed to tell stories on each other and I never have until today, even though this is what Alice has been doing all along. I said, "Alice, you are lying. You have not been acting the way you say, at all. You have been telling everyone that it was Martha, then it is me, and it is everybody but yourself. You act like you never make any mistakes of your own. Well, maybe that is because nobody ever squeals on you. You remember that time you put those insulators you make into the annealing oven at 550 degrees and they all bent? They should have been at 450 degrees. I knew that was soft glass, and I told you that, but I didn't say anything to anybody about that until just now. Why can't you do the same?"

She started to cry then, and she should have. Martha told her some things, too. Later, Ralph asked us if we would forget everything and start over again, being friendly with one another. I said I would and Martha said she would too, but Alice said she wanted to quit. I know what she was doing. She stayed on to talk to Ralph after Sally and I left, and now I can see she thinks she has won some kind of battle. Since lunch, she's been going all around the room, talking to all her friends, going yak, yak, yak, giggle, giggle, and I just sit at my bench—[pause]. Oh, I don't know what I'm going to do. I haven't slept for weeks thinking about all this and every day at work it's been terrible.

Late in the afternoon Ralph Langley invited the casewriter into his office to talk about the meeting that had been held there that morning. He sketched out events that had happened as follows:

Ralph Langley: *This whole thing came as somewhat of a surprise to me. I had known for quite a while that there was bad feeling beginning to develop in the room over the leaking stems. We've had that sort of thing crop up from time to time then work itself out. We've had this very bad leaking stem situation for eight weeks anyway and we've been giving attention to the problem from time to time, but it's not a real crisis. At one time we went for six weeks without producing a single tube of one particular variety because of a problem we were having with it. That was real money. By way of contrast, we have suffered about a 25* *percent to 30 percent drop 1n production on the stem production for the one type of tube, and the final department output of finished tubes hasn't been affected to even that extent. Neither Sally nor myself have ever said there was anything critical or pressing about this stem thing from management's position.*

The last few days, I could see that Alice and Sylvia were pretty tense; and you noticed the other day how I tried to cool Martha off. I also knew that the whole department's efficiency had slipped noticeably during the previous week. Yesterday afternoon I asked Sally what was wrong. She said, "Nothing is wrong, Ralph, we're okay in here." "Aw, come on now, Sally, tell me," I said, "what's going on in here? You know I know there's something brewing. Why is the volume falling off in everything?"

Then Sally began to bring me up to date on Alice and Sylvia. She said, "I guess Alice and Sylvia are at just about the hairpulling stage. Every little thing is being blown up into something serious. The tension is terrible. Martha is in the middle of it, too. The whole group is upset." I asked her if she felt it would help things if I got the girls together and talked to them. She did. "Okay," I said, "let's get it out on the table." It was after this meeting that the big blow-up between Alice and Sylvia happened.

When we all got together, I told them that I understood how everyone had gotten so tense and nervous over those stems. Then I said, "It has spread to every girl in the room, and the whole department is suffering." "Now," I said, "let's face it, you're acting like a bunch of children. You're not children; you're grown, mature women, and isn't it time you stopped all this and started to build up your relations with one another?" I had led up to this slowly, giving them every impression that I understood what their feelings were, not denying them, but telling them also that it was time to stop and to do something about it. I sat back and let it explode, and boy, did it, all over the place! There were feelings being spilled in every direction. They all said things they were going to regret later but it had to happen that way.

When I thought it had gone on long enough, I said, "Okay, hold it just a minute. I would like to make a suggestion." I outlined a proposition whereby Alice and Sylvia could each make up a batch of stems in their own way and determine in this manner once and for all, whether one was right and the other was wrong or both wrong or both right. I told them the outcome didn't matter to me. This would be for their benefit, to find out something. I didn't get a big response, so I let it go.

Feelings were still running high so I let it rage on again for a while and then told them in no uncertain terms that this was going to have to stop. I asked them if they were willing to forget all this and start fresh. Martha said she would and so did Sylvia, but Alice said she couldn't. About this time Martha had to leave, and shortly after that Sally picked up my cue that I would like to talk to Alice and left with Sylvia. Alice had a lot of emotions that hadn't gotten expressed yet. I listened to her and gave her every chance to tell me how things were. I told her how important it was for the department and to me, personally, that she stay on. Alice was very much calmed down when we broke up but I still didn't know for sure what she would do about staying or not.

Have you noticed how she's been acting this afternoon? You wouldn't know she's the same person she was this morning. I was talking with Sally about something a little earlier when Alice walked over to me with the springiest step and said, "Ralph, I only want to say one thing. I feel wonderful." At that she turned and walked off. Isn't that the darndest thing? She had been visiting with other girls and working with real spirit. I think it'll work out now.

The thing to do now is to let things take their natural course. I think Martha's all right, but Sylvia's not back into shape. It will take a little more time with her. I think she feels she's lost some kind of battle and the only thing that will correct that is to let the girls begin to work their way back to one another again. One thing will lead to another and they'll all be good friends again. It will never be the same as it was, but this does not necessarily mean it is all bad. There might even be some real good come of this. The important thing is that nothing interferes with the healing process.

About one week later the casewriter had a conversation with Sylvia Johns in which he asked her if any recent incidents had given her real satisfaction. She commented on a good batch of tubes, and then said, "One thing, Alice has started speaking to me again. That makes me feel good. It's just a little at a time, you know, but it's something."

The following day, he asked the same question of Alice Homart. She said, "You know, as far as the big fight is concerned, I think that will work out in the end all right. Things won't ever really be the same again but some real good might come of it. Look at what it has done for production. We're all of us really working, have been ever since this all came to a head. I know I'll never be able to be friends with either Sylvia or Martha the way we once were—not after the things they accused me of and did. I could never forget that, but somehow little by little we're working our way back on to speaking terms and eventually we'll all be okay."

Two days later, the casewriter was passing by Nellie's working station when she called to him:

Nellie MacDonald: Have you noticed how they're back talking to one another again? [Indicating Alice and Sylvia] And I don't mean just about work, either. It had to come about. We can't operate with a chasm in the department. We wouldn't have stood for it.

Casewriter: If that had happened, would you have done something about it?

Nellie MacDonald: Sure. Why do you think they're back together? We helped it. Monday at lunch we got it to start. I knew if we could just get one to do something for the other, it might make a difference. So, when Alice asked me at lunch if I had change for a $5 bill, I said, no. I did, but I also knew that Sylvia had it, too. I wanted to make Alice ask Sylvia for it. There was no one else there at the time. So, Alice asked Sylvia. Sylvia said, "Yes, I think I have it. If I don't, what do you need? A dollar? I'll lend it to you." She had the change so she gave it to Alice. I knew they needed some help to get started so I gave it to them.

Casewriter: Had you talked about this with anyone before that particular lunch?

Nellie MacDonald: Sure, just that morning, Sally and I talked about what we might do, even what we might do at lunch sometime. That's when we're all together and can really talk. That just happened to be the one day when Sally didn't go to lunch. But she asked me when I got back if anything happened at lunch. I said, "I think it's on its way." Then I told her what had happened. "That's good," she said. "Now we'll wait and see." And sure enough there it is. Tuesday, they were beginning to speak again. We all pretty much agree that things are back on track again.

Case 10–3
Product Management at United Brands*

They are the chosen few . . . the MBA Club. They're on the fastest track in the company.

They're a bunch of young, bright, and terribly egotistical guys.

It's the Momma's-chicken-soup syndrome. These guys assume they know how to do it best.

What they call creative thinking would be called B.S. any other place.

That department brings people in from the outside all the time; because they don't know their own business. They can't develop their own people; they promote them instead.

They have charisma. They are always great personalities . . . a bunch of actors . . . a superior race. They're the prestigious group, the comers.

All these statements are about Product Managers. They were made by people in the various departments of the Butternut Division of United Brands, Inc. Only the last statement was made by a Product Manager.

THE DEVELOPMENT OF PRODUCT MANAGEMENT
AT UNITED BRANDS

Established in the late 1920s through the merger and acquisition of a number of independent packaged food producers, United Brands was one of the United States' first multiproduct packaged food marketers. United Brands was also a pioneer in the use of the product management form of organization.

Originally, at United Brands, as in most companies, each function—production, research, marketing, and financial services—played a specialized role in the total operation of the company. The General Manager of a division coordinated the work of the functions in

---

* Disguised name, which has no relationship to the real company of the same name.

implementing the corporate strategy. However, as the number of products each division produced and sold increased, the job of coordination became increasingly complex. The product-management type of organization was United Brand's response to this complexity in coordinating the functional departments in the development, production, and marketing of a large number of products.

The product management organization was superimposed over the traditional functional organization, cutting across functional lines, as shown in the accompanying matrix.

Product Group	Functions				
	Market research	Sales	Production	Accounting and control	Product research
A					
B					
C					
D					
E					

Each Product Manager played a role similar to that of the Division General Manager, coordinating the work of people in the functional departments in implementing the strategy for the product (or products) for which he was responsible. An important difference, however, was that he had no structural authority over the people whose work he coordinated, as did the General Manager. In fact, a Product Manager sometimes had to compete with other Product Managers for the services of the functional departments. For example, in the Butternut Division of United Brands, the same sales force handled all the products of all five Product Groups. In other departments, such as financial services and, to some extent, market research, employees were assigned to work with particular Product Groups, while at the same time working for their superiors within the function.

In 1970, United Brands marketed a wide range of packaged food products in the United States through four operating divisions, each of which was treated as a relatively autonomous unit.

THE BUTTERNUT DIVISION

The Butternut Division of United Brands maintained its own production facilities, sales organization, product management section, marketing research group, research and development organization, raw food stuffs purchasing group, and personnel and controllership functions. (See organization chart and division headquarters floor plan, Exhibits 1 and 2.) Its products include peanut butter, jams and jellies, honey and maple syrup.

According to Mr. Lee Edwards, Butternut's Marketing Manager, the Butternut Division had traditionally been United Brands' largest division and the Butternut Division accounted for 37 percent of domestic sales.

However, although Butternut sales had continued to increase steadily over the past five years, their share of United Brands' total and domestic sales had decreased over the same period. This was due to a leveling off of the market for their group of products, United Brands' renewed acquisition program, and United Brands' increased activity in the institutional and international markets.

According to United Brands' 1970 annual report, the business of the Butternut Division would "remain a dependable and profitable business, but will account for a relatively smaller share of overall sales and earnings as other areas of the company grow more rapidly."

Product management in the Butternut Division

According to Mr. Edwards, Butternut's Marketing Manager, the Product Manager's role was a key one in the operations of the division. Characterizing them as "little General Managers" he described how the Product Managers were central to the planning and execution of marketing strategies:

> The Product Groups, with the advice of the various functional departments, formulate the marketing strategies and then pass them up the line of management for modification and/or concurrence. When agreement on the strategy is finally achieved, responsibility for the execution of the strategy rests with the product manager. This approach keeps senior management in control of policy and strategy, but it puts the burden of "managing" on the Product Manager. It also serves as a built-in manpower development program, as the Product Manager must constantly think up solutions to business problems and accomplish their successful execution.

Butternut Division organization chart

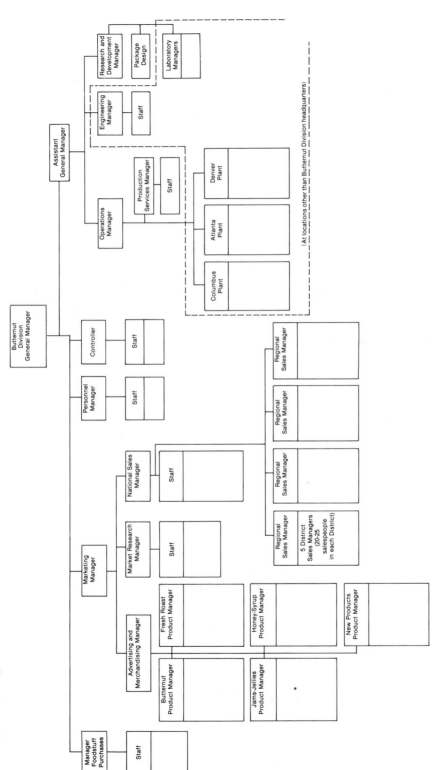

* Each Product Group was made up of a Product Manager and, usually, two Associate Product Managers and two Assistant Product Managers.

EXHIBIT 2
Floor plan of Butternut Division headquarters*

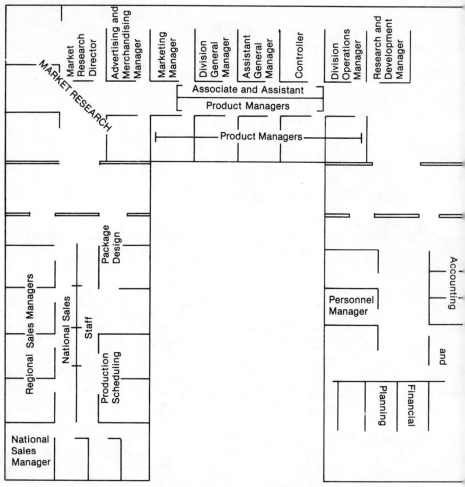

* The production plants and research laboratory were at separate facilities.

The Product Manager's work in executing the product strategy could be divided into two broad categories:

1.   The administration of trade discounts on current products.

Butternut management considered most of their products to be commodities in the packaged food business. Therefore, in terms of marketing expenditures, the division's marketing emphasis was on price competition. Three-fourths of the division's marketing expenditures were spent on trade deals.[1] Trade deals were administered on a district-by-district basis over the 20 sales districts. (The four Regional Sales Managers each had five District Sales Managers working for them, who in turn each had 20 to 25 salespeople.) Managing trade deals required negotiating the types and amounts of the trade deals for each district with the Regional Sales Managers and coordinating the volume requirements with Production. In the negotiations with the Regional Sales Manager, the Product Manager had the final say as to how and where the marketing money would be spent; the Product Manager controlled the purse strings.

2. Managing advertising and product changes.

This could entail introducing a new product, changing a current product, or changing its advertising. These activities required working together with the Product Research Group, the Market Researchers, the Product Group's advertising agency, Sales, and Production. An extremely simplified example of the process follows: Product Management and Market Research determined what could sell. This had to be reconciled with what Product Research could create and what Production could produce within cost limits. Production was then established on a limited basis. Product Management, Market Research, and the advertising agency then developed selling concepts and introduced them through the sales force to test market the product. Test market data were evaluated and decisions were made on a final strategy. The Controller was involved in financial analysis throughout the complete process.

While this example is sequential, in actuality all the different functional departments were involved in the process at all points along the way to some degree. A large number of unforeseen problems would come up in coordinating the work of the functional departments. Much of the Product Manager's job involved getting these cross-functional conflicts resolved and getting decisions made, so that schedules and objectives could be met. The Product Group served as the focal point of most coordination and decision making.

When the casewriter asked Mr. Edwards, the Division Marketing Manager, the basis on which Product Managers were evaluated, he answered, "On how well they did their job." He was reluctant to be

---

[1] Trade deals were promotional expenditures aimed at distributors and retailers, rather than directly at the customer. They included discounts off regular trade prices and allowances to retailers for running special newspaper advertising and retail coupon offers. These expenditures were often made with the intent that price reductions be passed on to the consumer. Sometimes trade discounts or dealer promotions required action by the retailer before the money was turned over; sometimes they did not. Trade deals did not include consumer promotions, such as sweepstakes contests, merchandise send-ins, etc.

more specific, explaining that, even though a Product Manager had met all the financial and market objectives of a product strategy, a Product Manager could still be judged as performing poorly because of other circumstances, such as momentum in the product before the Manager's arrival, or ineffectiveness in dealing with other people.

A successful Product Manager, he pointed out, must be able not only to coordinate the work of others, but must also be able to get good ideas from them and motivate them to carry out the decisions the Product Manager ultimately makes, following the established timetable.

The casewriter discovered that product management in the Butternut Division had traditionally been the route to top management positions in the company. The Chairman and the President of United Brands and 12 of the corporation's 16 top nonproduction operating officers were once Product Managers in the Butternut Division.[2]

On the whole, people in the product management group were younger and more highly paid than their counterparts in the other departments of the division. Most of them had MBAs.

Product management as seen by the other departments

The casewriter arranged to talk with people in each of the functional departments and with representatives of the advertising agency, with whom the Product Managers came in contact. The intent was to find out what constituted "effective dealings" with each of the groups. The casewriter asked these people two questions: (1) What are the basic conflicts between your department and product management? (2) In terms of helping you do your own job more effectively, what constitutes a good Product Manager and what constitutes a poor Product Manager?

Representative answers to the two questions appear below:

Question 1: *What are the basic conflicts between your department and product management?*

Advertising agency

The thing that's always bothered me about Butternut is, where their businesses are so huge and the funds are there, they don't try new approaches to advertising enough. They spend too much time on the day-to-day operations, making sure the deals are effective, making sure they meet their monthly share objectives. Product management simply does not experiment enough.

---

[2] Division Managers, Marketing Managers, National Sales Managers, Advertising and Merchandising Managers.

Production

Plants are basically big thick machines. Product management is constantly thinking of ways to market the products that don't fit those big machines, that require a significant amount of change. These big machines don't like to get changed. So this basic plant wish—in an ideal world, to produce everything in a one-pound jar—is basically at odds with product management, which is trying to make up exotic things to sell, exotic ways to make products, and exotic ways to package it.

The product management people seem to continually come up with new ideas that the plant cannot do.

One conflict is the speed with which product management would like to react. Once they have an idea, our cycling times to get that idea from a drawing board into a package is usually far too long for product management; and they try their damndest to get us somehow to commit to a date that's unrealistic.

Market research

What keeps competent people in this department is the opportunity for being personally creative, the opportunity to develop new market research techniques. Too often product management gets in the way of that. They're constantly sending us out to put out brush fires—little projects, the same kind of things all the time. What's worse is when they ignore your research results, because they don't fit the Product Manager's preconceived conclusions.

Controllership

Our main job is helping Product Managers project the results of their programs and then tracking what they've done and determining how successful it's been. They've got so many programs going at the same time—and these programs overlap—that it makes our job very difficult. And there's always something new and different that doesn't fit our ways of doing it. It's really a can of worms. But, then, that's what we're paid for. I shouldn't really complain about that.

Product management has traditionally not paid close enough attention to profits and has emphasized market share. They have rationalized that they were buying future profits; but until recently they haven't tried to cash in on their past investment. That's beginning to change now. Mr. Parkes, the new Division General Manager, is putting increasing emphasis on the profitability of brand strategy; and the Product Managers are catching on. But it is still something of a problem.

Sales

Some of the Product Managers are inexperienced. They don't know what the hell they're talking about. For the most part, they're trained to think profits and how to increase profits and spend the least amount of money. Or maybe it's the reverse—spend the least amount of money and, therefore, get more profits. Unfortunately it doesn't work out that way.

Product management's job is to make sure the consumer wants our product. Sales' job is to make sure the products are there. That means Sales has to know what is the best way to present it to the trade, which is the key execution in getting the product to the shelf.

Every market is different. But our salespeople are in each and every market. So we know our customers' needs; we have accumulated knowledge of those markets. Given our intimate knowledge of each of these markets, we can recommend to the product management people how they should spend their promotion money. Sometimes they follow our recommendation; sometimes they won't: When they don't, they there's conflict.

The major complaint in sales is that we don't handle the money. Product management has complete control of the purse strings. We try to get X amount of dollars from the Product Group for a program we feel will be beneficial to the division. They may not give it to us. And they have the final say.

Product research

The overriding basic conflict is we can't make what they want as cheaply as they want it. And they don't want what we can make. Of course that's an overexaggeration. But the conflict is there.

There's a tendency on the part of the product management people to theorize and postulate, etc. They see themselves as being very creative. They'd much rather argue than go out and try to get the information, to run the experiment. They shouldn't be creative to the point that they neglect facts. There's too great a tendency, I think, to fly by the seat of their pants, and not to get the facts.

Question 2:   *In terms of helping you do your own job more effectively, what constitutes a good Product Manager and what constitutes a poor Product Manager?*

Advertising agency

A good Product Manager doesn't use me just for working up copy. The Product Manager includes me in on the full range of marketing strategy formulation. That makes it very satisfying for me personally. It also insures that what we're thinking at the agency is in sync with what's brewing in the division. And, occasionally, I'm able to contribute something valuable that may have been overlooked by the product management people.

Production

A good Product Manager is a guy who understands the production function. So when we are unable to meet some of the timetables, the Manager better understands the situation. The Product Manager should be a person who's quite open-minded, quite willing to listen, and perhaps give some part of his day, or some importance, to Production.

Some product management people are honest and aboveboard. They tell you what they want, their reasons, and the impact on the company if they get it and if they don't get it. Others, you feel they're not really being honest with you. Their objective is to make short-term heroes out of themselves at the expense of long-term gains. They are in such competition with each other. There's a lot of backbiting.

Production persons will bust their rear ends to get something for a product person if they know it's in the interests of the division or the corporation. But if they think it's just to make the person look like a hero, they're not going to.

A good Product Manager is willing to make a decision and stand by it.

Marketing research

They will ask the staff to make recommendations on how best to solve a problem. They will *not* tell them what test to use, what kind of sample, etc. Instead, they will allow market researchers to do their jobs and make recommendations. Of course, they have the right to question the program—you know . . . "Is this question really answered?" But they won't tell you what to do; they will define the problem and then await your recommendations.

A good Product Manager gives us the opportunity to be directly involved in the formulation of marketing strategy, the chance to make and defend our own recommendations.

What I don't like in a Product Manager is indecisiveness. If I work out a program with a Product Manager, and he or she likes it and has bought it, I think he or she should support me in his or her recommendations to senior management. If there are points of conflict, he or she should be willing to let the market researcher into the discussion, where senior management is present, and let him or her defend it, too.

Controllership

The person who fails as a Product Manager is the one who is not able to meet schedules and timetables.

The good Product Manager is not only good at dictating, he or she is also a good listener.

Sales

A good Product Manager has to have a good personality—almost a sales-type personality. The individual has to be able to come down like he or she has just stepped out of the shower, and give an amusing, enlightened presentation to the sales force. He or she has got to be an extrovert, to be able to project a good image.

I have never seen a negative, or introverted, or nasty dispositioned Product Manager make it.

A good Product Manager will come right out and tell it like it is. "Here's how much I have. I'm sorry I can't give you more," rather than "We feel this strategy would be better for you."

My approach to them is, "Tell me what your story is and, if you don't have the funds, I can sit down and explain that to them." But I can't tell them we didn't get X promotion dollars because product management didn't think we were right. Because we know we were right!

You've got to have people to deal with who will act, who will make decisions, not the ones who think "If I don't do anything, it will go away."

A good Product Manager can develop a strong point of view, articulate it correctly, and stand up to his or her superior with it.

Product research

The ineffective Product Managers tend to look down on people in the other departments—like "you're my lackey."

A Product Manager must be able to speak the languages of the people he or she deals with, which is quite different from technical research, operations, or financial people.

He or she must have a basic desire to communicate with the different functions and be sympathetic to their needs as they relate to the total business. Not to cater to their gripes, but to really try to understand and appreciate the problems a person is trying to explain. The Product Manager must be willing to give up valuable time to communicate to these people what he or she is trying to do and the reasons why.

Product management as seen by subordinates of the Product Managers

Another group each Product Manager dealt with was his or her own subordinates. The casewriter asked several junior members of the product management group what kind of Product Manager they preferred working for. Some of their answers appear below:

A good Product Manager will give his or her subordinates new chances to develop their skills and new types of things to work on. I don't want to stay on one thing for too long after I've learned it. Then I'm just wasting time. I want to move on and up in the business. To do that I've got to learn all aspects of the business. A good Product Manager won't hold me back.

A good boss will always be ready to help you out with a problem; but he or she won't hover so closely over you that you can't grow through overcoming the difficulties of the problem yourself. The boss will be there when needed.

He or she will include me in on what's happening in the Product Group, beyond the particular project I'm working on; so I know where my work fits in.

Product management as seen by Product Managers

The casewriter also asked two Product Managers to describe what they thought differentiated the successful Product Manager from a less successful counterpart:

Product Manager 1:

The most difficult part of the job is to get the uninvolved, the not-interested people to be involved and interested in the business, like the production and packaging people, the nine to fives, the people who have no future in their jobs. A good Product Manager can do that.

You have to understand what the person needs—a kick in the rear or a pat on the back. Some fellows like to be loved. So you ask "How's your dog today? Did your wife sleep well last night?" He'll think "Hey, there's a nice guy. I'm going to take care of him next time." If you're sending pen and pencil sets to retailers as a promotion gimmick, you send him one. So he feels he's part of the brand. Others you have to lean on, get tough with, threaten. It depends on the guy.

Let me give you an example—Bob Jones, the purchaser in the Production department. If you don't get his attention, and you miss your target date, you may have the best program, but without glass to pack the product in, you don't have *any* program. And he is the guy who orders glass. He is the guy who can make supply work extra hard for you. But he works for five Product Groups, seven brands, and 30 different sizes. If he doesn't like you, you're in trouble.

So it's a function of how you show your respect for him, and how you communicate with him, how you build up this rapport.

If you need to get something done in three weeks, and the book says it takes four to six weeks to get it done, but you know if he wants to help you he can do it in three weeks, then it's that critical area of whether he's going to help you that makes or breaks you, or makes you look good.

That's why it's important to know how to deal with each person.

There are other things too, of course. If individuals can't handle the complexity of many things going at the same time, they'll never make it.

Also, there are some people who have great ideas; but can't sell them. They're just poor salespeople. They will yield right away when the boss gives them the pressure treatment, even if it's just to test them. They don't last.

There's another type that is extremely competent, but won't succeed because they can't live within the system; they won't observe all the protocols, they won't follow the procedures. If you want to succeed, you can step out of bounds only once in a while to show you're a tiger. You can be sort of a bastard; but not much, just sort of. You step on people's toes only once in a while.

The organization demands that its people be good Christian soldiers. That also means that you may stay in a position longer than you should, or take a job that you don't want; but you don't say no, you say "Yes, but." You have to strike the right balance between independence and compliance.

Product Manager 2:

To become a Product Manager, you have to be smart, aggressive, and creative. The smarter you are, the better. By aggressive, I'm referring to a people-oriented aggressiveness. To get ahead and succeed as a Product Manager, that aggressiveness must be attached to a commitment to get things done. Creativity is very important; but it's not necessary that you yourself be creative with new and appropriate ideas. It's more important that you be able to recognize appropriate creativity in others when you see it. You should continually be running across things others do with the reaction, "Gee, I wish I'd thought of that." The important thing is that even if you didn't come up with the idea it doesn't bother you—that you are delighted to accept an idea someone else has.

To get ahead as a Product Manager, you have to have a commitment to the results rather than to a particular technique or to a personality or to the source of the ideas. You have to show aggressiveness and a toughness, a tenacity that doesn't stop when somebody says "No, you can't do it." You try to figure out another way to do it.

Another thing you need to get ahead in product management is the broadest scope view of the job possible—that means you go beyond the requirements of your own job. There are three kinds of people who start off in product management: (1) Those who look upon the job as a crappy job; that go through the motions, not wanting to do it. The job suffers. (2) Those who manage to do the job adequately; that are committed to it; that want to do it well, so they can move on to something else more fun and exciting. (3) Those who do the job adequately and have the time—no, make the time—to do other things as well, that they think are important. They are the ones who go beyond their jobs. They are the ones who will succeed in product management.

Another important factor is what I call public relations (the cynic would probably call it politics). The fact that someone is using a great new idea in his or her work doesn't do any good unless the right people know about it. That is the job of the Product Manager. I am continually sending things up just to keep them posted as to what people in my Product Group are doing that is good.

Finally, a little humility goes a long way. That's trying to know as much as you possibly can without flaunting it. The person who says "I've been in this business 20 years, so I ought to know more about it than you do"—that's categorically wrong. The person knows more about his or her job; but I know more about how this job relates to what I'm trying to do—which is what we are sitting down to talk about.

So this person's attitude is wrong, if that's his or her attitude. But making him or her see that does not move the ball ahead. Playing "gotcha" is sometimes satisfying; but it doesn't help much.

Case 10–4
David Alpert (A)*

In 1971 David Alpert was the product manager for Butternut Peanut Butter in the Butternut Division of United Brands, Inc. (see organization chart, Exhibit 1). The previous year, five years out of the Harvard Business School, he had assumed responsibility for Butternut Peanut Butter, one of United Brands' top selling products. (Over the previous five years, Butternut sales and profits had been 9.1 percent and 15.4 percent of corporate sales and profits, respectively.)

Evaluation of David Alpert as a Product Manager

As far as the casewriter could tell, David Alpert was doing well in his work as Product Manager. Lee Edwards, Butternut Division Marketing Manager, had referred Alpert to the casewriter as a good example of a strong, effective Product Manager. Other people from the various functional areas in the division described Alpert in the following terms:

> Flexible . . . prompt . . . decisive . . . a decision maker (Sales); receptive to different ways of looking at the business (Control); sympathetic to problems we might have in accomplishing our task . . . tries to understand . . . a good communicator (Product Research); very fair-minded person . . . generally given to listening to all sides of a thing, given to letting people express their opinions . . . parochial in terms of pushing

---

* All names have been disguised.

EXHIBIT 1
Butternut Division organization chart

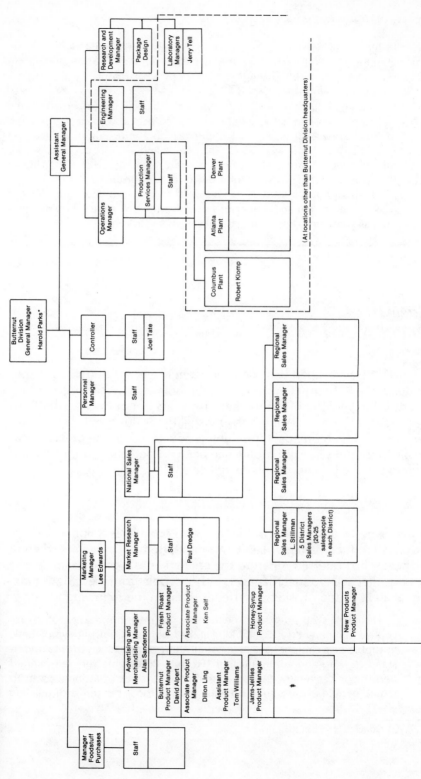

* Only names mentioned in the case are given.

for his brand's priorities, but easy to work with (Market Research); excellent . . . a good listener . . . keeps us informed as to how we fit into the overall picture (Production).

David Alpert's evaluation of the job

David Alpert told the casewriter he liked his job. He listed a number of reasons why:

First, I like the responsibility the job entails and I like the fact that I can measure my accomplishments. There are measures like market share targets and return on investment. There is also a certain measurement in the sense that we deal with programs that can be completed. We've just completed a successful program that involved spending an awful lot of money. It had a lot of little pieces to it. It was a real executional nightmare. It was satisfying to fit all these pieces together.

Second, I find a lot of personal satisfaction in being responsible for the expenditure of a lot of money and spending it well. I guess beneath that is the fact that I like to be looked upon as a guy who has things under control. It means something to me to have that reputation in the company.

Another thing about project work that is fairly appealing to me is the fact that on no given Tuesday do I have the same thing to do from week to week. There are no routines in the work.

Then I guess that I would have to say that there are people that I like to work with. First, there are those outside the product group. I find a great deal of satisfaction in cranking these people up to get a job done. Secondly, within the product group I have four people working for me, and I think I'm relatively good at getting them to progress—getting them to feel they are progressing.

There are two aspects to this. The first one is the training aspect. I enjoy working with my people and helping them to develop along the lines that I think are important for product manager types to have.

David then paused for a moment before he went on.

The second aspect you might call the public relations job. I like to insure that my people will have their day in court and be exposed in the way that will help them to get promoted. I think I'm pretty good at that.

Finally, the material rewards—the money—are, of course, very important. It's strange how you are consistently able to live just beyond your income; so that you're looking forward to each raise as it comes. I guess that's very much the American way of life. In any case, my salary progression has been fairly dramatic. My salary has increased fourfold since coming to United Brands. I am making in the high 30s now; and that's pretty damned important. Especially when it comes by doing something I like—that I'm making progress by doing things I enjoy doing.

Of course, it's not all a bed of roses.

It's aggravating to any Product Manager who wants to get the job done to sit and listen to somebody else tell you about their problems. If they didn't have problems they wouldn't have a job; and because they've got problems, they become one of your problems. On the other hand, if reciting their problems to you helps to solve their problems through some ego satisfaction or whatever, and your job is to solve their problems, then you are doing your job by listening to them talk about it.

But that's really not the most important part of our job—listening to somebody create a problem before your very eyes, which he or she will then proceed to solve and be a great big hero. When they do that, it's a fairly obvious ploy.

David Alpert's dealings with others in the Butternut Division

The casewriter spent three days with David Alpert, recording his dealings with others in the Butternut Division. Later David was asked to comment on these exchanges.

Monday—Task Force meeting

Among his other duties at this time, David Alpert headed a special temporary Task Force which had been formed to make up the five-year plan for the two peanut butter brands sold by the Butternut Division. Alpert represented Butternut Peanut Butter, United Brand's popularly priced line. Representing Fresh Roast Peanut Butter, United Brand's premium brand, was Ken Self, an Associate Product Manager in the Fresh Roast Product Group. Other members of the Task Force representing other groups in the division were:

Production, Robert Klomp
Control, Joel Tate
Sales, Larry Stillman
Market Research, Paul Dredge
Product Research, Jerry Tell
Advertising agency representative, Ned Ashby

Below are excerpts from one of the Task Force meetings (the Control and Sales representatives were absent):

The meeting began at 9:00 A.M. Jerry Tell (Product Research) summarized to the group the results of a meeting with higher management on Task Force objectives. He had attended the meeting representing David Alpert, who had been on vacation. Fifteen minutes into the presentation, Ned Ashby, the advertising agency representative, walked into the meeting late. He made a short apology and excuse and took a seat.

David Alpert answered his apology:

Alpert: *I told the secretaries there were two things we were missing—Ned Ashby and the coffee—and I wasn't sure which we were missing most.*

Ashby: *You're being polite.* [Everybody laughs]

The meeting then continued. Jerry Tell finished his summary with a comment on the use of market research in the division:

Tell: *The next issue was that, in a business that is as consumer oriented as ours is, we are not spending really enough time, money, or effort on basic marketing research, so that we can improve our ability to communicate with and to the consumer. The comment was generally made that there should be a great deal more effort in this area.*

Alpert: *Did you make the comment or did higher management?*

Tell: *I did. That's a personal thing I've been carrying around for quite a while. . . .*

Alpert: *You got that off your chest?* [joking tone]

Tell: *Yes, I felt a lot better. I slept very well that night.*

Later, the discussion turned to looking into areas of peanut products other than peanut butter, such as peanut candy bars, peanut cake frosting mixes. Several possibilities got batted around by the group in an animated discussion for about ten minutes. During that time, David Alpert remained silent. He then cut the discussion off, saying that what they were discussing were areas for the division to look into, but that they were probably more appropriate for the New Products Group— that the Peanut Butter Group would not have to worry about them.

Alpert then went through the five-year plan point by point with the group. All members of the Task Force participated freely in the discussion.

Robert Klomp (Production) raised the question of whether changes in taste preferences were going to come about in the next ten years, or whether it had been assumed that tastes would stay the same. Klomp suggested that it should be possible to project future changes in taste preferences on the basis of changes over the past ten years. Alpert answered him in a roundabout way:

Alpert: *Well, you've gotta have some givens—you've got to establish some base objectives. And the easiest ones to establish are markets and margins.*
You just can't cope with all the variables.
You have no control or relatively no control over what the market's gonna be. We hope we can expand it, but we made the best guess we can. [Jerry Tell joined in the discussion.]

Tell: *With our share of market, we have more control than I think we tend to exercise.*

Alpert: *Well, we don't know how to exercise it.*

Tell: *But with margins . . . .*

Alpert: *Yes, we've gotten some control over margins. But if the cost of peanuts is 70 percent of cost of goods sold, and if Fred [the raw foodstuffs buyer] doesn't know* *what the cost of peanuts is one day to the next, let alone one week or month to the next, then all you can do is assume you will take an active pricing action and adjust it as you go along.*

The casewriter noticed that during the meeting, Ken Self, the Associate Product Manager from the Fresh Roast Group, challenged Alpert a number of times on points such as use of merchandising methods, perceptions of the consumer, and advertisability of the brands. Each time, when Alpert answered his challenge with a milder response, Self backed off.

The meeting concluded at 12:15 P.M.

After the Task Force meeting was over, the casewriter asked Alpert about aspects of the meeting that intrigued him:

Rivalry and competition among Product Managers

Casewriter: *I thought what I saw going on between you and Self was friendly rivalry. Was it?*

Alpert: *No, it wasn't. I haven't been in a position to develop a lot of respect for his talent. The guys he works with think he's pretty good. I just haven't seen it. He hasn't really been any help on the Task Force. I thought it was nit-picking.*

Casewriter: *How did you try to handle it?*

Alpert: *Just as briefly as possible without being rude. Because, obviously, any obvious dissension between Product Manager and Associate Product Manager in a group like that would be picked up by the other functions. Probably with some relish; even though they are pretty mature people. There was nothing there to call for his being put down. In meetings like that, when somebody like Ken brings up something, I just tend to lose interest in the conversation. I let it wander around for a while, then pick it up again after a few minutes.*

Casewriter: *But, still, it looked like rivalry. Is there much competition among the product management people?*

Alpert: *Not really. I can't think of any. There is no reason to be. United Brands needs all the good Product Managers it can get.*

Use of humor

Casewriter: *Let's turn to something else in the meeting. I noticed you used humor a number of times.*

Alpert: *Humor goes a long way.*

Casewriter: *Like when you asked Tell if it felt good to have it off his chest, after his analysis of the marketing situation. It seemed to me he wanted to get involved in marketing decisions.*

Alpert: *Nearly everyone does. That's where they think the action is. It's where the status is.*

Jerry Tell is very easy to work with. He is far and away the most competent man at the laboratory from my standpoint. He thinks more like a manager than a technician. He evaluates a proposal on rational return on investment criteria rather than on whether it would be technically fun. He is a delight to talk to, a real breath of fresh air in the organization. But there are others who don't act that way. Really, he is the exception.

Dealings with Product Research

Casewriter: *How do you deal with others in Product Research?*

Alpert: *Those are the kind of guys you coddle. They have just as much education as you do. But they need experience on the job before they become effective. We spring full blown from Business School as "marketing experts." They don't; so our counterparts there are generally older than we are. Therefore, we tend to exclaim loudly and make a terribly big fuss over their accomplishments.*

For example, I'll call a guy down in the bowels of the laboratory someplace and congratulate him, and make it very clear that a product improvement was his accomplishment. Which it was.

Dealings with Production

Casewriter: *How about the production man, Robert Klomp? His major contribution was some speculations on the probability of taste preferences changing. It seemed he wanted to play marketer too, perhaps.*

Alpert: *Could be. He was really here primarily so the production people would feel included. Although there could be some things come up where I could use his knowledge.*

I've simply learned that bridges built to the plant will pay innumerable dividends. Primarily the junior Product Managers deal with them; but I try to keep in touch because they can screw us up so bad.

And those are the kinds of people that, if they want to, will ruin an entire plan just to prove that they're right and you're wrong. And they can do it.

I have no idea what goes on down there in the plants. And most of it, I suspect, would horrify me if I did. But that's not really important, so long as I can get them to do what needs doing for us. And change is by definition bad at the plants. So it's very important that I win them over to my side. It is important that they feel that they can come into my office and tell me that they are not able to do what I want them to do. If they don't come, but shove the problem under the rug, we can't work things out before it's too late. So the key there is communication—direct and easy communication and access. When they come to me with a problem, we sit down and try to figure out what we can do to overcome the problem.

Dealings with Market Research

Casewriter: *What about Paul Dredge, the market researcher?*

Alpert: *He is a bit parochial, but that's what he's paid to be. When he says he'll go away and think about ways we can incorporate research into our Task Force presentation and make it a little more research oriented, he'll probably be back* *in here first thing Tuesday morning with a bunch of ideas about how to do it. He's a good man. I've got few worries in that department. I was the Market Research Director for four months before I got this position. Now they're convinced true or false that I know enough of what's going on down there that they can't fool me. The key there is to kep them informed about the business so that they can keep their research program up to date. They don't need a lot of guidance.*

Casewriter: *Your sales and control people were not at the meeting.*

Alpert: *They are both out of town. I'll be meeting with Joel Tate, the accounting guy, tomorrow morning to discuss ROI calculations. I have to find out how United Brands does it before the next Task Force meeting. Our sales representative is a very good man for this job. He worked in product management for a while and has a broader view of things than most of those guys.*

Dealings with Sales

Casewriter: *Tell me about your dealings with Sales.*

Alpert: *The day-to-day dealings are handled almost exclusively by our junior people in product management. I usually get involved when they can't get a problem worked out.*

The sales people resent us. And yet maybe they are the most crucial people we have to work with. That whole relationship is a difficult one from their point of view. The Regional Sales Manager sees you as younger and less experienced than him—which we are. And yet as his volume and sales promotion planners, his success depends on our ability to get him his share of the total dollars for promotion and spending. So I can certainly understand the resentment—particularly against the people who don't do well at it.

We treat them with a combination of deference—because they are a little older, and particularly when we are junior—and candor. Candor is the key to the thing. They like to deal with decision makers. It's good for their own self-image, plus it saves time—which is an important commodity for any person.

When they make a request for a program that they think is necessary, they would far prefer they be told that we don't have enough money to do it. Whether it's a good idea or a bad idea, it's wasting time to debate it when you don't have the funds.

But if you don't think it is a good idea and you can convince the Sales Manager yourself, that can take you miles. If you can disagree and give reasons and really communicate, so that you end up working out something that you agree to, or at least the Sales Manager can understand your position, then that's very good. There's a lot of respect built in that kind of relationship. Say "I can't afford it" when you can't afford it, and say "I don't agree" when you don't agree.

Tuesday—meeting with Control

The next morning, Alpert had a short meeting with Joel Tate, the control representative to the Task Force, to talk about ROI calculations for the five-year plan. Alpert needed the material for a meeting with his superiors, Alan Sanderson, the Advertising and Merchandising Manager, and Lee Edwards, the Marketing Manager.

Alpert: *Where are your ROI calculations for the five-year plan? I've got to get some by Thursday. I need at least one, and perhaps several exhibits on that subject. Because they're probably the most important numbers—at least the second most important after share—that we'll talk about. And I can't just go say to Edwards it ought to be approximately 35 percent.*

Tate: *I'll have to do some work on it. I'm not too sure I can have all the data and all the . . . things together by Thursday.*

Alpert: *I mean we've got something, haven't we, we've got . . . .*

Tate [cuts in]: *Oh, I have the actual of how we came up with fiscal 1970—the 35 percent.*

Alpert: *Well . . . [acts impatient].*

Tate: *And, and I just got pieces for the other years.*

Alpert: *I'd like to see what those pieces are. [spoken firmly]*

Tate: *OK . . . as far as projections. We can maintain, I'm sure we can . . . . We should say that minimum is 35 percent.*

Alpert: *I mean over the last three years, can I see the calculations? [more impatient]*

Tate: *Sure . . . I'll bring them in. [Tate leaves]*

After Tate had left, Alpert turned to the casewriter and volunteered:

Alpert: *You needn't worry about stifling creative ideas that the elves down in accounting may have; because they don't have any. I think the secret with those people is that you not deal with them at the middle management level, that is Tate's level. Because I think that the truth of that department is that they occasionally get lucky and hire somebody that's good. But they can't keep them long enough to promote them through the ranks to get them to Tate's position. It's only the relative dullards, like Joel, that stay. I suppose he is a capable guy in his own right. He is not really stupid. He's not awfully smart; he can add a column of figures. But he is not going to become treasurer of the corporation or controller of the division or anything else.*

The best way to get real performance there is to latch on to a young guy who's aggressive and good and very junior in the organization and just have him working his rear off for you.

We've got a financial analyst under Joel who's assigned directly to Butternut. He is very good. He's the guy through whom we get things done. He is practically a member of the Product Group. A very, very junior member; because he doesn't create anything, he just does what he is told. But he is a tremendous help.

Tuesday—meeting with subordinates

Later that same day, Alpert met with Dillion Ling and Tom Williams, Associate and Assistant Product Managers on Butternut, about a test-market they were proposing in Atlanta. Ling was Chinese; Williams was a black. Alpert listened quietly to the presentation, now and then probing their assumptions, asking extra questions to see how well they had thought things out. After Williams finished his last points, Alpert said:

Alpert: *That's a very thorough way to go about analyzing what it ought to be . . . . The only question I have . . . . We've traditionally gone from a northeastern test market like Albany South and West without any compunctions. If it tested well in Albany, Syracuse, or Indianapolis, we'd take it South. We haven't got any experience with anything testing it in the South and taking it North.*

Ling: *We don't?*

Alpert: *I don't see any radical differences. But we don't want to get ourselves into situations where we've selected test markets that rationally people would think okay, but when it comes right down to it, they won't accept it emotionally . . . .*

They discussed that issue. Ling pushed for Atlanta, citing advantages with media and outlet control.

Alpert: *OK, let's assume it will be Atlanta. In the meantime, I'll do a little spade work across the hall with the Advertising and Merchandising Manager and the Marketing Manager and see if that makes people uncomfortable. Because I think it clearly is the best market. But I think we ought to be pragmatic about it. We want it, not because it's Atlanta, but because it's the best way we can think of to test our product.*

Williams: *We had a couple minor positives and negatives to going into Atlanta.*

Alpert: *OK, I'm convinced.*

Williams: *I think you want to hear these, though. One thing, a positive, is I'd go to the Hyatt House; I've never seen it.*
Another, a negative one, it's not a great area for minority groups to take their field trips. [Williams laughs cautiously]

Alpert: *Well, Atlanta's all right; but I'm not so sure about eastern Tennessee.* [everyone laughs]

Ling: *Johnny Cash is the spokesperson for Nashville.*

Alpert: *Yes. For eastern Tennessee, you want to send your white Anglo-Saxon Protestants; and we ain't got any of those kind of people.*

Williams: *Buy somebody some cut-off Levi's and get a rope to tie 'em up and a T-shirt, and send the person to eastern Tennessee.* [everyone laughs]

Ling: *The introductory promotion in March could be a shotgun; then for 50 cents you can get the shot and shoot the revenuer.* [laughter]

Alpert: *Make the ammunition the continuity.* [laughter]

After the meeting, the casewriter asked Alpert about his dealings with the subordinates in his Product Group.

Casewriter: *How do you train your people?*

Alpert: *A lot of the training is in your expectations.*

Junior Product Managers are, in their individual ways, terribly anxious to please. You don't have to give them orders, you just have to make known simply what you want and be clear about what it is you want done, and then stay out of their way, because they will go to great lengths and work terribly hard to get it done just the way they think you would want it done. That's awfully important. That's a characteristic of the good Junior Product Manager. The thing that separates the good ones from the excellent ones is that the good ones get it done just the way they think you want it done, and the excellent ones will get it done that way, unless they think there might be a better way—and they'll stop and think about it. They will come back to you and say, I heard you, but this is a better idea, that's sort of a step beyond. I think my people know about the distinction, because we've discussed it and will continue to discuss it. The key is initiative.

The most important thing is getting the job done, achieving the objectives. I don't have a lot of pride of authorship. I'm not really creative in bringing up new ideas of my own. I'm better at being able to take other people's ideas and adapting things that have been done before to problems that we have now.

Wednesday—meeting with superiors

On the morning of the third day, Alpert met with his two immediate superiors, Alan Sanderson (Advertising and Merchandising Manager) and Lee Edwards (Marketing Manager), to discuss the final stages of the five-year plan. Alpert was concise in his remarks and candid in his presentation. Several times the Marketing Manager disagreed with market assumptions Alpert had made. Alpert defended his ideas, saying that he thought the issues were more complicated than the Marketing Manager perceived them. He suggested that they look into them further.

After the meeting, the casewriter commented on Alpert's skill in making a persuasive, concise presentation. Alpert said:

Alpert: *I've learned most of that from Alan* [the Advertising and Merchandising Manager]. *He's a very good businessman and he's hard-nosed. And he doesn't like to beat around the bush. If you start to give him something in a roundabout sort of fashion, he's very good at cutting right through to the meat of it. And, he will do it disapprovingly, because he doesn't like you to be wasting his time telling him something in five sentences when you should be able to tell him in one. He doesn't like you to take five minutes on justification when one minute will do. He's a terribly busy guy. He has an incredibly time-consuming job. He can't afford the luxury of people who can't afford to talk straight, and his style is blunt enough; he'll tell you if you're wasting his time.*

Casewriter: *You were pretty candid in the meeting yourself.*

Alpert: *Ed and Alan encourage that. They encourage opposition. They're open enough so that if they don't agree with you, and you tell them you think they're wrong, they'll very quickly admit it if they agree with you. Alan in particular.*

He'll sometimes test you to see whether you've thought things out. He'll ask for five reasons you feel the way you do, and very often, he will cut you off after reason number 2 and say "OK."

That starts, of course, with the General Manager—to tell people what you think. That's Harold Parks' style.

Case 10–5
David Alpert (B)*

David Alpert and the casewriter went to a small French restaurant on the outskirts of Dayton, Ohio, to cap off a three-day visit the casewriter had spent with Alpert at United Brands. (See David Alpert (A).) As the evening wore on, the conversation turned to Alpert's personal life. The casewriter was interested in learning more of his background, his life-style, and his aspirations.

Casewriter: *Let me ask you two questions together, David. First, what is it about yourself—your personal skills, your likes and dislikes—that keeps you in product management? And second, what kinds of things in your upbringing, family life, and education helped develop these skills and made these likes and dislikes important?*

Alpert: *Well I guess the basic ingredient is a good sense for dealing with people, and a liking for it. That's what really sends someone into this area of business. At least that is the most valid reason for me. Sociability, having friends, being with them, enjoying them, making sure they enjoy me—this is something that is important to me and always has been, and manifests itself in different ways at different stages of life.*

I was the oldest of two children. (I have a sister who is seven years younger; which I always thought was a natural interval between children—until I started having them.)

When I was very young, there were very few children in my neighborhood. I didn't have very many close friends, in terms of neighbors that I could play with all the time, the way my kids do. I find that just absolutely delightful that we're falling over children at our house all the time (Usually I find that delightful; sometimes, I get sick of it.) But I can remember that as being rather significant. I could go three or four blocks before finding friends to play with. I don't know . . . I have no idea if this made me more outgoing when I was with people or what.

That was probably a pretty good summary through grade school. I had friends, not a great many. I don't remember a great many. I remember a couple

---

* All names have been disguised.

of them. We didn't live too close; we weren't together constantly. I don't remember myself as being much of a leader when I was younger, in grade school.

I'm not sure what denotes a "leader" in grade school anyway. But I became one in high school. It was a small school for boys. And my parents thought it would be a good thing for me to go to a private school; which turned out to be very wise of them. I didn't think it was a very good idea at the time; but I think so now. I got very close to one of my English instructors, who was also the dramatic coach; and I played the lead in my high school play as a sophomore. It just happened that the role fit me. The play was "The Man Who Came to Dinner." I played Sheridan Whiteside's part, which was a great deal of fun, and I guess tended to single me out in a very favorable way, because it was a very successful play and a lot of fun to do. A lot of people enjoyed watching it. It made me known as someone with a good sense of humor—which I think is pretty true anyway. It just magnified the thing and called it to everybody's attention all at once.

I worked on the school newspaper and the student council and ended up editor of the paper and president of the student council. There were 36 in the class; and there were two or three of us who were running the organizations at the school. I think we were well liked, without any question; but we were not the social leaders to the same degree as we were the organizational leaders. We weren't outcasts in any sense. An interesting part of that was that two of the three of us were the only two Jewish students in the class (No, there were three Jewish boys in the class.) One of them, a fellow that is still my best friend, was president of the senior class and I was president of the student body.

I guess that's an issue, religion, which is something that will crop up occasionally, because it's important. Here and there more important in some places than in others. I don't really think it was the drawback. I'm sure it was not a drawback; because the offices that I held were elective, the friends that I made in high school are still among my closest friends. But it was something that was there; and it tended to set the three of us apart a little bit. More so in the minds of some parents than in the minds of their children.

Casewriter: *After high school, you went to Harvard College, didn't you?*

Alpert: *Yes.*

Casewriter: *What are the most important things you remember from your college days, in terms of friendships made and things that had an impact on your future?*

Alpert: *For some reason, my closest friends in college were Jewish. In high school they hadn't been; but in high school there hadn't been as many Jewish boys to choose from. In college I didn't seek Jewish friends out. I really don't understand why that occurred; although my roommate was Jewish, and I met some of them through him (his father was Chairman of the Board of the Continental Publishing Company). The guys that I knew were rich and Jewish and generally from New York and the East.*

Casewriter: *Were you rich?*

Alpert: *No.*

Casewriter: *Were you a Harvard son?*

Alpert: *Yes.*

Casewriter: *What about important activities during your college days?*

Alpert: *I was involved in a couple of them. The best of them (which was a great thing I did; because, at the Business School, I needed it to put on that application) was that I ran the combined charity drive at Harvard College, the United Fund drive, with another guy in our junior year. It was a big undertaking. We had a couple of hundred people working for us through this organization that we set up. Compared to the previous year, we were quite successful. And I made some very close friends in the process.*

Casewriter: *Do you miss the fellowship of your college days?*

Alpert: *Yes, I do, to a degree. At the same time, the product management system gives ample outlet to anyone who wants to be with people and wants to get things done on a basis of forming friendly relationships with people. That, I guess, as I work myself around your original question, is probably as good a reason as any for why this job fills some important needs for me. I enjoy those kinds of relationships with people even though they are a smaller portion of my total life now than they were in college—even if it is with a Regional Sales Manager, for example, that I don't really spend a lot of time with, that I see occasionally at the office. They are not my kind of people, really, I mean, I wouldn't seek them out socially . . . some of them. But there's a couple that I would.*

Casewriter: *After you graduated from college, you went to the Harvard Business School, didn't you?*

Alpert: *Yes.*

Casewriter: *Why did you pick business as a profession?*

Alpert: *Partly because I eliminated the other professions for one reason or another; but also because I had some fairly positive attitudes toward business. I had spent summers working for various family businesses. I worked for my Dad first when I was about 15. At the time, he was a wholesale distributor for a large company. He did this for about eight or nine years.*

He has had, that I remember, I guess, about four different jobs since he's gotten out of Business School. He worked for a stationery and envelope company in St. Louis. It's a national company, but with its headquarters in St. Louis. Started out when he graduated from Business School. He started out hauling paper from the dock to the envelope machines in 1933, and thought he was very lucky to get the job. But he was eventually to become a vice president or something or other; but one of their three or four top employees. But the two or three above him happened to have the same name as the president. So he decided that was as far as he was going to go. He was with them about 15 years.

Casewriter: *He had gone to Harvard College and Harvard Business School?*

Alpert: *Yes. I guess he must have been a little better at that system than I was; because he graduated from Harvard College when he was 16 and graduated from the Business School when he was 18.*

After he left the stationery and envelope company, he acquired and ran a charcoal briquette business for another part of his family. He did pretty well with that business for a while; but the intrafamily relationship, as often happens, proved to be a difficult one. He was running a piece of the business that they weren't really close to; they were buying and selling grain on the floor of the Board of Trade, in St. Louis. And that led to frictions. And I think basic to the whole thing was that my father enjoyed being his own boss and he wasn't in that kind of situation. And when they did call that fact to his attention, it was over things that they were generally wrong about and he was generally right, and he knew that. So he got out in plenty of time to keep the family together, because he thought that was more important than the business relationship. And they continued the business on a good deal smaller scale than it was when he was there.

When he left there he bought a stationery office supply company in downtown St. Louis. He sells office supplies to offices in the area and has a retail store, and has done that for the last six or seven years, and has been very happy about it. It's been hard work.

Casewriter: How old is he now, David?

Alpert: Fifty-nine.

Casewriter: Are you in pretty close communication with him on business kinds of decisions and other kinds of things?

Alpert: Yes. We talk every Sunday. They call. Primarily now to talk to the children. They call nonetheless; and they ask us what's new before they ask if the children are there.

Whenever we're in St. Louis . . . I was in St. Louis last week for the sales meeting we had out there. I figured as long as I was running the sales meeting—we were having it for the whole midwestern area—we should jolly well have it in a place like St. Louis. It was fun. I invited Dad to come to the sales meeting. He sat in the back and enjoyed himself thoroughly. We had about 125 salespeople. Put on a hell of a fancy show.

We generally take some time to sit down and talk about things. I think we stay pretty close.

Casewriter: Tell me what it was like to work for your father.

Alpert: It was a pretty successful circumstance for me; because what I set out to do was to get people to say "He's pretty good in spite of the family relationship." And I really had the same thing going for me for the next four or five summers when I worked for the same family milling and grain company that my father eventually worked for. The most important thing to me was to be thought of by peers and superiors as one who could carry his own weight even if he had a different name and belonged to a different family.

But I guess it was also important in making a longer term decision not to be involved in a company your family owns; that you make it on your own without worrying about that. I wouldn't really be interested, I think, in a family business.

Casewriter: What kind of relationship did you have with your parents?

Alpert: I think the relationship with my parents was always pretty candid. We sought to make it that way. Our rules with the family would always err toward the side of communicating with each other. "We don't care if you smoke but if you smoke, smoke at home. We don't care if you drink, but if you drink, drink at home. Make up your own mind but don't try and do something when we are not here that's different than when we're here." I think that was a good description of our relationship.

Casewriter: What about their hopes and expectations of what you'll be professionally?

Alpert: They're convinced, my mother in particular, that I will be president of United Brands. And I don't do much to dissuade her. I don't suppose I could.

Casewriter: What about your own personal goals? Do you plan to stay in this business; or is there perhaps something else you'd like to get involved in?

Alpert: At times I've thought I'd like to get involved in politics. I did do some work in St. Louis for the John Kennedy campaign the summer he was running for president. I had gone to Washington right after school let out to try to get in on the campaign at the national level; but it was before the convention and they weren't hiring anybody.

Getting involved in politics wouldn't be as much of a change as you may think; because, in many respects, politics is what product management is. A good Product Manager, I think, would be a good politician, in the way politics ought to be. Staying with United Brands, I should progress to positions where the emphasis is less on marketing and more on management. The fact that you could be moving up to a point where you are spending most of your time worrying about and concerned with showing your interest in people seems like something really worth working for to me.

The problems we are dealing with are fascinating. But I get a little sick of the peanut butter business once in a while. I think it can only take you just so far. Peanut butter will come and go; but people will be around for a while.

Casewriter: How was it that you decided originally to work for United Brands?

Alpert: Several factors counted in making the decision. On the one hand, it was the big leagues. If I hadn't tried it in the big league, I would always wonder if I could have made it. On the other hand, although it looked like a high-risk place, it was actually pretty safe, in terms of going to a known quantity and going to a company that knew how to use the talent I had developed. The third factor was location; Dayton seemed like a nice place to live.

Casewriter: We have talked about your father; but we haven't talked about your mother. Do you have a Jewish mother?

Alpert: Oh, yes.

Casewriter: Is she like the one in the television commercials?

Alpert: Yes, oh yes. She's close. I thoroughly enjoy those commercials. I identify with that guy. But my mother can be put down, and goes down with a great deal of grace and style when necessary. I have a Jewish mother; but I don't have a Jewish wife. And that sometimes befuddles my mother.

Casewriter: How do you mean?

Alpert: Well, my mother is terribly carefully about stepping on my wife's toes. She doesn't mix in. Sometimes I know she's biting her tongue. As a matter of fact, the last time we were in St. Louis we all sat down and talked about it, because I thought she was frustrating herself unnecessarily, holding back. Because, so long as she realized that we were perfectly free to ignore her advice, I thought she should know we valued her advice as along as it was given in the spirit of, "Here's some free advice, which is worth what you paid for it."

EXHIBIT 1

IF

If you can keep your head when all about you
Are losing theirs and blaming it on you,
If you can trust yourself when all men doubt you,
But make allowance for their doubting too;
If you can wait and not be tired by waiting,
Or being lied about, don't deal in lies,
Or being hated don't give way to hating,
And yet don't look too good, nor talk too wise:
If you can dream—and not make dreams your master;
If you can think—and not make thoughts your aim,
If you can meet with Triumph and Disaster
And treat those two impostors just the same;
If you can bear to have the truth you've spoken
Twisted by knaves to make a trap for fools,
Or watch the things you gave your life to, broken,
And stoop and build'em up with worn-out tools:
If you can make one heap of all your winnings;
And risk it on one turn of pitch-and-toss,
And lose, and start again at your beginnings
And never breathe a word about your loss;
If you can force your heart and nerve and sinew
To serve your turn long after they are gone
And so hold on when there is nothing in you
Except the Will which says to them: "Hold on!"
If you can talk with crowds and keep your virtue,
Or walk with Kings—nor lose the common touch,
If neither foes nor loving friends can hurt you
If all men count with you, but none too much;
If you can fill the unforgiving minute
With sixty seconds' worth of distance run,
Yours is the Earth and everything that's in it,
And—which is more—you'll be a Man, my son!

Rudyard Kipling

Casewriter: *To me there seems to be a similarity between that kind of conversation and the kind of conversations you have every day at United Brands. Does it strike you the same way?*

Alpert: *Never had before. Well, I guess to the extent that I feel a lot more comfortable in being candid with people; because people respond so well when they know* *you are. It's really a very selfish thing. I like to be candid with people because I know people like it. Because people like it, our bonds are closer; and I enjoy that. I do it only partly because it is good for the other side, too. With that aspect of it, it's very true.*

Casewriter: *Sitting in your office, I noticed the poem "If" framed and on your wall. [Exhibit 1] The last line caught my eye, and it said something like . . . .*

Alpert [breaks in] *"Be a Man, my son!"*

It's really the first verse of that poem that has always seemed the most appropriate to me, which . . . . I don't remember the words . . . but it's something about keeping your cool when things are going adversely. If you can accept blame when it really isn't yours, or if you can keep your head when all those about you are losing theirs—that's really what the poem is about. Product management, when it's working right, should always be the eye of the storm. And that fits very well with my disposition. I don't tend to get excited; I roll with the punches.

On the other hand, there is a lack of great emotional involvement either on the high side or the low side that accompanies that. It is a fairly steady, even disposition. I am pleased when things are going well; but I don't reach the heights that some people do. I don't reach the depths, either. And I'd just as soon have it that way.

That obviously extends to more than business—it's a personal thing too. It bothers my wife sometimes. She says I don't get enthusiastic enough about the things that happen with the children or us, or whatever; but by the same token, I don't get as dejected.

I really don't think that's a qualification that you need for the job. It could be helpful.

Casewriter: *Would you like to be different? Or is that a moot question?*

Alpert: *Well, it's pretty much a moot question the way I go about things; because I'm . . . a . . . one of the outgrowths of that disposition or attitude is pragmatism. I try to recognize things as they are and make the best of them, instead of wasting a lot of time wishing things weren't that way. I guess it would be nice to get more enthusiastic about successful things and get more involved and excited, but then you're opening yourself up to a lot of stuff that's got to come on the other side of the coin. On balance, I'm satisfied with it the way it is.*

Part VI

Individual behavior and self-management

The primary purpose of the foregoing chapters has been to help the practicing manager perform his or her work responsibilities. The approach has been to view the organization as a total social and technical system, consisting of structural channels, forces, and processes which a manager must understand, guide, and sometimes change in order to affect the behavior of individuals and achieve results. In previous chapters the strictly individual, internal characteristics of people which cause their behavior were generally considered secondary in importance, compared to causes originating in organizational structures and social relationships. This has been done for the sake of clarity and to present the more objective aspects of the manager's work environment first.

In Part VI we shall round out the picture. Chapter 11 presents several concepts of individual personality structure which, in conjunction with other structures and forces, go into a determination of motivation in an individual.

In Chapter 12 we shall examine the criticism by Maccoby in his book, *The Gamesman* (1976), of the long-term effects of certain organizational environments on management personality. We shall recognize the face validity of the problem he defines, and deal with the problem as a challenge to be met in part by "self-management."

In Part VI the most important learning is highly individualized: what one reader can most use will differ from others. The cases each present a picture of an organizational situation almost exclusively from one individual's perspective, and raise questions of career and personal choice as well as managerial action.

Chapter 11

PERSONALITY, MANAGERIAL MOTIVATION, AND THE ORGANIZATIONAL GAME

"The fault, dear Brutus, is not in our stars, but in ourselves. . . ."

William Shakespeare
Julius Caesar, act I, sc. 2.

The importance of an individual's personality in affecting his or her behavior in organizations has been mentioned at several points earlier in the book. In Chapter 5 we highlighted the fact that a purely *objective* contingent approach to the implementation of organizational change was unreasonable: the personality and preferred style of the managers responsible for the change must also be taken into account. In Chapters 6 and 7, individual needs and traits were mentioned as having important effects on the characteristics of emergent work groups and managerial groups. In Chapters 9 and 10 we came even closer to the personal psychological inputs to perspective and behavior in describing interpersonal conflict and what lies behind management style. Given these separate treatments of aspects of individual personality, it remains for us now to put personality in the foreground and the social and organizational aspects in the background, in order to complete our treatment of important forces on perspective and behavior.

Another purpose here is to focus particularly on personality structure and motivation of managers themselves. Thus, although our concepts of personality are applicable to all employees, our illustrations and emphasis will be on the application of these concepts to managers' personalities. The reason for this is to suggest the relevance of personality factors by presenting them in a context close to the reader's own personal experience or expectations. In so doing, we invite the reader to engage in an exercise of self-assessment using these concepts.

In this chapter we shall first discuss three concepts useful for understanding personality as an intraindividual system of forces and structures. These are: (1) motives, (2) identity, and (3) cognitive style. We shall then turn to a particular way of characterizing the work setting facing the individual in complex organizations, namely the analogy of a "game." Particular aspects of the game for managers consist of diverse roles which must be taken on in pursuit of organizational ends. In Chapter 12 we shall pick up this theme by discussing conflicts between individual needs and organizational requirements, the *effects* on personality of playing the organizational game, and present some ideas for dealing with these conflicts and the ill-effects.

Figure 11–1 shows the overview model with emphasis placed on the elements and topics in this and the next chapters.

FIGURE 11–1
Overview model with emphasis on personality inputs

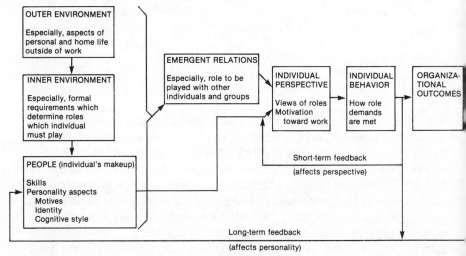

PERSONALITY ISSUES FACING MANAGERS

Why do we need to deal with personality in a treatment of organizational behavior for managers? Basically, the answer is that personality accounts for too much of people's behavior to be ignored. Although much of a person's perspective and behavior can be explained by influences from the formal organization and emergent relationships, much cannot. For example, a manager finds that no matter how much he or she encourages a supervisor to be more sympathetic to hourly workers, and despite the fact that other supervisors under this manager are able to do so, the supervisor—even though the desire is there—seems unable to change. It is important for the manager to have a vocabulary and some experience in assessing when such a situation can be explained in terms of personality forces.

Moreover, an understanding of the inner forces acting to affect people can help explain why people react differently to the external forces in their organizational environment. Why is it that one colleague avoids meetings and works best alone, while another seems to relish group discussion and goals set by others? An understanding of basic differences in makeup can help a manager plan how best to exercise influence to make use of the human resources at his or her disposal.

Each organizational member brings to work a unique genetic self and a unique set of experiences that go back to childhood. These factors have helped form each person's skills and personality up to that time. It is possible for a person's skills to be measured or assessed in some way, whether by a validated test, a thorough check of references and work accomplishments, or a careful job interview. On the other hand, personality attributes are much more difficult to assess. This difficulty arises from the fact that while skills and abilities have straightforward manifestations in behavior, such as typing speed, quality and speed at programming, analytical ability, quality of decisions, persuasiveness in dealing with others, and so on, the deeper intraindividual aspects of personality typically have less direct manifestations. Personality is an abstract concept, measurable only indirectly.

The human personality may be viewed as a system. Like other systems, such as the physical body or organizations, personality has structure, processes, and states of equilibrium and change. Personality is an open system in the sense of being in an exchange relationship with the physical human body and with the individual's total environment. Unlike most other systems it is extremely difficult to define and specify the elements of the personality system. This is because of its inherently abstract nature. Thus, instead of there being a physically observable set of elements, such as the pipes and valves of a plumbing system, we must develop constructs or concepts to define the structural elements and processes of personality. As one can imagine, this stage of affairs has given rise to a host of personality theories.[1] From a practical point of view, our problem here is to choose from a vast array of concepts used to define the personality the smallest necessary number of concepts. We should have a set which helps explain the motivation and behavior of

---

[1] For an extensive overview of personality theories, see Maddi (1971).

employees and managers in organizations, and which make sense intuitively to a person reflecting on his or her own personality.

THE CONCEPTUAL PIECES OF PERSONALITY

For managers who wish to understand something about the makeup of personality of themselves and others, three concepts of personality are important. The first is an explanation of the sources of forces that drive or motivate individuals from within. For this we shall use the concept of *motive*. Basically, motives are inner needs which a person seeks to satisfy. Material things or psychic events which satisfy motives are rewards. The second is *identity*. Identity may be defined as the set of traits and values which a person holds as a preferred set for himself or herself. One's identity may take the form of traits typically found in some occupational or career role, such as a leader of a firm or a teacher. It may also take the form of a particular individual in one's past (especially one's father or mother) or present (an inspiring leader or admired spouse). The third essential concept is that of *cognitive style* which a person uses for processing information. Cognitive style ranges on a continuum from highly intuitive to highly systematic.

A person's tendency to behave in an organizational setting, in the absence of any external forces or direct influence, comes from his or her personality, made up of these three conceptual pieces. Motives are in a sense the fuel or driving force that pushes the person to behave in some way. Identity and cognitive style are the structures which channel and guide these forces. Identity and cognitive style reflect our values and behavioral preferences for seeking the rewards which satisfy our motives. One person may seek to gratify a high need for affiliation, for example, through a career in which an identity is built as a counselor. A person with a highly systematic cognitive style may seek to satisfy a need for achievement through engineering or accounting as a career.

We turn next to an elaboration of these three personality concepts; the links among them, and their effect on individual perspectives.

Motives

The most basic and universal motives are biological: needs for food, shelter, safety, and sexual gratification. Other needs may be thought of either as derivatives of these biological needs or as independent of them and of a very different nature. These include the higher order needs in Maslow's (1954) hierarchy, namely social, ego, and self-fulfillment.

A slightly different way of conceptualizing these needs is suggested by McClelland (1975), who proposes that three motives can explain much of adult behavior. They are particularly economical as concepts to explain organizational behavior.[2] These are *need for affiliation, need for achievement,* and *need for power.* Need for affiliation is a social need; a person with high need for affiliation wants to be liked and is often sensitive and responsive to others. Need for achievement is the drive for individual accomplishment, for getting results that are measurable and visible and which provide feedback that the person can perceive. This is typically what motivates the inventor, the entrepreneur, or the salesperson on commission. The rewards are the recognition for accomplishment and money as a symbol of accomplishment. Need for power is the need to exercise influence. It can take two forms.[3] One is *personalized* power, in which one seeks personal control over others for self-aggrandizement. The other is *social* power, whereby one seeks to control the efforts of others for ends that are outside one's self and beyond the goal of controlling others. The individual exercising social power seeks to achieve goals which are common with others, toward the end of building something tangible or intangible. Rewards for the need for power are recognition for leadership, attainment of positions of influence, and money as a symbol of organizational or social status. Having some degree of social power as a motivating force is obviously of value to a manager responsible for achieving organizational results by influencing the behavior of others.

Identity

Identity and cognitive style in effect define the arenas and the methods by which individuals seek need satisfaction. Assuming one has the opportunities and skills to make a choice, whether one chooses a career in business or dentistry, nursing or teaching, farming or social work will depend in part on one's perception of the rewards available. This is part of what Schein (1978) refers to as one's "career anchor." It will also depend on one's identity, the implicit sense of self and of the ideal person one aspires to become.

A great deal of attention, both professional and popular, has been given to the concept of identity since Erikson used it as a central concept in his articulation of adult psychology.[4] Erikson recognized, along with the Freudian psychoanalysts, that our behavior patterns as adults are constrained by the particular identity formulation of our earliest years. At the same time Erikson noted that adult identity is changeable and that identity formulation is a continuing process, marked by reasonably predictable stages and transition points. At the transition

---

[2] See McClelland and Burnham (1976).

[3] See McClelland (1975).

[4] For a discussion of the concept of identity and Erikson's use of it, see Coles (1970).

points people have unsettling and often inexplicable feelings of uncertainty and loss of motivation. These periods are referred to as "crises" or "passages." Two recent works which have built upon the idea of changes in identity in adult life are those of Vaillant (1977) and Levinson (1978). Both these researchers studied adult men who were generally normal in psychological health. They describe the ways in which their subjects dealt with internal changes of identity and how external events both affected and were affected by the behavior deriving out of these internal changes.

A key point for our purposes is that adult personality undergoes change due to inevitable shifts in identity and the consequent rechanneling of motives. Because of this, personality lends itself to change and *self*-management. Thus, the person as a whole can at key times and under the right conditions grow and change in desirable directions.

Cognitive style

Motives and identity are concepts which describe inner drives and basic emotional or affective aspects of the personality. Physiologically, the source of energy from motives may lie in the more instinctual parts of the brain. By contrast, cognitive style refers to an aspect of personality which appears to be controlled from the neocortex, the part of the brain which has evolved more recently. There is evidence that the left and right hemispheres of the brain may be responsible for different styles of cognitive functioning. It appears as though the left hemisphere, which controls the right side of the body, is the seat of speech and writing and the development of systematic and logical thinking and ability at calculation. The right hemisphere, which controls the left side of the body, is where development of spatial relations, parallel thought, and artistic abilities occur.[5] Thus, it may well be that differences in cognitive style result from early encouragement of the development of one or the other of these hemispheres by home and educational environments.

Whatever the source and causes of differences in cognitive styles, it is quite easy to see these differences manifest themselves in people's behavior patterns and preferences. Of course, some people show a pretty good balance between the styles, and are able to work both systematically at times and intuitively at others. Most people seem to have a preference for one style or the other, and sometimes this is a strong force affecting career choices, the ways they perceive the world, and their abilities to deal with organizational work.

---

[5] For a discussion of the implications of the left-brain, right-brain dichotomy, see Sagan (1978).

One manager whom we know was a very good technical specialist in a computer department. Because of his success at technical jobs he was promoted to the head of the technical services unit. In this job he was expected to delegate specific technical work and to deal with the difficult relationships between his unit and users of the department's services, people in computer operations, and top management. His approach to this ambiguous job was to attempt to devise a flowchart and set of rules for all communications and relationships, an effort doomed to failure. Eventually, he was moved to a staff position, which made him and those he had worked with much happier.

Of course, people are not locked in to one particular cognitive style. Indeed, just as identity can change and be managed in adult life, so too can many individuals expand their competence for approaching problems using alternative styles.

Some implications for management

Before turning to a discussion of how aspects of personality come together in perspective, let us consider, in light of these concepts, what managers can do about what are euphemistically called "personality problems."

All too often managers blame low motivation or interpersonal conflict on "personality problems." As should by now be clear, such difficulties may represent problems of communications and misunderstanding (Chapter 9), problems of pressures from emergent groups (Chapters 6 and 7), or problems of formal structure, as well as from within personality. The first rule in dealing with personality problems and other personal problems of others is to make certain the other possible causes are *not* responsible. It can be embarrassing and dangerous to the reputations of the persons involved for a mislabeling to take place.

At the same time, it is our experience that most managers bend over backward to *avoid* labeling a person as having a personality problem. Indeed, we have provided personal counseling to several managers who are concerned about the behavior of a boss or peer or subordinate who question their *own* mental stability before questioning that of the other person. In several such instances, irrational behavior was being exhibited by others, with the source lying in some personality disorder. It is of great benefit in situations of this kind to have a confidential chat with a trusted third party.

Very few managers are qualified to make a diagnosis of another's psychological or other personal problems. To be able to identify that there is problem is a very big step, for it means one can at least recognize that reality. Whether the other person can be helped by some professional assistance is a question a manager should ask of a qualified expert, such as a psychiatrist. Short of that, however, it is advisable to take the view that most such problems are *relative* rather than absolute, and that the environment of a person with such problems can be an aid to helping them. The manager who takes this view adopts the philosophy that "everyone is a little nuts," that time alone can often heal, and that changes in environment and simply an understanding relationship provide the kind of support often needed.

No matter how understanding and helpful, however, extreme cases of these kinds of problems are all too frequent. The manager facing such a problem in others needs to keep a close vigil and be attentive to when the risk of injury to another's reputation is offset by the risk of permanent mental or physical harm. When that vague line is crossed, professional help is imperative.

PERSONALITY, PERSPECTIVE, AND MOTIVATION

The three pieces of personality come together as an important part of the individual person's perspective. It is in the perspective that motives are felt, that one's identity becomes compared with one's current experience, that cognitive style affects what we perceive and how we process information to come up with assumptions and beliefs. In general, perspective is the meeting place of these internal personality forces and all the external forces from the individual's environment.

Although one's motives are internal to the personality, we consider *motivation* to be one of the products of the meeting of forces in perspective, as discussed in Chapter 10. Motivation is the strength toward some behavioral act or behavioral pattern which an individual has at any point in time. It is the result of inner motive strength, channeled by values and patterns of preferred behavior arising out of identity, and affected by the person's perceptions of external forces.

There is a particular kind of motivation which has been proposed by White (1963) which has usefulness as a way of thinking about managerial behavior. This is "competence motivation," the pressure to work which derives from the experience of having mastered a task or challenge. This may include not only a *particular* task, but a professional series of tasks as a part of one's career. The inner motives involved here are the higher order needs for ego gratification and fulfillment—the need for achievement and the need for power. But the motivation per se also comes from the experience, in one's perspective, of learning and getting positive feedback. Thus, even when the inner motive is satisfied, a high competence motivation generally sustains energy toward further effort. Competence motivation has been elaborated on in the organizational context by Lorsch and Morse (1974).

THE WORK ENVIRONMENT: THE GAME

What is the nature of the typical work environment of people in organizations and particularly of a manager? The purpose of this section is to describe and characterize key dimensions of the work environment for managers in a way that will permit an analysis of the effects of the meeting of typical managerial motivation with this job environment. This will be the basis for the discussion in Chapter 12 of problems which arise in motivated managers as they deal with their jobs.

Formal managerial rewards

In general, organizations can offer managers role positions (jobs) which consist of two kinds of formal attractions and rewards. First, jobs can provide a structured opportunity for learning new skills and gaining experience. Through the exercise of those skills, managerial jobs offer opportunities for satisfaction of competence motivation. It may seem strange in this age of humanistic psychology and movements toward self-expression to suggest that external structure is an inducement rather than a detraction. And indeed many organizations do overstructure and inhibit the talents and contributions of managers who would be loyal and more productive if given additional freedom and autonomy. Nevertheless, a basic attraction and inducement of organizations for professionals and managers is the potential for structuring and guiding the work of others and having some degree of structure and guidance for oneself.

The opportunity to exercise mastery explicitly requires opportunities to learn skills and meet challenges provided by some external source. Organizations thus provide the opportunity to attain skills (ability to sell, to produce, to organize, and to influence others) which only the rare individual can provide for himself or herself.

The second formal inducement is more tangible. It is the rewards available for satisfying need for affiliation, need for achievement, and need for power. Organizations offer people a social environment, feedback, and means to influence others. The opportunity for pay and promotion are the essential rewards for these natural and inherent motives. Thus, in its structure and formal rewards organizations set up the stage, the rules, and the spoils for the game which managers and others *need* to play.

These opportunities and inducements are those of the formal organization in any typical environment where the organization must perform to a certain standard in order to survive. Business competition, legislative and public scrutiny, and the like are all external demands which put most organizations into the position of requiring of its members their energy, therefore offering opportunities for the formal game to be played.

Informal managerial rewards and their effects

In addition, however, organizations also offer informal inducements, or those which arise from the emergent system. The context of this was covered in Chapter 7. These demands and inducements take the form of *informal* role requirements which managers are expected to fill, such as being a member of a particular coalition and thereby being loyal to its members and cagey with nonmembers. The political side of organizational life is for some managers an inherent challenge and attraction, for others a distasteful and demeaning engagement. Working to achieve ends for which the institution stands can require working around the rigidity of the formal system. This is the necessary but informal, unwritten side of the game required for success in most complex organizations. The game aspect is inherent to the nature of organizational requirements, and must be dealt with by individuals who, choose managerial careers in organizations.

The higher the individual goes up in an organizational hierarchy, in general the greater the uncertainty and subjectivity of decisions that have to be made. Although the particular requirements of expertise and skills in the sense of specific technical knowledge needed to accomplish organizations' goals is probably evenly distributed across hierarchical levels, the absence of particular constraints to judgmental decisions increases the higher one moves as a manager. Therefore, success at higher levels generally requires, first, at least an adequate or in some instances a superior knowledge of the key technical or functional aspects of the business. That is a necessary but by itself insufficient condition for the organization to succeed. Also required is an interaction among organizational leaders which improves the quality of subjective decisions. This in turn implies a climate in which such decisions can be reached, where individuals with a particular mix of motives, identity, and decision-making style work to fulfill themselves. In short, it requires managers who know the territory, have the personal characteristics which enable them to play the game that awaits them, and who can thrive and respond to the game in ways that give their organization an edge in its environment.

For their survival and success, organizations thus require managers who can work and grow within a formal structure, enjoy their formal rewards, and do not back away from exercising direct influence on others. At a later point in their careers they need to initiate their own structures and thrive on influencing peers as well as subordinates in political processes. In particular, as the manager moves up, playing the game means taking on different roles and managerial styles and at some point having to be in charge of subordinates whose personalities and job requirements differ from the manager's own. The manager in this position must frequently exercise a contingent management style. As described in Chapter 10, this position, which corresponds to moving into general management in a complex organization, is a crucial promotional point. The key to the game is to recognize that it must be played as much with skills and motivations suitable to the political aspects of organizational functioning as with those suitable to the substantive or technical aspects.

CONCLUSION

The fit of a person having the appropriate motive pattern, identity, and decision-making style in an organization usually benefits both the individual and the organization. Many managers describe no greater turn-on than the sense of fulfillment that comes from learning the key skills and performing them; competing in healthy rivalry with one's peers; and eventually being motivated from the exercise of mastery, competence, and creativity. Needless to say, these personal rewards and growth can most often mean fulfillment of the organization's aims as well. At the same time, however, a number of risks and problems arise from the standpoint of criteria of personality development, organizational ends, and societal goals. We shall raise and discuss these in Chapter 12.

QUESTIONS FOR STUDY AND DISCUSSION

1. For a person who is important to you in your work or school, what would you say are the strongest motives or needs in terms of McClelland's three categories (achievement, affiliation, power)?

    Answer the same question for yourself.

    For the other person and yourself, what would you say are the characteristics of your predominant cognitive styles?

2. What kinds of jobs would make the best fit for a person high on each of McClelland's three needs and the different types of cognitive styles described in this chapter?

3. Times of identity change are stressful and unsettling. Can you describe such an era in your own life? What resources, mechanisms, etc. were responsible for your successful emergence in the next stage? What were the obstacles?

    Apply the same analysis to your organization.

Case 11–1
Hans Brauner*

On January 7, 1972, Hans Brauner was fired from his job as national service manager for Bakeomatic, Inc. Except for some part-time consulting, Brauner was unemployed until September 10, 1972. He was 38 and lived with his wife, Luisa, and two small children in their home in Weston, Massachusetts.

Exhibit 1 is a copy of the résumé Brauner used during his period of job search in 1972.

Brauner's parents were of German descent. His father was a successful executive, reaching the level of vice president of a medium-sized drug firm with headquarters in New York.

In school Brauner's interests were in science and math much more than subjects like English and history. He attended a private preparatory school. At 17 he entered college to study engineering, but switched to economics on the advice of guidance counselors. In the middle of his second year Brauner flunked out of college and enlisted in the U.S. Navy. There he became very motivated by technician training and enjoyed his associations with people, but felt "underchallenged." He returned to college at age 20 and graduated in electrical engineering at age 25.

Upon graduation from college Brauner returned to the Navy and served as an engineering officer for three years, mostly at sea.

Brauner's professional career began in 1962. During the ten years until he was fired from his job at the Bakeomatic Company he worked for five different firms, mostly in engineering. When he went to work for the first of these, Chase and Company, it had just been acquired by a larger company. Brauner and many others were laid off within a year of his joining the company. After less than a year in his second job, with Amp-Scale Engineering, he was again laid off. In this case again, he was one of a large number of engineers who lost their jobs at the same time.

Brauner next deliberately chose to work for a small firm, General Thermionics. Here he felt much happier. As he described it later, this was because, "now I was part of the operating team rather than being a tiny frog in a giant mud puddle." He left this job of his own volition after 1½ years. His next job was at Circuit Innovations, another small firm which was family owned and managed by the sons of the two founders. He worked for three years in the engineering development of a new product, electric radiant heating panels. Sales of the product

---

* All names have been disguised.

EXHIBIT 1

Résumé

Hans Brauner
384 Maple Street
Weston, Massachusetts 02193
(617) 123-5542

Personal	Married (two children); excellent health
Job objective	To have a major staff responsibility relating to the engineering or technical service department of an organization in the marine/oceanographic field.
Business experience	BAKEOMATIC INCORPORATED—National Service Manager Waltham, Mass. Product: Custom-made commercial ovens

Coordinated all service functions including installations in hotels, hospitals, universities, and passenger ships (*S.S. Rotterdam, S.S. United States,* and *S.S. Constitution*).

Upgraded new service personnel through improved training and hiring procedures.

1969–1972   Initiated the revision of service manuals to extend their function to that of a marketing and training aid.

Originated an expediting system that reduced late spare parts order volume to 2 percent of original figures.

Enlarged three field offices to serve as regional warehouses.

Sparked an incentive program that motivated service technicians to sell service contracts with a resulting 300 percent increase in revenue.

Increased the number of service agencies from 79 to 110.

CIRCUIT INNOVATIONS CORPORATION—Director of Engineering
Boston, Mass.
Product: Architectural lighting fixtures

Founded the Radiant Heat Division.

1965–1969   Re-engineered existing radiant electric heating element design to reduce cost of production.

Initiated new heating element design to broaden line.

Managed production for on-time delivery of products while maintaining inventory balances within strict budget levels.

Procured all materials used in production of electric radiant heating elements.

EXHIBIT 1 (*continued*)

	GENERAL THERMIONICS INCORPORATED—Chief Engineer Cambridge, Mass. Product: Electric lighting elements
1964–1965	Supervised the design of flexible electric lighting elements used in such applications as medical instruments and aircraft systems.
	Developed new construction methods for unique lighting elements.
	AMP-SCALE ENGINEERING CORPORATION—Product Engineer Needham, Mass. Product: Particle accelerators
1963–1964	Developed a low-cost system for the metering of a 200 kilovolt power supply.
	Improved a method for specifying and controlling the quality of magnet castings.
	CHASE AND COMPANY—Engineering Trainee Lexington, Mass. Product: Bio-medical electronic equipment
1962–1963	Participated in the following segments of the engineering training program: test equipment engineering, technical writing, and component testing.
Military	U.S. NAVY—Engineer Officer
	Supervised operation of engineering department consisting of three officers and 60 enlisted men aboard a diesel-electric-powered icebreaker. Ship operations consisted of oceanographic and meteorological studies in area of Alaska.
1958–1961	Responsible for the maintenance of gyros, fathometers, roll systems, desalination plant, diesel-electric generators, main engines, and all other electro-mechanical equipment related to control and operation of an icebreaker and a tank landing ship.
	Qualified as officer of the deck in all types of weather; logged 3,000 miles of day and night steaming.
	Supervised three-month shipyard overhaul of icebreaker.
Education	RENSSELAER POLYTECHNIC INSTITUTE Troy, N.Y.
1954–1958	Majored in electrical engineering.
	In addition to electrical engineering courses also studied celestial navigation, coastal piloting, and marine propulsion systems.

EXHIBIT 1 (*concluded*)

	Elected to Tau Beta Pi and Eta Kappa Nu scholastic honor societies; President of engineering club; NROTC scholarship student.
	Graduated in 1958—Bachelor of Electrical Engineering.
Background	Involved with naval and maritime subjects for 19 years beginning with my enlistment in the U.S. Navy in 1963.
	As enlisted man studied the maintenance of gunfire control systems and was graduated second in a class of 25.
	Brief stay in Germany in 1961–1962 where I learned to speak German and worked for a firm making depth gauges.
	Taught sailing in Charles River for two summers.
	Presently own small sloop used for family cruising in lakes and coastal waters.
Publication	Author of article published in *New England Electrical Magazine*. Title: "Radiant Heat Elements for Commercial Comfort."

were poor, however, and Brauner was offered a position elsewhere in the firm. He chose to leave because as he put it, "I wanted to make a change." He then began the job search that led to his being hired in 1969 as the national service manager for Bakeomatic. He held that position for three years until he was fired.

During the eight months he was out of work Brauner had several long discussions with John Campbell, a friend who happened to work as a casewriter at the Harvard Business School. In suggesting the interviews to Brauner, Campbell pointed out the potential value of Brauner's experience as a case. Their discussions were tape recorded. Verbatim excerpts are given below.

Discussion on April 19, 1972

Brauner: *You know, one very important thing that should be in the B-School curriculum is to teach a guy how to get a job. . . . In a sense Lyndon Johnson was fired. Bunky Knudsen was fired a couple of times. Both of these people are highly talented. The anguish and the shock that the people and their families go through when this occurs is such that this training is, I believe, a responsibility of someone administering a high-quality education.*

There have been four suicides in the Boston area as a result of recent tremendous engineer layoffs. This is a very high human price to pay for whatever the benefits are, namely keeping the company solvent, I suppose. I think this kind of remark will probably fall on more receptive ears these days than it would have two years ago. . . .

Campbell: *Maybe a good place for us to start would be what happened to you at Bakeomatic. Then we can go back and talk about your previous job history and whatever other personal history you think is relevant.*

Brauner: *OK, OK! It has been a spotty job history, in that the beast has been fired or laid off no less than three times! But to begin with Bakeomatic, I got my job through a methodical telephone process. I took a long list of companies who had Underwriters Laboratories' approved products and were located within a reasonable commute, and starting with A and working through Z, I called every one of them looking for work. The call to Bakeomatic resulted in an interview, and later an offer.*

Briefly, the work sounded interesting. The starting salary was very good: $15,000. It was a $3,200 raise over my previous position. My salary at the end was $17,500. And it presented an opportunity to build up an organization. In both this job and the previous job at Circuit Innovations, as opposed to two earlier ones I will talk about, the work was so intensely interesting that I could not stop myself at 5 o'clock and I could barely stop for lunch. But at Bakeomatic this petered out, which may have led to my firing. . . . Maybe they saw me starting to fall back into a pattern of disinterest. . . .

By the way, at some point I want to get into the process of how to choose a job. There's a lot written about it, and I've become an expert [laughs].

Campbell: *How about right now? We don't have to stick to a . . . .*

Baumer: *Well, no. I'd kind of like to finish on Bakeomatic and get back to the other later.*

Bakeomatic makes large commercial ovens that are sold to the hotel, restaurant, and institution trade. Sales run about $8 million a year. The customer's building has to be customed to the oven. The product is really interesting to me. . . .

I took over the national service department, which was grotesquely larger than anything I had ever run before in my life, and in a field that I knew nothing about [laughs]. I was the national service manager. As I look back on it, I wonder what the hell I was doing there!

Campbell: *What were some of the particular tasks and problems you faced in the service department at Bakeomatic?*

Brauner: *In the beginning there were several problems facing me. There was no uniformity in the company image, in what the service trucks looked like. There was no service manual.*

The service manager whom I replaced was the man I had to learn from. I was hired on top of him, in a most awkward situation. I would sit on a camp stool in his office and literally look at his desk as he sat behind it and wonder when he was going to get up from behind it! It was a peculiar battle that nobody understood. Finally, one day about a month after I came in he walked into the office and said, "I'm leaving. I just gave my two weeks notice. I'm quitting." He hung around for two weeks, gave me a little bit of help, and then became a printing press repair man. He still is to this day. He's happy as a lark.

I then began overhauling the service manuals, buying new trucks, and adding staff members in accordance with where the sales manager felt they were needed. And I tried to get a good secretary.

I'll discuss the secretarial position first. For the first woman I hired I looked basically for aggressiveness, because I wanted a secretary who could help to reshape the office. The woman I chose was certainly aggressive but not much else. She picked fights with our superiors, which reflected poorly on me.

It took me four months to screw up my courage to fire her. This was the first time in my life that I ever had to "do a person in" in any manner, and it was exceedingly distasteful. When I finally did fire her I gave the reason that I didn't feel that she was very happy in her job. Actually, I couldn't stand the son-of-a-bitch was the real reason.

After she left I was bound and determined not to hire an overly aggressive secretary and I was also determined that I would dominate her within an inch of her life. This secretary came to me with virtually straight As, well dressed, good typing skills, and an unbelieveable body. She was the showpiece of the corporation. However, I bore down on her so heavily in my reaction to the other secretary that she quit.

As a result of this I took a great deal of stock in myself and decided that "you catch more flies with honey than vinegar" is pretty true. I decided that with the next secretary I would pitch and court and woo and essentially treat her as though I loved her. So I hired the third one.

The third secretary lasted till I got thrown out which was just about a year. The first two had lasted about as long as I did in my first jobs: six to nine months. I think a comparison between them and me might be worthwhile. . . .

But to get back to me, starting in the beginning [at Bakeomatic] I was extremely eager, working from six in the morning to nine at night my first year. I was building my own empire, which, to be perfectly honest, is the greatest fun in the world.

An insidious thing happened to me. The previous head of the service department had been a very sloppy operator, whereas I tend to be picky and meticulous to the point of pissing off a lot of people, if I'm not careful.

Amongst my faults I tend to go in this direction: I worry about the little things. Now, unfortunately, I was egged on to using one of my shortcomings to propel myself. Upper management repeated to me how the previous service manager had been so sloppy and had no sense of order. The result was that I badgered people to fill in their expense accounts, I relentlessly built up the details and the nitpickies that had been left out. This got to the point where, and this is important, I made a great many enemies in the field. . . .

But the sequence of events and personnel shifts may be significant in what eventually happened to me. About a year ago, I had to fire the Ohio serviceman, Barrett Cole, whose father Wilson Cole, who was the highest paid and most capable salesman in the company. A few months later Wilson Cole, the father of the fellow that I had fired, became my boss.

Now, I like to think that he never held it against me, and he probably didn't, but I was too closely associated with firing his son for it to be comfortable. He also didn't like the salespeople's complaints about the strictness with which I operated on the field personnel. But he did admit to me that he had great respect for my administrative ability. He did tell me that before he fired me he had tried *very hard to sell me to the engineering department. But this did not seem to work.*

OK. That's it. That takes us up through the firing. I think the next thing is what to do after one is fired, and what I went through afterward.

Campbell: *OK. I think we should also talk about your job history some more, and about your background.*

Brauner: *OK. For now, let me give you this résumé* [Exhibit 1], *which I mailed out to a few companies back in January.*

I also have the results of a number of psychological tests, taken at various times, but mainly in the last couple of months as a result of my going to Brimmer Wycoff, a career-counseling psychologist-type. I have finished up with him. He sent me a summary letter of the results of all these tests. After dropping $250 on Wycoff, I'm not sure it was money well spent.

At this point I've already sunk $250 into Wycoff, plus the fact that I've read all these books on the subject of finding a job, selling yourself, all that garbage. . . . I've got as good a grip on this ballgame as I'm ever going to have.

One reason I have doubts about Wycoff is the shrink part of his work. . . .

Campbell: *You mean Wycoff comes across like a shrink, and going to a shrink . . . there's a kind of norm in our society against doing that?*

Brauner: *Yeah. One doesn't deal with a shrink. It is not done. . . .*

Well, uh . . . . I don't quite know what to say next. . . .

Discussion on May 1, 1972

Brauner: *Let me talk about the big psychological problem of having been fired. It's intriguing. When you have been fired from what you are doing, from what is almost your entire life except for your marriage, it is stupendous in its weight. Being fired is like really being thrown in jail. It's just unbelievably depressive.*

Now maybe to a guy who isn't a big bellybutton watcher, like your basic salesman, you know, it's not. But to a fairly introspective character like me, it weighs heavily. It's a real _____. And when you consult with job counselors and when you read the books, they say don't worry about being fired, it doesn't make a damn bit of difference. Hah! It's very hard to believe this no matter how often you hear it. Because the difference will always remain between a person who's been fired and one who hasn't; the one who hasn't been fired just plain looks more successful than one who has. . . .

It can knock you down to the point of making you move slower. I've had days lately where I did literally nothing. I would appear active. My wife and my kids would think I was doing something all day long but I was carrying coals to Newcastle and then back to the mine. Such things as going to the library to look up prospects and actually sitting there and reading Popular Mechanix. Getting up late, wasting time, doing a little bit of typing, and then going downstairs and making myself a chocolate milk or something like this. Gearing down to very low power, where there's two hours of productive work in the morning and two hours in the afternoon and a lot of TV at night and a lot of playing with the kids.

[Discussion wanders to Brauner's ethnic background.]

. . . in the family lore we were descended from Leonard Brauner, who was a scientist born in Switzerland, who operated between Moscow and the great university in Berlin. I grew up under the impression I was descended from this great guy, and believed it as my father had. But when I got to Germany I met some of my relatives who had been forced by Hitler to trace their family tree to prove they were not Jewish. It turned out that the family extended pretty much back to the time of Leonard Brauner, but instead of Switzerland they came from Mainz, Frankfurt, and Dieborg, and therefore I may be descended from a cousin or something like that.

Campbell: Do you think there were any ethnic reasons for your being fired from Bakeomatic?

Brauner: There were not ethnic forces, really, although one aggressive director is Jewish. And the one he was very much against was my boss, the Boston Brahmin. It didn't appear as though there was any fight there. It was mainly an investment thing. . . . If there was an ethnic thing all I can say is it was as subtle as any ethnic thing today. . . .

I don't know whether it's common or uncommon in things like this but it seemed that after the change in management everybody who was at all associated with the previous team, the one I was in, was in trouble.

And, . . . uh . . . my problem is, you know, is to ask myself is this just a rationalization on my part or was that really it? And I think maybe it's a rationalization to some extent, because if they didn't like me because of my association with the team they threw out they would have had somebody they could have really replaced me with goddamn quick, whereas in fact I was one of the last to go. . . .

As it was I saw the changeover and saw I had to correct problems I had created in the field. I knew how to straighten these things out, and I was beginning to take steps, but unfortunately, and this is the thing I'm really bitter about, I didn't get the chance.

So it was a great lesson for me, personally, in politics. . . .

Campbell: I don't see you and Luisa as being in any kind of long-term financial bind. I wonder if the problem of losing your job, being fired, is much more a psychological problem, a threat to your identity, than it is a financial problem.

Brauner: Yes, it is. And yes, it is not. It's a mixture of both. Our net worth comes to a shade under $100,000. . . .

Now, this brings up something else. Because of my father's checkered career, I have always been extremely wary of my own career and have always oriented myself in a very, very defensive manner. . . . I've always been an intense but very informal student of individual ventures because I realize that someday when I'm over 40, I probably will get fired. I've felt this in my bones.

Some of Wycoff's tests convince me that this is true. I have characteristics that make me probably the world's most abysmal employee. And while I am not a natural entrepreneur like Colonel Sanders, I may be forced into that position. This has been my feeling and it was confirmed by the psychological tests. The Edwards Personal Preference test and the Arnold S. Daniels test show almost zero natural aggressiveness and a great deal of what they called succorance, which means you're always asking for help.

Now the only way to cure these two very heavy psychological handicaps is for me to throw myself out in the position of having to fend for myself. Because I do not gravitate to these things naturally in the corporation.

I tend to get lazy after a while, which is lack of aggressiveness, and I tend to become very much of the type that always asks the boss, "Which way next?" instead of figuring it out for myself. And I suppose somewhere in the psychological stuff, although Wycoff didn't reveal it, this gets back to depending on mother, father, or some sort of _____ like that. I don't know what the hell it is. . . .

Somewhere in my life I became very dependent, I looked to other people for leadership. I'm a real good follower. I fit into a system like a jewel, to a certain extent. Until I get to the point where my goal is to get out. At a point I will chafe at it because I love freedom. As an enlisted man in the Navy, I just went bonkers.

Campbell: Do you think by any chance that there's anything in your German heritage that is behind this?

Brauner: I've often thought so.

People don't like to believe these things anymore, but, uh . . . I believe niggers are lazy, Jews are aggressive, and so on.

You should see my report cards from the first through sixth grades. The first grade report card says "Hans is quarrelsome and uses force undeemed as necessary." I am in some respects the stereotype and I can see it in myself.

Another thing about the Germans that I don't think Americans are aware of, they're great adventurers. . . . I'll never forget my Strong test, number three was "adventure."

Campbell: Was what?

Brauner: Number three. They were Mechanical, Medical Service, and Adventure.

And you'll see for the job objective on the new résumé: marine and oceanographic.

Do I like a racing sailboat? Competitive? No, I like a cruising sailboat . . . I, I suffer from the fact that I have great confidence in my ability to get out, but I don't have the guts to get into something. . . .

Give me some more cues. What do you want to know?

[Discussion moves to techniques of gaining entry and conducting job interviews when one is looking for a job.]

I've spent a lot of time reading the self-improvement books. . . . One of my ideas was to start a consulting business. I could go to a corporation and if they have any goddamn heart at all they would pay me a couple of bucks when they've fired a guy for me to help them be sure he doesn't go drink himself to death or shoot himself. Four people have done that within the last two years in the Boston area as a result of the terrific Route 128 engineer layoffs. But I see that this is impractical. . . .

Coming back to my original belief that job searching is a haphazard thing. . . . How do you know what the guy is going to think when he sees the résumé? You don't know. . . . So what the hell do you do?

Campbell: You've got to somehow know your audience before you know them. . . .

Brauner: *And you* can't. *So therefore it becomes a haphazard thing. Or you go through the techniques that these books advocate.*

Now I've done this in a couple of interviews and it actually works.

I'll give you an example, I went down to Plymouth Marine Corporation and spoke with the owner who graduated from the B-School six years ago. He asked about salary right away. I told him that I didn't want to talk about salary yet, and he got a look on his face that kind of said, "Oh, my god! I've been caught asking a person a question before I should have." But the great advantage that I felt was that I had some control over him. This subtlety of control is something that is totally alien to me as a person. I'm an open-faced sandwich. Premeditated defensive deviousness is something I just don't have the imagination for to the degree that I have it for mechanical things. In other words . . . .

Campbell: *What do you mean by defensive deviousness? Give me an example.*

Brauner: *Aggressive deviousness is when you plan ahead of time to try to control the interview. Now, I would never control an interview. I would walk in and say, "Here I am looking for a job, what's your question?"*

So there's a lot to learning this process. . . .

Campbell: *How is your current mood, or the way you spend your days?*

Brauner: *My attitude now is refreshed. I've written myself a new résumé. I have it directed in conformity with some of the things from the Strong test, where I have it pitched along scientific lines and blended with my 19 years of experience with nautical topics. . . .*

Say, something just popped into my mind here, and that is that I don't like dropping a thread of conversation and having to pick it up a long time later. I find myself saying, "Holy cow, now I'm going off on a different tangent!" And, "Is this bad?" And, "It's probably bad, because I'm indecisive." But then I think I'm learning more this way, and therefore this is good. It's a really funny thing. . . .

You said something to me once, about a year ago. You said that you get started on a project and later on you work up what it's going to look like. This is a basic Campbell, right?

Campbell: *Yeah.*

Brauner: *But Brauner operates a different way. Brauner can't tolerate that aspect of the Campbell. Brauner wants to work the whole _____ thing out ahead of time, and then let everything fall into place. Brauner does not believe it can be worked out unless the ducks are all lined up.*

Campbell: *Yeah. I see what you mean. So with respect to our discussions, you want to have some notion of precisely what's going into it before you start to talk, or when you talk you want to feel sure that it's going to make sense. And I appreciate that, I respect that. . . .*

Brauner: *But the thing is that I see from talking to Wycoff that even though I have these psychological characteristics and I cannot control them as much as I should, at least from talking to him I realize that they are there. In the case of being too picky or something like that I can bring myself up short and say, "Oooooooop!" That's the bad thing in me being picky! And I can let it slide. . . .*

Campbell: *This is a good benefit. I knew a guy once who said you should go to a psychiatrist once a year, just like to a doctor.*

Brauner: *Yeah, but I don't think just talking it out would really get at the problem. Louisa said to me that I don't come across as unaggressive as these tests show. And I said to her, "Well that may be true." But think about being competitive. Some people, I suppose this is true of probably most people, enjoy a little bit of competition. I just don't give a damn about competing in a game. There's no purpose!*

Campbell: *Did you ever play any sports at all?*

Brauner: *I've always avoided them, avoided them, unbelieveable! I've done everything in my power to avoid sports. They are the source of infinite embarrassment to me. . . .*

Discussion on May 8, 1972

Campbell: *Maybe we could concentrate tonight on what you've done in the way of a job search.*

Brauner: *OK. The first thing I did was to go on vacation down in the Caribbean. Now in the books they tell you not to go on vacation after being fired, but I did. . . .*

I had a good time. But the problem was there as it is here: the fact that I have no work is all-pervasive. Eight hours a day I don't have any real professional purpose other than to find a real, new, live job. So it weights pretty heavily at times, and at times I'll get a knot in my stomach, and I get almost a little frantic feeling. Like a caged animal. The only manifestation of this is perhaps sleeplessness. Occasionally, once a week, I really toss and turn. . . .

Oh, I did get involved in some consulting with Circuit Innovations Corporations, where I had worked before Bakeomatic. It involves designing a purchasing specification for a new consumer product. So this stretched the time out and I don't think I really got organized and started on a job search until mid-February. . . .

Well, after the first three interviews I reviewed Wycoff's advice once more and restructured my résumé to make it even more narrow: I wanted technical service department work in a company that was marine or oceanographic oriented. . . .

Psychological testing to me does nothing more than professionally corroborate suspicions you've had about cracks in your own personal plaster. But something like a Rorschach ink blot test is not a self-interpretation. But, if you have any curiosity at all you'll probably go to a library and look the Rorschach up and you'll learn how to answer it. If I were to take a Rorschach ink blot test for a sales position at Chase Manhattan Bank or General Electric right now, I would see in all those butterflies the large, powerful tigers and elephants and things like that, because that is what a salesperson sees.

Campbell: *Did you take the TAT?*

Brauner: *Yeah, I was given two series, one to take home and write a paragraph on. They include in there a picture of a silhouette of someone in a stance with one leg up on what appears to be an opening. Now this can be a back door that he is* *leaving after having slept with the boss's daughter, which is what the B-School student sees. To a highly depressed person, this is a window on the top of the Empire State Building out of which he is jumping.*

In my case, I described it as just someone in a sort of nebulous situation jumping out of a window into a flower bed. And then I followed it up by saying he may stay there or he may run across a large lawn, indicating indecisiveness and sort of reinforcing my indecision trait. This may be related to my current floundering . . . I know myself as not being brutally decisive . . . but not awfully indecisive either. . . .

Well, at any rate, that's some of my insights on the psychological testing.

Campbell: *Tell me about the job prospect up in Maine.*

Brauner: *OK. Pine Electronics is the only interview that brought forth anything resembling an offer. The location of the plant was an hour from Portland, Maine. But it's in the sticks, and I just can't stand the idea of being in isolation. The reason is because I know that what happens in an area like that is that you get this Peyton Place syndrome where people don't do anything but talk about each other. . . . When human beings are idle, they turn into monsters . . . at least I feel they do. . . .*

I was very impressed with the leadership of this corporation. I'm very impressed as a result of this being owned by a huge conglomerate. It sounds like a very well-run thing.

Campbell: *What impressed you about the leadership? Who did you meet up there?*

Brauner: *I met the general manager. He struck me as a very sharp, dedicated man. Truly a professional manager, and all professional managers to me are like monks in the Catholic Church in that they are heavily dedicated to their work. To the exclusion of a lot of other things. . . .*

I admire that, but my job searches and career orientation have been very much oriented toward where I am and what sort of people are in the neighborhood where I'm going to live. It's got to be an interesting town. . . .

Even your most dyed-in-the-wool corporate ladder freak doesn't really want to live in a place like Pine Falls unless what he is doing is there. But I will enjoy living in Boston even if I'm sweeping the streets. . . .

Campbell: *So what happened?*

Brauner: *I courted the hell out of 'em to the point where they finally gave me an offer of a temporary consulting job. . . .*

When I called he said, "We would like you to do a market survey and work with our marketing chief, and this way we can get to know each other better." And I said that sounded terrific and I'd be up next week on Thursday morning at 10:00 A.M. to discuss this with the marketing chief.

Now this is being positive to the last minute.

I knew I was lying even when I said this, way down inside of me. I really had a talk with myself, and something of a talk with Louisa. I decided that this was a sort of bird in the bush and not a bird in the hand at all and this combined with the fact that it would break my stride in looking for other jobs. In other words, I want a job offer or nothing. . . .

So, I accepted this thing. But all it proved was that I was operating the way the book said, which is not the essence of me. Then I did the really bad thing. I wrote 'em a letter saying that after heavy thought I am not going to be up there. And to some extent it was true. But all along, even from the very beginning, before I went up for the interview I looked at Pine Falls on the map and said, "Oh, _____!," it was an act, the whole thing was an act. But it had some therapeutic value just in the fact that I was so down in the dumps that to go some place where somebody more or less wanted me, felt good. . . .

Campbell: So you backed off with Pine Electronics.

Brauner: I reneged. . . .

But I liked the president. He was a ladder freak who works his tail off. I think like so many successful things a great deal of it is just intense interest and dedication and really giving a damn about it.

Campbell: Has the buoyancy from the Pine Electronics thing been lasting?

Brauner: Oh, no. It's a momentary thing. Now I'm back looking for more interviews. Each one has some therapeutic value. You're out in the environment . . . you're doing something, not around the house with babies and kids and stuff like that.

But if I succeed in getting the kind of job I want now I would probably be happier than I was before. The product at Bakeomatic, ovens, never really held my interest. They were too passive a device. I'm going to apply to Woods Hole [Oceanographic Institute], but I'm going for the administrative. The only thing I can possibly be is Woods Hole's purchasing agent.

Campbell: [Looks at empty beer bottles.] Well, we've killed a lot of Indians!

Brauner: In vino veritas!

Campbell: The other thing I was going to ask you about was the swing set business. Have you looked into that again?

Brauner: Yes. Yes. What's happened is this. I've sold the first one. Got paid for it. Got an order for a second one.

Louisa and I talked about my going into this full time, starting off on a Mom and Pop sort of basis. Mom will be very interested in participating 'cause she has her father's "make-a-buck" traits and she has the kind of organized mind to be a help.

Now I'm getting to the point where having been out of work for four months, I begin to look like an undesirable. It's a terribly long time by some standards. . . . And it's nothing by other standards. The thing is, if you have enough capital to keep the household more or less operating, the pressure is off you to settle for just anything. The boredom is more the problem than anything else. . . .

So that in starting this swing set company I have got the beginnings of something that requires virtually no investment. It's my insurance, my unemployment insurance. . . .

Discussion on May 16, 1972

Brauner: OK. Let's start out the next tape on the deeper feelings of what I would really like to do.

The thing that is complex is what do I want to do and what can I do? And I think this is where the problem lies . . . I think being fired makes me feel that *whatever I was doing I'm no good at. I probably got into problems with not handling people well and also I think that in a certain sense I got bored by the job, either because it actually was boring or I made it so by not venturing forth into different fields.*

I enjoy working by myself. I don't enjoy manipulating a bunch of people. I would never want to be a regional manager for Electrolux with seven sales-people reporting to me and having to listen to all their problems and complaints. I'm actually very happy doing what I am now which is designing children's swing sets. Designing them is a mental juggling act. This intrigues me. . . .

The other thing I like about a job is to have people around me—I suppose anybody likes this—who think the same, pretty much the same way as I do. And I suppose by this I pretty much mean scientists, engineers, teachers, doctors. This was brought out in my Strong test. . . .

Is this on the tape now, what we're saying?

Campbell: *Yeah.*

Brauner: *OK. Did I make the point before on these tapes that I'm conscious of the fact that I'm approaching 40?*

Campbell: *I think so. You mentioned your age once.*

Brauner: *Well, what it means to me is it just gets tough to get a job.*

The other thing is approaching 40 makes me very suspicious of not very profitable ventures. The company that gets into trouble is the one that's going to look for people to thin out. They're going to come gunning for me I figure, because I've gotten sensitive after I've been thrown out of three places, and thrown out of college once. I see a "Brauner-is-a-guy-who-gets-thrown-out" sort of pattern developing. Just like some people are success-oriented, I find myself sort of failure-oriented. . . .

Since then in the companies that I've worked for I've seen people who perform far [worse] than me who are still hanging around the company. So I don't say that I'm a total horrible employee or something like that. I'm just saying that I've hit upon a couple pieces of really bad kinds of luck. . . .

Discussion on August 9, 1972

Campbell: *Why don't you go back a month or so and describe the events that have happened.*

Brauner: *There were two job prospects down in Rhode Island, one of which was with Eastern Instruments and seems definitely out of the question for me now and the other is still open . . . [goes on to describe these].*

Campbell: *A lot of your early efforts were toward sending out a broadcast letter without including a résumé. What particular type of letter or opening seems to be most successful?*

Brauner: *The best thing I think really is some sort of knowledge of the people inside. I think that any sale is a skirmish which doesn't end until the two people involved in the deal trust each other. This is what you're heading for as you work your way through a sales pitch. . . .*

A real bit of depression and melancholia has sort of set over me and to answer your question before, "What works?" well, nothing has seemed to work. And it's just gone on and on and on.

And now with this consulting job at Circuit Innovations I am working about 35 hours a week at $8 an hour, which is a potential $300. I can't even get really juiced up on this thing. . . .

So far, I've been offered three jobs by the people at Circuit Innovations that are sort of temporary and terminate, plus one permanent thing. The result is that I said, "Now look, I don't know where this is going. You've offered me all sorts of opportunities here. There's a great mish-mash of things to be done in this company and what I'm looking for is my own salary, $17,500, and three weeks' vacation." So there it ended.

There you have me right now. . . .

Now there's one other thing that I want to go into here which we touched on before, and I didn't go into it before because I wanted to get the whole thing really into focus. Wycoff sent me to see a shrink. And I think it's good now 'cause as I look back in retrospect on this thing, I'm coming up with the opinion that it was really of little value.

Essentially what it boils down to is this. I have what is called an obsessive-compulsive reaction. Ever heard of that?

Campbell: I know what it means. I don't know the clinical definition.

Brauner: It's kind of a nervous guy who's always double checking things. Sort of unsure of himself. This kind of thing. And the treatment consisted of teaching me self-hypnosis where, now let me stop and go back. . . . This thing is to me very awkward and unbearably confidential. I haven't . . . Louisa's the only one who knows. Her parents don't know. My parents . . . my one parent doesn't know.

Now, his name is Childers and he's spent his life shrinking executive brains and students'. At any rate, what the guy said was, "Your problem is not asserting yourself." So I said, "Okay, that's true." His approach was two things. First of all was the self-hypnosis bit—what you may have heard of as autogenesis or something. . . . You sit in a chair and you relax. Just kind of flop like that. Take a breath. And just pretend everything's all sort of fat and heavy and your butt is all made out of sandbags, and then you concentrate on a thought. For example, asserting myself where I really have to write a letter and snap off the television set and run upstairs and write that thank you note to dear old Aunt Ermie for the stuffed pillow. So you're supposed to do maybe ten of these things three times a day while you're in this trance state. . . . You follow this with another one like that. And you go through these things. You're daydreaming, secret life of Walter Mitty-ing yourself, fantasizing yourself into this assertive, powerful person until you have become accustomed to this as a normal operating method—after many, many, many sessions of this.

And uhm. The second thing is the same thing as television advertising. What you do is you take one of these thoughts and you envision yourself turning off the TV set, going upstairs, writing a letter, and then you think of something that's really fun—eating a piece of chocolate cake, or sitting on top of a mountain you've climbed and looking at the view through clear air. Boy, that's a helluva *sensation. It's really great! And you'll notice that in a television ad, which is a hypnotic thing, you get the fact and then the funny at the end. . . .*

Campbell: *Uh hmm. I get it. It's a reward for doing what you need to learn to do.*

Brauner: *Yeah. Well, at any rate, I screwed around with this stuff for a while, and I kinda got tangled up in it all. There's Hans, the zombie, sittin' in the chair. I just couldn't make myself do it. . . . I didn't have enough incentive, I guess deep down inside I didn't really think I was that damned crazy. I mean there isn't enough incentive there. I just figured, "This is infant science." You know, "This guy's really sticking me for $30 an hour." You should advise your kids to be a shrink. It's a good life.*

After going through all of this stuff . . . I felt that it wasn't worth the effort. I just don't believe that even if he did succeed to some extent that he could really change me. I figured that somehow I'll muddle through life with the problems that I have. This was my decision. . . .

Campbell: *How did you decide to take Wycoff's advice and go to this guy in the first place?*

Brauner: *The shock of being fired is so bad. It really is so incredibly bad that you'll do anything. Uhm. To quote Wycoff, there's two things that drive a man to the shrink. Trouble in love and trouble in work. . . .*

So, as a result of this now, I see myself as a person who gets hung up in details or other characteristics, not wanting to make decisions, which is bad for an executive. Bad for anybody, but worse for an executive. I've always been aware of this to some extent, but now I recognize it as a pattern of this specific mental description called obsessive-compulsive. They are not decision makers. . . .

The other thing about an obsessive-compulsive is that he is a fearsome worker. Grrrr! Hammer and nail, gluing things, reading, doing some damned thing. Can't just do nothing. So I think it was worth it, you know. My life is complete now, I've gotten laid and seen a shrink. [chuckle]

So, I'm getting tired of not working, I'll tell ya that. It's a real pain in the tail. And I'm thinking that I can't be so choosy as to say I don't want to work at such and such a place because somebody already works there. . . .

My father-in-law offered me a position in his company a few years back, but I just didn't want to get involved. But now as time goes on I'm starting to think differently and I say, Gee, you know, here's a helluva guy to learn from. Here's a guy who really knows how to turn a buck. He never loses. Or, when he loses he compensates by an even greater win. And, I'm a fool not to take advantage of this thing. . . .

But there's a lot to be said for your own independence. When the day is done and the moon and the sun all set, you're going to come out of it clean.

I've got to go pretty soon.

Campbell: *You gotta report to the consulting job at nine in the morning?*

Brauner: *No. I'm just going to go. It doesn't matter when I get to that job. . . .*
[chuckle]

It's an awful sensation. Whenever I have an unproductive hour it just kills me to bill 'em for it. [Laughs] Hell. It's a real sleepy company. The product doesn't excite me. But the guys who run it are real nice guys, and they want to make it grow. They're good managers. It's a family company and I think they always make money on the thing. One of the jobs they proposed to me was where I would analyze all the competition, analyze all their lines, and teach the salespeople about it at seminars. I bet our salespeople are really stupid. . . .

Discussion on November 18, 1972

Brauner: *Let me tell you what's happened lately.*

I consulted through the month of August for Circuit Innovations. . . .

And at that point, with the termination of the project, they offered me a job at $17,500, which I was getting at Bakeomatic, plus three weeks' vacation instead of two and fully paid medical plan. And I took it.

During the course of the consulting I was very consciously soft selling myself at every opportunity. And I think they saw a person with whom they could work well and everybody would be relatively happy, so they then started to cast about for an excuse to bring me in. I say this because the job that I was offered was most extraordinary. It has three components to it:

a. *Searching the marketplace for the correct way to make a new type of burglar security circuitry that architects need.*
b. *Developing quality control where there has been none.*
c. *Developing safety engineering in the plant where there has been none.*

There are about 100 employees in the company. So far the job has been to concentrate entirely on the safety engineering, which I have done.

Campbell: *Give me an example of how you did the soft selling of your capabilities during the consulting.*

Brauner: *OK. The soft selling was, first of all, doing the consulting job right. . . . So the soft sell consisted of having this presentation meeting, which was very impressive to them. And I say this was a soft sell because I really wasn't trying to sell myself at this meeting, I was simply trying to do a good job. The meeting took place approximately August 15th, and they offered me the job shortly after Labor Day.*

The other part of the soft sell consisted of at various times having lunch with the president, or one of the two vice presidents, or all three together, and simply shooting the breeze with them about the company and making a maximum of intelligent remarks and a minimum of stupid ones. Really, it was just as simple as that. . . .

The other thing that I did was, and this was totally repulsive, was a premeditated soft sell. The president told me that his wife has analyzed him, in his tremendous success at racing 210 class sailboats, as a person who wins because he puts himself early in the competition in the position of a loser and this juices him up and gives him the incentive to become a winner. I filed this in my head and let it rest.

I then later on happened to hear him talking to someone he was very impressed with, and one of the things he mentioned was that Mr. X had made Tau

Beta Pi in his junior year in college. Now, I made Tau Beta Pi in my junior year in college and I filed this in my head.

Then three or four days later, on the way back from lunch, I jiggled the conversation into the motivation toward winning in competitive circumstances. And I simply told him that I also did like he, in that when I found myself behind the eightball, this is where I perform the best and this is how I got into Tau Beta Pi in my junior year. Now I fed him two pieces of highly digestible material in one pill and I think that this had some effect. . . .

Campbell: *Didn't you say this company was family-owned and run?*

Brauner: *Yes, it is a family company. There is no future for me here. Uhm. But this doesn't bother me. Because I don't really want to go any higher . . . it's not that I don't want to go any higher, but . . . I've been feeling very 40 recently. My eyes kind of went on the fritz, I can't focus closely.*

While I'm not saying that I'm not striving any harder, I've been batted down so much that I think there may be something of an element of truth in here and that if I kind of shift over, rather than trying to climb a ladder, just doing a job at what I'm doing and being conscious of Wycoff and the shrink's comments, analyses, and what not, and truly concentrating on doing a good job, life will take care of itself. . . . Uhm, this, this would be hard for some people to understand and a little bit hard for me to swallow but I think it also may be realistic. . . .

But we are going to need a bigger house. We are feeling pinched with two kids as they grow. I can see a problem arising there. Our yacht is too small. [laughs] So we got to get a bigger boat. So this will require more money. Maybe this will give me a goose in the tail. . . .

Campbell: *You know, you're saying things about yourself that you couldn't say before, I think. You're saying, "I'm the type of person who really prefers an interesting job that will give me a reasonable level of income."*

Brauner: *Well, it's not only am I in a job, but I've also gone through this psychological hash here, uhm, and I see that my job is to learn to work within the psychological limitations I know and which were pointed out by these guys and this is my challenge more than anything else, because if I can work around these things I will avoid getting fired again. You see, unlike an awful lot of people around us, I've been sort of thrown out of it. I'm punchy.*

Campbell: *Yeah.*

Brauner: *And, deep within me it's really traceable to these psychological limitations. For example, maybe not doing anything decisive or really constructive until I can get the whole thing figured out. Or getting all shook up about what the boss will think about it rather than just plain doing it and getting it done.*

I guess probably the most succinct of these is programming in the time element. I was never as conscious of time before as I am now. Not from the sense of hurrying up but from the sense of rather than struggle with the thing until it's exactly right, cut if off and get it done, and move on to the next one. Which is something I have been previously in my life totally unconscious of. . . . I'd struggle with the damned thing all _____ night rather than say, "I can't," and move over to something else. Perhaps to a larger degree than a lot of other people. And now I'm really trying to handle these things.

Campbell: *I see.*

Brauner: *My problem's just to hold on to one* _____ *rung as long as I can.*

Campbell: *You've got to hold on to that rung to keep your self-respect.*

Brauner: *Keep my self-respect? Uhm, no, it's not that . . . it's just plain not get fired again. It's just* _____ *awful. . . .*

Campbell: *You know, as you've said, and I'm just rephrasing it, this new job for you is a kind of a stage on which you can work out what kind of a person you are and you can, as you put it, smooth out a lump or two.*

Brauner: *Not, "Work out what kind of a person" I am. That sounds too much like the teenage identity crises. It's to work with the kind of a person that I have already become. I see that it's been going on so long and, uhm . . . and I never have changed. I've never changed my spots. And I don't think people radically change in their lives.*

Wycoff suggested a job in liaison between the workers and more sophisticated people, scientists and engineers. This is true in safety, although you have to substitute managers for scientists and engineers. I might do well to stay in safety and just make myself more comfortable. This is not ladder climbing, this is just to make myself more attractive to a larger company. And being something of the rule freak certainly fits in with safety. This might be a move later on.

I don't know. It is sort of silly to talk about getting out of the job just after you are getting into it!

Case 11–2
Leif Johansen*

"Leif, I hate to tell you what Tom did when it was announced in the meeting that the computer implementation project was drawing to a close and that your consulting would be finished by the end of the year."

"Let me have it."

"He *applauded . . . .*"

"That's about what I would expect at this point," said Leif.

The report on the behavior of Tom Brimmer, president of Billsworth Manufacturing Company, was just another reason why Leif Johansen felt it was important for him to make some choices about what should come next in his career. He had known for a long time that top management at Billsworth was not committed to the project, although there had never been a problem in funding and the evaluation of project by Dwight Nichols, a third party consultant, six months ago had been very favorable. "After all," Leif reasoned, "there was no need for top management to be committed so long as I am here to push the project

---

* All names have been disguised.

through . . . ." Moreover, he had had great success with the middle management people at Billsworth. He felt that those who were going to be directly and most dramatically affected by the computer were enthusiastic about it.

But now Leif had begun to feel uneasy about the politics of the situation, and he wondered how and when would be the best time to terminate his work at Billsworth, and what he should turn to next. In particular, if he chose to expand his consulting business he would need a strong success story behind him. This would not be as important if he chose to continue at about the same level of business he now experienced, which was running one or two projects at a time.

The more he thought about it, the more Leif felt that this career decision, at age 34, was the most important in his life.

EARLY YEARS AND CAREER BEGINNINGS

Johansen was born in 1939 in Brooklyn, the first son of Norwegian immigrant parents. While he was growing up his father worked as a sales manager of marine lubrication products for a large oil company. Leif remembered that his father occasionally complained about the bureaucracy of a big company and talked about going into business for himself, although he continued with the company until retirement. Leif recalled that his mother always dampened these suggestions. In 1973 his parents lived comfortably and modestly in what had been the family summer resort in upstate New York, surrounded by old friends, mostly Norwegian-Americans.

Johansen did well in school from a early age, in what he described as, "competing with highly motivated Jewish guys." He had a scholarship for private school, and was admitted to Yale with a scholarship in 1956. In that same year he met and fell in love with Deborah Martin. The two were married four years later.

Johansen remembers being very impressed with Yale, particularly the "intellectual atmosphere" and "the idea of a liberal arts education as it was espoused by Whitney Griswold." Nevertheless, his academic record was "erratic," as he put it. He majored in math with a minor in philosophy, but found that his ability and interest waned as mathematics became more and more abstract. In his senior year he faced what he recalled as a difficult decision of what job to take. In the summer of 1959 he had worked for IBM on a piece of the new "Sage II" simulator, coded in 704 machine language, and had found it challenging and interesting. As he described it, "I was intrigued by the power, elegance, and versatility of electronic computers. It was the beginning of my love affair with the machines . . . ."

After interviewing several departments of IBM in Poughkeepsie,

Johansen took a job at a salary of $6,500 a year with the group developing software for the Stretch Computer. Stretch was an ambitious project. It was advertised publicly by IBM as a major improvement in computing technology. Johansen reflected that he chose that job largely because he was attracted to the glamour of working on the "super computer."

He continued, "I was all fired up when I took the IBM job. I guess I saw myself at age 21 as a thinking man, a liberally educated man, getting in on the forefront of an important development."

Upon graduation from Barnard, Deborah Martin also took a job with IBM in Poughkeepsie, and soon became a very competent commercial machine systems programmer on the 1401, 1460, 7080, and 1410. Deborah and Leif were married in November 1960.

Johansen's work on Stretch was successful and rewarding, and his duties expanded until by 1962 he was recognized as the number one expert on the control program. He was sent to a number of installation sites including Los Alamos, where the first Stretch computer was installed. He took on increasing responsibilities in training user personnel and in testing and integrating the control program, and at one point single-handedly reduced the core requirements by 33 percent. His site work put him in contact with engineers, whose typical job was to find a problem with the machine and call him in to diagnose and remedy it. This involved first determining whether it was a hardware or software problem. As Johansen put it:

> I had a nose for the thing. I went about it in an intuitive, unstructured way, depending on my knowledge of the machine. This was in contrast to some of my colleagues. One of these in particular would lay out steps of analysis in advance, and go through a checkout procedure step by step. He would eventually get the job done, but I found my method more comfortable for me and generally a lot faster . . . .
>
> I was further impressed with the power and versatility of computers which were able to do everything from global weather simulations to airline reservations to playing checkers . . . I was having a ball, getting paid for it and getting raises at decent intervals.

Around 1961 the Stretch program began to run into difficulties. Although advertised as being 100 times faster than the 704, the speed of Stretch never exceeded 40 times the 704. When this became known, the price was reduced from $13 million to $8 million, which was below cost. Johansen recalled that the program became a public embarrassment to IBM, and Johansen recalled that a number of top experts and managers were demoted, one becoming a programmer.

The failure of Stretch as a commercial venture affected him. He began to feel that he knew more and more about less and less, and that this specialized knowledge was highly "perishable." He was coming into competition with a lot of very bright people at IBM who had advanced technical degrees, and he didn't want to compete with them on their terms. Although his career goals were unclear, Johansen had the general feeling that he would probably spend his life in a large corporation. He felt he needed to know more about business, and decided to apply to business schools. A further reason for this step was his feeling that he wanted to improve his last academic record, a rather mediocre senior year in college.

HARVARD BUSINESS SCHOOL AND RETURN TO IBM

Johansen was accepted at all three of the schools he applied to, MIT, Stanford, and Harvard. He chose Harvard because he felt "up to my ears in math" and wanted a nonquantitative approach. He applied for an IBM fellowship. Although this was turned down, he was granted a leave of absence for two years to get his MBA.

Johansen recalled the first year at HBS as a very broadening and intellectually stimulating experience for him, although he underwent something of a "culture shock" in the first weeks:

> At registration I turned up in jeans and a polo shirt. Everybody else had a suit and tie and briefcase . . . . I just wanted to learn something about business . . . I was very comfortable, very self-confident. I remember a section party where I met the wife of a classmate from the Midwest who said, "Tom and I figure you've got to make it by the time you're 40, or you'll never make it." I said, "What do you mean, 'make it?'" She and her husband looked at me as if I'd said, "What do you mean by sliced bread?"

Meanwhile, Deborah was able to get a transfer to the Boston branch office of IBM, and spent the two years working as a technical representative to a large insurance company.

Johansen thrived on the first-year classes and the case method. He quickly got a reputation as the section "computer jock" and something of a wit. Although he saw himself not taking all of HBS as seriously as many of his classmates, he finished the first year in the top third of the class and received a letter from the Doctoral program inviting him to apply. He sent a copy of his grades and the letter to IBM with a second application for a fellowship, and this time it was granted. It consisted of full salary and tuition.

During the summer between years at Harvard Johansen took a job with IBM working at a large "think tank" firm on their Stretch computer. He described the job as "probably a mistake" in that it did not teach him anything new, although it paid very well. The Johansens bought a sports car.

Johansen found the second year more of a drag than the first. As it came closer to the time to get a job he found himself "in something of an identity crisis." As he put it:

> Although I had enjoyed technical work, it seemed unthinkable to return to a technician's job. Nor could I see myself plodding rung-by-rung up the corporate ladder. I was increasingly concerned with career planning, yet I never could crystallize my personal career goals. In Business Policy we were supposed to write a "career strategy" paper. I simply couldn't write it! I went in to the instructor and told him I just couldn't
> . . . .
>
> I couldn't imagine myself doing anything. At HBS they train you to be a corporation president, but I was half-hearted about that kind of a future. I began to see myself as more of entrepreneur, especially in the role of applying innovative technology and systems. Entrepreneurship was very attractive in terms of independence and potential dollar rewards. A lot of this was reinforced by meeting people in the New Enterprises course . . . .
>
> My head was going in two different directions. I interviewed big companies with the vague idea that I might prepare for a future entrepreneurial thing by working for a few more years. I was kind of screwed up . . . I went to the HBS psychologist. It was helpful to verbalize all this, but I didn't follow up with other visits. I figured I should be able to handle this myself . . . .

Johansen looked seriously at several opportunities within IBM and one with another large company where two of his former superiors on Stretch, Guy Heller and Stan Caldwell, had gone and wanted him to do marketing and technical planning. With IBM he was offered a job in direct sales in the Cambridge office. He recognized it would the the "fastest track" in the company, but he was not turned on by the prospect of being a salesman. Another opportunity was market planning for the new 360 software system. This was a mainstream activity for the company, but it was staffed with a "cast of hundreds." Johansen could not see himself having a major impact in such a setting. Still another opportunity was in a group staff job doing pricing. He rejected this because it was "too bureaucratic."

During the course of an interview for one of the IBM jobs Johansen was told, "You must be quite a guy if you can still hold your head up after working on the Stretch job." Johansen recalled that his own feeling about his experience on Stretch was that the total project failure was not his fault, but that in retrospect his own feelings of satisfaction were "considerably less than what I could have felt if the whole project had been a success."

Johansen finally decided on a job in the Advanced System Development Division (ASDD) at IBM, at a salary of $11,000. The job involved developing new business opportunities for IBM by exploring new markets and technologies and assessing commercial and technical feasibility. Johansen saw it as broad gauge and demanding a full range of his talents. In taking this alternative he recalled, "I wanted a job where I could consolidate my HBS experience and leave my options open for the future. I was pretty enthusiastic about this job. . . ."

In the summer of 1964 Leif and Deborah Johansen moved to New York, where Leif would begin the new job. They bought a house and prepared to start a family.

THE ASDD EXPERIENCE

Johansen's first assignment in the Advanced Systems Development Division was as market planner for new "assembly shop" information systems, such as a system which would collect data at machines on the shop floor, feed into a centralized file, and produce reports on inventory, costs, times compared to standard, and so on. In support of this work he developed a model for estimating the market for such applications, based on census data and SIC data as inputs. The model produced a profile of aggregate needs for these kinds of systems in manufacturing and assembly plants. In giving seminars on the model Johansen developed something of a reputation in the division for the success of the model. He was also engaged in a variety of market surveys, case studies, and contract proposal writing.

Although he found the work interesting and broadening, and leading to good professional recognition, Johansen recalled that it was "my most staffy period" and that he missed a feeling of concrete accomplishment, of producing "anything tangible." Johansen also recalled being disappointed in the level of professional management in the division:

> I suppose this is a fairly common feeling among a lot of MBAs when they first go to work . . . I had the impression that the people never really were committed to the market-planning concept. Rather, it seemed the division was dominated by a bunch of technical guys who paid lip-service to the planning concept as a way of justifying development funds.

In mid-1965 IBM expanded its manufacturing facilities to cope with the new 360. This meant building new plants, each of which would specialize in a particular component of the machine and ship them to installations to be field-assembled. This event created the opportunity for ASDD to demonstrate the practicality of one of its shop systems, and it negotiated with the manufacturing division to do this in a new plant in Boulder, Colorado. Johansen and two colleagues were sent to Boulder in March 1966 to gather data and design the system for that particular application.

On returning to New York in September, Johansen was offered two jobs. One was a division staff job. The other was to become the head of the team of programmers for the Boulder project. The major problem with this job, which would put him in a mangement position for the first time in his career, was that the manager who had been in charge and who would be his boss had made a commitment to implementing the system by December. "I saw no hope of meeting that," recalled Johansen. Then I talked to *his* boss and was told not to worry about it, that this type of thing always slips its schedule." Despite these problems, after only "one night of soul-searching" Johansen accepted the job.

From October 1966 to June 1967, Johansen worked in New York on the Boulder project. He had 12 programmers and analysts reporting to him. At the time of acceptance tests the system "passed with flying colors." This was considered by all involved to be a major achievement, in view of the fact that it was a new system and new applications for the 360. Hardware consisted of the 360/40 with 1050 and 1070 terminals. Software was the OS modified for multi-tasking, and the newly released ISAM and BTAM packages.

Johansen remembered this job as one of the most rewarding of his entire career. It provided a "terrific sense of accomplishment" in a "real turnaround" situation. He found that he enjoyed thoroughly the management aspects of the work, and especially the opportunity to give subordinates their heads and let them show what they could do. Johansen was particularly gratified by the comments from the Boulder plant people, who noted how his team was strongly motivated and successful in its on-site work. He recalled the occasional fights with peers and superiors, but he considered these "part of the game."

COMPUTER GRAPHICS

Just after completion of the Boulder project, with only documentation and clean-up remaining, Johansen got a call from John Dwyer, who had been his boss during the last year or so of his work on Stretch. Dwyer told him he had just quit IBM and was going to form a new company, Computer Graphics, with Guy Heller and Stan Caldwell, whom they both knew from the Stretch project. He invited Johansen to join. Dwyer was to establish an information services division for the new company, which would eventually have as its principal product an entirely new machine for transmitting television pictures through regular telephone lines. Johansen asked, "What would I be doing?," to which Dwyer replied, "I don't know yet."

The next day Johansen flew to see the founders of the new company. He was offered 1,200 shares of stock in the yet-to-be formed company, and a salary of $13,000. This represented a significant cut from his current salary at IBM, which was $16,000. As Dwyer explained it, however, "We're all taking cuts . . . Caldwell was earning $60,000 before he decided to get into this . . . ." Johansen asked for more stock, and went so far as to say he would take a little less salary to get it. They agreed on 2,000 shares and the salary of $12,500, and Johansen took the job the next day, on July 6, 1967. The Johansens were expecting their second child in August.

On August 14th Dwyer and Johansen had their first contract for the information services division, an airlines reservation system project. Johansen was the only available body to work on the project, and was thrown in with many others in the customer's offices in what was referred to in the industry as "body shopping." "My ego was somewhat bruised," Johansen recalled, "because I had just come off my own successful job, now here everyone seemed to have more knowledge and authority than I."

The discomfort of the work on the project, however, was largely offset by the performance of the stock of Computer Graphics. Before the company began operations it offered 401,000 shares of common stock, representing 49 percent of the company, to the public at $10 a share. The offering went on the market in September 1967. On the first day the stock traded at $30, then continued to rise until it reached a high of $130 a share in 1969, riding the crest of the investment craze for glamour stocks.

In November 1967, Johansen learned from a friend who had worked under him on the Boulder project that their information system had been scrapped by IBM, to be replaced by a system developed by the manufacturing division itself. His friend told Johansen, "You were smart. You kept us rowing that boat hard, then jumped off just before the waterfall . . . ." Johansen remembered that he had misgivings about the permanence of the system even while he was working on it, but that his attitude had been, "What the hell. The challenges of this job are enough for me . . . ."

By March of 1968 Dwyer had managed to hire five more programmers and analysts for the airline reservations job, and Johansen returned to New York. At this time the stock was trading for $50. Johansen recalled that for the first time in his life, he began to think of the possibility of becoming wealthy. At the same time, he was becoming more concerned with "the intrinsic merits of money-earning activities," and recognized that he did not want to jerk his family around. Leif Johansen and Deborah were able to communicate in detail about his work, and although Johansen felt he was "bouncing my way through the computer industry," Deborah assured him that what was most important was that he choose what he was most interested in doing.

Although he found working on many projects unexciting, often due to the mediocrity of technical understanding by most users, Johansen resolved to dedicate himself to the information services business, and in particular to concentrate on learning to sell and land contracts, which he saw as the key to the business at that time. In August 1968, he landed a big contract for an on-line order entry system. He went to work managing the project for a few months, then turned it over to a subordinate. All in all, Johansen was able to bring in over $200,000 worth of new business in 1968 and 1969.

Meanwhile, he began to get involved in another division of Computer Graphics, the leasing business, and also in continuing problems of manufacturing and assembly in the plant set up to produce the company's product. About this time, the on-line order entry project began to be plagued by turnover of personnel, reflecting a growing trend in the computer software industry for people to leave and take their contracts with them. The Computer Graphics stock seemed to be leveling out, and began what was to be a long downward slide.

In September 1969, Johansen resolved to resign from Computer Graphics as soon as his employment contract terminated at the end of 1969. He was concerned about the apparent strategy of the company of using the information services division and the leasing division as temporary money earners which would be phased out when the company's product was self-sufficient. He could see no major role for himself in a "product only" company. In November he went to a lawyer to arrange for disencumbering his 2,000 shares of unregistered stock. When the lawyer asked him what he would do after he left the company, Johansen remembered that he answered, "I'm not sure. I may go into business for myself." The lawyer replied, "If you decide to do that, let me know. That would help us in getting approval for you to sell your stock."

That same day, Johansen decided to go into business for himself. He resigned on January 1, 1970, as did Dwyer and two others of the founding group of the company. In February he received permission from the SEC to sell his stock, on which he netted close to $100,000. The stock slipped to a low of $10 later in the year.

Johansen recalled that although the future was uncertain for him and he did not like the idea of leaving friends at Computer Graphics, his overall sense was one of having made a wise and timely move, particularly with respect to conserving capital. "In a nutshell," he recalled, "the value of my stock was going down $2,000 a week. That's why I started my own business."

In July 1970, Computer Graphics terminated the businesses of all its divisions except the one devoted to making the company's product.

LEIF JOHANSEN ASSOCIATES

Business was good for the new firm. Johansen landed three contracts, and hired two employees from Computer Graphics. He recalled being concerned during this period to build a "quality firm" with a strong reputation. He loved the independence and prestige of having his own firm. At the same time, Johansen remembered, there was an element of fright in the process. He would wake up sometimes at four in the morning, asking himself, "How do you build a business?" Although he wanted to give his business a full and fair chance to succeed, he was increasingly concerned with family questions. He wanted to build an estate as well as spend more time with his family and provide "a quality life and upbringing for his children."

In 1971 some of Johansen's fears about the business began to prove real. Several contracts "bombed out." He was forced to get rid of one employee, a very painful process for him, and he placed the other on a subcontract which he learned about from contacts on previous jobs. Business became so slow that Johansen remembers one period when he would come to the office for a few hours, then go to the movies to take his mind off the problem.

At about this same time, Deborah was experiencing pain in her back and was undergoing extensive treatments.

In September 1971, Johansen landed a contract with the Billsworth Manufacturing Company to install the firm's first computer system, with initial applications in sales reporting, production planning, and inventory management. For the rest of the year he worked on the project, hiring Gene Floyd for the company and laying out two-year objectives for the project. His feelings about the project, he recalled, were that it was his first chance to "combine an artistic and a commercial success":

> It was an opportunity to implement the lessons I had learned and the lessons of other firms who had installed computers in the 1960s. It was an opportunity to do it right the first time, to make a computer system pay off by attacking the right problems in a professional manner.

At the end of January 1972, Johansen submitted a detailed two-year plan for the implementation of the computer to top management at Billsworth. At this point he had recruited his old friend, John Dwyer, and the two of them began working closely with Floyd on the project. Lacking immediate response from management, they moved ahead with the project as planned.

Responding to Johansen's suggestion, Billsworth management decided to invite an outside consultant from a large and reputable management consulting firm to evaluate the plans Johansen had suggested.

Johansen recalled that he had several things in mind in making the suggestion:

> I felt top management here was fickle, and didn't really have what it took to make a proper evaluation of what we had presented. So, the first thing I wanted to do was to counter and ward off the other influences that would be operating on management, like IBM salespeople and auditors from the accounting firm. Of course, I also wanted to get an independent verification that our approach was sound. Then, I hoped whoever did the job would help top management to be patient about the project, and realize it was a reasonably long-term commitment before there was a big observable payoff. Finally, I wanted to get some visibility and exposure to other job possibilities and other contract possibilities, and getting to know someone from this consulting firm would help that.

In April 1972, Johansen met Dwight Nichols, the consultant who would be evaluating the plans for Billsworth's computer systems. Nichols recalled the meeting as a unique experience:

> A perspiring Johansen burst into my office five minutes before the scheduled time of our meeting. He began pacing back and forth while describing his activities at Billsworth in short choppy phrases, amply emphasized with facial and hand gestures. The meeting quickly moved to specifics, and at one point Johansen quizzed me on the cost of the programming for the Billsworth bill-of-materials system. After I faltered a bit, Johansen revealed an extraordinary low cost. Both the low cost and my inability to guess it seemed to please him. After this, the meeting took on a more relaxed atmosphere.

On the return plane ride from the meeting, Johansen felt exhilarated and pleased.

> First, I felt I was technically better than Nichols, I could handle any tough questions he might raise. Second, I felt that I could communicate with him, I was confident that Nichols was going to give me "high marks."

Later that month Nichols made his presentation to Billsworth management, and recommended acceptance of Johansen's plans.

Although the work at Billsworth and a few smaller contracts seemed to be going well, Johansen was increasingly concerned about Deborah and his family. Deborah had undergone major surgery for the pain in her spine, but after recovery the pain had returned and was a constant problem for her. Johansen found himself having to do family chores, and faced with "two sets of problems—those at Billsworth and those at home."

THE PRESENT

In August 1973, as Johansen thought about his career and what he should do next, he saw several alternatives. He could make a major effort to expand his business. The Billsworth job was becoming increasingly frustrating as top management continued to show lack of interest and little appreciation for what he was doing. Johansen felt it would be possible to get other contracts, particularly since his relationship with Nichols was continuing (the two were writing articles together) and Nichols was in a position to refer him to several leads.

Another alternative would be to take a job as an MIS manager for a large company. Johansen felt this was the least attractive opportunity professionally, since it would mean giving up his independence and getting entangled in company politics again. On the other hand, he recognized that such a job might make the most sense in terms of balancing his professional life with family life and hobbies. He felt more and more concern for his family as time went on.

Another alternative would be to pursue his entrepreneurial interests further. This might involve, for example, going into a totally new field and managing a small firm with a product to make and sell. Johansen had a friend in the venture capital business who had suggested this to him.

Finally, Johansen considered that he might continue at about his current level of activity, with only one or two employees, doing a lot of work on projects himself. This might be the most relaxing alternative.

Chapter 12

THE MANAGER IN THE ORGANIZATION: CHALLENGES OF THE GAME

. . . I was into *the process before I was* aware *of the process.* . . .

John Dean
Senate Watergate Hearings
June 1973

In the previous chapter we discussed how it is possible for people with certain motives to find stimulation of their motivation in the typical organizatioal environment for managers. That is all well and good. However, a number of authors and critics of capitalism and bureaucracy have pointed out some inherent conflicts between the individual and the organization. For example, Argyris (1957) describes the contradictions between social norms encouraging growth toward independence and the realities of most organizations, which encourage dependence. Another critic is Maccoby (1976*b*), whose book, *The Gamesman: The New Corporate Leaders,* raises basic doubts about the benefits to the individual and to society of the kind of motivating fit described in Chapter 11.[1]

---

[1] For a concise statement of his findings and arguments, see Maccoby (1976a).

624

THE GAMESMAN AND HIS PROBLEM

In his book, Maccoby reports on empirical research on managers in U.S. companies in the electronics and computer manufacturing industries. Out of interviews with the managers, their colleagues and subordinates, and their spouses, he develops categories of four basic character types of people in managerial roles in organizations. These are:

1.   The Craftsman.
2.   The Jungle Fighter.
3.   The Organization Man.
4.   The Gamesman.

In Figure 12–1 we show the approximate relationships which may be inferred between each of the four character types and the three motive

FIGURE 12–1
Maccoby's character types of managers and their relationships to motive patterns

Character types	Need for affiliation	Need for achievement	Need for power	
			Personal power	Social power
The Craftsman		√		
The Jungle Fighter		√	√	
The Organization Man	√			
The Gamesman		√		√

categories of McClelland, which were discussed in Chapter 11. Maccoby warns, appropriately in our view, that one should be careful not to use these four categories directly to stereotype managers. In this sense the types are *ideal* types, and no one manager is likely to fit precisely into one category. It is our experience that these four types are very suggestive and intuitively appealing to practicing managers. Used properly and not too rigidly, they can be valuable tools to use as an operational starting point for understanding one's own—as well as others'—manifest personality.

Maccoby found that the Gamesman type was best suited to the demands of the organizations he studied. These organizations, it should be noted, are in industries which presently are in great states of change, growth, and vigor. Organization structures are often the matrix form, organizational changes frequent, and managers are confronted with formal and emergent role demands which are highly diverse and require contingent management styles. The Gamesman, motivated to win and to achieve goals through influencing others, is ideally suited to this organizational environment. He or she knows how to build a power base and make it work.

Maccoby found, however, that as he or she works and is rewarded by promotions and a sense of success over the years, the Gamesman becomes increasingly conditioned in a certain way. That is, qualities of the *head* are improved while qualities of the *heart* atrophy. In other words, successful managerial behavior has long-term effects on personality. (This process is illustrated by the feedback arrows in the diagram in Chapter 11, Figure 11–1.) Success promotes the development of substantive knowledge and skills of the business, and also skills in the techniques of influencing people and solving problems as they arise, one at a time. At the same time, there are few opportunities or demands to help the development of one's sense of self and sense of more permanent and enduring values which make up one's identity.

What Maccoby describes are the effects that can result when a manager is caught up in a challenging and motivating process, a process best dealt with in contingent and pragmatic ways. In such situations, a person who has a firm sense of identity which is manifested in his or her behavior, such as a prototype Craftsman or Jungle Fighter, may be unsuited to the variety and pressures of the work. On the other hand, the Gamesman, who is so suited, experiences a growth of skills and techniques which outstrip the development of values and identity. The manager confronted with different roles to play becomes a role player, an actor on the stage whose self is no deeper than those roles.

Maccoby has pointed out explicitly that if this type of Gamesman comes to positions of power in corporations (or, we may add, in government), some real problems can arise for the individual, the organization, and society. The individual loses capability for love and feeling, the more human qualities of the self. The mere organization develops information processors whose decisions reflect their experience and may have no basis in a broader value context. Society cannot depend on its organizations, particularly private corporations, to make societally relevant decisions but rather only corporate and individually self-interested ones. We may add that the forces described here can lead to a perspective which concentrates on "winning" at the game and which leads to illegal and unethical behavior outside the organization as well as in political struggles within it.

It is important in a nonevaluative way to recognize the validity of the syndrome and problem Maccoby has described. As a matter subject to empirical verification, we believe our society and any complex society require (and probably *have* required throughout history) complex organizations to accomplish their main tasks, that these in turn set role demands like games, and that individuals rise and serve these organizations and indirectly the social good by effectively playing these games. The catch, the paradox, is that there is a real possibility (and, according to Maccoby, empirical evidence) that the process develops managers whose focus in life is on the game per se, on technique and means, not on larger ends, and whose personal development is stunted. A reverse of this paradox arises when we consider one alternative type of manager, say one with a firm identity around his or her technical expertise (Maccoby's Craftsman seems to fit this). Such a manager may maintain personal identity and values, but be unable to build power and exercise the interpersonal influence necessary to meet the role requirements of a dynamic organization which must be responsive to its environment. Such a person is characteristically strong on identity, heart, and values but too rigid and uncompromising for effective leadership.

This analysis leads to some fundamental dilemmas and paradoxes. From the point of view of societal goals and individual values, it is attractive to have organizations develop managers who look beyond organizational ends to the needs of society and to the effects of their work on themselves and those who depend on them, both within and outside the organization. On the other hand, the vitality of those organizations requires that their structure and processes be sufficiently flexible and attractive to induce gamelike behavior from middle and upper management. The seduction of that activity leads to character development which emphasizes technique, cerebral activities, and short-term problems solution at the expense of the development of an awareness of process and a perspective on broader ends, on one's life and the development of a firm identity.

THE GAMESMAN PROBLEM AS A CHALLENGE—AND SOME SOLUTIONS

Maccoby tends to be pessimistic about this state of affairs, and calls for major revolutions in the structure of organizations as a way of making them places where the whole person can be developed.

We take a different course. We believe it is the necessary nature of complex organizations that managers capable of playing the game come to the fore. While changes aimed at humanizing organizations are desirable and important, the basic demands for influence and gamesmanship will and should always be there, particularly in the organizations most crucial to a society in terms of growth, innovation, and vital responsibilities for the public good. We look on the problems Maccoby has described as a challenge calling for innovative solutions

which do not risk the destruction of organizational structures which
have evolved in a relatively free market outer environment.

In order to suggest solutions to the challenges and paradoxes, we
choose to turn partly to the organizations and wider society, but also
to focus our attention on the individual manager.

Social and organizational solutions

Part of an approach to solutions for these issues should be directed at
society, at top management, and at owners of organizations. To a large
extent, it is appropriate that society set the rules of the games in which
organizations engage in their environments. These rules, in turn, are
reflected in the incentives and forces which act on individual managers
through the input structures. By making regulations, laws, and economic incentives, government can have a great effect. It is important to
note that this does not mean more regulation and more restriction on
organizational goals and ends. Indeed, restrictions and regulations
which move from setting the external environmental stage and begin
to impose on the daily behavior of managers at work are almost sure to
have long-run negative effects on the flexibility and responsiveness of
organizations with respect to their achieving fundamental social needs.
Thus, restrictive limitation on hiring practices, restrictions on other
personnel policies, and pollution and environmental and health
impacts—as important as their aims are—may in the long run be coun-
terproductive means to achieve those aims. Much more appropriate, in
our view, is government action which emphasizes deregulation and
structuring of financial incentives in the environment to induce the
firm or agency to encourage its managers to take into account ends
other than strictly short-term organizational ones.

In a quite different way, society can affect the management of an
individual's values through its educational and communications system. We have argued that managers within firms should recognize
their roles for what they are, namely positions of influence over others
which should be used for appropriate ends rather than avoided or ignored. So, too, it is with governments and the influence which they play
in the development of their citizens. Preprofessional education which
emphasizes thinking rather than technique, appreciation of values,
and the development of the ability to distance oneself from immediate
activity and to view the larger historical and social context of one's
behavior can contribute to a solution of the managerial dilemmas we
have described.

This is an argument for broader, liberal arts-oriented curricula at
the undergraduate level. In our view, there is also a need for adjustment of emphasis in the pedagogy of some of our most prestigious

professional schools. Two books which represent firsthand accounts of educational experiences at the Harvard Business School and the Harvard Law School provide documentation which shows how those schools emphasize gamesmanlike qualities.[2] In one describing the Harvard Business School experience, the author states at one point:

> For seven and a half months now, following the dictates of curriculum and crushing workload, our concern has been with *technique*. How to solve this. How to deal with that. (Cohen, 1973)

What is needed is not less technique and problem-solving orientation at the professional level, but more of an educational experience which helps students learn how to be aware of the context of their work. This can be done partly through substantive courses and required summer reading. It can also be done through a teaching approach which, while maintaining the emphasis on professional skills and technique, also presents the student with the challenge of articulating in class his or her broader perspective. Such an approach in effect demands of the student an awareness of his or her personal values. It requires teachers in all subjects who know themselves, know what their values are, and who are unafraid of exposing those values and clues to their own identity.

In no way, however, can the issues we have raised be dealt with only through public policy and education.

At the level of top management and ownership a great deal can be done. Top management establishes the formal inputs which, we have argued, largely determine the nature of the emergent relationships and the perspectives of organizational members, including particularly middle managers. Incentives and rewards can be structured in ways to encourage behavior that is appropriate to ends other than expedient ones and to encourage the development of a perspective broader than merely accomplishing the job at any cost. Moreover, top management's own behavior in these respects is often more important than the formal system of structures. By setting examples for appropriate behavior, stating publicly and in writing the ethical and legal principles and living up to them, top managers can influence the emergent relationships within the firm while reflecting social and humanistic values of importance to the individual managers themselves.

But there are important limitations on how far top management can go in this regard. By the very nature of changes in the incentives or other input structures toward the broader and more personal goals and values we have described, top management risks a shift away from or at least a dilution of those inputs designed to achieve organizational ends. For the manager promoted for being a good scout, the more effec-

---

[2] These are Cohen (1973) and Thurow (1977).

tive negotiator or expert may be passed up. Eventually, the essential conflict must be faced between organizational ends which are appropriate for organizational survival, flexibility, and growth and ends which aim toward the development of the full human potential of managers and social ends. We are not of the school which argues that these types of purposes are ultimately compatible, nor do we argue for the abolition of the organization as the key element in achieving the basic needs of modern societies. Moreover, it is very doubtful whether society would be served by top management setting and deliberately influencing the value systems of its members.

While steps can be taken at the societal and the top management level, they cannot be sufficient for solving problems which arise at the individual level for middle managers. From their perspective, the issue may be stated as a challenge: how does one pursue the attractions of an organizational career and achieve the satisfactions available in that environment only and, at the same time, develop a strong sense of self and identity which is in keeping with values beyond those of the organizational game?

Self-management for the manager

From the perspective of the middle manager the personal problems and challenges which arise from engagement in organizational games result in part from the necessary treatment of organizational *ends* as separate from *means*. Managers face the necessity to achieve organizational results (ends) with less attention to the implications of the means. In other words, the manager generally has to behave as though he or she were assuming that the organization's ends were valid and appropriate as measured by some set of values. This necessity arises from the fact that a manager's job at middle levels, where the Gamesmen are developed, is more intraorganizational than extraorganizational, more concerned with carrying out strategy than with setting strategy. The problems of loss of heart which Maccoby refers to, or more generally the problem of loss of wider perspectives on one's behavior and of a firm sense of identity, comes about in part from a concentration on achieving the outcomes prescribed by the organization confronting the manager. This set of roles takes the form, as we noted above, of a demanding and rewarding game.

An immediate implication of this analysis of the issue is the importance of the individual's examination and understanding of his or her assumptions regarding the organization's goals and his or her roles in that organization. This is the first step. Managers must know where their behavior will lead, and what effects a recent decision will have on later events, both to the managers and to the organization and outer society. This is a prescription for awareness of oneself and of the process in which one is engaged. A dose of this should put us in the state where "the readiness is all," that is, where we are prepared for the seductive and overt aspects of behavior which would violate the behavioral code to which we ascribe. Awareness leading to readiness should help us avoid becoming part of a process before we are aware of its nature and to what it may lead. This was what John Dean claimed happened to him, as revealed in his quote at the beginning of this chapter.

Awareness of the context of organizational ends and of one's position in organizational processes implies measuring ends and measuring oneself by standards other than those of the required game itself. Thus, the manager needs to look to other standards and structures besides the organizational ones, for example religion or some other external code, and to reflect that in a personal value system. In our terminology, the locus of those values is the identity, and having an operational set of values, whether they are conscious or not, is tantamount to having a firm personal identity. But here is where the prescription becomes difficult in a number of ways.

We have already noted that success at the organizational game requires flexibility in behavior, and the ability in most instances to assume different and often conflicting roles. The sense of identity which one has is in part a product of how one behaves, and the danger for most individuals is that multiple role playing, requiring to a large extent ability as an actor, itself diffuses the identity. Thus, in addition to the sheer energy and time demands of the game, which militate against opportunity for reflection and insight leading to awareness and a sense of values, the roles imposed and the consequent variety of management styles work against the establishment of a firm identity. Conversely, if an identity or sense of values is too rigid, it may impair success at the managerial game.

The potential to overcome the problems of the Gamesman is in itself a variable which, we shall argue, differs across the population of middle managers. That is, some individuals will by virtue of their own personality (be it a firm sense of identity well established or a cognitive style conducive to awareness and the evolution of a sense of self) be able to cope with the challenges of the game and at the same time keep their sense of perspective by the time they reach middle management positions. At the other extreme, some individuals may have no desire for the challenges of the game itself, for their motive pattern does not incline them toward a career in management in complex organizations. Still others may be so inclined, or already in a career which they want to pursue, but have little potential to develop the sense of self we are talking about here. We shall assume that this group is very small in number, and that the majority of middle managers can, under appropriate circumstances, pursue careers in which there is a potential for achieving the rewards of management and simultaneously developing a strong sense of identity, conducive both to satisfaction in personal life and satisfaction of societal goals.

The validity of our assumption is a matter open to investigation. The notion of career and personal life stages, identified by Erikson and pursued by the research of Levinson (1978) and others, raises the prospect of identity shift during adult years. At the critical periods of change, the opportunity or indeed the necessity for reestablishment of identity is a paramount issue for the individual. These authors argue it cannot be avoided. If the situation is recognized for what it is, then these "crises" really become opportunities for the individual manager who experiences them to become reestablished. To the extent this life-stage theory proves valid, then the assumption that most individuals have the potential for establishment of an identity to help guide their adult behavior is also more valid.

For the individual aware and concerned with this issue, knowledge of potential pitfalls is a necessary first step toward their solution. This sounds simple but should not be taken too lightly for it has implications. Mature human development in a complex modern organization is not, for the vast majority of managers, something which "comes naturally" or can be accomplished without systematic attention to the forces, internal and external, which affect one's behavior and identity. Of course, prescription that one should "be aware" begs the question of how one attains awareness. It is beyond the scope of this chapter and this book to try to suggest how to increase awareness of oneself and of behavioral processes in the work place, but our experience gives us cause for believing that the vast majority of managers can develop such awareness regardless of their sensitivities to these sorts of issues earlier in their lives. Effective management development courses and in-house training can and do help. Indeed, there is currently a general social climate of acceptance and interest in "consciousness raising," a side benefit of which is the effect of making individuals more aware of themselves, their communications, and the processes they are involved in.

There are important limitations to this prescriptive advice. Taken earnestly or lightly, a commitment to becoming more aware, particularly self-aware, can potentially lead to self-absorption and to a diverting expenditure of personal energy away from work commitment. It is partly for this reason that the enthusiasm for so-called T-group training or sensitivity training has lost much of its appeal of the 1960s and early 1970s.[3] Those experiences often had so powerful an effect on the

---

[3] See Calame (1969).

perspective of participating managers that their whole lives were changed. In many instances this might well have been for the better, but in sufficient instances it was to the detriment of their employing organization and of themselves.

A total lack of awareness leads to a sense of drifting and a potential for poor decisions in organizational settings, as well as poor consequences for the individual and for society. Taken to the other extreme, too much awareness or an excess of self-absorption can paralyze the process of identity formulation. Managers need to develop self-awareness and awareness of behavioral and organizational processes in order to achieve results and to establish and develop their identity within an organizational game which both absorbs energies and provides them with important psychic material rewards. On the other hand, techniques or activities which lead to extreme self-awareness can become, particularly for this audience, all-absorbing. They can detract from engagement in relationships and work. Paradoxically, it is these very aspects of the organizational situation, the game, which we see as necessary for one who would become an effective and mature manager. The manager who embarks on this quest must both maintain his or her energy for work and evolve an additional dimension of understanding and sensitivity. In this endeavor a tension exits between action and reflection, between the application of an intuitive or a systematic approach.

Managers we have known to be successful in this quest describe techniques helpful for them. One method is to seek out those educational endeavors which recognize the tension between doing and thinking, and which do not attempt to destroy the motives and denigrate the attractions of the organizational world to which these managers are committed and from which they draw their motivation and their reward. Training which forces the manager to make an either-or choice between personal satisfaction and achievement and power satisfaction will either be rejected as unrealistic or lead to disquietude more problematical than the original problem.

Another technique is to take on the more humanizing or people-oriented parts of roles in one's work. Of particular importance to many young managers is the availability of a mentor, a more senior manager who informally takes on the leadership, development, and sponsorship roles for that younger individual. Most managers in the upper and middle levels have opportunities to be a mentor or sponsor. Taking them on can in itself lead to an engagement which increases one's sense of awareness. Personal growth comes from the generative process of giving and helping.

Finally, managers find success from simply exercising their will in what they want to accomplish. That is, they report learning how to manage themselves and how to influence themselves and change their way of thinking, their self-awareness, and their way of being. Communications with one or more other persons can facilitate this. Becoming interested in outside activities and hobbies or peripheral lines of activity within the organization can help. Some report that transcendental meditation, in addition to beneficial physiological results, leads them to a new, nondebilitating perspective on themselves and their work. The important point is that these men and women of action find that their gifts for influencing others can work on themselves; that their skills at understanding and exercising power can be applied to themselves.[4]

CONCLUSION

We have argued in this chapter that the individual manager in the organization is confronted with a work situation likened to a game, and that engagement in the organizational game has important rewards and some potential pitfalls. It is important for a manager to develop a balance between work absorption and self-absorption in order to achieve maturity and full potential for effectiveness. In a sense, the mature and effective manager is engaged in a game, and might even be referred to as a Gamesman, except the rules and nature of the game are different from the strictly organizational game. The mature manager's game is one which includes the organizational game as one part, but exists within a larger and contextually broader game which includes dealing with one's entire environment and oneself.

QUESTIONS FOR STUDY AND DISCUSSION

1. Which of the managerial categories delineated in this chapter most nearly fits you? What attributes of the other categories also describe you?
    Are there any attributes you do not have, but would like to?
2. Does your current work or the role of any other person in your organization with whom you are familiar require wide variation in style in order to be successful?
    How well do you or the other individual adapt to the needs for this variation in behavior?
    To what extent would you say you or the other individual is sufficiently aware of the differences between behavior and internal identity to avoid the problems of loss of integrity which Maccoby describes in *The Gamesman*?
    What steps can you or the other individual or the organization take to

---

[4] For discussions of the importance of will in personal action, see May (1973) and Wheelis (1973).

improve this awareness without compromising the need for the variation in behavior?

3. Give your own definition of "manipulation." In your view is it ever justifiable?

    Do the same for "lying."

4. Do you think your preprofessional education has been adequate to help you keep some insight into and detachment from the perils of the use of techniques?

    What particular aspects of that education do you most appreciate? What do you most strongly feel the lack of?

Case 12–1
James Short*

Early in 1953, David C. Davis, a management consultant, received a phone call from his friend, James A. Short, executive vice president of the Hudson Corporation, requesting a personal conference at the close of business that day. Although Mr. Davis had some social engagements for the evening that would need adjustment, he was glad to meet Mr. Short's request because he had been on the point of arranging a meeting for himself with Mr. Short.

Mr. Davis felt that he could guess what Mr. Short had on his mind. About seven years earlier, when his close acquaintance with Mr. Short began, Mr. Davis had assisted Mr. Short in locating a new job after he had resigned abruptly from the Hudson Corporation. Mr. Short had been persuaded to return to the Hudson Corporation about two years later. The new job in his old company was a marked improvement for him in terms of remuneration, explicit definition of responsibilities and authority, and a title designation that clearly indicated his post as number two man in the company hierarchy. Mr. Davis knew that matters had gone much more satisfactorily, from Mr. Short's point of view, during the years since his return, although Mr. Davis recently had heard indirectly that some of the earlier difficulties between Mr. Short and the president of Hudson Corporation had arisen once more.

The meeting between the two men began in Mr. Davis' club not long after five o'clock and continued through dinner and into the evening. The information that follows, together with the gist of the conversations reproduced, were written out by Mr. Davis, at the request of a case-writer from the Harvard Business School, soon after the conference occurred. The case was cleared for accuracy and disguise with Mr. Short by Mr. Davis.

Mr. Short opened the conversation immediately upon his appearance with the remark, "I expect you know what's up—J. G. can't keep his hands off any longer, and this time if I quit it'll be for good, and I want to plan ahead for it a bit more than I did last time."

Mr. Davis smiled. "How long can you hold onto yourself? You act teed off."

"I am," Short replied, "but I managed to finish the day and get up here without calling for a showdown. And tonight is Friday night, so there's the weekend ahead of me. Furthermore, I've had two good offers recently that still stand open waiting for my answer."

"That ought to help," Davis said. "Added to which, I have a third

---

* All names have been disguised.

offer that was specifically drawn up to appeal to you and about which I was planning to see you next week. Shall we move over to the dining room and get into all this over dinner?"

Settled at their table, Mr. Davis urged Mr. Short to bring him up to date on what had been happening in the Hudson Corporation since their last meeting about six months earlier. "I thought you had your troubles pretty well cleared up. At least you made no complaints at that time."

Short: *That's the devil of it. They were cleared up until somewhere around 12 or 15 months ago. Beginning then J. G. [Connell, the president of Hudson Corporation] has made my job increasingly difficult by postponing decisions I put to him— ones that required his approval and quickly too, to be worth acting on, by questioning a lot of my smaller decisions—ones I've been making for years without his objection, and really aren't important by themselves but only as a symptom of his intentional meddling, by making more and more suggestions about how I ought to handle my personnel—suggestions he knows damn well I won't accept. They concern the way he treats people, and are the ways I never have and never will use.*

Well, that's the way it's been going for more than a year. This morning when I went in to go over the next budget for my divisions he said he'd been studying it and thought I ought to cut the figure for promotion and advertising $1 million. I said, "Not unless I cut the figure for projected sales several times more." He didn't like that, but he wouldn't argue with me about it. We've gone to the mat on that one too often. So he went back to the $1 million he said I could save. I wouldn't take it without a proportionate cutback in sales. Finally, he said, "You aren't the president around here yet." I wanted to say, "Damn lucky for you I'm not." But I held onto it, and merely said, "That's right." He said, "I think you ought to cut 1 million out of that one figure. Think it over." I said, "I will," and walked out. And here I am.

Davis: *What's he want?*

Short: [slowly, after a long pause] *I hate to say this because it ought not to be true, but I think he's afraid of me. He ought not to be. He's the biggest figure in the industry, one of the old-timers, too, out of the rough-and-tumble era. He owns a lot of the stock, he controls a solid majority of the company directors, he's a very wealthy man and has been for years. It's taken a long time for me to admit this to myself, but it's the only explanation that fits the pattern of his recent behavior.*

The figures for my divisions are coming out the way I predicted them to him almost two years ago—I have lifted two of our perennial money losers out of the red. They're in the black now and next year they'll both be solid money makers. I think he's afraid to allow the company stockholders and directors, the bankers and the employees to see the transformation from perpetual red to dependable black as a result of the work I have been doing for the last four years. He fears they might figure he wasn't needed, and he's becoming more touchy every day about that since he passed the 70-year mark some time ago.

Davis: *He can't last forever, and you're the only possible successor he's got in the whole organization. Everyone in the company knows that, from top to bottom,* and a good many are praying for the day. You've put in 25 years all over the company, abroad and at home, getting ready for a takeover when the old man retires—the last ten years as the heir apparent, chosen and trained by himself. You think you can't take the punishment any longer?

Short: It isn't that simple, Dave. I've never taken any "punishment" from him, except lots of hard work and tough assignments—and I've asked for those. It's most of the other executives in the company who have taken the punishment—that is, the ones who stayed on for the sake of the high salaries he pays. The ones who wouldn't, left. I guess I'm the only one who wouldn't put up with his galley-slave tactics who stayed with him.

Davis: Maybe that's the reason you're the only one he has groomed as his successor.

Short: He groomed me as his successor because I always studied my problems until I was certain what the trouble was. Once that was done, a promising solution or two were never hard to find. When I went in to him I always took along my recommendations, and then fought for them. Usually I won, because I double-checked and triple-checked on everything. I never minded those combats and I don't think he did either. The other guys generally took only the problems to him and then asked him what to do about them. That's where they got into trouble. He'd tell them, and at the same time call them stupid or dumb or incompetent. Right in front of their own people, too. It used to make me sick at times, but I'd tell them afterwards, when they came to see me, that they'd asked for it by going in that way. I'd try to get them to see the only way to avoid a public horsewhipping was to go in with their own plan and battle for it.

You know he lives for nothing but his business. He lives in a hotel in the center of town so as to be close to the office. He and his wife don't own a home anywhere. They have no children. She's been a confirmed neurasthenic for decades, going from doctor to doctor. She shifted some time ago to cults and fads and healers.

Any time of night, or on weekends, or on vacations, he'll phone any officer in the company he wants to and either order them in for an afternoon or evening of work while the office is closed, or else keep them on the phone as long as he wants to bat a problem around. He tried that on me not long after I got back from that foreign assignment. I was expecting it, because some of the other men had complained about it to me—or, rather, their wives had to my wife. I told our maid to tell him I was busy entertaining our guests and that I would be in to see him first thing in the morning. He never mentioned it and never tried it again.

No, I'm not the one who's had to take that sort of punishment—it's the other men, the whole executive structure in fact.

Davis: We've gone over some of this before, but I'm still a little puzzled. Between bonus and salary you went well over the $100,000 bracket two years ago. You don't put up with the bully-ragging old Connell has been notorious for; on the contrary, you're almost indispensable to him. You've worked hard a long time for what you've almost got in your hand. It can't be so far off now. Why can't you go along until the ship is yours?

Short: [after another long pause] Age is one angle—his and mine. I've just touched 50 and if I'm going to accomplish anything particularly noteworthy in an organization as big as ours I've got to get a really free hand soon. Ten years is hardly *enough. Fifteen may be. At least I'm still ready to try hard. I may not feel that same way when the time gets shorter.*

He is over 70, but all his close relatives—uncles, cousins, parents were long-lived, many into their 90s. I believe he's going to hold on as long as he can. I may be wrong on this. He often talked with me about his retirement and I think he meant it. But not during the past two or three years has he mentioned it again. I don't know whether it was his 70th birthday, or my breaking into the black with the losers he could never rescue that made him clam up.

He still works like a horse, though he is slowing down and won't admit it. He may keel over one of these days—but I just don't know. It's a question mark, Dave: his retirement. I've speculated over that ever since he got over 65 and stayed on to 70. Now I'm 50 and I've concluded that I'm the fellow who's got to make the decision.

Davis: *Jim, what if a taxi ran him down this evening? What would you like to try for most with the Hudson Corporation? Why would you stay there rather than to go to any of the three openings we are going to look over later on? What's Hudson got that I can't top on behalf of Casper?*

Short: *[startled] Have you got an offer from Casper?*

Davis: *I've got the executive vice presidency for you. Not at once, but explicitly inside one year, to give Gene Darnell a decent interval in which to move back to the chairmanship. With it goes a salary, bonus, deferred payments, and pension tentatively proposed to meet your wishes, and with full authorization to me to meet any offer you get from any firm in the industry on each of the points I mentioned—salary, bonus, and so on.*

Short sat silent. He was not prepared for such an offer from the chief rival in his field. His thoughts had been so much preoccupied with the tangled difficulties of his own situation at Hudson that he found it hard to grasp Davis' statements. Finally he asked, "Is that true?"

Davis gestured toward his brief case, "I have the papers in there when you're ready to look them over. Now, how about my question: 'What's Hudson got for you that I can't top for Casper?'"

Short: *Well, for one thing I know Hudson like the inside of my own house. I know every move I want to make, who I want to make the moves, and when, and how. I know what our weaknesses are and many remedies I am sure will help correct them. I know also where we have unrealized sources of strength which I am confident could be developed to such a degree that, before I am through, we could attain a commanding lead in the industry. And that means [he said with a glance at Davis] that we could overtake Casper's present 10 percent lead in sales and go 20 percent to 25 percent ahead of them.*

That's one thing Hudson's got for me.

Another is—and I should have put it first—I think I could release the energies and capabilities of a lot of good men that J. G. has used as chore boys. I think I could attract and hold a lot of good men who would never enter our doors so long as Connell's practices are followed. And this is something I've wanted to do in Hudson longer than anything else. I sort of feel I owe it to a lot of men who

*never got a decent chance to show what they could do in an encouraging
atmosphere. I owe it to some friends of mine whose spirits or whose health was
broken, and to some whose lives were shortened because they worked in
Hudson.*

*That is a serious thing to say, but I mean it. And the funny thing is that I owe
more to J. G. than I owe to any man alive. He gave me my chance in sales when I
asked to transfer out of the accounting department 20 years ago. He sent me
abroad in charge of sales when our subsidiary in Austria looked weak. He put
me in full charge in less than one year when they had to replace their general
manager there. He gave me a free hand over the whole outfit for nearly a decade
before the war ended that operation. He asked for results, sure, but I would do
exactly the same thing. During his two visits per year we took our operations
apart down to the last penny and I learned as much about running my own show
during his inspections as I did during the rest of the year.*

*He's a rough and often ruthless man, but you've got to remember the period
when he was growing up. He was at work selling at the time of the Spanish
American war! I've told him a good many times that he is a holdover from the
old robbers barons who built our railroads and steel mills.*

Davis: *Quite a compliment to pay your boss. How did he take it?*

Short: *Sometimes he'd frown, sometimes he'd grin. Don't forget he is perhaps the
greatest promoter and one of the greatest salesmen our industry has produced.
Nobody could touch him ten years ago. Remember he merged the first truly
national organization in our field, just as he was the first to move aggressively
into the foreign field in a really big way—at least from an American base. And he
carried competition to every market that could be made to pay. In our field
there's no personality like him left on the scene.*

Davis: *Sounds like hero worship to me.*

Short: *Why, yes, I guess it does. I guess I've felt that way about him for years. But I
don't any longer. At least not much. Not since I've been continually at headquarters where I've seen him in action every day with the personnel of the organization. I was in Europe nearly ten years, you know, and after I came back he sent
me out again to put the southern subsidiary on its feet. I didn't really get to know
him, or the situation in the home office, until the war was over, scarcely eight
years ago.*

*I think maybe he's changed, too. I'm pretty sure he has in the last two or three
years. He lies to me now. He goes behind my back and then denies it. He never
used to do that. I've lost my respect for him.*

Davis: *Well, are you ready to look over the material I've got on Casper?*

Short: *Not yet, Dave, I can't swing around that fast. Nor that far.*

*What I mean is I never expected that kind of an offer from that source. Except
for two years I've worked all my life for Hudson. I can't get up out of the trenches
and walk straight across to the principal enemy I've spent most of my business
years fighting all over the globe. It sort of makes me feel like a deserter.*

*It would be a whale of a kick in the pants to the old man, though. Maybe it
would jar some perspective back into him. Still, he treated me awfully right that
first time I resigned. I just walked out. You remember?*

Well, he said I had to keep my title and my office until I made a connection. He wanted to pay my salary too, but I wouldn't take that. Furthermore, he met my terms when I was willing to go back and he kept them, until these past months.

Davis: *Well, what about the two offers you mentioned earlier? What have they got?*

Short: *You'll laugh when I tell you about the first one. Annual sales are barely over $10 million a year. Isn't that something, when both Hudson and Casper's sales run over $300 million a year?*

Still, they made it awfully attractive for me personally. And for my family, too. It's the M. B. Madison Co. You know the wonderful country club location they have built for themselves well out in one of the nicest unspoiled suburbs in the whole metropolitan area? I could live a country life—and you know I like the country—and not have more than a pleasant 20-minute drive to and from the office. I could live with my family once more, which I haven't been doing these past four or five years while I've put in about 12 hours a day trying to pull those divisions out of the red. My boy and girl are in college now, but if my wife and I don't make every opportunity to see as much of them as possible while we can it will soon be too late.

I owe something to my wife in all this: We were close together in Europe and nearly as much as so when we went South. But since this last deal got underway she must think I'm beginning to resemble J. G. She hasn't said much but I know how she looks at the way those two have lived their lives. Our years in Europe gave us a lot of interests that I've had to neglect recently. There really isn't much point in working yourself like J. G. does, especially since they tax it away nearly as fast as you can make it.

I'll never get her to make the choice, and I wouldn't want her to, but the M. B. Madison setup is closer to what we both feel makes all-around sense than anything I've got in sight. Let me tell you a bit more about it.

The presidency is opening soon and that is what they're offering me. The salary is $40,000 with a profit-sharing arrangement which I figure could make me an additional $30,000 after the two or three years we would need in which to substantially increase their sales. There is a capital gains opportunity through an option on 5 percent of their total stock which is attractive. The stock is low currently but has a growth potential that I believe could triple its price before I needed to sell—all in all, I see almost a quarter million dollar gain between the buying and selling price. The pension possibility for me is limited, and I'll have to build my own estate along the other lines.

The salary drop is severe, especially over the next five years, so money-wise I have to balance the near-term versus the long-run considerations in this offer against the immediate gains in the other openings.

Probably I'd have a freer hand in that organization because of its size, for one thing. In a year I'd know its people as well—maybe better—than I do my own now. Its officers are decent people; the company has an excellent reputation for its business standards. It's one of the oldest in our line and I'm confident there is a fine base for doubling its share of the market. Most of all, right now, I'd be on my own again, and the directors who have talked with me are ready to accept any reasonable conditions I want to set in regard to running my own show.

It's a temptation all right: the country, my wife and family once more, a sure chance to make a good record a dependable nest egg—all without killing myself as I have been doing.

Davis: What about the other offer?

Short: It's another presidency, after a year. I'll go in as executive vice president at $60,000, which will go up somewhere around $80,000 when I take over the president's office. There is a bonus which runs around 10 percent of the salary each year. The pension would enable me to retire with $30,000 annually from that source alone. The stock option proposal is a complicated formula but it works out so that I can buy stock on a basis which virtually assures me of doubling my money, and if the stock increases further in value I would secure that additional increment.

From a financial angle it would be hard to beat from my point of view. The salary and bonus are a reduction from what I'm getting now, but about three years ago I found that the huge bonus I got that year melted down to just a few thousand dollars after the Treasury took its bit. As a matter of fact, I bought tax anticipation warrants with what was left simply to remind myself that a big bonus often doesn't mean a thing.

It's the Martin Brachall Company. A fine old reputable concern with a name for honesty and integrity—a factor that appeals to me more and more as time passes. All the officers are gentlemen. I've known many of them for years, and I've admired the atmosphere of goodwill and cooperation they work in. They know what teamwork means and it is an asset I am definitely counting on when I estimate what I can do for the company.

They have a line of staple products, some of them virtual monopolies, not only because of worldwide consumer preference and brand prestige, but also because of entrenched marketing arrangements. As an old marketeer, I have a deep hunch that there is a tremendous potential, both in the company's position as well as in its products, that is ready for a long-pull expansion. The stock is closely held and hasn't missed a dividend in over two generations. The financial standing is gilt-edged. Actually all that is needed a period of concentration on promotion and sales—the very kind of assignments I've handled successfully three times straight at Hudson. Sales are running close to $30 million annually and I can see a dozen ways to begin lifting that figure nearly 10 percent a year.

Davis: I can't tell whether the Madison Company or the Brachall Company excites you the most. Aren't there any catches in the last one?

Short: That's the question, Dave, I asked myself after my confidential talk with Mr. McKee [president of Brachall Company]. I'm sure there is, but I haven't found it yet and I've gone over it a dozen times. All I've found, in fact, are some more pluses. Their offices occupy part of their own building—which leaves room for a convenient expansion. It is in the part of town I like best. It's very handy for me to reach from where we live now—and where we're really taking roots in the community at last. Even the president's office has exactly the view I like best in all the city, and it combines with an executive office layout that creates a mood in which I feel good and do good work. Maybe I'm oversensitive to such things just now, and perhaps it's silly to mention it, but I'll bet there are a lot of similar hidden considerations that lie deep in these kinds of decisions. I'm only trying to look at mine, and to me the building location and the offices I'll occupy are a clear plus.

Davis: Is it any use to look over the draft proposals I've got from Casper for you?

Short: I don't see why. At least not this evening, Dave. It's getting late and I've got a lot of thinking and deciding to do this weekend. I know the gist of the proposition: they will write me a better ticket financially than I can. . . .

Davis: They'll go further than that. They're ready to. . . .

Short: [interrupting] I know a big organization, Dave. I know what they can and can't deliver. Money they can—the rest is only a chance to try to turn a whale around. Maybe I'll want to, it's the kind of animal I'm most familiar with. Maybe these smaller organizations are simply "greener pastures" to me right now. I'm grateful to Casper—perhaps I ought to say to you; because you're probably the prime mover here—but it's good for my morale, coming from my friends the enemy.   [Short arose]

"Thanks for the evening, Dave. I did all the talking but I've found that helps clear up my thinking a lot if I find someone who is able to listen. Somebody besides my wife, that is. I didn't want to pour all this out to her without a preliminary run-through on you, you see, because this time she's more thoroughly involved than in any other single decision in my whole business career. This time her opinion isn't what I need. I want her to say frankly what kind of life she would like a part of for the next 15 years—from there on it's up to me to make the choice that meets her wishes, and mine too. Doesn't that make sense to you.

Davis smiled. "It makes sense to me all right, but I'm not the one you have to make sense to from here on. Good luck, and call me up any time I can be of use again."

JAMES A. SHORT

James A. Short was born in Minnesota in 1903; worked part of his expenses off in going through college and graduated from the University of Iowa in 1924 with Phi Beta Kappa honors. He majored in Business Administration and specialized in Accounting. He married in 1925. In 1933, after it was clear that children of their own would not be forthcoming, he and his wife adopted two babies, a boy and a girl, born eights days apart.

Mr. Short began work in 1924 as a cost accountant for a firm in Chicago that was merged with several others in 1927 to create the Hudson Corporation. His work with company figures soon disclosed to him that progress upward in the ranks of management was slow in his department and was most rapid then in Foreign Sales. He requested a transfer to that department which was effected in 1931. The years 1926–1931 were spent in Domestic Sales to prepare for entrance into Foreign Sales.

From 1931 to 1939 he was briefly sales manager for, and then general manager of, the Austrian subsidiary of Hudson Corporation. During his managership sales increased from approximately $100,000 a year to more than $5 million. The outbreak of war terminated operations in Austria and Mr. Short returned to the American headquarters of Hudson Corporation, now substantially large, and located in the New York metropolitan area. Shortly thereafter he was sent South to liquidate an old-line subsidiary of Hudson that had defied years of effort to make it profitable. Close attention to its accounts suggested ways in which money could be saved. These were instituted by Mr. Short and together with increased sales produced results that led the president of Hudson to encourage Mr. Short to continue his efforts. Between 1940 and 1943 sales rose from $5.0 million to $7.5 million, though net profits rose much more steeply.

Mr. Short was called back to headquarters in 1943 and made assistant to the president with the title of vice president. He was given trouble-shooting assignments throughout the whole corporation—a position he quickly grew to dislike. He requested, on several occasions, some definite responsibilities on which he could make his own record, pointing out that if he found trouble when dispatched on such missions it made other vice presidents look bad, whereas if he did not, it made him look bad. Once or twice he was dissuaded from pushing his request, thereafter it was agreed to, but fulfillment was frequently postponed. Mr. Short, at this point, resigned abruptly and worked for the two years, 1945–1946, with a smaller concern in the same industry which was only obliquely a competitor of Hudson.

Upon his return to Hudson in 1946, which was negotiated with Mr. J. G. Connell, Mr. Short was made vice president of the whole company and soon thereafter executive vice president and, in addition, was given direct responsibility, in 1948, for the two most difficult divisions in the corporation. Mr. Short began his conversation with Mr. Davis over events that derived from that assignment.

Case 12-2
Robert Harcourt*

In December 1974, Robert Harcourt had just completed the 14-week Program for Management Development (PMD) at the Harvard Business School and was looking forward with his customary eagerness to returning to his job. Harcourt, who was 39 years old, was one of the 175

* All names have been disguised.

officers at the group head level of Martin, Daley and Stevens (MDS), a leading international accounting firm. MDS offered a diverse range of services from accounting-based specialties (audit, taxation, conversion to data-processed bookkeeping, etc.) to management consulting in areas such as production control, working capital management, resource allocation, and marketing strategy. MDS had billings of almost $200 million in 1974 and employed 15,000 people, including 1,200 who worked in its headquarters office in Chicago where Harcourt worked. MDS's clients were in nearly 1,000 industrial categories and varied in size from small family businesses to large multinationals.

Harcourt was the group head for the Operations Research Advisory Services (ORAS) within the Management Consulting Division of MDS. (See organization chart, Exhibit 1.) His department applied analytical

XHIBIT 1
Martin, Daley, and Stevens-partial organization chart

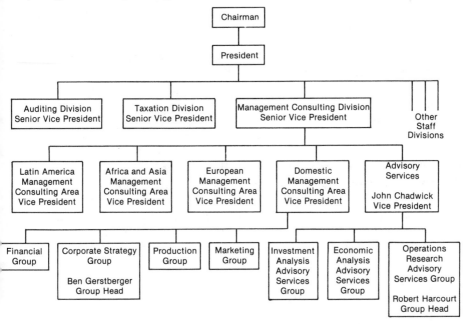

skills and tools to such problems as operations analysis, manufacturing control, inventory management, financial and budgetary control, and marketing distribution. ORAS offered advice both to clients and other departments within MDS on problems to which operations research could be applied. Eight professionals worked under Harcourt in ORAS. As he sorted through the mounds of material accumulated during the PMD course, Harcourt selected a few articles and notes of his own which he thought would be most useful to apply to his situation and which he could review on the flight home.

Harcourt thought that material from marketing, control, and organizational behavior would help him particularly in dealing with what he described as the "two problems that keep me awake nights." One was the need for a "product policy" for ORAS and for their unique services which would set them apart from other operations research consultants. An important new tool available to him was a computer simulation model which Harcourt had purchased the previous August, in hopes that it would provide an attractive new offering to clients. Just prior to coming to PMD in September, Harcourt had hired Rod Tracy, an experienced applied systems analyst. He had put Tracy to work developing product definitions and product policy for all of the existing and new services of ORAS to potential clients and users.

As he saw it, Harcourt's second problem was a need to reconsider his own "management style" in his dealings with his subordinates and perhaps even with his boss, John Chadwick. Harcourt was proud of the growth and success ORAS had achieved since his takeover two years previously. He felt that a large portion of the success was due to the close and informal work relationships of the professional team he had put together. Following an unsteady start the department had become well established and respected at MDS, and was currently growing both in size and responsibility. As a direct result of this growth, however, were increasing demands on Harcourt's time. These demands included traveling to most of the 235 offices in 53 countries to publicize the services ORAS could offer and to conduct training seminars for MDS managers, consultants, and their clients. Harcourt realized that these demands represented personal and professional opportunities for himself as well as means to further the success of ORAS. Although he normally spent one out of every six weeks away from Chicago, the 14-week period at PMD was by far the longest he had been away. Harcourt considered the 14-week absence an opportunity to see how well things would run without him.

OPERATIONS RESEARCH ADVISORY SERVICES IN RELATION TO MDS

ORAS did not charge clients for the services it performed. From a companywide standpoint the purpose of its work was to generate business for other parts of MDS. These included primarily the Domestic Management Consulting Area. For example, a U.S. machine tool manufacturer might seek the advice of ORAS on a particular production scheduling or inventory problem. This service could easily lead to the financial service department of the Domestic Consulting Area devising and implementing a total working capital system for the client's operation. In addition, continued ORAS services to the client could elicit contracts for additional services offered by the Consulting Division. The revenues to MDS would be derived then from the consulting fees of the services provided.

Harcourt was aware of the difficulty of judging the amount of ORAS business which resulted directly from the work of his applied systems analysts, the professionals under him who had the most extensive contact with clients and other MDS people. Most of the large corporate customers did business with other parts of MDS regularly; and this was not the result of their ORAS contact. From time to time another group leader would mention that a client had made reference to ORAS. Harcourt made a special effort to keep in touch with other managers who might be in a position to get feedback, because this was one of the few ways to evaluate the work of individuals in his department. He estimated that the value of contracts which came as a result of ORAS effort on the outside was some $20 to 30 million annually.

ORAS was an expense center in MDS, as were the other groups within the Advisory Services Area and some other staff divisions. Groups engaged directly in consulting and traditional accounting services were profit centers. Seventy percent of the ORAS budget (amounting to $275,000 in 1974) was charged to Domestic Management Consulting Area of MDS, which in turn provided some 25 percent of total corporate revenues. Another 15 percent of the ORAS budget was charged to other areas and 15 percent to corporate overhead. The working relationships between ORAS and specific consulting areas were sufficiently close that each of Harcourt's client contact analysts worked with one or more of the consulting project managers in those areas to service particular clients. It was from Ben Gerstberger, head of the Corporate Strategy Group in Domestic Management Consulting, that Harcourt obtained most of the information which he used in evaluating his analysts.

There were other relationships between ORAS and MDS as a whole beside the mutual client contacts in the Domestic Management Consulting Area. ORAS was usually involved in so many different projects of an innovative nature that its analysts frequently could transfer applied methods to new areas with surprising results. Of particular importance, Harcourt felt, was the relationship between ORAS and the small group of systems analysts and business analysts in the MDS data processing department. Harcourt and others in ORAS were frequently in contact with MDS offices all over the world and were typically the first people in the Chicago office to learn of new developments and leads for new consulting opportunities. Harcourt had even developed ORAS as a training group for consulting project managers for overseas offices. Two recent "graduates" of ORAS had been promoted to account officers, one in Tokyo and one to a new office in Iran.

The question of ORAS's relationship within MDS came into sharper focus for Harcourt on the day in October when he returned to his office during a PMD vacation break. A staff planner in the Domestic Management Consulting Area had made it known that he was considering a bid to bring ORAS into that area. His basis for this was partly the fact that, since 70 percent of ORAS expenses were being charged to his area, it should have more control over ORAS's costs. Moreover, the planner argued that this change would be consistent with a major reorganization study of the Management Consulting Division being conducted by a corporate committee. The concept of this reorganization involved movement away from the current functional organization and toward a customer or industry orientation. The planner felt that bringing ORAS's expertise in the application of operations research methods closer together with the Consulting Division's knowledge of the individual industries would reflect well the philosophy of the reorganization. Harcourt gathered this information secondhand from people in his group during his one-day visit. In his brief talk with Chadwick, his boss, no mention had been made of any overtures to reorganize.

THE APPLIED SYSTEMS ANALYST FUNCTION IN ORAS

The eight professionals under Harcourt in ORAS fell into three major units: analysts, mathematicians, and data processing specialists (Exhibit 2). Each of the four analysts was expected to be responsible for 8 to 12

EXHIBIT 2
Operating Research Advisory Services organization chart

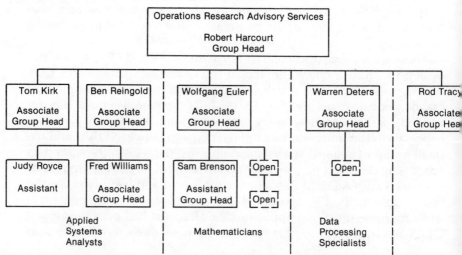

major clients, and to be in touch with each one at least once a week with information and advice. They spent over half their time with area specialists working on applications. The pace of the work varied from subdued and theoretical to frenetic. In order to make sound judgments, the analysts were expected to communicate with other MDS offices to learn of possible applications. Moreover, the analysts were to be in touch with industry specialists in different groups to ascertain the feasibility of methods. So as to keep abreast of the advances in their field, they also needed contact with professional operations research associates outside MDS.

Harcourt believed that experience as a consultant was excellent training for an analyst. He himself had been a consultant in the Financial Consulting Area for two of his ten years at MDS, while working overseas for the European Management Consulting Area. None of the analysts currently working for him had had consulting experience. Attracting good consultants to work in ORAS was extremely difficult due to the high demand for experienced consultants. Harcourt had hired three of the four analysts, all but Tom Kirk, within the past two years. He believed that Reingold, the most aggressive and outspoken, had the most promising potential of the four. Reingold had joined ORAS six months previously, after Harcourt had "fought for a year and a half to get him transferred from MDS Europe."

The most recent addition to ORAS was Rod Tracy, who had worked as an operations research specialist in a large management consulting firm in New York before coming on board in January. Hiring Tracy had been very gratifying to Harcourt, for he saw Tracy as "a real journeyman" in the field and as potentially his best analyst. Harcourt assigned Tracy the job of developing product definitions of ORAS services in the form of advertising brochures of ORAS offerings, rather than putting him to work immediately as an analyst. Harcourt reached this decision in part because of his impending departure for PMD as well as because of the pressing need for a product definition of ORAS services. During his October visit, Harcourt had been pleased by the excellent drafts of these brochures, and he knew that they would be ready for publication upon his return to Chicago. He recognized that as an analyst Tracy could be most valuable to ORAS, since his background at MDS was extensively in the "dirty" or applied area of operations research in diverse situations. But Harcourt had not settled on how he should arrange the reporting relationships. The organization of ORAS had become increasingly "flat" thus requiring a greater span of control than he thought was either necessary or beneficial. To make the organization more vertical he considered creating a "senior analyst" to whom the others would report. Kirk and Reingold had considerable MDS and ORAS seniority over Tracy, and Harcourt had given both of them, especially Reingold, very favorable performance reviews in each of the last two quarters. Their salaries, in the low 30s, were about as high as possible for associate group heads. Nevertheless, Tracy had been hired at that level of title and salary, and Harcourt could not imagine a man of Tracy's experience and competence settling for a subordinate position.

The mathematician function

At the time Harcourt attended PMD the mathematicians within ORAS consisted of only two people, despite the active search for two more which Harcourt and his head mathematician, Wolfgang Euler, had been conducting for several months. Euler and his assistant Sam Brenson were responsible for transferring problems into mathematical form; devising new methodology and models that might apply to specific problems; and informing both analysts and clients of the varying parameters, constraints, and functional limitations of mathematical modeling. They published a biweekly newsletter called "ORAS Facts," which summarized this information and served as a tool for communication between management scientists and practicing managers. The newsletter had gone on sale in mid-1974, and already had a circulation of several thousand. They also worked closely with Warren Deters, the data processing specialist at ORAS, to get many of their models on to the computer. Over the past few months Euler and Brenson had been developing a composite manual, to be updated in monthly additions, which described present and potential applications of operations research models to different industries. This would be particularly valuable to users and clients, Harcourt thought, because it would contain the basic assumptions and benefits of ORAS techniques with specific trouble shooting guidelines for systems presently in use.

Harcourt had hired Euler, a Swiss citizen and an internationally known operations research mathematician from the Science and Technology Committee of the United Nations in Paris only 14 months before. He thought of Euler as a "free spirit," eager to "do his own thing" and desirous of autonomy within ORAS. Harcourt was initially dubious, but had been subsequently pleased with the success of his efforts to get Euler to harness his free-form approach to the particular needs of ORAS users and clients.

Harcourt was pleased with the quality and productivity of the output of Euler and Brenson, whom he realized were the most overworked people in his group. In October, he learned that work on the new manual was six weeks behind the schedule Euler and he had charted in August. At that time he was reminded moreover of the nagging and persistent problem which had begun to develop in 1973 between Euler and the analysts, particularly Reingold. The problem concerned the use of the information in the biweekly newsletter. Prior to its publication, much of the analysts' time with clients had been devoted to explanations of the modeling concepts and applications, somewhat to the detriment of exploration of future applications and in-depth analysis of upcoming client needs. The purpose of the newsletter was to communicate concepts to other MDS and client users and to allow more time for diagnosis. Initially the analysts had resisted having a major part of their job taken over. While acceptance and use of the newsletter by the analysts seemed to be growing, a few heated exchanges between Reingold and Euler over the matter had occurred. In October, Harcourt found that the two men were "not on speaking terms again" but he did not have time to find out exactly what had ensued between them.

Data processing

The data processing area in ORAS consisted of one employee, Warren Deters. Deters' main task was to facilitate the use of the computer within ORAS in all possible ways, especially in ways useful to clients. In addition, he handled budgeting estimates and controls for the group. In the last few months he had worked to refine and maintain the new computer simulation model, purchased from a "think tank" for the complete optimization of entire working capital needs, and to relate these needs to the cost of funds, funds availability, and liquidity of the firm. Harcourt took a personal interest in Deters' work with the new model because it represented a source of tangible "product" or service which was a unique offering to clients and to MDS. This model was valuable not only because it produced a recommended working capital structure and funds flow when all cash, securities, inventories, and short-term sources were inputted, but also because it could be used as a training device for analysts, consultants, auditors, client treasurers, and controllers in firms. Moreover, Harcourt was anxious to see some concrete results from this model which, up until then, had just been in the "initial start-up" phase. He had originally contracted with the consulting think tank in Boston to develop the model using $15,000 out of his ORAS budget. By the time the model had been set up and proved operable, Harcourt was so convinced of its potential that he decided ORAS and MDS should own it exclusively. He and the consultants agreed on a price of $300,000. Harcourt had gone all the way to the MDS chairman to advocate the purchase, and after four months of effort he succeeded in June 1974 in obtaining approval and the sole rights to the model.

Deters had improved dramatically in performance and enthusiasm from the previous year. In 1973, Deters, who had emigrated from Poland to Canada and joined MDS as a clerk in a Canadian office in 1955, had been an administrative assistant in ORAS, earning $12,000. At that time he reported to Horace Clark, then head of the data processing function. Deters had no college degree, and had gained his knowledge of computers in nightschool and through experience in other MDS departments. Harcourt recalled Clark as "a genius with systems and the computer, a master's in computer science, but having no concept of marketing, what was relevant to the clients, and no interest in dealing with clients directly." Early in 1974, while Harcourt was out of town, Deters went to Chadwick and requested a transfer out of ORAS, a request which Chadwick dutifully began processing. When Harcourt returned, he stopped the transfer. A few months later Clark left ORAS, as Harcourt put it, "by our mutual consent," and Harcourt managed to arrange for Deters a promotion to assistant group head and a significant raise. Deters currently earned nearly $20,000. Harcourt perceived him as someone who had pulled himself up by his own bootstraps and who had "blossomed" in recent months. Harcourt felt that Deters had responded well to his own view of the computer as a tool for the group's and client's use and as a means to get ORAS closer to customer needs. In his last performance review, Deters had told Harcourt he was now "very pleased" with his work and responsibilities in ORAS.

BOB HARCOURT'S GROUP

Harcourt knew that ORAS was referred to as "Bob Harcourt's Group" by the officers in the Domestic Management Consulting Area. This characterization seemed to reflect the fact that John Chadwick was virtually never involved in the activities in ORAS and that Harcourt was usually involved in the details of consulting relationships by his analysts. Harcourt worried that his close involvement in ORAS could perhaps reduce the incentive of the group. Nevertheless, almost all the feedback on his analysts' performance from the Domestic Management Consulting Area was favorable, and his own judgment as well as outside indicators confirmed that Euler's and Deters' efforts were also successful.

Before he left for PMD, Harcourt had recommended to Chadwick that no one be put in charge of ORAS during his absence. Chadwick had concurred. Three weeks before his departure, Harcourt told the group his decision. He emphasized the increasing importance of their working together as a team. During his absence Harcourt delegated most of his normal duties. He asked Kirk to be the "catalyst for department opinion" on new applications, Reingold to coordinate client contacts and appointments, Deters to handle internal budget and control matters, and Euler and Deters to do their part in product planning and definition. The only function not delegated was personnel evaluation.

In October Harcourt had been satisfied that, individually, these functions had been well handled. Nevertheless, he did see two areas that might indicate problems. The analysts, although energetic and busy, seemed to lack direction and were neither functioning as foci of ORAS developments nor sharing their ideas with one another. It seemed to Harcourt that the analysts had done more work on individual problems and interests, and had avoided work which required extensive teamwork and coordination. The second problem, related to the first, was that of the interference between Euler's task of developing and publishing material for use by clients and the task of developing descriptive materials for analysts. As Harcourt saw it, this problem was exacerbated by the fact that Reingold and Euler just didn't get along.

In describing his own role in ORAS, Harcourt said:

> Professionally, I see myself first and foremost as an analyst. I believe, quite objectively, that I am the best analyst in the group. The others recognize this, and they bring their clients and their problems to me freely, on a professional-to-professional basis. With my training in operations research [Bachelor's degree from Johns Hopkins] and my ten years' experience in MDS, six of them in some sort of consulting role, I feel comfortable with that function. Finally, I lived and breathed that simulation model, so I know best its capabilities and potential.

Reflecting on the question of how he might change the management of ORAS, Harcourt said:

> I'm basically not happy sitting back and letting the world go by. My experience and, I believe, my success to date in business have largely been because I love to get involved. I take the initiative in a meeting. I simply like to run things when I know what's going on as much or more than anyone else. . . .
>
> Right now I want to satisfy more of the *creative* energies I have. I want more writing and teaching, and there are plenty of opportunities for this that can benefit the group as well.
>
> I think I know now, from having seen the results of being away for 14 weeks, that I can safely delegate more tasks, more functions to my people. The real question is more of what type of style do I adopt to help them work together and develop as individuals. . . .
>
> I've always depended on my people for inputs to a decision. My style has been to involve them up to the point where I know what ought to be done. . . . What I'd like to do now, as one of the faculty said the other day, is to get them to "learn without my having to teach them."

Harcourt and John Chadwick

Harcourt considered his boss an "ultimate politician," with a nonassertive, very "Theory Y" approach to managing. On the one hand, this gave Harcourt a free rein to make his own decisions; he could do anything he wanted within his budget without necessarily advising Chadwick. Harcourt had received Chadwick's approval for every single request for a raise or promotion for his people in the two years since he had taken over ORAS. On some matters Chadwick would typically agree to Harcourt's request rather quickly and quietly, then slowly turn in his chair, gaze out the window pensively, and say, "I think it would help matters, Bobby, if you yourself thought about going ahead to some of the chaps up the line on this. . . ."

On other occasions, sometimes for more serious requests, Chadwick himself would grant the final approval after a period of a week or more. Harcourt pictured the process as indirect, muddled decision making, not allowing for tests or challenges of ideas. Although Harcourt was never really sure how Chadwick reached his decisions on these matters, it seemed to Harcourt that he was part of a network of old hands at MDS, a sort of club where one's name counted far more than the substance of one's ideas. To Harcourt it was all rather inefficient and slightly amusing.

Harcourt also felt he had learned something indirectly from Chadwick, who was 58 years old and had been in MDS for 35 years. That "something" was a way of managing very differently from earlier styles Harcourt had known. Indeed, compared to Chadwick, his previous boss had been "the polar opposite, the complete Theory X. . . ." He felt that he had developed his basic approach to management through the influence of his previous boss.

Harcourt frequently felt mildly frustrated by Chadwick: "That man will not take a strong position on anything. There's no movement there, no initiative. Frankly, he seems not to think about taking the initiative."

Despite MDS policy that performance reviews be given every six months, Harcourt knew that Chadwick had given no one a face-to-face appraisal in four years. He was reminded of the significance of this as he got to know his PMD classmates: it seemed that all but a few of them had either been told directly that they were going to be promoted or had learned it through the grapevine. Harcourt could only assume that he was doing well and that he was not slated for a job change in the near future. His promotion to group head two years ago had put him on the same level as his previous boss. In the two years under Chadwick he had received salary increases at every opportunity, and was now 65 percent ahead of his level two years ago. Moreover, he and Chadwick's secretary of many years were friends, and he had picked up "favorable signals" from her of Chadwick's opinion of him.

One of the few times that Chadwick had expressed himself negatively came after Harcourt had asked if he could withdraw from PMD the previous July. It had seemed to Harcourt that in view of the pressure of work, new products, and new people in ORAS, it was the worst possible time to be away. Chadwick had sat up and thought for a moment. Then, looking directly at Harcourt, he said, "I believe it would be *unwise* for you to withdraw." The year before Chadwick had withdrawn his nominee for the PMD, to which at least one MDS manager a year had always been sent. Harcourt reasoned that Chadwick's relative firmness in denying him was out of a desire "not to be embarrassed" among his top management colleagues.

*   *   *   *   *

Harcourt was in early on the Monday morning of his return to the office. At five after nine, John Chadwick came by and welcomed him back. Sitting down, with a broad smile, he said, "Well, Bobby, what did you learn back at Harvard?"

BIBLIOGRAPHY

Albanese, A. *Management: Toward Accountability for Performance.* Homewood, Ill.: Richard D. Irwin, Inc., 1975.

Andrews, K. A. *The Concept of Corporate Strategy.* Homewood, Ill.: Dow-Jones, Irwin, Inc., 1971.

Ansoff, H. I., and **Brandenburg, R. G.** "A Language for Organization Design," Part I and Part II. *Management Science,* vol. 17 (August 1971).

Anthony, R. N. *Planning and Central Systems: A Framework for Analysis.* Cambridge, Mass.: Harvard Business School, Studies in Management Control, 1965.

Anthony, R. N.; Dearden, J.; and **Vancil, R. F.** *Management Control Systems.* Homewood, Ill.: Richard D. Irwin, Inc., 1976.

Argyris, C. *Personality and Organization.* New York: Harper & Row, 1957.

Ashby, W. R. *Design for a Brain: The Origin of Adaptive Behavior.* London: Chapman & Hall, Ltd., and Science Paperbacks, 1960. (First published in 1950.)

Athos, A. G., and **Coffey, R. E.** *Behavior in Organizations: A Multidimensional View.* Englewood Cliffs, N.J.: Prentice-Hall, 1968.

————, and **Gabarro, J. J.** *Interpersonal Behavior: Communication and Understanding in Relationships.* Englewood Cliffs, N.J.: Prentice-Hall, Inc., 1978.

Bales, F. F. *Interaction Process Analysis.* Cambridge, Mass.: Addison-Wesley, 1950.

Becker, H. S.; Geer, B.; Hughes, E. C.; and Strauss, A. *Boys in White: Student Culture in Medical School.* Chicago: University of Chicago Press, 1961.

Bennis, W. G. *Changing Organizations.* New York: McGraw-Hill Book Co., 1966.

Blake, R. R., and Mouton, J. S. *The Managerial Grid.* Houston, Tex.: Gulf Publishing Co., 1964.

Blau, P. M. *The Dynamics of Bureaucracy.* Chicago: University of Chicago Press, 1955.

Burns, T., and Stalker, G. M. *The Management of Innovation.* London: Tavistock Publications, 1961.

Calame, B. E. "The Truth Hurts: Some Companies See More Harm Than Good in Sensitivity Training." *The Wall Street Journal,* July 14, 1969.

Cass, E. L., and Zimmer, F. G. (eds) *Man and Work in Society.* New York: Van Nostrand Reinhold Co., 1975.

Chandler, A. *Strategy and Structure.* Garden City, N.Y.: Anchor Books, 1966.

Cohen, P. *The Gospel According to the Harvard Business School.* New York: Doubleday & Co., Inc., 1973.

Coles, R. *Erik H. Erikson: The Growth of His Work.* Boston: Little, Brown and Co., 1970.

Cummings, L. L., and Berger, C. J. "Organization Structure: How Does It Influence Attitudes and Performance?" *Organizational Dynamics,* Autumn 1976.

Cyert, R. M., and March, J. G. *A Behavioral Theory of the Firm.* Englewood Cliffs, N.J.: Prentice-Hall, 1963.

Dalton, G. W. "Influence and Organizational Change." In *Organizational Change and Development,* eds. G. W. Dalton, P. R. Lawrence, and L. E. Greiner. Homewood, Ill.: Richard D. Irwin, Inc., and The Dorsey Press, 1970.

Davis, S. M., and Lawrence, P. R. *Matrix.* Reading, Mass.: Addison-Wesley, 1977.

Drucker, P. F. *Managing by Results.* New York: Harper & Row, 1964.

du Jardin, P., and Gibson, C. F. "The PMD Alumnus: Summary Results of a Survey of PMD 29, PMD 30, and PMD 31." Working paper. Boston, Mass.: Harvard Business School, 1976.

Fayol, H. *Administration Industrielle et Generale.* Paris: Dunod, 1950. (First published in 1916.)

French, R. P., and Raven, B. "The Bases of Social Power." In *Group Dynamics: Research and Theory,* eds. D. Cartwright and A. Zander. 3d ed. New York: Harper & Row, 1968.

Gabarro, J. J., and Morley, E. "Increasing Our Understanding of Persons in Relationship." Boston, Mass.: Harvard Business School, 1972.

Galbraith, J. *Designing Complex Organizations.* Reading, Mass.: Addison-Wesley, 1973.

Gibson, C. F., and **Nolan, R. N.** "Managing the Four Stages of EDP Growth." *Harvard Business Review,* January–February 1974.

Greiner, L. E. "Evolution and Revolution as Organizations Grow." *Harvard Business Review,* July–August 1972.

Groggin, W. C. "How the Multidimensional Structure Works at Dow Corning." *Harvard Business Review,* January–February 1974.

Gulick, L. H. "Notes on the Theory of Organization." In *Papers on the Science of Administration,* eds. L. H. Gulick and L. F. Urwick. New York: Columbia University Press, 1937.

Hackman, J. R. "On the Coming Demise of Job Enrichment." In *Man and Work in Society,* eds. E. L. Cass and F. G. Zimmer. New York: Van Nostrand Reinhold Co., 1975.

————. "Work Design." In *Improving Life at Work,* eds. J. R. Hackman and J. L. Suttle. Santa Monica, Calif.: Goodyear Publishing Co., 1977.

Hackman, J. R., and **Kaplan, R. E.** "Interventions into Group Processes: An Approach to Improving the Effectiveness of Groups." In *Decision Sciences—Behavioral Science Contributions,* ed. E. E. Cummings. (Special edition of the *Journal for the American Institute for Decision Sciences,* December 1974.)

Harris, T. A. *I'm OK—You're OK: A Practical Guide to Transactional Analysis.* New York: Harper & Row, 1969.

Hersey, P., and **Blanchard, K. H.** *Management of Organizational Behavior: Utilizing Human Resources.* 2d ed. Englewood Cliffs, N.J.: Prentice-Hall, 1972.

Herzberg, F. *Work and the Nature of Man.* New York: World Publishing Co., 1966.

Hickson, D. J.; Hinings, C. R.; Lee, C. A.; Schneck, R. E.; and **Pennings J. M.** "A Strategic Contingencies' Theory of Intraorganizational Power." *Administrative Science Quarterly,* vol. 19 (1974), pp. 216–29.

Hollander, E. P. and **Julian, J. W.** "Contemporary Trends in The Analysis of Leadership Processes." *Psychological Bulletin,* vol. 71 (1969), pp. 387–97.

Homans, G. C. *The Human Group.* New York: Harcourt, Brace, & World, Inc., 1950.

House, R. J. and **Mitchell, T. R.** "Path-Goal Theory of Leadership." *Journal of Contemporary Business,* Autumn 1974, pp. 81–97.

Janis, I. L., and **Mann, L.** *Decision Making: A Psychological Analysis of Conflict, Choice, and Commitment.* New York: Free Press, 1977.

Jay, A. "How to Run a Meeting." *Harvard Business Review,* March–April 1976.

Katz, D., and **Kahn, R. L.** *The Social Psychology of Organizations.* New York: John Wiley & Sons, Inc., 1966.

Keen, P. G. W., and **Scott-Morton, M. S.** *Decision Support Systems: An Organizational Perspective.* Reading, Mass.: Addison-Wesley, 1978.

Kelley, H. H., and **Thibaut, J. W.** "Group Problem Solving." In *The Handbook of Social Psychology,* vol. 4, eds. G. Lindzey and E. Aronson. Reading, Mass.: Addison-Wesley, 1969.

Kolb, D. A., and **Frohman, A. L.** "An Organization Development Approach to Consulting." *Sloan Management Review,* vol. 12, no. 1 (Fall 1970), pp. 51–65.

Korda, M. *Power! How to Get It, How to Use It.* New York: Random House, 1975.

Korman, A. K. "'Consideration,' 'Initiating Structure,' and Organizational Criteria—a Review." *Personnel Psychology,* vol. 19, no. 4 (Winter 1966).

Kotter, J. P. "Power, Dependence and Effective Management." *Harvard Business Review,* July–August 1977.

————. "The Psychological Contract: Managing the Joining-Up Process." *California Management Review,* Spring 1973.

Lawrence, P. R., and **Lorsch, J. W.** *Organization and Environment.* Boston: Division of Research, Harvard Business School, 1967.

Learned, E. P.; Christensen, C. R.; Andrews, K. R.; and **Guth, W. D.** *Business Policy: Text and Cases.* Homewood, Ill.: Richard D. Irwin, Inc., 1965.

Leavitt, H. J. "Suppose We Took Groups Seriously." In *Man and Work in Society,* eds. E. L. Cass and F. G. Zimmer. New York: Van Nostrand Reinhold Co., 1975.

Levinson, D. J. *The Seasons of a Man's Life.* New York: Ballantine Books, 1978.

Lewin, K. "Group Decision and Social Change." In *Readings in Social Psychology,* eds. G. E. Swanson, T. M. Newcomb, and E. L. Hartley. New York: Holt Rinehart, 1952.

Likert, R. *The Human Organization.* New York: McGraw-Hill Book Co., 1967.

Lorsch, J. W. "Managing Change." Boston, Mass.: Harvard Business School, 1974.

Lorsch, J. W., and **Morse, J. J.** *Organizations and Their Members: A Contingency Approach.* New York: Harper & Row, 1974.

Lorsch, J. W., and **Sheldon, A.** "The Individual in the Organization: A Systems View." In *Organizational Behavior and Administration: Cases and Readings,* 3d ed., eds. P. R. Lawrence, L. B. Barnes, and J. W. Lorsch. Homewood, Ill.: Richard D. Irwin, Inc., 1976.

Maccoby, M. "The Corporate Climber Has to Find His Heart." *Fortune,* December 1976*a*.

————. *The Gamesman: The New Corporate Leaders.* New York: Simon and Schuster, 1976*b*.

Maddi, S. R. (ed) *Perspectives on Personality: A Comparative Approach.* Boston: Little, Brown and Co., 1971.

Maier, N. R. F. "Assets and Liabilities in Group Problem Solving." *Psychological Review,* vol. 74, no. 4 (July 1967).

March, J. G., and **Olsen, J. P.** *Ambiguity and Choice in Organizations.* Bergen, Norway: Universitets Forlaget, 1976.

March, J. G., and **Simon, H. A.** *Organizations.* New York: John Wiley & Sons, Inc., 1958.

Maslow, A. H. *Motivation and Personality.* New York: Harper & Row, 1954.

May, R. *Love and Will.* New York: Dell Publishing Co., 1973.

McClelland, D. C. *Power, The Inner Experience.* New York: Irvington Publishers, Inc., 1975.

————, and **Burnham, D. H.** "Power Is the Great Motivator." *Harvard Business Review,* March–April 1976.

McGregor, D. *The Human Side of Enterprise.* New York: McGraw-Hill Book Co., 1960.

Mintzberg, H. *The Nature of Managerial Work.* New York: Harper & Row, 1973.

Nystrom, P. C.; Hedberg, B. L. T.; and **Starbuck, W. H.** "Interacting Processes as Organizational Designs." In *The Management of Organization Design, Vol. I: Strategies and Implementation,* eds. Kilmann, Pondy, and Slevin. New York: Elsevier North-Holland, 1976.

Perrow, C. "Bureaucratic Paradox: The Efficient Organization Centralizes in Order to Decentralize." *Organizational Dynamics,* Spring 1977.

————. "Is Business Really Changing?" *Organizational Dynamics,* Spring 1974.

Porter, L. W. "Turning Work into Nonwork: The Rewarding Environment." In *Work and Nonwork in the Year 2001,* ed. M. D. Dunnette. Monterey, Calif.: Brooks-Cole Publishing Co., 1973, pp. 113–33.

Pugh, D. S.; Hickson, D. J.; Hinings, C. R.; and **Turner, C.** "The Context of Organization Structures." *Administrative Science Quarterly,* vol. 14 (1969).

Rice, A. K. *The Enterprise and Its Environment.* London: Tavistock Publications, 1963.

Rockhart, J. F. "Chief Executives Define Their Own Information Needs." *Harvard Business Review,* February–March 1979.

Roethlisberger, F., and **Dickson, W.** *Management and the Worker.* Cambridge: Harvard University Press, 1939.

Sagan, C. *The Dragons of Eden.* New York: Ballantine Books, 1978. (First published by Random House, 1977.)

Salancik, G. R., and **Pfeffer, J.** "Who Gets Power—and How They Hold on to It: A Strategic-Contingency Model of Power," *Organizational Dynamics,* Winter 1977.

Schein, E. H. *Brainwashing.* Cambridge, Mass.: Center for International Studies, 1961.

————. *Career Dynamics.* Reading, Mass.: Addison-Wesley, 1978.

————. *Organizational Psychology.* 2d ed. Englewood Cliffs, N.J.: Prentice-Hall, 1970.

Scott, W. R. "Effectiveness of Organizational Effectiveness Studies." In *New Perspectives on Organizational Effectiveness,* eds. P. S. Goodman and J. M. Pennings. San Francisco: Jossey-Bass, 1977.

Scott-Morton, M. S. *Management Decision Systems: Computer-Based Support for Decision Making.* Cambridge, Mass.: Division of Research, Harvard Business School, 1971.

Seashore, S. E. "Group Cohesiveness in the Industrial Work Group." Ann Arbor: Institute for Social Research, University of Michigan, 1954.

Seeger, J. A. "Changing Problem-Solving Behavior in Management Meetings." Boston, Mass.: Ph.D. diss., Harvard Business School, 1978.

Seiler, J. A. *Systems Analysis in Organizational Behavior.* Homewood, Ill.: Richard D. Irwin, Inc. and The Dorsey Press, 1967.

Shull, F. A., Jr.; Delbecq, A. L.; and Cummings, L. L. *Organizational Decision-Making.* New York: McGraw-Hill Book Co., 1970.

Simon, H. A. *Administrative Behavior.* 2d ed. New York: Macmillan, 1957.

Smith, Adam. *The Wealth of Nations.* New York: Dutton, 1978. (Originally published 1776.)

Solomon, S. "How a Whole Company Earned Itself a Roman Holiday." *Fortune,* January 15, 1979.

Tagiuri, R. "A Note on Communication." Boston, Mass.: Intercollegiate Case Clearing House, Harvard Business School, 1972.

Tannenbaum, R., and Schmidt, W. H. "How to Choose a Leadership Pattern." *Harvard Business Review,* May–June 1973.

Taylor, F. W. *The Principles of Scientific Management.* New York: Harper, 1923.

Thomas, R. R., Jr. "Managing the Psychological Contract." Boston, Mass.: Harvard Business School, International Case Clearing House, 1974.

Thurow, S. *One L.* New York: G. P. Putnam's Sons, 1977.

Turner, A. N., and Lombard, G. F. F. *Interpersonal Behavior and Administration.* New York: Free Press, 1969.

Vaillant, G. E. *Adaptation to Life.* Boston: Little, Brown, 1977.

Vroom, V. H., and Yetton, P. W. *Leadership and Decision-Making.* Pittsburgh, Pa.: University of Pittsburgh Press, 1973.

Walton, R. E. "From Hawthorne to Topeka and Kalmar." In *Man and Work in Society,* eds. E. L. Cass and F. G. Zimmer. New York: Van Nostrand Reinhold Co., 1975.

Weick, K. E. "Re-Punctuating the Problem." In *New Perspectives on Organizational Effectiveness,* eds. P. S. Goodman and J. M. Pennings. San Francisco: Jossey-Bass, 1977.

Wheelis, A. *How People Change.* New York: Harper & Row, 1973.

White, R. W. "Ego and Reality in Psychoanalytic Theory." *Psychological Issues,* vol. 3, 1963.

Wilson, S. *Informal Groups.* Englewood Cliffs, N.J.: Prentice-Hall, 1978.

Woodward, J. *Industrial Organization: Theory and Practice.* London: Oxford University Press, 1965.

Yuchtman, E., and **Seashore, S. E.** "A System Resource Approach to Organizational Effectiveness." *American Sociological Review,* vol. 23, no. 6 (December 1967).

Zander, A. *Groups at Work.* San Francisco, Calif.: Jossey-Bass, 1977.

INDEX

W

Walton, R. E., 286
Weber, M., 107
Weick, K. E., 8
Wheelis, A., 634
White, R. W., 590
Wilson, S., 339–40
Woodward, J., 101

Y

Yetton, P. W., 336, 344
Yuchtman, F., 8

Z

Zander, A., 341
Zimmer, F. G., 659, 661

This book has been set VIP in 10 and 9 point Century Schoolbook, leaded 2 points. Part and Chapter numbers are 36 point Optima. Part titles are 14 point Optima and chapter titles are 16 point Optima. The size of the type page is 27 × 45½ picas.